IMMIGRATION: New Americans, Old Questions

IMMIGRATION:
New Americans,
Old Questions

Edited by Melinda Maidens

Facts On File
460 Park Ave. So., New York, N.Y. 10016

IMMIGRATION:
New Americans,
Old Questions

Published by Facts On File, Inc.
460 Park Avenue South, New York, N.Y. 10016
© Copyright 1981 by Facts On File, Inc.

Library of Congress Cataloging in Publication Data

Maidens, Melinda.
    Immigration: New Americans, Old Questions

    Includes index.
    1.   United States—Emigration and immigration—
Addresses, essays, lectures.   I.   Facts on File, Inc.
II. Title.
JV6455.M3   325.73   81-9914
ISBN 0-87196-598-4   AACR2

International Standard Book Number: 0-87196-598-4
Library of Congress Catalog Card Number: 81-9914
9 8 7 6 5 4 3 2 1
PRINTED IN THE UNITED STATES OF AMERICA

Contents

Preface

... "Give me your tired, your poor,
Your huddled masses yearning to breathe free,
The wretched refuse of your teeming shore,
Send these, the homeless, tempest-tossed to me,
I lift my lamp beside the golden door!"

No discussion of immigration can fail to refer to Emma Lazarus' famous lines, and the reader will frequently encounter them in the editorials in this book. Inscribed on the Statue of Liberty in New York Harbor, they aptly express what America has meant to many millions of people. Our nation's founders conceived of America as a refuge for the world's outcasts, and that "wretched refuse" eagerly flocked to our shores. They were desperate, ambitious, adventurous or simply restless, but America's "golden door" was wide open to all.

This is why immigration policy remains such a sensitive topic among Americans. It cuts deeply into our national psyche, touching our personal and family histories. Everyone who lives here came from somewhere else. We cannot discuss immigration control without a twinge of guilt, for our forebears were victims of earlier attempts to exclude newcomers. Still, we owe it to ourselves and future immigrants to formulate a coherent policy on admissions into this country. Ideals must be balanced against reality, and a compromise must be found that will not betray conscience or defy reason.

Recent events make it all the more urgent that we create a new immigration policy. Our laws are at least 15 years out of date, and conditions have changed radically since the last major overhaul of immigration laws in 1965. In 1979, the last year for which precise figures are available from the U.S. Immigration and Naturalization Service, 677,900 immigrants and refugees were admitted into the country. Indications are that the 1980 figure is much higher. Estimates of illegal aliens run as high as six million, more than the entire population of Massachusetts. The problems of immigration, illegal aliens and refugee resettlement concern local communities across the nation, as the following editorials will show. Chosen from major newspapers in all 50 states and Canada, they represent a wide range of views. They are included in this volume without regard to balancing or favoring points of view. They were written to stimulate public awareness of an issue that goes to the heart of our identity as a nation.

August, 1981   Melinda Maidens

Part I: Immigration

A "nation of immigrants," America has been the destination of peoples from every country in the world. The U.S. is unique among countries created by immigrants in its conscious decision to become a "melting pot" society, where people of all nationalities would be judged by their abilities, not their backgrounds. With vast expanses of land to settle, the U.S. had no interest in establishing immigration controls until 1882. Betraying its ideals, the U.S. that year passed the Chinese Exclusion Act, which barred Chinese from joining their half-million countrymen who had flocked to the West. It was the first indication that the "melting pot" theory had its limits. Despite ever-growing restrictions, immigrants continued to come. They confounded the expectations of the prejudiced by successfully integrating into American life.

Today, a new wave of immigrants has once again revived old fears. The Hispanics from Central and South America are this country's fastest-growing immigrant group and are forecast to become our largest minority group in the near future. Unlike past immigrants, who left the "old country" beyond the ocean, Hispanics are very close to their homelands in the Western Hemisphere. The psychological and cultural distances that former immigrants had to travel does not exist for the Hispanics, whose native countries are a relatively short distance away. Such proximity hinders the pull of assimilation and increases the pressure for bilingualism.

Illegal immigration in the U.S. has existed side-by-side with legal. The sheer length of America's boundaries with Canada and Mexico ensured that illegal crossings would be a fact of life. In the 19th century, illegal immigration was limited to felons eluding police. As Congress began to erect barriers to legal immigration in the early 20th century, illegal immigration increased. It rose sharply after the 1924 Immigration and Nationality Act, which restricted immigrants by nationality. The illegal alien problem persisted alongside the "bracero" program of World War II, which permitted temporary entry to Mexicans to work on U.S. farms. Perceptions of a manpower shortage encouraged the U.S. government to take a lax attitude toward controlling illegal immigration during the 1940s–1950s. That perception has long since changed, but law-enforcement efforts have lagged behind. Those years of neglect have taken their toll by permitting illegal aliens to become so integrated into the U.S. economy that an attempt to deport them would result in substantial expense and economic dislocation.

Hispanics in America: A Newly Discovered Minority

The U.S. is situated in a Hispanic hemisphere, but that did not attract general notice until the 1970s. The 1980 census was the first in history to include Hispanics as a separate category, and the resulting figures were a revelation: 14.6 million people listed themselves as Spanish in origin. Hispanics are America's fastest-growing minority and are figured to become the largest minority group in the country by the end of the 1980s.

This large category embraces many people of different cultures but one language, Spanish. The majority are Mexicans, seven million, including an unknown proportion of illegal aliens. Puerto Ricans account for 1.8 million, and Cubans comprise 700,000. These three largest groups, plus others from elsewhere in Latin and South America present the U.S. with one of the hardest "melting pot" challenges in its history.

The Hartford Courant

Hartford, Conn., November 28, 1977

The new census of Hartford's schools shows that the number of Spanish-speaking students continues to rise, to the point that one high school — Hartford Public — now is predominantly Hispanic. The city and its environs must pay strict attention to the message conveyed by this report.

The message is a mandate for greatly improved services to the Spanish-speaking persons new to this area, to help them become oriented to the ways of the English-speaking community they have moved into. For while the census is specifically a count of school children, it points to the needs of their families and draws attention to how many more Hispanics now are here in Connecticut. In Hartford's public schools, they are almost one-third of the total enrollment — precisely 32.6 per cent, and still climbing.

As important as it is to acknowledge the growing number, it is also essential that we realize that the Spanish-speaking peoples who are migrating here are not all alike. They do not all come from the same place, or the same background, and they cannot all be expected to adapt to life here at the same pace.

According to recent studies in New York City, with its comparable — but larger — influx of Spanish-speaking residents, these immigrants come from many cultures in South and Central America, and not solely from Puerto Rico. This fact compounds the problems of dealing with them and giving them assistance.

Mainlanders tend to cast all Hispanics into the single assumption that they all come from Puerto Rico with a recognized cultural background and customs. New York found that its people come from the Dominican Republic, Colombia, Ecuador, Peru, Mexico, Venezuela, Bolivia, Argentina, Cuba and elsewhere, each with different ways of life and expectations.

While they all speak Spanish, it is with varying degrees of speed and different dialects, almost as foreign to one another as to persons who speak only English. Some come from the mountains, some from the plains, some from the city or from rural areas. Putting them into one mold is simply wrong, and it creates trouble for them and for the country.

According to one New York official, some of the immigrants are scarcely educated, and some are well educated. Many Cubans have been here for a generation and have found good jobs and established themselves as functioning Americans.

But for most of the immigrants, problems outweigh the positive aspects of their move to this country. Moreover, their troubles are made more difficult by the immigrants' tendency to pretend to be from Puerto Rico so that they need not observe the rules for aliens.

One common factor among all the Hispanics is the discrimination they face when they get here. Their influx and increase cannot be taken lightly. They are here to stay, and this land of immigrants must be ready to welcome them with services that help them adjust to their new surroundings — and help the communities and neighborhoods into which they move.

The Washington Post

Washington, D. C., April 11, 1978

A nation within the nation is emerging....

THAT IS THE startling but inescapable conclusion of a recent series in this newspaper on the Mexican American community in the southwestern United States. Along the border from California to Texas, and in such non-border cities as Los Angeles, Houston and Denver, Mexican Americans make up an increasingly larger share of the Southwest's residents. In 1976, according to Census Bureau statistics, there were about 6.5 million Mexican Americans in the United States. Today the Mexican American population in the Southwest alone is believed to number more than 7 million. Whatever the precise number, the growth of the Mexican American community constitutes the most significant new social fact of the Southwest.

Some Mexican American families lived on this side of the border before the Southwest became U.S. territory. But most have immigrated in the last two decades. It is the continuing heavy immigration—legal and illegal—that underlies both the community's potential and its problems. Its potential is simply stated: The Mexican American community can become the dominant minority group in racially and ethnically diverse cities and states throughout the Southwest. Its problems are low levels of education, poverty, unfamiliarity with the English language and the general "Anglo" culture, and a disposition to political apathy. The last characteristic is particularly telling, for without involving itself in politics, the Mexican American community will remain unnecessarily dependent. For example, Los Angeles's 1.5 million Mexican American citizens have not had one of their community elected to the city council for 15 years.

However, Mexican Americans in some communities are beginning to flex political muscles (as they've done in New Mexico for years) and to speak up for their own interests. In a number of communities that has led to conflicts with police departments, school officials, and other elements of the prevailing order. Those conflicts are reminiscent of the racial conflicts in the South a decade ago. It is a matter of an emerging group demanding the benefits of full citizenship —benefits largely denied in the past.

We have no ready solutions to the severe economic problems of the Mexican American community. They will probably have to be treated within the context of the region's, and the country's, overall economic policies. But we are certain of one role federal and state governments should play in the full emergence of that community: Ensure Mexican Americans the same civil and political rights due all Americans. Thus, we welcome the Justice Department's challenge last week of the lenient and "entirely inappropriate" sentences a federal district judge in Houston handed out to three former city policemen. The judge sentenced the men—convicted of violating the civil rights of a Mexican American who died while in their custody—to one year in prison. As the Justice Department action illustrates, ensuring those rights need not involve, at either level, creating new agencies or policies. Rather, it's a matter of using existing ones in ways that spread benefits to that "new" community.

THE DENVER POST

Denver, Colo., September 9, 1979

AS NATIONAL Hispanic Heritage Week gets under way — it starts Monday and climaxes with the Sept. 16 observance of Mexican Independence Day — it appears that President Carter is making a greater effort to recognize Americans of Spanish heritage. But there still is a feeling that he could do more.

A low point in Hispanic perception of the president's support came after his Cabinet shakeup in July. Carter had given many Hispanic leaders the impression that he was about to appoint an Hispano to the Cabinet.

But Carter disappointed many Hispanics when he named Moon Landrieu to head the Department of Housing and Urban Development and Neil Goldschmidt as secretary of Transportation.

Now Carter has regained some credibility by appointing Esteban Torres, U. S. representative to UNESCO — an eminently qualified leader who appears to appeal to all factions of the Hispano community — as his special assistant for Hispanic affairs, effective Saturday. In a more political realm, Lon Saavedra, a young aide to Denver's Democratic Rep. Patricia Schroeder, was named last month as coordinator for the Carter-Mondale re-election campaign in 11 Western states, including Colorado and California.

The president's recent appointments still are scant recognition of the role and contributions of the nation's largest linguistic minority group — 12 million Americans nationally and close to one-fifth of Colorado's population — but at least it's a start.

The Wichita Eagle and Wichita Beacon

Wichita, Kans., August 19, 1979

Society sometimes creates invisible people. For decades it often has seemed the best way to deal with an uncomfortable situation was to ignore it. Such has been the lot of many of the poor, the elderly, blacks, Indians, Vietnam refugees, and even the majority of people in this country: women. Sometimes it has taken social upheaval to restore 20-20 vision to the American conscience: the civil rights and women's liberation movements, the anti-war demonstrations of the '60s, and the horrors of the "boat people."

Now, a new breed of invisible people is demanding to be seen and heard: the more than 12 million people of Hispanic descent living in the United States, not including an unknown number of illegal aliens.

Hispanics comprise 17 percent of the population in California, 20 percent in Texas and 10 percent in New York state. By 1985, aided by a steady tide of unlawful immigrants, it is estimated that people of Hispanic origin will be the largest minority in America.

The manner in which Hispanic Americans demand recognition and the degree of responsiveness shown by other Americans will help shape the nation's destiny. Ruben Bonilla, president of the League of United Latin American Citizens, when he was in Wichita last week, spoke of the former isolation of Hispanic Americans from the American mainstream. Now, he said, their growing numbers and sophistication are certain to reverse that trend.

Mr. Bonilla's comments about job discrimination, civil rights abuses, and the problems of poor community-police relations were reminiscent of the complaints of other groups that have sought and continue to seek the elusive goal of full citizenship.

The Hispanic leader endorsed the inclusion of "undocumented workers," or illegal aliens, in the 1980 census, while expressing concern for the plight of the migrant worker generally. He made the telling point that this country is spending millions to rescue the "boat people" of Southeast Asia — and rightly so — but is "dispatching dogs" to keep Mexican laborers from entering this country illegally.

The important thing for Kansans and for all Americans is that an honest and sincere effort be made to address the needs and concerns of Hispanic Americans. Hindsight now should serve the country well. There is no need to re-enact the emotional turbulence and violent disruptions of the past, when the country anguished over its dealing with other neglected minorities.

Hispanic Americans exist. They must be seen, and they must be heard. They no longer are "invisible." And how America at large meets this challenge will help determine what kind of society we have in the approaching 1980s.

Court's 1974 Bilingualism Decision Creates Bureaucratic Confusion

Bilingual education is usually thought of in connection with Spanish-speaking children, but it was upheld in a 1974 Supreme Court ruling involving Chinese students in the San Francisco area. Since the late 1960s, Washington had appropriated funds for voluntary bilingual education, but on Jan. 21, 1974, the Supreme Court unanimously ruled that schools had an obligation to provide bilingual services. Reversing a lower court, the justices found the San Francisco school system guilty of violating the 1964 Civil Rights Act by failing to offer special instruction to 1,800 Chinese pupils who could not speak English. "There is no equality of treatment merely by providing . . . students with the same facilities, textbooks, teachers and curriculum," the court wrote, because "students who do not understand English are effectively foreclosed from any meaningful education." The Department of Justice cited the ruling in seeking help for the estimated two million Spanish-speaking schoolchildren in the U.S.

Acting on the ruling, the Department of Health, Education and Welfare in 1975 ordered schools to provide bilingual education for non-English-speaking children, under the threat of losing federal funds. Public school districts that had a significant population of such children were required to give students instruction in their native languages in basic subjects as well as special classes in English. Early in 1976, however, HEW modified the order, explaining that it had "misinterpreted" the Supreme Court's decision as a requirement for bilingual education. HEW said the ruling would serve as a voluntary guideline to school districts, which would be allowed to adopt their own programs for non-English-speaking students.

BUFFALO EVENING NEWS
Buffalo, N. Y., April 22, 1976

The Department of Health Education & Welfare has rightly modified the policy it laid down last year of forcing bilingualism on certain school districts in the nation. This meant that children's regular classes were conducted in languages other than English, which was taught only as a second language. Under its revised policy, HEW does not insist on bilingual classes.

The original HEW order was the result of a misinterpretation of a 1974 Supreme Court ruling that special education was required for some 1.1 million students in 26 states whose primary language was not English.

Apparently it never occurred to HEW that the best thing it could do for children who couldn't speak English would be to teach them English — not as a sort of optional "second language" but as the main language of instruction.

In an English-speaking country, HEW does no favor to children by encouraging them to grow up without a good grasp of English. America is known as a melting pot of peoples, and President Ford has rightly spoken of the "great treasure" of the U.S. "ethnic heritage." But our common language is one of the major cultural influences that draws us together, and without that there would have been not a melting pot but a series of linguistic and cultural enclaves, resistant to change.

So HEW would be better attuned to the American tradition if it revised its policies further. Instead of merely not insisting on bilingual classes, it should be insisting that every school child learn English as part of his American heritage — and provide the non-English-speaking with extra aid and enrichment to facilitate this.

Houston Chronicle
Houston, Texas, April 23, 1976

Our sympathy is extended to school administrators who must deal with the U.S. Department of Health, Education and Welfare on the bilingual issue.

In a 1974 case, the U.S. Supreme Court decided that children have the right to be taught in a language they understand. The educators, who long recognized the problem, of course, waited for an explanation of how this ruling would be interpreted. HEW came out with an emphatic document which was taken to mean bilingual programs were mandated. The understanding was that Washington was telling school districts that students whose primary language is not English must be taught history, math and other subjects for years in their mother tongues rather than let the schools stress special English instruction.

This order caused considerable consternation and much debate. Educators were looking at expenditures of millions of dollars and questioning what the results would be in terms of learning and culture.

Costs of bilingual education are considerably higher—up to $400 per student. Competent teachers are difficult to find and there is the expense of training others. Critics also questioned whether education in a language other than English would tend to polarize the students and asked what had happened to the "melting pot" approach to immigrant children. If a student remains dependent upon the foreign language, would he not be handicapped in dealing with all the other aspects of American life?

The federal government, which has appropriated up to $450 million for bilingual education through a variety of agencies, kept the issue clouded with regional directives.

Now, HEW has come out with an internal memo saying that the earlier policy satement was a matter of guidelines and should not be considered mandatory. Each district with a bilingual education problem is expected to show "that the remedies submitted will be effective to cure the violations." At the same time, an HEW official acknowledged that there are no conclusive studies showing the effects of bilingual education.

So educators have to be somewhat confused by what HEW expects. The ability of a bureaucrat to compound confusion is once again proven.

Actually, Texas is way ahead of the U.S. Supreme Court and HEW in this field. The Chronicle has supported bilingual education programs such as the ones approved by the Texas legislature.

The thrust of the Texas plan is to provide bilingual education until such a time as a student's mastery of English can allow education to proceed in that language.

Regardless of what some bureaucrat down the line in HEW writes in a memo, bilingual programs should be designed to help students get started and should work to eliminate a language barrier that could shut students out of the mainstream where they can learn, compete and hopefully prosper on equal footing with the rest of the citizens.

The Hartford Courant

Hartford, Conn., May 17, 1976

Because of anticipated education budget cuts Hartford's school children now may be denied some vital bilingual programs which only recently got underway. These teach non-English-speaking youngsters the academic subjects necessary for all children in the lower grades while they also are taught to speak English in special classes. By the time they are in fourth grade, if there has been continuity, the youngster should be ready to drop English classes and complete his education in English. In Hartford the greatest need is for teachers bilingual in Spanish but in other parts of the state other languages are involved.

If the City Council cuts up to $3 million from the Board of Education's $54.68 million budget request, it could mean a layoff for about 78 teachers. Under the rules of seniority, it can be expected that the last hired will be the first fired. Those bearing the brunt of the layoffs would be blacks and Puerto Ricans because they have the least seniority. Spanish-speaking teachers' removal could threaten the bilingual classes and create real problems for Superintendent Dr. Edythe J. Gaines who recently promised her commitment to a full and effective bilingual program despite the changed interpretation of the requirements for such programs by the Department of Health, Education and Welfare. HEW reversed its earlier mandate of bilingual classes saying the rule resulted from a "misunderstanding."

Fortunately for Hartford and its Spanish-speaking students, the local board and superintendent refuse to lower their standards just because the federal agency would diminish its emphasis on the special needs of some 5 million of the nation's Spanish-speaking children. Considering the resultant loss of job preparation, of financial independence and of opportunity to raise the standard of living for that many persons, the importance of bilingual education is put into better perspective.

In Hartford's school population, 24 per cent have Spanish surnames. That does not necessarily mean that they all cannot understand English but it does illustrate the potential for trouble.

The recent backtracking by HEW is a neat way to relieve the federal government from subsidizing bilingual education. However, that must not stop the state or local communities from making every effort to help their school children become English-speakers, whether they are among the Spanish, Italian, Portuguese or some other lingual background.

Educational research shows that schools allowing pupils to speak their native language in the primary grades and have teachers who can converse in this language have fewer dropouts than schools that insist on a single language from day one.

The situation serves to remind us that Americans are among the few peoples who are primarily single-language populations. In Aruba, by the time children have reached the tenth grade they know five languages. In this nation, too many Americans never even learn to speak English.

RAPID CITY JOURNAL—

Rapid City, S. D., April 23, 1976

Another example of a federal agency exceeding its authority by going beyond the intent of a law or court decision has come to light.

The incident helps explain some of the mistrust of federal government which is a factor in this political year.

In 1974 the U.S. Supreme Court ruled on a case involving Chinese-speaking students in San Francisco's public schools. The issue was whether the students should be required to learn in English or should there be special programs for them in Chinese.

The Supreme Court ruled that teaching English to children of Chinese ancestry was one choice. Giving them instruction in Chinese was another. The court also said there may be other choices to afford equal educational opportunity.

The Department of Health, Education and Welfare interpreted the opinion as a mandate for bilingual education. A task force whose members were admitted advocates of bilingualism drew up a document calling for "remedies" to achieve equal educational opportunities for minorities. The document made it appear teaching in two languages was required.

More than a million students in some 333 school districts stood to be affected, including Indian youngsters in Rapid City.

Now that many school officials have been led to believe that pupils of foreign language groups had to be taught in two tongues, HEW has moved to clear up the confusion. It has circulated a memo affirming that it is not mandatory for school districts to provide bilingual instruction to children whose primary language is not English.

The bilingual-bicultural program in the Rapid City schools is still under study. It may be implemented if it is felt that such a program will contribute to an equal learning opportunity for Indian children.

But in view of the clarification by HEW, the decision will be a local one. It will be based on local conditions and resources rather than a bureaucratic mandate rising out of a faulty interpretation of a Supreme Court decision.

The incident points up the need for Congress to curb the power of federal agencies to write regulations, guidelines and remedies which have only a tenuous basis, or no basis at all, in law.

Failure to do so will contribute to the "anti-Washington" feeling becoming a permanent and harmful ingredient of national thought.

DESERET NEWS

Salt Lake City, Utah, April 8, 1976

Are children discriminated against and denied equal educational opportunities if their primary language is not English and they are not instructed in their own language?

The Department of Health, Education and Welfare says so, and is busily finding examples of supposed laxness in Utah. And the result is promising to increase difficulties for many of Utah's school districts.

In Davis County, for instance, several Thai children have moved in who are dependents of members of the Air Force wing shifted from Thailand to Hill Air Force Base. A Thai-speaking instructor must be found so they can be taught in their native tongue.

HEW's rules constitute an experiment without precedent either in the world or in history. Even at the height of English colonialism, those who went to English schools were expected to learn and be taught in English.

Throughout U.S. history, the "melting pot" idea worked well as those immigrants who hoped to find jobs had to learn English or work at such menial tasks a knowledge of English was not essential.

That should help point out some of the absurdities of the present law. If students are taught in their native language, where and when will they learn English? And how will they be assimilated into the job market at their true potential?

Furthermore, is delaying the time when they must learn English not a discrimination in itself?

Certainly instruction in their native language can be helpful, but only if it's a step toward learning to speak and write English as soon as possible.

The Washington Star

Washington, D. C., April 21, 1976

After working school officials all over the country into a lather over the possibility of losing federal aid if they didn't provide bilingual instruction for students whose mother tongue isn't English, the Department of Health, Education and Welfare has decided that such instruction is not mandatory.

It seems that an HEW task force, whose members were big on bilingual education, decided that a 1974 Supreme Court ruling required bilingual programs so that children who spoke little or no English would receive equal education opportunity. With a policy paper drafted by the task force, HEW officials began to warn school juridictions that if they didn't get with it on bilingual instruction, they were going to be cut off from the education money tree.

Never mind that it would be enormously expensive for jurisdictions like Arlington, Fairfax and Prince Georges Counties, and hundreds of others across the nation, to provide bilingual instruction. Arlington, for example, has only a few hundred non-English speaking students but among them are children who speak a total of 52 different languages. Requiring the county to set up special classes to teach each of these students in their native tongues would be a gross imposition on the school system and the taxpayers.

Most school systems do try to identify students who have trouble speaking English and to give special tutoring to those who have difficulty keeping up. But that was not satisfactory to the powers at HEW.

Well, it turns out that the Supreme Court didn't mandate bilingual education. The court said that bilingual instruction is one approach that might be applied, that giving special instruction in speaking English is another, and that there may be others.

HEW has sent out a memo to "clarify" a "misunderstanding." A department official said the new memo "is intended to point out that the legal obligation is to eliminate the language barrier and the method is up to the school district."

This is another example of Washington bureaucrats, who didn't know what they were talking about — or worse, knew but proceeded as they pleased — trying to tell local boards of education how to run their schools.

The Des Moines Register

Des Moines, Iowa, April 1, 1976

The Governor's Spanish-Speaking Task Force has issued a report which concludes that the 30,000 Spanish-speaking Iowans have been victims of discrimination and neglect. They are more likely than most Iowans to drop out of high school, fall below the poverty line, live in inadequate housing and have difficulty obtaining assistance from the government.

The task force suggests that many of the problems stem from inadequate education. Some of the children of Spanish-speaking parents have difficulty speaking English when they first come to school. The task force found that Iowa schools generally fail to recognize the unique adjustment problems created by the Spanish-speaking pupils' cultural background. This failure helps explains why a disproportionate number of Spanish-speaking students are classified as slow learners. The 1970 Census reported that 42 per cent of Spanish-speaking Iowans between the ages of 18 and 24 had not completed high school.

Lack of an adequate education traps many Spanish-speaking Iowans in low-paying jobs (35 per cent of Spanish-speaking families in Iowa earn less than the poverty level) and poor housing. Thus they are more likely to be eligible for government social assistance. But the task force found that because of the linguistic barrier and other obstacles, Spanish-speaking Iowans actually receive proportionately less aid.

The task force recommends that Iowa create a commission to address the needs of Spanish-speaking people. Such a commission has been approved by the House Committee on State Government. It would be a positive step toward overcoming the neglect that has narrowed the lives of thousands of Spanish-speaking Iowans.

The Houston Post

Houston, Texas, December 1, 1976

The United States is an English-speaking nation and must guard this heritage. But it would be tremendously useful for Houston to become bilingual. All of us, Spanish and English speakers alike. We should see it as an opportunity for a fuller, more interesting life In fits and starts, the Houston public schools have led in the right direction, but we have a long way to go.

Back in the 1950s Houston began to offer early-morning Spanish classes to children whose parents had been clamoring for foreign language study to begin in elementary school. The classes were so popular that they were incorporated into the school day in several schools. By the time the children who began Spanish in second grade got to high school, they were so advanced that they forced a complete revision of the high school Spanish courses. Then, suddenly, the school board cut the program as an unnecessary frill. Ever since, Houston children have had to wait until junior high for their first foreign language training. This is too late for most students to perfect an accent.

Meanwhile, the Houston school administration saw that increasing numbers of first graders spoke Spanish with no knowledge of English. Long before the Supreme Court ruling required American school systems to provide bilingual education, Houston schools began recruiting bilingual teachers to help give a good start in kindergarten and first grade to Spanish-speaking pupils. This work goes on.

But Houston has many lacks. A survey of 54 city departments showed that only half have Spanish-speaking staff members to answer queries from callers who speak only Spanish. The Chicana Association for Reform and Advocacy found that 81 per cent of the questions asked in English were answered in three minutes, compared to only 14 per cent of those in Spanish. In Six departments that cope with emergencies, only one could offer someone who spoke Spanish — the Rabies Control Department after five transfers.

Houston is not only a gateway city for Spanish America, but a host city to thousands of Spanish-speaking visitors coming to the Texas Medical Center and surrounding clinics, to our universities or to do business or shop. Many employes in the Medical Center are trying to learn Spanish because they feel the need in their work. But the Houston Intercontinental Airport offers scant help to Spanish-speaking arrivals. The airport needs more signs in Spanish and more Spanish-speaking employes in information booths and other parts of the airport.

But — and this is an important point — in our schools, our first goal must be to teach English to Spanish-speaking children and adults. It will be to their advantage as well as ours. English is the world's most useful language. More technical and scientific knowledge can be found in English than in any other language. But for the enrichment of Houston's culture and for our enjoyment of the Spanish Americans who come here, English-speaking Houstonians need to learn Spanish. *Se habla espanol.*

Bilingual Programs Multiply; So Do Doubts Over Effectiveness

After the 1974 Supreme Court decision declaring bilingual education a student's right, school districts throughout the nation organized programs in a variety of languages, including American Indian and Eskimo. By far the largest number of bilingually taught pupils were Spanish-speaking. The 1968 Bilingual Education Act was renewed in 1974, spurring numerous lawsuits by Hispanic groups to institute bilingual education programs in local schools. The result was a bewildering array of programs, which lacked consistency and were often taught by poorly trained educators. Bilingual programs produced enormous controversy over the legitimacy of teaching children in a foreign language in a country whose national tongue was English. In addition, they were not warmly received by local school boards annoyed over the added expense. Washington had issued the guidelines but provided only minimal funds for implementing them.

THE INDIANAPOLIS STAR
Indianapolis, Ind., September 22, 1977

At a time when it's fashionable to promote bilingualism in education, David Gonzalez, a native of Puerto Rico, has sounded a welcome note.

As welfare director of Bridgeport, Conn., Gonzalez has ordered all able-bodied non-English-speaking welfare recipients to enroll in free English classes or lose their welfare checks.

This naturally has created an uproar.

State welfare officials are questioning the legality of the order, and several civil rights organizations are threatening court action against it.

However, we find Gonzalez's reasoning flawless.

It's all but impossible for anyone who can't speak English to find a job, he says. Anyone who won't take whatever steps are necessary to find a job isn't deserving of welfare.

About 150 Spanish-speaking men and women have already signed up for the free English classes. Whether it's because they don't want Gonzalez to kick them off welfare or because they realize Gonzalez is right about the difficulty they will have getting a job unless they learn English, we don't know.

We hope it's the latter.

Minneapolis Tribune
Minneapolis, Minn., January 22, 1977

To understand the complaints of some Mexican-American parents about the difficulties their children have in school, imagine a low-income English-speaking family moving to Greece without knowing how to read Greek. The school authorities there would insist that the children learn Greek at the same time that they were trying to keep up with their classmates in literature, science and social studies. There would be no instruction in those subjects in English, however, so the children would be at a disadvantage not only in the classroom, but also after they left school and went looking for jobs.

In the Twin Cities, many Spanish-speaking parents say — correctly, we believe — that the failure of schools to start their children's instruction in their first spoken language harms the children. A group of St. Paul parents last year sued the school district for not providing an adequate bilingual-bicultural program. It is unfortunate that such efforts come at a time when school districts, including St. Paul, are strapped for money, but they are valid nonetheless.

The U.S. Supreme Court's landmark Brown vs. Board of Education decision requires that states compensate for inequities among children. Because some foreign-language-speaking children in Minnesota have been hampered by language and cultural barriers, they have not had equal access to educational resources. Gov. Rudy Perpich is an example of how a non-English-speaking child can overcome that handicap, but such examples are too rare. In today's society, most children without a background of spoken English at home need help. The goal of a bilingual-bicultural program is to teach them to communicate, relate and learn in English.

The cost of a bilingual-bicultural program for Minneapolis's 450 students from non-English-speaking homes would be about $900,000. Because federal aid is not available for such a small number (the federal government seeks to fund districts with much heavier concentrations of such students), it is up to the state to provide funds. So the Minneapolis school district has joined the Spanish-speaking community in supporting a bilingual-bicultural bill in the Legislature. The Legislature this year is expected to be cautious about approving new programs, but as it considers the dollar costs of attacking this special-education problem, it should also consider the intangible social costs of not helping.

The Cleveland Press
Cleveland, Ohio, May 4, 1977

For several years the Federal Government has been pouring tens of millions of dollars into special classes — taught in Spanish, Chinese, Navajo or some other language — for children from non-English-speaking backgrounds who have difficulty with English in the public schools.

The object of the program is to ease children into English instruction gradually so they don't become discouraged and perhaps, even drop out of school.

Yet a new study of bilingual education seems to show that these children do as well or better when they're thrust into regular classes and required to learn English as quickly as possible.

The study, conducted by the American Institutes for Research among 7700 students in 300 elementary schools, uncovered little evidence that teaching in a foreign language is beneficial.

In fact, students taught in these special classes often tended to learn English more slowly than students from similar backgrounds who attended regular classes from the beginning.

By all means, a student who has difficulty reading, writing or speaking English should have the extra tutoring he needs to catch up.

But for all practical purposes — from earning a living to shopping in a store — this is an English-speaking society. And the sooner a child is able to master the English language, the better off he's likely to be.

Anchorage Daily Times

Anchorage, Alas., October 16, 1977

THE U.S. OFFICE for Civil Rights seems determined to play the villain in the continuing controversy over bilingual education in Alaska's schools.

The inane struggle reached the farce level recently when Marshall Lind, Alaska's commissioner of education, wrote the office's director in Washington, D.C., "I can only conclude that OCR has decided to act in a manner directly contrary to the law."

Mr. Lind's decision to do battle with the intransigent agency resulted from a recent federal court ruling that it cannot penalize the innocent along with the guilty in withholding education funds.

About $18 million in federal funds has been received by 16 Alaska school districts allegedly in noncompliance with federal regulations. Millions in additional aid will be in jeopardy if the agency refuses to come to its senses.

COMMISSIONER LIND profiled the nightmare world of bureaucracy when he reported to the civil rights director that "The entire basis for OCR's imposition of sanctions (is) its allegations that the former Alaska Unorganized Borough School District failed to provide OCR with certain timely and accurate data."

Because an agency which no longer existed failed to meet a request, which may or may not have been reasonable, the federal civil rights agency began issuing its noncompliance rulings in November 1975.

The State of Alaska subsequently developed three handbooks for bilingual education, all of which were rejected by the civil rights office. A fourth is now being developed by the state's Department of Education in the hope that it will win the federal agency's blessing.

Although it claims that the bilingual programs in scores of Alaska schools have been "infected by illegal discrimination," the federal czars have refused to make district-by-district findings on just what the illegalities are. The districts find themselves hard-pressed to defend themselves against charges which aren't spelled out.

Many of the districts involved are dominated by native school boards that can be expected to demand that their children get the bilingual education which in their judgment is at a proper level.

THE FRUSTRATION of Alaskans in the northwest with the state-federal bilingual battle was demonstrated at a recent hearing in Kotzebue when witnesses testified that the school district there has a bilingual program better than the one proposed in the state's 200-page handbook.

They argued that giving the handbook preference over the locally developed guidelines would usurp the school board's authority.

The Kotzebue hearing also disclosed that the school district, which is in a fund-losing position, has never been investigated for noncompliance.

Resolution of the ridiculous two-year-old controversy may come only after a federal administrative hearing officer takes testimony on the matter at an Anchorage hearing on Oct. 31.

We hope the boldness demonstrated by Commissioner Lind in challenging the arbitrary actions of these unknowing and arbitrary federal bureaucrats will continue when Alaskan witnesses appear at the hearing. The bilingual farce has demonstrated that patience, consideration and reasonableness are negative virtues when dealing with an autocratic federal agency.

Rocky Mountain News

Denver, Colo., February 14, 1977

WE HAVE BEEN hard pressed to find a legitimate reason for the Colorado Legislature's grossly insensitive mauling of the state's bilingual-bicultural education program.

Rarely has a program offered so much promise of educational achievement for so little money. Bilingual-bicultural education is as important to Colorado Chicanos in 1977 as desegregation of schools was to southern blacks in the 1960s.

It is a proven method of overcoming the monumental learning problems of children whose first language is not English.

And yet, attempts have been made in the House to severely cripple the program by making it optional rather than mandatory. And the legislative Joint Budget Committee, complaining about inadequate data, slashed $1 million from the program's meager $3.1 million budget request.

We are as opposed as anyone to government mismanagement and wasteful spending. But such concerns don't adequately explain the intensity of some of the legislative opposition to the bilingual program.

Sen. Paul Sandoval, D-Denver, one of the primary sponsors of the two-year-old program, has labeled attempts to weaken bilingual education as "racist."

Perhaps. But we prefer the explanation of Ernest Andrade, director of the bilingual-bicultural education program for the Greeley Public Schools. He says those who are against the program either don't understand it or have a "deep prejudice" that can't be shaken.

If the legislators would bother to visit a bilingual school they would find that Colorado's largest minority is at last being given an equal educational opportunity – for the first time in the history of the state.

Nationally it is estimated there are five million children unable to compete successfully in school because of their difficulty with English. And the Spanish-speaking minority – the country's largest language minority – has the worst record of academic achievement.

But it is not merely the Chicano children who benefit from a bilingual program. The Anglo children, the black children, also gain. They can be exposed to another culture, another language – yet never at the expense of their own.

It's time for legislators to end their mindless bickering and realize that bilingual education is a rare opportunity to free thousands of Colorado children from almost certain failure in a system they can't understand.

Denver, Colo., June 2, 1977

THE COLORADO HOUSE deserves credit for accepting a compromise aimed at salvaging the state's bilingual-bicultural education program and ending one of the session's most bitter controversies.

The compromise was engineered by House Minority Leader Ruben Valdez, D-Denver, with assistance from House Speaker Ron Strahle, R-Fort Collins. Hopefully the agreement will now be accepted by the Senate and signed into law by Gov. Dick Lamm.

Lamm correctly vetoed an earlier GOP effort to change the bilingual program, noting that it deserved at least a two-year track record before being altered.

But the Senate then attached the proposal to the program's appropriation request in an attempt to force Lamm to approve the bill or kill the entire funding.

This backhanded scheme made it through two committees in the House when Valdez fashioned a compromise which appears to satisfy major Republican objections to the program without crippling it.

The agreement is a good one in that it clarifies several ambiguities in the original bilingual law while retaining safeguards to prevent children from being removed from the program prematurely.

We are disappointed the House rejected Valdez's attempt to increase the program's funding from $2.5 million to last year's level of $3.1 million.

Nevertheless, the compromise – if agreed to by the Senate – will at least insure that thousands of Colorado youngsters will not be denied the bilingual assistance they so desperately need to succeed in school.

We would have preferred no changes at all in the bilingual program this year. But demands from Republican legislators – traditional guardians of the status quo – to alter the program were not to be denied.

In the face of such opposition, the Valdez compromise is the best supporters of bilingual education can expect from this year's Legislature.

WORCESTER TELEGRAM
Worcester, Mass., September 9, 1977

It's been nearly a decade since Congress enacted the Bilingual Education Act. Since then, it has become a common yet controversial feature of American education.

Its critics, including many educators, say that bilingual education magnifies differences among ethnic groups and hinders rather than facilitates the assimilation of non-English speaking persons. Others are concerned about its cost at a time when schools are forced to cut back on music, art, athletics and other special programs.

Supporters of bilingual education dismiss these claims as exaggerated. Says Don Wong, director of the Chinese American Heritage Projects in San Francisco: "It's not an attempt to compete with the English language. It's a bridge for language minorities to gain equal access and participation in American society."

The U.S. Office of Education estimates that as many as 3.6 million school-age children have English-language difficulties. Despite the growth of bilingual programs — and the amount of public money being spent on them — there is little evidence of the effectiveness of bilingual education. A recent study conducted by the American Institute for Research in the Behavioral Sciences found that Spanish-speaking children enrolled in 38 bilingual programs were not learning to speak and read English as quickly as students who were picking it up on their own.

There is a shortage of textbooks and qualified teachers. According to a recent report by the General Accounting Office, only 27 per cent of the teachers involved in the projects the GAO surveyed had received any college training to teach in bilingual classrooms. What's more, only about 65 per cent were bilingual themselves.

Most bilingual programs fall into one of two categories. So-called "transitional" programs are designed to bring the language-minority child into the mainstream of society as quickly as possible. Such an education is considered temporary, to be used only until the child is "caught up" with English-speaking children.

"Maintenance programs," on the other hand, have a much broader purpose. They strive to educate the students as "bilingual-bicultural" citizens. The two languages and cultures are given equal importance and both languages are used, permanently, as mediums of instruction.

Supporters of bilingual education say nothing short of the maintenance approach will do. They advocate "cultural pluralism."

The results so far indicate no need for escalation. It is not the federal government's responsibility to finance and promote the teaching of ethnic languages and culture on a permanent basis. Prof. William G. Milan of Columbia University sums up the views of many in the field when he states that maintenance education "much too often sets as its primary goal the preservation of the mother tongue at the expense of a good quality education."

It is one thing to help a non-English-speaking youngster learn the language of the land as quickly as possible. But relegating him or her to permanent second-class citizenship through easy-way-out bilingual programs is another. Leaders of ethnic groups should be the first to realize that.

Sooner or later educational authorities in this country will sit down and sort out the problems of classroom teaching and declining standards. When they do, bilingual studies ought to be given a lot of attention.

THE MILWAUKEE JOURNAL
Milwaukee, Wisc., June 26, 1977

Officially supported bilingualism is new in this country — a policy that government grabbed at in response to the wave of ethnic awareness that has hit the US. Now it is time to think about where the nation should go with this program. Some of the long range consequences of official bilingualism could be severe.

We are not implying that bilingualism is bad per se. On the contrary, it is deplorable that, as the world grows smaller, most Americans are able to communicate only in English. The nation should become more aware of other languages and how to use them.

Nor are we claiming that bilingualism never was present in the US. This is a nation of immigrants. Little Mexicos, Polands, Italys and Germanys have always existed in many cities and in some rural areas. Bilingualism informally has been with us since Europeans first landed here.

But until 1968 the federal government never deliberately promoted bilingualism. Even then, Congress did not intend a drastic departure when it approved the Bilingual Education Act. In a multiethnic, multiracial society, English was viewed as the unifying force. Bilingual education was meant to bridge the gap for non-English speaking children until they could learn English and use it effectively. However, it is not clear that this has been the result.

Much confusion exists in practical application of the program. In some cases, the original legislative goal is twisted. Instead of acting as a bridge to English proficiency, the program is primarily used to maintain the other language and culture as a divergent force.

And even where bilingual programs are applied as originally intended, nationwide evidence so far casts doubt on effectiveness. Non-English speaking pupils may not be "catching up" any faster than if the programs did not exist. Thus it should be asked whether there are other ways to attack this legitimate educational problem.

Surely there are perils in using a bilingual policy to perpetuate cultural separatism, based on language. Americans need only look north to Canada and the French speaking province of Quebec. Canadian political unity is being stretched to the breaking point by the divisions between English and French speaking cultures.

A similar potential exists in this country. Present bilingual programs are chiefly aimed at Spanish speaking Americans. The Census Bureau estimates that there are about 11.2 million people of Latin descent in the country, with about 60% of them concentrated in the Southwest. The total is growing at about 300,000 a year. However, the bureau admits its figures are conservative because of the unknown numbers of illegal aliens in the country, many of whom enter from Mexico. The estimates for illegal aliens range from 2 million to 12 million, though the number who actually stay permanently in the US is believed near the lower figure. Most "illegals" seek moneymaking jobs and then return home.

In any case, the danger is that the nation could one day find itself with a large Latin enclave with cultural and language aspirations similar to Quebec's. True, the growing dispersion of Spanish speaking residents away from the Southwest mitigates against a geographic enclave. Nevertheless, national bilingual policy, while properly supporting cultural diversity, should not promote excessive cultural separation.

A good, tough look needs to be taken at what bilingual policy is achieving and where it is heading. Whatever form bilingual programs may take in the future, the goals should not deviate from initial intent — providing transition to English fluency. This does not mean destruction of cultural pluralism or ethnic pride. There is plenty of room for them to grow. Nor does it mean that bilingual capability should be de-emphasized. All of this enriches the American experience and an integrated society. What a national bilingual policy should recognize is that a multiethnic, multicultural America can best flourish through use of one unifying language.

THE DENVER POST

Denver, Colo., May 5, 1977

The Colorado Senate has joined the House of Representatives in making changes in Colorado's two-year-old bilingual education law. Despite heated debate, the changes do not greatly alter the scope of the program.

If the assembly now funds the program adequately, the changes can be useful by providing more specific guidelines to the state's bilingual policy.

Since the 1975 act was passed there has been debate over its aims.

Some thought it required the state to finance in a positive way an ongoing program emphasizing other languages besides English throughout the pupil's school years.

Other people insisted the state's involvement, through state appropriations to local school districts, was to be transitional. It was to help pupils with linguistic differences to achieve better facility in English.

House Bill 1146, now passed by both houses, mandates the State Board of Education, which supervises the program, to make the program transitional.

Another ambiguity involved the question of qualification of pupils for a state-funded program. One section of the 1975 law said programs were required of districts on the basis of cultural "and" linguistic differences.

Another section bridged the two qualifications with the word "or." The difference is quite significant.

Many Hispano-surnamed youngsters have little linguistic difference from other pupils but their surname can be interpreted as a cultural difference.

The assembly has decided the matter by saying in all instances that a program shall be provided where both differences are present.

Otherwise, the qualification is unchanged. Under the new wording a school district must offer a bilingual education program if 50 students or 10 per cent of its kindergarten through third-grade enrollment is identified as "linguistically *and* culturally different."

By saying a school district must reach these threshold levels with pupils who have both language and cultural differences the number of qualified schools drop from about 187 to 144.

The number of Colorado pupils who will no longer receive a state-ordered bilingual program drops by 1,300 from the present 13,000.

This is not a great number. Importantly another section of the 1975 law remains intact: Anywhere in Colorado where a pupil has major difficulties in schooling because of language, a special effort, somewhat like tutoring, will be provided. But the program won't have to be schoolwide if the percentage of pupils is small.

The change does make the law more specific in its intentions. And if the assembly will maintain a good level of funding the reductions need not hurt.

Above all, the changes should not be used as an excuse for reduction of funds. The present budget of $3.1 million is a good budget. Keeping the spending at that level, instead of slashing it as the assembly has proposed, will insure the program can go forward in a constructive way.

A good level of funding would demonstrate that the assembly's intention is to maintain a good level of bilingual instruction in Colorado, while curbing some of the more exploratory efforts some people are asking of the program.

The program is working. It is bringing parental involvement into school programs to a heartening degree. It would be a shame to undo any of the good things the program has done.

Chicago Tribune

Chicago, Ill., September 11, 1977

The latest eruptions of bilingual education as an issue in Canada and in New York should be taken as a warning in Chicago, where the issue has arisen in a so far much less virulent form.

In Chicago, the official goal is clear and sensible: namely to offer bilingual education only as an auxiliary measure to help Spanish-speaking children keep up with their schoolwork while they are learning English. In theory, at least, it is a temporary program which will be phased out when and if there is an end to the flood of Spanish-speaking immigrants [many of whom have entered the country illegally].

But there are many who, shortsightedly, prefer to look on bilingual education as a permanent feature of a bilingual society. In Brentwood, N.Y., a Long Island suburb with a large concentration of Puerto Ricans, the issue at the moment is whether to keep what has become an almost wholly autonomous Spanish-speaking school program started four years ago with federal aid.

The issue arises because voters have refused to provide more tax money for their schools but have protested the school's resulting effort to trim its teaching staff. The teachers who would be dismissed are those with low seniority and include most of the Spanish-speaking teachers. In a temporary ruling, a federal court has enjoined the schools from thus crippling the bilingual program.

But in practice, the program can hardly be called bilingual. Large segments of school life are carried on solely in Spanish; English is treated rather as a second language. Some graduates are so poor at English they are having trouble getting in to American universities.

Meanwhile in Canada, where the federal government has tried to appease the French-speaking people of Quebec by making both French and English the official languages throughout the country, Quebec has responded by outlawing English-speaking schools except for those already in them; in the future English-speaking newcomers will have to go to French schools. There are already rumbles of rebellion, and this, in turn, has strengthened the French movement for independence.

The world offers few successful examples of multilingualism; Switzerland is the only one, in fact, that comes immediately to mind. Elsewhere, linguistic minorities have become political minorities as well, sometimes even calling for separatism: the Basques in France and Spain, the Tyroleans in Italy; the Welsh in Britain; the Flemish in Belgium. The Soviet Union has had trouble suppressing the national feelings of its linguistic minorities—and suppressing the news of its failures. India has tried in vain to establish a national language to do away with a multitude of local dialects.

On the other hand there are a number of examples where, as in the United States, immigrants have been successfully assimilated linguistically while often retaining other cultural traditions: the Germans in Brazil, the Italians in Argentina, and the Irish in Chile 'Chile's national hero is its founder, Bernardo O'Higgins].

Those who come to this country in search of freedom, and then seek to perpetuate their isolation from the rest of the country, forget that our freedoms have thrived because our union was secure. When a country is threatened by ethnic unrest and separatist movements, freedom is likely to suffer.

The Evening Gazette

Worcester, Mass., June 21, 1977

The Worcester public school system has about 600 students enrolled in bilingual classes. Of those, about 425 speak Spanish and about 125 speak Greek as a first language.

The program — mandated by a 1972 state law — will be beefed up next year and shifted to the schools in the Great Brook Valley area. Clark Street School already has bilingual classes. St. Nicholas Avenue School will start bilingual classes in the fall. There has been a considerable migration of Hispanic families from the Main South neighborhood to Great Brook Valley.

But is bilingualism the best way to go?

A recent report by Noel Epstein in The Washington Post told of the mixed marks the national bilingual education program has been getting from evaluators.

According to Epstein, some studies show that children in bilingual programs advance more slowly than children in straight English programs, at least in some schools. And in some places the bilingual program is seen by Hispanic parents as more a means to maintain the use of Spanish than a transition step to English.

John Corcoran, who heads up Worcester's bilingual program, is aware of the criticisms. But he firmly believes that the program here has proved its value. He points to the improved school attendance record of Hispanic students, and the academic progress they are making, as strong indications that the program should be continued.

Millions of Americans whose ancestors had to struggle as best they could to learn English feel that the sink-or-swim method is the best. They would make no concession to any other language. But educators disagree. No one knows, they say, how many new immigrants failed the brutal language test and were shunted aside into less productive lives.

The key point, it seems to us, is that the bilingual program be understood as transitional — a bridge between the use of Spanish (or Greek) and the use of English. Some Spanish-speaking parents feel otherwise. They want the Spanish language and culture to be maintained by the schools. But this is impractical. That part of it must be done in the home, as has always been the case.

We Americans seldom refer to the "melting pot" any longer. We have come to understand that ethnic and cultural diversity is possible and desirable in this large and easy-going country.

But it is also clear to most that English is and will be the essential tongue for the American people. There is no substitute, and no one should pretend otherwise. Competency in more than one language is an excellent thing, and should be encouraged. But the primary purpose of any school bilingual program must be proficiency in English.

Education Office Report Criticizes Bilingual Program

Evaluation of bilingual education followed slowly in the wake of the outpouring of guidelines and funds. The first official study did not appear until May 1978. It was issued by the Office of Education (of the Health, Education and Welfare Department) and surveyed 38 Spanish-language programs during the 1975–76 school year. The EO found several "shortcomings" in the programs, among them the discovery that only one-third of the students had major problems with English and 85% of them were kept in bilingual classes even after they had mastered enough English to join regular classes. A private study released at the same time reported little difference between the achievements of Hispanic students in regular and bilingual programs, except that the bilingual students were slightly ahead in mathematics and slightly behind in English.

The EO quickly tightened regulations for bilingual programs as a result of its findings. Students in bilingual classes had to be "significantly limited" in using English, not just accustomed to speaking a foreign language. The focus of bilingual education was narrowed to giving non-English-speaking children competence in English, rather than helping them with the rest of their school subjects. The EO also authorized funds for developing bilingual curriculums. Annual spending on bilingual education had mushroomed in 10 years to $150 million from $7.5 million.

The Miami Herald
Miami, Fla., June 4, 1978

IT IS HARDLY surprising that Hispanic students in Dade County's eight "bilingual" elementary schools are learning English faster than English-speaking students are learning Spanish. What is disappointing is that some Anglo parents see this limited success in teaching Spanish as reason for doing away with bilingualism.

That would be a serious mistake. Although we do not advocate mandatory bilingualism, we do believe bilingualism should be encouraged wherever possible. Bilingualism helps each culture to appreciate the other, to obvious advantage. Its importance in the marketplace is increasing, an obvious spur to learning both languages.

We submit that the disparity in rates of learning in the bilingual schools is attributable less to the schools' shortcomings than to the county's cultural mix. While nearly a third of Dade County's population is Spanish-speaking, English remains the dominant cultural force.

So most students, Latin or Anglo, encounter more English than Spanish language throughout the day. Thus a Spanish-speaking student will tend to learn more English by cultural osmosis, so to speak, than an English-speaking student will learn Spanish.

We agree with Dade School Board member Holmes Braddock that "learning Spanish is a survival skill." As the flow of Latin American tourists into Dade County increases, and as Dade's business ties with Latin America get stronger, the bilingual job applicant will have a distinct advantage. This alone will motivate more young people of both cultures to become bilingual.

There are, of course, persons in both cultures who resent the other's language. While this resentment is perhaps understandable, it is also short-sighted. For resentment cannot alter the fact that Dade County is a bicultural community and that each culture is here to stay.

Therefore, whatever the schools can do to encourage bilingualism deserves encouragement, patience, and support.

THE SAGINAW NEWS
Saginaw, Mich., January 8, 1978

A new infusion of federal funds amounting to millions statewide for bilingual education programs is one of the nicest pieces of news we know of to begin a new year.

We're particularly encouraged by the amount of money coming into this area from the state as part of a nationwide $84 million federal appropriation.

Bringing it to the bottom line, the Saginaw School District will get just under $166,000.

Buena Vista, Carrollton and Bay City schools will share $178,000 for an experimental program aimed at kindergarten and first grade youngsters.

Equally important, Saginaw Valley State College will get a part of $400,000 to be distributed to five state colleges and universities for training certified bilingual education teachers.

The latter is vital for two reasons. Certification is required by 1974 state law which established bilingual education in the public schools. And a lack of certified teachers in the early stages of the program in Saginaw was one of the things that concerned the U.S. Department of Health, Education and Welfare.

The lower schools which have to provide this program where there are significant numbers students who speak essentially Spanish, for example, will welcome continued federal support to the colleges who train teachers in bilingualism.

While the grant for Saginaw schools is not quite as large as requested, what is due this year will help strengthen city bilingual education.

As we've said so often before, this is a most worthy program.

For the student who comes to school with limited or no real acquaintance of English — only because Spanish is spoken in the home — bilingual teaching bridges the gap that has historically trapped too many young people in educational failure at the outset.

The Providence Journal

Providence, R. I., May 17, 1978

Before anyone categorically denounces bilingual education programs and demands an end to federal financing on the basis of a recent report released by the U.S. Office of Education, it might be smart to stop and count to 10 ... and then breathe deeply:

1. While the study found that students taught in their native language did no better than others of similar background enrolled in traditional classes, the sample was relatively small and both successful and unsuccessful programs were lumped together.

2. The study found that fewer than a third of the students enrolled in bilingual programs were "significantly limited in their command of the English language." But only 5,300 students were surveyed out of 253,000 enrolled nationwide and several million in all with language problems.

3. In 1975 and 1976, the years covered by the study, 85 percent were kept in bilingual classes after they were capable of learning in English. But since then regulations have been tightened, limiting programs to those with significant language problems.

4. It would be as absurd to expect children who don't speak English to learn from an English-speaking teacher as it would be to put a hearing-disabled student in a class with a teacher who didn't know sign language.

5. While it is true that making language demands upon a foreign student will help him or her to learn English, such demands ought to be balanced to facilitate academic achievement.

6. In Rhode Island, students of a foreign tongue are taught English in one class and all other subjects in their native language.

7. Some 2,000 students in Rhode Island are enrolled in Portuguese and Spanish bilingual programs in 10 communities.

8. Uncle Sam provides about $1.5 million a year to help youngsters in this state bridge the language gap.

9. There is no question that bilingual programs around the country can be improved; the Office of Education's $1.5-million study makes that clear.

10. Clear also is the misleading nature of the study's findings which seems to suggest that bilingual education is a waste of time. It simply isn't true.

Now, breathe deeply.

THE DAILY OKLAHOMAN

Oklahoma City, Okla., July 14, 1978

NOT that more horrible examples were needed, but evidence continues to accumulate that many of the dollars we have expended on various social welfare and education programs have been wasted.

Usually the horror stories have been revealed by investigative reporters and, increasingly in recent years, by documented studies conducted by scholars and research institutions with impeccable academic credentials.

Now even the federal bureaucracy itself is beginning to wake up and concede some of its glaring failures. A recent example is a $1.5 million study, released by the U.S. Office of Education, which casts serious doubt about whether bilingual education projects have been successful or even necessary.

The idea was that Chicano and Puerto Rican children, and a few other minority groups whose primary home language was other than English, would benefit from a dual language approach in the classroom. Toward this end the federal government this year is spending $135 million and is budgeting $150 million for 564 bilingual projects that will enroll 253,000 children next year.

But the study indicates that fewer than a third of those enrolled in previous bilingual programs were significantly limited in their ability to speak and comprehend English, and that 85 percent of them were kept in special classes even after they were capable of learning in English.

Nor did the subsequent academic achievement of the bilingual class students indicate any improvement over those who were taught in traditional classes.

Foreign language instruction certainly has a place in our schools. But this study confirms the judgment of those who have insisted all along that the teaching emphasis should be in the dominant language of our country.

Detroit Free Press

Detroit, Mich., January 15, 1978

NOW THAT Michigan is into the third year of its bilingual education program, it seems clear that major renovations are in order. In our view, the main fault is not that the program is underfunded, as it clearly is, but that it was badly drawn in the first place.

The state law says that any school district with as many as 20 students whose primary language is not English, and who speak the same language, must provide them with a bilingual education program. That is without regard for their grade levels or how scattered they may be in the school district.

This is a bad requirement. Because of inadequate funding, it almost inevitably results in many school districts' going through the motions on bilingual education without doing what the law seems to really require. The bilingual programs now reach 18,000 students, of 23 language groups, in 62 school systems. The state director of the program, Renato Gonzalez, says the state now spends about $3 million annually on this but should spend at least $12 million to do the job well.

Is this a good allocation of dollars, even for the students involved? We doubt it, especially for Detroit, where apparently almost half the affected students are. The Detroit system's shortcomings simply in providing basic education suggest that the money could be used more wisely.

There also is a fundamental question about how far the schools should go in formal programs addressed to individual language groups. Under the present law, a system may be required to put teachers in the classroom to instruct students by using both English and, for instance, Icelandic, Arabic or Chaldean. A more practical approach would be to provide special help for these students to speak English without trying to do it through employing so many of their own languages.

Where there are large numbers of students from a particular language group—Spanish, for instance—that perhaps can be done best by having instructors who know both English and Spanish. But there should be room for some common-sense judgments on such matters.

What is happening, we think, is far beyond what the Legislature thought would result from its 20-student requirement. It should re-examine that number, as well as its specific requirements for how the program is to be conducted.

The Houston Post

Houston, Texas, July 9, 1978

Bilingual education is simple as an idea, incredibly complex to carry out. It was mandated in early 1974 by the Supreme Court on a case that began with Chinese children in San Francisco. But in Texas, New York City, Miami and such central cities as Chicago, bilingual education applies chiefly to Spanish-speaking children. The United States had more than 10 million Spanish-speaking people in 1975 — the fifth largest Spanish-speaking population in the world.

Foreseeing the need long ago, the Houston Independent School District made its start on bilingual education five years before the mandate. Then, and ever since, HISD has met and struggled with the complexities. Bilingual teachers, essential to the task, are small in number. It takes time to develop more. Bilingual classroom material does not grow on neighborhood bushes. The whole program is caught up in the diverse and often conflicting opinions of ethnic leaders. Withal, any school district hoping for federal aid must comply with the precise regulations laid down by federal agencies.

In 1973-74, HISD was busy teaching teachers to speak Spanish in special classes of 80 at a time. It was working with local universities to develop undergraduate and graduate programs leading to degrees in bilingual education. Intense though they were, these staffing efforts lost ground before the tidal wave of Spanish-speaking children flowing into Houston schools.

The Department of Health, Education and Welfare has declared Houston one of 50 Texas districts failing to meet HEW's standards in bilingual education. The district must find 50 or 60 more teachers to move from school to school where there are too few Spanish-speaking pupils or students to justify a full-time teacher. The district must spend an additional $750,000 to avoid losing as much as $3.5 million in federal funds. Superintendent Billy Reagan and the Houston School Board will surely do the best they can to come to terms with the federal department.

In all this brouhaha, both Houston and the federal agencies need to keep their goal in mind: To teach these children English as quickly as possible. No other generation of immigrants has been so favored. Germans, Czechs, Poles, Swedes, Chinese and Japanese have come to this country and learned English the hard way, thereby becoming Americans. Our Spanish-speaking immigrants, whether kindergartners or of high school age, must do the same. Nobody can hope to become a part of business, industry, the professions or community affairs without a complete command of the English language. English is the most important gift public education can offer.

Nevada State Journal

Reno, Nev., March 19, 1978

Sometimes it takes an extreme opinion to awaken people to a problem. It's not that they agree — it's that it alerts them to certain dangers.

Earlier this month, a Humboldt County school trustee complained of the growing number of children in Winnemucca schools who can't speak English.

He said he was tired of paying school taxes and seeing the education of his own children slowed by the growing number of Hispanic-American children in the system.

He suggested that Hispanics be segregated into special classes so that other children's education would not suffer.

The remark has been contested by J. Esteban Valle, executive director of the Latin American information Center in Reno.

He pointed to the value of the Hispanic labor force to the Winnemucca economy. "On the one hand they take advantage of this labor and on the other they indcit it for disrupting the schools. They want to take advantage of the situation without paying for it."

Valle is absolutely right. Nevada cannot reap the advantages of Hispanic-American labor and not shoulder their social burdens as well. And one of the first social burdens is education, particularly in the English language.

In Humboldt County the problem in all its aspects is shown as if beneath magnifying glass. Since 1970, almost 25,000 acres surrounding Winnemucca have been planted in potatoes. Inexpensive labor is required to harvest the potatoes and to pack and process them. It's estimated that of a population of about 7,500 in Humboldt County, 1,000 are Hispanic-American — and not all are legal immigrants.

Last fall, 50 Spanish-speaking students registered in Humboldt County schools. Few could speak English.

Valle of the Latin American Information Center estimates there are 15,000 Hispanics in Washoe County. He thinks the number will grow and with good reason.

With the growth of the Northern Nevada casino industry the numbers of low-paying jobs in the area will soar. Many Hispanics, particularly recent arrivals from Mexico, do not speak English. Many have no job training. They will inevitably fill the lowest rungs of the job market.

Others will arrive from California cities such as San Francisco, Los Angeles and San Diego which have large Hispanic-American neighborhoods. A Hispanic who does not speak English can live comfortably in these neighborhoods. But they will be disoriented in Nevada.

California is a state which has already been forced to cope with large numbers of migrant Hispanics who come to harvest crops. It has coped poorly. The native Mexicans are usually employed to harvest crops in the San Joaquin Valley and then rounded up by the thousands and returned to Mexico.

Those who do become American citizens usually hit the welfare roles once harvest is over. Naturally, the fact that many cannot speak English makes welfare inevitable.

The experience in Winnemucca is a sign that Nevada could soon have a problem similar to California's. But there is time to avoid it.

Nevada schools should immediately embark on a program which will make teachers available to instruct students who do not speak the langauge.

Federal money is available for these programs through the Department of Health, Education and Welfare and some state money is also avilable.

Nevada schools can get a handle on the problem before it becomes a major source of concern. And they don't need to segregate students.

According to Valle, the Latin American Information Center has established a home-bound tutorial program and employs six language teachers under a federal grant. Since many Hispanics work two jobs and also have difficulty moving around town, the home-bound program is a good one. But the real thrust should take place in the schools.

One factor which has limited the amount of federal money which Nevada schools can receive is that no one really knows how many Hispanics or non-English speaking persons there are in the state. The only figures now available are taken from the 1970 census and there has been an enormous increase in the minority population in Nevada since then.

The Nevada Department of Human Resources is conducting a survey which should update these figures. And speaking at a convention of Hispanic leaders in Las Vegas recently, both leading gubernatorial candidates, Lt. Gov. Bob Rose and Attorney General Bob List supported bilingual education programs.

These are good signs.

We hope all Nevadans realize quickly that in a democracy, students cannot be segregated soley because of language problems. The faster they are brought nto the mainstream of education, the better for the student, and the better for society as well.

Roanoke Times & World-News

Roanoke, Va., March 6, 1978

President Carter's increased intrusion of the federal government into public education would add more funds for bilingual education. That is, more Spanish teachers, teachers of Oriental languages and even of the Indian languages. The move is in accord with the established vogue of having registration forms and ballots printed in some language other than English.

Mr. Carter said that the federal support of bilingual education would be increased "with emphasis on teaching English as a primary and over-riding goal." Huh? It must simply be out of fashion to assume that if the primary and over-riding goal were English, the instruction would be in how to use the English language.

Back in the bad old days, immigrants arrived at Ellis Island and other places and had one bad time because they could not speak English; but they had desire, discipline and they learned English after a fashion. Their children learned it very well. To use a word fashionable 100 years later they "integrated" themselves into the American culture. Today is different.

The Topeka Capital Journal

Topeka, Kans., March 5, 1978

The Carter administration is to be commended on its intention to de-emphasize federal encouragement of bilingual education in the schools.

It will place primary emphasis on teaching children to use English, rather than on teaching other subjects in foreign languages.

In some parts of the nation, students of various ethnic groups have been kept in bilingual classes long after they were fluent in English.

In Topeka bilingual teaching has been transitional — while children learn English.

Some bilingual education proponents scoff at America's "melting pot theory," under which people of many races have given up primary loyalty to their homelands and have become English-speaking Americans.

But this has benefited those of all backgrounds. Descendants of Poles, Mexicans, Irish, Scots or Frenchmen are proud of their ancestry, even though they can't speak a word of the mother tongue.

But they are even prouder to be Americans. Most of us trace our "roots" to people of diverse nationalities.

In this sense, America is much more fortunate than Canada, where the French of Quebec are a tightly knit ethnic group, demanding to use their own language and agitating for independence.

Such a break-away state would be far less prosperous and happy than it would be as a part of the union. Its departure would hurt Canada badly.

Canada some day may wish it could have induced Quebec's citizens to be Canadians first and Frenchmen second.

Topeka schools have sought to help children who could not speak English to learn the language as a necessary tool for becoming Americans. Last year it completed a two-year program for Vietnamese, after those in Topeka had learned English. Most children of other ethnic groups know English better than the ancestral tongue.

It is proper, of course, for schools to teach modern foreign languages to any students, where there is a demand.

But teaching academic subjects in a foreign tongue may cost up to one-third more than regular classwork. This is wasteful where students know English.

THE ARIZONA REPUBLIC
Phoenix, Ariz., November 10, 1978

THE signs in front of the voting booths were clear enough:

VOTE HERE
VOTE AQUI

Inside the polling places there were equally clear signs:

NO SMOKING
FAVOR DE NO FUMAR

Large sheets of instructions could not be misunderstood. They were headed:

INSTRUCTIONS
INSTRUCCIONES

And the ballots themselves were careful to print everything in two languages, English and Spanish. With one exception. While "Yes" was translated into "Si," someone decided that the English "No" didn't have to be translated to the Spanish "No." That word only appeared once when it came to disapproving the three propositions on the ballot.

Is this bilingualism necessary in the voting booth? We doubt it. What person qualified to vote can't understand the meaning of "Vote Here"?

Probably the most expensive application of bilingualism in this election dealt with the publicity pamphlet that the secretary of state is required to publish. It describes in detail, with arguments for and against, propositions that are referred to the voters by the Legislature or that are the result of initiative petitions. English and Spanish pamphlets were printed separately. As a result, there weren't enough of either to go to every voter.

Mexican-Americans form the biggest ethnic group in Arizona. They also turn out in small numbers for most elections. But printing ballots in two languages won't get a larger turnout.

Because it reduces the amount of money available for instructing the voters in English, it probably results in a more poorly informed, not a better informed, electorate. Bilingualism is a crutch that impedes good citizenship.

And it irritates those whose ethnic backgrounds do not rate the favorable treatment given to Mexican-Americans.

Actually, no one is being discriminated against if only English is used. Those who are hurt the most are those who will never learn English, because they can use Spanish, and who hence miss most of the history and culture of America.

Chicago Tribune
Chicago, Ill., October 21, 1978

Mrs. William L. Rohter, a member of the Chicago Board of Education, says that some teachers in bilingual education programs in the Chicago public schools are unable to speak English. She reports personally encountering "more than a dozen" such teachers, and says, "If it's only one teacher, the problem is critical. That one teacher may touch the lives of several hundred children."

Bilingual education is supported by a lobby which has been effective in getting legislative mandates and appropriations. In Illinois, state law requires school districts to establish bilingual programs wherever as many as 20 pupils with a single non-English primary language are enrolled. The current state appropriation for bilingual education provides Chicago with millions, though both the Illinois Board of Education and the General Assembly cut original requests. The federal Office of Bilingual Education sponsors 700 programs in 41 states and 5 territories, at considerable expense.

This effort to help children from non-English-speaking families is new. The federal program dates from only 1974, the state mandate from 1976. Earlier, children without English entered regular classes on a sink-or-swim basis — and they generally swam.

A key term in the Illinois bilingual education law is "transitional" — "a program in transitional bilingual education." The legislative intent is clear — that bilingual education encourage and hasten pupils' mastery of English. But if children have a teacher who is not fluent in English, what chance do they have for any transition, let alone a swift one? And if the economic advantages to teachers depend on large enrollments in bilingual classes, what incentive is there for teachers to hasten this transition? Small wonder that some say pupils are entered or retained in bilingual programs even if they are fortunate enough to have learned English.

Parents upset by their children's lack of progress in English should realize that Illinois law gives them an "absolute right, if they so wish, to withdraw" their children from bilingual education programs. Enrollments this fall in Chicago bilingual programs ran far behind expectations, suggesting that many parents of children eligible for such programs prefer regular classes.

State law also says that teachers in bilingual programs must have "communicative skills in English." Mrs. Rohter's observations are that this requirement is not always met.

It should be. The whole bilingual education idea, nationally as well as here, should be critically reconsidered — by educators, parents, and general public —to see if it is worth what it costs, if it indeed may not be doing more harm than good.

Democrat and Chronicle
Rochester, N. Y., October 24, 1978

THE IMPORTANCE of learning a foreign language has been emphasized and neglected, depending upon the school. This wishy-washy attitude among educators, then, doesn't make it surprising that there is still resistance to bi-lingual programs in public schools.

In fact, even the experts are still far from reaching a consensus on the subject.

Take Wallace Lambert, a Canadian psychologist and proponent of bi-lingual programs. He told 30 educators here that "languages can be liberating."

"They can help students feel better about themselves," he said, ". . . that beneath the differences in language and culture, people are basically the same."

Lambert bases his opinions on a case study in northern Maine. Teachers used to wash out the mouths of French-speaking Americans if they were caught speaking French in the schoolyard.

But once those students were encouraged to speak French in school and received one-third of their instruction in French, their performance on tests given in the English language as well as their self-image improved dramatically.

A DIFFERENT emphasis is provided by Rochester Teachers Association President Joseph Pasquarella's opinions outlined in a WXXI radio commentary.

Pasquarella is all for bi-lingual education, but says that "the major effort of the program . . . should be to help children learn to speak English . . ." to ". . . provide a comfortable transition for children who speak little or no English (at home) so that they may as quickly as possible join their English-speaking schoolmates."

Whatever specific uses educators see for bi-lingual education, it can be used as a transition from one language to another. But it also can be used to remove barriers and promote human understanding.

The Cincinnati Post
Cincinnati, Ohio, September 7, 1978

If an "Anglo" politician had said it, scorn and derision would immediately have been heaped on his head.

S. I. Hayakawa can get away with it because he belongs to one of America's smallest minorities and because the elderly junior senator from California unfortunately doesn't seem to be taken seriously by many people.

This is a great pit, because Hayakawa, distinguished scholar of languages, issued an important warning to Americans recently.

Asked why, as a Japanese-American, he had expressed doubts about bilingual education (much of it federally funded), he said:

"What I'm really nervous about—it's a very, very distant fear, of course —but if you push the bilingualism process too far, especially in the states with a heavy Mexican population like Texas or California, you could some day find yourself in a situation with the problems of Quebec."

It may not be all that distant. Numbering an estimated 12 million today, Mexican-Americans and other Spanish-speaking people are expected to be the country's largest minority by the end of the century. Some Hispanic organizations are already demanding that Spanish be accorded equality with English in their schools and communities.

It would be, we submit, a tragic day for America if bilingualism were ever written into law, and this is no reflection on the Spanish language or Spanish-American culture.

If anything is abundantly clear in this world, it is that linguistic rivalry is one of the most divisive elements in human affairs, and is most divisive and embittering where it is combined with religious, ethnic or racial differences.

It is doing no favor to the children of Spanish-speaking parents—or of those who speak any other language, for that matter—for well-meaning educators to hinder or delay the earliest possible mastery of English, which is spoken by the overwhelming majority of Americans and is the closest thing the world has to an international language.

New Bilingual Regulations Set as Local Battles Continue

In June 1979, the Health, Education and Welfare Department issued new regulations for schools that desired federal bilingual education funds. School districts were ordered to provide figures on the number and proportion of students in the programs and an estimate of the district's financial situation after federal funds ran out. The new requirements also called for evaluating the students' progress every two years and determining what specific skills they would need to enter the regular curriculum. Previously, HEW grants for bilingual education had gone to school districts employing noteworthy or innovative teaching methods. Federal funds in general played a small role in bilingual programs; they were kept going by state and local grants. This led to lively legislative battles around the country, as the following editorials will show.

Hispanic success in promoting bilingualism inspired swarms of suits by other minority groups for special schooling. The Office of Education soon found that it had to extend its regulations (and funds) to the handicapped, the gifted and the delinquent. In one case, a U.S. district judge in Ann Arbor, Mich. ordered the school system to establish a special program for children who spoke "black English," to prepare them for schoolwork in standard English.

THE KANSAS CITY STAR
Kansas City, Mo., July 12, 1979

To set up special language classes, thereby tacitly admitting that foreign-born students have been illegally deprived of an equal education, or not set up classes and allow youngsters to lag behind their American-born neighbors: That is a ridiculous dilemma to hand any school district.

A new Kansas law provides that districts can be reimbursed for students in such classes, yet state education officials indicate districts that deal with the need take a risk because it means admitting they have educationally deprived students. It's akin to the knot private industry faced, unable to proceed with affirmative action programs prior to being found guilty of discrimination, until the recent Weber Supreme Court decision. Perhaps that will be a guidepost for education.

In the schools, it should not be a question of setting up programs of dual language instruction but of reasonable assistance to youngsters, transplanted from another land and culture, so growth can proceed while they make the change to a second language. Because English will be the communication medium of their play, social activity and work, there should be no hedging that the nature of the classes is transitional. Instruction in English should be part of or paired with other classwork, and when sufficient proficiency in the adopted tongue is achieved, the foreign language instruction should cease.

This country has enough stumbling blocks to progress as one people without promoting bilingual education as an end in itself that will build another barrier between diverse groups.

THE
DENVER POST

Denver, Colo., April 12, 1979

THE COLORADO Senate did the right thing early this month when it killed a bill that would have repealed the state's 1975 law requiring bilingual-bicultural education in many school districts.

The controversial program appears to be working. Early this year, a Texas-based educational organization set up to evaluate bilingual programs said Colorado was "way ahead of any other state." Russ Goldsmith, head of the National Dissemination and Assessment Center for Bilingual Education, said he had "never encountered a set of evaluation findings... that evidenced as high a degree of success as I found in the evaluation of the Colorado programs."

Perhaps, as Colorado critics of the program have charged, that kind of praise is to be expected from an organization supportive of bilingual education.

But an analysis from the state auditor's office, which approaches everything with a healthy skepticism, suggests clearly that the program has helped some Spanish-speaking students learn English and become better students. That is perhaps the most important of the four goals of the 1975 law.

Admittedly, there was a lack of information to analyze the program's effectiveness in reducing dropouts, developing students' self-esteem and increasing parental participation in school programs—other goals of the four-year-old law.

The limited information the auditors could find showed that in 20 of the 182 grades in which the program is offered, children showed "significant" academic progress attributable to bilingual education. Children in another 30 grades probably benefited from the program, the report said.

This year, the program is costing the state about $2.1 million. The year before, when the appropriation was $2.5 million in state tax dollars, 20,306 students were enrolled in bilingual-bicultural programs. That included 6,536 who needed help learning English, usually because they came from homes where a different language was spoken. Another 2,500 students received tutorial help, and 11,270 English-speaking students enrolled, as the law permits, for "cultural enrichment."

Critics, including Sen. Hugh Fowler, R-Littleton, chairman of the Senate Education Committee, have questioned whether the program is effective and whether it's a waste of money to allow English-speaking students to use it as a way to learn a foreign language.

The present system requires school districts to offer bilingual-bicultural programs if 10 percent of a school's enrollment or at least 50 students come from homes where English isn't the primary language. Fowler introduced the bill, SB 85, that would have replaced that system with a tutorial program. Only 10 of the 35 senators voted for his bill when it got to the floor, and only 12 voted for an alternative that would have ended the program in July 1980.

One of the leading figures in the fight for bilingual education, Sen. Paul Sandoval, D-Denver, has told his colleagues that he is as interested as they are in seeing that the program is effective. During debate on Fowler's bill, he promised his fellow senators that he personally would move to eliminate the program two years from now if it is found conclusively not to be working.

While the evidence so far couldn't be called conclusive, it certainly is positive rather than negative. Bilingual-bicultural education clearly deserves at least two more years of trial.

THE SACRAMENTO BEE

Sacramento, Calif., July 19, 1979

Bilingual education was designed to allow non-English-speaking and limited-English-speaking public school students to learn the basic subjects in their primary language — usually Spanish — until such time as they could function in English. At the same time, as the state Legislature declared when the bilingual program was adopted here, the ultimate object was to "develop in each child fluency in English so that he may then be enrolled in the regular program."

After several years of experience, however, the results of bilingual education programs remain inconclusive at best. The most extensive national surveys indicate that as often as not children labeled "limited English speaking" or "non-English speaking" have done as well in the regular school program as in bilingual programs. Those conclusions have themselves been subject to challenge, yet insofar as they are correct no one has been fully able to explain them.

Recently, however, a team of researchers working for the state Board of Education came up with some startling observations. Reviewing reports from various school districts in California and published studies in the field, they discovered data indicating that roughly half the 260,000 children enrolled last year in bilingual education programs in California speak their "primary" language even less well than English. In many instances, indeed, they can't speak the "primary" language at all. The Riverside Unified School District found, for example, that of the 470 "limited-English-speaking" students in its Spanish bilingual program, only 131 speak Spanish fluently and 223, nearly half, speak no Spanish at all.

* * *

The researchers, Marina K. Burt and Heidi C. Dulay, point out that in most instances teachers with "English dominant" students will automatically conduct their "bilingual" classes in English, but since the law requires tests to be given in Spanish, one doesn't have to look far to understand why achievement scores are low. Burt and Dulay also point out that where bilingual programs enroll only children who are more proficient in their primary language than in English the bilingual curriculum generally proves to be more successful than regular classes.

To remedy such absurdities, the state board is now backing major revisions in the California law that sets criteria for entrance and discharge from bilingual programs. Any student found to be "limited English speaking" on a test who comes from a home where anyone speaks a language other than English is now placed in a bilingual program. Although the student is tested for proficiency in English, he is not examined for proficiency in the foreign language that is assumed to be primary.

* * *

Under the proposed revision, AB 690 being carried by Assemblyman Richard Alatorre, students would be tested in both languages: Those "limited-English-speaking" students found to be more proficient in English than in the "primary" foreign language would be placed in one of two programs in which English is either the primary or the only language of instruction and where extra help is provided in English. Non-English-speaking or limited-English-speaking students who are more proficient in a foreign language would be placed in a "core" bilingual program conducted in the foreign language. Similarly, the Alatorre bill would establish specific "exit criteria" that would encourage the movement of students into classes conducted in English.

* * *

The bill is bitterly opposed by elements of the bilingual establishment who argue that it will weaken the program and that it represents only a cover for an attempt to create jobs for English-speaking teachers at the expense of bilingual teachers. It is also argued that the bill reflects bias against minorities and particularly against Chicanos.

The latter argument is simply wrong; there can be no greater form of discrimination than a rule requiring a child to take a test in a language he doesn't speak. The other argument is irrelevant, a claim overwhelmed by the absurdity of the situation it seeks to perpetuate. If the state board's data are correct — and other sources seem to confirm that — then nothing would make more sense than to limit the program to those who really need it and to exclude those who, common sense suggests, will do far better if they are allowed and encouraged to operate in English. The Alatorre bill merely moves toward what bilingual education was supposed to have provided in the first place: giving children a chance to learn in the language they know best and, beyond that, to learn English as fast as possible.

Sacramento, Calif., September 10, 1979

A bill instituting major reforms in the state's bilingual education program has been resurrected in the Legislature and is scheduled for a vote in the Senate today.

In essence the bill, which had been regarded as all but dead, would eliminate definitions and categories in existing law that now capriciously place tens of thousands of children who speak English better than their so-called "primary language" into bilingual programs. As a consequence, such children — estimated to comprise more than half the enrollment in bilingual classes statewide — are often taught, tested and evaluated in a foreign language (generally Spanish) which they either speak less well than English or don't speak at all.

To remedy that situation, the new bill, resurrected as AB 1254 and sponsored by Assemblyman Dennis Mangers of Huntington Beach, would require children being considered for bilingual programs to be tested in their "primary" language as well as English and would encourage instruction in the language they understand better. Heretofore, if a child from a Hispanic background (for example) was deemed to have an inadequate command of English, the child would automatically be placed in a bilingual program. It is for that reason that so many have been misplaced.

In its original version, AB 1254, then sponsored by Assemblyman Richard Alatorre as AB 690, ran into vehement opposition from groups of professional Chicano educators who charged that it would result in a sharp reduction in the number of bilingual teachers and that, in general, it reflected bias against Chicanos. It was partly that opposition and partly sheer ignorance of the provisions of the reform bill that blocked its passage a couple of weeks ago.

It would be unfortunate if the bill failed again. Even if this legislation costs some bilingual teachers jobs — something which, given the existing severe shortage, it will not — the job argument is irrelevant. The teachers are there to help children learn; the program was not created to create jobs or benefit particular teachers. More significantly, the bill would take the troubled bilingual program one large step toward the objective for which it was created in the first place: helping children function in school until they have sufficient fluency in English to learn in the regular classroom. The faster children can be placed in the regular program, the more successful bilingual education will be.

The Evening Gazette

Worcester, Mass., August 10, 1979

With a Hispanic population which may be as many as 15 million persons in the United States, the stated aims of bilingualism are far from reality.

The most recent official census of the Spanish-speaking population sets the figure at 6,000,000. But those figures are four years old and don't include illegal immigrants, children, recent arrivals and many others missed by census takers.

Bilingualism in some form is a fact of life in just about every American community. Affirmative action programs, education requirements and economic practices indicate the presence of Hispanics in most cities and many smaller towns. Bilingual signs, long prevalent in Spanish Harlem, little Cubas in Florida and the Mexican barrios of Texas and California are not unusual in public buildings in most parts of the country. Commercial radio stations broadcasting in Spanish are heard in most larger cities and nearly all public broadcasting facilities present at least some Spanish programs. Supermarkets in this area cater to the special food tastes of Hispanic customers.

But the sharing of two languages — bilingualism means equal proficiency in any two tongues but has come to be synonymous with Spanish and English in most uses — is still an unreached goal, despite government policies which support it.

Since 1970, when the Hispanics became the largest linguistic minority in the United States, replacing Italians, millions of dollars have been spent trying to educate this population in two languages. More funds have been spent teaching Spanish to those who work with Hispanics in schools, agencies and institutions.

Yet there has always been a dichotomy in the underlying philosophy. Is bilingualism just a balance of two languages or a bridge between two cultures? For Puerto Ricans, who are not immigrants but American citizens, there is a tug-of-war between the desire to retain their own language and the need to accept the official language of the United States in order to succeed.

And the need for bilingualism varies from one group of Hispanics to another. Cubans, Ecuadoreans and other South Americans who fled repressive political regimes tend to be middle-class professionals, many of whom already speak English and

other languages. Mexican and Jamaican farm laborers, Puerto Rican factory and service workers, Haitian domestics and those who arrive in the United States for economic reasons tend to have had less opportunity to learn English.

The dilemma for the schools is that a Spanish-speaking child can't learn in English, but if he is taught in Spanish, that youngster isn't learning English with his peers. The problem has been intensified by government insistence that not only language but cultural programs be provided. And there is a shortage of teachers able to provide transitional training from Spanish to English and cultural background as well. The Worcester School Department proposes to recruit such teachers in Puerto Rico.

The goal of proficiency in two languages is admirable. In practice, though, it is a difficult one for school children who must bear the brunt of learning in two languages and two cultures.

Nevada State Journal

Reno, Nev., August 20, 1979

Nevada's Board of Education decided last week to take a much-needed step toward helping out the state's rapidly growing number of migrant workers' children.

The board voted to seek federal funds to pay for bilingual teachers aides and special materials for the youngsters who do not speak English.

The step is the result of several petitions for aid by minority advocates from Nevada's rural counties, and a study of the situation by the state's education department.

During the last school year, advocates from Elko County appeared before the board to outline the problem. Many children were not attending public school, they said, because of parental fears about deportation. Local school officials at the time were requiring documentation proving the families were legal residents of the United States. For those who were turning up in school, very little help was available, even in the form of a bilingual teacher.

The board's response at the time was both compassionate and sensible. It took the position that educators are in the business of educating, not serving as immigration officers. It required local school officials to admit the youngsters, and pledged to seek federal aid to supplement the local educational system.

MIGRANT CHILDREN

The department study found nearly 600 children of migrant workers in the state, mostly in Clark, Humboldt and Elko counties. Most of them speak only Spanish, and most are isolated by both language and culture within their communities.

Similar problems are to be found here in Washoe County, with current estimates placing the Hispanic population at 10 percent of the total, or perhaps 20,000 persons. They are hard-working people with strong family ties who are also helping to pay for their children's public school education through taxes. They are as essential to the health of the local tourism-based economy as are their counterparts who help harvest the crops on Nevada's rural farms.

Unfortunately, too often their youngsters find themselves adrift in an educational sea of foreign sounds they do not comprehend, and customs they do not understand.

Washoe County is, however, considerably ahead of rural school districts in having an English as a Second Language (ESL) program. The program emphasizes the use of English as the medium of communication and teaching within the classroom. The student's native language is used only when absolutely needed.

BILINGUAL PROGRAMS

While many educators believe bilingual programs are the quickest road to assimilation, minority advocates say students would learn more through a strong bilingual, bicultural program, which they are not getting in Nevada school districts. And existing programs are not offered uniformly in the district, they add.

While the differing viewpoints about meeting minority students' needs have yet to be resolved, it is encouraging to see the state's education board pursuing avenues for financial aid.

Without much fanfare, the board has remained constant in backing up its promise so find ways to effectively educate all children of public school age in Nevada.

Los Angeles Times

Los Angeles, Calif., August 28, 1979

The Senate Finance Committee is trying to compromise conflicting bills to improve California's bilingual education program; the hybrid that it has produced may end up compromising the program itself.

Last Thursday, the committee took up rival measures to amend the state's Bilingual Bicultural Education Act of 1976. The bills are aimed at meeting criticisms that students whose first language is not English are remaining in bilingual classes longer than need be, and that too many teachers are required to win certification as bilingual instructors. The measure that we support, sponsored by Assemblyman Peter R. Chacon (D-San Diego), would build on existing law. The other, by Assemblyman Richard Alatorre (D-Los Angeles) and Dennis Mangers (D-Huntington Beach), would shift the focus toward more instruction in English only.

The Senate Education Committee passed out both bills. To try to avoid making the Finance Committee pick one or the other, the Legislature's Chicano caucus proposed that the Chacon bill be approved, with an amendment making the Alatorre-Mangers

approach a pilot project that could be field-tested in six areas over the next two years.

Instead of this eminently sensible compromise, the committee, chaired by Sen. Albert S. Rodda (D-Sacramento), tied the measures together in such a way that school distrcts may choose whichever format they prefer. That means that children with limited ability to speak English may get instruction from bilingual teachers in one part of the state and not in another. The resulting confusion could doom the program to failure, and thus extinction, when it comes up for review in 1984.

The committee will meet Wednesday. The curious amalgam on which it will vote will be no clearer to school districts than English is to some foreign-born students. If this measure sends any understandable signal at all, it is that the state will not make a firm effort to see that bilingual education works. The proposal would also indicate that the state will not accept its responsibility, under the 1974 Lau v. Nichols Supreme Court case, to ensure that non-English-speaking students have access to the education that they need to succeed. □

WORCESTER TELEGRAM.
Worcester, Mass., September 15, 1979

The manner in which the School Committee handled the hiring of six bilingual teachers from Puerto Rico was shameful. It involved back-room maneuvering and personality clashes that didn't serve the public interest.

The administration presented convincing arguments that it needed to go to Puerto Rico in order to find qualified bilingual teachers. The superintendent says there are no locally-qualified candidates. But that's not the point.

The point is the shameless politicking that surrounded the School Committee "deliberations."

After recommending a slate of six teachers from Puerto Rico, a School Committee faction led by Raymond Mariano managed to hold up the hirings based on claims that local persons were overlooked. A volcano of charges and counter charges erupted.

On one side, School Supt. John Connor asserted that Mariano is "ruining the school system" for political reasons. Committee member Elizabeth Price said she had been told one of the local candidates overlooked was a campaign worker for Mariano. Connor said that was the least of his problems with Mariano. He said in 25 years of working here he had not seen anyone "manipulate" the committee for personal ends as much as Mariano. He added that Mariano "has harassed members of the administration, making their positions very uncomfortable."

Mariano denied all, saying he never promised a job to anyone, and added that Connor "is trying to influence the election."

The people don't really know what the facts are. Not enough of the matter has been done up front for public scrutiny.

The School Committee functions as the chief executive body of the school system. It meets as a body and directs the school superintendent to carry out its policies. But it acts as a body. No one school committee member is authorized to act as an administrator on his own.

Connor's charge that Mariano has "harassed members of the administration" is a serious one. He should come forward with more documentation than he has. Did Mariano's role amount to meddling in administrative matters or was it merely zealous research?

It's too bad all this has cropped up on the eve of city elections. The rhetoric becomes fueled by heightened emotionalism. Be that as it may, some serious questions have been raised. They must be answered.

Pittsburgh Post-Gazette
Pittsburgh, Pa., August 22, 1979

In simpler times, when the assimilationist metaphor of the "melting pot" was celebrated by native-born Americans and immigrants alike, the suggestion that one could be an American and not speak — or desire to speak — English would have been dismissed as absurd.

Not so today. The presence of a growing (and politically influential) Spanish-speaking population in the United States — a Special Report published in the Post-Gazette this week estimated their numbers at 15 million — poses the real possibility that the United States will become a nation divided by language. And educators, politicians and Spanish-speaking Americans themselves cannot agree about whether such a prospect should be welcomed or, if possible, averted.

That debate should be resolved clearly in favor of the second course. True bilingualism, in an individual or in a social group, is obviously an asset. Something else entirely is what might be called "bi-monolingualism," a situation in which society is divided into two groups, each of which speaks it own language and has little or no command of the other. That sort of linguistic *apartheid* has a sorry history and continues to bedevil modern societies like Belgium and Canada as well as more than a few developing ones. One needn't be a cultural imperialist to hope that the United States can be spared a similar divisiveness.

The obvious answer to the problem of language division is bilingual education for Spanish-speaking immigrants and their children. Indeed, in cases involving Chinese-Americans and speakers of the dialect known as Black English, the courts have rightly held that public schools have a positive duty to provide remedial bilingual instruction. The practical problem with such special help for non-English speaking pupils is that school authorities, teachers and parents can be easily tempted to postpone the transition from classes in Spanish (or some other language) to classes in English. And there is a growing political and philosophical constituency for such hesitance. Its central tenets are that choice of a language is a constitutional right, and that the government should incur whatever expenses are necessary to protect the exercise of that right.

That thesis, attractive as it might be to believers in cultural pluralism, is ultimately dangerous. The fact is that even if the Spanish-speaking population of the United States were to double, English would remain the dominant language and a command of it would still be a passkey to educational, economic and social mobility. In holding school segregation unconstitutional 25 years ago, the Supreme Court said that "separate is inherently unequal." That axiom also applies to linguistic segregation.

The United States has been immeasurably enriched by its ethnic, racial and cultural diversity. But in diversity there must also be unity, and for 200 years a common national language has been the chief symbol and safeguard of that necessary unity. It should not be undermined now.

Rockford Register Star
Rockford, Ill., December 11, 1979

The problems of those forced to move to a foreign land with a strange language and different customs must always remain a matter of deep concern for Americans.

In this nation, formed and dedicated to be a haven for the oppressed seeking liberty and a better life, we must never forget this historic role for our country. We must never forget that this nation is the product of the merging of the many different cultures which have been brought to our land from other nations.

We also must remember that those coming to this nation from other cultures come in confusion and fear — facing an uncertain future. There always have been and there must continue to be certain concessions made to welcome these people to our nation, concessions taking into acount their different language and cultural background.

And it is from these perspectives that we must view those problems which are growing with the increased numbers of Spanish-speaking peoples coming to America.

However, it also is incumbent upon those joining us in this land to accept the fact that our customs result from decades of striving for individual freedom and equality in America — the result of majority rule while still protecting the rights of individuals.

And this fact would appear to be involved in the dispute between parents of children enrolled in Rockford's bilingual program and the local school system — a dispute which has led to Spanish-speaking children being withheld from school by their parents as a "strike" against the local school system.

Because of language difficulties, the federal government has mandated and the local school system implemented special bilingual programs for Spanish-speaking youngsters in two local elementary schools — New Milford and Gregory. Under this program, the children work with both Spanish-speaking and English-speaking teachers as they attempt to both learn a new language and keep up with the educational achievements of others in their age groups.

It is not an easy program; nor is it an inexpensive one.

That is background, but what are the facts in the present "strike"? Is the local school system being unfair to the Spanish-speaking minority, or is this group, organized as the Parent Advisory Council, asking too much?

The Spanish-speaking PAC — representing parents of the 156 pupils in the bilingual program — is demanding that school bus routes be changed so that their kindergarten and first grade pupils can catch a bus within a block of their homes. School policy (providing better service than required by state law) offers bus service to within four to six blocks of the homes of elementary pupils for all 33,000 pupils in the local district.

So the PAC and its leader, Rosa Gerdes, are asking something for their children not available to any other children here.

Local school officials have not been unbending in the dispute. They have met with PAC parents and offered a variety of alternatives. The PAC has refused to temper its demands.

Even local law officials, while pointing out the parent group is violating the law by withholding their children from class, has tempered its reaction and is ignoring the legal violation while a solution is sought — but also is warning that the violations cannot continue forever.

School officials also have studied specific cases involved and have found only one case where a child was being asked to walk farther than the normal distance to catch a bus. That route has been corrected.

There really seems nothing more the school officials can do unless they believe this one group should have special services not available to every other child — a position the School Board obviously cannot take.

Meanwhile, there are victims who continue to suffer through the "strike" — the children being withheld from school. These Spanish-speaking pupils obviously have enough difficulties keeping up with class work while struggling with a foreign language. They can ill afford the lost time from school.

It simply makes no sense for their own parents to penalize these children while continuing an uncompromising position.

Guidelines for Bilingual Classes Issued by Education Agency

In August, the Department of Education issued detailed rules for schools to observe in providing bilingual education to children whose native language was not English. Education Secretary Shirley Hufstedler Aug. 6 said all schools that had two or more classes composed of at least 25 non-English-speaking children must provide bilingual classes to help those children learn English as well as their regular subjects. Hufstedler said the children should be tested for English competency periodically and should not remain in bilingual programs for more than five years. Teachers of the bilingual classes were required to be proficient in English as well as in the foreign languages they taught.

The DOE's recommendations were made in response to complaints of inadequate bilingual education in parts of the country. The 1974 Supreme Court decision that mandated bilingual education for foreign-born children left it up to the individual schools to implement bilingual programs. The DOE standardized requirements for bilingual programs, and in the process, was criticized for exceeding its authority to tell local schools what to do.

Opposition to bilingual education was outspoken from the start and appeared to be gaining ground. Voters in Dade County, Fla. Nov. 4 approved the repeal of a statute that had established Spanish as the county's second official language. The referendum ended six years of bilingualism in the county, which had a population of 600,000 Spanish-speaking Cuban immigrants.

The Kansas City Times

Kansas City, Mo., October 16, 1980

Children have the right to a full education in traditional public school classes in this country. In the storm and rhetoric over new Education Department regulations on bilingual teaching, that simple idea is too often forgotten. The department expects districts to provide non-English speaking-students education in their own language until special classes in English allow them to slip into seats next to their American-born peers. Some members of Congress and other opponents prefer no bilingual education at all.

There is a legitimate concern that once established, such classes might become permanent rather than transitory as prescribed in the regulations, eventually leading to a double track in education and perhaps other areas of American life. That would be counterproductive. It is a direction that should be strongly opposed. The other fear of some is that this is a sneaky intervention ploy of the department into state and local educational systems.

That's a major feeling behind the Rep. John Ashbrook, R-Ohio, amendment to the education bill barring the department from requiring anything other than "intensive instruction in English" for non-English-speaking pupils. It passed the House narrowly and has yet to be accepted by the Senate.

Interpreting the 1974 Lau decision of the Supreme Court which mandated remedial instruction for needful students, the Department of Education regulations do overlook the fact that the court allowed either intensive English instruction or bilingual classes in stipulating a specific remedy for the literacy gap. It was necessary. We do not need children floundering in a morass of indecision and do-nothing discussions on the part of administrators who cannot make up their minds to remedy the situation by any method. Lost time is lost opportunity for too many young people. Doors may never be opened again in exactly the same way.

If properly carried out as an interim measure, these regulations will give children a chance for access to educational systems, then to the adult world of work, social activities, and full participation in a democracy. True, thousands have made it without special help. But thousands have suffered, slipped and failed in trying. It must not happen to any more generations of Americans, whether Hispanic, Asian or other nationalities, and there is no good reason why it should. Bilingual classes, so long as their temporary nature is as assured as their quality, are a good addition to America's public school system.

The Evening Gazette

Worcester, Mass., September 12, 1980

Credit Shirley M. Hufstedler with one important achievement: She has brought the hush-hush scandal of bilingual education out into the light of day where it can be seen and judged on its merits.

True, that was not Mrs. Hufstedler's intention. As the first secretary of the new Department of Education, she tried to spell out rules for a national policy on teaching children who know little or no English.

As might have been expected, she went whole-hog for bilingual education, and ruled that even small school systems will be required to teach in two languages.

Bilingual education means swollen teacher staffs, more administrative jobs and more directives from Washington when the system does not function properly. And bilingual education functions properly practically nowhere. Some educators think it is exactly the wrong way to go.

Mrs. Hufstedler has been hit with a barrage of angry criticism ever since she laid down the rules. Albert Shanker, president of the American Federation of Teachers, says her directive would be "an unmitigated disaster." The National School Boards Association, the Council of Chief State School Officers and the national associations of elementary and secondary school principals all have attacked the idea.

Mrs. Hufstedler, defending herself, says that 3.5 million school children in the United States use English poorly or not at all. There is a real problem and no one denies it.

But no one really knows how best to attack the problem. In some instances, bilingual education works pretty well in moving children from their native language to a proficiency in English. But in many other cases, according to educators, it does not work well at all. It often seems to be counter-productive, in that it becomes a crutch. This is especially true when an ethnic group demands that its "culture" as well as its language be preserved in the public schools. There is no clear evidence that this can be done.

Mrs. Hufstedler's blunder is just the sort of thing that critics of the new Department of Education anticipated. When a Washington bureaucracy tries to become the Big School Committee to all of the nation's hundreds of thousands of schools, what happens to local initiative, responsibility and control?

And what happens when Washington, in its myopia, tries to force on the nation's schools a policy as badly flawed as bilingual education?

Chicago Defender

Chicago, Ill., October 21, 1980

Bilingual education has become a national matter in the educational world and for that matter in the daily life of millions of Hispanics and other millions of English-speaking citizens.

In some areas of the country, where the Hispanic population is large, or a majority, bilingual studies have made considerable inroads.

The fact is, however, that this is an English-speaking country and will remain such for a long time, and unless immigrants of whatever national origin learn to speak and write English fluently, they will handicap themselves for advancement in the American economy.

This condition is similar to the "black English" issue in white-black relations, in schooling and communication generally. But the Blacks who have advanced most have been those who have mastered standard English. The same will probably hold true for the Hispanic citizenry.

The Providence Journal

Providence, R.I., October 27, 1980

Bilingual education is on the defensive. Bills to repeal or revise it are now before Congress. Locally, the president of the Providence Teachers Union has called for an end to the program in an opinion column written for these newspapers. *Fortune* magazine last month argued similarly, in an article reprinted on today's Commentary page.

Few would argue against sensible programs designed to keep public school students from falling behind or dropping out because of language difficulties. Indeed, school systems in larger metropolitan areas, where newly arrived Americans tend to congregate, have for years provided supplemental English-language classes to meet this need.

To the degree that such help was not available to newly arrived Americans, the Supreme Court was justified in its 1974 ruling (*Lau v. Nichols*) that this violated the civil rights of foreign-speaking students. The court, however, did not specify *how* such help should be given. Presumably it would have been satisfied simply to have all public school systems provide English-language reinforcement classes where the need exists.

But HEW, under pressure mainly from Hispanic minority groups, went far beyond that. It convinced Congress to appropriate $7.5 million for a demonstration project in which children would be taught *all* subjects in their native tongue.

This approach is a radical departure from the traditional American meltingpot idea of one nation bonded together by one language. If that alone does not make it undesirable, the costs involved may well do so.

Providence, already hard put to meet its school budget, does not have a huge problem. But cosmopolitan cities like New York, Washington and Los Angeles, where a dozen or more ethnic groups may be congregated, do. Fairfax County, Virginia, a suburb of Washington, D.C., for example, has 15 minority groups that qualify for bilingual programs in Spanish, Vietnamese, Korean, Urdu, Farsi and Swahili, among other tongues.

The cost, complexity and confusion of the bilingual approach in such situations are reason enough to reject it. Already the initial $7.5 million appropriated by Congress in 1974 for a pilot program has swelled into $200 million a year, and a total of $1 billion has been spent so far.

With what results? Evaluation studies of some programs have been made, with varying estimates of their effectiveness. But one massive study done for the federal Department of Education is discouraging. After tracking 11,500 Hispanic students in bilingual programs and comparing them to Hispanic students in regular classrooms over four years, it found the scholastic performance of those in the special programs little better than that of their peers in regular classes, and all of them far behind the national average. Most egregiously, the bilingual program students showed no noticeable improvement in English.

The fast-growing number of ethnic minorities in the United States do pose new problems which may require new solutions. But those who attempt to meet these problems ought to approach them modestly, building on the proven practices of the past, at the same time maintaining the national ethos of one country, held together by one tongue.

ARKANSAS DEMOCRAT

Little Rock, Ark., October 18, 1980

If it's high costs that's killing the Arkansas Education Assn.'s initiated amendment for quality education, what about the cost of bi-lingual education that the U.S. Department of Education is trying to slap on the public schools?

If as few as 25 pupils in a school are having problems with their English because it isn't their born tongue, then the school must teach them all the basic courses in both their native languages and English.

Shirley Hufstedler & Co. say they're only following a Supreme Court decision that declares that it's unconstitutional not to school youngsters properly simply because English isn't their native tongue. "Properly" doesn't necessarily mean wholesale bi-lingualism – but we'd guess that the court was thinking mainly of the Spanish-speaking. They would indeed present the biggest problem, but also the one most easily solved. There are plenty of Spanish-speaking teachers to whom Spanish is native.

But the problem of bi-lingual teaching is much bigger than that. It turns out that a lot of schools have foreign students for whom no bilingual teacher can easily be found. Washington, D.C. – probably the worst case – needs teachers who can teach Thai, for instance, and Farsi (Persian) and a dozen or more unusual tongues. The likeliest recourse it to foreign-born Americans who know these languages, but how many of them are teachers? As for native Americans, most of them simply aren't bi-lingual or interested in being so. So finding teacher prospects is no easy matter.

Even such Americans as do become foreign-language teachers – and quite sensibly these people attain languages that are most offered in the schools – often aren't so proficient even in Spanish and French that they can readily teach in it. So even if there's a run on out-of-the-way tongues, we'll still face the same problem of proficiency.

We'd like to think that sheer necessity will force many teachers to become really proficient – which would be no bad thing for either them or their foreign pupils. But if we really are going to have federally ordered bi-lingual teaching in public schools, many foreign-tongued kids are simply going to get just a lick and a promise in the way of learning basic subjects in their own languages.

The federal argument is that that's all they're getting now by way of English instruction, but that doesn't have to be. The language-learning faculty is at its highest in pre-teen years. Why not – instead of speaking broken Persian or whatever to the foreign-tongued youngster – school him, really school him, in the English that's being spoken all around him anyway?

Not only will the child acquire a foreign tongue – maybe the one he'll need the rest of his life – but public schools will be spared untold wasted millions in trying to do the impossible.

Who can judge whether a teacher hired to teach in a certain language is able to do so – unless it's another teacher born to the language, or the kids that will be subjected to this sort of thing? In many cases, the kids won't have enough English even to complain that their "teacher" isn't coming across to them.

The Evening Bulletin
Philadelphia, Pa., August 12, 1980

Shirley Hufstedler, secretary of the new U.S. Department of Education, is trying to right a wrong with some proposed regulations on bilingual education. The question is whether a blanket directive is the best approach. We say no.

The issue came before Mrs. Hufstedler back in 1973 when she was a judge on the U.S. Circuit Court of Appeals in Los Angeles. In a dissent to a court decision, she held that the civil rights of Chinese speaking students in San Francisco were violated when they were given instruction in English only.

The next year the U.S. Supreme Court agreed with her. Her department, for the first time, now seeks to implement the high-court ruling.

Mrs. Hufstedler says the thrust of the regulations is to have kids who speak other languages learn English "as quickly as possible." Fine. One of the strengths of this country has been a single tongue. Unlike Canada or South Africa, we haven't had to wrestle with divisions born of language diversity.

The department's proposal is that, if there are enough pupils of the one language, schools must offer courses in that language for a transition period. A pupil would not be allowed to stay in those classes for more than five years.

One question is whether schools should go ahead with courses, say, in history and biology taught in Spanish rather than teaching the students English first and then history and biology in English. We say the emphasis should be on teaching English as quickly as possible so that all instruction in other courses can be in that language. Why not first teach english to those who do not have the language? The other subjects could wait until the students are able to be instructed in english.

Then there's the sweeping-directive matter. The proposals are very specific, down to number of pupils to be instructed and time periods and so on. But what may apply for Laredo, Texas, is likely not to apply to Kennett Square, Pa., to mention two communities with Spanish-speaking residents.

There is a national problem. Government officials say that 60 percent of the students eligibile for bilingual instruction are not receiving it and presumably are being denied equality of opportunity. That needs to be remedied.

In the hearings on confirming her nomination as secretary, Shirley Hufstedler said she would work to minimize federal "disruption and domination of the nation's schools. This is an area, we'd say, where an injustice can be corrected by a flexible, not a dogmatic, approach.

Los Angeles Times
Los Angeles, Calif., August 10, 1980

The battle over bilingual education saw action on two fronts last week—in Washington as well as in Sacramento.

In proposing regulations for bilingual-education programs, the federal government moved to help state and local districts draw a sharper bead on what is required of them. For its efforts, the new Department of Education is probably going to find itself caught in a crossfire.

But in Sacramento, this year's controversy over changing the state's bilingual-education legislation took a step nearer resolution. The Senate Finance Committee revived measures to improve the program after its chairman, Sen. Albert S. Rodda (D-Sacramento), and Gov. Jerry Brown worked with most of the forces involved to forge a compromise.

The state bill, sponsored by Assemblyman Peter R. Chacon (D-San Diego), would establish clearer standards for moving children in and out of bilingual programs. It also would extend the deadline for teachers to obtain bilingual training, and would allow districts to experiment with various techniques for teaching English. At Rodda's insistence, the bill was amended to make it clear that the purpose of bilingual education is to help youngsters learn English as quickly as possible. We supported Chacon's bill earlier in the session; we think it looks even better now.

If the measure is passed by the full Legislature, it will make much of the anticipated federal debate over bilingual education moot as far as California is concerned, because this state's program already does much of what the federal government's proposal would require. Nevertheless, that debate is important as an element of national policy.

The Education Department proposals are the first formal rules outlining how school systems should comply with a 1974 Supreme Court decision. The ruling, in the San Francisco case of Lau v. Nichols, held that students with limited proficiency in English are being denied equal educations unless schools offer them special assistance. Many educators and representatives of language minorities say that the informal guidelines in effect since that decision are too fuzzy. Even though these groups and others are just starting to analyze the proposals, they are finding substantial targets at which to aim in a series of hearings next month in six cities, including San Francisco.

There will be extensive arguments over what kind of testing should be conducted to determine the need for bilingual programs, over how many bilingual teachers should be required, over the requirement that children leave the programs after five years regardless of their language proficiency, over what alternative programs would be acceptable, over the cost of the programs and—from some—over whether the programs are necessary at all.

There are those who argue that, during earlier waves of immigration, people learned English without extensive government-financed help. Many immigrants did in fact learn English—in publicly supported schools. The need to master English reading and writing skills is much greater in today's society, where so much depends on the ability to read everything from classified job ads to computer manuals, so children deserve all the help they can get.

Richmond Times-Dispatch
Richmond, Va., August 17, 1980

The new federal Department of Education has proved, in its first major test, to be just as dictatorial and as destructive of sound educational practice as its critics had feared.

The issue furnishing the test was bilingual education. In its 1974 Lau v. Nichols decision, the United States Supreme Court said special remedies must be undertaken for non-English-speaking pupils to insure that they have equal educational opportunity.

But the court did not presume to say what those special programs should be. It left that to the discretion of local school boards and administrators.

Now, however, Secretary of Education Shirley M. Hufstedler, a former federal judge, has decreed how all the nation's public schools ought to teach foreign-born students whose knowledge of English is limited.

The schools must, according to Ms. Hufstedler, teach those students basic subjects, such as mathematics and science, in their native tongues until they have mastered English through remedial instruction. The schools would test the pupils' command of English within two years and annually thereafter to see if they should be removed from the "transitional bilingual program" and placed in regular, English-language classes. No pupil would remain in the program for more than five years, according to the education department regulations.

The Hufstedler ukase is objectionable on both practical and philosophical grounds. As Virginia's superintendent of public instruction, Dr. S. John Davis, notes, this state already enrolls children who speak more than 100 foreign languages. Finding qualified teachers to accommodate this babel would be an administrative nightmare.

Aside from that practical problem, no justification exists for the federal bureaucrats telling local educators in Virginia and elsewhere that they have to junk their "English as a Second Language" approach to assimilating foreign-born children into the education mainstream. In ESL, English-speaking teachers with special training intensively teach English to the foreign born until they are able to take their regular courses in English. A four-year evaluation of bilingual education made under contract with the U. S. Office of Education shows no educational advantages for that approach over ESL.

English is the dominant language in the United States, and it does the immigrant youngsters no favor to push back the time they must come to grips with this reality and to encourage them to believe that their native tongues will enable them to get by.

THE BLADE

Toledo, Ohio, August 31, 1980

ANY new federal guidelines for bilingual education in the United States should be based on one simple precept — that English is the common and official language of all Americans.

A U.S. Supreme Court decision in 1974 ruled that the rights of all children to a free public education could not be realized if those who lacked ability to use English were denied instruction in their mother tongue. This has led to a burgeoning program of federal aid to school districts to implement bilingual education for linguistic minorities. Plainly, like so many other federal-aid projects, bilingual education has become something of a boondoggle.

New proposed guidelines issued by the Department of Education, however, seem to address this problem in a constructive way. Secretary of Education Shirley Hufstedler commented: "First, students must be taught English as quickly as possible. Second, they should not be permitted to fall behind their English-speaking classmates while they are learning English."

The department suggests a five-year limit on any pupil's enrollment in a course taught in a language other than English. Some educators think the ceiling should be no more than two or three years, but a five-year limit presumably is better than none. There are bilingual-education activists who feel it is an inherent constitutional right to learn — or to teach — in some language other than English all the way through high school.

Obviously, this is a ruinous course financially for hard-pressed school districts, but more important, it simply delays a student in his ability to converse and study in English, to his disadvantage. This notion also smacks of ethnic or linguistic politics. Any minority large enough to command public attention would have an advantage over refugees from, say, an Asian country whose native language is not spoken by anyone competent to give instruction in school subjects. What usually happens in such cases is that a pupil, thrown into an English-speaking environment, rapidly learns the language of his classmates, as generations of young immigrant children did before him.

From the standpoint of efficiency in the schools, a certain amount of bilingual education can be defended. But it should not be perceived as a "civil right" or as a source of employment for non-English-speaking teachers.

That does not mean that a person must abandon his culture or native tongue as so many immigrants did throughout much of American history — a trend which now is being abandoned as people delve into the roots, language, and culture of their forebears. Nor does it mean that persons with little or no ability to speak English should be denied the fruits of society. Earlier generations of immigrants could live and die in this country without having much contact with public agencies. In today's society that is not possible, and assistance should be provided such persons.

But the assistance should be transitory — aimed at providing a bridge for those who are learning to use English as the indispensable key for unlocking the door to opportunity in the United States. Many cultures but one official language is a time-tested American doctrine. There is no reason to abandon it.

Chicago Tribune

Chicago, Ill., August 7, 1980

The Department of Education has proposed new regulations for bilingual education. They inspire a sigh of relief, because they are by no means as bad as we had been lead to fear.

According to Secretary Shirley Hufstedler, the regulations emphasize the principle that "students must be taught English as quickly as possible." That of course will disappoint those who want instruction in Spanish, for example, from kindergarten through high school. The regulations set a five-year limit on any pupil's participation in a bilingual program. Any limit is better than none, but five years is far longer than any child of normal intelligence requires to learn a language. If the Department of Education were in earnest about "as quickly as possible," it could have set the limit at two years or even less.

The requirement that teachers in bilingual programs must themselves be proficient in English is welcome. The criteria for a pupil's participation are limited proficiency in English and greater proficiency in a non-English language than in English—better criteria than the rejected ones of having a native language other than English and being in the lower half of the student population in proficiency in English. The proposed regulations should make for better teachers and fewer pupils in bilingual programs than the tentative rules reported earlier.

Of course the basic theory of bilingual programs is open to serious challenge. Generations of immigrants to the United States, from every quarter of the globe, learned English successfully [and speedily] without such programs. The theory underlying present bilingual education is that under the Civil Rights Act of 1964, as interpreted by the Supreme Court in 1974 in Lau v. Nichols, it is a violation of civil rights to provide for no instruction other than in English.

Obviously, children who neither speak nor hear English in their homes are at a disadvantage in an English-only school. But it by no means follows that bilingual programs that have grown without pattern or reason to become a costly, crippling, and divisive burden on big city school systems are the best way of dealing with this handicap.

Still, the law is what the Supreme Court says it is. Bilingual education is now a legal necessity if not an educational one. Federal bureaucrats will be examining school systems for compliance with the bilingual education regulations, and threatening withholding of federal money from systems found out of compliance. As only 60 per cent of pupils eligible for bilingual education are now enrolled in it, the bilingual programs are headed for higher costs and longer payrolls, even though the proposed regulations are much better than they might have been.

If, as is entirely conceivable, it was not the intent of Congress in enacting the Civil Rights Act of 1964 to call into being a vast program of bilingual education, Congress might do well to speak on the subject in the near future. Until it does, the Department of Education is justified in issuing regulations for bilingual education and policing compliance with those regulations. It is good that the regulations are as sensible as they are.

They will become effective after public hearings—which we hope will not leave them less sensible.

The Virginian-Pilot

Norfolk, Va., September 5, 1980

In an effort to woo Hispanic and other ethnic voters, the Carter administration is prepared to trample on the liberties of state and local schools.

Those who swore the new federal Department of Education would be a "hands-off" bureaucracy were foolish. Already, its hands have been laid on local school curricula.

The issue now is bilingual education. New federal regulations demand that localities instruct foreign-born children in their native languages if two or more classes have 25 such children enrolled. For the two to five years the children receive such instruction, they are expected to get remedial English on the side.

The new regulations go beyond anything the Supreme Court has required. They appear to violate the statute under which the Department of Education was created. Certainly they flout every assurance of non-intrusion that the Department's backers gave.

But Jimmy Carter thinks bilingual education is what Hispanic, Vietnamese, Korean, and other ethnic voters want. We think if Jimmy Carter were looking for a way to divide this country, he couldn't have done a better job.

Bilingualism postpones the day many minorities will enter the linguistic mainstream. It prolongs their condition of linguistic "illiteracy." Rather than bilingualism for non-English speaking children, we should be immersing them in English from the moment they arrive at our schoolhouse doors.

That's the view of Virginia School Superintendent S. John Davis, who plans to challenge the new regulations at a public hearing in Chicago on September 17. That's the view too of Virginia Attorney General J. Marshall Coleman who pledges to contest their enforcement in federal court.

Mr. Davis advocates what educators call the ESL (English-as-a-second-language) approach. This approach argues sensibly that the more English is used in schools, the faster children will learn to speak it. Fairfax County alone has an ESL population of more than 2,500 students representing 50 different languages. Tests, says Dr. Davis, have repeatedly proved ESL's educational effectiveness.

Dr. Davis has one other reason for resisting federal mandates: money. Implementing bilingualism would cost the taxpayers of Virginia an extra $10 million each year.

Implementation, says Virginia Education Secretary Wade Gilley, also means "that in addition to the more common languages such as French, German, or Spanish, we might have to find teachers who could teach in Vietnamese or even Swahili."

It's sad when presidential politics outlaws common sense. It's tragic when such politics mortgages the common destiny of a nation.

By 1990, Spanish-speaking Americans will surpass blacks as our most numerous minority. What feelings and loyalties will they develop toward a country whose dominant tongue many but dimly understand?

The compassionate course is to teach them English, the sooner the better. The principled course is to preserve the option of localities to do so, in the face of this latest federal power grab.

If defending these principles means going to court, then Virginia should.

Newsday

Long Island, N.Y., September 2, 1980

The task of educating non-English-speaking children in American public schools is not a simple one, as many school officials can testify: In the past couple of years, two Long Island school disticts (Central Islip and Patchogue-Medford) that taught English as a second language to Hispanic pupils have been told that their efforts did not meet federal standards.

The problem is that when the U.S. Supreme Court ruled in 1974 that children who don't speak English must have equal access to education with those who do, it left unclear how that standard could be met.

Now the U.S. Department of Education has offered guidelines to clear up the uncertainty, so that school districts won't try to meet pupils' needs in one way, only to be told they must do it in another.

Basically, the department is proposing that children who are more competent in another language be taught school subjects in that language while they are also being taught English. When they are fluent enough, they are to be shifted into English-speaking classes.

We like that approach. It ensures that children won't waste time in classes conducted in a language they don't understand. At this point, however, the proposal has two real defects: It's unclear whether children will move into the regular classroom quickly enough; and it's all too clear who will pay the costs.

The department has purposely left some details vague, pending hearings this month. For example, it has yet to decide just how limited a child must be in English to be assigned to a bilingual program. And there's room for debate over whether the proposed two-to-five-year stint in bilingual classes is needed.

When it comes to such questions, we think the underlying principle is clear: The guidelines should be written to put pupils in English-speaking classes as early as possible.

That won't please parents who want the schools to foster their cultural traditions. But we don't think that's a task the schools can afford to do and still perform their primary job: preparing all youngsters to function as effective, informed adults in this country.

Which raises the second point—the cost. The Department of Education estimates that bilingual programs will cost several hundred million dollars a year nationally. It proposes to pay one-third.

That's not enough. Few local school districts can afford new and costly projects; those with large non-English-speaking populations are likely to be more hard-pressed than others. If Washington is going to define their responsibilities, it should be prepared to pay more of the cost of meeting them.

Roanoke Times & World-News

Roanoke, Va., July 23, 1980

Relatively commonplace in the 19th century, bilingual education in the United States almost died in the Americanization hysteria of the World War I era, only to be revived as a promising "new" experiment to teach the children of Cuban refugees in the late 1950s.

But not until 1974 was bilingual education elevated from a matter of state or local school policy to a nationwide civil right for non-English-speaking children. That elevation occurred via a U. S. Supreme Court decision that appeared to go far beyond the intent of the 1964 Civil Rights Act on which the ruling was based.

As legal doctrine, the decision was questionable; educationally, it was tragic. It diverted attention from the question of whether bilingual education has practical value and instead focused attention on the propriety of forcing English-language taxpayers to subsidize programs that maintained minority languages. As a result, two fundamental points got lost:

● It is in the national interest for all Americans to share a common language, for non-English-speaking children to learn English as quickly and as well as possible.

● It is also in the national interest for Americans to be fluent in foreign languages, for English-speaking children to learn to speak one or more foreign languages as fluently as possible.

On both scores, the situation today is worrisome. As many as 3.6 million children in the United States, mostly Spanish-speaking, have trouble with English. Until they are fluent in English, they will be unable to communicate with most of their countrymen. They will be condemned to second-class status politically, economically and socially. They are done

no service by a bilingual education program that downplays the need to learn English or reduces their motivation to do so.

As for the English-speaking majority, only 15 percent study a foreign language before college, compared to 36 percent before World War I. Only eight percent of American colleges and universities require a foreign language for admission, compared to 34 percent 15 years ago. There are 10,000 English-speaking Japanese businessmen in New York City, but only a handful of the 900 American businessmen in Japan speak Japanese. The American automobile industry might be in marginally better shape if cars marked "Body by Fisher" had not been translated in Belgian advertisements as "Corpse by Fisher."

The vital question is whether bilingual programs can meet those problems. The concept of bilingual education — early, large doses of instruction in languages other than English — is broad enough to include a wide range in the quality, scope and design of individual programs. That's probably one reason why the evidence is mixed as to how well those programs lead non-English-speaking children into learning English. And bilingual education is seldom even thought of as an opportunity for English-speaking children to learn foreign languages.

But more evidence won't help much if there is no clear idea as to what bilingual education is supposed to be doing. It should be judged a failure if it does not help produce English-speaking citizens, regardless of whether bilingual education preserves minority languages. And it should be judged a failure if it makes no attempt to improve fluency in the major foreign languages of the English-speaking majority.

ST. LOUIS POST-DISPATCH

St. Louis, Mo., August 22, 1980

New guidelines promulgated by the Department of Education could bring more coherence to bilingual education programs in the U.S. Currently, the federal government provides aid for language education without many regulations. This was done in large part because of the continuing controversy over whether a child should be taught English as quickly as possible or should be given instruction for the most part in his primary language, with English taught as a foreign language. The proposed regulations try to combine the two approaches.

Without strict guidelines, most large bilingual programs have developed in the latter fashion, largely out of a fear that forcing quick assimilation into a new language would injure the child's cultural development. But what has often happened is that the child fails to attain a command of English and hence his social development and occupational opportunities are limited.

The proposed revisions would limit bilingual programs to those who need them, rather than having them as a place for anyone with a Hispanic surname, for instance, regardless of proficiency in English. They would also limit the special language services to five years for each student, so that integration in the larger school environment would eventually take place. Each school will have to develop its own program to ensure that children whose primary language is not English are not harassed and do not lose their cultural heritage. The new regulations make sense and should help students for whom English, for all purposes, is a foreign language.

The Cleveland Press

Cleveland, Ohio, August 11, 1980

Secretary of Education Shirley Hufstedler's commitment to state and local control of education didn't last long.

When she took over the new Department of Education last May, she said: "There isn't going to be any dominance of education by the federal government. I am firmly committed to the proposition that control in education rests with the states and localities."

Yet one of her first major acts was to propose the other day a regulation that would force bilingual education on the nation's schools.

Nor is imposition of this federal authority on local school districts the only aspect of Secretary Hufstedler's bilingual rule that ought to be questioned.

It has not been proven that bilingual education — the teaching of non-English speaking students in their native language — is a benefit to youngsters. Indeed, there are some studies that suggest it slows down their progress toward functioning well in American schools.

Another reason to be leery of bilingual education is that too many are pushing it for reasons other than the education of children. Some use it as an issue to gain power within minority blocs and to create jobs for themselves and associations. Others are mainly interested in maintaining native cultures.

Preserving some native customs and traditions can be a good thing but it can be overdone in the American melting pot.

There is reason to suspect that in the spread of bilingual education lie too many seeds of separatism. One need only look northward to Canada and the Quebec separatist movement to see the problems caused by too much emphasis on maintaining separate customs and language.

This is the United States. It is not Mexico, or Vietnam, or Korea or any of the dozens of other countries whose languages would be involved in Secretary Hufstedler's regulation.

The English language is one of the glues that hold the United States together. The sooner a child learns it, the better equipped he or she will be to function in and become a productive member of this society.

Pittsburgh Post-Gazette

Pittsburgh, Pa., November 8, 1980

Of all the ballot questions across the nation in Tuesday's election, probably the most overdrawn belonged to Dade County, Fla. There the electorate approved an ordinance that prohibits county officials from spending tax money to promote any language except English or any culture except American.

As its critics have pointed out, the broad scope of the ordinance gives the Dade County attorney the rather awesome power to decide what is American. And if he follows a strict interpretation, then such aids as multilingual directional signs at the Miami International Airport might be the first victims of Dade County's drive for cultural purity. The teaching of French, German, Spanish and other foreign languages in Dade County schools also could be threatened.

The detailed changes forced by the vote are still being contemplated. Yet the new ordinance is already expected to have a polarizing impact.

Traditionally, Dade County has had a large Latin American population. The referendum was aimed unmistakably at the recent influx of Cuban boat people. And the ordinance would eliminate services that have been developed to foster Miami's role as the gateway to the Caribbean, such as translation and public-information services in the county's Office of Latin Affairs.

But the referendum's passage also has caused anxiety because of its possible financial consequences. It could eliminate a county-supported Spanish-language advertising campaign aimed at the half million South American tourists who vacation in Miami Beach each year.

To overcome any impression that Dade County now wants free-spending South American tourists to stay home, the Miami Beach Visitor and Convention Authority, which is funded by that city rather than the county, will spend about $200,000 next year to convince Latin tourists that Miami Beach still wants them. The ads will be published, of course, in Spanish.

The Miami Herald

Miami, Fla., November 6, 1980

Long after the divisive and hurtful first effects of the English-only ordinance have been lessened by time and common sense, Cuban-born Paul Cejas will remain as a member, and possibly as chairman, of the Dade School Board. That fact shines as a beacon of optimism in a community that had seemed overwhelmed by frustration and tension.

Cejas

Mr. Cejas Tuesday became the first Cuban-American ever to be elected to countywide office in Dade. He conducted a campaign of unity that touched the common wish of all parents for a well-managed, educationally sound school system for their children.

The same voters who simultaneously were expressing their frustration over the prevalence of Spanish in the community wisely ignored ethnic differences to keep Mr. Cejas in office. Election of the Cuban-born certified public accountant was an important affirmation that Dade voters will embrace well-qualified candidates without regard for their ethnic background.

In contrast to that clarity, the meaning of the 3-2 approval of the muddled English-only ordinance is murky at best. A survey of voters leaving the polls showed widespread confusion about the ordinance that was promoted as "anti-bilingual." A near majority of those who supported the measure acknowledged that it is a bad law but saw in it a handy vehicle for protest. Sixty-one per cent mistakenly believed that the ordinance would prevent the county from printing ballots in Spanish.

Most voters said they agreed that information about essential county services such as hurricane evacuations should be translated into Spanish. Further, 66 per cent denied that passage of the ordinance would be an insult to Hispanics. Yet, it's likely that at least some of those needed services no longer will be provided with county funds, and there is little doubt that many Hispanics do consider the referendum a personal insult.

The survey exposed a deep confusion about the ordinance and an even deeper anxiety on the part of non-Hispanics. That anxiety is understandable even though its expression through an ill-conceived ordinance against bilingualism is regrettable.

The decisive success of Mr. Cejas's campaign, however, helps keep voter attitudes in perspective. The community is staggering under burdens that were imposed by forces beyond its control. Yet, its voters proved that they can and will support positive efforts for unity.

That demonstration should be viewed as the first application of healing balm to the divisions that the English-only referendum symbolized.

CHARLESTON EVENING POST

Charleston, S. C., November 24, 1980

Washington's new Department of Education is back in the middle of another brouhaha. It issued a 25-page proposed regulation that would require public school, bilingual education for schoolchildren who cannot speak English. The controversy is so heated that Congress has barred Education from using any federal funds to enforce the regulation until after new hearings on the subject. (In passing, it's interesting to note there are no federal funds tied to *implementing* the program since it is classified as civil rights legislation and therefore locally funded.)

Opponents argue for local school district autonomy on such subjects. Said one, "If these regulations are passed, what would stop the Education Department from setting math and history guildelines?" And there is a rare-language problem. In Hawaii, 6,000 students speak limited English and 41 different native tongues; in Guam, students speak nine languages and three Filipino dialects.

Proponents, on the other hand, and the National Education Association is in the fore, cite equal opportunity as the driving need, and that, they say, is not a local responsibility but a federal one.

While we believe the idea of America being a perfect "melting pot" is foolish, we can be consistent and disagree with those who feel they are providing more "opportunity" to a child by teaching in some language other than English. Those who would embrace teaching in a foreign language, or "black English" for that matter, are not preparing that child for a realistic environment in the post-school world.

We suggest that educators place emphasis (and spend money) on giving special assistance to children who speak limited or no English. Help them first to learn English, then proceed with teaching other subjects.

The Washington Post

Washington, D. C., October 28, 1980

ONE BY ONE, the area's local governments are weighing in against the proposed federal rules on bilingual education. Alexandria was the most recent to do so. In a letter to the Department of Education, its school board urged the newest federal bureaucracy to drop its proposal and to let local school districts decide for themselves how best to educate non-English-speaking students.

That is good advice. It is much like the message being delivered by other school boards here and around the country. Most of them have told the department that the proposal to require them to provide bilingual courses if they have a substantial number of non-English-speaking students is educationally unwise and economically unfeasible.

The fight over bilingual education is emotional and highly political. In its narrow terms, it is a dispute over whether children for whom English is a second language should be taught other subjects in their native language while they are learning English or whether they should be immersed in English and brought into the regular curriculum as quickly as possible. In its broader terms, it is a dispute over whether the public schools should be used to preserve the language and culture of large minority groups.

Given this nation's long tradition of leaving matters of educational policy in the hands of state and local governments, the Department of Education should never have decided to resolve those disputes nationally. There is no single policy on bilingual education that has demonstrated its effectiveness sufficiently to deserve being adopted nationwide.

The only standard the Department of Education should insist be met is that a local district provide all its students with an equal opportunity to learn. Such a standard does not ignore the legitimate concern that the special needs of some non-English-speaking students are now being ignored. Instead, it focuses that concern where it belongs—on the local school boards.

In some school districts, equal opportunity may best be provided through bilingual classes. In other districts, other techniques may work as well or better; the record of this area's schools indicates that non-English-speaking students can be integrated quickly and successfully into the regular curriculum without bilingual classes when school boards and teachers take the problem seriously.

The proper role for the federal government is to see that the goal is reached, not to prescribe the route that must be taken. If the Department of Education persists in trying to do otherwise, it will provoke an unnecessary showdown on Capitol Hill next year over what is essentially a matter for state and local governments.

St. Petersburg Times

St. Petersburg, Fla., December 16, 1980

Bilingualism, you might assume, means the ability to use two languages. It is hard to be against that. But when educators talk about bilingualism they mean something else. They refer to a teaching practice that may actually deter Spanish-speaking and other foreign-born students from ever becoming proficient in English.

Under this concept of bilingualism, immigrant pupils who show up for school unable to understand English are taught basic subjects in Urdu, Vietnamese, or more likely Spanish, whatever language they speak. They are presumed to get in addition, and usually do get, instruction in English, in the hope they can eventually move into regular classes.

SO BILINGUALISM refers more to the school than the student. The school (assuming it can find the qualified teachers) offers all the usual instruction in two or more languages. The student initially can handle just one, and experience has been that because he can get by in the bilingual school without English, he may never actually master a second.

Traditionally, through America's earlier waves of immigration, public education has gone the melting pot route. The kids were thrown into school without a whole lot of help. It was the hard way, but they learned to speak English, or else.

That may not have been fair, and it didn't always work. Many immigrant youngsters have gone through life without ever mastering English, forever doomed to an uphill struggle and a second-class citizenship. Bilingualism, unfortunately, could produce a whole generation of such English dropouts.

THE SUPREME COURT, properly, has ruled out the old-fashioned cold turkey treatment for today's new waves of immigrant children. It says they deserve a leg up on the same education the natives are getting. Just how this would work was left to the schools.

Or, as it turned out, to the U.S. Department of Education, which of course has drafted new rules. Under the department's proposals public schools will be required to go the bilingual route, wherever any substantial group of foreign-speaking students enroll.

School systems everywhere are distressed about that. And one of Ronald Reagan's advisory groups has recommended against it, a pretty good indication the new president may want to have it revoked.

THAT'S FINE, provided Reagan's school people don't drop the matter with that. Maybe most school systems won't need prodding, or help, in handling their immigrant pupils. But many will need both.

Even if it takes federal rules and government money, the foreign born kids deserve assurance they won't be simply flunked out or left behind because they only half understand what they are hearing or reading.

Maybe they'll need a crash course in nothing but English for starters, then a quick merger into the main stream of the regular courses. Or at the very least, as they struggle to make sense of what the teachers and other students are saying about arithmetic, geography, and American history, they will need special help to become proficient in English.

Maybe that way bilingualism can be restored, with the least possible pain, to its original meaning. The ability to speak two languages fluently will give the immigrants a head start over all but a few of their peers. And the melting pot can continue to bubble.

The Washington Star

Washington, D. C., August 9, 1980

Among the points of controversy raised by Education Secretary Shirley Hufstedler's new regulations about bilingual teaching, the pros and cons of bilingual teaching may turn out to be the less important. To begin with, here again are all those old questions about federal control of education. The ones that made so many people dubious about adding a Department of Education to the bureaucratic leviathon in the first place.

Everybody knows that "guidelines" mean "Do it or else." Everybody also knows that "or else" means taking away the Washington money local school systems have come more and more to depend upon. So much for a community's authority over what its children will be taught and how.

Secretary Hufstedler and her department came to Washington trailing clouds of reassurance about local control of education. But the dynamics of a federal agency will not be denied. It *must* tell them what to do out there.

So now it is no longer up to individual school systems to find individual solutions to the problems of students whose first language is not English. Classes in basic subjects, taught by bilingual instructors, must be offered to those whom testing determines to be more proficient in their original language than in English.

Enter the next set of issues. Bilingual educa-

tion challenges the melting pot concept of absorbing immigrants into American society by Americanizing them. It raises fears of divisiveness and even eventual separatist movements like that of the French in Canada.

There is also uncertainty about how far the cultural fragmentation might go. While the largest group at issue is Hispanic, the number of Asians in the United States is growing. And black English is still around making its claims for curricular recognition.

Privately sponsored bilingualism has kept the ancestral culture alive for more than one immigrant group in this country while English-speaking public schools and Americanization classes for adults pressed newcomers to enter the national mainstream. People as disparate as the Chinese and the Lithuanians have shown how the old values can be kept with after-school classes sponsored by parents. For the other side of the coin, the early part of this century gave rise to a whole literature illustrating the comedy and romance of immigrants learning to be Americans.

Many aliens coming here now still have the kind of naive zest for becoming American that emerges so vividly from the old stories about Hyman Kaplan trying to move from Yiddish to English and understand George Washington

along the way. Outgrowing the chauvinistic narrowness that once made them take it for granted that anything Anglo-Saxon must be the best, some Americans have lost the old pride of identity that once made them assume wihout argument that anyone living in this country would be better off adopting its ways and values.

Beyond such philosophical debating points, the new directives on bilingual education raise practical issues that are equally formidable. Where are the bilingual teachers coming from? What about textbooks? How well does a child learn any language when more than one are taught in school?

There will be public hearings around the country in the next two months before Secretary Hufstedler's rules take on legal force. Such hearings are designed partly to build support for what a government agency wants to do. They can also turn attention to what is really at stake in a turn of policy.

Perhaps the greatest contribution these can make to the national interest would be to suggest that federal funds would be better used on classes in English as a second language than on bilingual classes. Or on the Department of Education.

The Evening Gazette

Worcester, Mass., August 9, 1980

The new federal Department of Education is putting out new guidelines for bilingual education this fall, emphasizing teaching English to non-English speaking students.

Until now, bilingual education has been interpreted differently at different government levels. The federal government, which mandated bilingual education back in 1964, never defined its purpose. Some supporters of bilingual education, particularly Hispanic leaders, insisted on an education in two languages and cultures. This often meant divided emphasis on Spanish and English, with English coming off second-best.

Now Secretary of Education Shirley M. Hufstedler says the guidelines and laws will state:

"First, students must be taught English as quickly as possible.

"Second, students must not be permitted to fall behind their English-speaking classmates (in other subjects) while they are learning English."

Students with a poor command of English, as determined by examinations to be administered by bilingual personnel, must be placed in bilingual classes. Bilingualism must be applied as school policy even in relatively small communities.

It is this sort of rigidity that raises all the old questions about the wisdom of having a federal Department of Education. Why should bilingualism be the only policy permitted?

Has it proved to be that effective? A lot of educators don't think so.

It is good to see the federal government at last declaring that the purpose of bilingual programs shall be to teach English better and faster. But as usual, the bureaucracy is trying to go too far in trying to put a federal straightjacket on all school departments.

There are approximately 3.5 million children of school age in the United States who are not proficient in English; 60 percent are Hispanic. The next largest group is Oriental (Chinese, Korean and Vietnamese.)

Bilingual education has been mired in many school systems because of the different interpretations of the fuzzy federal guidelines. Let's hope the new federal guidelines solve more problems than they create.

Worcester, Mass., October 23, 1980

In Worcester, Hispanic leaders are claiming credit for forcing the School Department to offer new services through the bilingual program to Spanish-speaking children.

In Leominster, School Committee members are demanding changes in the bilingual program to reduce discrimination against non-Hispanic students.

In Worcester, the program is seen as not doing enough for Hispanic children. In Leominster, it is seen as doing too much.

The controversy over bilingual teaching is nationwide, but it is particularly sharp in communities with Spanish-speaking people, particularly Puerto Ricans. The reasons are worth examining.

The national policy is to use bilingualism for one main purpose — to teach children of other tongues to speak and write English.

But many Puerto Ricans are ambivalent about that goal. They want bilingualism also to sustain and broaden Hispanic speech and culture. To some, the mastery of English may be secondary.

Thse who argue that Puerto Ricans should be treated "just like other immigrants" miss an important point; Puerto Ricans aren't immigrants. They are American citizens.

But for many years, Puerto Ricans have resisted being absorbed by American culture. Many think of themselves first as Puerto Ricans, second as Americans. Unlike the immigrants from Europe, Puerto Ricans

maintain close ties with their home island and often visit there. Many of them plan to go back to stay eventually.

This conflict of cultures puts a heavy load on the bilingual program in the schools. The issue raised is really broader than language teaching, and should be debated and decided in different terms and perspectives.

As far as the schools go, the bilingual effort — for Puerto Ricans and all others of another language — should be aimed at teaching the children English as rapidly as possible. It is unfair to the children not to use the schools for that primary purpose. Anything less will not prepare them properly for life in America. Of all the handicaps people face in this country, the inability to use English ranks near the top.

Puerto Ricans have every right to have their children maintain their language and culture. But that really should be the province of other agencies and efforts, beginning in the home. The public schools cannot handle that task properly nor should they be asked to.

AKRON BEACON JOURNAL

Akron, Ohio, September 8, 1980

THOSE WHO believed that a new Department of Education would bring new support for public schools did not have to wait long to learn that the support and new programs will be on Washington's terms — as most federal programs are.

With the department now about four months old, the new Secretary of Education, Shirley Hufstedler, has already set a high priority on a controversial program: bilingual education.

In August, she proposed rules that would force schools to teach in their native language children whose primary language is something other than English and who test below the 40th percentile on an English test.

Secretary Hufstedler said more than 3.5 million youngsters have limited English proficiency. Of those, 70 percent are Hispanic.

Her proposal, said Albert Shanker, president of the American Federation of Teachers, "is an unmitigated disaster. It threatens the fabric of American education and the future of our country."

Mrs. Hufstedler

Many agree with Mr. Shanker, including leaders of the National School Boards Association, the Council of Chief State School Officers and organizations of elementary and secondary principals.

It has been possible, since the nation was founded, for children of any background — Greek, Italian, German, Asian, Spanish, Polish — to come to the United States, unable to speak a word of English, and rise to the top of their profession and to leadership roles in their communities and in the nation.

But the first thing they did was learn to speak English, generally in English-speaking classrooms. A second, or a third language was an advantage to them, as it would be to American children if they were taught other languages as a routine part of their education.

English is the key

But for all of them, born here or abroad, probably the greatest single service schools have performed for children over the years is to teach them to speak and write grammatically correct and lucid English and to read English with understanding. That is the key that unlocks every other educational door.

But Mrs. Hufstedler insists that things should be reversed, and proposes that the child first be taught in his or her native language.

Of course the non-English-speaking immigrants need help — lots of it from understanding teachers and special teachers and from local agencies such as Akron's International Institute. Even Mr. Shanker, who spoke only Yiddish and could not ask directions to the lavatory when he started

school in New York City, says he would have loved to have had someone to speak with. But he adds that if he had not been forced to learn English, he would not be "functioning in our society today."

Bilingual education is not a new idea and, by many accounts, it is not a very successful one. Since the Bilingual Education Act was passed in 1968, the federal government has funded bilingual projects in 46 languages — even in Punjabi, Cambodian, Arabic, Korean, Pennsylvania Dutch, Samoan and 20 native American Indian tongues.

An expensive idea

Federal funds appropriated for such programs rose from $7.5 million in 1969 to $115 million in 1977 and $169 million last year. The cost for Secretary Hufstedler's regulations would add up to $592 million on top of that.

The thousands of Cubans coming into America and the Vietnamese and other nationalities who have been pouring into the United States presumably want to be U. S. citizens and to take advantage of the opportunities they find here. It is as ridiculous to think that they can do that

without learning English first as it is to assume that the average American could find employment and happiness in, for instance, France or Japan without learning to speak and read French or Japanese. It is hard to become a real part of any group or nation without being able to communicate with its people.

Opponents of bilingual education have some arguments. They believe it will weaken American unity, make children less competent and less able to deal with a competitive society, preserve the child's mother tongue at the expense of a good quality education, make poor use of limited education funds and tend to segregate children.

Furthermore, education officials say there are not nearly enough qualified teachers for bilingual education classes.

Mrs. Hufstedler is correct to encourage more language instruction, but the effort for all American children in U. S. schools should be in English first and a foreign language second.

Bilingual education, as she proposes it, does not meet that goal, and it is a poor cause on which to launch the new Department of Education.

Chicago, Ill., June 24, 1980

Penny-wise members of the Illinois House the other day killed an appropriation to fund bilingual education throughout the state. That's not as damning as the fact that Gov. Thompson actually encouraged them to do so.

Fortunately, Sen. Philip J. Rock (D-Oak Park) revived the appropriation in committee, and we urge Thompson now to rethink his priorities, write "bilingualism is Americanism" 100 times and start pushing.

Chicago will hurt most if he doesn't.

Should the state withhold the $16 million the city's poverty-stricken Board of Education seeks, the board will have to find it else-

where. There's no choice. The board is obligated under federal regulations to continue the highly successful, 19-language program it operates for 32,000 pupils.

Bilingual education has a bad name among the uninformed because it somehow connotes un-Americanism. Actually it speeds the Americanization process. Records show that 96.5 percent of bilingual pupils here advance to all-English classes after three years of transition from their native tongues. Class attendance and graduation rates both rise with bilingualism.

Color it *rojo, blanco y azul.*

Wichita, Kans., June 2, 1980

A federal district judge in New Jersey recently ruled that bilingual education teachers in that state must be proficient in both languages, and the new U.S. Department of Education is proposing a regulation that would apply such standards nationwide.

In Kansas, under legislation passed last year, the employment of non-certificated instructors in bilingual education programs is permitted.

New York apparently interprets existing federal equal educational opportunity requirements even more casually. A New York Times writer recently noted that blackboards in bilingual classrooms in New York City frequently are filled with uncorrected misspellings of English and Spanish words. He reported some critics fear that New York's program may, instead of teaching Hispanic pupils to be fluent in English, simply be making them semiliterate in both languages.

Certainly, pupils who do not understand much English are not going to get as much out of classes taught in English as the regular English-speaking pupils do. That is why federal regulations require that bilingual instruction be available in all school districts that contain children not fluent in English.

The situation in Kansas has been brought to

a head by the filing of a federal court lawsuit against the Garden City school district. In it, the Mexican American Council on Education, (MACE), an organization of Spanish-speaking parents, has accused the district of deliberately neglecting to meet the educational needs of Hispanic students, and thus violating both the equal protection clause of the 14th Amendment, the 1964 Civil Rights Act, and the 1974 Equal Educational Opportunity Act.

MACE estimates that 855, or about 21 percent, of the Garden City school system's pupils are of Hispanic origin, and contends that of the 700 pupils MACE estimate need bilingual instruction, less than half are getting it.

If so, that's a shame. Children usually are fast learners. Childhood is an ideal time to pick up a new language. Unless the new language is adequately taught, other learning is bound to be slowed, too.

We doubt Garden City's shortcomings are deliberate. Its school superintendent, Horace Good, says the system has tried to recruit more bilingual teachers and just can't find them. Other systems undoubtedly run into the same difficulty, which is one reason the 1978 Legislature enacted the provision permitting the hiring of non-certified personnel.

But it may be that some school districts still aren't taking advantage of the resources

available to them. Last year's legislators also appropriated $300,000 to help school districts pay the costs of bilingual instruction. The money was supposed to take care of the 2,000 most educationally deprived Spanish-speaking children in the state, at the rate of $150 per child. Although it had been estimated that at least 5,000 Kansas pupils might be from Spanish-speaking homes, school district claims against the $300,000 fund fell somewhat short of expectations.

The Kansas Advisory Committee for the U.S. Commission on Civil Rights now has announced plans for an extensive survey to see how well local schools and local governments in the state are serving residents whose main language is not English.

But meanwhile, it is obvious that a need exists both for teachers who are fluent in more than one language and for better utilization of the funding that is available.

When 1980 Census figures are added up, they no doubt will reveal that Kansas has become an increasingly multilingual state. Yet, since English is the basic language — the language of government, business, education and most everyday life — newcomers from many other parts of the world must be helped to bridge the communication gap as rapidly as possible.

THE CHRISTIAN SCIENCE MONITOR

Boston, Mass., August 7, 1980

The federal mandating of bilingual education is such a watershed question for the United States that the public ought to make full use of the present invitation to let Washington know its views. The Department of Education has set Oct. 6 as the deadline for accepting comments on proposed regulations specifying when primary and secondary school systems are required to offer classes in languages other than English. In addition, there will be hearings in several cities next month before the rules are put in final form.

The need for clarification of what schools must do has been evident ever since the US Supreme Court's 1974 decision in Lau v. Nichols. The court ruled that the San Francisco school system had violated the Civil Rights Act of 1964 by failing to take positive action to help students (in this case Chinese-Americans) who were not fluent in English.

But the court did not spell out remedies, leaving such options as extra teaching of English or instruction in the student's first language. Circuit appeals court decisions have included upholding a New Mexico bilingual program ordered by a lower court and striking down a detailed Denver one as an unwarranted incursion into local authority.

For a time federal civil rights enforcers appeared to interpret the Supreme Court decision as requiring instruction in languages other than English. A 1975 report by the US Civil Rights Commission favored bilingual instruction: "Evidence gathered by the commission and others documents that language-minority students badly need an alternative to education in the monolingual English school system."

But later federal civil rights enforcers were instructed that bilingual education was not necessarily required to carry out the law. School systems have understandably felt some confusion. The news has dealt mainly with the large numbers of Spanish-speaking students, but there are also many others including those of Asian origin and the recent inflow of French-speaking Haitians.

So a clear set of guidelines, arrived at through vigorous public participation, will be welcome. And Education Secretary Shirley Hufstedler has offered sound principles for the pending regulations: "First, students must be taught English as quickly as possible. Second, they should not be permitted to fall

behind their English-speaking classmates while they are learning English."

How best to implement such principles will be the question for discussion. The new Republican platform says that "there should be local educational programs which enable those who grew up learning another language such as Spanish to become proficient in English while also maintaining their own language and cultural heritage." How far should local programs be outlined by Washington? How far can Washington avoid outlining local programs without failing to enforce the law? The proposed rules would require that students clearly less proficient in English than in another language be offered classes in the other language; they would shift to regular classes as they improve their English. Still undecided is whether the same provision should be made for students performing at the same relatively weak level in both languages. Here is where it will be particularly important to reach conclusions that will encourage students to move forward in English, the language they will have to have to realize the opportunities offered by America.

Bilingual Education Proposals Revoked by Secretary Bell

In his first official act, Education Secretary Terrel Bell Feb. 2 revoked proposed regulations that would have required public schools to teach non-English-speaking students in their native languages. Calling the rules "harsh, inflexible, burdensome, unworkable and incredibly costly," Bell said they were "symbolic of the many ills that have plagued the federal government" and the Education Department (which President Reagan was intent on abolishing). The rules, issued in August 1980 by former Education Secretary Shirley Hufstedler, would have required school districts with more than 25% foreign-speaking children to provide them with instruction in their native languages in basic subjects such as mathematics, reading and social studies as well as extra classes in learning English. Bell said the Education Department would issue new bilingual guidelines that would give more leeway to individual school districts. "We will protect the rights of children who do not speak English well," Bell asserted, "but we will do so by permitting school districts to use any way that has proved successful." About 500 U.S. school districts had some kind of bilingual program, mainly to serve the estimated 3.5 million Hispanic children living in the U.S. Bell's decision drew strong criticism from Ruben Bonilla, president of the League of United Latin American Citizens, who called the decision "one more example of the Reagan administration trying to disembowel the Hispanic community."

SYRACUSE
HERALD-JOURNAL
Syracuse, N.Y., February 4, 1981

Education Secretary Bell earned his pay during the first week on the job. He scrapped the Carter administration's extravagant orders to school districts to provide courses of instruction in students' native tongues.

Otherwise, Uncle Sam would cut off funding.

Bell thus lived up to President Reagan's publicized intention, quickly and definitely.

Estimated cost of the mandated two-language instruction (native tongue and English) runs to a billion dollars and, as Bell noted, really hurt civil rights efforts because of their "heavy-handed misdirection."

That's readily discernible.

If students didn't have to learn English, why would they? By not doing so, they insure permanent minority status for themselves.

The two-language orders ignored this country's history as well. Millions of Americans arrived in this country knowing scarcely a word of English. They survived and prospered. In fact, they're the proud products of this country's public school system.

As a postscript, we believe firmly all Americans should know a second language, second to English, a communication skill common to citizens of Euorpe and to the educated in Asia.

ALBUQUERQUE JOURNAL
Albuquerque, N.M., February 4, 1981

When Education Secretary Terrel Bell recently scuttled the federal bilingual program, he not only saved taxpayers some big money. He restored some national tradition to the area of public education.

The United States has long left matters of educational policy up to state and local governments. The new federal Department of Education defied this tradition last August, proposing sweeping regulations in bilingual education. Those regulations would have had the force of law come next June. Bell rejected them in part, he said, because they were "unworkable and incredibly costly."

Local school districts were apprehensive about a federal takeover of a matter that should have been expressly in their domain. They are applauding Bell's move, with good reason. Had they defied the law, the federal government could, and probably would, have taken them to court.

The feds thought they had court backing since the 1974 Supreme Court decision, Lau vs. Nichols. It was a landmark case in which the court ruled that public schools were obliged to provide special help to non-English-speaking students. It did not specify what form that help should take. Nor did it address the broader issue of federal involvement in an area that the Tenth Amendment would seem to leave to local districts.

In New Mexico, the state Department of Education provided the help in its own way. Today its bilingual program is underfunded but does meet the needs of many non-English-speaking New Mexicans. It is designed to help everyone learn English. When help is needed to meet that purpose, it is provided.

New Mexico officials, when asked their reaction to the federal regulations last fall, went on record as opposing them because they were too rigid, prescriptive and dictatorial. Bell's recent move seconded that and is supported by the state's congressional delegation.

Bilingual education is a commendable idea. The challenge is to provide help to those who need it in order to secure an education and compete in the American mainstream — a part of the "melting pot" ideal that gives strength to this republic.

A full-scale program of bilingual education may or may not be the ideal way to meet that challenge. But the Tenth Amendment to the U.S. Constitution seems to leave the decision up to local districts when it says: "the powers not delegated to the United States by the Constitution nor prohibited by it to the states, are reserved to the states respectively or to the people."

Sentinel Star

Orlando, Fla., February 2, 1981

TO TEACH English to a non-English-speaking public school student do you: (1) throw him into an all-English curriculum in the hope that he will float up to the scholastic average; (2) bombard him with intensive English classes at the expense of grade-level studies or; (3) attempt to teach him English while he receives classwork in his native tongue?

That not-so-simple question has placed school districts and educators across the country squarely in the middle of what may be the biggest educational quandary of the year. In Florida the problem is especially acute.

The Civil Rights Act of 1964 was interpreted to mean that every child is entitled to an equal education, regardless of his proficiency in the English language. There were no official guidelines on how it was to be accomplished, only that it work.

Most schools have used one of the three approaches above to get students who can't speak English into the mainstream. Each method, of course, has its pros and cons. The first is the cheapest and simplest approach. The non-English-speaking student is treated no differently from his American counterpart; he either learns or he doesn't. Many don't.

The second method — commonly known as English as a Second Language — gives the student the opportunity to grasp the fundamentals of English before being thrust into highly verbal classroom situations. The student may learn the language adequately in, say, a year. Meanwhile, he may slip behind in other academic studies, a situation opponents call discriminatory and inequitable.

The third method — called bilingual education — is costly and controversial. Extra bilingual teachers must be hired, often straining already-tight school budgets. And detractors point out that bilingual programs further segregate the students, both culturally and educationally, by fostering a dependence on their native language.

It was into this morass of conflicting opinions that the federal government stepped last year attempting to standardize the nation's approach. When the Department of Education proposed regulations to mandate expensive and highly restrictive bilingual programs, it raised a nationwide protest.

School districts argued that the department was usurping local autonomy by mandating how individual schools must teach its students who don't speak English. In addition to being highly restrictive, the program was also so costly that most school systems couldn't afford it.

Congress has placed the department's plan on ice until June 1. Chances are good, given the Reagan administration's less-government-the-better stance, the proposed regulations may never be defrosted.

Still, the nagging problem remains: Which is the best way to educate students who don't speak English? It is a need that has to be met.

The answer is probably best found within individual school districts, based on the ethnic characters and individual needs of their student populations. For certain, they should not be forced to implement bilingual programs. The ultimate test, of course, is whether the district's educational program works. There has to be some standardized system of testing to measure that success.

By stepping out of the picture now, the federal government is putting the burden on local systems to produce their own programs. If the systems don't meet that challenge, they are failing in their own responsibility and inviting federal intervention once again.

The Des Moines Register

Des Moines, Iowa, February 9, 1981

The furor over the bilingual-education regulations proposed last year by the U.S. Department of Education, frozen by Congress and withdrawn by the Reagan administration last week might lead one to think that federal involvement in this subject is new and has now been ended.

The issue is not new, and, if an act of Congress and a decision of the U.S. Supreme Court mean anything, Education Secretary Terrel Bell's withdrawal cannot become a full-scale retreat.

The 1964 Civil Rights Act bars schools from receiving federal aid if they discriminate against racial groups. The Supreme Court ruled in 1974 that the San Francisco school system's refusal to provide special English instruction to 1,800 of its Chinese-speaking pupils constituted such discrimination.

To implement the decision, the Department of Health, Education and Welfare drafted guidelines requiring not only special English instruction but transitional help in the pupils' own language wherever their number makes it feasible. This requirement has been upheld in federal courts.

All the denunciation of federal dictation notwithstanding, a school that does no more than dump its non-English-speaking pupils into one special English class a day is not meeting those pupils' needs. We hope that Bell doesn't intend to let schools qualify for federal aid merely by going through the motions that way.

Transitional help for Asian and Spanish-speaking youngsters to set them on the path toward fruitful citizenchip is an idea that should not be cast aside simply because it will not be required. School boards often say they don't need Big Brother in Washington to tell them what they ought to do. Here is a chance for them to prove it.

The Dispatch

Columbus, Ohio, February 9, 1981

INCREASING numbers of Spanish-speaking immigrants in America have presented the public education system with a problem — whether to teach school children in their native tongue or rely on the traditional "melting pot" and provide instruction in English.

The Carter administration, heeding a U.S. Supreme Court ruling that schools were obliged to provide special help for non-English speaking children, proposed they be taught in their native tongues.

But the Reagan administration has revoked that proposal, saying the five-year $1 billion cost was unwarranted, although it warned school officials about discriminating against children facing a language barrier.

The logical answer may be in a program at Ohio State University which last fall received a $380,000 federal grant to develop teachers specializing in bilingual education. A requirement was that they be fluent in Spanish.

That leads to the question of why a bilingual teacher cannot satisfactorily teach a Spanish-speaking pupil in English, rather than in the learner's native tongue. The melting pot worked for earlier generations of immigrants. It can work as well today.

The Dallas Morning News

Dallas, Texas, February 4, 1981

"IT'S A step backward," says State Sen. Carlos Truan.

"I'm very disappointed about it," says State Rep. Gonzalo Barrientos.

"This is but one more example that the Reagan administration is trying to disembowel the Hispanic community," says President Ruben Bonilla of the League of United Latin American Citizens (LULAC).

The gentlemen should calm down. They are seriously overheated. So the Reagan administration has scrapped the previous administration's guidelines for bilingual education. That in no way constitutes a victory for racism, or whatever — rather, a victory for common sense and, to use a quaint old expression, constitutional government.

Last August, the Carter administration proposed permanent rules requiring a school district with as few as 25 non-English-speaking students to teach these students in their "primary" language.

Five months later, the Carter administration packed and left town. The new secretary of Education, Terrel Bell, this week said the guidelines likewise had to go. Bell called them "harsh, inflexible, burdensome, unworkable and incredibly costly" which is perhaps the ultimate that can be said against any government regulation.

Bell said the new administration's approach would be to support bilingual education all right but to let the states come up with their own programs.

"I would like," he said, "to use this regulation, symbolic of many of the ills that have plagued the federal government and this fledgling department, to telegraph a message to the American people. We will produce fewer and more reasonable rules and provide a more civil service."

If we read the election returns rightly, it was to do just this that Reagan was elected. The myth routed at the polls last November was that only federal programs and federal directives suffice for the righting of wrongs. The reality is that no government can always legislate wisely for a country so large and diverse as this one. Texas' needs are not Connecticut's. For that matter, Dallas' needs are not necessarily Houston's.

Of course there should be no abandoning of bilingual education. But it makes sense to design such education to meet local needs.

Bell's decision, be it noted, does not automatically free Texas to do what is right for Texans. An imprudent decision by U.S. Dist. Judge William Wayne Justice would compel the state to do much more in the bilingual education line than really needs doing. Fortunately Justice's isn't the last word. Let us hope the higher courts reverse him so Texas can join the ranks of states newly liberated from a suffocating imposition that only zealots should mourn.

The Seattle Times

Seattle, Wash., February 3, 1981

CARTER-administration regulations that would have required schools to teach foreign-speaking pupils in their native languages are a classic example of bureaucratic theory triumphing over common sense.

Terrel Bell, the new education secretary, calls the regulations "harsh, inflexible, burdensome, unworkable and incredibly costly." That covers all the bases and adds up to reason enough to junk the regulations, as Bell did yesterday.

The rules, which were to have taken effect in June, would have been particularly burdensome to a school district such as Seattle's, which has a smorgasbord of foreign languages represented among its pupil population.

Bell says his department will "protect the rights of children who do not speak English well, but will do so by permitting school districts to use any way that has proven successful."

That is in line with Seattle School Supt. David L. Moberly's contention that the federal government should have no role in mandating instructional methods.

There remains some unfinished business in Olympia. There, three Seattle-area legislators have drafted a bill to abolish mandatory bilingual instruction in Washington schools.

Yesterday's action at the federal level ought to make it easy for the Legislature to act.

The bill's sponsors — Representatives Helen Sommers and John Eng, Seattle Democrats, and Dan McDonald, Bellevue Republican — correctly point out that bilingual instruction actually is a handicap to a child who eventually must live and compete in an English-speaking society.

Los Angeles Times

Los Angeles, Calif., February 5, 1981

The Reagan Administration's decision to discard proposed rules on bilingual education may mean little practically and a lot politically.

Many states with substantial non-English-speaking populations either already have bilingual education programs, as California does, or are under federal court order to provide or improve them, as Texas now is.

Education Secretary Terrel H. Bell remains under court order himself to issue rules to help school districts know how to obey a 1974 U.S. Supreme Court decision. That decision, in the San Francisco case of Lau v. Nichols, held that children's equal opportunity to obtain a public education was denied them if they could not understand the language in which that education was being conducted. Bell's predecessor, Shirley M. Hufstedler, was trying to clarify the existing but imprecise guidelines with the new rules.

The rules were controversial. No one will ever know now whether they would have worked. What is important for the future is whether Bell encourages school districts to follow the existing voluntary guidelines while he writes what in his mind would be less harsh, less costly, more workable rules. He says he will. And he says he will continue financing experiments in how best to teach children English, which should, after all, be the goal of the whole affair.

Many people disagree with the concept of bilingual education. They think that children can be taught English by hearing English; in many cases they are correct. But with vast groups of immigrants, such as Latinos here in California who are often immersed at home and on the street in Spanish only, the bilingual approach often works better. It requires well-trained teachers, however, and there is a shortage of them.

The idea is that children can be learning mathematics and science as they are also learning English. They will stay more or less abreast of their English-speaking schoolmates, not get frustrated and not drop out. The goal is not to preserve their native language but to teach them English while not penalizing them for not knowing it for other subjects.

That brings us to the political and symbolic implications of Bell's decision. Only two weeks in office, the Reagan Administration has angered or at least disappointed many Latinos. In some areas they are the prime users of the public schools. The Reagan Administration does not realize that, to many Latinos, bilingual education is their civil-rights act, their access to getting ahead. This was the first major decision of Reagan's education secretary, and it was not handled well politically. It would have been wiser to have turned the thrust of the decision around, emphasizing what will still be done and what can be saved from the proposed rules.

While some Latinos simply use bilingual education as a political rallying cry, many others genuinely perceive that the door to educational opportunity has again been closed in their faces. It is a perception with which Bell and his department must wrestle when deciding what to do next.

The Hartford Courant
Hartford, Conn., February 10, 1981

Education Secretary Terrel H. Bell's decision to scrap his department's rules on bilingual education should not, indeed must not, eliminate bilingual instruction.

Mr. Bell argues that the regulations — ordering bilingual classes in school districts with more than 25 non-English-speaking students of one language group — were "harsh, inflexible, burdensome, unworkable and incredibly costly."

His objections are based more on his dislike of federal intervention in local educational matters than on any intrinsic unhappiness with bilingual instruction.

He has not, in other words, resolved the emotional national debate on bilingual education, affecting some 3.5 million students. The conflict remains between the people — and school districts — who believe children should be taught only in English and those who believe that children should be allowed to make a gradual transition from their own language to English.

The U.S. Supreme Court ruled unanimously in 1974 that failing to give non-English-speaking children special language instruction deprived them of an equal education. "There is no equality of treatment merely by providing students with the same facilities, textbooks, teachers and curriculum, for students who do not understand English are effectively foreclosed from any meaningful education," Justice William O. Douglas wrote in the case of Lau vs. Nichols, which involved Chinese-speaking children in San Francisco.

The court, however, never specified what sort of language instruction should be offered. A number of states, meanwhile, approved their own bilingual education laws. Connecticut, for example, requires that bilingual instruction be offered in school districts where 20 or more children speak the same foreign language. Parents do not have to enroll their children in bilingual classes if they do not want to. About 10,000 children, most of them Spanish-speaking, receive bilingual instruction in Connecticut.

The federal regulations were aimed at states and school districts which had not acted to carry out the Supreme Court decision. These regulations were frozen by Congress last summer, and finally killed by Mr. Bell last week.

School districts still have an obligation to educate children who do not speak English. States and local school boards simply have the option of deciding which method they prefer. School districts with small numbers of non-English-speaking students may choose to immerse those youngsters in English more quickly because they will need English skills immediately to survive in their environment. Other cities, like Hartford, Bridgeport, New York or Chicago, with large ethnic communities, may find bilingual education more effective, to prevent children from falling behind in other subjects while they learn a new language.

The danger is that without federal prodding in some school districts, no language instruction will be offered, or that states which now require bilingual education will no longer feel compelled to do so.

Historically, immigrants to this country have been expected to survive in an all-English environment. People tend to forget the trauma of not being able to communicate and keep up in school. Bilingual education tries to ease the shock of a new language and culture by teaching children basic subjects in their own language, while they achieve fluency in English. Bilingual classes seek to bridge the old life and the new, to allow a person to integrate past and present experience.

Mr. Bell's action does not negate the value of bilingual education. It simply returns decisions about curriculum to local governments. The Supreme Court insistence remains, that non-English-speaking youngsters be given special language instruction.

The Birmingham News
Birmingham, Ala., February 3, 1981

New Education Secretary T.H. Bell has, rightly, put an end to the notion of federally required bilingual education with a firm and clearly understandable English "No."

Rules developed by the Education Department during the Carter administration would have forced the nation's schools to teach children who aren't native speakers of English in both their native tongue and English. The requirement would have cost schools from $180 to $591 million a year, according to the department's own estimates.

Bell, however, called the new policies "harsh, inflexible, burdensome, unworkable and incredibly costly." He used as his justification for dismantling the policies — which already had been put on hold by Congress — that they would be "an intrusion on state and local responsibility," a theme emphasized by President Reagan in his Inaugural address.

Secretary Bell is of course right in that observation, but he might as well have added that bilingual education offers a greater potential harm in the disservice it would do the students for whom it supposedly was brought into being. By relegating English to the status of second language, bilingual education can, in effect, condemn such students to lives outside the mainstream of American life, hobbled perpetually by their inability to communicate as effectively as they should.

Local school boards will still be able, if they wish, to institute special programs for students whose native tongue is a foreign language, as is only right. They deserve extra help in mastering English while attending to other studies. But, this is best done through immersion into the American language as well as culture, not through an artificial program of instruction which can only result in fettered English-speaking abilities.

And, in a land where foreign languages remain, in fact, "foreign," such would be an unfair burden to place on the backs of students who should be receiving the most effective training possible.

The Burlington Free Press
Burlington, Vt., February 4, 1981

In tossing out the Carter administration's bilingual education proposals in favor of other approaches to teaching students who do not speak English, Education Secretary T.H. Bell has taken a step to avert serious problems for the nation's school districts.

His move also will save taxpayers an estimated $1 billion in the next five years.

Under harsh guidelines drawn up by his predecessor, Shirley M. Hufstedler, and blocked by Congress last year, school districts with more than 25 foreign-speaking students would have been required to offer them instruction in their native language as well as in English. Children with limited or no ability to speak English were to be taught basic courses — reading, mathematics and science — in their native language. Only by obtaining a waiver from the Department of Education could the schools deviate from the requirements.

"Nothing in the law or the Constitution anoints the Department of Education to be national school teacher, national school superintendent or national school board," Bell said in making his announcement that the rules would be discarded.

Aside from the added burdens that would be imposed on taxpayers by the proposals, they would have created an untenable situation in schools by slowing the shift from native languages to English. Such a step might have created a problem of language disabilities among youngsters who might be reluctant to learn English.

Since one of the most difficult obstacles to overcome in learning a second language is the ability to think in its terms, the possibility would exist that the basic courses which were taught in the child's native language might have to be relearned when the transition to English was made. Just where the shift to English would begin was not made clear by the Hufstedler proposals.

But one thing is certain: Foreign-speaking students must begin to learn English as soon as possible in the schools or they will be penalized intellectually and socially for that failure.

Champions of bilingual education must realize that their support of such programs could be doing incalculable harm to those youngsters who need the most help if they are to cope with the problems of an English-speaking society.

TULSA WORLD
Tulsa, Okla., February 4, 1981

THE Reagan Administration has junked the ill-advised plan to force U. S. schools to instruct children whose primary language isn't English in both their native tongue and English.

The new Secretary of Education T. H. Bell said the plan, offered in the closing days of the Carter Administration, is "harsh, inflexible, burdensome, unworkable and incredibly costly."

He's exactly right, of course.

Already there are screams of outrage from so-called civil rights leaders who see in his action an offense against minorities, presumably those whose native tongue isn't English.

It is nothing of the sort.

There is nothing to stop schools across the nation from giving non-English speaking students special instruction in English to prepare them for classes to be taught in English. In fact, this will be encouraged by Bell's discarding the bilingual instruction rule.

The undeniable fact is that English is the language of the United States. Wave after wave of immigrants have been called upon to learn the language of their new country and succeeded admirably.

Bilingual instruction would have in many cases delayed that learning to the detriment of not only the individuals involved but the country as well.

One of, some say the most, important unifying factors in the U. S. is the commonality of language. The important thing is not that the language happens to be English. If the common tongue were Spanish or French the principle would be the same; everyone should be encouraged (and helped) to speak the language of the country.

Schools can now turn to a reasonable course that all should support. Let's spend whatever is needed (and it will be far less than teaching courses in a variety of languages spoken by a small percentage of the population) to see that every student learns English to prepare him for an education and a productive role in an English-speaking society.

The Salt Lake Tribune
Salt Lake City, Utah, February 5, 1981

In revoking federal regulations that would have required public schools to teach foreign-speaking students in their native language, Secretary of Education T. H. Bell was not abandoning the underlying concept upon which the regulation rested.

Instead, the former Utahn was opting for a new, less structured approach to educating foreign speaking children.

The regulation which Dr. Bell revoked was the federal government's belated response to a 1974 U.S. Supreme Court decision which held that Chinese-speaking students in San Francisco public schools were being discriminated against under civil rights laws by being taught only in English. The court did not spell out an acceptable remedy but the then Department of Health, Education and Welfare went to work drafting a response which would meet court objections. It was this effort — it had not yet gone into effect — which Dr. Bell jettisoned because he found it too inflexible and expensive.

In revoking the old regulation, the secretary pledged that he and his staff would rewrite the regulations to provide greater leeway for local school districts. Meanwhile, the department will follow guidelines issued in 1975 which call for bilingual education in some instances but do not have the force of law.

Although the bilingual education issue directly affects only an estimated 3.5 million children who speak little English, its seeming affront to the hallowed "melting pot" image of public education has made it an issue of interest far and wide. And with the influx of new refugee and illegal alien waves, the controversy can be expected to build.

Some ethnic groups meet the language dilemma by maintaining private instruction facilities which teach the old country language while the same children are encouraged to learn English and American ways in the public schools. The idea of teaching them in public schools in their native tongue appears to go against absorption into the mainstream but it doesn't have to.

Even under the now-revoked regulations, English would have been taught all students although instructors spoke the native language in the early stages. Such a system facilitates instruction in other fields than language in the first years of school while a knowledge of English is being phased in. Dr. Bell's new guidelines will presumably encourage, without mandating, a continuation of this design.

As with many federal programs applied to the nation as a whole, local authorities are in a better position to judge the degree of application necessary to achieve desired results and should have a relatively free hand to do so. Where bilingual instruction is needed, there should be some outside pressure to see that it is provided. But the pressure should take the form of enlightened guidance instead of blanket fiat.

THE CHRISTIAN SCIENCE MONITOR
Boston, Mass., February 4, 1981

The new secretary of education's first major action — dropping proposed bilingual education rules — is a signal of reducing specific federal requirements on states and localities. It is not a signal of abandoning federal responsibility for protecting the rights of American children, including those who enter school with a primary language other than English. These points were made quite clear by Secretary Bell in announcing his controversial decision. They should be kept in mind as he and his staff go ahead with preparing what he described as more flexible regulations to meet the needs of the nation's estimated 3.6 million school-age children who are not proficient in English.

Some 70 percent of these children are Spanish speaking. And Mr. Bell is starting right off in the spirit of the platform endorsed by the President who appointed him: "There should be local educational programs which enable those who grew up learning another language such as Spanish to become proficient in English while also maintaining their own language and cultural heritage."

It was to reduce confusion about the civil rights requirements for local programs — and to give rules for implementing them the force of law — that the Department of Education offered the now rejected proposals last year. They were attacked and supported from many sides. Some welcomed the fact that, for the first time, a maximum limit (five years) was placed on the extent of bilingual education provided a given student, and that the teachers in other languages were required to be fluent in English. Some complained that the identification of eligible students was prescribed only below the ninth grade, and that bilingual classes were not required unless there were at least 25 eligible students of the same primary non-English language in two consecutive grades of a given school. Among all the matters spelled out, one question left dangling was what should be required to serve children found equally lacking in both English and their native tongue.

The need to dispel confusion remains. As does the basic object of the rules described by former Secretary Hufstedler: to teach English as quickly as possible to children of other languages while teaching them other subjects in a language they can understand so that they do not fall behind their English-speaking classmates in the meantime.

Therefore Secretary Bell should not delay in fashioning regulations to ensure that all schools know what they are expected to accomplish under civil rights legislation — and under the 1974 Supreme Court decision interpreting it to require positive action on behalf of students not fluent in English. Since the court did not specify remedies, schools need guidance on what is acceptable — without being stifled from the local initiative, energy, and inventiveness to reach the most appropriate and efficient solutions for local circumstances. For example, considering the quickness of young children in assimilating language, a program of intensified English instruction might be found a satisfactory alternative to teaching in another language.

The costs of any effective program must be seen in the perspective of the enormous loss to the nation of allowing a significant segment of its young people to fail to reach their potential because of language barriers. In helping them, the greatest care must be taken not to worsen those barriers by locking individuals or parts of the country into any other language as an encouraged alternative to English. They must be brought into the mainstream of America's official language both for their own sakes and to prevent a linguistic fragmentation that could go beyond healthy pluralism and feed divisiveness.

THE SACRAMENTO BEE
Sacramento, Calif., February 9, 1981

The Reagan administration's repeal of proposed federal regulations on bilingual education was more symbol than substance, not only in places like California whose program already exceeds the proposed federal standards, but in many other places where, with some modification, they might have had some benefit. In any case, since Congress had already blocked their implementation, probably forever, there was a great deal less in the revocation than the big headlines suggested.

The regulations, announced last summer by former Secretary of Education Shirley Hufstedler, would have required school districts with more than 25 non-English- or limited-English-speaking students to offer those students instruction in their native language as well as in English. Alternative programs or other variances from the rules were permitted, but would have required a waiver from the Department of Education.

The rules were probably too rigid, particularly since the success of bilingual education in getting students into the academic mainstream has never been clear enough to commend it over intense, special instruction in English or other alternative approaches. It's, of course, that questionable record, combined with the flexibility for local school districts that it seems to require, which underlies the administration's rationale for revoking the guidelines. Indeed, there is an argument to be made that the flexible approach the Reagan administration favors is more consistent with the U.S. Supreme Court's ruling in *Lau v. Nichols*, the San Francisco case which mandated special efforts for non-English-speaking students but did not specify what techniques should be used. It was *Lau* which created the need for such guidelines in the first place.

Nonetheless, as a definition of objectives and standards of bilingual education, the now-revoked guidelines made good sense. They established "exit criteria," for example, that would have encouraged schools to move students out of the bilingual program and into regular classes as rapidly as possible. Had the Department of Education retained those definitions while giving local disticts greater flexibility in approach, the guidelines could have been extremely useful, particularly in places like Arizona and Texas, where local option in this field is, more often than not, exercised by doing nothing.

In many places in the Southwest, the practices haven't changed much — which is, of course, why at least some states and local school officials were so adamantly opposed to the Hufstedler guidelines. Thus, while the federal government has now opted for greater flexibility, it cannot choose to abandon its responsibility, moral and legal under the *Lau* decision, to make certain that children who do not speak English get the educational services that will allow them to enter the mainstream — through bilingual education, through English-as-a-second-language programs, or through other means. Local discretion cannot be allowed to become a cover for local neglect. The administration has undone something in this area. It has yet to do something.

The Idaho STATESMAN
Boise, Idaho, February 5, 1981

Education Secretary T.H. Bell's decision to toss out the Carter administration's bilingual education proposals is good, but should not be taken as a complete disavowal of any federal role in ensuring good education for children who do not speak English well.

Rather, it is — or at least should be — a retreat to a proper federal role, one in which Washington does not set local policy but serves as an enforcer of last resort for those who suffer because of racial or linguistic discrimination.

Under the Carter proposal, the Education Department would have mandated when, where and under what circumstances local school districts would have had to provide bilingual instruction — classes in which students who don't speak or read English very well are taught basic skills in their primary language.

Such rules just aren't necessary. Under the Civil Rights Act of 1964 and a Supreme Court decision rendered in 1974, schools must provide equal education for children who don't speak English.

The Education Department has — and will continue to have — considerable clout to enforce such rulings through the threat of withholding federal funds. Burley schools, for example, were forced to provide bilingual instruction after inspectors discovered the district was not providing adequate education for Spanish-speaking students.

Ontario, Ore., schools also were forced to re-evaluate and upgrade their programs after federal officials determined Spanish-speaking students there were not receiving adequate instruction.

In such cases a little federal prodding probably is necessary. Sometimes local officials just won't admit there is a problem unless somebody slaps them with an action. Such prodding, however, should be done on a case-by-case basis, rather than through a blanket mandate for bilingual programs.

That way, local school officials can react to local problems with solutions designed to meet local needs.

The Philadelphia Inquirer
Philadelphia, Pa., February 4, 1981

The language Americans speak is English, or anyway, a version of it. Anyone who intends to function in American society, to get ahead in his work or profession, had better be fluent in the American language (unless he is a foreigner with an established reputation in, say, ballet).

That is why Secretary of Education Terrel Bell, in his first official act, was right in revoking the controversial rules proposed by his predecessor, Shirley Hufstedler, to require public schools to teach non-English speaking students in their native languages.

Mr. Bell seemed to emphasize ideological rather than linguistic factors. "Nothing in the law or the Constitution," he declared, "annoints the Department of Education to be national school teacher, national school superintendent or national school board."

But there is something in the law, the Civil Rights Act of 1964, which forbids discrimination on the basis of "national origin," and the U.S. Supreme Court, in 1974, ruled that that meant schools were obliged to provide equal educational opportunity to students unfamiliar with the American language. The court did not, however, prescribe how that was to be provided. That's where the Carter administration, with good motives, came up with a bad prescription.

The point is not so much that the proposed rules were, as Mr. Bell put it in rather purple prose, "harsh, inflexible, burdensome, unworkable and incredibly costly." The point is that the Carter administration was not doing a favor to the estimated 3.5 million children in the country, about 70 percent of them Hispanics, who speak little or no English.

The public schools have traditionally been the place where immigrant children learn the language Americans speak. To require those children to be taught in the language of their parents is to delay if not obstruct them in their ability to assimilate into and function in American society.

This is not to say they should be encouraged to forget the language of their parents. Quite the contrary: The bilingual person has an advantage. It is to say that the way to equalize educational opportunity is to provide special training in English to non-English-speaking children. That will have its costs, too, but it is cheaper for the schools than finding teachers who speak Spanish or Chinese or whatever, and better for the children.

NEW YORK POST

New York, N.Y., February 3, 1981

The first action of the extravagant new Dept. of Education set up last year by the Carter Administration was to propose nationwide regulations for bilingual education and the first substantial action of the Reagan Administration has been to scrap them.

Should we cheer? No more than half a cheer.

The new Education Secretary, Terrel Bell, declares: "The policies were harsh, inflexible, burdensome, unworkable and incredibly costly."

They were much worse than that. They would have encouraged divisiveness and fragmentation.

One of the main purposes of the public schools has been to Americanize waves of immigrants. In New York City, for example, almost half the population has a mother tongue other than English — 25 major languages are spoken by fairly large blocs.

The real menace of bilingualism in education is that, while appearing to help newcomers assimilate, it actually insures that they will be handicapped later by an inability to speak English and get skilled jobs.

Every course, from mathematics to music, would have required two teachers. Soon there would have been two sets of teachers and administrators in every school district.

When President Reagan named Bell Education Secretary, we were the first to ask, given his long career in education, if he were the right man to close the department, which now has a $15 billion budget.

Today we offer him only half a cheer because he has not scrapped the bilingual program, as he should have. His staff is simply rewriting the rules to make them more "flexible." Meanwhile, the department is switching to guidelines issued in 1975 which, as U.S. Education Commissioner, the same Terrel Bell wrote.

Once again, we must ask, is he likely in the long run to scrap this completely unnecessary program in its entirety and, even more important, this completely unnecessary department?

The News and Courier

Charleston, S.C., February 4, 1981

When he announced the scrapping of the Carter administration's bilingual education proposals, Education Secretary T. H. Bell labeled the rules that would have implemented them "harsh, inflexible, burdensome, unworkable and incredibly costly." Mr. Bell's assessment was accurate. The rules were all that, and more.

Take the cost alone. Requiring the nation's public schools to teach non-English speaking youngsters in their own languages would have added from $176 million to $596 million to annual operating costs — that was the Education Department's own estimate at the time Mr. Bell's predecessor wrote the proposed rules.

Something else was wrong with the bilingual education plan that Secretary Bell could have cited, too. It might have helped some non-English speaking pupils in the short run. It would have done none a favor in the long run. It would have done them a disservice.

The proposed program would have set them apart. It would have accentuated their differences. It could have stifled the incentive to learn the country's primary language. It would have provided a crutch that pupils later would have wished they had not depended on. In short in might have had an effect opposite what presumably was intended.

Among Americans are many whose grandparents or parents came to these shores unable to speak English. They and their sponsors didn't ask for bilingual classes. They accepted the learning challenge because they wanted to communicate, to be part of the business or community circle. Most buckled down and learned English; many excelled. It was not easy, but they did it on their own, without adding to the burdens of others.

Herald News

Fall River, Mass., February 4, 1981

Some confusion has arisen because Education Secretary T.H. Bell has announced the Reagan administration will not implement guidelines for bilingual education which the Carter administration recommended.

School Superintendent Correiro has pointed out that Bell's announcement does not affect the state-mandated, bi-lingual program here, nor the federal funding the city receives for this purpose under Title Seven.

In point of fact, all that it does is make plain that the administration will not try to implement Carter's proposal to force any community with more than 20 students who do not speak English to institute a bi-lingual program.

The superintendent did indicate that it is unclear what, if any, effect Proposition 2½ will have on the state-mandated program here, or whether the federal Department of Education, which President Reagan has previously announced he will dismantle, will change its rules regarding funding for bilingual purposes under Title Seven.

In other words, the statement by Secretary Bell has no local implications, but the superintendent, like everyone else, is at present uncertain about what future cutbacks on the federal or state levels will entail.

It was never at all certain that a separate, cabinet-level Department of Education was a good idea. The Carter administration fought for its creation and won the fight, but the department, which has not been in existence long enough as a separate entity to justify itself, may well be dissolved and its functions returned to some other department such as HUD.

If so, the motive will be less educational than economic, and will not in itself indicate what the administration's attitude is toward bi-lingual education.

Everywhere in the country there is uncertainty about the administration's intentions in respect to many federally funded programs in education and other fields. That uncertainty is compounded in Massachusetts by Proposition 2½, and it extends to the future of bilingual education.

But Secretary Bell's statement, in itself, does not indicate what that future will be.

THE PLAIN DEALER

Cleveland, Ohio, February 4, 1981

We endorse the Reagan administration's revocation of proposed regulations that would have required public schools to instruct foreign-language pupils in whatever tongue they happened to speak.

The rules would have applied to all school districts that enroll more than 25 foreign-language pupils. Secretary of Education T. H. Bell said the cost over five years would have been about $1 billion — not to mention about $175 million in federal funds already spent annually on bilingual education.

This is not to say that the rights of foreign-speaking pupils are any less than those of pupils who speak English. To the contrary; what it does say is that it is not right for the U.S. government to subsidize — indeed, to sponsor! — a program that in effect encourages a minority of youngsters to remain linguistically separate from the majority of U.S. society. That isolation could greatly inhibit their opportunities — economic, social, political or otherwise.

Bell said he would go back to the drawing board to determine how the regulations, which would cover about 3.5 million children in the nation who speak little or no English, might be reworked. The emphasis should be on teaching the youngsters to reason and communicate in English, the language of the United States. Such an approach would foster equality of opportunity, not promote a doctrine of separate but equal, as did the regulations set aside.

It is valuable for ethnic and nationality groups to hold onto customs and cultures, and these need not be sacrificed in the approach we favor. Many persons who would be affected by the regulations are Hispanics. They need look only at the immigrant groups that preceded them to this country to see that learning a common language need not mean abandonment of a way of life.

New regulations and guidelines should allow for as much local decision-making as possible. What works in Miami, El Paso or San Diego might be wrong for Cleveland, Chicago or Detroit. It no doubt would be reasonable to retain certain bilingual programs. But to ensure that all children are prepared to function as equally as they can in society, they should be able to reason and communicate in the common tongue.

THE SAGINAW NEWS
Saginaw, Mich., February 4, 1981

The dumping of proposed regulations on bilingual education is not the blow some members of the Hispanic community now believe it is.

It could even help more kids.

Education Secretary Terrel Bell did not, and could not, dump court rulings asserting the right of all children to equal educational opportunity.

Nor did he, or could he, overturn state laws. Michigan already insists on special instruction in districts with a large foreign-speaking community. In most cases, but not all, that means Spanish.

Bilingual education is a good way to help many youngsters keep up their studies while they learn English. It has been around since the 1960s. It has not been dumped. Its value, contrary to the gist of some reaction to Bell's decision, wasn't the issue.

The question was whether the federal government or local school people can better decide how programs are taught.

In our view, the federal regulations were too strict, too costly and went too far. Even local efforts that work would have been scrapped if they deviated from Washington's version of what's best.

That sort of attitude has proved a failure in many instances of federal regulation. It is an insult to the judgment of local communities.

In the Saginaw area, we believe there is real concern for the educational success of children whose native language is not English. Our thousands of Hispanic citizens should make sure that concern continues.

Secretary Bell said the responsibility is now back where it belongs. Local educators, from school boards on down, should show they accept that responsibility.

Pablo Ruiz, director of bilingual education for Saginaw schools, wisely noted that some districts, freed from arbitrary regulations, may now take their own steps to better serve students who need special help with language transition.

The goal should be to help students learn to understand and use English. The proposed federal rules would have retarded this process by making instruction in a foreign language a "right" and not a transition.

Ethnic diversity is highly important. It helps us know ourselves and understand each other.

But English is still the social and economic glue of this society. Without it, anyone can expect to be handicapped through life.

The purpose of bilingual education is to eliminate handicaps to equal opportunity. That purpose can be reached better without federal regulators acting like a national school board.

Roanoke Times & World-News
Roanoke, Va., February 6, 1981

The Carter administration's bilingual education proposals, requiring the nation's schools to teach non-English-speaking children in their native languages, are dead. May they rest in peace, for a good long time.

As he sounded the death knell, Reagan administration Education Secretary T. H. Bell stated the matter succinctly. "Nothing in the law or the Constitution," Bell said, "anoints the Department of Education to be National School Teacher, National School Superintendent or National School Board."

Secretary Bell said he sees the death of the proposal as a symbol "to telegraph a message of change to the American people." Message received, Mr. Bell. Thanks.

The Charlotte Observer
Charlotte, N.C., February 5, 1981

The Carter administration no doubt had good intentions when it proposed requiring schools to teach children in their native languages. In this country, a child has a right to education, but if the child can't speak the language in which the education is offered, the "right" becomes difficult to claim.

Despite those good intentions, the Reagan administration was right to scrap the plan this week. It would have required school districts with more than 25 foreign-speaking students to teach them in their own languages until they learned English.

For many school systems, that would have been all but impossible, and prohibitively expensive. In Charlotte-Mecklenburg this year, for example, students come from homes where 64 different languages are spoken, including Farsi, Tagalog and Urdu.

And even where it was possible, it was the wrong approach when it diminished the incentive for children to learn English and assimilate into the American melting pot, whose glue is a common language: English.

Many schools already provide adequate help for foreign-speaking students. In Charlotte, students are taught English as a second language, and teachers receive special training in communicating with students who don't speak English yet.

The problems of students in English-speaking schools who are just beginning to learn the language are real, and school systems ought to address those problems — under government pressure, if necessary. Likewise, the schools ought to be required to display and encourage respect for a variety of ethnic backgrounds.

But none of that should require any school system to provide teachers fluent in all the native languages represented in a large metropolitan area. The greater emphasis ought to be on encouraging all students who don't speak English to learn it.

THE ARIZONA REPUBLIC
Phoenix, Ariz., February 5, 1981

BILINGUAL education is back where it belongs, in the hands of local school officials.

That happened when Secretary of Education Terrel Bell withdrew bilingual regulations proposed by his predecessor, Shirley Hufstedler.

For Arizona and the rest of the American Southwest, that amounts to exorcism of an especially pernicious federal specter.

Local school districts had been trying for decades to cope with the problem of drawing youngsters into the English-speaking mainstream from homes and neighborhoods where another language, usually Spanish, predominated.

The approaches varied. Some districts offered the three R's in Spanish, while transitional language courses brought the students into English fluency by the middle of elementary school.

Others used the total-immersion technique.

Other districts did nothing. It was up to parents to prepare youngsters for school in the national language.

That led to federal intervention in the name of civil rights.

Failure to educate non-English speaking students, said the Supreme Court, amounted to discrimination against them. To the cheers of the National Education Association, which saw the potential for thousands of new jobs in a nationwide bilingual-education program, the Carter administration drew up the rules by which local educators would have to live, reporting to Washington at every step of the way.

To carry out those regulations would have cost the country's taxpayers $1 billion over five years. Now that the Reagan administration has discarded those rules, local districts remain free to deal with their students' language problems as they'd like.

That doesn't free them of their responsibility of educating those students, however. They can co-opt parents into the teaching process, they can try the transitional approach, or they can blitz the youngsters in the Berlitz fashion.

But educate them they must — and should.

Failure to educate speakers of broken English today would all but guarantee serious social problems tomorrow.

Rockford Register Star

Rockford, Ill., February 6, 1981

Quite aside from the $1 billion in additional costs the plan would have foisted on American schools, mandatory expanded bilingual education deserved its demise on humanitarian grounds.

The Reagan administration, in its first major decision affecting students, correctly has scuttled Carter proposed standards requiring foreign-language speaking students be tutored in their own tongue while they were being taught English.

Local school districts can elect to do this, as Rockford's Board of Education does. However, the Washington edict makes clear that such an option is exactly that, that a nationwide rule demanding dual language instruction would be ''harsh, inflexible, burdensome, unworkable and incredibly costly.''

That's the view of the new Education Secretary T.H. Bell.

And Bell said something else that speaks for the outlook of the new Washington regime: ''Nothing in the law or the Constitution anoints the Department of Education to be national school teacher, national school superintendent or national school board.''

In this stand, he has the support of the National Association of Elementary School Principals, the National School Board Association, and the American Federation of Teachers. All have opposed the mandatory bilingual standards proposed by Bell's predecessor, Shirley F. Hufstedler.

Even so, some florid and undeserved flak is being fired Bell's way.

Rep. Shirley Chisholm, D-N.Y., said of Bell's stance, ''This new racism is as invidious and destructive as the racial attitudes that have marred our history.''

Racism it is not. Indeed, Bell reaffirmed his commitment to civil rights in these words, ''I am committed to civil rights . . . and no school administrator should misread this action as an invitation to discriminate against children who face language barriers.''

Another over-reaction came from Rep. Robert Garcia, D-N.Y., who said, ''My God! If this is the first major educational decision of the Reagan administration, then this country is in for absolute disaster.''

Quite the opposite is true.

Had the standards gone forward, that would have been disaster. It would have said, implicitly and insidiously, that English is not the first language of this nation, which it happens to be. Mandating that math and science and reading be taught in French or Farsi or Senegalese, while also offering English, splays the reality of lingual discourse in this country.

To mandate full schooling in a second language would only perpetuate racial schisms in this country. It could only end forever the boast of the United States as the great melting pot of the world's people.

We use English as the instrument of communication and commerce. Why suggest otherwise? Why confuse youngsters as to what's expected of them? It is expected they will make the transition from a foreign language into English. This need not cancel a native language. It is a cultural plus. And, happily, these native languages frequently are spoken in the family home.

But a policy, promulgated in Washington, telling every school system in the country to gear its program to all foreign languages extant in the student population is something else again.

And where would be the limits of such a program? What would be the cost, for instance, of hiring an expert in the Mohawk language for only one Mohawk Indian in a class? Or one expert in Pushtun for one Iranian? Or one expert in Bambara for one student from the Republic of Mali?

Nor did Washington intend to help underwrite such exotic expenses. Indeed, Congress specifically withheld funds from bilinguistics.

So it is happily scuttled as a lockstep national rule. As an enlightened local option (Rockford serves 18 different language groups on a bilingual basis in five schools — offering help during a two-year language transitional period), that's something else again — a decision for the forgotten folks back home.

Let's leave it there.

THE DAILY HERALD

Biloxi, Miss., February 5, 1981

When newly appointed U. S. Secretary of Education Terrel H. Bell announced cancellation this week of department rules requiring school districts to provide bilingual education to children whose native tongue is not English, a vast sigh of relief was breathed by public school officials across the land.

The rules, adopted after the Department of Education was created by the Carter administration as a Cabinet-level entity, were flawed in concept and it is good they have been set aside.

It has been estimated that enforcing the rules to teach children reading, writing and other primary subjects in two languages — English and their native tongue — could have cost school districts from $180 million to $591 million a year. From a financial standpoint, given today's hard-pressed economy, it would have been a luxury few districts could afford.

But the objections are more basic than cost.

First, there is deep resentment among local educators of bureaucrats at the national level presuming to require the curriculum to be offered in their schools, and the manner in which it is presented. Traditionally, and logically, this is a matter for local boards to determine within boundaries set by professional accrediting associations.

Secondly, there is a danger, in our opinion, in the concept that non-English speaking children must, by federal dictate, be educated in their native tongue. We are a land of immigrants, and the process of absorption, so far as public schools are concerned, has been the presumption of Americanization and schooling in our historically-dictated language, English.

While multi-lingualism is an advantage to an individual and is easily accomodated within the private sector of this nation, the official stance, we believe, should enforce the position of English as the national language.

The U. S. Supreme Court in 1973 ruled that public schools must provide instruction to non-English-speaking students, but did not specify how they should be taught. According to Bell, setting aside of the department's bilingual regulations means schools can now revert to 1975 guidelines based on the Supreme Court ruling.

This leaves flexibility of method of instruction in the hands of local boards, consistent with Civil Rights law.

Bilingual instruction is primarily a significant issue today in those states bordering Mexico which have a large number of Spanish-speaking peoples. Certainly, efforts should be made to provide their children with educational opportunities, with state and federal financial assistance supplementing local programs as justified.

But while ethnic variations provide a rich strain in American culture, we do not need federal dictates which, in so basic a matter as language, could promote divisions rather than absorption among our peoples.

WORCESTER TELEGRAM.

Worcester, Mass., February 12, 1981

U.S. Education Secretary Terrel Bell has reversed the Carter administration's mandatory policy on bilingual education.

To require thousands of school departments to set up bilingual instruction, even when there were few students who needed it, would be "harsh, inflexible, burdensome, unworkable and incredibly costly," Bell said.

Of those five adjectives, "unworkable" is the most pertinent. For all the effort and money that has been put into bilingual education, it has seldom worked as hoped.

Bilingual classes have been least effective among groups with a strong affinity for another culture and language. If bilingualism is used not primarily to teach children English but to support a non-English tradition, it can become a crutch that slows the child's mastery of English rather than speeds it.

Bilingualism in some form will continue to be a useful tool for some school departments, as long as its primary aim is to expedite the teaching of English. But other school systems may want to try other methods.

The new ruling by Bell permits the sort of flexibility that local schools systems need to deal with this complex challenge.

THE COMMERCIAL APPEAL
Memphis, Tenn., February 10, 1981

THE PROPOSITION that foreign-born children in American schools must be taught in their native language according to strict national guidelines denies the remarkable achievement of cultural adjustment made by similar children down through the years.

It mocks the dreams of millions of other immigrants in the past who struggled to learn English so they could take advantage of the opportunities this country offered.

And it promotes the pompous, meddling, unworkable idea that the federal government can fix every problem by mandate.

So the news was encouraging last week that Secretary of Education T. H. Bell had revoked proposed regulations that would have required school districts with more than 25 foreign-speaking students to offer the students instruction in their native languages as well as in English.

The regulations, Bell said, would have cost the taxpayers about $1 billion over the next five years. He called them "symbolic of the many ills that plagued the federal government."

Supporters of bilingual education argue that many of the 3.5 million children in this country who speak little or no English face severe learning handicaps if they're taught only in English. But they face even greater handicaps if they don't master English.

These children undoubtedly need help, such as intense instruction in English. But the best and fastest way to learn any foreign language is through total immersion. That's why serious students of another language try to visit the country where the language is spoken. That's why some teachers of French, for instance, only allow French to be used in their classes. That's why many immigrants in the past banned their native languages in their homes.

The sons and daughters of those earlier immigrants were able to become productive members of this society without bilingual education. Why should things be so different today?

BELL'S ACTION doesn't abandon foreign-speaking students. Local school systems will still be able to have bilingual programs if they want to. About 500 systems already do. And, Bell said, "We will protect the rights of children who do not speak English well, but we will do so by permitting school districts to use any way that has proved successful."

The goal should be to teach English as quickly and effectively as possible. Then, even in school districts with 25 or fewer foreign-speaking students, lack of English would be much less of a handicap.

The Cincinnati Post
Cincinnati, Ohio, February 4, 1981

Secretary of Education Terrel Bell has wisely scrapped the Carter administration's proposal to force local schools to teach non-English-speaking students in their native tongues.

Not only would the bilingual education plan have been enormously expensive, but also there was no clear evidence that it would have been better for the students.

To the contrary, some educators argue that such students make more progress and are assimilated into American society more easily if they attend regular classes and are given extra help in learning English.

Bell aptly described the plan drafted by his predecessor, Secretary Shirley Hufstedler, as "harsh, inflexible, burdensome, unworkable and incredibly costly."

It would have required school districts that had more than 25 students

with a first language other than English to teach the youngsters in their native language. Some major metropolitan areas would have had to establish special classes in dozens of languages and find teachers capable of teaching classroom subjects in those tongues.

Besides the controversy over the value of bilingual education, a major reason for Bell's scrubbing Hufstedler's proposed regulation was to give local officials more say in how students shall be taught.

His action does not relieve local schools of the need to give proper education to non-English-speaking students. The Supreme Court ruled in 1974 that equal educational opportunity must be afforded them.

What Bell has done is give local officials leeway to choose the method of instruction they think best and not be dictated to by Washington. That is as it should be.

The Morning News
Wilmington, Del., February 8, 1981

A WELL-DESERVED death blow was dealt last week to the Carter administration's complex and overbearing regulations for bilingual education. This does not mean, however, that the federal government will henceforth shirk its responsibility toward non-English speaking students. Even if the Reagan administration wished to do so, the 1967 Bilingual Education Act, the Supreme Court Lau decision and civil rights laws would promptly summon the federal government to its obligation to ensure equal educational opportunities for all.

Few would dispute the idea that a first grader who speaks only Spanish will have immense difficulties learning how to read English. Similarly, a 15-year-old youngster fresh from Vietnam will face great obstacles in learning history, chemistry or any other high school subject when he barely knows how to say "hello" in English. If these students and an estimated 3.5 million like them across the United States are to get a proper education, they will need prompt and appropriate assistance in learning English. That much is clear.

But educators, government officials and English- and non-English-speaking citizens cannot agree on what constitutes "prompt and appropriate assistance." Former Secretary of Education Shirley Hufstedler wanted to issue a definition of "non-English speaking." Her proposed regulations also stipulated instruction in the student's native language for possibly as long as five years. These regulations have now been countermanded by T. H. Bell, the new secretary of education. He classified them as "inflexible, burdensome, unworkable and incredibly costly." And he promised to issue new guidelines to ensure equal educational opportunities for all, without interfering with local educational prerogatives.

Among the criteria Secretary Bell should bear in mind are:
● The goal must be to master English as quickly as possible.
● Different age groups must be treated differently. For instance, elementary school children may learn English best by being immersed in an English-speaking classroom where the teacher or a teacher's aide is available to assist with translation. Older students may require a period of intensive instruction in English before they go on to take regular schoolwork.
● The schools have no obligation to help students maintain fluency in their native language. Responsibility for that rests with the family and the private sector, just as religious instruction belongs in the home and the religious organization of one's choice.
● Different schools should be allowed to devise their own programs, depending not only on the needs of the student population but also on the teacher skills that can be secured.
● Consideration should be given to whether it is wise to keep foreign-speaking students grouped together, as is now the case with Hispanics in New Castle County, or whether these students would do better when grouped heterogeneously.
● The degree of federal funding obligation for any special program for non-English speaking students should be specified.

Parents who send their children to school in the United States must understand that knowledge of English is fundamental to getting an education. The schools have an obligation to assist non-English speaking students in acquiring skills in English. But that obligation is limited to a reasonable time period during which special instruction is provided and allowances are made.

As long as English is our country's language anyone wishing to live and work here has to do everything possible to learn to communicate in English. The earlier in school that task is undertaken, and the more swiftly it is carried out, the better will these non-English speaking persons be able to cope with life in the United States.

Hispanics Face Discrimination, A Familiar Immigrant Problem

New populations establishing themselves in the U.S. usually have to contend with intolerance, and the Hispanic community is no exception. Spanish-Americans suffer additional pressure because they are identified with illegal aliens. Most illegal aliens are Mexicans or other Latin Americans, and law enforcement officials often assume that anyone with a Spanish name is likely to be an illegal alien. This has resulted in unjustified detentions, warrantless house searches and other indignities.

Legal Hispanic-American citizens—even if American-born—are not immune from mistreatment. Mexican-American community leaders in Texas charge that state and local police use excessive violence against Hispanics. In the late 1970s, a number of investigations were launched into charges of police brutality against Mexican-American prisoners. In the most famous case, the Justice Department fought unsuccessfully from 1977–79 to increase the sentences of four ex-Houston policemen charged in the death of Joe Campos Torres. Three days after his arrest in May 1977 on a disorderly-conduct charge, the 23-year-old was found beaten and drowned in a Houston bayou. Two policemen received suspended one-year sentences in October 1977. The following March, after a Justice Department appeal, their sentences were reinstated, a third officer was sentenced to one year in prison, and all three received suspended 10-year sentences and five years' probation. The Justice Department again appealed on grounds the sentences were too lenient, but the court merely handed down additional one-year terms in October 1979 and allowed those terms to run concurrently with the 1978 sentences. Ruben Bonilla of the League of United Latin American Citizens called the case "a shocking, obnoxious misuse of federal power" and demanded the dismissal of the judge who handed down the sentences.

The Idaho STATESMAN
Boise, Idaho, August 10, 1978

The trial of Melton Garcia illustrates the turmoil to which aliens in this country are sometimes subjected. If you're Mexican, or even look like you could be, you can have your whole life rearranged by a knock on the door in the middle of the night.

Garcia and his wife were in their Caldwell apartment when immigration officers arrived. Acting on a tip, they were in search of six illegal aliens. The lawmen, according to testimony during a preliminary hearing, asked Garcia for his alien registration card and a fight resulted. Garcia suffered a broken jaw. A witness testified Garcia was hit over the head with a flashlight and struck repeatedly.

We won't speculate on who hit whom. Little will be accomplished by trying to surmise what happened, much less place blame, in view of the conflicting accounts that have surfaced and the ongoing judicial proceedings. We do know some things for certain, though, and what we know is disturbing.

The officer who "arrested" Garcia never told him he was being arrested. This blunder changes the whole complexion of the case. A man who thinks he is merely having a disagreement with a law enforcement officer is likely to act quite differently than one who is being arrested. Being arrested has a decidedly sobering effect.

Garcia is not an illegal alien. His registration card was found the next day.

What we have then is a case of immigration officials, in search of illegal aliens, entering the apartment of a legal alien and hauling him away without bothering to officially arrest him. Most of the faux pax, it would seem, were committed by the gendarmes. But it's the legal alien who ended up with a broken jaw and a chance of being removed from the U.S., fined $5,000 and sentenced to three years in jail.

If there is justice here, it isn't very obvious. From what we can see, the worst thing Garcia did was put up a struggle against what he considered a rude intrusion. He may have gone overboard, but so might a lot of people in similar circumstances.

If he had had blue eyes and blond hair, we suspect, the incident would have ended abruptly with profuse apologies by the immigration officials. But he doesn't have blue eyes and blond hair. He is a Mexican, and Mexicans sometimes get a different view of the law.

THE CHRISTIAN SCIENCE MONITOR
Boston, Mass., February 1, 1978

Time was that no one would have been surprised by Mexican-Americans being treated insensitively at school, whether intentionally or not. Time was that nothing would have been done about it anyway. But the Community Relations Service of the Justice Department is ameliorating such situations among many unsung achievements since the early days of its prominence in easing black-white conflicts during the 1960s. Cut back under the Nixon administration, the CRS nevertheless has been dealing with a growing number of cases in recent years, reaching some 650 in fiscal 1977. Its spirit of seeking solutions through a cooperative rather than adversarial approach deserves every support.

In the Mexican-American case resolved this month, a memorandum of understanding was obtained through mediation by the CRS. Parents had alleged that teachers and administrators in California's Coalinga Unified School District were insensitive to Mexican-American pupils and their culture. Under the memorandum, school officials agreed to points like promoting participation by teachers and other staff in courses in Mexican-American history, culture, and sociology such as those available at a nearby college.

Progress has been seen, according to the CRS, in a variety of other instances where agreements have been in effect for a couple of years or more. These involved such problems as racial fights in prison, police-minority relations, discrimination in the use of revenue-sharing funds, withholding city services from black families, and locating a fast-food chain restaurant in a black neighborhood where residents feared it would worsen traffic and become a center for delinquency near their homes. In the latter case, for example, the CRS helped bring about an agreement pledging the restaurant management to work with community leaders.

These may seem like small steps but they all involve people and the effort to live together. Multiply them and extend them over the whole country. They add up to no small contribution toward oiling the gears of America.

DAYTON DAILY NEWS
Dayton, Ohio, May 9, 1978

It is not surprising that Mexican-Americans rioted in Houston the other night; it is surprising only that they had not rioted before. When people are denied even the appearance of justice, nobody should be shocked when they vent their frustration and anger.

About a year ago three Houston policemen had in their custody a young Mexican-American. They apparently beat him brutally, and somehow he drowned in a bayou.

Imagine what would have happened if the situation had been reversed and a Houston policeman had drowned in the company of three young Mexican-Americans after having been beaten.

But the U.S. District judge apparently figured that, well, cops will be cops, and after all the dead man was only a greaser. The policemen were convicted on charges of violating the civil rights of the dead man — under a federal law often used when local authorities refuse to prosecute what is suspected to be far more serious crimes. The judge gave them suspended sentences and probation and only a few months in jail.

The police are supposed to be society's protection against barbarism. When they themselves become barbarians, it is up to the courts to restrain them. In the Houston case it appears the court, too, was part of the barbarity.

Attorney General Griffin Bell is looking for a way to bypass that court and have the sentence increased. Good for him.

Houston Chronicle
Houston, Texas, May 17, 1978

The leadership of Houston's Mexican-American community deserves praise for its endeavors of recent days.

The community itself has responded with dignity and restraint following the outburst of violence on May 7.

In a tense period, the Mexican-American community in general chose to follow leaders of their own selection and chose to present their views in peaceful fashion. Instead of rampages, there have been peace marches.

Political leaders, religious leaders, neighborhood leaders and individual example have all worked for the best interest of the Mexican-American community and our city as a whole. In the process, these groups have peacefully and forcefully stated their concerns about our city, its services and its recreational facilities.

Commendation should also be extended to Police Chief Harry Caldwell and the individual police officers who have shown restraint under provocation. The police department, with the full support of city officials, has demonstrated both a determination to enforce the law and a sensitivity to community feelings.

This is not to say that all our problems are behind us. While there is much to be done, we can be thankful for the type of leadership being exhibited.

The Houston Post
Houston, Texas, May 17, 1978

The Sunday prayer march in the Moody Park neighborhood typified all that Houston has come to expect of its Mexican-American community. It seemed to represent the spirit of the neighborhood majority. It was the public demonstration of the wisdom that prompted the Mexican-American leaders to go from house to house, asking neighbors to continue the moderation that is the most effective form of responsible citizenship.

This spirit, coupled with the self-discipline of the Houston police, has tamped down a fuse that extremists tried to light. The police had promised to keep the peace in Moody Park, and by their presence and policy, protected the prayer march from new efforts at disruption. In this special mood of cooperation, we must hope that the city and the Mexican-American community can discuss in depth the legitimate complaints and grievances of the community. As the Rev. Edward Salazar said: "The Mexican-American community is serious about restoring the community in peace, but we also have rights as taxpayers. We come as prayerful people to demand our city fathers listen to us." It is important now that the mayor and City Council listen to the pleas for better city services. This plea, made not in violence but in quiet and dignity, deserves priority attention.

Arkansas Gazette.
Little Rock, Ark., May 13, 1978

We haven't seen much of urban riots lately, of the kind that ripped American cities in the '60s with fire and bloody battling in the streets. In Houston last Sunday, though, there it was again, a lurid replay of years gone by. Cars burning, stores smashed, a crowd charging the police. When it was all over, 15 persons had been injured and 22 arrested, and damage was staggering. Thank goodness no one was killed, and we can only hope that Houston can learn something from the episode.

Sadly enough, that opulent city still has a great deal to learn, from all accounts, about treatment of its Mexican-American citizens. This was their first big riot, and of course it had to be put down with force, and fortunately, this time around, the police were restrained enough not to shoot anybody. They may be gaining a better perception of proper conduct from all the national publicity which has come Houston's way as a result of their past mistakes and excesses. The most notable of these, of course, had to do with the cruel death of Joe Campos Torres, a Mexican-American who was thrown into Buffalo Bayou after questioning by city policemen, and couldn't swim. Finally, efforts to achieve justice for this prevailed, after a fashion, but almost as incredible as the act was loathsome were the light sentences given three policemen convicted in the case.

Last Sunday just happened to be the first anniversary of Joe Torres' drowning. Hence, among a crowd of Mexican-American citizens who gathered in a park for a fiesta, some small spark started a riot against the police which finally engaged thousands of people. It was inexcusable, of course, and lamentable in that two television newsmen were stabbed and that actually the rioters destroyed the small stores of many Mexican-American merchants. But Houston, behind its vast wealth and skyscraper sheen, is a tinderbox, homemade. The long toleration of mistreatment of Mexican-Americans by its police has created pent-up anger which may very well explode again if assurance isn't given, unmistakably, that those Latin citizens — by and large a gentle people — henceforth are to be treated humanely, with respect, by every policeman, at risk of losing his job immediately if he acts otherwise.

What a shame it is that this still has to be learned in any city in America, after all we've been through. What a shame it is that Joe Torres had to gain fame by becoming a symbol of what's wrong, a name chanted in fury by marchers who have had enough of imposed degradation.

Illegal Aliens Illustrate U.S. Strength and Weakness

The U.S. is a fortunate country in having the most open borders and the fewest internal checks. This privilege has its price, however, in the unknown millions of people who live here illegally. They slip through controls on the Mexican-American border or outstay their visas and simply "disappear." They accept the risks of staying here for the same reason that legal immigrants come: the promise of a better future. Their presence provokes passionate arguments. On the one hand, they take jobs from Americans; on the other, they take only the lowest-level jobs, which Americans refuse. On the one hand, they burden government services; on the other, their wages are taxed, but they receive no benefits in return. Suggestions for dealing with illegal aliens depends considerably on one's perception of them.

THE DENVER POST
Denver, Colo., May 27, 1978

CONGRESS ONCE AGAIN is fencing with that old late-in-the-session bugaboo, illegal alien legislation. Whether anything will be done is—again this year—very much in doubt.

For years the object has been to control the flow of aliens by controlling their employment in the United States. AFL-CIO has argued that Congress should simply make it illegal to hire them.

That means, from the union view, that criminal sanctions ultimately could be applied to the employer who fails to verify the citizenship of those he employs.

Obviously, this has brought many objections and the Carter administration, trying to respond to them, last August unveiled a proposal with three parts:

• Employment of illegals would bring civil penalties, including injunctive action where employment of aliens is so persistent as to constitute a pattern.

• Aliens who entered illegally before 1970 and were continuously resident since then could become permanent residents.

• Aliens who came here before 1977 could remain as resident aliens for five years pending congressional determination of their status.

One can understand the reluctance of Congress to take action on so sensitive a subject in an election year (or any other year) but the proposals listed above contain at least a start toward dealing with a growing social crisis.

A New York Times study of Los Angeles' demographic patterns revealed last week that there may be as many as 400,000 illegal Latin aliens—mostly Mexican citizens—in California's largest city.

While the aliens contribute substantially to industrial and service labor needs there are accompanying problems. The Times report says undocumented workers cost $50 million annually in free Los Angeles medical service. Similar costs are showing up in public school budgets.

Politically, too, there are important ramifications which need to be understood. The cultural impact is a difficult equation. It is getting far less attention than it deserves.

The immediate issue is the legislative package proposed by President Carter. It is modest enough but it would be a step toward better control of the flood of aliens. If the influx continues unchecked it could boomerang on those who seek its short-term benefits, along with the aliens themselves.

THE INDIANAPOLIS NEWS
Indianapolis, Ind., July 17, 1978

Catholic Bishop James S. Rausch is incensed at the way 200 Mexicans are being held in American jails.

He has written a letter to Vice President Walter Mondale to complain about the treatment of these prisoners who are being held as material witnesses in Federal cases against the smugglers who brought them in.

What makes things doubly bad is the fact that the smugglers, who are charged with violating the law, are out on bond. But the prisoners, who are not charged with any violation of the law, are confined in crowded prison cells so that they can testify when the smugglers' cases come up in court. Sometimes the witnesses spend more time in jail than the smugglers who are found guilty.

While we can sympathize with their plight, especially the lack of amenities provided the detainees, we think Rausch is failing to see the forest for the trees.

The imprisoned Mexicans are among perhaps 12 million aliens who are in the United States illegally. They paid the smugglers to get them into this country because their own country doesn't provide them a chance to make a decent living. If they get the jobs they seek, they will probably be replacing American citizens. They send their children to schools which are supported by local taxes.

President Carter was going to solve the illegal alien problem, but after a few speeches and an ill-timed suggestion about amnesty for the illegals, he seems to have forgotten the matter.

The question of illegals in this country, particularly Mexican illegals, is tremendous. Nowhere else in the world is there such a disparity in income between two countries which have a common border.

The pull of the American standard of living is almost irresistable for the underfed, underpaid and underclothed Mexicans.

The population growth in Mexico does not make the problem any easier. Reputable demographers say the population of Mexico will surpass that of the United States during the first half of the next century. All of the underprivileged Mexicans obviously cannot be provided homes and jobs and schools on the American side of the border.

America's illegal immigration problem can best be solved by eliminating Mexico's emigration problem. Perhaps that is where the U.S. should be making its major effort.

The Dallas Morning News
Dallas, Texas, May 20, 1978

President Carter has the most comprehensive plan for dealing with the illegal alien problem ever presented. But it isn't perfect by any means.

The problem: Most critics just don't want to do anything. Many small businessmen cater to illegal aliens because the immigrants do menial jobs that domestic workers won't touch. While the employer may treat the illegal alien fairly—some don't—the immigrant is still subject to all types of pressure from unscrupulous landlords and others he comes in contact with.

Illegal aliens are a fact of life in the United States. They come because they want work, and the U.S. economy needs their labors. Otherwise, there wouldn't be an attractive job market for them.

In this respect, we are no different from other Western industrial countries. Unlike the others, however, the United States has no "guest worker" program. And that would be the solution to the major problem of illegal aliens—their exploitation.

Studies have indicated that the average stay of an illegal alien, particularly the alien from Mexico, is only four to six months, although he may return annually.

A system of registration could be set up to monitor the flow. But the immigrants would be given legal status, although they would be subject to return to their home country in times of national economic distress.

Too much of the argument about illegal aliens fails to face these basic problems. And it is time we did. Illegal aliens are human beings and should be treated as such. For this reason, the status quo is totally unacceptable.

Houston Chronicle

Houston, Texas, May 12, 1978

We cannot concur with the State Department's opinion that President Carter's legislative package to deal with illegal aliens will help keep the country's "international image" from being undermined.

On the contrary, we believe it would be a blow to that image if Congress were to create the type of second-class resident that is a key part of the proposals.

This is the temporary amnesty and non-deportable status for illegal aliens who were in the United States before 1977 but not before 1970. They could register and work legally but would have practically no rights and no one will say what would happen to them after the five years specified for that non-person status.

What kind of image would it be for the United States of America to formally legislate what would surely be labeled in foreign minds as an inferior subclass? We hate to think of how much propaganda could be made of this.

Besides, what has "image" got to do with the illegal alien problem anyway? It may be properly the State Department's mission to be worrying about image, but it seems to us that image is pretty far down on the list of problems the illegal alien situation presents.

The Morning Star

Rockford, Ill., September 15, 1978

The "torch held high beside the golden door" was dimmed some years ago, but the stream of immigrants into the United States continues, only now through illicit channels in many instances.

Despite the many problems we, as a nation, may feel we are afflicted by, this nation still has much of its glitter as a mecca for those who see no way to improve their lot in their native land.

Increasingly restrictive immigration laws, some dating back to the 1920s, have slowed the legal tide, but the illegal flow of persons — mostly from Mexico — continues.

While in one way we could feel ourselves honored that anyone would take that much trouble to come to the United States — or more specifically Northern Illinois — local authorities are experiencing quiet frustration as they attempt to comply with what is supposed to be federal law.

Local police can't hold illegal aliens without some charge. Immigration officials, swamped in their efforts to stem the tide, don't want to be bothered unless they can deal in busload quantities of aliens.

Meanwhile, persons in Mexico, faced with unemployment or inadequate wages, spend their last pesos to pay "contractors" to smuggle them into the United States and arrange for them to find work.

Strangers in a strange land, unable to speak the language in many cases, the newcomers are targets for most every type of exploitation. Sub-minimum wages, deductions for Social Security and income taxes which never are paid to the government and quick calls to the federal officials to report the illegal aliens so they can be deported before payday — with the informant collecting a reward to boot — all too often is the "American dream" as it comes true for the alien.

Adding to the problem, the illegal aliens in many cases take jobs which otherwise would go to our own low-income or unemployed workers.

However, the problem has other complications. Farm interests point out, with some justification, that many of the "stoop labor" jobs — such as picking tomatoes — will go begging before anyone here will put up with that drudgery and low pay. If the pay were raised to make the jobs more attractive, the price of food would go up.

The whole sad situation is similar to the problems out society has with prostitution, drug use and similar "victimless crimes" where the person who commits the crime does so of his own choice, and also suffers the biggest loss. The law is almost, but not quite, strict enough to stop the illegal alien trade, possibly because many really do not want it stopped.

If the United States government really wanted to do so, it could effectively seal our borders to illegal immigration. If immigrants could not be physically stopped, a few simple changes in federal or state law would make it impossible for them to get jobs once they arrived.

For example, if we wanted such a thing, there could be a system of national identification cards to allow an employer to quickly determine exactly who he was hiring. The ID card scheme has been proposed, and rejected, as an obvious curtailment of freedom.

There could be penalties for employers who knowingly hire illegal aliens. So far, this idea has been scotched on the grounds it is too hard to be sure a person is here legally. On the other hand, the state appears to have little trouble enforcing a law that says you can't sell liquor to minors — leaving it up to the bartender to tell the customer's age, or face a penalty.

The laws we have on the books are just strict enough so illegal aliens can be sent packing if they get in the way, but not strict enough to eliminate this sad human tide — possibly because if it was eliminated something drastic might happen, like an increase in the price of canned tomatoes.

THE DAILY OKLAHOMAN

Oklahoma City, Okla., March 9, 1978

THE problem of illegal aliens in our midst is a lot like the weather. Everybody talks about it but nobody, least of all Congress, seems to be able or willing to do anything about it.

But the problem won't go away. It is a spreading socio-economic fungus that is already costing U.S. taxpayers untold millions and threatens to blight our entire society if left unchecked.

Hardly anybody saluted when President Carter ran his proposed "solution" up the flagpole — and with good reason. His suggested amnesty for all illegal aliens who could prove they were here prior to 1970 and legal resident status for those who arrived afterward merely bows to the problem.

It is a confession that the political leadership of this country lacks the courage to face facts and take the actions that must be started now if we are to avoid being inundated by the silent invasion within a few more years.

At least our new commissioner of the Immigration and Naturalization Service, Leonel Castillo, recognizes that unless something is done we will have to "build fences such as this country has never seen." A Chicano himself, Castillo is no advocate of unconditional amnesty or wide-open borders.

As he said in a recent U.S. News & World Report interview, "The United States has to preserve the integrity of its own laws by deciding who can come in and who can't. We simply haven't been doing it as well as we should."

In all the public dialogue about aliens, there has been far too much emotional rhetoric about the plight of poor Mexicans risking unlawful entry because they lack opportunity at home and too little rational analysis about the consequences to our own country if the tide is not stemmed.

Nobody really has a proven statistical handle on the total impact of the 6 to 8 million illegals currently estimated to be among us. But from the sketchy studies available, it is far worse than many suppose.

It is true that many of the Mexican illegals are drawn by the availability of work at unskilled, menial jobs which, thanks to the benevolence of our welfare and support programs, are going begging on the domestic labor market. But upwards of a million aliens are holding well-paid jobs and depriving U.S. citizens of employment, according to former INS Commissioner Leonard Chapman.

Another loophole is abuse of welfare payments by aliens, which a recent General Accounting Office study estimated is costing more than $72 million a year in five states alone.

There may be more truth than sarcasm in the recent comment by former Central Intelligence Agency chief William Colby to the effect that it would be cheaper to send U.S. food stamps to Mexico and keep the illegals at home than let them continue to swarm over our borders.

Whatever the U.S. responsibility for alleviating global poverty may be — and we have been generous beyond measure on that score — it cannot take precedence over the security and economic interests of our own citizens. Congress should keep that priority in mind when hearings open next week on illegal alien control legislation.

Roanoke Times & World-News

Roanoke, Va., April 29, 1979

In contrast with the prevailing view, that illegal aliens pose a problem of crisis proportions, there is another opinion: that the problem is poorly understood, has been blown out of proportion, and that there is no need to deal with it as if the nation were about to be taken over by people who covet the American way of life.

This contradictory view is voiced in an article in the spring issue of *The Journal/The Institute for Socioeconomic Studies*. The author is Elliott Abrams, administrative assistant to U.S. Sen. Daniel P. Moynihan, D-N.Y. Among the points Abrams makes:

● Aliens contribute more to the public purse withheld through Social Security and income tax payments than they take out. Labor Department studies seem to document the extent of such payments. They also suggest that fewer than 8 percent of illegals have children in school and only 1 percent are on welfare.

● At least four major studies indicate that most illegal aliens get the minimum wage or better and thus do not depress U.S. pay or working conditions.

● However, many of them do take the jobs that few Americans want, such as dishwashing, cleaning motel rooms or harvesting crops. Welfare and unemployment benefits make these jobs much less attractive to out-of-work citizens than they might be otherwise.

● Migrants tend to come for temporary work, enabling them to save money for a fresh start when they return home — most often to Mexico.

● If the border with Mexico could be sealed off — in fact, an impossibility — it would wreck the Mexican economy and our relations with that border country.

Since hard facts on the scope of the illegal alien problem are difficult to find, some skepticism may be warranted about the studies Elliott cites. At least one of his contentions, though, seems rooted not only in history but also in common sense:

America has always needed and has made good use of immigrant labor for its "dirty work." . . . Just as foreign workers were vital to our economy in the 19th century, so they may be again soon. If present birth rates continue, some demographers forecast a labor shortage in the coming decades. Immigrant workers may once again be — and be recognized as — a key to economic growth in America.

Along this line, one measure Elliott suggests is "a large temporary worker program," cousin to the bracero program outlawed in 1965. This, he says, would allow for much greater control over entering aliens, who might then be routed to labor-scarce areas or industries.

On its face, it is not a bad idea. It is embarrassing to state the obvious: that immigration made America what it is today. It is also embarrassing to consider that it might take an influx of hungry foreigners to restore the work ethic to its old status

Democrat and Chronicle

Rochester, N. Y., May 14, 1979

DO WE exaggerate the economic and other threats posed by the tide of illegal immigrants from Mexico and other countries?

Is this but one more of those streams of immigration that have made this country what it is today?

Certainly there's reason to ponder the arguments made by Elliott Abrams in the course of his finding that the illegal alien situation is a problem but not a crisis.

Writing in the forthcoming spring issue of The Journal of the Institute for Socioeconomic Studies, Abrams, administrative assistant to Sen. Moynihan, says it's a myth that illegal aliens are displacing Americans from jobs.

He quotes one observer as saying in 1978 that if the Mexican border were sealed off, there would be "no great rush of unemployed people on the West Coast to pick onions in 100 degree heat for three weeks."

It's a fact, certainly, that substantial numbers of illegal aliens are doing the worst jobs that our economy has to offer.

"Is it clear," asks Abrams, "that in their absence Americans would crowd forward to be maids, or to wash dishes in restaurants, or to spend a few months in a temporary and dead-end job as field hands?"

Indeed, there's a distinct disincentive for Americans to take such jobs when public assistance and unemployment compensation pay more than the low-skill jobs accepted by the illegal aliens.

ABRAMS also rejects the idea that aliens not only depress wages but also exploit the social welfare program.

There is, he maintains, no hard evidence to support such claims.

U.S. Department of Labor studies show that 77 percent of illegal aliens pay Social Security taxes, and very few collect any benefits; 73 percent of illegal aliens have income taxes withheld from their wages.

Rather than try to seal our borders, we should, suggests Abrams, concentrate on improving economic conditions in those areas of Mexico and Latin America from which so many of the aliens come.

"It is time," he says, "to see this problem for what it is: not a crisis demanding urgent responses but a problem with deep roots in American economic history, likely to be with us as long as we are richer than our neighbors."

Perhaps we have indeed been pushing the panic button needlessly.

THE INDIANAPOLIS NEWS

Indianapolis, Ind., August 3, 1979

In a classic case of governmental ignorance, illegal aliens have become political assets.

For years we have been wondering how to deal with the increasingly weighty problem of illegal aliens. Hundreds of thousands, mostly Mexicans, pour into the country annually. Federal immigration authorities regularly round up aliens and send them back to their homelands, but investigations show that deportation is merely an inconvenience for the immigrants. After a day's rest, many aliens cross the gaping U.S. border again.

Undaunted, Texas is investing heavily in the "Tortilla Curtain," a highly controversial wall along its Mexican border. But in light of recent findings by the United States Census bureau, Texas might reverse itself and follow California's lead of covertly encouraging alien migration.

Illegal aliens suddenly have become an important source of political power for states with large alien populations. Since revenue-sharing funds and many other Federal grants are based on population, the more people on paper the better. And as far as the census is concerned, aliens are just as much citizens as the President himself. The political punch goes further: Population changes affect voting district reapportionments, and illegal immigrants could have a significant effect on the number of 1982 congressional seats and, therefore, the number of presidential electors in 1984.

The bottom line is this: Because the political machine is tied directly to the census, illegal aliens could find themselves represented in Congress and state legislatures.

Giving illegal immigrants equal rights in the very framework of our political process is not only wrong, it also encourages governmental leaders to disregard the impropriety in favor of potential political advantages. California is a case in point. In an effort to include as many aliens in the 1980 census as possible, Gov. Jerry Brown and his Democratic legislature have set aside $800,000 to get out the count. The Census Bureau, too, has allocated a portion of its billion-dollar budget to convince illegal aliens and welfare recipients that census takers are only interested in numbers, not IDs.

The rewards for such a misdirected effort can be great for states swollen with the immigrants. The Federal bureaucracy spends more than $50 billion annually on government projects allocated by the census. These projects include affirmative action programs, school and busing aid, and housing improvements.

In the final analysis, though, this governmental tangle shows a loss of economic and political strength for states less affected by alien influx. But, more important, it shows a loss of moral strength to tackle the real issue at hand, that of dealing with immigrants living in this country illegally.

TULSA WORLD

Tulsa, Okla., August 8, 1980

THE CONTINUING flood of illegal immigrants into this country may well be the most serious single social problem now facing the United States. And, as Columnist William Raspberry asserts on the opposite page, the national response has been less than realistic.

Raspberry treads on dangerous ground, however, when he seems to reduce the misfortune to a conflict between aliens and American blacks for low-paying jobs.

The competition for jobs cannot be fully ignored. It is part of the problem. It has become almost a cliche to blame the recent rioting by blacks in Miami, Fla., on the fact that they have been crowded out of menial jobs by Cuban refugees.

But to emphasize this competition to the extent of villainizing the aliens and depicting them as a major cause of black unemployment is bound to be self-defeating in the long run.

Black unemployment is a nationwide problem — not limited to Miami or one or two other Cities with an extraordinarily high alien population.

Even if you assume, for argument's sake, that aliens are crowding a large number blacks out of jobs, the problem would not be solved by fueling a new wave of racial/ethnic ill will between the nation's most deprived groups of people. Nor could the disaster be whipped by outlawing the employment of illegal aliens and trying to starve them out of this country — even if Americans were cold-blooded enough to invoke starvation as a national policy.

The notion that immigrants are a terrible threat to native American workers has an ugly history. It has always worked against the interests of the poorest people.

The Know-Nothing movement of the 19th Century directed hatred, religious bigotry and violence against the Irish, Italians and other poor immigrants of the day. It was fueled by precisely the same charge of job-theft now being thrown at Spanish-speaking and Asian immigrants.

Our own observation is that many illegal aliens are taking jobs that most Americans — whether black or white — wouldn't touch with a 10-foot pole. How many native Americans who could qualify for a welfare check or by unemployment pay would want a minimum-wage job in the food processing industry, for example?

In any case, black Americans should be the last group on earth to help fuel a new wave of nativism and anti-foreign bigotry. The same Know-Nothing spirit that made life tough for latter-day European immigrants well up into the middle of this century was vented with special fury against blacks.

The Dallas Morning News

Dallas, Texas, June 2, 1980

FOR MORE than a decade the tide of illegal aliens, especially from Mexico, has risen in the United States. Yet Congress has been hamstrung. Neither will it change the immigration laws nor will it provide adequate funding to enforce existing laws to solve the problem.

The reason, William Chambers, Dallas regional director of the U.S. Immigration and Naturalization Service, told Ann Atterberry of *The Dallas Morning News*, is that the constituents of the congressmen from states most affected by the flow benefit from the illegal immigration.

Only recently have we seen Texas lawmakers even acknowledge the problem. Now Sen. Lloyd Bentsen, for example, feels the aliens must be given legal status. And that seems to be the emerging attitude. It should be.

In recent weeks, *The News* has uncovered numerous horror stories about the mistreatment of illegal aliens by employers. They are underpaid or subjected to extortion. And other forms of exploitation have been found.

The economic climate, particularly in the Southwestern states, explains why the aliens are coming. Texas, for example, is booming, despite the downturn in the national economy. Its unemployment rate stood at 4.8 percent in April, well below the national average. And by most standards, that figure represents full employment, even if 3 million illegal aliens are in the state as Gov. Clements contends.

In the metroplex, the labor market is even tighter, with the unemployment rate standing at 3.8 percent. And this figure is attained even with Chambers' estimate of 100,000 illegal aliens here.

If, as some citizens contend, the aliens should be sent home, what would become of our economy? The aliens take menial jobs — as dishwashers and busboys — that Americans won't accept. And they also take "blood-and-sweat" jobs in the construction industry that are anathema to many U.S. workers. After observing a Dallas County road project recently, a *Dallas News* editorial writer quipped that there weren't enough citizens on the crew to play a hand of bridge. An exaggeration? Maybe. And maybe not.

Fact is that there is a basic need for the aliens' labor, even if they are paid the minimum wage and above. And that's why a visiting worker law that provides them with legal status and protection is desperately needed today.

The illegal aliens are willing to work to support their families and to improve their lot in life. We need to quit penalizing this residual work ethic.

The Houston Post

Houston, Texas, October 24, 1980

The Mexicans who come into this country leave a corresponding space at home. They cannot appear here without noticeably disappearing there. And a three-year study of migration by the Mexican government suggests that the United States has vastly overestimated the number of undocumented Mexicans living in this country. The Nixon administration used to speak of 6 million to 12 million illegals. The Carter administration halved that with an estimate of from 3 million to 6 million. The Mexican tabulators, using methods endorsed by the U.S. Census Bureau, offer a calculation of 400,000 to 1.22 million, depending on the season.

In 1977, after President Carter's first immigration package lost impetus in Congress, the United States and Mexico agreed to work together on estimates and policies. The American select committee, which is due to recommend policies on migration by the year's end, concentrated on devising ways to keep undocumented Mexicans from getting jobs by a national labor identification card or by sanctions against employers. But Mexico's Labor Ministry focused on the migrants themselves. Starting in 1977 the researchers interviewed 10,000 Mexicans being returned by the U.S. Border Patrol. They interviewed another 75,000 in 1978 and 1979. Interviewers went to 58,000 households in rural and urban communities. They collected information on 350,000 people.

Their findings confirmed earlier studies. More than half the migrants come from four northern and central Mexican states. More than half head for California, 20 percent for Texas. Few expect to stay. Six out of seven are men. Most are between the ages of 15 and 34. They usually leave three to four family members in Mexico dependent on money they send back. The migrants are not from the pool of Mexico's poorest and least educated. A majority had jobs before leaving but hoped to find higher pay. They were slightly above the Mexican national average of 3.1 years of schooling. But because their educational average is below that of American minorities, the Mexican Labor Ministry believes, they offer little job competition for most Americans.

The big point of the survey seems to be that whatever their numbers, few of the migrants wish to move here permanently. A Christmas-New Year survey found that all but 405,000 Mexicans had come home for the holidays. And of those surveyed throughout, only 28 percent had been away for longer than one year. A Mexican demographer said, "This is the first time a massive household survey has been carried out." It is always useful to have facts, and to have data from both sides of the border before shaping national and international policies.

America's Illegal Alien Problem Is Mexico's Population Solution

An old saying observes that "One man's meat is another man's poison." This, in a nutshell, describes America's illegal alien problem viewed from Mexico City and from Washington. The overwhelming majority of illegal aliens slip back and forth across the 1,810-mile U.S.-Mexican border to work in the Southwest. All are men, and many support families in Mexico with their U.S. earnings, which can amount to more after one day than after a week back home, despite sub-minimum wages usually paid to illegals. U.S. efforts to stop illegal aliens at the source run up against the practical problems of encouraging Mexicans to stay home when unemployment tops 50%. In 1977, Mexico's population was estimated at more than 65 million and growing at 3.6% a year. In contrast, economic growth that year amounted to 2.8%, nowhere near enough to absorb the new entrants into the workforce.

Clearly, the illegal alien problem cannot be controlled in isolation from Mexico's problems of economic development. Presidents Jimmy Carter and Jose Lopez Portillo recognized this during their meetings in February and September 1979. The subject of illegal aliens took a back seat in the light of Mexico's new-found energy wealth. Washington was obliged to consider Mexico as something more than just a source of wetbacks.

The Dallas Morning News

Dallas, Texas, May 6, 1978

"FOREIGN AID" is in low repute in Washington. And with good reasons.

But Rep. James Scheuer flouted the concept recently. The chairman of the House Select Committee on Population asserted that Mexico needs special treatment. Without agricultural and industrial trade preferences, grants and loans, up to 20 million new illegal aliens could disrupt the U.S. economy in their flight from economic problems in Mexico.

No one has a firm count. Recent estimates are that between 3 million-6 million illegal aliens are now in this country. And we can count on more. They want jobs that aren't to be had at home, particularly in Mexico.

The reason? Mexico must create 600,000-800,000 new jobs each year to accommodate its growing population. These workers are already born. They come into the job market annually.

A Mexican official pointed out last year that his country needed either direct or indirect economic aid. Mexico is at a 2-to-1 trade disadvantage with the United States.

The "foreign aid" sought is not necessarily a handout. Officials have suggested that custom regulations could be changed and that "fair prices" be paid for natural resources that are taken from Mexico.

Yet while the Carter administration has professed concern about the illegal alien problem and Mexico's economic difficulties, it has been erratic in its efforts at solutions.

Recall, Pemex, Mexico's national oil company, arranged to sell 2 billion cubic feet of natural gas a day to U.S. companies last year. But the Carter administration nixed the $2.60 per-thousand-cubic-feet selling price because it was higher than the bureaucrats wanted to pay domestic producers. So an arrangement between willing buyers and a willing seller was scotched. A "fair price" for a natural resource was rejected.

It is inconsistencies like these between policy and action in Washington that complicate the illegal alien problem on both sides of the border.

This point for sure: Mexico's economic health must be a foreign policy priority. It is our only immediate neighbor to the south, and our security, as well as our economic well-being, may be at stake.

THE  SUN

Baltimore, Md., May 7, 1978

Secretary of State Vance brought a nice diplomatic counterattack on his overdue visit to Mexico City. Mexico's President Jose Lopez Portillo has been crusading for lower American trade barriers to Mexican products as the price for co-operation toward halting illegal Mexican immigration to the United States. But now Washington is turning the tables and asking for lower barriers the other way.

After all, Mexico has gone from a huge trade deficit with the United States to a small one, because of burgeoning oil exports. In a few years, with greater oil and probably gas sales, it should go into surplus. The United States is in an immense world trade deficit because of an oil dependency which shows no sign of abating. Unemployment is still high (for the United States). We are not in a beneficent national mood. The State Department's reaction to protectionist domestic clamors is as a classic free trader. It opposes higher barriers here while trying to batter them down abroad. This is the approach taken toward Japan. Taking the same line with Mexico creates a coherent policy.

But there is a problem with all this. And the investigation by *The Sun's* Gilbert A. Lewthwaite into Mexico City's metropolitan morass vividly highlights one side of it. Compared to the environs for most of the 13.5 million souls who live on what was once a lake protecting the Aztec fortress, New York is a garden city. About four million refugees from the parched Mexican countryside live in shanty-towns without utilities, jobs or hope. An estimated thousand country cousins, often illiterate, join them every day. Glamorous, charming, colonial Mexico City faces, in Mr. Lewthwaite's words, the danger of urban, social or environmental collapse. This peril results from the same rural exodus that propels uncountable millions of illegal immigrants across the 2,000-mile border with the United States. Mexico cannot feed or employ its 63 million people.

No single lever will halt this tide. Curbing the 3.5 per cent birthrate (which officials told Mr. Lewthwaite is now down to 3.1 per cent) would help. So would opening American markets even wider to goods made in Mexico by cheap labor. And so would industrial expansion in southern Mexico based on the huge oil and gas reserves still being discovered. In their dispute with Washington over the price for gas to be piped to the gas-starved United States, Mexican officials are threatening to keep theirs at home. If it fueled job creation, this would lessen one American problem while worsening another.

The State Department is right to insist that Mexico is no longer a poor little country. It is a great, middle income, nation of rich resources and poor people. Its problems are more fundamental than those of the United States which create Washington's tough bargaining posture. Presidents Carter and Lopez Portillo have created a friendly atmosphere of close consultations, of which Mr. Vance's visit is a part. These are not so far producing solutions to economic and social difficulties which will outlast the Carter and Lopez Portillo presidencies.

THE SACRAMENTO BEE
Sacramento, Calif., June 11, 1978

Former CIA Director William E. Colby put things in perspective the other day when he told a Los Angeles Times reporter that the United States faces a greater threat from Mexico than from the Soviet Union.

Of course, he wasn't speaking in military terms. The Mexican threat comes because that nation is exporting its economic problems to the United States.

Those problems are bad now and are likely to get worse. The combined unemployment and underemployment rate in Mexico is about 40 percent. This has driven millions of Mexicans to seek employment in the United States as illegal aliens.

Meanwhile, the population growth rate in Mexico continues to skyrocket. The 65 million people of today will become 125 million by the year 2000. As a result, Colby estimates, 20 million more illegal aliens will swarm into the United States in a search of employment.

His solution — and indeed the solution of many of those knowledgeable in the matter — is for the United States to help Mexico expand its industry and agriculture to absorb its jobless people.

The Carter administration last year was said to be considering such a plan — a $1 billion fund to stimulate industry in Mexico and create jobs. This sum would be matched by Mexico if that country agreed.

There hasn't been much talk about the proposal lately. Maybe the administration is waiting to see if Mexican President Jose Lopez Portillo can do anything to reverse the disastrous economic policies of his predecessor, Luis Echeverria. Under Echeverria, Mexico was forced to import corn, beans and other staples that easily could have been grown there. The nation also racked up a huge foreign debt under Echeverria.

Lopez Portillo promised austerity and more realistic economic policies. In the meantime, time is running out both for Mexico and the United States.

The Idaho STATESMAN
Boise, Idaho, June 30, 1978

We in the United States wonder and worry at the flood of illegal aliens coming across the Mexican border to work in the fields and shops of California, Idaho and other western states. We shouldn't.

An incident in Mexico City Monday demonstrates why Mexican citizens are so anxious to get into our country. Upon the order of the mayor of Mexico City, 18,000 persons were routed from their shanties on the outskirts of the city, and the shanty town was burned to the ground by flame-throwing helicopters.

Mind you these people had no right to the land. They were squatters. But what, we wonder, will become of them now? Certainly the people and their problems do not disappear simply because their shanties are burned. The mayor seems afflicted by the "out of sight, out of mind" syndrome.

And perhaps it is beyond his control. The same story that related the burning of shanty town gave statistics on unemployment in Mexico. According to the dispatch, from 40 to 60 percent of the Mexican work force is out of work or underemployed. And we think 6 or 7 percent is high!

Can we wonder, then, that Mexicans stream across our border? Would we do any less if our families were in such financial distress? Certainly the United States cannot absorb all of Mexico's unemployed citizens. The answer, or at least part of the answer, appears to be for Mexico to get its economic house in order.

Unless and until Mexico can offer its citizens the kind of opportunities available to them here, we will continue to see an unending stream of Mexicans attempting to enter the United States. President Carter has proposed a program for slowing the tide by imposing restrictions on employers who hire aliens, allowing amnesty to those who have been in this country for some time, and improving law enforcement efforts to catch the illegals at the border. We have also seen a crackdown on those who prey on the illegals by transporting them into this country or delivering them to labor contractors.

But Carter's plan has not budged, even though it was sent to Congress almost a year ago. And even if it were enacted, it has a quality to it much like the burning of shanty town: Fewer Mexicans would be in the United States to remind us of their financial distress, but distressed they would remain.

At some point, someone must take responsibility for improving the lot of these people in their own country. That task falls, of course, to the Mexican government. We certainly hope Mexican officials are able to come up with more humanitarian and effective ways of dealing with their unemployed than burning shanty towns. If not, and if the United States crackdown makes it more difficult for Mexico to use us as a safety valve, we suspect it will not be the shanty towns that are burning in a few years, but the buildings of the bureaucrats, as the Mexican left takes matters into its own hands.

Democrat and Chronicle
Rochester, N. Y., November 19, 1978

MEXICAN President Jose Lopez Portillo, while on a recent official visit to China, made some pointed remarks on the flow of Mexicans across the border to the United States:

"Our compatriots continue their painful exodus northward and now they go, not only to be exploited, but to be rejected," he said. "Now the doors are closed and they cannot work despite the fact' . . . many Mexicans went to the United States to contribute to its progress."

The contribution to progress comes later. The immigrant's first instinct is to escape a life of grinding poverty and joblessness in Mexico.

Since many illegal immigrants are caught, deported and enter the U.S. again and again, the cruel fact should be obvious to Portillo that they have decided that exploitation is preferable to poverty.

One way to cut the exploitation is to crack down on illegal immigration, yet Portillo complains when the U.S. rejects his countrymen.

But he did say elsewhere in his speech that Mexico must find a way to create jobs to stop the exodus — that's another important part of the solution to the immigration problem.

A third part of the solution, proposed by President Carter last year but not acted upon by Congress, would increase punishment for smugglers as well as employers who knowingly hire illegal aliens.

Both the blame and the solutions for the illegal immigration problem must be shared by the United States and Mexico. Cooperation will be needed to eliminate the conditions under which there is profit to be made from poverty and suffering.

The Miami Herald

Miami, Fla., November 27, 1978

THE PRESIDENT of Mexico, Jose Lopez Portillo, was one of President Carter's first foreign guests as this Administration began with optimistic pronouncements about rebuilding cordial relations within the hemisphere.

In case you haven't noticed — and you might not have, because the events meriting notice have been few and far between — here's what Mr. Lopez Portillo said last month: "Mexico is neither on the list of United States' priorities, nor on that of United States' respect."

It truly seemed that a new dawn was coming in North-South relations as President and Mrs. Carter visited Latin America and, particularly, since Mexico announced oil reserves that may be as much as 300 billion barrels — more than those of Saudi Arabia.

The comment of U.S. Ambassador Patrick Lucey about all this was, "It would be a serious mistake for us to focus our attention solely on the impact of Mexican oil in assessing the future course of U.S.-Mexican relations."

True. But the United States seems not to have focused its attention on Mexico at all.

While Congress worked to increase the price of natural gas produced in the United States, the Administration haggled over the financing and marketing of Mexican gas. This occurred even though the price had been accepted by the U.S. corporations that would be directly involved. American pressure blocked financing of gas pipelines through the Export-Import bank, so Mexican officials went to Europe for the money. The pipeline was diverted.

Mr. Lopez Portillo decided if the United States was going to take such a cavalier attitude toward his petroleum products, he'd go elsewhere. He did — and oil-starved Japan gave him a favorable reception.

The Immigration and Naturalization Service had its own unique proposal for improving U.S.-Mexican relations: a 12-foot-high wall all along the border at El Paso. How silly can the Administration's minions get?

The National Security Council has been working on a study of bilateral relations, and Mr. Carter has announced a state visit to Mexico next February.

That's good, for without attention and pressure from the White House and the Secretary of State, the crucial decisions in U.S.-Mexican relations will be left to the kind of lower-level functionaries who think up 12-foot walls as solutions to complex diplomatic and economic problems.

We hope Mr. Carter's visit will produce actions that will help deal with the problems that are driving two close neighbors apart.

Roanoke Times & World-News

Roanoke, Va., November 27, 1978

Perhaps, as some demographers contend, the global birth rate is declining; the claim arouses controversy. Even if it is, the world will face additional population problems in only a decade or two.

One of these problems is the growth of metropolitan cities to proportions that stagger the mind. The annual report of the United Nations Fund for Population Activities looks to the year 2000 and sees Tokyo-Yokohama, which had nearly 15 million inhabitants in 1970, with as many as 26 million; greater Cairo (5.6 million in 1970) with 16.3 million; Lagos (1.4 million in 1970) with 9.4 million; and Mexico City (8.5 million in 1970) with 31.6 million.

In this technological age, there is not much mystery about why cities in underdeveloped nations grow. As people find it harder to scratch out an existence in rural areas and small towns, they migrate to the metropolis in search of opportunity and supportive communities. Some find what they seek; most end up in worse squalor than they left. It beggars imagination how any city, no matter how wealthy, could provide even minimal services for more than 30 million people.

As the U.N. agency's report points out, countries need to develop "growth poles" to divert migration from metropolitan areas. If Mexico in particular does not offer alternative attractions within its own borders, millions of its jobless and hungry will head northward — following the endless stream of illegal immigrants already bound toward the United States.

For our part, this country ought to encourage Mexico to undertake such planning and development by whatever means possible. We need oil, and Mexico is emerging as one of the world's great new petroleum reserves. Aside from agricultural products, our chief item for export — to pay for imports like oil — is technology. We have a ready-made customer in our next-door neighbor.

The Evening Gazette

Worcester, Mass., August 21, 1978

President Carter will face a variety of problems and issues during his upcoming visit to Mexico, but the most important among them will go a long way toward shaping the tenor of relations between our two countries for a long time to come.

We desperately need to establish a workable immigration policy with Mexico.

The United States Border Patrol has the difficult job of preventing Mexicans from illegally crossing the border. That's a thankless task. Economic conditions in northern and interior Mexico drive thousands to seek work in southern California. There is a thriving business in smuggling people into this country, with the smugglers reaping huge profits from their illegal business.

People who pay out what little money they have for a promise of passage into this country are sometimes abandoned in the desert, sometimes left behind and sometimes killed. But the hope that they might cross the border and find work is a powerful lure.

The Border Patrol says the section of our border that reaches from the Pacific Ocean into the mountains of southeast California has become a combat zone where helicopters and electronic snooping devices are used to guard the night against border crossings. The patrol is building a new, five-mile fence which some worry will only force the desperate farther into the desert.

We don't know what the answer is, but we've got to do better than we're doing now.

George Bush, candidate for the GOP presidential nomination and a man with close ties to Mexico (his daughter-in-law is Mexican) suggests a return to the temporary work permit system that used to be used for migrant workers.

President Carter cannot afford to travel to Mexico in search of oil and gas, which this nation badly needs, without paying primary attention to the greater question of how the people of the United States relate to their neighbors to the South.

Leonel J. Castillo, the first Hispanic to hold the job of commissioner of Immigration and Naturalization, says that the United States offers the migrants a "half-open door and a half-open wallet."

He says we don't want to open the door so people can walk in "fully and properly." So "we let them kind of squeeze their way in through the door, and then we hire them with our half-open wallet. We pay them less than we pay other people.

"We have opened the gates in such a way that we legally let in the people who are almost the exact opposite of what is said on the Statue of Liberty," he says. That is, it's easier for the well-educated and well-trained to get in than those without skills or schooling.

President Carter should go to Mexico prepared to deal forthrightly and imaginatively with President Lopez Portillo on this enormous human problem.

Perhaps a willingness to encourage more American investment in northern Mexico would be part of a solution. Perhaps a lowering of tariffs and restrictions on Mexican farm products would make it possible for more Mexicans to be gainfully employed in their own country.

But we cannot continue to wage quasi-warfare along our southern border with impoverished people looking for work. It's not in the American grain to use barbed wire and watchtowers to keep desperate people from going where they want to go.

THE CHRISTIAN SCIENCE MONITOR

Boston, Mass., September 25, 1979

There was a time when a visit to the United States by the President of Mexico would have drawn yawns or, at the least, indifference. No longer. The days when the US could adopt a somewhat condescending attitude toward its southern neighbor are gone. Not only is Mexico now an oil power, whose sizable resources make it an increasingly attractive economic partner for the US. Its dynamic growth — and accompanying population pressure — is impacting strongly on US society. In these circumstances it becomes crucial that Mexico and the United States put their relations on a solid, mature, mutually respectful footing. President Carter has an opportunity to do this with the visit to Washington this week of President José López Portillo.

The conclusion of an agreement on the sale of Mexican natural gas to the US, after more than two years of difficult negotiations, augurs well. There apparently is a difference of opinion over whether the deal proved better or worse for the US than the one which former Energy Secretary James Schlesinger so imperially turned down in 1977. But the consensus seems to be that at this juncture the agreement is mutually advantageous and, perhaps most importantly, paves the way to long-range cooperation on energy matters. The US public certainly cannot fault the Mexicans, struggling to lift their country, for extracting maximum advantage from their oil; Americans would do no less.

Other sensitive issues remain, however. Mexico is concerned about the increased salinity of the Colorado River, whose waters are damaging Mexican crops and soil. It is also unhappy about US trade restrictions on Mexican imports of farm products and semimanufactures. The United States, for its part, worries about oil spills, narcotics, Mexico's own protectionist policies, and — most troubling of all — the explosion of illegal immigration of Mexicans into the US.

It is the immigration issue which arouses the most passion and will be the most difficult to deal with. The López Portillo government is vigorously pursuing a family planning program to bring down Mexico's high rate of population growth. But it could be 10 to 15 years before Mexico's economy is able to provide enough jobs for the growing pool of unemployed. Meantime any draconian US action to curb the rising flow of Mexicans over the border could cause instability in Mexico itself and impinge on the US in even less desirable form. Clearly some accommodation has to be reached until there is a market solution to the problem and Mexicans will want to stay home.

The difficulty is that the US Government and the American public in general are in disarray on the subject. There seems to be no consensus on how many so-called "undocumented aliens" are now in the US (some figures go as high as 6 million) let alone on whether they are or are not making an economic contribution, especially when welfare and other social burdens are taken into account. One thing might be said: if it is recognized, as it is, that the US cannot simply build a fence to keep out the illegal entrants, then a policy must be devised of letting in temporary immigrants in an organized, rational way.

Nor does this absolve Mexico of responsibility for the problem. With the growth in the number of Hispanics in the US and corresponding growth of Hispanic political power, Mexico can all too easily ignore the situation and cite its "population problem" as an excuse to do nothing. Yet surely the American people have a right to ask whether Mexico is indeed carrying out social and economic policies that benefit the lower and working classes, or whether the nation's wealth is merely enriching the elite. US society is being appreciably affected by what some call the trend toward Latinization, with growing demands for bilingual education and other rights not previously accorded immigrants. If mutual understandings are not reached on this critical issue, therefore, ugly tensions could develop across a now-peaceful and open border.

President Carter thus cannot afford to treat the López Portillo visit lightly. Efforts must be bent by the two sides to eliminate the strains which today beset Mexican-US relations and to move toward a partnership which benefits both countries and cements the underlying friendship. Patience and understanding will be required toward this end.

SAN JOSE NEWS

San Jose, Calif., September 28, 1979

AT the conclusion of President Carter's three-day visit to Mexico City last February, he and Mexican President Jose Lopez Portillo pledged in a joint communique "to carry out close, bilateral cooperation in order to find realistic and long-term solutions which will respect the dignity and human rights of (Mexican migrant) workers."

Now the president of Mexico is visiting the president of the United States in Washington. Over the weekend they are scheduled to meet twice in the White House. They will sign agreements formalizing Mexico's sale of natural gas to the United States; they will probably discuss Lopez Portillo's United Nations energy address, and they may explore the prospects of the United States buying more oil from Mexico.

If they get around to talking about the continuing flood of undocumented immigrants from Mexico, the discussions are likely to be couched in diplomatically correct (and non-committal) language. The subject is a hot potato for both presidents because the problem is an emotionally-loaded one for both countries.

It is also a problem that can't be ignored away. Federal officials guess that as many as 8.2 million Mexicans are living and working in the United States at any given time. The yearly influx is estimated at between 500,000 and 2 million.

These immigrants are mostly landless peasants who cannot find work at home. The wealth produced by Mexico's new oil and gas discoveries has not trickled down to them yet; 40 percent of the nation's work force is still unemployed or underemployed.

They come north to work in our fields and canneries, in service industries such as restaurants, in all manner of menial tasks. Those who object to this tide of immigration say the Mexicans are taking jobs away from Americans and/or sending welfare costs through the roof.

What few studies have been conducted offer little evidence to justify these fears. To the contrary, they suggest undocumented workers pay taxes and stay away from welfare offices for fear of being deported. Further, say the studies, the Mexicans take the dirty, low-paying jobs Americans don't want and can't be induced to take.

Even granting the assumption that these immigrants contribute more to the American economy than they take from it, they pose moral and legal problems. Who is responsible, for example, when an illegal immigrant is robbed and beaten by the man he has paid to smuggle him into this country? It happens.

Should anybody have to work for less than the legal minimum wage because he fears deportation if he asks for more?

What are the responsibilities of the U.S. and Mexican governments in dealing with these essentially human rights issues?

The Carter administration two years ago offered a limited amnesty program which got nowhere in Congress. Now two California Republicans, Sen. S.I. Hayakawa and Rep. Dan Lungren, want to legalize what is already going on.

They propose, essentially, an expanded bracero program. The old braceros, literally the "strong-armed ones," were seasonal farm laborers. They helped harvest American crops during and after World War II. The new braceros would not be restricted to farm work or to a particular employer. They would be admitted for 6-month periods in response to unfilled domestic labor needs.

The concept is valid, though the details need to be spelled out carefully. Presidents Carter and Lopez Portillo should explore the idea over the weekend.

By all accounts, the Mexican government has no intention of discouraging the northward migration. That being so, it might be asked to consider more favorable oil export terms in exchange for a generous U.S. policy on immigration.

We hope President Carter raises that possibility — diplomatically, of course — with President Lopez Portillo this weekend.

'Tortilla Curtain,' Border Fence, Considered Briefly, Then Dropped

The U.S. Immigration and Naturalization Service briefly entertained a plan to build a fence along the border between El Paso, Texas, and Juarez, Mexico, to thwart illegal alien crossings. When the INS announced the plan in October 1978, the fence was immediately criticized and dubbed the "Tortilla Curtain." The 6½-mile, 12-foot-high steel fence "will be very much like the fence ... between East and West Berlin," in the words of Gaston de Bayona, director of international relations for Juarez. The $1.4-million project was to be a concrete-based, five-foot steel fence topped with seven feet of small hard-mesh flexible chain that would be difficult to climb. The fence was never built; the Justice Department announced the following April that economic and diplomatic considerations made the fence impractical. At the same time, the department said eight miles of existing fence along portions of the border near El Paso and San Diego would be replaced.

The Dispatch

Columbus, Ohio, November 26, 1978

A PLAN for a steel mesh fence, 12 feet high, to discourage the illegal aliens flooding this country from Mexico has come under public fire.

Frankly, we do not understand the furor. The so-called "tortilla curtain" is a far cry from the infamous Berlin Wall. The latter is designed to hold East Germans in, while the proposed fence along the Mexican border would help keep illegal aliens out.

It is quite clear that the continuing flow of illegal immigrants to the U.S. poses serious problems, and the political leadership in Washington has avoided necessary actions. Under Immigration and Naturalization Service director Leonel Castillo, the situation seems to have grown worse. There are a number of reports that INS morale is at an all-time low and that top border patrol officials seem unconcerned with stemming the flow.

We would be the first to acknowledge that the problem is a complicated one. In recent years Mexican-American groups have developed an articulate and effective lobby in Washington to protect their own interests.

It is simply not feasible to round up and remove the estimated eight million illegals currently living and working in the U.S. But, without vigorous enforcement of existing laws there is little question millions of others will cross the frontier surreptitiously to join them in search of economic opportunity.

To continue tolerating this illicit migration is unfair to those foreigners who scrupulously apply for admission to this country and to the millions of Americans whose ancestors entered this country lawfully in years past.

As in the past, America continues to welcome many of the world's poor and disadvantaged who qualify for entrance under existing immigration laws. But it is not our national obligation, or national interest, to have an open frontier.

The "tortilla curtain" may not be the best solution—but it is one solution likely to work. To construct a fence along a nation's frontiers is not a signal of repression. Rather it is clear indication that officials expect those who would enter the U.S. to obey our laws.

The Morning News

Wilmington, Del., July 26, 1978

It certainly wasn't very cheerful news the other day about U.S. plans for a five-mile, $3 million fence separating us from one of our neighbors.

Our neighbor to the south certainly can't call the barrier, which will be started later this year, a spite fence. Neither can Mexico very well deny that we have a need for such an obstacle to the flow of illegal aliens into this country from that one.

The problem of illegal aliens entering and living in this country is a very serious one. There are an estimated six million to eight million "illegals" in the country right now, and many people are concerned that they are making demands on the job market that keep U.S. citizens and other legal residents out of work.

Mexico's border is by no means the only trouble spot. Folks are entering the country from every direction. For example, people from the Dominican Republic are reported to be flying to Puerto Rico and taking advantage of the easy access from that U.S. island commonwealth to the "mainland" states. South Americans reportedly are being smuggled across our border from Canada.

The area around San Diego, California, is, however, one of the main highways for the illegal traffic. The Chula Vista sector near San Diego is a particularly bad area. Hundreds upon hundreds of robberies, knifings, shootings and rapes connected with the flow of illegal immigrants were reported last year. (In fact, at one point a Border Patrol spokesman described that sector as too dangerous for his patrolmen to operate in. Nonetheless in that sector 45,036 aliens were apprehended in April of this year alone. (That compared to 5,925 in the corresponding month of 1971, an indication of how much the traffic has picked up and how it is now estimated to add half a million to the total of illegal aliens each year.)

It is in that area that the new "fence" is going to be built, a five-mile long steel bar barrier running eastward from the ocean.

Of course, we can point with some satisfaction to the fact that the United States is reluctantly building a barrier to keep folks *out*. On the same day that news of the plans for the fence was reported in this paper, there was a news story of two young men disguised in homemade border guard uniforms climbing over the Berlin Wall and escaping to the — comparative, if you like — freedom of the West. That's an old Communist barrier to escape *from* a repressive regime.

There may be other approaches to the problem of illegal residents in this country. We hope they'll be found soon. Meanwhile, all we can say, reluctantly, is that perhaps "good fences" do make good neighbors."

The Kansas City Times

Kansas City, Mo., April 30, 1979

There have been few more tangible examples of confused United States foreign policy than the infamous fence on the Mexican border. Ill-conceived from the start, the fence stands as a symbol of diplomatic idiocy rather than a barrier to illegal immigrations.

The fence originally was to be 12 miles long and be of the type that could slice off the fingers and toes of anyone trying to climb over it. The Immigration and Naturalization people logically figured that if they were supposed to build a fence to keep Mexicans out, then they would indeed build a fence to keep Mexicans out. It was a hasty decision. Mexico discovered massive oil deposits. U.S. Hispanic groups complaining about the fence suddenly were given consideration. There were some second thoughts high up in the INS.

Now the fence is going to be only 8 miles long and, incredibly, be constructed in such a way that it "won't be dangerous to anyone trying to climb over."

The next story we expect to read will be about some INS engineer explaining that the fence will be zero miles long and invisible. And that will be the best idea of all, for immigration problems are better solved by negotiation and not chain links. As far as Mexico and the U.S. are concerned, it finally should be apparent to all that fences definitely do not make good neighbors.

The Boston Herald American

Boston, Mass., December 2, 1978

That dark cloud you saw over Mexico City recently was the ruckus kicked up by the fence along the Mexican-American border. For 20 years there has been a 27-mile fence between the two nations, to keep out illegal aliens, and until now no one has uttered scarcely a peep about it.

What stirred the storm was an announcement by the U.S. Immigration and Nationalization Service (INS) that it is about to rebuild six miles of the old fence, and tack on six miles of new. Whereupon an argument erupted, and the argument, like the fence it is about, has two sides.

On the side of those critical of the fence-building is the United States Embassy in Mexico City, which was furious for not being told in advance what INS had in mind. Also furious was Mexico President Jose Lopez Portillo, who couldn't wait to get back from Peking before criticizing the U.S.A. for lack of "the slightest concern for human rights."

The move was viewed by the Mexican press as an "insult." Dr. Jorge Bustamante, chief adviser to the Mexican government on emigration, said: "At the very least the affair represents a severe breakdown in communication between the U.S. and Mexico." Some call the barrier "a tortilla curtain" or "Berlin wall," and insist it doesn't serve its purpose of preventing farm workers, or "braceros," from drifting north.

On the other side of the fence are those who see dangerous consequences in the emigration of a million illegal aliens a year. The Mexicans take jobs away from Americans, a complaint American labor unions have been making for years.

Leonel Castillo, the commissioner of INS, wonders what all the fuss is about, noting that the fence has been around for a long time without anyone getting perturbed about it. Castillo's predecessor, former Marine Corps Commandant Leonard Chapman, called the Mexican migration an "invasion," and another critic, worried about loss of jobs in this country, accused Mexico of "exporting unemployment."

Although good fences haven't made good neighbors of Mexico and America, but no major crisis is expected. The INS may have blundered in its communication, but it was doing what it thought good for the country. Unemployment in Mexico is serious, but the solution is not shipping it to the United States.

The San Diego Union

San Diego, Calif., November 16, 1978

Immigration Commissioner Leonel Castillo got off on the wrong foot with his plan to erect new fences at points along the Mexican border where there is the greatest concentration of aliens slipping past the Border Patrol. Obviously it was a mistake to have considered a type of fence that could cause serious injury to people trying to climb over it.

Mr. Castillo has ordered the fencing to be redesigned. But he is under pressure to abandon the project altogether, and we think that also would be a mistake.

The Border Patrol believes its task would be easier if there were higher, sturdier fences in areas where it is having the hardest time coping with illegal border crossings. The plan initially is to erect these 10-foot fences along six-mile stretches of the border at San Ysidro and El Paso, Tex. Present fences in these areas are torn and sagging and in some spots breached altogether.

If the people responsible for enforcing our immigration laws see a practical value in these fences, then the fences deserve serious consideration. Even at a cost of $3.5 million, this is more economical than hiring more patrolmen — a thousand, in Mr. Castillo's estimation — to accomplish the same amount of protection.

When the Border Patrol is facing a freeze if not a cutback in personnel due to efforts to hold down the federal payroll, Mr. Castillo's interest in fences is understandable.

We also understand why Mexican-American organizations, and others speaking out on both sides of the border, see such fencing as a symbol of "repression" like the Berlin wall. High fences along an international border have a certain symbolism, but in this case they are inevitable results of U.S. policy. These fences are symbols of failure. On the one hand, they symbolize the failure of U.S. immigration policy to deal with the reality of what is happening in one corner of our labor market — the employment opportunities which undocumented aliens are eager to exploit with the connivance of smugglers and employers. On the other hand, they symbolize the failure of Mexico and many other countries to offer more of their people a chance to make a decent living at home.

Those failures are creating the problem for the Border Patrol at San Ysidro, El Paso and other pressure-points along the border. Fences in these areas are used to control immigration much as the turnstiles found at any immigration station in any country.

Like the uniforms of patrolmen and inspectors, like the passports, visas and identification papers that are the stuff of entrances and exits along international boundaries, they represent the authority of a government to control traffic across its own border.

Mr. Castillo's proposed fences would be simply an extension of the authority the U.S. government is trying to exercise — inadequately, perhaps — to deal with the illegal alien problem. When they're built, pictures of them should be laid on the desks of President Carter and each member of the incoming 96th Congress, and on the desks of their counterparts in Mexico.

Six miles of chain-link fence should symbolize the cost of their collective failure to attack those conditions in both countries which have made it a necessity.

FORT WORTH STAR-TELEGRAM
Fort Worth, Texas, May 1, 1979

A fence is a fence is a fence. No matter what it looks like or what it is called, a fence is a fence.

The United States Immigration and Naturalization Service is going ahead with plans to build a wall between the United States and Mexico in two sections of the country where there have been serious problems with illegal aliens. One of the areas is in El Paso.

The federal government originally had planned 12 miles of fences but the length has been reduced to 8 miles. Originally, the fence was to have been constructed of material that could injure a person trying to climb it. The new fence will not be dangerous, the INS says.

But the fence is going up. It is going up while Mexican-American relations are going down. Where is our diplomacy? How on earth can a government hope to improve relations with a nation by building fences between itself and that nation?

The old farm saying, "Good fences make good neighbors," is not true in our relations with Mexico. There is a problem with illegal aliens. The immigration service said that about 500,000 of the 862,000 border patrol arrests for attempted illegal crossing in 1978 were made at the two points where the fences are being built.

At a time when we should have open minds and be working to solve our border problems with Mexico through mutual action, we erect obstacles. A fence is an obstacle, both physical and mental.

There are other ways to handle the alien problem. It is a problem that requires tact and mutual effort. There is some indication, principally from the Carter trip to Mexico, that mutual effort is being considered. We wish that our government would show some sign of tact and diplomacy.

The Salt Lake Tribune
Salt Lake City, Utah, June 28, 1979

Federal policy makers sometimes go out of their way to stir up resentment against the United States.

A fence being built along two short sections of the Mexican-American border in Texas and California is that kind of thing.

The fence is supposed to aid the Immigration and Naturalization Service in controlling the flow of illegal aliens into this country from Mexico. And that it might do although there is serious doubt about its overall effectiveness.

Even if it keeps out a few thousand poor Mexicans (who would be welcome in Utah cherry orchards) the fence is an open invitation to worsening relations with Mexico.

More damaging is the symbol it hands anti-American agitators around the world. That fence is potentially many times more costly than the $2 million being spent to build it.

The United States, for example, is in a poor position to urge Thailand and Malaysia to accommodate hordes of Vietnamese refugees when it is building a 10-foot-high chain-link fence to keep out refugees from Mexican poverty.

The illegal alien problem is a challenging one. Trying to solve it, even in part, by throwing up an American version of the Berlin Wall can only make a solution more difficult. The fence should be stopped.

Los Angeles Times
Los Angeles, Calif., April 29, 1979

Despite protests from Mexican-American organizations, the U.S. Immigration and Naturalization Service intends to build a higher, stronger fence along 5.6 miles of international boundary separating San Ysidro and Tijuana. The work will start next month.

A similar barrier will be built between El Paso and Ciudad Juarez, and for the same reason—to slow the increasing movement of illegal aliens into this country.

San Ysidro and El Paso are the major crossing points for illegals, accounting for 60% of 862,000 apprehensions by the Border Patrol in 1978.

The present fences are useless because, in the words of one agent, they "are as full of holes as Swiss cheese." The patrol must pull officers away from wide-open sections of the border to guard what ought to be fairly secure sectors.

The Immigration and Naturalization Service got off to a bad start with the project late last year by announcing that the replacement fences would be built of sharp steel latticework that could sever the fingers and toes of climbers. It was a terrible concept, and it was thrown out at the insistence of President Carter. The new fences, to be built of close-mesh chain-link, will pose no hazards.

But Chicano activists continue to insist that the very existence of a fence on the border "is an insult to the Mexican-American community. Symbolically, it is still a very offensive thing."

We disagree. To demand that the replacement fences not be built is tantamount to demanding an open border. The fact is that the Border Patrol lacks the personnel to guard the 2,000-mile international boundary effectively, and the fences are the most economical way to slow the pace of illegal immigration at key points. The barriers are not a symbol of oppression against Mexican nationals trying to cross the border illegally, but are a symbol of the patrol's impossible assignment.

The question of border controls is also a critical issue in relations between this country and Mexico. We want more of their oil and natural gas and, as part of the exchange, they want us to accept more of their citizens eager to come to this country to escape unemployment and poverty in their homeland.

It is entirely possible that the Carter Administration will agree to accept more Mexican nationals, possibly as temporary workers. But the necessity for controlling the border will always exist. Those who insist that the fences must go could argue, with equal logic, that the Border Patrol must also go.

The Courier-Journal
Louisville, Ky., July 7, 1979

Good fences make good neighbors . . .

— Robert Frost in "Mending Fences," 1914.

POET FROST probably was right in his perception of a useful way to preserve good neighborliness. But even a Vermonter might see red if the folks next door erected a chain-link fence, 9 to 10 feet high, and posted signs warning of what would happen to those who try to cross it.

That's what our nation is doing, however, at two key points on the Mexican border, where a total of eight miles of sheathed fencing may very well look to Mexicans — and a lot of Americans — like a Berlin Wall in reverse. This can only sour an already poor relationship between our nations.

Mexico wants the migrant labor question high on the agenda of negotiations promised after President Carter's trip there last winter. The U.S. decision to go ahead with fences at the two most popular crossing points for illegal aliens, El Paso, Texas, and San Ysidro, California, seems to be closing off, not only the border, but the question as well.

The fences themselves may help our understaffed Border Patrol repulse more than the estimated one of every three aliens who are stopped now. But those who want jobs badly enough will find other passages along the 1,900-mile border. What seems to be behind the construction is the widespread American misperception that hoards of Mexicans are draining dry the U.S. welfare system and sopping up jobs Americans want. There is little statistical evidence to support either fear.

First of all, the assertion that there are 12 million illegal aliens in the U.S., originally made by a Immigration and Naturalization Service commissioner, is admittedly based on guesswork, estimating those coming in while ignoring the millions that go back out. Others put the figure at around 4 million, with well over half coming from Mexico. They come to find work, frequently leaving at the end of the season or when dollar savings from U.S. employment will tide them over for a longer time back home.

While here, most illegal laborers pay Social Security taxes they will never collect. Sales taxes also assure that some of their dollars stay north of the border. They have come here for work, not welfare, since welfare investigations would soon uncover their illegal status.

The job-displacement fear also seems largely unfounded. A few skilled workers cross the border illegally. But most are the rural poor, unable to find jobs at home. The kind of low-paid work they get in the United States — stoop labor in the fields, restaurant jobs and tedious hand assembly in clothing factories — is not popular with many Americans who would rather go on welfare. And, in some cases, factory owners could move south of the border in pursuit of cheap labor if the workers no longer could come to them.

The irony of the fear of illegals is that it is less their numbers that are disturbing than their status. Through most of the last century, black Americans and the poor of Europe and Asia performed the kinds of tasks Mexican and Caribbean laborers do now. From 1942 until 1964, the bracero program made migration for that purpose legal and partially controllable. But no alternative to the bracero program has been worked out with Mexico, although American employers still need the kind of labor it provided.

Mexico is well aware of these facts. But the U.S. ignores them at its own peril. While the futile fences may please voters north of the border, the huge nation to the south no longer need swallow such indignities. Its vast reserves of oil assure that its days as a Third World power, necessarily deferring to the affluent Yankees, are coming to an end. In the long run, Mexico may even be able to find jobs for its too-swiftly-expanding population. That will require investing oil revenues in light industries dispersed among depressed rural areas.

Now is the time for the United States — both the public and private sectors — to recognize both the promise and the problems of Mexico. Cooperative ventures, in line with Mexico's long-term development plans, should benefit both countries. Closing off the safety valve of migrant labor might create internal pressure the Mexican government couldn't control. The offending fences aren't fatal, but they will make understanding and cooperation more difficult. They, and the attitudes that support them, should come down.

SAN JOSE NEWS
San Jose, Calif., June 25, 1979

THROWING good money after bad is nothing new to the federal government, but paying $3.5 million to fence 12 miles of the Mexican border may be a record, even for Washington.

The Anchor Fence Co., of Baltimore, Md., is scheduled to begin construction today on six miles of fence along the border south of San Diego. Another six miles will go up along the Rio Grande at El Paso, Tex. By the time the project is completed in January, it will have set the taxpayers back $3.5 million.

The idea is as dumb as it is expensive.

The estimated 8 million "undocumented immigrants" from Mexico now in the United States are mute testimony to the lack of any real desire in Washington and Mexico City to seal the border. The Border Patrol concedes it apprehends and returns only a small fraction of those who enter this country illegally.

It passes understanding why anyone would suppose 12 miles of fence will make much of a dent in the problem; the incentives to come north are too great.

Despite its new-found oil wealth, Mexico cannot yet provide jobs for all who want to work; five out of nine Mexicans don't earn enough at home to feed their families. They go north because that's where the jobs are.

The issue was put into clear, if bitter, perspective last October by Jesus Cuellar, a store clerk in Juarez, the Mexican city just over the Rio Grande from El Paso. The announcement of the Border Patrol's fence project prompted Cuellar to observe:

"I don't care how high they build this wall, the Mexican people will get across it. A man can work on a construction job here in Juarez for 10 hours, maybe more, and all he will earn is $4 or $5. If he can earn $1.50 an hour on the other side, he can make three days' wages in one day."

Twelve miles of fence may slow down these job-seekers from Mexico, but it won't stop them.

Senators Suggest Revival of 1940s Guest-Worker Program

Sen. Harrison Schmitt (R, N.M.), joined by Sens. S.I. Hayakawa (R, Calif.) and Barry Goldwater (R, Ariz.), introduced a bill in June 1979 to grant Mexicans temporary work visas in the U.S. Citing U.S. job opportunities as "the root cause of illegal migration from Mexico" and noting the difficulties of patrolling the border, the senators suggested that the Immigration and Naturalization Service grant Mexican applicants visas for six months of each year, which would give them unrestricted opportunity to seek jobs in the U.S. The INS would establish quotas for the temporary workers, and they could be barred from a job if it was proved that they displaced Americans. The senators said the program would benefit both Mexico and the U.S. and would prevent aliens from becoming permanent illegal residents. A similar bill had been introduced in the House of Representatives by Rep. Hamilton Fish (R, N.Y.) in January.

A number of Western European countries had guest-worker programs, which employed thousands of Arabs, Turks and Yugoslavs in France, Switzerland, West Germany, Scandinavia and elsewhere. The U.S. had had its own guest-worker program from 1942–64 under which more than four million Mexican "braceros" had worked in agriculture. The program was terminated because of union hostility. A report released in February 1980 by Sen. Edward Kennedy (D, Mass.) cited the "dangers" of a guest-worker program. The study said temporary workers would drive down U.S. wages and working conditions, since they would be willing to work under worse conditions and for less pay than Americans. The study added that Western Europe's experience with guest workers showed that they inevitably became a permanent "underclass" in the host country.

The Dallas Morning News

Dallas, Texas, November 9, 1979

Let's hope that Gov. Clements hasn't let his natural optimism run away with him. He thinks that within a year the federal government will come up with a solution to the decade-old illegal alien problem.

The solution, as the governor outlined to the Dallas Citizens Council, is to issue Mexican workers visas good for three, six or 12 months so they can enter this country legally. They also would be issued Social Security cards, enjoy municipal benefits and be paid a fair wage under Clements' plan.

Those are wise changes. Certainly we need a rational plan to legalize status of the Mexican workers who come to the United States by the millions today. Already they pay taxes for which they receive no benefits. Studies indicate that most of the illegal aliens already pay Social Security taxes, income taxes, state taxes and local taxes. But few use any government services. They are afraid of being sent back home if they apply.

Our only concern is the governor's timetable. Congress has dawdled and procrastinated for more than 10 years without coming up with a solution to the problem — and some solutions are fairly obvious.

But as the governor noted, the key to the problem is to provide the illegal aliens with some legal status. After that first step, many other parts of the problem will work themselves out.

ALBUQUERQUE JOURNAL

Albuquerque, N. M., June 8, 1979

Sen. Harrison "Jack" Schmitt, R-N.M., is proposing the revival of the discredited and long-abandoned "bracero" program as a short-term answer to the problem centered around the flow of illegal aliens into the United States from Mexico.

The bracero program was initiated during World War II, ostensibly to alleviate a wartime shortage of agricultural workers in this country. It was abandoned under fire in 1964. A close look at its history will reveal so many pitfalls as to convince almost everyone that it should be permitted, now and eternally, to "rest in peace."

It is significant that one of the strongest critics of the old program was the American GI Forum, a nationwide organization of Spanish-speaking and bilingual war veterans whose membership felt a strong empathy for the farm workers imported from Mexico. Especially deplored was the failure and apparent inability of the federal government to enforce minimal standards for the shelter and feeding of the workers. Exploitation of workers by labor contractors through practices reminiscent of the proverbial "company store" also aroused bitter criticism.

Farmers, ranchers and agricultural leaders were able to keep the program alive after the war by convincing Congress that U.S. citizens were either unavailable or unwilling to perform the menial tasks assigned to imported workers. Time has proved that those same menial tasks have been performed annually since the bracero program was terminated — but at appreciably higher wage rates.

Unfortunately, nothing thus far advanced in Sen. Schmitt's proposal presumes to forestall any of the abuses of the old program. The old program was discreetly restricted to agricultural labor, and that proved too hot to handle. Schmitt apparently would extend work visas to laborers in any industry which could not clearly prove an ample supply of U.S. citizens willing and able to do the work.

Sen. Schmitt envisions his proposal as a means of alleviating the pressures of illegal aliens at the nation's borders. What was then called the "wetback" problem was given strong impetus by the bracero program, which actually provided a convenient cover for those who succeeded in entering this country illegally.

Sen. Schmitt is right in his view that the long-term solution to the illegal Mexican alien problem lies in "the total development of the economy of Mexico." It is suggested that the best conceivable short-term solution is an early start on the long-term solution.

THE SACRAMENTO BEE
Sacramento, Calif., July 5, 1979

The timing, if nothing else, would give cause for a long, hard look at U.S. Sen. S.I. Hayakawa's bill to restore a modified bracero program, which would permit Mexican nationals to work legally in the United States for up to 180 days.

The bill was introduced at a time the United Farm Workers union has been complaining that illegal aliens have been hired by growers to break the UFW strike in the lettuce fields of California. The bill contains no restrictions on hiring braceros to replace striking workers.

The bracero program, inaugurated during World War II when farm workers were desperately needed, was discontinued in 1965 over the protests of growers who complained that agriculture, especially in California, would be ruined without the braceros. Nothing of the sort happened. Instead, there was more mechanization on the farms, and more permanent jobs for farm workers.

And it was precisely because there were more permanent farm jobs and no bracero program that Cesar Chavez had success in organizing farm workers.

Hayakawa has said several times since his election that he feels the bracero program should be reinstated to help solve the twin problems of high unemployment in Mexico and the influx of millions of illegal aliens into the United States. There should be a third reason: that there is an unmet need for additional farm workers here.

If, indeed, the bracero program would discourage the flow of illegal aliens across the border, it would take on some merit. There is no question but that many of the illegal aliens are exploited and sometimes forced to live in subhuman conditions — for example, sleeping on cardboard between the rows of grapevines. The illegals are afraid to seek medical help, afraid to complain of mistreatment, and, most of all, afraid they will be caught and sent back to Mexico. Hayakawa said that with passage of his bill the illegal aliens would be transformed automatically into legal workers who could complain about subpar wages and working conditions.

His bill also would permit restrictions to be placed on the hiring of braceros if it could be shown that the aliens would replace "available, qualified and willing" workers.

If there have been recent cases where farm workers could not be recruited and the farmers suffered losses because of it, we have not been aware of them. Therefore, we remain unconvinced that this nation needs to bring in unskilled foreign workers to perform menial jobs while the unemployment rates across the country are so high. And we are totally unconvinced that bringing in braceros would even slightly impede the flow of illegal aliens.

St. Louis Globe-Democrat
St. Louis, Mo., August 28, 1979

The experience of Mexican migrant workers harvesting the Illinois peach crop again illustrates the folly of treating these productive people as "illegal aliens."

Jim Eckert, produce manager of a popular orchard operation, makes no bones about the value of the Mexican fruit pickers. "Without the illegal aliens in this country these produce crops would be in sorry shape," Eckert said.

Illinois growers cannot find local workers willing to stay on the job until the harvesting is complete, Eckert contends, whereas the Mexicans are willing, able and reliable.

No one is making trouble for the aliens at present, but legislation is pending to make it illegal for growers to hire them. That would be an act of stupidity.

A sensible approach would be for the government to issue temporary work permits to Mexican field hands, thus assuring them of a welcome. The government should be concerned with seeing to it that employers are not deprived of a work force and that the workers are not exploited.

Migrants willing to perform needed tasks shunned by able-bodied Americans should not be barred from the opportunity to be of useful service.

FORT WORTH STAR-TELEGRAM
Fort Worth, Texas, September 13, 1979

Reason again raises its level head to propose that President Carter urge enactment of a new documented worker program in the United States.

Such documentation would do exactly what needs to be done to minimize the problem of illegal aliens from Mexico.

House Majority Leader Jim Wright and Fort Worth City Councilman Louis Zapata propose that Mexican nationals be given permits to work in the United States.

This would eliminate the ridiculous situation of the United States closing its eyes to the wholesale violation of the law

The illegal alien problem exists because there are not enough jobs in Mexico, even as many unwanted jobs go begging in the United States.

A shallow river isn't enough to discourage an unemployed Mexican from wading across to take a job so readily available. The Mexican becomes an illegal alien.

Zapata said he became concerned about the problem when he realized that 35,000 to 40,000 illegal aliens live in Fort Worth.

And one of the complications can be seen in the present controversy over whether public schools in the United States should educate the children of workers who are in the United States illegally.

"They (illegal aliens) are ripped off when they cash their checks, they are discriminated against in housing and jobs and they are afraid to complain because they might be deported," Zapata said.

The official United States view is that the illegal aliens are outlaws, but in reality the law turns its head and the nation tolerates them.

Wright's observation is right on target: "a certain number will come either legally or illegally, and it's better to have certain controls on them."

A documented worker — Wright prefers to call them guest workers — would have most advantages of U.S. citizenship while in this country and, most important, the worker would be here legally.

They could then complain about criminal acts against them or about discrimination without fear of deportation.

Only illegal aliens would have fear of deportation.

We have stated editorially that it is better to document foreign workers and know where they are and what they are doing than to ignore a flood of undocumented workers because we simply cannot deal with the problem.

Wright and Zapata offer an alternative that could work to the advantages of Mexico and the United States and to the people of both nations.

Chicago Tribune

Chicago, Ill., September 6, 1979

Native-born Americans are turning lazy and have nearly lost their work ethic and spirit, said Leonel Castillo, commissioner of the Immigration and Naturalization Service, the other day. Therefore, he urged, immigration policies should be liberalized to give American society an infusion of "human capital." In particular, he wants to increase the annual quota of Mexicans from 20,000 to 50,000.

Mr. Castillo's assumptions are troubling. So is his remedy.

We agree with Mr. Castillo that most immigrants do work hard. Generations of immigrants have started with the poorest paid and hardest jobs and worked their way, or their childrens' way, up the socioeconomic ladder, enriching us all in the process. But the decline in the productivity of American workers probably results more from a slowdown in capital investment—resulting, in turn, from government tax policies—than from what Mr. Castillo described as "two-a-day coffee breaks and two-martini lunches."

In any event, the remedy is not to import immigrants to do Americans' dirty jobs for them. To do so is to denigrate immigrants, to give credence to charges that lazy Americans fill welfare rolls because they won't take undesireable jobs, and to encourage the kind of plantation mentality that brought enslaved blacks from Africa to pick the southern cotton.

What the United States needs — and what Mr. Castillo and the Carter administration have failed to do — is to get control of immigration. The problem is not legal Mexican immigrants, but illegal. An estimated 8 million Mexican aliens now live illegally in the United States — a growing class of working poor, difficult even to count let alone to educate, furnish with health care, and assimilate into the American population.

Never before have so many illegal immigrants flooded into a country with so little protest. Never before has one nation pushed its excess population into another on such an enormous scale while failing to control its own birth rate, now one of the highest in the world. Never before in our nation's history has a group of immigrants been so insistent on perpetuating its own language and customs, on affirmative action programs that push its people ahead of native-born Americans for jobs and schools, and on turning many large cities into bilingual communities.

Mr. Castillo is resigning his job as head of the Immigration and Naturalization Service in October. It's unfortunate he hasn't left behind a more reasoned and workable immigration policy. The United States must, of course, continue to open its doors to newcomers, particularly to the politically oppressed. But we do have a right to control immigration and should, especially when we have made substantial efforts to reduce our own birth rate. And while those who do come may reasonably want to retain some of their cultural heritage, we should insist that they come with the intention of becoming part of the American society and economy, not remaining a contentious minority calling for special treatment.

The San Diego Union

San Diego, Calif., July 18, 1979

Reports in the news media of the primitive and unsanitary conditions forced upon undocumented aliens who labor in the farm fields of San Diego County point once again to the need to give legal status to foreign workers.

The now-defunct Bracero program brought thousands of aliens to the fields and orchards of this country under contracts covering their pay and welfare and their return home. There were, it is true, some complaints of unsatisfactory living and working conditions, but nothing happened to them that could match the inhuman treatment of the farm workers who now come here illegally.

Afraid to reveal their presence by complaining, some are forced to live under makeshift shelters in remote canyons. There they lack the most rudimentary sanitary facilities, clean water and medical care.

Their employers accept no responsibility for their living conditions and even cite their illegal status as reason why facilities should not be provided for them.

The exposure of helpless people to these conditions is unconscionable. Because their illegal presence invites exploitation, and they fill an acknowledged need in the labor market, the apparent solution is to remove from them the cloud of illegality.

In the meanwhile, public agencies should enforce the law vigorously to see that alien migrants are provided with the basic sanitary necessities, at least. It is being demonstrated that this can be done under the police powers of the county Health Department which has mandated the cleanup of McGonigle Canyon.

Perhaps the exposure of the degrading condition of alien workers will hasten the day when national immigration policy grants legal recognition to temporary immigrant workers. This would extend to them the protections enjoyed by other workers in this country and remove a blot from the nation's conscience.

San Francisco Chronicle

San Francisco, Calif., September 3, 1979

SENATOR S. I. HAYAKAWA has lately been making appearances up and down the state asking for a show of interest in and support for his plan for dealing with what he calls the "large and uncontrolled influx of undocumented workers from Mexico."

This is one of the most intractable problems on the American agenda. Its solution has apparently defied President Carter, but we believe the senator may be able to make a case for Congress' accepting his approach. It looks like a hopeful way to handle a flow of illegal immigration that is admittedly quite out of hand.

WE START WITH the formidable fact that the man who should know best, Leonel J. Castillo, commissioner of the Immigration and Naturalization Service, can only estimate the dimensions of the problem. He puts the number of illegal aliens now in the country at between 6 million and 12 million. Tens of thousands of Mexicans attempt to come over the border each month to add to this number. Last year the Border Patrol logged 862,000 arrests.

This large number of illegals was willing to face the risk of arrest in order to get jobs paying up to 13 times as much as could be earned in their own country. Hayakawa proposes to establish a temporary worker's visa program which, by offering legality for temporary employment, could reduce the flood of immigration. He and Senator Harrison Schmitt, R-New Mexico, have presented the Mexican-American Good Neighbor Act to admit Mexicans as non-immigrants on visas allowing them to work in the United States for 180 days a year.

This measure, the senators say, assumes that such workers from Mexico would not want to stay permanently in this country; that they have a short term need to supplement their incomes, and that legalizing entry to available jobs for which farmers and business are unable to find domestic workers at the minimum wage would end the pressure to settle here.

TO INDUCE COMPLIANCE with the 180-days-only rule, the senator proposes requiring a monetary deposit on the issuance of a visa, the deposit to be held in escrow by the Mexican government and refunded on the worker's return home.

It would be foolish to predict total success for this approach, but since we have to try something, why not legalize what otherwise would be illegal and see if the free operation of the law of supply and demand for labor would not cure the depressing, unscrupulous traffic in human beings that now goes on?

An Extreme Solution: Opening U.S.-Mexican Border

The Register

Santa Ana, Calif., January 8, 1981

We're not privy to everything president-elect Reagan and Mexican president Jose Lopez Portillo discussed during their meeting in Juarez. We presume that they dealt more in formalities and generalities than specific policy matters.

Reagan aides have suggested that the talks were designed to set the stage for an informal "North American accord" that would embody increased trade and cooperation with both Mexico and Canada. An anonymous aide noted that the first steps would have to be informal because "both Canada and Mexico have become cynical after years of neglect of their interests by the United States."

Probably the worst thing the United States could do would be to announce that it was suddenly going to look after the interests of Canada and Mexico. We have enough trouble defining what our own interests are and then acting on our understanding. Presumably, Mexico is more capable of looking after its own interests than we are.

However, declining to formulate policy on the basis of our perception of somebody else's interests doesn't mean there aren't steps we can take to improve relations. We should take those steps not because they fit some State Department specialist's vision of Mexican interests, but because they are in our own best interests and in line with the best aspects of American tradition. Coincidentally, they should improve relations with Mexico, but we should take them whether they do or not.

We refer specifically to the idea of an open border and unrestricted immigration. We would prefer completely unrestricted immigration and elimination of such absurd restrictions as customs inspections and limitations on what people may carry into this country. If the United States is not yet ready for this libertarian approach, we might start by opening up the border with Mexico.

All the restrictions and border guards we now have have done little more than throw a few inconveniences and indignities in the way of the flood of illegal aliens. If there's a chance of a better life in the United States and money to be earned to send back home to the family, people from Mexico will continue to seize that opportunity. The immigration restrictions simply create an aura of illegitimacy about what should be a natural and welcome flow of willing workers.

For the most part "undocumented workers" create an economic boon for the United States. The jobs they take are most often those few Americans want to do, but which still need to be done. Some industries would probably die without them.

The principal reason for opening our borders, however, does not revolve around economic pluses and minuses. It is that a nation that claims to have a unique concern for personal liberty shouldn't be throwing up walls around its borders and establishing quotas for people who want to move here. Such policies are a travesty on our traditions.

Some will complain that foreigners come to America just to live on welfare. The studies we've seen indicate that's a myth — that undocumented workers generally pay social security taxes and income taxes through deductions, and collect little in welfare for fear of being deported. But myth or not, there's a simple solution. Simply pass a law establishing a residency requirement for welfare or any other form of public assistance. It should be a substantial time period, at least five years. We think most immigrants come to the U.S. to work and have a chance to get ahead, not to collect welfare. We see no need to push welfare on people.

An open border policy with Mexico could have substantial benefits. For starters, it would eliminate the psychological feeling that Mexico and anything Mexican (including returning American tourists) are somehow undesirable and deserving of a body search before being allowed into the glorious U.S.A. It would encourage more substantial trade, and might set the tone for some sharing of what appears to be an oil bonanza into which Mexico has fallen.

But the step should be taken because it is right, not in expectation of some *quid pro quo.* A free country should have open borders. Period.

WORCESTER TELEGRAM

Worcester, Mass., May 27, 1979

Paul F. Oreffice, president of the Dow Chemical Company, has come up with an idea majestic in scope and yet basically simple.

He wants to unite Mexico, the United States and Canada into a political alliance and an economic customs union. Although the three would retain their separate political independence and identity, national barriers would be lowered, including the fence between Mexico and the United States. People, goods and capital would move freely across the borders. North America would become the most dynamic economic unit on the globe by far.

There are two ways to look at this proposal: One can feel overwhelmed by the immense political difficulties it would entail; or one can sense the enormous possibilities it encompasses.

It would resolve the problem of illegal Mexican immigration in perhaps the only possible way: by making it legal.

It would make feasible a continental energy system, utilizing Mexican oil, Canadian tar sands, U.S. coal and Alaskan natural gas in a rational way, unhampered by political boundaries.

It would let down the bars, north and south, to U.S. capital and technology, to the benefit of everybody.

It would permit the enormous food-producing capacity of the three nations to be developed and enhanced to the benefit of all.

The Oreffice plan is perhaps the most revolutionary idea the New World has produced in a long time.

Of course, there are at least 10,000 reasons why it will be deemed impossible.

The Mexicans will suspect another Yanqui plot to get U.S. hands on their oil.

Canada, in the shaky hands of a new Progressive Conservative government led by an inexperienced young man, will think this is not the time for grand experiments.

Some fatuous Americans, living in a dream world, will see no need to make any concessions to the neighbors we have so long taken for granted.

And so on.

Oreffice's plan perhaps will have to be put on the shelf along with Benjamin Franklin's Albany Plan of Union in 1754. Franklin proposed that the 13 colonies combine into one federation to better protect their common interests.

The notion was obviously impractical. That's why it never got anywhere.

Texas Schools Ordered to Accept Illegal Alien Children

Thousands of children of illegal aliens began attending Texas public schools in September as the result of a July court decision. District Judge Woodrow Seals overturned a state law that barred the use of state funds for educating children of illegal immigrants, citing the equal protection provision of the Fourteenth Amendment to the Constitution. "Equal protection of the laws is meaningless," he wrote, "unless it applies to the unpopular as well as the popular, the weak as well as the strong. The undocumented children residing in the state of Texas are entitled to that protection." The state law, enacted in 1975, had led many public schools to bar children of illegal aliens, while others imposed high tuition fees on illegal aliens who wanted to send their children to school.

The Oregonian
Portland, Ore., July 26, 1980

Texas belatedly joined most of the world July 21 in being forced to affirm a child's right to free primary education whether or not the child is an illegal alien. In fact, that right has been affirmed in international agreements written decades ago.

Foreign residents, legal and illegal alike, contribute to United States society in the form of state taxes and productive work. They should, therefore, have access to a state's social services, according to a ruling by a Texas federal District Court.

In his ruling, the judge relied on the 14th Amendment to the Constitution, which applies to persons — not necessarily citizens — living in the United States. However, he failed to mention that the right to free primary education is explicitly assured in international agreements as well — in both the United Nations Universal Declaration of Human Rights and the charter of the Organization of American States. The United States is a member of both bodies.

Defendants argued that the presence of thousands of undocumented workers placed an unfair burden on Texas school district budgets. But since undocumented workers are required to pay sales and property taxes, the state law requiring illegal aliens to pay additionally for primary schooling was not only unconstitutional but smacked of racism as well.

Undocumented aliens certainly take some jobs from U.S. citizens. But people who cannot work in this country legally will migrate here as long as jobs are available. The United States cannot secure thousands of miles of borders against illegal entry. Illegal immigration will stop only when work is unavailable.

However, if it is true, as recent studies show, that many illegal aliens serve an indispensable role in the U.S. economy, their role should be formally recognized. Secretary of Labor Ray Marshall, a Texas college professor who has specialized in the undocumented alien issue, believes a work permit system can be devised that could provide foreign labor to U.S. businesses without displacing American workers; that would preserve constitutional rights of all residents in this country; that would not place undue burdens on any locality; and that could lubricate the sticky relations this country has with its hemispheric neighbors over the undocumented immigrant issue.

Ultimately, the solutions to this problem lie among the tangled roots of the imbalance between the poverty and wealth of different nations. It is a national-international problem, not a state-local one. The federal government must untie the knots. States and school districts cannot do it.

Houston Chronicle
Houston, Texas, July 25, 1980

There is something fundamentally wrong with a court decision saying that people who have no legal right to be in this country nevertheless have a legal right to a free education at the taxpayers' expense. This is turning rationality on its head; the two facts are mutually exclusive.

That point is so basic, so undeniable, and yet so puzzlingly lost in U. S. District Judge Woodrow Seals ruling this week that illegal alien children have a constitutional right to a tuition-free education in this state.

No amount of legalistic or sociological argument can get around the simple fact that illegal aliens are by definition not entitled to be present in this country at all, therefore how can they be entitled to the public services of the country? Does citizenship and legal residency mean nothing any more? What kind of Pandora's box is opened by such an interpretation of the law?

If a federal court is just to sidestep the underlying question of illegal presence here and note, as Judge Seals did, that illegal aliens "enjoy a form of de facto amnesty" because Congress has not allocated sufficient funds to stem the tide of immigration, that seems to us an invitation to legal chaos over all other public services.

By all means this decision should be appealed, as Attorney General Mark White is moving to do. We trust that on appeal higher courts will address themselves to the real issue involved — illegal aliens have no right to be here in the first place.

FORT WORTH STAR-TELEGRAM
Fort Worth, Texas, July 24, 1980

By his decision opening the doors of the public schools of Texas to the children of undocumented workers U. S. District Judge Woodrow Seals has rendered all the residents of this state, the legal residents, as well as the illegal ones, a tremendous public service.

He ruled correctly that the Texas law passed in 1975 that bars the state from spending tax money to educate the children of undocumented workers violated the U. S. Constitution's guarantees of due process and equal protection under the laws.

Basing his ruling on the 14th Amendment, the judge said: "The Constitution does not permit the states to deny access to education to a discrete group of children within its borders when it has undertaken to provide public education."

Texas was the only state in the nation that had passed such a law. This ruling should preclude any other states doing so.

To appeal the decision would appear to be pointless. The school districts of this state should have anticipated what the ruling would be and have made preparations to admit the children. The state should not delay making its share of the funding available to the school districts.

Undoubtedly there will be considerable additional costs involved in admitting these children to the public schools, but Judge Seals said he found no evidence that the state or the school districts "lack the necessary funds."

He brought home a point in his ruling that we have emphasized on several occasions — that the cost of not educating them could prove heavier in a few years than this state will have to pay now. He pointed out that most of the children will become permanent residents of this country and that by denying them an education "we insure that most of them will become wards of our society."

It is understandable that Gov. Bill Clements would have preferred to have seen this problem solved within the context of his proposed system of legalized residency for work purposes. But, if that program is ever to be established it will be years before it comes to fruition, and the problem of the school children demanded attention now.

It is fortunate that Judge Seals has issued his ruling in time for preparations to be made to admit the children this fall. Like School Board President Dr. Richard O'Neal, we are "relieved" at the decision. As O'Neal said, "We know where we stand now."

And, more importantly, so do the children.

The Dallas Morning News

Dallas, Texas, September 9, 1980

School doors will open for many children of illegal aliens in Texas this fall thanks to U.S. Supreme Court Justice Lewis Powell's ruling that they can attend classes while a federal district court decision is appealed.

"The harm caused these children by lack of education needs little elucidation," the justice said. And that sums up the ramification of the 1975 Texas law that bars them from a public education.

These children are the prime victims of a breakdown in U.S. immigration policy that has opened the borders for any aliens who want the jobs willingly offered by American businessmen. Unable to bring itself to attack the source of the problem — employers who invite aliens into this country — the Texas Legislature jumped on the kids.

Testimony in the initial trial showed that illegal aliens pay the same taxes that Americans do. Through their state and local property taxes, sales taxes, gasoline taxes and other levies they subsidize the education of American children while their own kids are denied the opportunity.

Justice Powell's action indicates that the Supreme Court will approach the case with an open mind. Now if the Congress would just do likewise and provide a rational guest worker program, that would be even better news for the illegal aliens' children and for all others concerned.

Dallas, Texas, November 29, 1980

No one is surprised that illegal alien students, attending Texas schools for the first time under a federal court order, are exhibiting special problems.

Brownsville school principal, Carlos Alvarado, after watching 53 illegal alien youngsters enroll in his elementary school, declared that "Some of them have had no schooling whatsoever. Socializing is even a problem. When they first come here, they don't understand the rules and regulations."

Compound this lack of experience with the language problem that many of the youngsters face, and the costs of educating them run far above that experienced with regular students.

And this is just another reason for the federal government to face the reality of the problems it has created for border states' schools by failing to enforce its immigration laws.

Special federal funding is needed to help educate these youngsters, who must in fairness be allowed to attend schools in the United States as long as their parents are free to immigrate, legally or illegally.

This funding should be part of a comprehensive package of immigration law reforms proposed as one of the Reagan administration's first programs.

THE SACRAMENTO BEE

Sacramento, Calif., July 29, 1980

In declaring unconstitutional a Texas law that bars illegal alien children from attending public schools, Federal District Judge Woodrow Seals gave new meaning to the equal protection clause of the 14th Amendment. And just as importantly, he reopened the classroom doors, which had been shut to these children for nearly five years.

Under the 1975 law — unique to Texas — the state withheld reimbursement funds to local school districts for the costs of educating illegal aliens, mostly Mexicans. Some schools charged prohibitive tuition — Houston's monthly fee for example was $162. Others simply barred them from attendance altogether. Consequently, thousands of youths stayed home or wandered idly in the streets.

In justifying the statute, the state contended that illegal aliens pay no taxes and overcrowd the schools, thus the need for tuition to meet the added expenses. Judge Seals correctly called that argument "nonsense." The people in question pay property taxes through rent, he reminded state officials. Furthermore, the state has collected a windfall in federal education funds based on census counts that include illegal aliens. The judge might have added that most also are subject to regular payroll deductions for federal income taxes and Social Security, as well as gasoline taxes and other sales and excise taxes, yet make little use of tax-supported public services.

More fundamentally, the ruling addressed for the first time the question whether the equal protection provision applies to illegal aliens. The clause must indeed embrace them too, Judge Seals ruled, if the law is to have any meaning. His ruling should be a clear message to other states with large illegal alien populations that may be considering laws similar to Texas'. In California, the ruling will have no significant impact, since school districts here already maintain an open-door policy with no questions asked about immigration status.

From a purely economic standpoint, the Texas law was shortsighted and self-defeating anyway. State officials, in prohibiting children of illegal aliens from attending school, may have saved a few dollars today, but would surely have borne serious financial and social costs tomorrow. Besides penalizing the children for their parents' actions, the state would have bred a generation of illiterates and wards of society. The children deserve better, and so does society.

Chicago Tribune

Chicago, Ill., July 24, 1980

A federal court in Houston has struck down as unconstitutional a Texas law denying illegal immigrant children access to free public education. In his long awaited decision, Judge Woodrow Seals held that the equal protection clause of the 14th Amendment "does not permit the states to deny ~ccess to education to a discrete group of children within its borders when it has undertaken to provide public education." Texas schools may not even charge undocumented alien children tuition. Given the poverty of many illegals, to charge tuition would be to exclude many of their children from school.

The school districts and states with large numbers of illegal immigrants may well feel aggrieved. They are bearing the cost of educating people with no right to be in the country, people whom the federal government might be expected to deport, since it failed to exclude them. Perhaps the concept of aid to "impacted districts" should be extended from districts serving army posts to ones with substantial numbers of undocumented aliens—though of course it is virtually impossible to get an accurate count of such aliens.

Yet the public interest surely is served by Judge Seals' decision. As he said, most of the children in question will spend their adult lives in this country. They need the basic skills required of anyone who is going to be an employable worker and a desirable neighbor. Clearly it would be cruel as well as irresponsible to condemn innocent children to an almost inevitable future as welfare clients if not prison inmates. As the judge rightly said, children excluded from school "suffer great harm." So does the community in which they live.

The state of Texas argued that it lacks the means to educate all children if undocumented aliens were admitted to the public schools. Judge Seals rejected this argument, saying there were "sufficient funds to educate the undocumented children."

The decision is important for a number of states, though Texas is the only one which has tried to exclude undocumented aliens by statute. Florida and all the states bordering Mexico have a problem. So do northern cities, such as Chicago, where illegals have tended to gravitate.

The schooling of the children of illegal immigrants is a national problem, a spin-off from the larger national problem of how to restrict illegal immigration and of what to do with those who evade what restrictions there are. The smaller problem posed by the school-age children can hardly be resolved as long as the larger problem of illegal immigration remains unsolved. Until then, Texas and the rest of us need to provide schooling for our resident population without trying to strain out those whose papers are not in proper order.

ARKANSAS DEMOCRAT

Little Rock, Ark., September 19, 1980

Poor Texas. She's all for having Mexican aliens count for political purposes but not at all keen about having to spend tax money on the children of those aliens. But on these two issues the courts appear to be singing the old song, "You can't have one without the other."

Texas insisted that the 1980 census count the aliens for purposes of congressional representation. That's been done and it will probably mean a new congressman or two after reapportionment – but does it follow that the state should be landed with court orders directing it to furnish free public school to the children of the aliens? Poetic justice, some say – but the the state declares that if the federal government can't do its job of keeping aliens out, then it's Washington, not Texas, that should pay for educating the children of the aliens.

That's sense – but the whole question of free education for these children makes sense only if they are treated as entirely separate from the legal problems of their parents. And that doesn't make sense.

Presumably, when an alien family is detected, all members are sent back to Mexico together. So which "children of aliens" qualify for schooling? Surely not those whose parents reveal themselves as such. We can't guess the ins and outs of a situation in which illegality is the first condition of a statutory social guarantee – schooling! But we don't doubt that when word of the free gringo education gets around Mexico, many an alien will drag his children across the border to take advantage of it. Some such parents will even treat or understand the guarantee as their own passport to lawful residency.

So what were the courts thinking about in issuing such an invitation? "Equal protection of the laws," they say – meaning that states must give aliens the same lawful benefits they give their own people. That's a far cry frym the original meaning of equal protection: that Southern states after the Civil War were not to discriminate statutorily against freed slaves or exclude them from the benefits of any laws passed generally. How that can be turned into a positive social benefit for foreigners beats us. The courts appear to be confusing criminal due process (which the Constitution guarantees unreservedly) with social benefits that aren't constitutionally guaranteed at all.

In any case, in the matter of aliens, the federal government is now fighting itself. The border patrol is hollering, "Stay where you are," and the federal judiciary is chanting, "Y'all come." It's easy to see that the courts will win out. If the free education principle is extended nationwide, the costs of such ruinous policy could run into billions.

The Charlotte Observer

Charlotte, N.C., July 24, 1980

In a watershed case regarding access to public education, a federal district judge in Texas ruled this week that a state can't deny schooling to the children of illegal aliens.

It was time someone told the news to the Texas legislature, which in 1975 enacted a harsh law barring use of state funds to educate the children of illegal aliens — the only such law in the nation. School districts where the children of so-called undocumented workers were enrolled — mostly in the poor border areas along the Rio Grande River and in the state's major metropolitan areas — had to find other ways to pay for teachers and supplies for uncounted thousands of children.

Some school districts began barring the children; others charged high tuition fees the parents could not afford. Some children went to inadequate alternative schools, but many simply did not go to school, spending their days roaming the streets.

The result, as U.S. District Judge Woodrow Seals pointed out, was to create a permanent underclass of uneducated children. Yet, as Judge Seals wrote in his opinion, "Equal protection of the laws is meaningless unless it applies to the unpopular as well as the popular, the weak as well as the strong. The undocumented children residing in the state of Texas are entitled to that protection."

U.S. laws give illegal aliens few rights. Workers who illegally enter this country can't receive Social Security benefits (although employers withhold taxes from their paychecks), Medicare, Medicaid, food stamps, employment training, unemployment compensation or housing benefits. Few undocumented workers seek services for which they are eligible (such as maternal and health care and education for their children) because they fear it could mean discovery and deportation.

If Texas wishes to avoid helping school districts educate the children of illegal immigrants, it should do what so far it has been unwilling to do: work to cut off the flow of illegal aliens who provide cheap labor for Texas businesses and homes.

Though 12 other states have enacted laws forbidding businesses to employ illegal aliens, Judge Seals noted in his opinion that the Texas legislature has refused to enact laws that would punish Texans for knowingly hiring of illegal aliens. (Unfortunately, neither of the Carolinas has such a law, either.)

Texas's 1975 law permits the community to benefit from the labor of illegal aliens while permanently damaging their children. The judge has ruled that if the community accepts the benefits of the illegal aliens' labor, it can't reject the responsibility of educating their children.

THE RICHMOND NEWS LEADER

Richmond, Va., July 31, 1980

● *There was only one catch, and that was Catch 22, which specified that a concern for one's own safety in the face of dangers that were real and immediate was the process of a rational mind. Orr was crazy and could be grounded. All he had to was ask; and as soon as he did, he would no longer be crazy and would have to fly more missions. . . . If he flew them he was crazy and didn't have to, but if he didn't want to he was sane and had to.*
—*Joseph Heller in 'Catch 22'*

That is the kind of Catch-22 situation that the state of Texas now finds itself in, as a result of a recent Federal District Court finding. The court ruled that Texas must provide free public education to the children of illegal aliens.

It is up to the federal government, of course, to enforce immigration laws, but the feds are notoriously lax in keeping illegal aliens from jumping the Mexican border into Texas and staying there. Once Congress repealed the bracero laws permitting Mexican workers to work legally on a temporary basis in this country, an influx of illegal immigrants from Mexico began to swamp the Southwest. In 1975, Texas passed a state law allowing school districts to charge illegal aliens $160 a month in tuition to public schools or to ban the children of illegal aliens from those schools.

The Justice Department filed suit, charging that the Texas law violated the aliens' right to equal protection of the law guaranteed by the 14th Amendment. The Justice Department, of course, is the parent bureaucracy of the Immigration and Naturalization Service, which is charged with keeping illegal aliens out. The District Court agreed with the Justice Department, casting the taxpayers of Texas as fall guys in Justice's con game.

The problem of educating the children of illegal aliens may not be a substantial one in states well removed from the Mexican border. In Texas, however, the court decision could swell public school enrollment by between 40,000 and 110,000 children. That is the extent to which the Immigration Service has neglected its enforcement duties. Admission of these thousands of children could cost Texas taxpayers as much as $200 million a year and seriously jeopardize the state's

bilingual educational programs. Texas already is having trouble finding enough bilingual teachers to serve the children of the state's legal aliens.

It is argued that illegal aliens pay taxes, and thus they should not be singled out for tuition charges. But few illegal aliens pay property taxes that provide the basis for most public school funding. The Texas legislature used that reasoning in the law permitting school districts to charge tuition: that property owners should not have to bear disproportionate school costs because the federal government was failing in its job of patrolling the border.

It also is argued that children of illegal aliens especially need the education provided by public schools to prepare them for citizenship, and that argument is persuasive. Nonetheless, Texas property owners naturally believe that the burden of financing this costly education should not be theirs alone to bear. It is far too easy for the federal government, ignoring its role in creating the problem, to pass the buck to Texas and its taxpayers, just because Texas — as a border state — proves an irresistible lure to illegal aliens.

There are several alternatives to putting the full costs of the federal government's failure on Texas taxpayers: (1) The Immigration Service needs to beef up its forces along the border and to enforce deportation procedures strictly. (2) Congress ought to reinstate the bracero program, allowing Mexicans to take temporary jobs in this country without settling here. And (3), Congress should redirect the funds now spent under the impact aid program (to reimburse communities for the imaginary costs of high federal or military employment) to states with many illegal alien children to educate.

If the federal government will not keep illegal aliens out or deport them when their illegal status is a matter of record, the feds should be sent the bill for their ineptitude. Perhaps if all taxpayers — instead of just a few — had to finance such folly, public indignation would persuade the feds to enforce the law against illegal immigration and stop the problem at its source.

Los Angeles Times

Los Angeles, Calif., July 23, 1980

In California the children of illegal immigrants are allowed to attend public schools like all other youngsters. But not in Texas—until Monday, when U.S. Dist. Judge Woodrow Seals struck down a state law that effectively barred such children from attending public schools.

Seals ruled that a law that forbade the use of state funds for the schooling of children whose parents are in the United States illegally was discriminatory and unconstitutional. The statute had prompted some school districts in Texas, like Dallas, to bar such pupils altogether. Other districts, including Houston, barred these children by charging prohibitively high tuitions.

Seals also ordered the state to begin enrolling and educating what he called "undocumented children" because preventing them from going to school violated the Constitution's guarantee of due process and equal protection of the law.

It appears likely that Texas will appeal Seals' decision, perhaps setting up a test case that may resolve the issue of whether people in the country illegally are entitled to the same constitutional protections as are citizens. Regardless of what higher courts may decide on that question, Seals' decision deserves praise because it enforces what is simply good public policy. There is no benefit to be gained by preventing children, who after all had no choice in the migration of their parents to this country, from receiving an education. Instead, it runs the risk, as Seals warned in his ruling, of creating a permanent underclass in this society.

Seals' decision will also be helpful if it serves as a reminder to local governments that they should be wary of trying to interpret or enforce immigration laws, which are properly a federal matter. Latino civil-rights groups have been warning for some time that a vigilante attitude toward illegal aliens by local governments is not only hazardous to the rights of Mexican-Americans and other citizens but is shortsighted as well. This is so whether it involves local police departments alienating Latino communities by arresting persons simply on suspicion that they are in the country illegally, or local health authorities turning persons away from county hospitals if there is some question as to their immigration status, thereby possibly endangering public health.

We can understand the frustration that prompts such local reactions. The federal government has created a vacuum by delaying for too long a thorough revision of this country's immigration and refugee laws. The continuing deliberations of the Select Commission on Immigration and Refugee Policy will, we hope, finally begin that process.

In the meantime, shortsighted "solutions" to immigration-related problems, like Texas' law on illegal-alien schoolchildren, cause more troubles than they resolve—which is why Seals' decision was both necessary and proper.

Gauging the Effect of Illegals on Welfare

It is maddeningly impossible to determine how much of a burden illegal aliens place on U.S. taxpayers. A study commissioned by the Immigration and Naturalization Service in 1975 estimated that illegals cost the public $13 billion a year. However, no other agency has been able to arrive at precise figures. Illegal aliens are understandably reluctant to apply openly for welfare because of the fear of discovery. A 1977 report by the General Accounting Office was forced to conclude that "insufficient data exist to estimate the extent of use or financial impact" of illegal aliens on the welfare system. The study acknowledged that illegals used public assistance, especially medical facilities, unemployment insurance and public education. State and local governments probably bore the brunt of the financial burden, the GAO concluded. The agency added that illegal aliens indirectly affected the welfare system by displacing American workers. Those aliens who managed to obtain direct assistance used false documents or went undetected through bureaucratic inefficiency. The GAO reported that illegals contributed to tax revenues by paying sales taxes, gasoline and property taxes and having Social Security and other taxes deducted from their paychecks. The GAO report concluded that it was impossible to determine whether illegal aliens received more or less in benefits than they paid out in taxes.

The Cleveland Press
Cleveland, Ohio, December 30, 1977

It's possible to disagree about the question of amnesty for illegal aliens. But one thing we're sure almost all Americans would agree on is that there should be no amnesty for people who sponsor legal aliens, pledging financial support of the aliens as a condition of entry, and then dump them on the public welfare rolls.

It happens, because after 30 days in the United States, aliens seeking permanent residence are eligible to receive $177.80 a month in federal Supplemental Security Income payments.

A survey by the General Accounting Office of the five states worst hit by this abuse — California, New York, Florida, New Jersey and Illinois — found that more than 37,000 aliens collected $72.3 million in SSI payments in 1976.

According to Sen. Charles Percy of Illinois, many of these aliens were the parents of American citizens and were brought into this country by their children, who had no intention of supporting them.

Percy intends to introduce legislation that would (1) require a five-year residency for SSI eligibility and (2) make a sponsor's affidavit promising support of an alien a legally enforceable contract.

We hope the bill is passed in the next session of Congress, so that those who have been honoring their fathers and mothers this way can start honoring their word to Uncle Sam.

THE RICHMOND NEWS LEADER
Richmond, Va., May 25, 1977

The problem of illegal aliens who are sneaking into the U.S. appears prominently in the news, but little attention is given to the problem of legal aliens who are adding to the nation's welfare burden.

The General Accounting Office reports that legal aliens currently are drawing $72 million a year in benefits under the Supplemental Security Income program. This program was designed to aid the aged, blind, or disabled who have not accumulated enough credits under the Social Security program to qualify for benefits; funds for SSI come from general revenues.

An alien entering this country legally usually has an American sponsor who guarantees the financial security of the alien for 30 days. This guarantee, however, does not have the force of law, and many aliens are applying for SSI benefits before the 30-day period expires. Having gained admittance to the land of plenty, they waste no time in going on the dole.

Congressman Paul Findley of Illinois has been trying to solve the problem for some time. His latest effort would require that an alien meet a five-year residency requirement before becoming eligible for SSI benefits. The sponsor's 30-day guarantee also would be considered a legal contract. So far Congress has ignored the need to tighten restrictions on welfare for legal aliens, but perhaps this time around Findley will be successful. A nation staggering under a heavy welfare burden has problems enough with its own mendicants. It needs no more takers from abroad.

Des Moines Tribune
Des Moines, Iowa, November 25, 1977

Millions of U.S. welfare dollars are being spent yearly on immigrants brought into this country through subterfuge, the U.S. General Accounting Office (GAO) has found. Senator Charles Percy (Rep., Ill.) is planning legislation to halt the welfare drain.

Immigration laws favor those who already have relatives in the U.S. The immigrant must have a job waiting or, if he is aged or disabled, his American sponsor must pledge support. Too often, the pledges are phony, the GAO found; each year, an estimated 42,000 immigrants arrive in the U.S. and promptly claim welfare benefits due the aged or disabled.

"Some of these people get off the plane and their first stop is the Social Security office," a GAO official said. In five states alone, such immigrants are receiving $72 million in welfare yearly, the GAO estimates.

Percy's plan would make the pledges of support signed by the immigrants' sponsors legally binding, and would require a five-year waiting period before an alien could receive welfare.

Promising support for an alien, then refusing support and dumping responsibility on the taxpayers is a cynical abuse of both the immigration and welfare laws. Percy's remedy is sound.

Honolulu Star-Bulletin

Honolulu, Ha., March 1, 1978

The General Accounting Office, an investigative arm of Congress, reports that 214,000 aliens are estimated to be receiving benefits under the Supplemental Security Income (SSI) program. Of this number, 42,000 have been in the United States less than five years.

Of the newly arrived aliens who collect SSI benefits, the GAO estimates that 8 percent enroll within 30 days of arrival in the United States, 41 percent enroll within six months, and 63 percent enroll within their first year in this country.

In Los Angeles County alone, the GAO estimates, newly arrived aliens collect more than $19 million annually under the Aid to Families with Dependent Children, Old Age Assistance, and Aid to the Totally Disabled programs. In five states studied by the GAO, newly arrived aliens receive more than $72 million annually under the SSI program.

Hawaii's Sen. Spark Matsunaga has cosponsored a proposed amendment to pending Social Security legislation aimed at correcting this problem. The amendment would make a sponsor's affidavit to provide support for immigrants a legally enforceable contract so that the alien does not become a public charge. If the sponsor reneges on his obligation and SSI payments are mistakenly made, the government could recover the payments from the sponsor.

The amendment, introduced by Sen. Charles Percy, R-Ill., would also establish a five-year residency requirement before most aliens could become eligible for SSI payments. Some aliens currently collect SSI benefits within 30 days of arrival for causes that arose prior to their entry.

The GAO report says "In most cases, aliens apply for SSI because their sponsors, who promised in affidavits of support to keep them off public assistance, do not keep their promise. The sponsors cannot be forced to pay assistance because the courts have ruled that the affidavits are unenforceable moral commitments."

Hawaii, one of the gateway states for immigrants, has a large alien population and is vulnerable to the sort of abuses described by the GAO. Gov. Ariyoshi has proposed residency requirements for welfare recipients but has encountered opposition. But the federal government could alleviate the problem by holding the immigrant's sponsor to his promise of support.

The Dispatch

Columbus, Ohio, March 22, 1978

INADEQUATE PROCEDURES for screening aliens and deficient Social Security laws are costing U.S. taxpayers millions of dollars annually.

That is the conclusion of a report by the U.S. Comptroller General, and it deserves prompt attention.

The study focuses on newly arrived aliens receiving supplemental security income—federal cash assistance to the needy aged, blind and disabled.

It indicates that about 37,50() newly arrived aliens receive about $72 million in government benefits —and the study concerns only those living in five large states.

Aliens too often become public charges when their sponsors fail to provide support promised in visa applications.

And, there are no residency requirements to prevent newly arrived aliens from obtaining public assistance.

What is the solution? The report suggests several practical remedies—more stringent income criteria for visa applicants and residency requirements for public assistance applications.

For too long the taxpayer's interest has been neglected. While it is important to treat all U.S. residents fairly and provide aid to the genuinely needy, this country should not have to support large numbers of elderly aliens. These people have worked abroad, and should not be permitted to become public wards in an adopted country.

Congress and the Executive should move speedily to impose realistic new standards.

THE INDIANAPOLIS STAR

Indianapolis, Ind., January 4, 1978

Thirty days after a foreigner who has been granted permanent residence status sets foot on American soil he can go to the nearest Social Security office to demand — and receive — a monthly government welfare pension.

Sen. Charles H. Percy (R-Ill.) explained how this raid on taxpayers' money by foreigners works. A welfare program called Supplemental Security Income, funded by the federal government and optionally by some states, distributes more than $6.4 billion each year. These payments of up to $117.80 per month go to poor people who are blind, disabled or aged.

Few Americans would oppose such aid to their fellow citizens too old or disabled to work. But Percy points out that, due to a gaping loophole in the law, aliens who have never contributed to the American economy can become eligible for such pensions after living in the U.S. a mere 30 days.

Many aliens receiving SSI payments were granted permanent-residence visas on the basis of promises by American sponsors to give them financial support so that they would not become wards of the state. However, the courts have decreed that such promises cannot be enforced.

Thus some Americans, including some affluent ones, apparently seize upon the law's loophole to bring relatives into the U.S., signing affidavits to the effect that they pledge financial support of the aliens. Some "sponsors" have fulfilled that pledge by guiding the aliens to the welfare office 30 days after they touch U.S. soil, Percy says.

"It is unfair to American taxpayers to have to foot the bill for foreign nationals who become public charges when their sponsors renege," Percy declared.

The General Accounting Office, an investigative arm of Congress, found that in just five states — California, New York, Illinois, New Jersey and Florida — some 37,000 newly arrived aliens are collecting more than $72 million annually. The GAO estimates that more than 15,000 started collecting SSI payments within six months of entry.

"No one knows exactly how much of this government money is shelled out to abusers of the system but it is clear that good news travels fast among immigrants," Percy said.

The loophole in this law should be closed. The American taxpayer is already being raided enough by his own government. Being raided by foreigners is a little too much to ask him to stomach.

Census Bureau Includes Illegal Aliens in 1980 Count

When the U.S. Bureau of the Census announced that it would count all U.S. residents without regard to immigration status, there was a chorus of protest. The Federation for American Immigration Reform, a private immigration lobby, brought suit in 1979 to block the future reapportionment of congressional seats on the basis of the Census figures. FAIR, which was joined in its suit by 28 congressmen, argued that the Census Bureau's procedure would distort population totals and result in the improper reapportionment of as many as 16 congressional seats. A Washington, D.C. federal court dismissed the suit in February 1980 on grounds that FAIR and the congressmen could not prove that they personally would suffer loss of representation because the Census Bureau had counted illegal aliens. In its unanimous decision, the three-judge panel said FAIR could bring suit after the seats had been reapportioned.

A separate Census Bureau study released early in February 1980 estimated that there were no more than six million illegal aliens in the U.S. The bureau said the figure might be as low as 3.5 million, including 1.5 million to two million Mexicans. (A previous estimate of the illegal alien population by the Immigration and Naturalization Service had put the total figure at four to 12 million.) The Census Bureau drew a distinction between Mexican and non-Mexican illegal aliens because of what it termed the "cyclical nature" of illegal immigration from Mexico. Mexican illegals, the study reported, were more likely than non-Mexicans to move back and forth across the border and stay in the U.S. for less than a year at a time. In contrast, the study said, non-Mexican illegals were more likely than Mexicans to remain permanently in the U.S., since they were concentrated on the East Coast, far from U.S. borders. The study concluded that there was little hope of arriving at a definite count of illegal aliens, and "policy options dependent on the size of this group must be evaluated in terms which recognize this uncertainty."

The Boston Globe
Boston, Mass., December 28, 1979

Virtually no public policy issue in recent years has proved more intractable than that of illegal aliens. A couple of years ago, President Carter proposed a program that went nowhere. A federal commission studying the whole range of American immigration policies has been stymied by the question of illegal aliens. And now there is a suit in federal court in Washington maintaining that the Census Bureau should exclude illegal aliens in its official 1980 census.

The suit raises a tangle of new legal questions related to the reapportionment of Congress and the distribution of federal funds that are allocated on the basis of population. The Constitution requires congressional districts to be drawn on the basis of "people," not citizens. However, when that language was drafted, virtually every person in the nation was entitled to become a citizen and there was thus no arguable need to make a distinction.

Ironically, one of the recent problems has been that no one knows for sure how many illegal aliens there are in the country; they have generally avoided being counted for the very reason that they fear identification will lead to deportation. For a long time unofficial estimates have placed their numbers at between three and 12 million, a range which suggests the lack of precise knowledge. Now, most estimates place the minimum number at five or six million.

Surely if the Census Bureau is compelled to make distinctions between legal and illegal aliens, any hope of getting a truer count will be lost. What the Census Bureau eventually does will, apparently, be decided in the courts. But as a matter of policy a serious effort should be made to count them. If this requires their indiscriminate inclusion in the general census — as it almost surely does — than so be it.

Legalistic distinctions aside, illegal aliens are people. They contribute to local economies and public coffers. And they utilize public services. Jurisdictions in which they are concentrated should not be denied federal funds because of uncertainties at the federal level, having to do with humanitarian, foreign policy and economic considerations, over how to treat them.

To argue that the inclusion of illegal aliens in the census will skew congressional apportionment is based on an unrealistic assessment of the Census Bureau's likely success in counting them. Further, it puts too much emphasis on mathematical precision and ignores the wide variances in congressional district populations that develop after each decennial census anyway.

The American system will not falter because Texas or California or New York gets an extra congressional seat. But, if there is an official decision to exclude illegal aliens from the 1980 census, the nation will be effectively granted another decade in which to ignore the problem and the need to craft a sensible and realistic policy toward those who live among us without legal status.

The Evening Bulletin
Philadelphia, Pa., December 26, 1979

There's a legal debate underway in Washington that is so incredible that you want to rub your ears to make sure you are hearing right.

Here's the issue: Should the eight or nine million aliens known to be illegally in the U.S. be counted as part of the 1980 federal census to start April 1?

Now, before you shout "no" or "yes," remember that the 435 seats in the U.S. House of Representatives are allocated on the basis of the census, as is some 50 billion dollars of various kinds of federal aid.

Pennsylvania once had 30 seats in the U.S. House. Now, with declining population, it has 25 and figures it will drop to 24 when the numbers from the 1980 count are in. New Jersey thinks it might hold its 15.

These forecasts are sent spinning, though, if you include illegal aliens for purposes of congressional reapportionment — the only constitutional reason for the once-in-10-years census. And count the illegals is what the Bureau of the Census says it will do since the U.S. Constitution only talks about counting "persons" and doesn't say anything about citizens.

If illegal aliens are counted in reapportioning congressional seats, Pennsylvania would lose three seats instead of one. But New York and New Jersey, because of the concentration of aliens in the New York City area, each might pick up one seat. The big winners, since most of the illegal aliens are of Hispanic origin, would be the "Sunbelt" states. California, in fact, could pick up as many as six additional seats in the U.S. House.

This means, of course, that some states will have undue power in Congress — at the expense of Pennsylvania and other states — because the Federal Government has been unable or unwilling to enforce the immigration laws. Besides, counting those who are actually violating federal law by being here makes a mockery of the generally accepted "one man, one vote" basis for legislative representation as set by the Supreme Court.

We can see changing the immigration law to make it easier for those who have been here a long time to become citizens. We agree the Federal Government needs to know how many people are in the country illegally. And we think those cities that have to spend their money to care for the illegal aliens should get help from Washington. But we don't think it's right, or just, to base our representation in Congress in any degree on those who are not citizens, do not vote, may evade taxes, don't serve on juries and are thus, by most measures, "ghosts" among us.

DAILY ☆ NEWS

New York, N. Y., August 17, 1979

Millions of illegal aliens are apt to go uncounted in the 1980 census unless the Catholic hierarchy responds affirmatively to a government appeal for aid.

The aliens, many of whom are Spanish-speaking and Catholic, are naturally leery of getting involved with census-takers. Most aren't aware—or don't believe—census data is confidential, and won't be used by immigration authorities. Federal officials believe those suspicions will be allayed if priests explain the law from the pulpit.

It is a sound and sensible suggestion, and we hope church leaders will go along for the good of their communities. The census count, taken every 10 years, determines representation in the House and also plays a large role in determining how federal grants are distributed under many programs.

An accurate tally is especially important for New York. The city stands to obtain sizable increases in reimbursements for health care and other social services if its alien population—estimated at up to 1 million—is registered.

The Philadelphia Inquirer

Philadelphia, Pa., December 23, 1979

A lawsuit has been filed which, in effect, asks the U.S. government to wear blinders when it conducts the 1980 census. Five congressmen and a private group called the Federation for American Immigration Reform are trying to undo the plans of the Census Bureau to include illegal aliens in next year's count of the population. They argue, speciously, that counting the illegal aliens will dilute the political strength of citizens and legal immigrants, diverting federal monies distributed on the basis of population.

The legal question raised in the suit is whether the Constitution requires only legal residents to be counted for purposes of legislative apportionment. Scholars seem to agree, as is the case with most constitutional issues, that reasonable arguments can be made on both sides. But the argument that the purpose of the census is to count all people, except visitors and diplomats, as has been the practice, is most persuasive. And the overwhelming practical fact is that illegal immigrants receive at least some social services and therefore, the realistic thing to do is to count them.

Even trying to find a way to identify and exclude the estimated 4 million to 12 million illegal aliens in this country would present the Census Bureau with innumerable practical problems, at a time when its effort has been directed toward the opposite — to try to get as accurate a count as possible of all residents, including illegal aliens.

At bottom, the question of what to do about illegal aliens, how and whether to count them for representation or distribution of funds, is separate from the census and should be addressed separately by the Congress. The census is to count people, all people, truthfully, not to manipulate public policy.

The Pittsburgh Press

Pittsburgh, Pa., August 4, 1979

California is toying with a novel — and ominous — approach to the problem of illegal aliens which would, in effect, tell them: We can't lick you, so we'll le you join us.

The California legislature has allocated $800,000 to promote participation by illegal aliens, as well as other previously uncounted or undercounted minority groups, in the 1980 census.

Because illegal aliens are treated the same as citizens for census purposes, California stands to benefit in three important ways:

✔ It would qualify for more congressmen when all the states redraw their congressional districts after the 1980 census.

✔ It would automatically be entitled to greater representation in the Electoral College, and hence carry more weight in presidential elections.

✔ It would be entitled to a greater portion of federal revenue-sharing funds and scores of other census-based programs.

California's gains, of course, would be at the expense of other states that do not harbor significant numbers of illegal aliens — thus making its action both cynical and reckless.

★ ★ ★

This country obviously has lost control of its own immigration policy. It is the aliens who decide if they are going to enter or not, and they apparently do so with ridiculous ease.

President Carter would grant them amnesty if they elude the authorities long enough. Now California Gov. Jerry Brown would enlist their bodies for political advantage.

Is it any wonder the tide of illegals continues to swell?

THE KANSAS CITY STAR

Kansas City, Mo., December 31, 1979

The federal government intends to count illegal aliens as American citizens in the 1980 census. It is a bad plan and could distort, among other things, the new congressional districts that will be based on that count.

An estimated four to 12 million persons, depending on the source of the figures, are in this country unlawfully. Spread among a population in the 220-million range, that might not appear to be a significant number. Many of them, however, are concentrated in a few areas — mainly New York, California and Texas. If they are included as citizens the U.S. House districts with a heavy population of the so-called illegals would have more weight in the Congress than those inhabited by legal residents. Federal aid also is keyed to the number of residents, thus some areas could receive a disproportionate share of grants.

This misguided plan has not gone unnoticed. A group that calls itself the Federation of American Immigration Reform (FAIR) is attempting to block it through court action.

The point is not whether the aliens should be counted. They should be, although that likely will be a difficult task because these nonresidents fear deportation. Nonetheless an attempt to get an accurate record should be attempted.

Crucial at this moment is the effort to exclude them from the count that would reflect on congressional districts and federal aid. Otherwise their presence in this country will be given a form of legitimacy.

That is an unacceptable contradiction. The fundamental law of voter representation can't be based on illegality.

The Salt Lake Tribune

Salt Lake City, Utah, December 30, 1979

Illegal aliens now are coming to public attention in a way that promises to break new legal ground.

With the 1980 Census due to begin April 1, 1980, a constitutional question has been raised over whether illegal aliens, whose numbers may top 8 million, should be included in the count for purposes of reapportioning the next Congress.

A lawsuit filed by the Federation for American Immigration Reform asserts that the government's plan to include illegal aliens in the count would dilute the political representation of citizens and lawful immigrants. Such a course, the suit says, would give an undue number of seats to states which have large populations of illegal aliens.

Although the suit alleges reapportionment abuse, its outcome could also influence the annual allocation of $50 billion in federal aid under 100 or so programs that are based on local population counts.

The U.S. Constitution is vague on the matter. As altered by the 14th Amendment, it states that representation should be based on "counting the whole number of persons in each state, excluding Indians not taxed."

An illegal alien is plainly a person and in one way or another most of them probably pay some taxes. But the best argument in the government's favor is that there is almost no practical way for census takers to determine the citizenship status of those they count. For one thing, much of the counting is done by mail.

Like it or not, illegal aliens constitute a significant though still relatively small segment of the overall population and there seems little chance that their numbers will decrease.

For reasons of their own, many illegals will shun the census taker anyway and won't be included in population totals. The advantages of identifying the rest of them would not justify the immense effort required. The illegals are here, they might as well be recognized.

THE SACRAMENTO BEE
Sacramento, Calif., February 19, 1980

Ever since 1790, the decennial census has tried to count every warm body in the United States. The Constitution provides for such a count of "persons" and bases congressional representation upon it. In addition, all sorts of federal funds are allocated according to population, a fact which makes the census much more than a statistical exercise of passing interest.

Now a group called FAIR, Federation for American Immigration Reform, is suing the federal government to force the Census Bureau to keep a separate count of illegal aliens — a measure which FAIR claims is necessary to keep regions with large numbers of illegal aliens, among them Southern California, from gaining a "windfall" in federal money and representation at the expense of places which do not have such concentrations.

Given the large number of illegal aliens in this country — a number estimated at anywhere between 5 million and 12 million people — it's argued by FAIR and a number of members of Congress who may be adversely affected that including illegals in the count would severely skew representation and deny voters in certain regions the representation to which they are entitled.

The government and various groups representing Hispanics in this country, among them the largest single number of illegal aliens, counter that such people require just as many public services, pay taxes and, in any case, are covered by the constitutional provisions which speak only about "persons" without making any distinctions among them.

Both sets of arguments have merit. The fact is that neither the framers of the Constitution nor, indeed, any generation of Americans before this century regarded immigration as a major problem. Until the end of the 19th century, most immigrants were generally welcome to this country without restriction, and there was thus no concept of "illegal" aliens. And it's only as their numbers have grown in the past generation that illegal aliens have become a serious issue.

Nonetheless, the growing questions associated with immigration policy should have no bearing on a count of "persons" in the United States. As a practical matter, it would be almost impossible to find and count people identified as "illegal." It will be hard enough to have illegal aliens stand still for the count even if they are assured that they won't immediately be seized by federal authorities and deported. Although the Census Bureau is making great efforts to encourage all persons to cooperate with the census, that fear may, in any case, lead to a serious underrepresentation not only of illegals but of many others who believe they have something to fear from agents of the government. That in itself may effectively minimize the impact of illegals on the census.

Yet even if that were not the case, the attempt accurately to count people separately as "illegals" would be administratively hopeless and, for most purposes, legally pointless. The result would create more problems than it solves: Should "illegals" then be counted for certain programs but not others? Should they be represented? A similar controversy once arose over representation of slaves, a controversy resolved in the Constitution by counting each slave as three-fifths of a whole person.

The unresolved questions of immigration policy obviously have to be confronted, but this is not the way to begin. The Constitution says count persons; let's count them.

The San Diego Union
San Diego, Calif., January 6, 1980

In accordance with the Constitution, common sense, and traditional practice, the U.S. Bureau of the Census plans to include everyone, citizen and undocumented resident alike, in next year's decennial count.

This prospect has upset five Republican congressmen, who in turn have filed suit challenging the bureau's right to include non-citizens in the census totals. Their argument strikes us, and the Census Bureau, as untenable.

The congressmen contend that counting non-citizens, including several million illegal aliens from Mexico, will "distort" congressional reapportionment and the distribution of federal funds through programs calculated in part on local population.

Yet, no one pretends that undocumented residents will disappear if only the Census Bureau ignores them. Like it or not, they are here and there is no realistic prospect of either a voluntary or compulsory mass departure.

The Constitution makes no distinction between citizens and others in its mandate of a census count every 10 years. Nor does the 14th Amendment exclude non-citizens from the population figures that serve as the basis of congressional apportionment.

As for the distribution of federal funds, they are supposed to be appropriated on the basis of need and population is a key index of that need. The systematic exclusion of non-citizens from any activity subsidized by federal funds is a practical impossibility even if it were legally and morally acceptable.

The issues at stake here are far broader than any political advantage accruing to states, including California, with large numbers of non-citizens. But it is politics, not principle, that seems to have motivated this unworthy challenge to a complete and equitable census.

Newsday
Long Island, N. Y., January 13, 1980

The 1980 census may have patronage problems on Long Island, but that's not the half of it. The count could actually be delayed a year because some people think it's wrong to include illegal aliens. Yet the growing costs these immigrants are forcing on the nation must not be ignored.

The Federation for American Immigration Reform is suing to prevent the Census Bureau from including illegal aliens in this year's count. States with many aliens, FAIR says, would get more members of Congress than they should because seats in the House depend on population, including legal and illegal aliens.

According to FAIR, New York State will lose four House seats after the census if aliens are not counted, but only one seat if they're included. It's estimated that between 750,000 and 1 million illegal aliens live in New York City, with as many as 200,000 in Queens alone.

Federal, state and city officials want all aliens included in the count. After all, they use schools, hospitals and other costly services. And because these are partly funded by federal aid grants figured according to population, an undercount would cost states and cities money.

The 1980 census must go ahead. It's required by the Constitution. It's a vital source of economic and social data. And as many aliens as possible should be counted—although the task won't be easy, because illegal aliens don't want to talk to government people of any kind.

But there is also a serious conflict with rational, long-term immigration policy here. According to some U.S. Department of Labor estimates, there may now be as many as 8 million illegal aliens in the country. Many of them are here because they are employed at depressed wages, by western or southwestern farmers or in squalid eastern factories. But federal and local governments shouldn't subsidize cheap labor by guaranteeing public services to illegal aliens as a matter of routine. Even if they could afford it—which they can't—it would be bad social policy.

Mass expulsion of millions of aliens is obviously out of the question. Immigration law is clear; so are the difficulties of enforcing it. Employers of cheap labor will not like a policy of stricter enforcement. Members of Congress whose districts include large illegal alien populations may not care for it either. But ultimately there is no other sound choice.

Sentinel Star
Orlando, Fla., January 7, 1980

FOLLOWING the 1790 census Thomas Jefferson expressed concern about aliens being included when apportioning seats in the House of Representatives, suggesting a separate count be taken for that purpose in later censuses. But, until now, the number of aliens, particularly those here illegally, had not been enough to cause debate on Jefferson's concern.

Now comes the Federation for American Immigration (FAIR) into federal district court to ask that the suggestion be revived and implemented, at least as concerns those here illegally. If it isn't, FAIR contends, as many as 10 congressional seats could be shifted to three large states, dozens of cities would lose or gain congressional and state representation, and billions of dollars in federal money would be awarded solely on the basis of the presence of illegal aliens.

While the suit smacks of partisan politics — the illegals tend to concentrate in areas that would tilt to Democrat — FAIR's charge does have a ring of fairness to it: After all, why should representation and the distribution of federal money be determined by millions of people living here illegally?

But the solution proposed by FAIR — that the Census Bureau identify those here illegally and exclude them in apportioning House seats — is impractical.

It is estimated that the number of illegals in the United States is somewhere between 4 million and 14 million, the most frequently agreed upon estimate being 8 million. If all these people were counted in this year's census, FAIR contends, California would get eight new congressional seats rather than the two predicted on the basis of the legal population; Texas would gain three rather than two, and New York would lose only one instead of the predicted four. Losers would be small states that have few or no illegal aliens.

It's not likely, of course, that all illegal aliens will be counted, although the Census Bureau says it will be making its best effort to count every one of them, and probably will do better than one might expect. Even so, census counters make no effort to determine if a person is alien, legal or otherwise.

It's not the bureau's business to determine that, a spokesman says, noting that the Constitution requires that "all persons" shall be counted (and, yes, that includes foreign students from Iran) and that House seats shall be apportioned on the basis of "persons counted."

This is not to ignore the unfairness to the political system the presence of so many illegal aliens could have, or the other problems they create, particularly in the job market. But it is impractical to expect the Census Bureau to enforce immigration laws while counting people.

The inequity cited by FAIR does, however, serve to focus attention on a serious problem that cries for solution: Either we should drop all bars to entry or find some effective way to control it.

ST. LOUIS POST-DISPATCH
St. Louis, Mo., January 5, 1980

With the support of mayors of large cities with minority populations, the U.S. Census Bureau plans to count illegal aliens in the 1980 census. Certainly they should be counted. The trouble with the bureau plan is that illegal entrants will be counted with the rest of the population, with no distinction.

That means, first, that states with large numbers of illegal residents would get an unfair advantage over others in the congressional redistricting that will be based on the census. California, says an immigration law reform group, might gain as many as six congressmen while Pennsylvania lost two. Secondly, the census distortion also would distort distribution of federal funds from more than 100 programs that depend in part on population figures. Again, states with the most illegal residents would gain unfairly.

Since there are somewhere between 4 million and 12 million aliens living illegally in this country, a case can be made for giving them some forms of welfare support; they cannot be allowed to starve. But in that case Congress ought to provide for them specifically. Aliens should not be encouraged to remain illegally by a deliberate Census Bureau effort to include them with citizens. That stamps illegality as legitimate.

St. Louis, Mo., February 9, 1980

Some time before April 1, the date of the next decennial census, the courts are expected to decide whether illegal aliens should be included in the count of the population. Millions of dollars in federal assistance and a probable increase in the number of seats in Congress for several states are among the things that will be determined by the ruling. The issue has produced several pairings of antagonists: state against state, urban areas against the countryside, blacks against Hispanic-Americans.

As it has since the first census in 1790, the government proposes to count all persons, with the exception of diplomats and tourists. To prevent it from doing so, an organization called Federation for American Immigration Reform (FAIR) and 26 members of Congress have filed suit to force the Census Bureau to keep a separate count of illegal immigrants. (Whether such a count would be possible poses still another question. FAIR proposes that persons declare in their census questionnaires whether they are citizens. Subtracting the number of legal, registered aliens from the total would give the number of illegals, says FAIR. But immigration service figures are so inadequate, the government rejoins, that if this technique had been used in 1970 the number of illegals would have been minus 623,000.)

Both sides have legitimate arguments at their disposal. FAIR contends that if illegals are counted, their totals will affect apportionment for Congress, giving states such as New York and California more representatives. That, in turn, says FAIR, would undermine the principle of one-man, one-vote, since the power of registered voters in those states would be enhanced at the expense of voters in states with small numbers of illegals. Rural politicians in Illinois fear that if Chicago receives more representatives, because of its large number of illegal aliens, their own congressional districts will be adversely affected. Black organizations contend that gains by Hispanic-Americans will come at the expense of their own progress in congressional representation.

The opposing arguments, we think, are even more impressive. First, there is the language of the law, mandating a "tabulation of total population" — a snapshot, if you will, of the entire country. Second, states with large numbers of illegals have increased responsibilities for providing vital public services, such as schools, fire protection, police, health care and emergency services. In that census statistics are the bedrock of more than 100 federal welfare and assistance programs, not counting illegals would add to the crushing state and local burdens of paying for these services.

Interestingly, the government points out that the Constitution allows states to permit even illegal aliens to vote, politically unlikely as that might be. But there are stronger constitutional arguments than that for counting illegals. Chief among them, we think, is the fact that the Constitution distinguishes between "citizens" and "persons," and it uses the latter as the basis for apportionment. Moreover, although illegal aliens may be subjected to certain specific penalties, the courts have not held that they are hence excluded from all government programs, including that of census taking.

At the time the relevant parts of the Constitution were written, of course, illegal immigration was not the problem that it is now, when as many as 12 million illegals may be in the country. Even so, the way to treat that development is by enacting laws that exclude illegals from being counted for purposes of apportionment; for surely a state's representation in Congress ought to be based on numbers of lawful residents, whether citizen or alien. Census figures, however, should be as accurate as possible and depict this country as it really is.

Lincoln Journal

Lincoln, Neb., January 15, 1980

An organization which calls itself the Federation for American Immigration Reform (FAIR) is trying to block the scheduled April 1 start of the 1980 census.

This is not an insignificant case. How, in what proportions and to whom the national government annually distributes $50 billion — repeating, $50 billion — to states and local governments may hang in the balance.

FAIR wants a three-judge panel to enjoin the decennial head-count unless the census concurrently identifies and locates the number of illegal aliens in the total. Congress could direct such a thing, of course, but the census couldn't then get untracked until 1981, officials contend.

FAIR's interest is not uncovering smuggled-in folk so their exportation could be speeded. Hardly.

There are an estimated 8 million illegal aliens in this country. Mainly they're located in big cities or Western or Southwestern states. It should be obvious their inclusion in census results will have a pronounced effect throughout the 1980s — between states and even within states — under formulae used to pass around goodies from the federal treasury.

Population is a major component of such formulae. States and cities with more people get more money.

Overall, Nebraska stands to be a financial loser if the illegal aliens are included, having put their faith in Census Bureau Director Vincent Barabba's assurance that no names will be supplied other agenices. Such as the immigration authorities.

As much as a self-interested Nebraskan yearns to endorse FAIR's creative litigation and its fiscal end result during the 1980s, it strikes us as probably futile.

The Constitution directs a census of "persons," not simply American nationals. Since 1790 onward, census figures have embraced aliens, without distinction. The 14th (equal protection) Amendment employs the word "person." The U.S. Supreme Court in 1971 interpreted the term "person" as encompassing aliens in the receipt of certain government benefits, such as welfare.

Ergo, FAIR seemingly has a puny case. If that's so, the sooner it is disposed of, the better.

The Houston Post

Houston, Texas, January 9, 1980

Illegal immigrants are pictured as people who come into the United States surreptitiously, swimming rivers, using back roads and trails, hiding in the trunks of cars. But every year the United States may be taking on from 500,000 to 700,000 new residents who traveled in style by transoceanic airline. However unknown and uncountable the arrivals by land may be, the arrivals by airline are just about equally unknown and, so far, unaccounted for.

In its population estimates, the Census Bureau has counted on a standard 400,000 legal migrants per year. Most demographers, counting both legal and illegal immigrants, accept a rule-of-thumb estimate of from 500,000 to 600,000. Considering this with our slightly waning birth rate, demographers have seen no reason to sound an alarm on overpopulation in the country. But Daniel R. Vining Jr., a University of Pennsylvania researcher, questions the estimates and the comfortable conclusion. He cites U.S. International Air Travel Statistics which show that the arrivals by air outnumber the departures by more than 1 million people a year. Vining then tempers that startling data with other statistics collected by individual airports and the International Air Transport Association.

The basic trouble is that we are more interested in counting arrivals at our border crossings, ports and airports than we are in counting the departures. We forget that not everyone who comes in will necessarily go out again. The United States expects 500 million border crossings a year — many of them vacationers shuttling across the Canadian and Mexican borders. Of these fewer than 1 percent come from overseas. Over 95 percent come by land. But it is impossible to know how many come, how many stay. Even if all movement were channeled through official border stations, we would not know because the United States takes no count of people leaving through these points.

Plane travelers are better documented. But Vining says, "The excess of arrivals over departures is not only consistently positive, as one would expect, but also astoundingly large." Vining estimates that migration into this country by air alone runs between 500,000 and 700,000 a year. Put these against Census Bureau estimates that our legal migrants total an average of 400,000 a year.

Long used to having room enough, land enough, resources enough to be hospitable, the United States has been casual about counting the ins and outs of migration. If we have managed to overlook half a million or more people a year, simply because they came by air, it is time that we find the facts and determine what should be done about them.

Los ANGELES HERALD EXAMINER

Los Angeles, Calif., January 2, 1980

Every ten years Americans get to find out all sorts of things about themselves — things like how many of us there are and what parts of the country we're congregating in. In 1980, however, if the Census Bureau has its way, the one thing we won't find out is how many illegal aliens there are in the U.S. The Census Bureau is planning to count everyone living in the U.S. and lump everyone together, whether they're here legally or illegally.

The Census Bureau claims that its instructions have always been to count everyone who's here and not ask to see immigration papers. Neither Congress nor the courts have ever directly stated whether or not the Census Bureau should be counting illegal aliens separately — or at all.

The courts may make that statement now that the Federation for American Immigration Reform has filed a suit to stop the Census Bureau from counting illegal aliens. The federation contends it's improper to include illegal aliens in the census figures because these figures will be used to apportion seats in Congress. Illegal aliens have no right to vote, so they shouldn't be included in determining congressional seats. Because illegal aliens are concentrated in places like Southern California, including them in the census could shift more than a dozen seats away from states with low illegal alien populations. Good for California, maybe, but is this in the best interests of the country?

The Census Bureau says it's impractical to distinguish between people on the basis of immigration status. According to one census official, why bother to ask about immigration status "since there is no feasible way of making sure you are getting an honest answer?" Furthermore, the Census Bureau claims its plans for the 1980 census are too far along to be changed now.

There are two things about the Census Bureau's plans that strike us as strange. First, what is the Census Bureau doing deciding that illegal aliens should be counted along with the rest of us for purposes of deciding congressional districts and how federal aid should be apportioned? Decisions about U.S. policy on illegal aliens should be made by Congress and the president, not by Census Bureau bureaucrats.

Actually, we shouldn't be blaming the Census Bureau for this one. Congress and several presidents have refused to make any decisions about illegal aliens and, in effect, forced the Census Bureau to decide for itself whether or not to count them.

The second thing we find strange about all this is that the Census Bureau is going to lump illegal aliens in with citizens and legal aliens. But what the country really needs is a count of illegal aliens separate from the rest of us. One of the barriers to decisions about illegal aliens is that no one has any idea how many of them there are.

We think the Census Bureau should count everyone, but divide the totals into people who are here legally and those who are in the U.S. illegally. We think the census people could count illegal aliens by asking to see proof of immigration status. But if the Census Bureau decides to do this, we want to see the Immigration and Naturalization Service announce ahead of time that no information given to census counters will be used to deport illegal aliens. Without this assurance, the integrity of the counting effort will surely be compromised.

The Chattanooga Times
Chattanooga, Tenn., January 14, 1980

The U.S. Census Bureau is right to count aliens living in this country when it conducts the decennial census this year. But its plan, backed by the mayors of several large cities not to distinguish any possible "illegals" from the rest of the population could result in a flawed count.

One obvious reason, of course, lies in the congressional redistricting that is based upon totals compiled during the census. States such as Texas or California, with a disproportionate share of illegal residents, would automatically receive an unfair advantage over other states in the apportionment of congressional seats. Similarly, states whose population totals are increased artificially through the inclusion of illegals would also benefit disproportionately from the distribution of federal funds from some 100 programs in which the outlays are tied to population figures.

No one knows for sure how many illegal aliens are living in this country; estimates range from 4 million to more than 10 million. Their presence here creates a need for increased welfare outlays, if only to keep them alive. Congress can do that through specific legislation if it chooses.

A Census Bureau decision to count any possible "illegals" along with the rest of the population, however, would undermine the federal government's efforts to expel those who enter this country illegally. It would, in effect, make their illegal status legitimate while distorting other federal actions, such as congressional representation and dispersal of funds. That's wrong.

FORT WORTH STAR-TELEGRAM
Fort Worth, Texas, February 7, 1980

Every now and then some good news comes down the pike.

Well, maybe it isn't exactly good news, not actually, but it is a hint or speculation about good news.

Some Census Bureau demographers have put their statistical heads together and speculated the United States just may have fewer illegal Mexican aliens than previously thought.

These experts say the total number of illegal aliens is almost certainly below 6 million and may be as low as 3.5 million. Some have placed the total many millions higher.

This analysis would mean that Texas might have only about 500,000 illegal Mexican aliens instead of the previously estimated 750,000.

The study also indicates much in-and-out movement on the part of illegal Mexican aliens. They tend to enter the United States, then return to Mexico. In contrast, illegal aliens from such places as Europe, South America and the Philippines are more likely to establish permanent residence in the United States.

The illegal aliens have raised all sorts of issues in this nation, such as whether to accept them in our schools and whether to count them in the upcoming census, an important consideration since population is used in determining distribution of federal money and in deciding political districting.

The report did not tell us why there might be fewer illegal aliens.

It did not even tell us for sure that there are.

It simply speculates there might be.

Which means we have less to worry about.

Maybe.

But in these days of trouble at every turn, it is nice to have somebody — anybody — tell us we have a little less to worry about regarding one of our big worries.

Such good news is alien to the steady diet of bad news that keeps zapping us.

And we are grateful for small favors.

DAYTON DAILY NEWS
Dayton, Ohio, January 28, 1980

According to the Constitution, the major purpose of a national census is to reapportion seats in Congress on the basis of a state's population. In that count, the Census Bureau has excluded foreign tourists and diplomats who happen to be around at the time.

But what about resident aliens? What about illegal resident aliens? And who'll admit he's an illegal alien?

Hispanic-American groups have persuaded the Census Bureau to attempt a count of all aliens in the 1980 census which begins April 1. Since such a count would affect the number of seats a state holds in the House of Representatives, several congressmen and a group called the Federation of American Immigration Reform have filed suit in federal district court to stop the counting of illigeal aliens. If they win, the census will have to be postponed until new forms are designed.

This calls for a Solomon's judgment. On the one hand, all aliens should be counted because population numbers help determine the distribution of federal funds, and states must care for residents even if they're aliens. But what alien would admit he's an illegal one?

On the other hand, non-citizens should not determine the voice of a state in the House of Representatives. Since the number of representatives can't rise above a certain level, growth in some states means a decrease in representatives in other states. California and New York probably would be big winners. Ohio would be among the losers. No state would acquiesce at losing representation because of aliens in another.

Is it possible Congress could, on the one hand, allow all aliens to be counted for every purpose expect political representation and on the other hand credibly guarantee confidentiality to ones who will admit they are here illegally?

Los Angeles Times
Los Angeles, Calif., March 3, 1980

A special panel of three federal court judges has upheld the decision of the Census Bureau to include illegal aliens in the decennial head count starting April 1.

Common sense and the Constitution left the court no choice. It would be impossible for the bureau to distinguish between citizens and non-citizens, as the plaintiffs demand. The count is taken mostly by mail, and the form contains no questions relating to citizenship. Even if it did, illegal residents would be unlikely to reveal their status.

Beyond that, the 14th Amendment specifies that the count, for purposes of congressional apportionment, shall include "the whole number of persons in each state . . ."

The court, sitting in Washington, said that "both the equities of the situation and the merits of the case" favor the inclusion of non-citizens in the general count. "The language of the Constitution is not ambiguous."

The plaintiffs in the case—26 members of Congress and the Federation for American Immigration Reform—argued that the inclusion of aliens would distort the next reapportionment of Congress, and would permit states with large populations of aliens to secure more than their share of federal funds for general revenue sharing, education, public health and law enforcement.

We question that non-citizens will respond to the count in large numbers. Despite the absolute confidentiality of the census, their fear of detection and deportation is too great.

But, even if the bureau were able to count every last illegal migrant, the arguments of the plaintiffs fail the test of equity. The federal grants to local governments are not gifts, but a sharing of tax revenues, on a population basis, with the localities where the taxes are paid.

Illegal migrants pay taxes just as all other residents do, and the tax collector does not ask them if they are citizens or not. They have a right to public services because they pay for them. To exclude them from the census count, and thus exclude their communities from a fair share of federal funds and from proportional representation in government, would punish citizens and non-citizens alike in states, including California, that have the largest number of illegal migrants.

Despite the plaintiffs' defeat before the special tribunal, they intend to appeal to higher courts, and to introduce legislation in Congress to achieve their ends.

It could prove expensive. The Justice Department told the court that a ruling against the Census Bureau could delay the count for many months, and add at least $150 million to its cost.

Fallout of Illegal Immigration: Smugglers and Desert Deaths

The deaths of 13 would-be immigrants from El Salvador in July 1980 brought to light one of the least savory aspects of illegal immigration: professional smuggling. The dead Salvadorans and 10 survivors were found in Arizona's Organ Pipe Desert by agents of the U.S. Border Patrol. With the help of four "coyotes," or professional smugglers, the Salvadorans had made their way into the U.S. via San Luis Rio Colorado, a Mexican town south of Arizona. The surviving Salvadorans and two of the smugglers were picked up July 5 by Border Patrol agents after having spent more than a week in the desert with less than a gallon of water each. The two other smugglers were arrested in Yuma, Arizona several days later and sentenced in October to five years' imprisonment. (The smugglers who were found with the Salvadorans were paroled because witnesses testified that they had tried to help the stranded band.)

When the case was first reported, Border Patrol Chief E. J. Scott said it was not unusual to find bodies of would-be immigrants in the desert. "Coyotes" were known to operate a flourishing business of guiding illegal aliens secretly across the border. Often, however, they robbed or assaulted their customers instead of bringing them to the U.S.

Roanoke Times & World-News

Roanoke, Va., July 11, 1980

Nothing more illustrates the desperation with which thousands of Latin Americans have sought entry into the United States than the recent deaths in the Arizona desert of 13 people, mostly El Salvadorans, after they were smuggled across the border from Mexico.

U.S. citizens might take a measure of pride in the knowledge that their 204-year-old republic, even after a history of rather shabby treatment toward its neighbors to the south, remains a symbol of hope throughout the hemisphere. But there is also a legitimate fear that the hope is encouraging a wave of illegal immigration threatening those very institutions and traditions in the United States that validate the symbolism.

At the moment, it is not unauthorized entrants from El Salvador but thousands of undocumented aliens from Cuba and Haiti who pose the most direct threat to one important tradition, the rule of law. Too often, the issue is sidetracked into an argument over whether the 15,000 new undocumented aliens from Haiti are victims of U.S. racism, treated less favorably than the 115,000 new undocumented Cuban immigrants because Haitian skins are darker.

The real question should be whether either Cubans or Haitians — and if so, which ones — qualify as political refugees who, under U.S. law, can be allowed to stay despite the unauthorized nature of their entry. As 6th District Rep. Caldwell Butler of Roanoke observes in his July 3 weekly report, the Refugee Act of 1980 defines who qualifies for such status as those "unable or unwilling to return to (their) homeland due to persecution or a well-founded fear of persecution on account of race, religion, nationality, membership in a particular social group, or political opinion." Adds the congressman, referring to both Cubans and Haitians: "Clearly, many of the new entrants do not fit the definition of refugee under the law and would not otherwise be admissible."

At one point, officials in the Carter administration displayed an understanding of the implications of winking at the immigration law. John A. Bushnell, deputy assistant secretary of state for inter-American affairs, was telling a House subcommittee as recently as June 17:

The population of the Caribbean, including Cuba, approaches 25 million. Despite the so-called "middle income" status of most of these countries, meaning per capita incomes little more than one-tenth of U.S. levels, the great majority of these people are poor, a significant portion of them desperately so. Most of them are potential emigrants to the United States, especially if there is a reasonable expectation of remaining and making a livelihood in this country.

Now, however, the administration seems set on a policy of accepting responsibility for resettling the undocumented aliens already here from Cuba and Haiti. The policy, in other words, is to ignore the law rather than to enforce it. The likeliest effect is an even larger flow of illegal immigration, as the message gets out to residents of poverty-stricken Latin American nations that emigration to the United States is, in effect, unrestricted.

DESERET NEWS

Salt Lake City, Utah, July 8, 1980

It mustn't be written off and forgotten as just another sad chapter in the history of man's inhumanity to man.

Rather, it should be carefully examined with an eye to seeing what can be done to prevent future such outrages.

We're referring to this week's episode in which smugglers brought illegal aliens from El Salvador across the U.S.-Mexico border, then robbed and left them to die in the desert of Arizona. At least 13 died, and other bodies still may be found.

This grisly event provides ammunition to the U.S. Immigration and Naturalization Service, which chronically complains of being under-funded and under-staffed. Though patrols can't keep a constant watch on every inch of the U.S. border with Mexico, maybe more patrols might have helped avert this tragedy. Maybe.

This episode likewise gives ammunition to those who insist that Congress made a mistake when it tightened U.S. immigration laws three years ago, stiffening entrance requirements for Latin Americans and thus increasing pressure to try to enter the U.S. illegally.

Or this week's tragedy in the Arizona desert could be cited by those who insist that the way to prevent a recurrence is to crack down on potential employers of illegal immigrants in the U.S. Penalties for hiring illegal aliens should be made so stiff, this argument goes, that employers could no longer absorb such fines as just another cost of doing business.

But whatever else is done, Mexican authorities cannot just rely on the U.S. to tighten its borders but ought to make every effort to track down the smuggling ring that committed this week's mass murder in the Arizona desert.

The ultimate cause of illegal immigration is the vast economic disparity between the industrialized nations of the world and their poorer neighbors. As long as these disparities exist, the rich countries will hold an irresistible attraction for the disadvantaged people of poor countries.

WORCESTER TELEGRAM

Worcester, Mass., July 9, 1980

Let's pray the United States and Mexican governments catch up with the body smugglers who brought some 40 to 50 people from El Salvador across our border and then robbed and abandoned them in an Arizona desert. Thirteen perished in the broiling desert. It's likely the death toll will go higher, since not all the group has been found.

The smugglers could have told their victims in which direction to walk to get to a main road. Instead, they left the people to die in 110-degree desert heat, without food or water.

Body smuggling is only too familiar to both U.S. and Mexican border authorities. It goes on all the time.

People seeking to escape repression, poverty and misery hand over life savings to be transported surreptitiously into the United States. The length of our border with Mexico makes it impossible to stop all such illegal entry.

But perhaps if the government agents make an all-out effort to track down those who perpetrated this vicious crime, an example could be made of them. That might ward off atrocities in the future. An American border officer interviewed about this incident said it wouldn't do much good to find the people responsible, since it's likely not much would be done to them anyway. That defeatist attitude is not a sufficient response.

Those body smugglers are brutal murderers. They must be caught and punished.

THE MILWAUKEE JOURNAL
Milwaukee, Wisc., July 8, 1980

There is no way to prevent the kind of grisly tragedy that befell the Salvadorans who were abandoned to die in the Arizona desert after being smuggled across the US-Mexican border. As long as the economic lure of America remains, there will be those trying to enter the US illegally, and those willing to exploit them in the process.

But there are ways of minimizing the repetition of tragedy. And that is what the president and Congress should be concentrating on. The nation needs a more coherent immigration policy, one that protects the national interest while dealing humanely with the people hungering to enter the country

Yes, America has an immigration policy. There are rules, regulations, visa requirements, country quotas. But what looks good on paper breaks down in practice. Immigration policy has been overwhelmed by the sheer number of people — millions annually — willing to risk entering the US illegally, mainly by crossing the US-Mexican border.

The key to gaining better control of immigration is effective enforcement. We don't advocate barbed wire and mines along the Mexican border. America isn't that kind of society. Furthermore, the people trying to cross illegally are not criminals, but mostly hard working, honest folks trying to better their lives. In that regard, they are reminiscent of our immigrant ancestors.

However, we do advocate altered regulations that would make effective enforcement easier. For one, there should be heavy civil fines, if not criminal charges, for employers who knowingly hire illegal immigrants. There is too much regulatory wrist-slapping today.

The minimal risks, in turn, encourage callous employers to hire and exploit illegal aliens, usually paying them considerably less than would be paid US citizens protected by law. The mere fact that the jobs are there, no matter how dismal the working conditions, spurs the illegals to come.

A second step that would make enforcement easier would be a broad "guest worker" program that would allow aliens to enter temporarily and legally to work in the US. That way the US would have better control of the people entering, and the foreign workers would have legal protections regarding entry, pay and working conditions.

Neither of these steps would completely stop illegal immigration. But they could help curb the numbers. They could save lives by reducing the chances that immigrants would risk the barbarous treatment that the Salvadorans encountered on the parched Arizona desert.

The Dispatch
Columbus, Ohio, July 10, 1980

THOSE TRAGIC deaths in an Arizona desert of Salvadorans being smuggled into the United States may have been the result of a grave blunder by smugglers who did not prepare for the desert ordeal.

Actually, it would be just one more blunder in this nation's sorry saga of dealing with illegal immigration flowing northward across the Mexican border.

Federal and state law officers are holding two suspected smugglers and criminal charges could be filed. Punishment is indeed appropriate.

But certain other facts are glaringly apparent. Congressional appropriations are so skimpy that only five border patrolmen are available to police the 70-mile line over which the hapless Salvadorans were smuggled.

And the U.S. Senate has paid little heed to a possible key to curbing the flow of illegal immigration. It is a House-passed bill sponsored by U.S. Rep. Chalmers Wylie of Columbus to ban American employers from hiring illegal immigrants. It is the attraction of easy jobs that ignites the northward flow of immigrants.

However inept the smugglers in the Arizona tragedy may have been, the fact remains that the federal government's continuing neglect of a long-standing problem has placed America in the inexcusable position of being an accomplice to the Arizona tragedy.

To the credit of the U.S. Immigration Service, its meager patrols are intercepting an estimated 700,000 illegal immigrants along the Mexican border a year.

And the Mexican government is seriously concerned about the flow, stationing its own patrols on the border. But Mexico's woefully weak economy and its high rate of unemployment continue to force Mexican eyes to look yearningly northward.

Until Latin countries are able to fashion more productive job-creation programs of their own, the illegal immigration problem will go unsolved. And unless this country's federal government takes the situation more seriously, there will be new opportunity for blunders and tragedies.

Rockford Register Star
Rockford, Ill., July 10, 1980

Somewhere in the murderous heat of the desert north of the Mexican border, a group of refugees from El Salvador have perished.

Their striving was for sanctuary in the United States. But they trusted guides who brought them illegally into this country and left them to die, once they had paid off the smugglers.

Traditionally, the smugglers' fees go as high as $750 a person. To this ill-fated group, such an amount would have been a fortune. But they paid it, whatever the sum was.

After all, most were young people. Their lives lay mostly ahead of them. And the enticement of the U.S. was as an old one: the land of hope. It was a dream exceeding all of El Salvador's dismal realities.

We recall this story, not because of the chicanery of those who cheated these refugees of their money and ultimately their lives.

Nor is the story singular because our border was breached by strangers. The Cuban exiles, more than 100,000 of them, similarly crossed into this nation, albeit with clearer signals of welcome and safety.

What we tend to forget, and must relearn through this kind of grievous adversity, is our own country's continuing appeal for the besieged and dispossessed.

We take our very liberty for granted. Not these exiles from El Salvador. Not those hordes from Castro's Marxist regime.

They do not — and did not — come here because of some textbook briefing on the life and times of the U.S.A. What they hungered for was opportunity and dignity and reprieve from the grinding oppression that enslaved them. What they gambled was their limited treasure, munificently matched by their lives.

The cause was that basic. The need, this compelling.

Our allies in Europe, of recent months, have begun to question the resolve and determination of this country in meeting its worldwide commitments. Naturally, our allies couple such speculation with their own irresolution, their own self-doubts, their own incapacity to act concertedly in the face of Russian aggression, Iranian revolution, and the continuing tyranny of an oil-rich Middle East.

But we would say to these latter-day friends, one thing: remember those nameless dead on that stretch of desert north of the Mexican border.

Recall that those refugees shed their very lives in pursuit of American freedoms, in pursuit of American respect for the individual.

Even in turbulent times such as these, with a president in the White House whose policies are often misconstrued abroad, the credibility of this land, its strength and purpose still reside amidst the greatness of its people.

That's what our European allies need to recall.

A disarming statement of such strength was stamped on the sweltering desert the day those refugees from El Salvador perished there.

THE ARIZONA REPUBLIC

Phoenix, Ariz., July 24, 1980

ARIZONA has not yet recovered from the shock of the horrible deaths of 13 Salvadorans in the Organ Pipe Cactus National Monument who were left to die by ghouls who had promised to get them into the United States.

The Salvadorans apparently were brought across Mexico by an alien smuggling ring known as *Las Munecas,* Spanish for The Dolls.

Each Salvadoran paid somewhere in the neighborhood of $1,200, but the pay-off wasn't limited to the Munecas.

Two former members of the ring, according to *Republic* reporter Randy Collier, said they paid regular amounts to Mexican immigration officials when they were in the smuggling business.

They testified against three Mexican officials, but the officials were turned loose because an appeals judge held there was insufficient evidence to justify a trial.

One of the officials has been reinstated in the Mexican immigration office in San Luis.

The job of enforcing U.S. immigration laws does not lie with the Mexicans. It must be done by Americans.

But a way should be found to persuade Mexico to stop Mexican officials from aiding and abetting smugglers of aliens, particularly those headed for jobs in the United States.

The most reasonable approach to the problem of undocumented immigrants would be an agreement between Mexico and the United States whereby unemployed Mexicans could be brought into the United States

to work for specified periods of time and then allowed to return home with their earnings.

This suggestion is usually met with cries of "slavery," but contract labor is used around the world. Italian workers enter Germany, Spaniards enter France, Filipinos go to Iraq, and North Koreans go to Guam.

Such contracts protect immigrants from being gouged by employers and provide them with health and educational services through regular channels.

Thirteen dead Salvadorans might be alive today if Mexico and the United States had agreed on a program for contract labor, and then had policed the border between the two countries.

St. Petersburg Times

St. Petersburg, Fla., July 9, 1980

The 13 people who perished last weekend in the Arizona desert were the victims of a notorious class of criminals. The "coyotes" who smuggle people across the Mexican border often rob and rape them, sometimes abandon them to be caught, and at times lead them, as in this case, into the desert to die.

Evil as they are, however, the smugglers are not the only ones to blame. They exploit a black market in human beings, but they did not create it.

SOME VERY substantial citizens did that.

Undocumented aliens wash dishes, make beds and change diapers in tens of thousands of America's most respectable homes. They cook the food, scrub the floors and clear the tables in the finest restaurants from Washington, D.C. to Washington state. They toil in sweatshops in every major city. They pick fruit in Florida, cotton in Texas and lettuce in California. If there's a dirty job to do, they do it; they do it for the minimum wage or less, and they do not complain of anything. "They work both scared and hard," says Secretary of Labor Ray Marshall. They also pay taxes whose benefits they never see.

They come by the millions, most of them because they are poor, hungry and jobless and because they know that jobs await them here despite U.S. law. The victims found this week were middle-class immigrants, but most of the coyotes' prey have nothing but the price of illegal passage. To such people, even slave wages are worth certain risks.

IT IS NOT just the employers who are responsible. The U.S. government lets it go on, refusing to reform immigration laws that are plainly unrealistic and pretending that an unfortified 2,000-mile border patrolled by a mere 2,000 officers can stop such an invasion.

Members of Congress have their own vested interests in this black market. Some have been suspected of employing illegal immigrants, and many of them take hefty campaign contributions from agricultural concerns that employ undocumented aliens.

What should be done is obvious, which is not to say that it will be simple. The law should be rewritten to rec-

ognize and legalize the contribution of foreign workers while limiting their number in an enforceable way. With its own population aging and its birth rate shrinking, the United States cannot afford to shut out these willing workers. Neither can it afford, morally, to continue exploiting them.

COMPREHENSIVE reform will entail amnesty for the millions who are already here, coupled with realistic annual employment quotas to protect the jobs and wages of U.S. citizens.

And what of the employers who persist in hiring aliens who have no work papers? That is now no federal crime. No reform will succeed without stiff federal fines and jail terms, but sanctions present practical difficulties.

Employers can't be held accountable without giving them some reliable and convenient way to confirm a job-seeker's eligibility. Lawful immigrants will have work papers, which have become relatively forgery-proof. But native-born citizens have no such documents. Those who give the appearance of foreign birth would be denied work on mere suspicion.

THE MOST plausible suggestion calls for issuing everyone a tamper-proof, serialized Social Security card — a large but not impossible job. States have already issued about 100-million drivers' licenses with pictures. The work force is not much larger. And a Social Security account already is the one thing that nearly all workers must have.

The danger, though, is of creating a national identity card that would erode civil liberties in a very real sense. No immigration reform could justify requiring Americans to carry the equivalent of a passport in their own land.

Yet it might be safe to rely upon a new Social Security card if there were very strong laws prohibiting its use for any purpose other than establishing employability. A presidential commission on immigration is leaning in this direction.

When the commission makes its report early next year the Congress will have absolutely no excuse left not to act. There can be no more prey for the coyotes. Decent Americans want no more deaths in the desert.

ALBUQUERQUE JOURNAL

Albuquerque, N. M., July 10, 1980

As Latin America's population explodes, the United States can brace itself for an ever-larger flood of illegal aliens until all involved countries find a solution.

The recent dehydration deaths of 13 illegals from El Salvador in the Arizona desert are a sickening and tragic offspring of this worsening problem.

Aliens entering the U.S. illegally, of course, do not wish to be discovered. So it would seem the U.S. could have done little to save them. But steps should be taken to prevent it from happening again.

Two things have kept the U.S. from sticking to any clear immigration policy. One is political pressure. The other is the collision of old American values — symbolized by the Statue of Liberty — and new economic and social feelings. The goal, then, is to establish a reasonable and humanitarian policy for all immigrants.

The policy makers (or non-makers, as it were) in Washington should give more help to the Immigration and Naturalization Service. The U.S. may not have a solid policy, but that is no reason to saddle the INS with underfunding and understaffing.

The U.S. should push this matter to the forefront of meetings like the just-concluded Mexico-U.S. Border Governors Conference.

The U.S. should also lean more heavily on Mexico for help. Mexico does not object strenuously to illegal immigration into the U.S. because it provides an economic "safety valve" for its poor people. But Mexico has been quite concerned about the inhumanity with which smugglers treat illegals.

The answers will be difficult and will dissatisfy a great many on both sides of the border. But the problem will never simply disappear. Future solutions cannot be found unless the involved parties talk about them now.

Chicago Tribune

Chicago, Ill., July 8, 1980

At least 13 refugees from El Salvador, trying to enter the United States illegally, have died in the baking heat of the Arizona desert. They were the immediate victims of the inhuman greed of professional people-smugglers who chaperone refugees across the border for extortionate sums of money and then abandon them, perhaps taking what money they have left before heading back for another consignment of potential victims.

But in a broader sense the dead were the victims of our own government's ambivalence toward its immigration laws. If a more consistent effort had been made to enforce the laws all these years — if they had not been allowed to degenerate into a state of near-fiction—then the number of "wetbacks" might have been held to tolerable limits and the career of people-smuggling would not have proved so attractive to human rats.

If on the other hand the government had yielded to the argument that the Mexican border cannot be patrolled adequately and given up the pretense of enforcing the laws, or perhaps changed the laws, then there would have been no need for these refugees to try to evade the law and they would not have condemned themselves to die on the desert.

The tragedy demands attention for several reasons. One is that it is by no means unique. Almost every day, illegal immigrants are the victims of one kind of misfortune or another, but they don't make headlines. They may involve only robbery. Or, like the many Haitians who try to escape to the United States or the Bahamas on makeshift boats and drown at sea, their fate may never be publicized.

A second reason for special concern is that because of political turbulence in El Salvador, Nicaragua, and Guatemala — coupled with a particularly bad harvest in Mexico — there will almost certainly be more demand this summer than ever for the services of people-smugglers along the Mexican border. And to make matters worse, the border patrol's attention has been diverted to the Cubans and Haitians in Florida. We can expect a record number of border crossings — and, if the heat in the Southwest keeps up, more deaths.

Nobody dares to pretend that there is a simple solution. It is always easier to prevent a situation from getting out of hand, as this one has, than it is to restore control once the barriers have been trampled down. Things are further complicated because many United States employers thrive on low-cost labor by men and women who, being here illegally, don't dare complain. Finally, a sudden crackdown would anger the Mexican government, which has been relying on emigration to relieve its problems of high unemployment and a high birth rate.

But even granting that illegal immigration can't be stopped overnight or before next year, there has been too little willingness to face the problem squarely. Frustration and a sense of resignation have delayed any action, and every day's delay makes the problem worse. Our traditions and instincts tempt us to welcome refugees from abroad, especially from political oppression. But as problems and populations grow in the rest of the world, we simply cannot open our borders to everybody who wants to come. Control will have to be restored; the border patrol is going to have to be strengthened; and, however reluctantly, we may have to make it clear that illegal immigrants will not be able to obtain jobs as easily as they have so far. This week's tragedy should remind us that the problem cannot much longer be ignored.

THE DENVER POST

Denver, Colo., July 8, 1980

THE TERROR-RIDDEN homeland they fled was named *El Salvador*, Spanish for "The Savior." But they found no salvation in their flight, only a private Calvary in the heat of the Arizona desert.

We don't even know yet how many of these pitiful men, women and children died, perhaps 30 to 40. Many of the 13 bodies already recovered from the Organ Pipe Cactus National Monument haven't yet been given even the residual dignity of a name. We haven't caught the devils who took their money to smuggle them from their war-torn homeland to the promised Eldorado of the United States — then robbed them and abandoned them without food or water in an area where the soil heats to 150 degrees.

But we do know a few things. We know that the group of 40 to 50 people paid up to $1,200 each to the smugglers, who were part of a well-organized traffic in human lives. We know that they are a small fraction of the refugees from war or economic deprivation who are struggling to get into this country. We know that in the agony of their betrayal and thirst they drank their own urine in the struggle to survive.

And we know there will be more of them — unless we change our immigration policies which increasingly stand as an affront to our professed national ideals.

The Salvadoreans caught the nation's attention only because so many died in one place. It's routine for desperate people to be exploited by unscrupulous smugglers. Some are robbed and abandoned as were the Salvadoreans. Others are actually murdered by the smugglers.

Some survive the passage of the border only to enter into bondage at the hands of unscrupulous labor contractors and employers. They make the news from time to time when they are found smothered in the back of locked trucks, or, the luckier ones, expelled by *la migra* because an employer or contractor found it more convenient to place an anonymous phone call than to pay what is due them.

Probably we can never completely eliminate such tragedies as the one in Arizona. We can't absorb all the tens of millions of people displaced by war, famine or persecution throughout the world. But a responsible policy for foreign laborers would go a long way to reducing the number of future catastrophes.

The blame for our present system is widely distributed. Undoubtedly, some ignore the problem out of racist motives — the victims are chiefly Hispanics and there are those who would like to keep "those people" out.

Liberals convinced that population growth is the world's prime evil fear a floodtide of immigrants if we humanize our policies. Labor unions fear the aliens will undercut wage rates.

But few of these motives withstand analysis. The laid-off auto worker in Detroit, drawing benefits totaling 95 percent of a compensation package which may be in excess of $30,000 a year, isn't facing competition from the Mexican national who hopes to pick fruit on Colorado's Western Slope for the minimum wage.

Nor would legal immigrants, licensed to work in the United States for specified periods, necessarily mean more residents. They would move back and forth across the border between their families and their seasonal jobs — as studies show the illegal laborers already do.

Other industrial nations, such as Germany, have been able to evolve civilized policies for handling foreign laborers, increasing or decreasing the number of permits issued in tempo with their economy.

Since abandoning the much criticized *bracero* program, which for all its faults at least gave workers legal standing and minimum dignity, the United States has not been able to draft a civilized replacement.

On balance, the chief problem with the "illegal aliens" who work in this country is simply that they are illegal. Until we face up to that fact squarely, we can expect more Calvaries on our borders.

The Kansas City Times

Kansas City, Mo., July 10, 1980

Lest we become inured to sorrowful news and the hard hearts of fellow human beings, events periodically occur to shake the public soul. Such was the unfolding tale of the El Salvadorean aliens smuggled into this country, half of whom died in the desert.

Neither the first nor the last instance of the current trade in men, women and children for profit, death shaded with horror the saga of a group of El Salvador natives trucked last weekend into the United States, then apparently misled into the desert near the Mexico-Arizona border. At least 13 people were the victims of inadequate clothing, no water or other provisions in the scorching heat and hostile sands.

The sun and earth might have buried the scheme with the victims had not survivors found their way back to civilization to tell the tale of monies paid, fights for any drops of liquid become precious, and death.

The tragic story does not erase the fact that the victims and survivors entered this country illegally. Nor does it give them preferred status over the unknown thousands of other Latin American aliens who have slipped more quietly into the fields and kitchens, factories and farms of the U.S. to escape economic or political poverty in their homelands. It does illustrate that the hands of more worldly, greedy individuals are often involved in the various ploys, usually at a high cost to the fleeing aliens. The case of the El Salvadoreans shows how far the traders in human souls will go to make a few bucks, to say nothing of the value they place on human life.

The aliens have already paid twice for their misdeeds. Immigration officials and the Justice Department should spare no effort to ensure that the smugglers also receive fair punishment. It is unfortunate that their freewheeling colleagues will continue to ply their illegal and dirty trade unless another dramatic tragedy rouses the public ire.

Part II: Refugees

George Washington conceived of America as "an asylum to the oppressed and needy of the earth." Refugees were indistinguishable from immigrants in the early years of America's history: the Irish and Chinese fled famines, and the Jews fled pogroms. They came when immigration into the U.S. was relatively uncontrolled. Subsequent immigration legislation made no distinction between immigrants and refugees. Only after World War II, which created refugees on a scale unprecedented in human history, did the U.S. begin to consider refugees as a separate case. President Harry S Truman initiated the effort by admitting 40,000 war refugees in 1945 and pushing a reluctant Congress to pass the Displaced Persons Act in 1948. President Dwight D. Eisenhower followed up Truman's efforts with the Refugee Relief Act of 1953. Both acts allowed more than 400,000 people into the U.S. during the 1950s.

When the country's immigration laws were overhauled in 1965, refugees were given last place in the seven-category immigrant preference system. No attempt was made to organize their admittance. They continued to be defined according to the Cold-War-inspired Immigration and Nationality Act of 1952 as persons "fleeing Communist or Communist-dominated countries, the Middle East, or areas struck by natural disaster." The 1965 act placed a quota of 17,400 on annual refugee admission, but the Justice Department's parole authority allowed it to admit additional refugees in emergency situations or when it suited "the public interest." Of the 38,000 Hungarian refugees resettled in the U.S. after 1956, 32,000 were admitted under parole authority.

After the Hungarian uprising, there was no spectacular outpouring of refugees until Indochina's holocaust of the late 1970s. The U.S. was obliged to reexamine its haphazard refugee policy and take note of the world refugee situation. The closer the look, the more refugees were found, from Indochina to Africa to the Caribbean. Political oppression emerged as only one of many reasons driving citizens from their homelands. A new term, "economic refugee," entered the picture. Is there a difference between people who flee political oppression and people who flee abject poverty?

When poverty and persecution are combined, as in Haiti, are the refugees "economic" or "political"? Making choices among the cries for asylum is an unpleasant task, but it must be done in the interests of practicality. An America that cannot function because of overpopulation will be of little help to refugees, now or in the future.

Steady Stream of Indochinese Flee Their Homes in Boats

Since the conquest of South Vietnam by North Vietnam in 1975, a steady stream of refugees had flowed out of Vietnam and neighboring Laos and Cambodia. At first, they were evacuated by the U.S. and international relief organizations. After the U.S. pullout, however, refugees were left to their own devices to escape the hardships of the new regimes. The exodus from Vietnam by boat picked up during the last part of 1977, despite a Vietnamese government crackdown on sea escapes. Meanwhile, refugees from war- and famine-torn Laos and Cambodia fled to neighboring Thailand. President Jimmy Carter announced in July that the U.S. would admit 15,000 Indochinese refugees, most of whom were awaiting a decision on their fates in overcrowded camps in Thailand and Malaysia. Estimates put the number of refugees in both countries at 87,000 Vietnamese, Laotians and Cambodians. France had been accepting Indochinese on a regular basis, and Australia, Canada, New Zealand, Belgium and Denmark promised to increase their refugee admissions quotas. Malaysia ended its ban on accepting refugees in August in light of the West's pledge to ease the refugee burden.

The Morning Union

Springfield, Mass., September 26, 1977

The plight of the "boat people," Vietnamese who fled the Communist regime in Vietnam but who were refused sanctuary elsewhere in Indochina, is being eased at last by the United States. The vanguard of the 15,000 expected to enter the country this year landed at San Francisco International Airport last week.

An additional 15,000 a year will enter the United States over the next three or four years under a program announced recently by President Carter. Meanwhile the State Department is urging an extension of the federal refugee aid program to handle the new arrivals. Their transportation here was paid for by a private international refugee aid group, with first priority given those who have had to exist in deprivation aboard boats, some so small they barely kept afloat.

The humane gesture of the United States is in contrast to the image of heartlessness imposed on it by some nations whose doors have remained closed to the Vietnamese refugees.

The Seattle Times

Seattle, Wash., September 16, 1977

THE Indochina Refugee Assistance Act, passed by Congress in 1975 to provide funds to help people who fled their homelands in the aftermath of the Vietnam war, is scheduled to expire September 30.

The federal government has spent about $550 million to assist some 150,000 refugees (6,000 in Washington State) who were granted asylum in this country after the Communist take-overs in Vietnam, Laos and Cambodia.

The bulk of the money, which amounts to less than $4,000 a refugee, went to reimburse state and local governments and volunteer agencies.

Many of the refugees, although members of political, social or economic elites in their own countries, have had difficulty adapting to American life.

The federal Department of Health, Education and Welfare's Refugee Task Force reported in May that 87 per cent of the male and 68 per cent of the female refugees who were heads of households were employed — but often in low-paying, menial jobs despite their experience or education.

Some have had problems learning English and fitting into a society that — in contrast to their own — shunts aside the elderly and gives children great freedom. A sense of rootlessness coupled with economic problems have meant anxiety, depression and even suicide for some refugees.

It will take a few more years before such problems are surmounted and the refugees are assimilated, according to those involved with refugee programs.

But unless Congress extends the refugee-assistance act, the entire burden will fall on local governments and charitable organizations. We urge Congress to continue federal funding, which seems a small price to pay to help those in such need.

In addition, we hope Congress passes a separate measure, now pending, that would give most Indochinese refugees the status of permanent resident aliens. This would open up employment opportunities and provide an important psychological boost to the refugees.

As Representative Joel Pritchard, a co-sponsor of the bill, has said:

"If there is one group which has come to this country which we should help, it is these people. We were involved in their coming here."

The refugee-assistance program — if it is continued — could turn out to be the only American success story of the Indochina-war era.

The Charlotte Observer

Charlotte, N. C., September 28, 1977

Two years ago Congress passed legislation designed to help Indochinese refugees cope with life in the United States. It has been a resounding success that deserves to be extended. It has given financial aid, educational and even psychiatric counseling to people sorely in need of whatever steadying hands could be offered.

The law has helped over 150,000 refugees, most from Vietnam, who are making places for themselves in American life. Sour predictions that refugees would simply form a welfare society and contribute nothing to the life of the nation have not, thus far, proven true. A government survey three months ago, in fact, found that the unemployment rate among refugees was just 7.9 per cent, down from 13 per cent last January.

The legislation providing the help that has made such encouraging figures possible is due to expire Friday. It deserves to be extended, but not in the form the Carter administration proposes. The administration's notion is poor policy, we think. It would reduce aid to refugees to a simple payout of cash. That's fine only if what you want is to encourage the welfare syndrome. The sensible course would be to extend good legislation that has already proven itself in the form in which it has proven itself.

The strength of the existing Refugee Assistance Act is the stress it places on things besides a simple check to pay the rent and buy some beans. Several senators, including Hubert Humphrey and Ted Kennedy, want to extend that bill for three more years. The Refugee Assistance Program has provided a variety of programs to help refugees learn English, acquire a trade and get on with productive lives. It has done its job for many refugees.

But 15,000 more will come to this country each year for several years, at least, and many of those who have been here for some time still need help. They need some financial help, to be sure. But they also need the training programs that help people get and hold jobs.

Remember that old, old story? Give a man a fish and you feed him a meal. Teach him how to fish and he feeds himself forever. The Carter administration is offering a fish.

The San Diego Union

San Diego, Calif., September 24, 1977

On Sept. 30 the Indochinese Refugee Assistance Program expires, and unless Congress acts posthaste, some state and local governments will have to start paying bills that clearly are the federal government's responsibility.

In 1975 the federal government instituted the program, under which welfare costs for refugees of the war in Southeast Asia who are living in the United States have been paid. The program expires next Friday.

An end to federal assistance would mean that this state would have to pick up $24 million in welfare costs, and various California counties about $15 million. San Diego County would have to pay $2.5 million.

What to do? A bill to extend the program has been proposed, by the administration, but because it offers less than full reimbursement of welfare and retraining costs, it is not wholly satisfactory. Obviously, time is short. However, the wisest course would be for Congress to extend the present program for at least another year. Thus the federal govern-ment would maintain its responsibility, and taxpayers of pertinent state and local governments would not be unfairly indebted. And, during the year of extension, Congress more calmly could assess the problems of refugees, the state and local governments, and the national interest.

Rocky Mountain News

Denver, Colo., September 28, 1977

SOME STORIES in the news are so heart-breaking that even we would prefer to skip over them.

We have in mind the arrival a few days ago of the first of an eventual 15,000 new Vietnamese refugees to this country – 7,000 of them "boat people" who escaped from former South Vietnam by sea in small, frail and uncertain craft, and 8,000 others who made their way overland to Thailand.

What is painful are not the individual or collective stories of these refugees. Though they involve an immense amount of suffering and sacrifice, they are, after all, 15,000 stories with happy endings.

No, the wrenching thought is that for every refugee who has made it safely to the United States, many others continue to languish in camps in Thailand or are buffeted from country to country seeking one that will give them sanctuary. Unknown numbers of boat people have perished in storms or, we are told, have been sunk by patrol boats.

No doubt this latest refugee movement in a century that has seen so many of them would have happened even if the United States had never become involved in Southeast Asia in an attempt to fill the vacuum left by the French and prevent the forcible absorption of South Vietnam by the Communist North.

But since we did become involved, transforming a small, bitter war into a large, terrible war, we bear a special responsibility toward the victims of that conflict and its aftermath. The 15,000 new refugees will make a total of 165,000 Indochinese who have entered the United States since the fall of Saigon in April 1975.

How many tens of thousands more will come knocking on our national conscience, no one can predict.

THE SACRAMENTO BEE

Sacramento, Calif., September 26, 1977

Here it is a few days before federal financing of aid for Indochinese refugees runs out and nobody can say for certain what Congress is going to do about it.

For California, it is a critical question. Half of the 150,000 who fled to this country from war-ravaged Southeast Asia settled in California. State officials estimate the cost to the state may run $39 million unless federal benefits are extended.

The end of the migration is far from over. The Carter administration has authorized another 15,000 to come in. It is expected the total will range somewhere between 45,000 and 75,000 in the next three to five years. On the basis of experience, more will prefer California to any other state as their second home.

Most of the recent refugees, at least, arrived with little money and no jobs, and many have large families to support. They need time and help to become rooted in a strange new society. But they are here because of federal initiative. They are a national problem. The solution should be national in scope to spread the costs evenly among all taxpayers.

The pending Carter administration bill seeks federal funds to pay for 75 per cent of state costs the first year, 50 per cent the second year and 25 per cent the third. While that seems reasonable enough, eligibility rules have been criticized as too narrow. Another source of controversy is the absence of funds to underwrite resettlement projects of churches and service organizations.

There also is a proposed stopgap measure which would continue 100 per cent federal financing for six months to allow Congress more time to work out its differences. However Congress goes about it, it canot dump the problem entirely on local property taxpayers, especially when the burden is unduly heavy in states like California.

Los Angeles Times

Los Angeles, Calif., September 21, 1977

The deadline is only days away, but Congress still has not passed legislation needed to continue assistance that was first provided in 1975 to help relocate Vietnamese war refugees and to reimburse states for the welfare assistance that they have provided.

If Congress doesn't act by the end of the month, when the current program is scheduled to expire, the burden will fall on state and county welfare agencies. If that happens, California, which houses about one-half (75,000) of all the refugees in the nation, will be hit hard. This will be particularly true in the southern counties, and especially Los Angeles and Orange, where most of California's refugees are concentrated.

Mario Obledo, California's health and welfare secretary, estimates that the expiration of the federal program would cost California $39 million a year. The cost to Los Angeles County taxpayers has been estimated at $5 million; in Orange County, the tax rate would have to be raised another 3 cents per $100 assessed valuation to cover refugee aid.

That's a financial burden that federal officials should not pass on to the states and counties; they do not have the funds to meet it.

Historically, welfare has not been a way of life in Vietnam. And most of the refugees, in the short time that they have been here, have made remarkable adjustments. Many, however, have serious health, education and housing problems, and do need help. About 35% of the refugees (22,000 in California) are presently receiving some form of public cash assistance. Their plight is a national, not a local, problem.

There are several bills pending in Congress. They come down to two approaches:

—One, being pushed by Sen. Hubert H. Humphrey (D-Minn.) and Rep. Fortney H. Stark (D-Calif.), would provide full federal funding for one year, then reduced reimbursement for the next two years. But its key point is a continuation of social services and special projects to provide funds for language and job-training programs to help make the refugees employable and self-sufficient. The estimated first-year cost is $118 million.

—The Administration measure would cost an estimated $72 million, but it is strictly a welfare bill that calls for reduced reimbursements over the three-year period, and no special funding for training programs.

The Humphrey-Stark approach is much better. And with 15,000 more refugees from Southeast Asia being admitted to the United States under a special program, it is only fair to continue the full federal financing for at least one more year.

The refugees pose a special problem. The more than 50,000 still on welfare rolls are a strong indication that they need more time and help to develop job and language skills they must have to take their places beside other refugees as productive, self-sufficient residents of the American community.

Refugee Outflow Mounts; International Aid Sought

The pace of refugee outflow from Vietnam, Cambodia and Laos picked up markedly during 1978. This gave rise to calls for increased efforts on the part of the U.S. and the international community to provide aid. Despite efforts by the Vietnamese government to ban escapes, almost 40,000 "boat people" had fled the country from January to September, according to the United Nations High Commissioner for Refugees. The flow was augmented by thousands of ethnic Chinese whose businesses in Vietnam had been nationalized by the Hanoi government.

The U.S. came under heavy pressure to absorb the bulk of the refugees, because of its 20-year involvement in Vietnam. In April, Washington said it would accept 25,000 during the next 12 months. Sympathy for the stranded refugees prompted the Administration to raise the quota by 22,000 in November, but Washington stalled at doing more. Undersecretary of State David Newsom told Congress that the U.S. limit on the number of refugee admissions was intended to put pressure on other governments to admit refugees. Attorney General Griffin Bell added that the Indochinese refugees were a world problem of serious dimensions, not merely a U.S. problem, and Congress should begin a review of U.S. refugee policy.

Shortly afterward in December, the U.N. High Commissioner for Refugees sponsored a conference in Geneva on Indochinese refugees. No practical solution emerged from the two days of talks among the 34 participating nations. The Vietnamese delegate dismissed the 200,000 Indochinese awaiting asylum throughout Southeast Asia as a small minority used to "unproductive consumption," who could not be integrated into the new government. The U.S. announced during the conference that it would increase its quota to a total of 50,000 through April 1979. By that time, 200,000 Indochinese refugees had been admitted into the U.S.

The Wichita Eagle

Wichita, Kans., March 6, 1978

The Indochinese refugees who have fled, and are fleeing, their ravaged homeland should be on the conscience and in the thoughts of every American. Kansas was one of the first states to open wide its doors to the influx of war-tossed humanity. But other areas were less generous, and thousands of refugees have begun new lives in America under the most adverse circumstances.

Still they survive, and many thrive, and — as Wichita and other Kansas cities may attest — those communities that have former refugees living in them are the richer for it.

But though the United States has provided emergency homes for nearly 170,000 refugees from Vietnam, Kampuchea and Laos, another 100,000 still await their fate in camps clustered along the borders of their former countries of residence.

And the refugee flood is growing; perhaps 1,500 monthly continue to flee the fratricidal regime in Kampuchea and the communist government in Vietnam. Many become "boat people" who are refused entry to neighboring countries' ports, and made to stay on their boats and survive on the most meager rations. Some even have been forced to return home,

which often means — in the case of Kampuchea, at least — certain death.

Last summer the Carter administration approved the entry of 15,000 Indochinese refugees, among half of whom were Vietnamese "boat people." The State Department later sought authority to admit 10,000 more of the boat dwellers, lest they perish in an aborted flight to freedom.

More recently the International Rescue Committee, which was formed during the awful days of the Nazi Holocaust to aid the exodus of European Jews to friendly countries, has entered the struggle to assure homes for the fleeing Indochinese.

The committee has urged the suspension of exclusionary criteria for the admission of refugees to this country, so that the remainder of Indochina's pitiful castaways may find haven in the land of their erstwhile protectors.

This is no more than right, or just. If this nation was willing to commit billions of dollars and 55,000 young Americans' lives to the defense of Vietnam, it should be willing now to offer its precious soil as sanctuary to those who were left behind.

ST. LOUIS POST-DISPATCH

St. Louis, Mo., March 25, 1978

Attorney General Griffin B. Bell seems to be the obstacle barring entrance to a safe harbor for the so-called boat people, Indochinese refugees who have fled their countries in vessels that may or may not be seaworthy. According to an article in *The New York Times*, Secretary of State Cyrus Vance has said he favors admitting all boat people to the U.S. who are rescued at sea, but are turned down by other countries, as well as all unplaced refugees from Vietnam and Cambodia. Mr. Bell apparently believes such admission would have to await congressional action, which might take a year.

In the opinion of the State Department, these refugees can be admitted now, without waiting for Congress, through the attorney general's "parole authority," the power to admit aliens in an emergency. The man who has the power, however, is said to believe that the parole authority is only to be used on an individual basis, rather than for a large group. The parole authority has been used to help large numbers of refugees before — Hungarians in 1956 and Cubans in the 1960s. The people fleeing Vietnam and especially Cambodia deserve equal compassion, particularly since actions of the United States contributed to the situation from which the refugees are trying to escape.

Waiting for Congress to act could be a death sentence for a great many people. The fairly high rate of unemployment here and guilt lingering from the war could well extend the time in which Congress might act and could cause that body to be less than generous. But surely the U.S. has the obligation to offer hope to those persons who are fleeing the destruction of their way of life due in some measure to American involvement. Mr. Vance's view should prevail, and we hope Mr. Bell is persuaded quickly.

St. Louis, Mo., April 6, 1978

The Carter administration has decided to do the humanitarian thing of admitting all Vietnamese refugees living on boats who have been refused entry by other countries, as well as many other Indochinese refugees who have family or political ties to the United States. This action would be taken under the attorney general's emergency parole authority, rather than waiting for new refugee legislation, which is not expected to be passed until next year.

Putting off admission of stranded refugees or those with ties to the U.S. could well have been the same as a death sentence for many of them. The number of persons expected to enter the country under this emergency authority is not enormous, approximately 25,000. Attorney General Bell, however, resisted using his authority for admission of a regular, predictable number of refugees rather than for persons who are in a sudden "emergency" situation. Mr. Carter disagreed, and rightly so. Many of the refugees fleeing Vietnam, Laos and Cambodia are in a state of emergency equivalent to that of the people who fled when Saigon fell; and they deserve the help that the U.S. can give with so little expense.

DESERET NEWS
Salt Lake City, Utah, August 12, 1978

Since the fall of Indochina in 1975, there has been a steady flow of refugees.

So far, well over a third of a million of them have chosen to risk their lives rather than live under communist domination in Southeast Asia.

Some of these refugees flee by land, mostly from Laos and Cambodia. Many others must crowd into small boats, then run the risk of sickness from drinking sea water and being robbed at sea by pirates from Thailand.

Until recently, the number of boat refugees — almost all of them from Vietnam — averaged 1,400 to 1,600 a month.

But now, the U.S. State Department reports, the number has climbed sharply to over 5,000 each month.

So much, then, for the notion that all is well in Vietnam now that the war is over and that the new leaders there are running a benign society.

What's to become of this new wave of people without homes and countries?

The Thais and Malaysians often push the refugees and their boats back into the sea. Some other Asian countries provide refuge only temporarily. Only a few countries — the U.S., Canada, France, Australia, and Israel — have been willing to help alleviate the suffering by permanently accepting Vietnamese refugees in sizeable numbers.

The U.S., of course, has a special obligation to these refugees. Many of them are regarded by the present communist rulers of Indochina as enemies because of their past association with American policies, programs, and personnel.

But no country can solve the world's welfare problems virtually single-handedly. This is a job for as many nations as possible, not just a handful of them.

For the most part, the Vietnamese refugees are desirable citizens — upper-middle class professionals who put little burden on the jobless and welfare rolls. In the U.S., 89% of Vietnamese refugee families are employed and only 11% are solely dependent on welfare.

The United Nations has a High Commissioner for Refugees. This office ought to convene an international conference on the resettlement of Indochina's swelling tide of refugees.

The Hartford Courant
Hartford, Conn.,
March 21, 1978

Secretary of State Cyrus R. Vance has indicated that he favors unlimited U.S. immigration rights for all Vietnamese and Cambodians who have escaped from their lands and cannot find refuge in other places.

Literally thousands of "boat people" escaping from the nightmarish aftermath of the Vietnam War are still trapped at sea, unwelcome in neighboring countries and uninvited by others more distant.

The United States has accepted more than 150,000 refugees from the area, most of them in the months immediately following the Communist takeover of South Vietnam in 1975. Congress and the Justice Department have resisted recent efforts to lift the normal immigration quotas and procedures, so additional Asians can be admitted immediately.

Mr. Vance and President Carter should press the case of the refugees. The nation's long and tragic involvement in Vietnam is reason enough to show special compassion for the refugees, a substantial number of whom cooperated with the American military and have reason to fear a return to their native land.

Under the provisions of the Immigration and Naturalization Act, the attorney general of the United States "may in his discretion parole into the United States temporarily, under such conditions as he may prescribe for emergency reasons or for reasons deemed strictly in the public interest, any alien applying for admission to the United States."

Although Attorney General Griffin Bell has argued that this provision was not intended to be used for mass immigration, other administrations have used it to take in Hungarian freedom fighters in the 1950s and Cubans in the 1960s.

The boat people look to us now, as millions of victims of other political, economic and social tragedies have looked to us in the past. They deserve American help.

Newsday
Long Island., N. Y., April 4, 1978

The United Nations defines a refugee as a person who is outside "the country of his former habitual residence because he has or had well-grounded fear of persecution by reason of his race, religion, nationality or political opinion." Those are human rights issues, so it follows that President Carter would want this country to treat refugees as compassionately and generously as possible.

This desire has been translated into an interim policy that would admit to this country all the "boat people" of Indochina and refugees from Vietnam, Laos and Cambodia who have family or political ties here. The vehicle for admitting them would be the Justice Department's emergency parole authority, which Attorney General Griffin Bell resisted and Secretary of State Cyrus Vance supported.

Legislation is pending in Congress to increase the number of refugees admitted on a regular basis, but it's not likely to see action until next year. That's a long time to wait on leaky boats or in overcrowded refugee camps. We're glad the administration chose to act now to lessen the misery of the thousands whose misfortune it was to be left with a regime they couldn't abide.

THE COMMERCIAL APPEAL
Memphis, Tenn., March 27, 1978

THE UNITED STATES welcome mat may have worn thin when it comes to helping aliens like the Indochinese "boat people."

But thin as it is, it should be put out to let the world know that this country takes a responsible moral view of the painful problem of refugees from Indochinese communism.

Secretary of State Cyrus Vance and others in the Carter administration recognize that adding Vietnamese and Cambodian refugees to our other national burdens won't win any popularity contests.

But Vance has testified, according to undenied reports, that the United States should find a way to admit the people fleeing Indochina in small boats when other nations turn them away or they are bypassed by ocean ships.

Other countries have, in a fact, done something to face the problem. Israel symbolically welcomed a few Vietnamese refugees last summer. They were given asylum after the Israeli ship which picked them up 30 miles off the Vietnamese coast could not, get Hong Kong, Taiwan or Japan to accept them.

Thailand has taken thousands of refugees until it felt it could take no more. Malasia, Australia, New Zealand and France have taken some. A handful have been accepted by Denmark and Belgium. But the continuing flow of escapees — running despite a ban imposed by the Vietnam Communists — has taxed the willingness of other countries to invite the problems refugees are certain to bring.

The United States knows those problems already. The difficulties in resettling the first wave of Vietnam refugees after collapse of the South Vietnamese government in April, 1975, has been felt in America, including Memphis. The barriers of language and custom, and the loneliness of a people torn away from their land and its history, are facts well known.

We know, too, that accepting Vietnamese "boat people" increases the pressure to absorb Mexicans who slip into the United States seeking jobs.

BUT THE FEAR of new burdens should not be the deciding factor. As Vance has stressed, this country has a large responsibility to a people in whose country we spared no expense to fight a costly and futile war.

We owe them something. We need to show others a humanitarianism that is more than rhetoric.

The Honolulu Advertiser
Honolulu, Ha., April 4, 1978

After months of debate within the administration, President Carter has approved a new policy on the admission of refugees that is humane and worthy of support.

He is committing the administration to seeking long-term legislation that would increase the number of refugees regularly allowed to enter each year from the present level of 17,400 to a new level of approximately 40,000. Prospects for favorable consideration would be improved at least in the Senate next year, with Edward Kennedy, who is more sympathetic, succeeding James Eastland as chairman of the Judiciary Committee.

MEANWHILE, Carter will use the current law's emergency "parole authority" to admit all Vietnamese "boat refugees" — people who fled in small boats — unable to find homes elsewhere. About 5,600 such refugees are believed to be stranded presently in various parts of Asia, and each month about 1,500 more have been leaving Vietnam. Many have died at sea after being turned away from one country or another.

Carter's emergency authority also will be used to admit all Indochinese refugees who escaped by land into Thailand and who have special family or political ties with the United States. Administration officials estimate that after an initial admission of several thousand such persons, about 1,000 a month will be coming to the United States in this category.

The emergency authority also will continue to be used to admit Eastern European refugees, mostly Jews, who want to come.

Most of the Indochinese refugees who come will be impoverished. They will need public assistance, which the federal government will be obligated to provide.

Some, perhaps many, Americans may not want the refugees, fearing their presence will add to economic and social strains in U.S. communities. But the alternative to admitting them appears to be condemn them to homelessness or death; we would lose much of what is good about this country if we let that happen.

RIGHTLY OR wrongly, many of the refugees once found themselves allied with the United States and as a result fear persecution in their home countries.

As the world's wealthiest nation, we can afford not only to admit them but also to welcome them and help give them a new start.

SAN JOSE NEWS
San Jose, Calif., August 11, 1978

In the three years since the fall of Saigon, the United States has admitted 172,000 refugees from Vietnam, Laos and Cambodia, and the exodus continues in significant numbers. These human beings constitute another, compelling kind of national debt.

The United States, for reasons of national interest, fought a bitter, bloody, expensive and losing war in Vietnam. When American troops pulled out finally, in 1975, that terminated this nation's military and political involvement in the affairs of Vietnam. Withdrawal did not — and cannot — dispense so abruptly with our moral responsibility to those who, with the United States, lost the war.

Once again, Congress and the Carter administration are being asked to make good on this particular national debt, on the need to resettle and assimilate into American society the refugees of the Vietnam war. The request should not be denied.

Pending in the Senate is legislation by Sen. Alan Cranston, D-Calif., that would continue full federal funding of all Vietnam refugee programs for another year. Cranston's measure is at odds with a Carter administration proposal to fund fully only programs for resettling "new" refugees. Santa Clara County's Washington lobbyist, Susanne Stout Elfving, testified in favor of the Cranston ap-proach Wednesday, pointing out that about 16 percent of all Vietnamese in California, 11,000, have settled here. Another 10,000 are expected to arrive within nine months, a hefty portion of the 25,000 or more the State Department expects to arrive from Vietnam annually in the next few years. Full federal funding for all Vietnamese refugee programs is a must for two principal reasons.

First, the refugee problem is a direct consequence of national policy; it is patently unfair to expect state and local governments to shoulder this burden. Second, Proposition 13 has restricted property tax revenues and placed additional strains on remaining state and local government revenues. There is no money for local refugees programs, too.

Last October, President Carter signed a bill providing $100 million for refugee assistance through fiscal 1978, with the aid, for medical and social programs, tapering off in subsequent years. That is not good enough so long as Vietnam continues to create refugees and so long as those Indochinese already here continue to need readjustment assistance.

Presidents Nixon and Ford insisted the United States found peace with honor at the conclusion of the Vietnam war. The refugees created by the war constitute a debt of honor that President Carter and the Congress cannot ignore.

The Boston Globe
Boston, Mass., July 29, 1978

The Government Printing Office has recently published the latest chapter in a central story of American history — the acceptance of refugees. It has not always been a cheering story, yet it has usually ended fairly happily. This would seem to be the case with the latest chapter, the account of the US receipt of Indochinese refugees.

Since the end of the Indochina war in 1975, more than 150,000 such refugees have come to the United States — about 130,000 from Vietnam, 10,000 from Laos and the remainder from Cambodia. They have settled around the nation — 35,000, the greatest number, in California, 1400 in Massachusetts and a few score in every state. And while there have been traumas, defeats, rebukes and much sadness, the overall picture reported by a study for the Senate Subcommittee on Refugees is encouraging.

While many refugees have had to take entry-level jobs, their rate of unemployment (5.9 percent last year) is lower than that for the population as a whole. Further, after reaching a peak in the summer of 1977, the number of refugees receiving cash assistance has steadily declined. A modest proportion of the refugees has received language training; Indochinese dentists and some doctors have managed to receive accreditation.

The successes were accomplished despite the fact that the refugees arrived in unprecedented numbers for such a short time, arrived when the economy was depressed and arrived in a place with a totally alien culture.

What the report demonstrates, however, is not that the US responsibility for Indochinese refugees is over; what it indicates is that the responsibility can be met. That is an important lesson because more needs to be done.

Indochinese refugees are admitted by special permission of the Attorney General, a cumbersome process that reflects the nation's uncertainty about how to deal with aliens. Recently, the Carter Administration has increased the number of Indochinese to be accepted through this process by next May by 25,000. And it has pointedly reaffirmed the US responsibility under international law to accept any refugees picked up on the high seas by US flag ships. But still more must be done.

Rather than waning, as has been widely predicted, the emigration from Indochina is intensifying. The 25,000 additional "parolees" the Administration has agreed to accept may well prove insufficient. The figure may have to be raised. Fortunately, it is a responsibility that we not only have a historic obligation to address, but, as the Senate report indicates, a current capacity to meet.

The Afro American
Baltimore, Md., December 26, 1978

Off the coasts of Southeast Asia, the so-called "boat people" are dying. These Vietnamese men, women and children refugees are too expensive to keep alive.

That is the fact. After years of war the area has difficulty feeding its own populations. Refugees from Vietnam have been taken in, by Thailand for example, but the absorption point seems to have been reached.

It is estimated that as many as 1500 people take to the sea from Vietnam every month in the hope that someone will allow them to land in safety. Half of them are left to die of exposure, of hunger, or drowning.

The United States admitted 7000 last summer and is admit-ting 10,000 more. What of the others? Dare we say how many shall live, how many shall perish?

The Catholic Conference, the charitable arm of the Roman Catholic Church in the United States, is asking the federal government to let these "boat people" come to our shores — shores that have before taken in those who fled from tyranny. They are so relatively few, compared to our population, that they would present no economic challenge, according to the charitable organization. What jobs they would take are those that no one here seems to want.

Of all seasons, this would seem to be the time to extend the hand of life and mercy to these unfortunates.

NEW YORK POST
New York, N. Y., March 17, 1978

Yesterday was the 10th anniversary of the My Lai massacre, an event that all Americans would probably rather forget. But it should serve as a reminder that we still bear a large measure of responsibility for desolation in Indochina, and especially for the stream of refugees still escaping on small boats.

It was heartening to hear Secretary of State Vance endorse the admission of all those Indochinese refugees who can find no other haven. But other forces in Washington, including Attorney General Bell and the discredited but still powerful House immigration subcommittee chairman, Joshua Eilberg, oppose offering the Indochinese the haven we have offered other large groups of refugees from Hungary and Cuba.

It is time that President Carter, in the name of human rights, resolved this intra-Administration dispute in favor of the "boat people"—and of American honor.

The Charlotte Observer
Charlotte, N. C., April 14, 1978

About six weeks ago, a Laotian mother and her two daughters fled across the Mekong River to Thailand. Thai officials forced them to get back into their small boat and return to Laos. When they landed on the muddy bank, Lao soldiers shot and killed them.

Cruel Thais? Yes, but there is a problem. Over 100,000 refugees from Cambodia, Laos and Vietnam are now stacked up in camps in Thailand.

Most of those refugees who survive their escape go to Thailand, which has been less and less willing to accept them. For Thailand has its own problems. They include finding a way to get along with the country's Communist neighbors, who are not delighted to see 3,500 citizens a month fleeing.

What is the American responsibility? It cannot be talked away: We have an open-ended commitment to find a chance at a decent future for the fleeing Indochinese, who have come to be known as "the boat people" because of the way many of them fled. The United States spent too many years in Indochina holding out the vision of a brighter tomorrow to turn from those refugees flattened by the collapse of U.S. policy there.

That does not necessarily mean every refugee must come here. Many of them will; the United States will continue diplomatic efforts to encourage other countries to welcome refugees. The critical thing is for the world to know that the United States will fulfill its responsibility.

That might end a frequent tragedy: refugees crammed in little fishing boats being ignored by steamships at sea or being refused safe harbor by other countries.

Since the Communist victories three years ago, some 172,000 Indochinese have settled in the United States. There are about 1,500 in North Carolina, about 1,300 in South Carolina. To be a refugee is very rough, but these newest immigrants have done well.

Fewer than 15 percent are now getting any sort of public aid in North Carolina. "They have been quite eager to get some kind of language training and to become self-supporting," says Judy Poston of the N.C. Dept. of Social Services.

South Carolina established a special office to aid in settling Indochinese refugees. The S.C. Indochinese Refugee Agency says 59 percent of the refugees are employed. That is a very high figure, since another 37 percent are housewives or disabled or aged.

Kay Rogers, who runs the S.C. office, thinks the refugees are doing well: "I feel comfortable with the degree of resilience that has been exhibited." She will be in Washington next week for a discussion of how to cope with the next influx of refugees.

The Carter administration is seeking congressional approval to accept up to 25,000 Indochinese refugees a year. Congress should grant that approval. Present law admits only 10,200 refugees a year from the Eastern Hemisphere. That quota, of course, includes China and the Soviet Union. The Indochinese have thus far been admitted under the parole authority of the attorney general. It would be far preferable for the Congress to authorize their admission. That would be an expression of the political will of the country.

The need is there; those refugees already here have generally proven themselves worthy additions to America. And there is no question about the responsibility.

THE MILWAUKEE JOURNAL
Milwaukee, Wisc., April 4, 1978

Pity the refugees from Indochina, seeking freedom in a deplorably unsympathetic world.

Today more than 100,000 refugees from Vietnam, Cambodia and Laos crowd squalid camps in Thailand. These escapees are treated like lepers by the surrounding countries of Asia. Horror stories abound of fleeing refugees being turned back to sea in overcrowded, leaking boats, or being forced to return across the borders from whence they just came. Yet in the face of such a hostile reception, they still flee their authoritarian homelands — a fact that illuminates the sturdy character of these people.

What has the US done? Far too little. Yes, America opened its doors to about 145,000 South Vietnamese at the close of the Vietnam War. About 20,000 more Indochinese have trickled in since. But that burst of humanitarianism hardly relieves us of a moral responsibility we bear after a decade of war in Southeast Asia.

It is time for the US to accept many more of Indochina's refugees. The relatively painless way this country absorbed the first group of refugees indicates that it need not be a disrupting experience. And the mechanics for quick entry are available. US Atty. Gen. Griffin Bell need only use his emergency authority to open the immigration gates.

To his credit, President Carter has told Bell to use his emergency powers more liberally. Thus all the Vietnamese "boat people" who aren't accepted by other countries will be allowed in; so will all refugees in Thailand who have family or other special ties to the US. But that still leaves thousands of these refugees in the "unwanted" category.

The problem all along has been official timidity over the refugee question. Bell has been very reluctant to use his authority — probably, in part, out of fear of ruffling the feathers of Rep. Joshua Eilberg of Pennsylvania, chairman of the House subcommittee on immigration. Eilberg is known to be adverse to repeating the first Vietnam refugee experience. Bell also argues that letting in large numbers of refugees would be an abuse of his emergency powers.

Technically, Bell may be right. To be tidy, perhaps new legislation is needed to handle the political refugee problems of the future. Carter supports this.

But there is plenty of precedent for the Carter administration to attack the present refugee problem with the powers it now has. A half-million Cubans and 170,000 Hungarians entered the US through use of the attorney general's emergency powers. Indochinese refugees are America's special moral burden. To neglect them is to betray the nation's humanitarian precepts.

Detroit Free Press

Detroit, Mich., December 10, 1978

TROY NGUYEN'S desperate attempt to learn the fate of his 11 Vietnamese refugee relatives tells us, as no pictures of nameless "boat people" could ever do, what is at stake in the refugee situation in Malaysia.

Mr. Nguyen, now a Hudson's executive, is trying to intervene personally, by going to Kuala Lumpur to try to find out about his relatives first-hand. He has heard from them over the last two months, but the information is fragmentary and unsatisfying. Meanwhile, the responses of the United States government to these particular refugees and the Vietnamese refugees in general are also fragmentary and unsatisfying.

There are now approximately 20,000 "boat people" a month, fleeing Vietnam to the only refuge they can find and taxing beyond effective management Malaysia's capacity to deal with them.

What we ought to be able to understand, from hearing of Mr. Nguyen's urgent efforts on behalf of his family, is that these are people, not numbers, and that we in the United States are involved in their fate. The subtleties and complications are less important than the human tragedy their predicament represents.

Other countries — Canada and France, for instance — have tried to respond to the needs of the refugees in Malaysia and to those trying to flee by boat from Vietnam. And President Carter has said that he will ask Congress to double the number of refugees that the United States can accept — to 30,000 by next May.

What seems to be lacking, though, is a real sense of the urgency of the plight of the refugees and of the moral obligation of the United States. In a very real sense, these are **our** refugees, victims of the war that we muddled around in and for which the Vietnamese people are continuing to pay the price.

Troy Nguyen said he must go to Malaysia because of his "moral obligation" to his only sister and the rest of his family. But the moral obligation is not his alone. It is America's — an obligation to remember not only the "lamp beside the golden door" and the "huddled masses yearning to breathe free," but the contribution our own involvement in Vietnam made to making these people victims of war and of international politics.

The responsibility for what is happening in Vietnam today is certainly not ours alone, or maybe even ours primarily any more. A lot of bad things are happening in Southeast Asia that are beyond our control.

But we can make a swift, honest, openhearted attempt to respond to those now piling up in the refugee camps of Malaysia. Like Troy Nguyen, we have a moral obligation to do so.

The States-Item

New Orleans, La., December 4, 1978

The flood of refugees, mostly Chinese, fleeing from the brutal Communist government in Vietnam is creating an increasingly serious problem that must be dealt with in some sort of systematic manner.

An estimated 500 "boat people" have been ferried across the South China Sea to Malaysia in recent days, often arriving in overcrowded, dangerous, vessels. About 42,000 refugees have found a haven in Malaysia. Hundreds more have been turned away and, in one case, most of the passengers on a boat towed back out to sea drowned when the vessel capsized.

Having to leave a country that has been home is difficult enough. In the case of the Vietnamese refugees, the exodus entails payment of substantial amounts of money. For those who succeed in getting out, the future is uncertain.

The United States has acted to ease the way for entry of 25,000 Indochina refugees between now and April. The 96th Congress will be asked to approve more immigrant slots for Vietnam refugees.

The pressure on Malaysia is growing and the solutions offered by liberalization of U.S. immigration regulations are in the future.

What is needed now is an international effort to deal with the Indochina immigration problem. It has been suggested that the United Nations might be the logical vehicle.

The United States certainly has an obligation to help in resettling the homeless thousands streaming out of Vietnam, but other nations should be willing to share some of the responsibility. The chaotic, often dangerous, conditions faced by the refugees must be resolved.

St. Petersburg Times

St. Petersburg, Fla., December 2, 1978

And still they flee Vietnam. By the thousands they sail their small, leaky boats into the South China Sea. Mostly they don't know where they are headed, and they wouldn't know what course to steer if they did. If not swamped or shipwrecked, they tend to wash up on the shores of Malaysia.

So don't be too righteous in denouncing the poor reception they get. More than 42,000 of these refugees already have been housed in pitiful Malaysian camps, and more are arriving at a rate of 1,000 a day.

Some boats are forcibly repulsed by the natives, who often see themselves as worse off than the unwanted immigrants. Police have turned some vessels around and towed them back out to sea. Recently, 200 drowned as their boat swamped when officials repelled it.

A FREIGHTER onto which 2,500 refugees had been jammed, with little food and water and virtually no sanitation, was held at anchor for weeks while Malaysian officials appealed to the world for help.

That help was slow and reluctant, partly because these refugees were ethnic Chinese who apparently had bought their release and chartered their boat. But they were refugees no less, victims of the latest manifestation of communist abuse in conquered South Vietnam.

Happily, U.S. authorities now have quit holding back. Never mind that these suffering people may have bribed their way out, Attorney General Griffin Bell said. And never mind that their plight may not stem directly from the Vietnam War. Bell said their desperation nevertheless must have been great.

Some already had been accepted by Canada and others by France. Bell urged other nations to help but said the United States would admit to this country whoever of this shipload was left.

BELL ALSO USED used his emergency powers to order admission of 4,375 persons who have escaped the killer regime in Cambodia, plus an additional 15,000 Vietnamese boat people languishing in refugee camps in Thailand and Indonesia as well as Malaysia.

Bell's action almost doubles the quota of fleeing boat people this country has agreed to accept. And it had previously resettled about 150,000 Vietnamese who escaped during the communist rout after the United States pulled out of the war.

But that leaves scores of thousands still homeless, unwanted and confined to refugee camps all over South Asia, under spartan conditions and with dwindling hope of rescue. Considering its well-intentioned but ill-advised role in a war that consigned their homes and lives to destruction, the United States has a special responsibility to continue its help.

FOR ETHNIC and cultural reasons, it may be that many or most of these refugees wouldn't be happy in the United States. And despite Emma Lazarus and the Statue of Liberty, the United States in this century obviously can't hold its door wide to all the poor huddled masses from over the world.

But it is worth recalling that the ancestors of all but a few Americans came through that same open door. It ill behooves this country now either to slam it or to crack it grudgingly in the admission of more of these long-suffering people.

Indochinese Exodus Reaches Crisis Proportions

War between Vietnam and Cambodia and Hanoi's expulsion of ethnic Chinese made 1979 the climax of the Indochinese refugee problem. More than 26,000 reached asylum during the first two weeks of June alone, while unknown thousands perished at sea. The number of "boat people" piling up at temporary camps in Thailand, Malaysia, Indonesia, Hong Kong and the Philippines neared 400,000. Efforts to enlist Vietnam's aid in establishing an orderly emigration procedure failed because of Hanoi's unwillingness to acknowledge the refugees as anything other than a minority of malcontents.

Several international conferences were held over the problem, and the industrialized nations came under heavy pressure to accept more refugees. Burdened by their own sluggish economies, they were slow to respond. The first meeting was held in May in Jakarta, Indonesia and sponsored by the Association of Southeast Asian Nations (Indonesia, Malaysia, Philippines, Singapore and Thailand). Vietnam told the conferees that it would allow people to leave the country only if the West gave a definite commitment to accept them. Two more conferences were held in late June and early July by ASEAN and the Australia, New Zealand, U.S. Treaty Organization, which sought in vain to pressure Vietnam to halt the refugee outflow. The ASEAN countries categorically refused to accept more "boat people" and threatened to expel those who had already arrived unless other countries granted them permanent asylum. The ANZUS nations urged ASEAN to delay its threat and give the developed nations more time to prepare for the Indochinese refugees. Shortly before the conferences, the U.S. had doubled its Indochina refugee quota to 14,000 a month from 7,000. A number of other countries responded to the pressure from ASEAN by increasing their refugee admissions quotas for 1979. Canada announced that it would accept 50,000 until the end of 1980.

A two-day U.N. conference in Geneva late in July produced pledges of asylum for 266,000 more Indochinese. The conference was attended by 65 nations and raised $190 million for refugee aid. China made its first entry onto the international-aid stage by offering to relocate 10,000 ethnic Chinese from Vietnam and donating $1 million to the U.N. Japan, although furnishing 50% of the U.N. Indochinese refugee budget, steadfastly refused to accept more than a handful of Vietnamese.

Refugee arrivals throughout Southeast Asia fell off noticeably during the second half of 1979; still, many Indochinese failed to find even temporary asylum. Thousands of Cambodians remained in semi-permanent residence in Thai border camps, where they were prey to the Vietnamese army. By far the majority of the "boat people" wound up in the U.S., which had taken more than 250,000 since 1975. State health and welfare services, particularly in California, were strained to the limit by the sudden influx, and friction broke out between newly resettled Indochinese and local natives. The refugees were viewed everywhere as competitors for either jobs or social services.

THE KANSAS CITY STAR
Kansas City, Mo., May 7, 1979

One wonders what Americans would do if 250,000 white, Anglo-Saxon Christians risked their lives to flee an oppressive communist country only to be shunned by their free-world neighbors and forced into overcrowded camps or allowed to die at sea. We'd open our arms, that's what. We'd bring them into our homes, give them clothes, food and jobs.

But the 250,000 Vietnamese, Laotians and Cambodians involved in the exodus from the Indochina holocaust seem to be a different matter. When Saigon fell we took in a relatively small number of refugees to assuage our guilt over losing the war. Then we turned our backs even though an estimated 6,000 Vietnamese a month continued to flee their hostile government.

To be fair, neither America nor any other country can be expected to immediately absorb all these "boat people." But our efforts and the efforts of our Asian friends have been less than impressive. An agreement between Vietnam and the United Nations High Commissioner for Refugees attempting to control the refugee flow has been ineffectual. Talks scheduled for next month in Jakarta, Indonesia, do not promise a quick solution.

It is never said in so many words, of course, but the problem apparently is that the boat people simply are undesirables — the great majority are relatively poor and unskilled. If they had any money at all, it was used in bribing officials to let them out of their country.

But they do have what Americans say they value most — a desire to be free.

We have a Vietnamese-American friend, one of the lucky ones to escape before the fall of Saigon, who in the last 30 years has been forced to start his life three separate times: first as a young man in Hanoi, then as an anti-communist in Saigon and now as a restaurant employee at Crown Center. His English, although he speaks three other languages, is not yet good. His American-orientated skills are somewhat limited.

Even so, he and his family have set up a neat, clean apartment in the area of Rockhurst College. He is proud of his children — "A" and "B" students who speak the language "like No. 1 GIs."

If this man and his family are undesirables, we should have more undesirables.

DAILY NEWS
New York, N. Y., June 30, 1979

President Carter acted in accordance with the oldest of American traditions when he opened the nation's door to more of Vietnam's pitiful political refugees. The decision will allow 14,000 Vietnamese a month into the country, double the previous quota.

It is unfortunate that other free world leaders in Tokyo declined to make similar firm commitments for sheltering more Vietnamese. Japan, which has given permanent shelter to just three refugees, would only agree to take a maximum of 500 more—hardly a generous gesture for the richest nation in Asia.

However, it is to Carter's credit that he did not measure America's response to the plight of the Vietnamese by what other nations were willing to do. Throughout our history, the miserable and oppressed of the world have looked to the U.S. for asylum. We could not in good conscience turn our backs now on the flood of poor, desperate people fleeing Communist tyranny in Vietnam.

The Union Leader
Manchester, N. H., June 26, 1979

Man's inhumanity to man is evident on the world stage in the daily news reports coming out of Malaysia, from which country thousands on thousands of Vietnamese "boat people" are being towed out to sea in their boats and left to die. It's a horrible spectacle, and one gathers that if U.S. senators and congressmen had sizable Vietnamese constituencies in the United States, something would be done in short order to aid these unfortunate souls.

The blunt truth of the matter is that America has a prime responsibility for the plight of these men, women and children. It is we who abandoned them to the Communist tyranny from which they are fleeing. It is America that has the capacity to assimilate them, even if that means that the rest of us might have to eat slightly lower off the hog.

Chicago Tribune

Chicago, Ill., June 4, 1979

Of all the miseries inflicted on Southeast Asia's "boat people" the most shocking has been the refusal of some governments and ship's captains to give them refuge. When we read of crowded boats being towed back to sea by inhospitable authorities or of ships steaming straight past sinking boats, we wonder how any human being could behave so heartlessly. It is estimated that as many as 200,000 refugees have drowned or died of dehydration in recent years, often because nobody would accept them ashore or because, when sinking or disabled on the high seas, no ship would go to their rescue.

But responsibility for the deaths of those boat people and for the sufferings of many in crowded camps ashore lies not only with the government officials and sea captains involved. It lies also with our own U.S. Congress, which is doing too little, too late.

A bill authorizing a $105 million supplemental appropriation to assist the refugees became ensnarled in a budgetary muddle unrelated to the problem, and only now is beginning to make its tortuous way toward approval. Other legislation giving the President authority to permit increased numbers of refugees to enter the country has also been plagued with delays.

It is beyond understanding why Congress is so slow in dealing with the problem. No powerful lobbies are battling the bills; there are no delicate foreign policy considerations; the cost is not prohibitive.

On the contrary, most Americans feel a deep sympathy for the refugees and are eager to be of assistance. More U.S. aid would be a foreign policy boon since it would ease the pressures on Asian nations now caring for the refugees and would put us in a stronger position to urge other nations to join in the humanitarian effort. The cost, though not inconsequential, is barely a fraction of what we spend for pet food every year.

Meanwhile the need for action is urgent and growing more so by the day. The war between China and Viet Nam has led to a racist witch-hunt by the Vietnamese authorities directed against the ethnic Chinese in their midst. The Chinese are fleeing in every imaginable kind of boat, including some that are unsafe on inland rivers to say nothing of the treacherous South China Sea. Fighting and famine in Cambodia is producing still more refugees.

But there is almost no place left for them to go. Refugee camps in such countries as Malaysia and the Philippines are hopelessly overcrowded, so much so that the authorities are towing boat people back out to sea simply because there is no room for them. Hong Kong is reluctantly accepting many, but the crown colony is already densely populated and cannot absorb the 1,000 now arriving daily [not to mention another 800 or so crossing over from China every day].

There are those who argue that the U.S. cannot accept refugees because they will go on welfare or steal jobs. That is nonsense. Most are ethnic Chinese known throughout Asia for their industriousness—only a tiny fraction of those now in this country are on the welfare rolls and in the long run their genius for business will create jobs, not destroy them.

The little that Congress is now doing still is not enough. Present legislation is intended to deal with conditions that existed some months ago when the exodus was not as great. Now, more than 45,000 are r e a c h i n g neighboring countries every month; there is no way of knowing how many more drown, but there is concern that thousands more, hundreds of thousands more, could die if conditions continue as they are.

Those numbers represent young mothers watching their babies die of dehydration and whole families being towed to sea in boats that probably will sink. Congress must bestir itself. We must not let these people die.

Wisconsin ⚜ State Journal

Madison, Wisc., July 30, 1979

The tragedy of the Vietnamese "boat people" is a poignant reminder of the Jewish exodus from Europe after World War II.

Humanitarian peoples are anguished by the brutality of the Vietnamese government in oppressing a segment of its people, without obvious ways to counteract it.

Other Southeast Asian nations are reluctant to accept the fleeing Vietnamese. Most refugees are ethnic Chinese who are not easily absorbed by nearby nations, particularly the many in Southeast Asia that already have a surplus of people.

Because the United States played a big part — through the Vietnam War — in creating the situation that has led to the exodus, it is up to the United States to help solve the problem. And it is responding.

The solution is not entirely governmental, although President Carter has acted correctly in expanding the number of Vietnamese that can enter the United States to 14,000 monthly.

In Wisconsin, state Rep. Milton Lorman, R-Fort Atkinson, has taken the lead in developing a plan for placing the refugees.

Much of the placement will be through private agencies such as churches, which have taken the lead in raising money, guiding the refugees and helping them find places to live and work.

"We are a nation of immigrants, found by people fleeing from oppression," Lorman noted. "Wisconsin, as a state settled by immigrants, proves that this dream works."

Lorman deserves credit for organizing the refugee effort, obtaining the support of Gov. Lee Dreyfus and tapping the successful Iowa Refugee Service for ideas on how the state can supplement private efforts at settling refugees.

Des Moines Tribune

Des Moines, Iowa, July 27, 1979

Congress has shown courage and speed in responding to the crisis posed by the boat people of Indochina.

Only hours after the administration made the request, two House subcommittees voted to add $207 million to a foreign-aid appropriation bill to care for additional Indochinese refugees. President Carter recently said he hoped to double, to 14,000, the number of such refugees allowed into this country each month, and Gov. Robert D. Ray has said Iowa will take as many more as it can accommodate.

The congressional action was particularly commendable in light of evidence that many Americans object to the rising number of Indochinese refugees being admitted to the United States. A recent New York Times-CBS News poll found that 62 percent disapproved of admitting more refugees while 34 percent approved.

Some object for racist reasons. Others argue that this country has many urgent domestic problems that need to be faced before it tries to cope with admitting thousands of new immigrants.

The nation certainly has unmet needs, but it need not be an either/or proposition. A country that seems willing to spend more than $30 billion for a nuclear missile it doesn't need ought to be willing to spend a fraction of that amount for those who need help — be they Indochinese boat people in Iowa, black teen-agers in New York, or migrant farm workers in California.

For more than 200 years, this country's economy and culture have been enriched by immigrants. The people of Indochina are the latest to become a part of that tradition. Americans should welcome them.

Newsday

Long Island, N. Y., June 20, 1979

It was hard to imagine how the plight of the Vietnamese "boat people" could get any worse—until Malaysia warned last week that they would be shot on sight if any more of them tried to come ashore.

That threat has now been withdrawn, but countless boat people have already died at sea. And Malaysia may well be serious about shipping out the 70,000 refugees who are already there—unless other countries take them in soon. Thailand has sent thousands of Cambodians back across the border, into the thick of a war between their own brutal ex-rulers and the invading armies of Vietnam.

Most of the world would probably be very pleased if all of the Indochinese refugees could be resettled in Thailand or Malaysia or some other nearby country. But these are have-not nations themselves, ill equipped to take on additional economic burdens.

Many of the refugees are ethnic Chinese, and China claims to have taken in 200,000 of them. At least that many— mostly South Vietnamese—have come to the United States. According to President Carter's refugee coordinator, the governor of Iowa has complained: "We've got houses rented. We've got jobs waiting for these people. Why aren't you raising the number?"

The solution is to move the refugees quickly out of their temporary camps in Southeast Asia more quickly. That may require new camps in the countries of ultimate settlement. If it takes an international conference to set quotas, so be it.

But there's no time to waste. Every generation knows what the previous one should have done about its refugees. Who is not ashamed, in hindsight, of the world's feeble response to the Nazi persecutions nearly half a century ago? Will our own children be any prouder of our response to Indochina's holocaust?

The States-Item

New Orleans, La., July 24, 1979

It now seems clear that only direct efforts by the United States can save thousands of Vietnamese boat people from prolonged agony and possibly death at sea.

World opinion has forced some Southeast Asian and European nations to display a somewhat more generous attitude toward the desperate refugees, and the United Nations studied the problem at a gathering last weekend in Geneva, but concerted international efforts might come too late.

Some 57,000 refugees have found temporary relief in the Indonesian archipelago and elsewhere, but another 20,000 to 60,000 are adrift in creaky boats and with dwindling food supplies.

The Carter administration's proposal to use U.S. Naval ships and planes in a massive and dramatic rescue at sea appears to be the only hope for the homeless refugees. Such an effort not only would be consistent with President Carter's human rights policy and humanitarianism, it would be consistent with our nation's historical response to desperate peoples of other nations.

The dreadful plight of the refugees — set adrift by a brutal Communist dictatorship in Vietnam and rejected by other Southeast Asian governments — is a glaring reminder of the lack of caring for human life in some parts of the world. So far, no other nation has come close to making the effort the U.S. has made to relieve the suffering of the castoff Vietnamese.

As Americans, we are going through a trying period of self-doubt, but without question ours remains the most generous nation on earth.

It is a point to be remembered when the U.S. is the target of criticism by friendly European countries as well as Communist and Third World nations.

Without the U.S., thousands of Vietnamese refugees would simply perish at sea.

Detroit Free Press

Detroit, Mich., July 21, 1979

THEY OFTEN ARE the waiters who flash broad smiles when they enter your hotel room, happy to be wearing dry clothes and to be in a clean room. They are refugees. Boat people. Indochinese. Theirs is a mounting problem that only our best and most sensitive efforts can resolve.

The U.S. has already taken in 220,000 Indochinese, most of them Vietnamese. That is more than all the other nations of the world combined. President Carter has promised to raise the number of Indochinese admitted to the U.S. from 7,000 to 14,000 a month. We have a responsibility to do this, but it must be done humanely.

Though nearly all of these mostly ethnic Chinese refugees long to come here, they do not spread evenly throughout the country on arrival. About one-half settle on the West Coast, where large numbers of Asians already live. The 2,500 arriving in San Francisco each month have begun straining that city's health services to the snapping point.

According to public health officials, the refugees have "significantly higher rates" of leprosy, tuberculosis, and skin and intestinal parasites. Even so, leprosy is rare among the refugees and is not easily transmitted. Tuberculosis responds quickly to antibiotics, and parasites generally disappear when living conditions improve. But such health problems do underscore the need for the special screening clinics, financed by the federal government, now being instituted on the West Coast. We must better anticipate such problems, and prepare for them now.

There is, of course, no way the U.S. can absorb all of the world's refugees. There are 14 million refugees worldwide, uprooted from old homesites and searching for new ones. The U.S. must give greater aid to socalled countries of first asylum, relatively stable nearby countries that could absorb refugees. It must also apply diplomatic and economic pressures to countries such as Cambodia, where genocidal policies are creating hundreds of thousands of homeless people.

And despite a national energy crunch, inflation and unemployment, we must embrace thousands more of the dispossessed. They would probably smile even in long gas lines.

The Evening Gazette

Worcester, Mass., June 30, 1979

The Environmental Fund people are still sending out copies of their big newspaper ad, just as if they were proud of it.

For those who missed it the first time around, the ad makes several recommendations for national policy including: "We must lower our birth rate; STOP illegal immigration; balance immigration with emigration, and reform our foreign aid programs."

It was that "STOP illegal immigration" that got to us. Apparently the Environmental Fund folks think we should station the Army along the Rio Grande, ready to shoot any wetback who comes over from Mexico.

We wonder what the organization thinks about the pitiful hordes of refugees from Vietnam and Cambodia who are trying to find some place to survive? Has President Carter committed an environmental crime in offering them haven? Are we to turn our backs on them, letting them die in their stinking, sinking boats?

So far we have accepted about 240,000 of them. Other countries have accepted about 100,000 more. But there are still more than 300,000 waiting in festering camps in Malaysia, Hong Kong, Indonesia and elsewhere. No one wants them. Japan has accepted three. That's right — three. Not 3,000.

The world has a choice. The United States has a choice. We can adopt the policy apparently favored by the Environmental Fund which is to let surplus people die.

Or we can stand true to our heritage and once again be the "last, best hope" of people who have no other hope. And we can encourage other nations to do likewise, as Carter is trying to do.

The Environmental Fund can take any stand it wants, but this particular position paper seems far out, to say the least.

The Birmingham News

Birmingham, Ala., July 29, 1979

At a time when many Americans seem to be doing some soul searching about whether their nation is truly one of the world's "good guys," one piece of evidence that should not be ignored is the operation now taking place in the South China Sea.

There, the U.S. Seventh Fleet, a mighty military force, is being used for a most important humanitarian purpose — helping thousands of innocent refugees who have been cast out of their homelands and sent to sea in floating death traps.

Four more ships were recently ordered into the area to help search for the floating victims of what some have called the second holocaust, other ships have been diverted from their regular routes for the hunt and long-range search planes are being dispatched daily to hunt and help the boat people.

Almost at the same time news leaked out that the Vietnamese had massacred 85 of those pathetic, suffering victims who have committed no crime against anyone, it was announced that the U.S. and other participants in a recent international conference had pledged to resettle 260,000 of the estimated 400,000 refugees now in Southeast Asia alone. They also promised $190 million to fund the effort.

In addition, the U.S. is trying earnestly to regularize the flow of refugees out of Vietnam and to reunite some 5,500 Vietnamese, currently living in Vietnam, with their relatives who have already fled to the U.S. So far, however, the Vietnamese government has allowed only 29 such people to emigrate.

In this pathetic tragedy, if the choice is between the U.S. and the callous, apparently shameless, leaders of Vietnam, there can be no doubt at all about who the "good guys" are.

THE ATLANTA CONSTITUTION

Atlanta, Ga., August 24, 1979

President Carter, during a "town meeting" at Burlington, Iowa, was asked a somewhat hostile question about his decision for the U.S. to accept 220,000 of the Vietnamese boat people. The president's answer was perfect.

"How many people here have ancestors who were native Americans?" he asked. "I see two or three hands back there whose parents were Indians."

Then, Carter added, "Whether your parents came here 300 years ago, or whether your parents came here one generation ago, or whether you've only been here a few months, the United States has always been a nation with an open heart and with open arms . . ."

The U.S. is the great nation it is because its people are so diverse, because we have always accepted immigrants by the hundreds of thousands. Unless you are 100 percent American Indian, there is immigrant blood flowing in your veins — the life-giving legacy of someone who came from "over there" within the past four centuries.

Unfortunately, a good number of Americans forget this — and always have. Over the years, there has been opposition to various waves of immigrants. But those immigrants have always, given time, merged into American humanity. The nation has always absorbed them, and then prospered even more.

The same will hold true for the Vietnamese. Many Vietnamese refugees are already here, having fled communism when the war ended. The merger into American life has been rather easy for some, difficult for others. But they're coping and, despite some problems, they're mostly succeeding.

As always when two cultures meet, there are misunderstandings — and adjustments have to be made. There have been, for example, problems with Vietnamese who took up fishing as a livelihood in the U.S. "Their" traditions of fishing and "our" traditions of fishing have collided, but the problems are being met and answers found.

Of course, America should accept the boat people, as many of them as possible. Otherwise, we would not be America.

The Charlotte Observer

Charlotte, N. C., August 3, 1979

The United States is a nation built on the strength and industry of immigrants. But as the country has matured Americans have been less willing to keep our shores open to others. Our sluggishness in admitting Jews fleeing from Hitler is a stain on our history. Our hostility to non-Caucasians was evident in our law banning Chinese immigrants from 1882 to 1943.

Against that background, the lukewarm welcome many Americans have given the Vietnam refugees is not surprising. But President Carter's policy is morally and politically right: We must help these desperate people.

Why help them, when we have problems of our own to solve?

Look at it this way: In the last decade, the world has witnessed — sometimes live on television — the acts of terrorist kidnapers. These terrorists, some of them with legitimate grievances, decide to seize and threaten innocent hostages until their demands are met.

Civilized people abhor such actions. Yet those are essentially the tactics a few Americans advocate in response to the desperate plight of Indochinese refugees. Do not let that rabble into this country, they say, until *our* demands have been met.

Thank God such people are few, for they are terrorists: Though they brandish no guns, they would help themselves at the risk of innocent people's lives.

Many Americans do have legitimate needs that remain unmet — health care, housing, education, employment. But meeting all the needs of everyone here should not be a precondition for rescuing Indochinese refugees.

Indochina's refugees aren't at sea on a whim. They set out in crowded, leaky boats because they believed that only death or a life not worth living was in store for them in Indochina. That matter of life or death pushed them into their desperate voyage without a destination.

The United States has agreed to help some of them. Jimmy Carter has pledged to step up those admitted to 14,000 a month from 7,000. The increased stream in the months ahead will seem all the more threatening to this country's own needy in the months ahead.

That dilemma can't be swept aside. The refugees will compete for housing and jobs and attention in an economy pinched by inflation and recession. Many, if not all, of them will need a share of the limited public assistance for the needy.

Yet would even the poorest of Americans be willing take a seat on one of those crowded boats? Of course not. We must offer the refugees a safe harbor. To do otherwise would betray everything this country stands for.

SAN JOSE NEWS

San Jose, Calif., August 3, 1979

ALL this week, readers of the Mercury and News have been introduced, intimately and extensively, to the "boat people." If compassion and self-interest still animate Americans, the acquaintance should ripen into an enduring relationship.

Staff writer John Askins and photography director J. Bruce Baumann went to Southeast Asia to meet and try to understand the Vietnamese refugees. What manner of men and women uproot themselves and their children, often paying their government in gold for the privilege of risking rape and plunder by pirates and drowning in the South China Sea?

Askins and Baumann took the measure of these exiles, many of them ethnic Chinese, in transit refugee camps in Hong Kong, on Pulau Bidong island off the Malaysian coast and in the Malaysian capital of Kuala Lumpur.

For more than a week, the journalists met, talked with and photographed some of the estimated 370,000 refugees and displaced persons that are adrift today in Southeast Asia. Askins and Baumann found courage, determination, patience, energy, intelligence and a touching faith in the essential goodness of man.

They found, in short, a testimonial to the human spirit.

The boat people are the newest of the world's dispossessed. They have been driven from their homes for a variety of political, racial and economic reasons. They challenge our conscience.

Here and there the challenge is being taken up. The U.S. government has pledged to admit 14,000 a month; together the industrialized nations pledged at Geneva last month to make room for 260,000 Indochinese refugees.

Americans, individually and in nongovernmental groups, are helping; the Los Gatos Christian Church, for example, has raised $23,000 to help refugees in transit camps. The church hopes to raise more. Other individuals and groups are volunteering to sponsor the resettlement of refugee families here.

That is good. The effort, individual as well as governmental, should be sustained. It is not only a matter of charity; it is also a matter of recognizing exceptionally valuable human potential.

A survey of changing immigration patterns, as reported in the Christian Science Monitor, found the new Vietnamese-Americans contributing fully — and quickly — to their new country. Of the 130,000 Vietnamese who were admitted to this country in 1975, after the collapse of South Vietnam, more than 90 percent are employed and most of the rest are in school, according to the report.

Askins, in his final report today, hypothesizes the life awaiting Van De Ty, a 32-year-old former coffee grower, his wife and son when they finally arrive in San Jose:

"They would live on welfare for about a year, maybe with relatives, maybe in a cheap apartment where they would be model tenants, learning American ways and the American language . . . And Van would find a job . . . electronics, perhaps . . . He would do well. He would work harder and longer than those whom life had not set so far behind. He would labor without talking, and he might irritate his American colleagues by his reluctance to observe breaks and mealtimes and quitting times. He would get a second-hand car and start saving for a house, He would pay back the $1,900 or so it had cost to fly his family to America."

Sounds familiar, doesn't it? America was built by such immigrants. We still need them.

Bring on the boat people.

The Idaho STATESMAN

Boise, Idaho, July 2, 1979

The world is experiencing a forced human exodus unparalleled for its toll in suffering and death since the Holocaust. Yet the best the seven leading industrialized nations of the western world can come up with is a vague statement urging Vietnam and other Indochinese countries to "take urgent and effective measures so that the present human hardship and suffering are eliminated." How selfishly, miserably inadequate that response.

Only one of those seven nations — the United States — did more. President Carter announced the United States would double its admission of refugees from 7,000 to 14,000 a month. Good for the United States and its president.

But the problem is too big, the suffering too great to be relieved by one nation's entrance quotas. The question is not just where to resettle the refugees; it also involves saving them from the ravages of the seas and caring for them while they await resettlement.

U.N. Secretary General Kurt Waldheim has called an international conference on the refugee problem for July 20. Waldheim is worried the conference will degenerate into a name-calling confrontation. We share his concern. At the very least the conference will not convene for another three weeks, and whatever solutions it arrives at will take more weeks to institute. We hope for a good outcome, but must wonder what will happen to thousands of refugees in the meantime.

Malaysia in the past two weeks has forced 15,000 persons in 77 ships out to sea. Malaysian authorities say they will not accept any more refugees until United Nations refugee camps are established in other nations. Of the 15,000 persons refused sanctuary to date, many certainly will die.

Indonesia and other Southeast Asian nations likewise are mounting a naval blockade to keep refugees from landing.

Thailand has forcibly repatriated 45,000 Cambodian refugees, which in effect is like sentencing many of them to death.

Estimates of the number of refugees who die at sea range from 20 to 50 percent. The emphasis on resettling those who reach Malaysia or other points will do nothing to help these poor souls.

The point is that something must be done immediately. After festering so many months, the refugee problem has come to the point of catastrophy. July 20 and polite talks in Geneva will be too late and too little for many suffering men, women and children.

The United States, it appears, must step into the breach alone. So be it. Let there be no repeat of the sad U.S. performance during the Holocaust when Jews were denied admission to the United States and shunted from place to place.

The Carter administration should seek immediate U.N. sanctions for temporary refugee camps on Guam and other American-controlled places in the Asian region.

Further, the first residents of these camps should be some of those now living in squalor on the island of Pulau Bidong. This would relieve crowding on that island and make it easier for U.N. officials to improve the sanitation. Such a move also should encourage the Malaysian government to accept more refugees.

Second, the United States should airlift from Thailand to refugee camps elsewhere a good number of Cambodian refugees, thus relieving the pressure on Thailand and hopefully forestalling more forced repatriations.

Moreover, the United States should enlist its Navy to intercept boat people early on their exodus from Vietnam to reduce the suffering of long boat journeys and ensure that fewer people fall victim to the sea.

There is an obvious danger in all of this: U.S. action would relieve pressure on the nations meeting in Geneva. That is a gamble, however, that we must take. Pressure, in the form of dead and dying human beings, is something we do not need on our conscience. We have the resources to relieve the suffering and the humanitarian tradition that suggests we must do it.

Chicago Defender

Chicago, Ill., July 11, 1979

Echoes of the post-World War II period are upon us. This time, they are primarily coming out of Southeast Asia where we are hearing of "boat people," refugees by the thousands looking for refuge somewhere in the world. All of it seems somehow a hangover from the sad Viet Nam war.

The entire region of Communist Indochina seems dominated by the inordinate exodus of hundreds of thousands of people without homes. Already more than 300,000 refugees are in Southeast Asian camps. Thousands of others are living on beaches. Two countries, Thailand and Malaysia, have taken harsh countermeasures against the refugees.

The United States already has taken in more than 200,000 refugees since 1975 and has agreed to take in another 50,000 this year.

This influx of Asians is viewed here by many as a complication of the problem that millions of people born here already have. It will add to the competitions in industry for thousands who already face a major problem of employment.

And yet, can this country — can any country that is in general "better off" than the harried nations of Indochina — fail to heed such an emergency, such a call for help from hundreds of thousands in such a plight?

Can we afford to repeat the errors of World War II? It seems to us that we cannot, and that this country must do all that it can to help the plight of people anywhere and everywhere. That is what is meant by a concern for human rights.

And as for those of us at home who have little or less than what we should have or think we should have, it is for us to utilize all the agencies of a relatively free society to make all the progress that is possible.

The Philadelphia Inquirer

Philadelphia, Pa., July 2, 1979

The decision to double the number of Indochinese refugees the U.S. accepts every month for a year is a humane response to the displaced Asians' desperate plight. It should mean some relief for the thousands of persons who have fled or been expelled from Vietnam and Cambodia and are languishing in bleak, makeshift camps or making their bid for freedom on rickety boats in unfriendly Southeast Asian waters.

The U.S. action alone will come nowhere near to relieving the problem, however. Much more needs to be done. It can be hoped that other countries at the Tokyo summit, where the American decision was announced, will soon announce specific commitments to take in more refugees and to contribute more money to the international resettlement effort coordinated through the United Nations. A general commitment to do so was made by the seven nations represented at the summit — Japan, Canada, Britain, France, West Germany and Italy — as well as the U.S. President Carter did well to disclose specific U.S. commitments within two hours after announcement of the general agreement; his action should serve as an example.

Another action taken at the Tokyo summit has the potential for directing more world attention toward the refugee problem and bringing more world resources to bear on solving it: The Tokyo delegates called for a U.N. conference on the refugees' plight.

Such a conference is expected to be convened in Geneva within a few weeks. It will concentrate on the humanitarian aspects of the refugee situation rather than its political origins, although some countries, most notably China, which is at odds politically with Vietnam, have called for a conference on the political aspects of the problem. The humanitarian side of the refugee situation is crucial enough, and rightfully demanding of solution, that a conference designed simply to rescue more human beings from boats, without the need to pass all kinds of resolutions of blame and political resposibility, is well worth doing.

Under the plan announced by President Carter, the number of Indochinese refugees admitted to the U.S. will go up from 7,000 monthly to 14,000, probably starting in the fall.

The U.S. has fallen a couple of thousand short of even its 7,000-person quota in recent months because the Congress has been slow to approve funds for refugees' relocation. Plans to increase the intake of refugees in the next few months to make up for that should be implemented; and Congress should see to it that money — an estimated additional $150 million a year — is made available to make good on Mr. Carter's promise in Tokyo.

For the U.S. to do anything less would be for this country to tarnish one of its finest traditions — that of being a haven for homeless people "yearning to be free."

The Sun Reporter

San Francisco, Calif., July 12, 1979

The refugee problem haunts the world. Despite the lowly status which Blacks continue to occupy as the base of the American democratico-capitalist societal pyramid, Blacks, who know suffering, reach out to these homeless people wandering the world's seas.

However, bitter experience tells us that the new wave of Asian refugees will be but one added burden placed on the heads, the backs and the broken bodies of Black America. The Cuban refugees in Florida, have created the third tier resting on the backs of Florida Blacks: white upper class and middle class, poor whites, Cuban exiles and Blacks. The "freedom fighter" of Hungary, after several years in the U.S.A. became the most vocal apostles of the myth of white supremacy.

Can the refugees from Vietnam be of any different ilk? Do they not represent the upper middle class persons who contributed much to the hoped-for defeat of the national liberation forces of North Vietnam, assisting the barbarous regimes of Diem, Ky and Thieu, as well as the U.S. military forces? Their Vietnamese predecessors have not been kindly disposed to assisting in the national struggle against racism, sexism and classism, the U.S.A's three scourges. Millions of illegal Mexican aliens in the Southwest these Asian refugees will deepen the economic crisis suffered by Blacks with whom they compete in the blue collar job market.

Yes, human life anywhere in the world is precious; but can any living body wandering the face of the world be any more precious than those native Americans who wander from one job to another, and wonder where the money will come from to pay for housing, food, clothing and medical care? Can the U.S. government in good conscience allow 14,000 Vietnamese refugees to come to America each month with guaranteed jobs provided by their sponsors, while not providing guaranteed jobs for the millions of Americans who are unemployed through no fault of their own? Humanism must be practiced at home with the natives sharing in America's bounties.

The Washington Star

Washington, D. C., July 2, 1979

As horror story followed horror story out of Southeast Asia, there seemed to be no ceiling on either the numbers of fleeing "boat people" or their misery. Now, however, with President Carter's announcement that the United States will double — to 14,000 — the total this country takes in each month, the tragic tide may be turning.

We still don't know how many more will escape or be driven out of Vietnam, Laos and Cambodia, and we are far from knowing how to solve all the problems of resettling them, but the president's bold gesture in Tokyo promises to mobilize international effort in their direction as it has not been mobilized thus far. Although the global refugee situation is worse than at any time since World War II, countries not directly touched by it have been slow to respond.

The United Nations is spending $30 million a month provisioning the camps in Hong Kong, Thailand, Singapore, Malaysia and Indonesia where some 325,000 people wait for the opportunity to start over in a new country. Except in comparison to the overcrowded and leaky boats that bring the refugees there, the camps are grim places where disease and hunger threaten and where the fight to stay alive may involve black marketeering and smuggling as well as scrounging to earn small sums at legitimate work.

The countries where the camps are all have large populations, fragile economies and political systems that are, at best, precariously balanced. In several of them, historic antipathies to the Chinese add to the reluctance of the temporary hospitality.

Many of the more distant nations that might receive the boat people on a longer-term basis can cite similar reasons for not doing so. And even those who can't have been finding excuses. Up to this point, only the United States, France, Australia and Canada have actually absorbed many of the boat people. However, President Carter's pledge, dramatizing the acuteness of the problem, has prompted Sweden, Israel, Japan and New Zealand, among others, to raise the numbers of refugees they will accommodate to a few hundred or a few thousand.

Overall, since World War II, the United States has admitted 1.9 million refugees as permanent residents. Thirty-two thousand Hungarians came in after the 1956 uprising. Since Fidel Castro took power, 260,000 Cubans have come in. There have also been some 28,500 Soviet and Eastern European refugees admitted along with the 250,000 Indochinese brought here in the last five years.

As the influx has swelled, the American government has tried to arrive at policies that would soften the abrasions of transition for all concerned. There has been an effort to distribute the Indochinese throughout the United States rather than to allow the buildup of such ethnic enclaves as the Cuban colonies of Florida.

Fate rather than policy dictated that the first wave of Vietnamese to relocate in the United States was made up of people most of whom were sufficiently educated, able and hard-working that they could put down new roots with relative ease. They, in turn, have been able to help the less skilled who came after them.

Transplanting these people to so alien an environment is still a tortuous and expensive process. Even after decisions have been made and money has been allocated, it takes time and art to re-establish the refugees. Happily, though, there appears to be a strong consensus behind the effort. Between the Sixties war protesters who think the boat people owe their plight to American support of the Thieu government, and Vietnam hawks who consider the boat people victims of communism, just about everybody would be impelled to help, even if these people's obvious suffering did not arouse the compassion it does.

THE DAILY HERALD

Biloxi, Miss.,
September 7, 1979

One of America's proudest traditions--the abundant capacity of our people to welcome "huddled masses yearning to breathe free"--is again being tested, this time in Biloxi and along the Mississippi Gulf Coast.

The tradition has been scarred whenever earlier immigrants were unable to cope effectively with the changes inherent in the process of assimilating later arrivals.

As each group of immigrants came, fleeing their native countries in search of surcease from the tempests that tossed them about, they have had to struggle. Struggle to begin new lives. Struggle to adapt to strange customs, to bewildering language barriers, to alien social mores, and to mazes of laws and regulations.

These struggles have sometimes been exacerbated by hostilities from earlier immigrants, those who had already substantially completed the assimilation process and sensed, or felt, the realization of their own dreams was somehow threatened by the newcomers.

The struggles have also been eased when the newcomers have been assisted by those who have been willing to share America's opportunities.

As Assistant City Editor Billy Ray Quave points out in *The Daily Herald's* series, New Ripple of Immigrants, the historical patterns are repeating themselves in our community.

Some reluctance to welcome the Vietnamese into our community has surfaced and seems to center in the fishing industry, where many Vietnamese are now working.

Problems invariably arise when newcomers move into a community. The assimilation process calls for a period of adjustment, both for the newer residents and for those whose roots are more firmly established.

These are best solved with generous measures of common sense, healthy doses of good neighborliness, avoiding prejudice, refraining from circulating baseless rumors that cause harm and incite emotions, sympathetic understanding of the plight of others and extensions of helping hands. These will help dissipate the problems.

Biloxi and Gulf Coast residents should recall our country's commitment to lift Liberty's lamp beside the golden door and rededicate ourselves to upholding America's proud tradition of sharing freedom's opportunities.

THE LOUISVILLE TIMES
Louisville, Ky., July 5, 1979

"Boat people" and the other refugees streaming out of Vietnam, Cambodia and Laos were the subject of talks by world leaders last weekend. Unfortunately, only the United States was forthcoming with major new assistance for them.

Of all the people who have fled political oppression in Indochina, about half, or more than 325,000, are now crowded into temporary camps in neighboring countries, waiting desperately for some country to offer them permanent homes.

But the patience of their seriously overburdened hosts is wearing thin. Recently Thailand forced 45,000 back into Cambodia, at gunpoint. Malaysia has put 57,000 boat people back to sea this year — about half will not live to set foot on land again. Last week the five countries which have received the bulk of the refugees said they will let no more in, and may send them back to their homelands unless other countries take them.

While such actions seem cruel at first glance, nothing else has gotten other nations to do much. Only five countries have accepted any appreciable numbers of refugees for resettlement — the United States, Canada, France, Australia and China. At last count Japan, the economic giant of Asia, had taken in six Vietnamese refugees and reluctantly offered to accept 500 more, pleading lack of space, traditional Japanese hostility toward outsiders and the difficulty of learning the Japanese language and customs. At least Japan did offer money for refugee services, which is more than other countries have done.

Refugees are not a new world phenomenon. Many countries, including the United States, were largely settled by people fleeing their native lands. It has only been in this century, though, that they have had so much travail, first in leaving their homelands, then in gaining admittance elsewhere.

Millions made homeless by two world wars and myriad other political upheavals have been resettled. Yet these activities have always been difficult because governments must volunteer money and places for refugees.

Early this year the United Nations raised its refugee budget by 30 per cent, but cannot find anybody to contribute most of it. United Nations support to countries which maintain refugee camps is often less than $1 per person per day.

And now, as before, the refugees are desperately waiting. To our credit, the United States is providing the lion's share. We have taken in 215,000 already, more than two-thirds of the Indochinese refugees who have been resettled. President Carter last week doubled our emergency quota to 14,000 a month.

We can probably take in many more. One of our nation's great strengths, and one of our blessings, too, has always been our willingness and ability to absorb immigrants. But we shouldn't have to carry the entire load. Asian countries could well afford to help, but haven't — Japan, Taiwan and South Korea, for starters. Great Britain, West Germany, Scandinavia, Latin America all have remained oblivious.

U. N. Secretary General Waldheim will convene an international conference on refugees in Geneva on July 20. We must fervently hope that other nations can be prodded, persuaded or shamed into sharing the burden. When Europe was torn by war twice in this century the rest of the world helped take in her homeless. This seems a fine time for that continent, now enjoying peace and prosperity, to do something in return.

Perhaps the U. N. conference can ease the refugee crisis in Southeast Asia and set up a system to cope with other crises from other wars. Almost 60 years ago the League of Nations took on the problem of World War I refugees, under the inspired leadership of Fridtjof Nansen, the great Arctic explorer turned statesman. His success won him the Nobel Peace Prize. A similar honor would be appropriate for anybody who can repeat his accomplishments.

CHARLESTON EVENING POST
Charleston, S. C., August 6, 1979

President Carter's order to the U.S. Navy directing it to assist in the rescue of the Vietnamese boat people is, if anything, long overdue. Those lost at sea, the shipwrecked, have always been the proper concern of mariners, if for no other reason than "There, but for the grace of God, go I."

Navy Regulations indeed require ship commanding officers to render assistance to those in distress at sea. If these regulations have been modified in any way by the enormity of the situation created by the Democratic Republic of Vietnam's expulsion of its ethnic Chinese population, we are unaware of it. Mr. Carter's order, apparently, simply means that rescue of the boat people by the Navy no longer will depend on chance encounter, and that a formal search and rescue operation is now or soon will be underway.

This will not be the first such operation by the Navy in Vietnamese waters. A little history: Twenty-five years ago, after the French defeat at Dienbienphu, a military demarcation line was established near the 17th parallel in Vietnam. A period of 300 days was set aside for the phased withdrawal of Viet Minh and French military forces to the north and south of that line respectively. During this same period, civilians residing in either zone were to be allowed complete freedom to move to the other zone.

In the north, warnings were scrawled on the walls of public buildings, urging the populace to flee in advance of the Viet Minh Army. The Roman Catholic Church advised its adherents to abandon ancestral homes and fields and seek sanctuary in the south. The streets of the two principal evacuation centers, Hanoi and Haiphong, were soon choked with masses of desperate people. Public services broke down in the crush. Personal possessions representing the savings of a lifetime were hawked fruitlessly from door to door.

French transport alone could not cope with the staggering demands placed upon it, and the assistance of the U.S. government was requested. Within three months, more than 100 U.S. Navy and MSTS ships and craft were ferrying refugees to the south. The operation was code named "Passage to Freedom," and when it ended in May, 1955, the Navy had evacuated some 310,000 people. Even more had made their way overland. In all, an estimated 800,000 fled the communist North.

Many of those evacuated by the Navy, no doubt — those who survived the years of horror that still lay ahead — are refugees again, but this time with no certain haven in sight.

Since the end of the Vietnam War, more than 550,000 refugees from Indochina have been resettled. Three countries — the United States, France and China — have taken 500,000 of them. Despite this, unwelcome hundreds of thousands still crowd refugee camps in Southeast Asia, with who knows how many more hundreds of thousands still to come.

The expulsion of the boat people is a major tragedy, ranking with the Holocaust in terms of man's inhumanity to man. Thus far, the American people have been generous in welcoming to these shores their share of the refugees and more. The refugees themselves, despite language and cultural differences, have compiled an enviable record as good and productive citizens.

America cannot, however, continue forever an open door policy in respect to the distressed and the poor of this world. As the recession looming ahead inevitably deepens, resentment of the new immigrants by the old, in this nation of immigrants, will surely grow. Their very success will be held against them, their jobs coveted by those who have no jobs. It is as predictable as tomorrow's sun, and as depressing as man's selfish nature — even in our own America.

Post-Tribune
Guarding Your Interests Daily

Gary, Indiana, June 24, 1979

Malaysia isn't going to be as tough on the Vietnamese "boat people" as it first sounded. That's good.

However, unless other nations begin to look with more pity on one of this decade's more poignant problems, Malaysia may get tough again. That would be bad.

What Malaysian Prime Minister Hussein Om first threatened was to send those who had fled the tyrannies of the Vietnamese government and landed on his shores back to sea in their leaky crafts. Others trying to land were warned they would face "shoot-to-kill" orders.

Some perceptive reporters interpreted the first warning as an attempt to call the pitiable plight of the Vietnamese refugees to wider world attention. The Malaysian chief's subsequent remarks indicate that interpretation was fairly accurate. True, some have since been turned back to sea, but those were newcomers, not the earlier refugees.

Still, Hussein further qualified his more recent remarks by saying he would expel those currently on his shores only if other nations refused to accept them in considerable numbers.

The United States has thus far done better than most in offering haven to some of the refugees. It probably should. It was to some extent a combination of its involvement in the Vietnamese War when that land was two nations and then its eventual withdrawal from the conflict that did much to precipitate the problem.

Yet neither Malaysia, because of its proximity, nor the United States, because of its culpability, can be expected to carry the whole load. People seeking asylum from tyranny in the land of their birth constitute a world problem.

We hope the rest of the world, like Malaysia, can find it in its collective conscience to soften the calloused attitude with which it has failed to face up to the problem to date.

Detroit Free Press

Detroit, Mich., July 8, 1979

NOBODY KNOWS how many boat people there have been in the last four years. They have gone down in the monsoons. They have starved and thirsted to death. They have been machine-gunned.

In Tokyo this week President Carter promised to raise the number of Indo-Chinese admitted to the United States to 14,000 monthly, from the present 7,000.

That's not going to be enough. There are 42,000 boat people cooped up on the island of Pulau Bidong alone, in an area the size of two city blocks.

Vietnam is already beginning to evict 1.1 million ethnic Chinese. Thailand has 40,000 Cambodians in temporary residence, but has begun escorting them back at gun point to grim fates in their onetime homeland.

Thousands of men, women and children are clumped around the impoverished nations bordering on Cambodia and Vietnam. The agony is beginning to approach that of the World War II Holocaust.

The world, and the United States with it, cannot turn away from this suffering. It will be difficult, but those fleeing for their lives must be given sanctuary. Those who choose freedom must be given it.

The responsibility of the United States goes beyond the mess we created by intervening in Vietnam and bombing Cambodia.

We have prided ourselves for decades for raising the lamp beside the golden door to guide huddled masses yearning to breathe free to our shores.

It is not as simple it was in the days when we had vast areas of undeveloped land to absorb the Irish and the Scandinavians and the Poles and the Italians and all the rest.

We are hard pressed to deal with the tide of legal immigration from Puerto Rico and illegal immigration from Mexico. Many of the newcomers burden our job market and our welfare system.

We have taken in 220,000 Indo-Chinese, mostly Vietnamese, more than all the other countries combined. Japan, with its crowded islands, has taken in only three.

We should not have to do it alone. This is a human responsibility, and every civilized country should be appalled, and help.

But we are the richest and most powerful large nation in the world, and have been the most proud to be able to share our good fortune. We have not come to the end of our resources to do this.

We must answer the cry for help. Oh, the empty eyes of the children of the boat people.

The Salt Lake Tribune

Salt Lake City, Utah, July 5, 1979

Since the Vietnam war the United States has accepted some 215,000 Indochinese refugees. Of the world's industrialized nations receiving Indochinese refugees, the United States takes about 70 percent.

Now President Carter will double that rate of acceptance, on a monthly basis. For the next 12 months the United States' intake of refugees from Indochina will be 14,000 a month, instead of the present 7,000.

That doubling means that by next July 168,000 more Indochinese, primarily Vietnamese, will have immigrated to the United States. That, in one year, will be about 78 percent of the number of Vietnamese who have already settled in this country since the Vietnam war ended four years ago.

President Carter has initiated this acceleration of America's acceptance of Indochinese refugees, as one U.S. official put it, in the hope "our actions would serve as the impetus or stimulus for similar actions on the part of others."

There is desperate need for "similar actions on the part of others." Since 1975, driven by war, hunger and oppression, more than 700,000 people have streamed out of Indochina.

America has done, or will have done, more than its share to rescue these people. By July of next year some 383,000 of these homeless and desperate men, women and children will have been received here. That is 54 percent of all the people who have fled the cruelties of life in Indochina.

If a single nation, the United States can absorb more than half these people, providing them the opportunity to live in freedom and security, there seems little excuse why the rest of the world's industrialized nations can't assume the remaining 46 percent of humanity's obligation to rescue these refugees from the squalor, danger and misery they now endure.

THE DAILY OKLAHOMAN

Oklahoma City, Okla., July 3, 1979

IN a surprise exercise of his power under existing laws, President Carter says he will immediately increase the number of Southeast Asian refugees accepted for resettlement in the United States from 7,000 to 14,000 per month.

It is contingent upon Congress providing another $150 million a year to finance their resettlement, and humanitarian and church agency groups already are calling for quick approval. But there is growing resentment and uncertainty in this country about the long-range consequences of taking in more of the world's unwanted.

The administration's program, as presented to Congress recently, calls for admission of 120,000 refugees a year above the normal immigration quota of 290,000. The expectation has been that this would permit acceptance of 36,000 a year from the Soviet Union and East Europe — most of them Soviet

Jews who exit their homeland with visas for emigration to Israel — and 7,000 a month from Southeast Asia.

Thus the Southeast Asia quota was already planned to be 84,000 out of a total from everywhere of only 120,000, in refugee status. It is not clear whether the additional numbers Carter proposes to accept will be added to the total or shifted from other countries of origin.

Carter's statement in Tokyo called on all other countries with respect for human life to take similar action. Especially in the Asian nations which might provide a more familiar environment for the Indochinese, that call may fall on deaf ears.

The Asian refugees face ethnic prejudices which are hard to understand in this country, where minority groups complain about the lack of equal opportunity but seldom claim they are actually hated or abused. In Asia, hatred of those who are different — although the actual differences are not always apparent to those of European origin — is common.

It feeds on economic fears and on the fact that, in many of the nations once part of the colonial systems of Europe, ethnic Chinese — the "overseas Chinese" — have been the energetic merchants, factory owners, bankers and other prospering engines of the local economies. Their success has generated envy.

Malaysia, when it became an independent federation, was especially fearful of its Chinese population. That was one reason for the breakaway of prosperous Singapore, now a self-ruled city-state. Australia only accepted Oriental races as immigrants in very recent times. And some of the other nations of Asia are unable to provide for their own people now.

Canada, Latin America and Australia seem to offer the best prospects for acceptance of the boat people and other refugees from that region today. But their lot will not be an easy one. Even those in this country several years report unhappiness, homesickness for Asian ways, and difficulty in making adjustments.

What is clear, however, is that the United States cannot be expected to do any more than it's already done. The scope of the boat people saga — with refugees being expelled or escaping from Vietnam at the rate of 60,000 a month — is beyond the ability of unilateral government action.

Cooperative sharing of the problem, with more than just a few countries assuming any of the burden, should be demanded by U.S. spokesmen at the forthcoming U.N. conference in Geneva.

The Sun

Vancouver, B. C., July 28, 1979

You don't have to be a whiz with figures or even terribly perceptive to realize that this community of ours is torn and troubled.

You have only to read the letters to the editor on the subject of the boat people.

The volume is tremendous, the message contained in 80 per cent of The Vancouver Sun's mail clear: We don't want the refugees.

Frankly, we find it disturbing that so many people, fine upstanding citizens all, should be so tortured and tormented by what the other 20 per cent see as a simple moral duty

But that is their dilemma and their right. We prefer to believe that these percentages do not extend through the population and that the first government planeload of Vietnamese refugees to reach Vancouver will be made as welcome as the last immigrant who passed through citizenship court.

The only difference in the two categories is that one has a choice. The boat people have none. They didn't ask to be uprooted from their homeland; they were cast out.

It doesn't do any good, either, to cast around for scapegoats or to wish that somehow the refugees would all go away. They won't go away because they can't —

unless countries like Canada give them a hand. And even then, what is 50,000 out of the hundreds of thousands crammed into the primitive camps of Southeast Asia and being forced to take their chances on the South China Sea?

The problem is bigger than any one country or possibly any combination of countries, but that, surely, is no reason to be negative.

What, we wonder, would be the reaction of the majority of our letter writers if the government suddenly decided it didn't like the color of their skin or their politics and cut them adrift?

We wouldn't wish it on them any more than they would wish it on themselves but the moral issue is the same: Do we ignore them? Pretend that they don't exist? Hope that they'll go away to some distant shore, not caring whether they sink or swim?

Our obligation is clear, even though our commitment seems still to be clouded.

Of the 201 refugees airlifted to Canada yesterday, 34 are destined for points in B.C. Twenty-nine of these are unsponsored, which means they will be looked after by the immigration department until such time as sponsors do come forward.

Remember, they didn't have a choice. We do.

Winnipeg Free Press

Winnipeg, Man., August 23, 1979

One of the arguments used by people who oppose any large-scale entry of boat people into Canada is that these Vietnamese and Chinese will take jobs from Canadians; and, with our present high unemployment rate, this is not desirable.

But a report from Ontario this week appears to knock this argument on the head. A resettlement officer of the Canadian Employment and Immigration Commission in Toronto says that the refugees are taking jobs that the employment centre has had on file for a long time; these are not high-paying jobs and are jobs that Canadians do not want.

Because most of the refugees do not yet speak English, they are in jobs where they do not meet the public; they are working as chambermaids, dishwashers and kitchen help. Many are training to work in trades, particularly those who already have experience with machines. Women who can sew are taking a course in industrial power sewing; others who were office workers in Vietnam are qualifying for similar work in Canada.

According to the officer, employers say that the refugees are hard working and good employees.

The situation in Ontario, *vis-a-vis* the boat people, is not so greatly different from that experienced at times in Western Canada. It was not long ago that hotels in the West had to import workers from Mexico to do jobs that Canadians would not do; and market gardeners have found it necessary to import field workers from outside the country. Undoubtedly the textile industry can use workers once they have been trained.

All in all, it would appear that the influx of boat people will be a boon, not a hindrance, to the Canadian economy.

The Toronto Star

Toronto, Ont., July 26, 1979

The benefits of immigration go deeper than most of us realize.

No matter how poor one's home country may be, no matter how desperate conditions may have become, not everyone has the courage to leave the land of one's birth to start life over again in strange and unfamiliar surroundings. Not everyone has the courage to learn a new language, a new trade and a new way of life in a faraway place.

Those that do tend to be special. They are people determined to break out of the cycle of poverty in their own countries to build a better life for themselves and their children.

A recent Star report on Metro's growing Korean community describes how hard some of its members worked to save enough to open their own small businesses. People like Mike Kim, Woo-San Back and Yung-Dai Kim put in 14 to 16 hours a day, seven days a week, 52 weeks a year for 10 years to make a success of their corner milk stores.

Others worked as welders, car-wash operators, waiters and waitresses to save enough to start their own small businesses.

They stayed open late and never closed on the weekend. They provided a service their customers needed and appreciated.

This is how it has always been with immigrants. Many of them take heavy, dirty jobs no one else wants. They work at tasks longtime Canadians consider beneath their dignity.

Fifty years ago there was a Chinese restaurant on

the main street of every Ontario town and a hand laundry on the side street. It was a lonely life, remote from other Chinese families. But this was where opportunity lay. This was where one could make enough of a living to send home for a wife, raise a family and see one's children move onto something better.

The same was true of Serbian miners, Polish farmers, Swedish lumbermen, Jewish tailors, Scottish textile workers, Irish bricklayers and English draymen.

They did not come to Canada to live off someone else's bounty. Instead they worked hard and dreamed of better days. They not only kept the wheels of industry turning, they used their imagination and experience to create new opportunities for themselves and others.

They expanded our tastes in food, they created new services, they opened up new industries.

So it is with this generation of West Indians, East Indians, Chinese, Koreans, Maltese, Filipinos and Latin Americans in Canada.

So it will be with the 50,000 Vietnamese boat people we have pledged to rescue from squalid camps in the Far East. Like all the others before them, they will not be taking jobs that Canadians might have filled, they will be taking those we scorn and cannot fill.

And in a few short years they will be creating fresh job opportunities for all of us. We will all be the richer for it.

The Evening Telegram

St. John's, Nfld.,

July 14, 1979

There is a rising wave of concern about the present condition and ultimate fate of the thousands of refugees from Indochina, especially Vietnam. They are the socalled Boat People who are fleeing from Communist cruelty and tyranny in whatever kind of craft that's available. In many instances they have had to part with their large or paltry life savings to get passage in one of those vessels.

Canada has a good record in assisting political and other types of refugees. The greatest modern effort was made during the Hungarian uprising against the Soviet Union in 1956 when more than 40,000 persons were brought to this country. In the current situation the government in Ottawa has made a commitment to take 8,000 people which, although a sizeable group, represents a very small percentage of the 500,000 now in United Nations refugee camps. The UN is holding an international conference on July 20 to deal with the horrendous problem.

Many sources are urging the government to move fast in accepting its quota. They suggest the process of health examinations could be speeded up if some doctors would volunteer their services. It was only a month ago the Canadian Medical Association passed a resolution urging the government to take in at least 30,000 a year. It's pointed out that the Canadian Armed Forces have a trained medical corps and a fleet of planes that could be pressed into immediate though temporary service.

The major problem of looking after the refugees as they arrive has prompted a heartwarming response across the country to a call for interested groups to sponsor these Boat People. The groups would be obliged to help newly-arrived families for at least a year, to get food and shelter, and find jobs

And there's the rub. With so many thousands of Canadians jobless, there is a natural resistance to any move to add more competition. But the small number the government has agreed to accept cannot have too serious an impact on the work force. Canada's part in repatriation of these hapless people may be small by comparison but it is vital. Any contribution we can make to this national effort will be well worthwhile.

Montreal, Que., July 5, 1979

Les journaux et la télévision nous ont sensibilisés de nouveau, au cours des derniers jours, au problème pathétique des réfugiés du Sud-Est asiatique.

C'est par dizaines de milliers notamment qu'on voit des Vietnamiens clamer leur détresse dans des camps de fortune malais où ils ont fui, au péril de leur vie, parce que leur patrie ne voulait plus d'eux. Ils sont évidemment à la recherche d'un pays qui voudra bien les accueillir de façon définitive et mettre ainsi fin à leur terrible cauchemar. La Malaisie peut paraître cruelle en refoulant à la mer nombre de ces exilés, mais, à la vérité, avec le peu d'aide qu'elle reçoit des organismes internationaux, il est bien difficile de lui lancer la pierre.

Certains diront qu'il faut d'abord s'attaquer au fond du problème qui relève d'une politique absolument inacceptable de la part des pays d'origine de ces réfugiés. Heureusement, ce n'est pas l'avis de la majorité. Certes, il faudra bien, et le plus tôt possible, amener les dirigeants des pays coupables de ce genre de génocide à mettre un terme à leurs pratiques discriminatoires, à leur persécution de caractère idéologique. Mais il est plus urgent, cela va de soi, de secourir ceux dont la vie est présentement en danger

Toutes les nations bien nanties ont un devoir de conscience d'aller à la limite de leurs possibilités pour soulager cette misère. Elles ne peuvent se contenter de vagues déclarations ou de voeux pieux. Le temps est à la concertation, à l'action.

Le Canada, jusqu'ici, se classe assez bien parmi ces nations bien nanties. On sait qu'il a accepté d'accroître sensiblement le nombre des réfugiés qu'il est prêt à accueillir en 1979. Il a également pris des mesures pour hâter la sélection des Indochinois qui répondront à ses critères d'admissibilité.

Mais on est en droit de se demander s'il ne pourrait pas faire encore davantage. Surtout que les provinces ont généralement fait savoir qu'elles étaient prêtes à apporter leur plus entière collaboration.

C'est d'ailleurs le cas du Québec. À cet égard, on ne peut pas ne pas se réjouir de l'attitude fort conciliante du ministre québécois de l'Immigration, M. Jacques Couture, qui s'est dit prêt, au nom de la province, à accueillir la moitié des réfugiés indochinois que le Canada entend accepter cette année. Et le Québec le fera sans chercher la moindre querelle de juridiction avec Ottawa.

Ceci témoigne d'un sens de la solidarité humaine qui devrait impressionner les autorités fédérales. Mais il existe un moyen encore plus puissant de forcer la main du gouvernement canadien: la réaction de la population elle-même.

C'est à celle-ci de faire savoir qu'elle est prête à entrer dans le jeu, à s'imposer des sacrifices qui lui feront mal au besoin pour traduire sa sympathie dans les faits. Une occasion en or lui en est offerte avec le programme de parrainage dont peuvent se prévaloir les paroisses ou groupes locaux.

Le parrainage est une formule qui facilite grandement l'action des particuliers. On a calculé qu'il pouvait en coûter environ $5,000 pour adopter une famille moyenne de réfugiés et assurer sa subsistance pendant la durée minimum d'un an prévue par la loi. Pareille somme dépasse en général les possibilités d'un seul individu, mais un groupe d'une vingtaine de personnes, par exemple, peut en disposer en se serrant un peu la ceinture.

Les pasteurs de toutes les Églises du Canada ont fortement incité leurs fidèles à entrer généreusement dans la ronde. Il faut espérer que leur appel sera entendu. Les questions d'idéologie ici doivent être laissées de côté. Qu'on soit de droite ou de gauche, on ne peut demeurer indifférent devant la souffrance de ses semblables.

Les gouvernements, c'est bien connu, peuvent difficilement aller plus loin que n'est prête à le tolérer l'opinion publique. Par contre, si cette même opinion les incite de toute évidence à se montrer plus généreux, leur tâche en sera facilitée d'autant.

Le Canada, bien sûr, ne peut à lui seul soulager toute la misère qui s'étale dans le Sud-Est asiatique. Le problème est à la dimension d'un monde. Mais chaque nation, en mesure d'apporter une aide quelconque, ne doit pas attendre que les autres lui donnent l'exemple. Elle ne doit surtout pas décider de ses initiatives exclusivement en fonction d'une rentabilité immédiate.

En d'autres termes, il faut accepter de témoigner d'une générosité qui n'attend pas nécessairement quoi que ce soit en retour. Il faut se laisser guider par le sens de la fraternité et du partage.

Nous nous plaignons facilement de nos conditions de vie. Elles pourraient être meilleures. Mais, au fond, nous savons que nous sommes des privilégiés et qu'il serait inhumain de notre part d'écarter de notre table ceux qui croupissent dans la plus grande misère dans des camps indignes de notre civilisation.

Cuba Offers to Free Prisoners If U.S. Takes Them

During 1978, the Carter Administration took cautious steps to improve relations with Cuba. This resulted in October in an unexpected offer from President Fidel Castro to free all political prisoners, about 3,600, if the U.S. would accept them. The U.S. took 46 former prisoners and their families immediately, including Antonio Cuesta Valle and Eugenio Enrique Zaldivar Cadenas, two prominent anti-Castro heroes of the Cuban community in Miami. Castro added that he was willing to allow 7,000 ex-prisoners and 40,000–50,000 Cubans with relatives in the U.S. to emigrate, provided Washington agreed. Citing President Jimmy Carter's human-rights stand, Castro said the U.S. had a "moral obligation" to accept the prisoners.

Chicago Tribune
Chicago, Ill., December 19, 1978

Fidel Castro complains that the United States is being too slow and picky about admitting the 3,000 or so political prisoners he is willing to free—if the U.S. will admit them. He says his amnesty demonstrates his concern for human rights, and he says that if Mr. Carter is sincere in all of his talk about human rights, he should be delighted to accept Mr. Castro's rejects.

This country's problem is that tens of thousands of refugees from Communist hell-holes all over the world have been admitted to this country or are still clamoring to come in. Millions of others, mainly from Mexico, have "admitted" themselves to this country illegally, and are generally getting away with it. Up to a point, this is in keeping with our tradition of sympathy for the world's oppressed; it is a tradition symbolized by the Statue of Liberty.

Not only that. The people most eager to escape from Communist "Utopias" are likely to be skilled and self-reliant—people who would rather sink or swim on their own than put their fate in the hands of the state. Mr. Castro's past "rejects" have already turned Miami into one of the fastest growing and most prosperous cities in the country.

But our hospitality has generally been tempered with rules and quotas, and we're glad to know that Atty. Gen. Bell and the immigration service are insisting that the Cubans be examined individually, each on his or her own merits.

The fact is that we are doing Mr. Castro a favor by admitting his prisoners at all. They are nothing but a burden on him, a constant source of potential rebellion. His willingness to free them is prompted neither by humanitarianism nor a desire for conciliation. On the contrary, it was timed so as to embarrass the Carter administration. The message to Mr. Carter was: "If you're so concerned about the human rights of prisoners in Cuba, you can show that concern by letting them into your country."

Nor can we ignore the possibility of "plants" among these prisoners recommended for admission—agents posing as prisoners or prioners-turned-agents.

So it's good to know that Mr. Castro has not succeeded in conning the Carter administration into letting him determine our immigration policies.

The Miami Herald
Miami, Fla., September 2, 1978

WHATEVER the reason for Fidel Castro's decision to release at least some of his political prisoners, the world can know it is not because of any concern for human rights. If he had any such concern, he would not have 4,000 people in jail for "crimes against the state."

Perhaps he is uncomfortable with the image that results from imprisoning his own people while continuing military incursions in Africa in the name of "liberation." Maybe, just

Castro

maybe, he would like to soften his contentions with the United States just a little to take attention away from his meddling in Puerto Rico as well as Africa. Perhaps he just wants to stop feeding prisoners he knows have committed no real crimes and are of little danger to his locked-up island.

Whatever the motive, the action dovetails with U.S. interests. Our national policy of furthering respect for human rights and the release of political prisoners everywhere is served by the decision and is to be welcomed — with caution.

There will be caution. A State Department team, accompanied by FBI agents and immigration officials will screen each of the first 48 released prisoners individually. They will have to meet the test of being truly political prisoners, not simply criminals whom Castro has re-labeled.

How many will pass the test and come to the United States is not known, but the number could be 500 to 1,000. Meanwhile, U.S. efforts will naturally continue to seek release of the remaining American prisoners, some with dual citizenship. Castro has set up a cruel chess game, using human beings as pawns, but this nation can afford to play as long as it wins freedom with every exchange.

A year ago, we supported the decision to establish diplomatic "interest sections" with an American presence in Havana and a Cuban contingent in Washington. The interest section in Havana implies no recognition or approval of Cuba's actions, but simply serves this nation's best interests.

The practical proof of that came with the opportunity this week to widen a crack of humanitarianism in a place where it has been walled up for too many years.

And we can hope the U.S. interest section in Havana will soon be overworked by the release of *all* political prisoners in Cuba.

The Providence Journal
Providence, R. I., September 6, 1978

Cuba's offer to allow 1,000 political prisoners to seek exile in the United States may be simply an act of good faith to show that the regime of Fidel Castro truly desires improved relations with this country. If so, the traditional openness that the United States has shown to political exiles from all quarters ought to be fully extended to the Cuban exiles.

But Washington is justifiably cautious about taking this unilateral offer from Havana at face value. Premier Castro is not known for his generosity either to those who oppose his politics at home or to those he likes to revile as Yankee imperialists.

Certainly President Carter's appeals to all countries to honor human rights are not likely to have stirred the milk of human kindness in the Castro breast. One is led to suspect, therefore, that either Mr. Castro is setting the stage for some as yet unknown *quid pro quo*, or he intends to infiltrate his "political prisoners" with spies, terrorists or common criminals.

A Justice Department spokesman says that a team of FBI, State Department and Immigration and Naturalization Service officials will prescreen each individual that Havana proposes to send, starting with 48 applications already received. No doubt the

federal files are well stocked with profiles of most if not all of the experienced Marxist-Cuban agents, and current contacts in Cuba as well as within the large anti-Castro Cuban community in Miami can be useful in helping detect undesirables among those who apply.

America still welcomes the tired, the poor and the oppressed, and may she always do so. But those who would abuse that hospitality or betray it are not welcome, and compassion needs to be tempered with wisdom to be sure that what is being offered here is not a Trojan horse.

Carter Orders Halt to Refugee Flow; Haitians Demand Asylum

Cuban refugees began reaching the shores of Key West in late April, after Premier Fidel Castro terminated a two-day airlift of refugees to Costa Rica. Private boats, bought or chartered by Cuban-Americans, headed for the port of Mariel to pick up relatives or other Cubans who had been allowed to leave the country. The refugee flood reached serious proportions by mid-May, prompting President Carter May 14 to reverse himself on his initial pledge to welcome the Cubans with "open arms." Carter ordered the U.S. Coast Guard to prevent boats from leaving Florida, and he called for measures to screen incoming Cubans in Miami. By May 15, a total of 46,000 Cubans had landed in Key West, and there were reports that criminals and mental patients were among them. Most were flown to U.S. military bases to await processing. Aside from the problem of handling such a large flood of refugees, there was fear that the influx of Cubans would give rise to anti-Hispanic sentiment in Florida, whose Cuban population was already quite large.

The refugee exodus stirred up anti-U.S. sentiment in Cuba. The U.S. May 4 closed its interests section in the Swiss Embassy in Havana and ordered all personnel to leave May 15. Cubans waiting to enter the interests section had been attacked by pro-Castro mobs.

Meanwhile, Haitians who had reached Miami by boat told a federal court judge May 7 that they should be classified as political refugees like the Cubans. The U.S. listed Haitians as economic refugees, which did not entitle them to asylum. About 26,000 Haitians had fled poverty and repression in their country to reach Miami, where they were considered illegal aliens and ineligible to work. Carter was criticized by labor, human rights and black groups for the different treatment of the Haitians. They charged the Administration with racial prejudice, noting that most of the Cubans were white, while the Haitians were black.

The Seattle Times

Seattle, Wash., May 9, 1980

THEY come in waves, sometimes thousands in a single day. There are Communist spies among them. And criminals and prostitutes. Nearly all are destitute.

Yet the United States has not barred the gates to this newest of the world's repeated floods of political refugees.

Cuba's "Freedom Flotilla" poses a wide array of problems for the U.S., including the urgently necessary one of screening out the spies and other undesirables. This country is being called upon to assimilate the new waves of refugees even while a similar task remains far from complete in regard to the transplanted Vietnamese and Cambodians.

Yet President Carter was reacting in line with the best of this country's traditions — and with majority American sentiment — when he pledged to accept thousands more Cuban refugees and declared that they are welcomed with "open arms and an open heart."

The earlier generation of Cuban refugees, who fled to these shores when Fidel Castro was first consolidating his power, has proven to be a national asset — a successful ethnic community not unlike the European ethnic communities that took root in the U.S. in the last century.

We have no doubt that the ultimate verdict on the newcomers will be the same.

For the short range, though, there is obvious validity in a federal official's observation that "Castro is jiggling us. He is playing games with us, is trying to embarrass us."

The U.S. is helping the Cuban Communist dictator ease his problems of overcrowding, political dissent and economic stagnation.

But the larger reality is an admission of failure on the part of the Castro revolution. In the last analysis, the U.S. — for all of its tactical blundering during more than two decades of indecision as to how to "handle" Castro — has a reason for pride.

THE MILWAUKEE JOURNAL

Milwaukee, Wisc., May 1, 1980

In attempting to cope with the flood of refugees from Fidel Castro's authoritarian Cuba, the US government should not forget this country's tradition of providing a haven for the disinherited and politically repressed.

Granted, Castro is cynically testing America's hospitality by urging hundreds of thousands of dissatisfied Cubans to move to the US. But the US government, which criticized Malaysia and Thailand for being reluctant to accommodate the boat people from Vietnam, will appear callous and hypocritical if it slams its "golden door" on Cuban refugees.

Confronted with a similar Cuban exodus in 1965, President Lyndon Johnson stood at the base of the Statue of Liberty and enunciated a policy that permitted 265,000 Cubans to systematically enter the US over an eight year period. As a group they have proved to be responsible and self-sufficient.

So far, the Carter administration's policy is confusing. Some officials have been threatening to fine boat owners who illegally transport refugees to the US; others seem mainly concerned with filtering out the criminals (Castro reportedly is emptying his prisons). Commendably, President Carter has at least decided to provide Navy escort for the boatlift.

There's no denying that the influx of Cubans, particularly if it comes too fast, can create problems in a country already worried about unemployment and perplexed over a growing population of illegal aliens. Therefore, it would be reasonable to try to stretch out the admission of Cubans over a period of time. It is also sensible to screen the refugees, seeking to distinguish between, say, a political dissident and a common criminal. And it is proper to call upon other countries to share the refugee burden.

The thing to avoid, however, is any suggestion that the US has forgotten its historic invitation to the "huddled masses yearning to breathe free."

The News and Courier
Charleston, S.C., May 8, 1980

President Carter's pledge that the United States will accept with "an open heart and open arms" tens of thousands of Cuban refugees typifies the humanitarian spirit that freedom-loving people in other lands long have associated with America. The president's promise of sanctuary, made as small boats continued to land refugees in Florida, puts in sharp contrast the ways of life in the U.S. and in Castro's Cuba. The exodus has made the differences stand out for the world — and especially for Latin Americans — to see.

Accepting thousands and thousands of Cubans fleeing a repressive regime is not without complications, however. Reaction to the stream of refugees has put U.S. immigration policies in disarray. Aliens without proper papers are welcomed, while the masters of the boats which brought them are fined. Laws bent or broken for reasons of compassion inevitably will invite charges of unfairness. How does a government justify taking in illegal aliens escaping oppression in one country, while turning away those fleeing another?

Beyond that are the strains imposed in receiving and absorbing the Cubans now joining the 800,000 who have come to this country since Castro came to power 20 years ago. Millions in federal funds are going to help Florida cope with the influx. The economic impact will, of course, spread, extending to employment and welfare fields where populations are concentrated. Job competition will create anomosities, if experience is any guide.

There is, additionally, a screening problem. Immigration officials say there is evidence Fidel Castro is unloading his jails, pushing criminals into the immigrant stream to the U.S. The scope of that problem can only be guessed at.

Welcoming refugees with open heart and open arms presents difficulties even in a nation as large as the United States, because most go not to the open spaces, but to overcrowded metropolitan areas.

The Cleveland Press
Cleveland, Ohio, May 1, 1980

The challenge flung down to the United States by Fidel Castro in the matter of the Cuban boat refugees demands a bold response.

Here is a chance to strike a telling psychological and propaganda blow against Cuba's Communist dictatorship. Here is an opportunity to wipe away some of the humiliation this country suffered in the hostage-rescue debacle in Iran.

In our fancy, we hear President Carter proclaiming, as President Johnson did during a similar opportunity in 1965, an "open door" policy for Cuban refugees.

We picture him going beyond Johnson's limited airlift and chartering a fleet of Caribbean cruise ships, each capable of carrying hundreds of passengers, and every other large ship he can, and sending them to Havana harbor in full view of the world.

We imagine the Voice of America saturating Cuban airwaves unto the remotest parts of the island with the news that transportation to freedom awaited everyone who could make his way to the coast.

Fanciful, of course. But the fact is that the Castro regime stands very close to being fatally discredited, for today's refugees, unlike the earlier great wave in the 1960s, are Cubans who have grown up under communism.

Sadly, this sincere champion of human rights around the world has so far mustered only a feeble, legalistic response to the greatest human rights challenge of his administration — one taking place right on the nation's doorstep.

U.S. authorities are seizing boats and fining their captains for bringing refugees to Miami. It is a field day for hucksters in human lives who are charging exorbitant boat rental fees. Caught in storms in tiny, unseaworthy craft, an unknown number of refugees have drowned.

We implore the president to rise to this challenge.

The London Free Press
London, Ont., May 7, 1980

The Communist dictatorship put together by Fidel Castro is still capable of bringing out hundreds of thousands of Cubans for a May Day propaganda rally in Havana. But the thousands of other Cubans fleeing the island in small boats at grave risk to their lives attest to the political oppression and economic inefficiency of this self-styled "paradise of socialism" in the Caribbean.

Judging from the number of requests for exit visas, diplomats in Havana estimate from 200,000 to 400,000 Cubans would like to quit the island. Most prefer to go to the United States, of course, but as the 10,000 would-be emigrants who jammed into the Peruvian embassy grounds last month indicated, many thousands of Cubans would be pleased to settle in almost any other impoverished Latin American country just to get out from under Castro's yoke.

To be sure, conditions in Cuba today are in many respects much improved over the injustices which existed under the previous Batista dictatorship. Unlike most other Latin American countries, few children in Cuba now go barefoot and almost all have an opportunity to attend school. In many Latin American countries, half the population goes hungry, but in Cuba, almost everyone has an adequate, if bland, diet as well as access to minimal health-care services.

So what's wrong with Cuba? The main problem seems to be that initial gains in social justice have given way to continuing economic stagnation and political oppression.

For 1976, the Castro regime admitted that production fell 2.2 per cent or $200 million below the planned target level. Corresponding figures have not been released for any year since — a good indication that no improvement in productivity has occurred.

Economic conditions would be much worse without support from the Soviet Union. U.S. experts estimate that out of a total gross national product for Cuba of a' out $10 billion a year, no less than $3 billion depends on Soviet subsidies. That's an expensive drain for the Kremlin, which already has serious economic difficulties to contend with at home.

Indeed, the economic problems of Cuba and the Soviet Union have an important common cause; namely, the collectivization of agriculture. Nowhere has this system of farming proven efficient in promoting long-term gains in food production. Not in the Soviet Union, not in Tanzania, and certainly not in Cuba.

Land reformers in Latin America and elsewhere would do better to look not to Cuba but to rural North America of the last century. There can be no doubt that in comparison with communal farming and large landed estates, a system of privately owned family farms is far more conducive to promoting social justice, economic growth and political freedom. The end results might not be utopia, but that's a delusion pursued by political fanatics like Castro at great expense in suffering for thousands of his countrymen.

THE SAGINAW NEWS
Saginaw, Mich., May 11, 1980

The flood of Cuban refugees braving death to reach America's shores says something about Fidel Castro's Cuba. It says more about America. And Americans should listen.

While paranoid ayatollahs and two-bit dictators are kicking our country around, the people they rule are still voting their own feelings. On the issue of America, their ballots are emphatically marked yes.

It's yes, also, that the refugees are coming while our nation is in an economic slump — although many of them gladly take menial jobs and seek only opportunities for advancement, not guarantees of it. It's true they create temporary settlement problems and that Castro is trying to foist criminals off on the U.S.

Even that is indicative of the spite of a dictator sharply rebuked by his own people in their eagerness to escape, to taste freedom, to make a new life in the one land where that more than anywhere else remains possible.

It's sad that so much of the world shares this yearning, one above and beyond political mouthings. But in our own malaise, it must be encouraging that Liberty's torch remains visible and bright beyond our shores. We cannot extinguish it without darkening the reflection it casts on us and our nation.

The Miami Herald

Miami, Fla., May 7, 1980

PRESIDENT CARTER'S change of heart on the Cuban refugee boatlift puts him slightly in the posture of the host who says "Welcome!" after the guests he didn't invite have battered down his door.

But that doesn't matter. What matters is that Mr. Carter's "open heart, open arms" declaration of Monday more than makes up for his Administration's initial inhumane efforts to stop this unstoppable yearning of repressed people to be free.

On Tuesday, the President gave more substance to his new policy by declaring Florida a disaster area. That legalism qualifies the state for Federal funds to lift the financial burden that the refugee onslaught would place on Dade County's taxpayers.

The President's decision to open the gates to freedom that his aides at first had tried to close is significant for another reason too. For the first time, Mr. Carter signaled that Haitians fleeing Jean-Claude Duvalier's dictatorship deserve haven as much as Cubans fleeing Fidel Castro's Communist regime.

Of all the words he has spoken about human rights, of all the actions he has taken against inhumane regimes near and far, none gives more vivid witness to the American tradition than these:

"Those of us who have been here for a generation, or six or eight generations, ought to have just as open a heart to receive the new refugees as our ancestors were received in the past.... We'll continue to provide an open heart and open arms to refugees seeking freedom from Communist domination and from the economic deprivation brought about primarily by Fidel Castro and his government."

Castro's revolution has failed. He knows it. The world knows it. Each Cuban who deserts his home and goes to Mariel, there to await a boat — any boat — to freedom testifies to it. Ever since the Havana 10,000 jammed the Peruvian embassy, Castro has used all his cunning and brutality to try to convert U.S. hesitation and immigration quotas into capital for his own morally bankrupt despotism.

It almost worked. But with his new declaration on refugees, President Carter has at last seized the initiative. More than that: The President has rekindled the flame of liberty at a time when it seemed in peril of flickering out.

Yet the new wave of Cubans, like the smaller but ceaseless wave of Haitians, has rekindled something else in South Florida: an unreasoning fear. Fear of being inundated by people speaking another language. Fear of job competition in a coming recession. Fear of the unknown numbers yet to come, of the unknown costs — financial and social — of their coming.

Unless this fear is allayed forthrightly and soon, it will dwarf the momentary disruption that the new tide of refugees has brought. The President took the first allaying step by designating Florida as a disaster area. It is imperative that the Federal Government apply this legal designation as quickly and broadly as possible. The agencies processing the Cuban refugees already are sending to other states those without immediate families in South Florida to take them in.

That policy is both wise and kind, and the President should back it with all the resources at his command. For it would be tragic indeed if, in opening the nation's heart and arms to these new refugees, the President allowed uncertainty to close Dade Countians' hearts and arms to them.

Miami, Fla., May 15, 1980

THE CARTER Administration, in opening its arms to the new wave of Cuban refugees, seems destined to slam an elbow into the teeth of the local governments — particularly Dade's — upon which they are descending.

That mustn't happen. If it should, it would pervert humanitarianism. Where is the humanitarianism in opening America's gates to all comers and then telling local taxpayers, "Here they are — you take care of them"?

Yet that could be the result of the President's apparent intention to grant the influx of Haitians and Cubans "asylum" rather than "refugee" status. Involved are some 20,000 to 25,000 Haitians already in Dade County, plus an exodus of Cubans that already has passed 40,000.

The President at long last acted Wednesday to try to stop the flotilla. The Government itself should transport the refugees from Cuba, because only then can U.S. authorities even begin to control those it allows to come here.

Granted, the Administration does face a Hobson's choice. If it granted refugee status to the Haitians and Cubans already here, the Government fears that might trigger a monumental rush toward Florida of people from impoverished lands throughout the Caribbean. Yet if it grants these newcomers asylum instead, it risks dumping the cost of caring for them upon the communities to which they gravitate.

The reason is that Federal law entitles refugees to Government assistance, but persons receiving asylum are not included. As refugees, the Haitians and Cubans would be entitled to Government relocation aid, subsistence and job-training benefits, and medical care. Conversely, the asylum option requires that Congress appropriate funds for these purposes. If Congress balks, local taxpayers will have to pick up the tab.

That clearly is unconscionable. It creates precisely the situation that Fidel Castro hopes to create: backlash against Cubans fleeing his regime. Added to the resentment and fear already generated by the mental defectives and convicts Castro has mixed among the Cubans awaiting transport from Mariel, it threatens to turn Castro's failures into an American domestic political crisis.

Let the President and Congress bear one fact clearly in mind: They and they alone created this problem, and they and they alone must bear the financial responsibility of their actions. South Florida's governments simply do not have the financial resources to pay the bills for chaos custom-ordered by their national Government.

Nor, purely on principle, should they. The Refugee Act of 1980 stipulates that after today, groups of people cannot be granted blanket refugee status; their applications must be evaluated one by one. That act did not envision the Havana 10,000 or the exodus from Mariel to Key West that Fidel Castro subsequently triggered. Nor did the President anticipate, when he declared his "open heart, open arms" policy toward these desperate human beings, that Castro would empty jails and asylums into the boats crossing the Straits of Florida.

But Congress wrote the Refugee Act of 1980; Dade Countians and Florida's state government didn't. And the President authored the policy that made a shambles of U.S. immigration law; Dade Countians and Florida's state government didn't.

Let Mr. Carter and Congress recognize where Federal responsibility requires Federal help. And let them do it by addressing to the local governments impacted by the refugees an unstinting policy whose first words are, "Pay to the order of..."

DESERET NEWS
Salt Lake City, Utah, May 14, 1980

Since their flight to freedom began last April 21, nearly 37,000 Cubans have arrived in the U.S. By the end of May, a total of 60,000 Cuban refugees are expected to have arrived on Florida's shores.

This influx confronts the U.S. in general and Florida in particular with some demanding challenges. Those challenges are magnified by the fact that among the refugees so far are eight cases of suspected tuberculosis, one of confirmed leprosy, two suspected airplane hijackers, and an unknown number of other possible criminals.

Granted that the U.S. could and should have done a better job of spelling out in advance the kind of Cuban refugees it would and would not accept, and must now do the most rigorous possible screening to reject the undesirables.

Granted that Washington needs to do a more vigorous job of persuading other Latin American nations to help absorb some of Castro's cast-offs.

Granted, too, that Congress will have to allocate extra funds to deal with the refugee influx.

Even so, there are sharp limits to how much the Carter administration can be faulted, or to how sweepingly the critics can legitimately portray the challenges involved.

To put the current influx in perspective, keep in mind that since 1959 when Castro came to power, more than 800,000 Cubans have fled to the U.S. The current exodus is only the third largest one.

That means the U.S. has been able to handle an average of some 40,000 Cuban refugees a year. Though that level already has been approached in just a few weeks of April and May, it's hard to believe such a heavy influx can continue much longer — particularly if the U.S. starts deporting the felons among these refugees.

The Cuban refugee problem pales in comparison with the 400,000 Cambodians who have crowded into Thailand, the 500,000 refugees from Ethiopia's disputed Ogaden region who have concentrated in Somalia, or the nearly one-million Afghans taking refuge in Pakistan.

Aside from the relatively few undesirables among the Cubans, the average refugee is usually among his country's most competent citizens and is ordinarily an asset to the host country in the long run.

Moreover, the influx of Cubans into the U.S. helps refute some harmful propaganda. If Cuba has become such a paradise under Castro, why do so many want out? Likewise, if the U.S. has really mistreated its Latin neighbors, why do so many of them look upon North America as a haven?

The current influx of Cubans should remind the world of America's wide streak of idealism and generosity. Let's look upon the refugees as a challenge to be mastered rather than as something irksome to be avoided.

THE DAILY OKLAHOMAN
Oklahoma City, Okla., May 6, 1980

IT'S beginning to look as if we've been played for a fool again by Fidel Castro.

The Cuban leader stunned the world by declaring that some 10,000 of his countrymen who took refuge in the Peruvian embassy in Havana could go to any country that would accept them. Then he offered the same deal to any others, prompting a wild exodus to Florida.

About 7,000 have arrived (we earlier agreed to take only 3,500) and the flow continues. Local facilities in Florida are unprepared and unable to handle such an influx in addition to an estimated 3,000 Haitian refugees who have arrived illegally in recent months.

U.S. authorities say 200 or more Cuban espionage agents have filtered in with the crowd. Not only that, but the "refugees" reportedly include a goodly number of criminals released from Cuban jails and other social undesirables, as well as bona fide seekers of freedom from Castro's communism.

Our government should order an immediate halt to this mess that is making a mockery of our immigration laws and discriminating against those in other lands who want to emigrate to the United States but are restricted by rigid quotas.

The Sun  Reporter

San Francisco, Calif., May 12, 1980

The USA has recently become the major refuge for the victims of war, usually those on the losing side. [who else?] Prior to World War I the nation's immigration laws were regulated so as to favor the caucasoid man, predominantly from Europe. However, after World War II the immigration laws were relaxed so that members of the Oriental race were allowed more freely into the continential USA. This trickle became a floodtide after the Democratic Republic of Vietnam crushed the South Vietnam–US military machine and finally won the Vietnamese War in 1975.

After World War II the "freedom fighters" of Hungary found sanctuary and a new life in the USA. After the "Bay of Pigs" in the early '60's, Castro opened the gates for the exit of anti-Communists, and tens of thousands of them now inhabit Florida and the southeastern USA. Then came the tens of thousands of Indochinese.

Within the last two weeks, it is estimated that approximately 37,000 Cubans have been received in the USA. Unfortunately, the escapees from Hungary, Cuba, Vietnam and now again Cuba, represent a most conservative and reactionary segment of their native populations, who lost in their native struggle against Communism. When these tens of thousands of refugees reach the USA they contribute little or nothing to our traditional liberalism, but coming from a privileged class in their native lands they represent the worst part of the racist, sexist and classist dimensions of our American social order. One common strain runs through all of these refugees: they stood firm on their native soil against "godless" Communism, and they are now beginning their second line of defense against Communism in the USA.

On the other hand, there are thousands of Haitians who have fled to Florida in an attempt to escape the evil political oppression and physical crimes of "Baby Doc" Duvalier. The propaganda value of the Haitians is nil in the international propaganda against the worldwide spread of Communism. Moreover, the Haitian refugees are predominantly Black.

President Carter and his administration have shown little enthusiasm for receiving Haitian escapees from a fascist dictatorship. Only the vigilance of the Black Press and the increasing clamor by masses of Black citizens the Carter administration to desist from turning these Haitians away. Not only must Black Americans struggle to blunt the present administration's policy of rejecting the Haitians, must also demand that the Haitians be given every opportunity, as given to the Hungarians, the Cubans and the Indochinese, including Vietnamese and Cambodians, to start life anew in the USA.

The covert injection of racism and red-baiting into the opening and the shutting of our doors to those who seek a new life on our shores, causes the Carter administration, the defender of "human rights," to appear as a charlatan before the world community.

The Pittsburgh Press

Pittsburgh, Pa., May 7, 1980

The United States is accepting several thousand refugees every month from Indochina.

It has taken in more than 800,000 Cubans who have fled Fidel Castro over the years. And the current exodus of refugees from Cuba no doubt will result in thousands more becoming U.S. residents.

This country also is taking in Jews from Russia and persons escaping tyranny elsewhere around the world.

Mexicans illegally cross the border in droves, and for the most part only perfunctory efforts are made by U.S. authorities to slow their influx.

But U.S. officials have taken an uncharacteristic hard-nosed attitude toward Haitians fleeing a woeful existence on their Caribbean island.

Estimates on how many Haitians have fled their homeland in the last decade range up to 25,000. Most of them have crossed 800 miles of open sea in flimsy boats to reach Florida, and the number who perished on the way will never be known.

The Immigration and Naturalization Service is trying to deport the Haitians on grounds they don't qualify for asylum. It argues that the Haitians are not trying to escape political persecution but are only fleeing economic conditions at home.

Certainly Haiti is among the most impoverished places of the world. But equally certain is the fact that the Duvaliers, who have ruled Haiti for more than 22 years, are among the world's less enlightened rulers.

President for Life Jean Claude "Baby Doc" Duvalier may not be the tyrant that his father Francois "Papa Doc" Duvalier was, but if he has many humanitarian impulses he has kept them well-hidden.

It is highly incongruous for the United States to accept refugees by the tens of thousands from around the globe yet close its heart to a few thousand Haitians seeking sanctuary at great personal risk.

The Wichita Eagle

Wichita, Kans., May 15, 1980

The continuing controversy over the status of thousands of Haitian refugees in this country is an embarrassment to the human rights policy of the Carter administration. There is no logical reason for the failure of U.S. officials to treat these people as legitimate victims of a corrupt and brutal dictatorship.

Today is the last opportunity for President Carter to grant the Haitian refugees asylum under the Refugee Act of 1980. If this is not done, then deportation procedures will begin, and death, torture or imprisonment will be the fate of Haitians forced to return to their native land.

The 23-year Haitian reign of terror — first under Francois "Papa Doc" Duvalier, and now under his son, President Jean-Claude Duvalier — rivals any degree of persecution experienced by the 37,000 Cuban refugees who are receiving preferential treatment by immigration authorities.

It is now up to President Carter to prove that the "open arms to the oppressed" policy of his administration is a sincere reality, and not a selective political gambit. The Haitian refugees should be given asylum today.

The Star-Ledger

Newark, N.J., May 10, 1980

The "open arms, open heart" compassionate gesture by President Carter for thousands of Cubans who have inundated southern Florida in recent weeks curiously has not been extended to Haitians who sought refuge in the United States from the political tyranny and economic misery of their homeland.

Where the Cubans are welcomed, thousands of Haitians are detained as illegal aliens, denied job opportunities and other minimal benefits they require for bare subsistence.

The double standard is defended by U.S. immigration officials on grounds that Cuban nationals are political refugees, whereas most Haitians are illegally entering this country for economic reasons, escaping from the grinding poverty of Haiti.

• • •

The fact is that thousands of Cubans, Vietnamese and Cambodians have come to the United States for the same reason. They have been accorded humane treatment, while 13,000 Haitians have been barely surviving in Florida, and living in fear of being returned to a repressive political climate back home.

Congress has been asked by the Carter Administration to underwrite the admission of more than 230,000 refugees. An estimated 90 per cent will come from Communist states in Eastern Europe, the Soviet Union, Cuba and Indochina. The quota for Latin America, including Cuba, is 40,000.

Some provision should be made in the new refugee admission program for the Haitians living in miserable circumstances in Florida. The granting of asylum would be an overdue humane acknowledgement they will not have to return to a repressive dictatorship back home.

THE ARIZONA REPUBLIC
Phoenix, Ariz., May 10, 1980

IS THERE anyone who can make head or tail of President Carter's policy on the boat people?

The president says he welcomes them.

At the same time, he says he will strictly enforce the immigration laws.

The result is confusion compounded.

The U.S. Navy is patrolling the Caribbean to help boats in trouble and escort them to Florida.

Ashore, U.S. Marines are setting up temporary shelters for the boat people.

Meanwhile, other U.S. authorities are notifying the boat captains that they face a fine of $1,000 for each of the Cubans they bring into the country.

This may make sense to the man who characterized the failure of the attempt to rescue the American hostages in Iran as "an incomplete." But it doesn't make sense to anyone else, least of all the boat captains.

They are simply disregarding the Customs officials.

Some of them already face fines of $200,000 or more, but they are going back to Cuba to pick up more refugees. They're certain that, when push comes to shove, the federal government will find itself unable to enforce the laws. And, of course, they're right.

There are now at least 1,500 boats engaged in carrying the Cubans to freedom. The Navy doesn't have enough ships to stop them, and it would be ridiculous to attempt to jail the captains.

It would create an uproar of volcanic proportions among the 500,000 Cubans already living in Miami. And it would make the United States an object of scorn and derision throughout the world.

Over the years, and especially since the Hungarian uprising in 1956, the U.S. has provided refuge for at least 2 million victims of communism, including 800,000 Cubans.

It cannot do less for the boat people, no matter what the immigration laws say.

Carter should recognize reality, and call off the officials. They are making him — and the nation — look ludicrous.

St. Petersburg Times
St. Petersburg, Fla., May 6, 1980

Putting out the welcome mat for Cuban refugees, while slamming the door for Haitian refugees raises serious questions about the morality of the United States' immigration policy.

The double standard is indisputable and unconscionable.

For many hungry and bedraggled Cubans, their first home in the United States will be a $1-million tent city, complete with hospital and dining facilities, erected overnight in North Florida by the military.

For many weary Haitians, their first home in the freedom land is a dingy jail cell where they are detained as long as several weeks awaiting medical checkups and further processing by immigration authorities who want to send them home.

WHEN THE Haitians are finally released from jail, the United States still treats them poorly, refusing to grant them the work permits they need to get decent jobs here.

The State Department's explanation of why the two groups are being treated so differently just doesn't ring true.

Immigration officials claim that Haitians who flee their country are only looking for a way out of crushing poverty, rather than escaping political persecution, and therefore do not deserve asylum.

Cuban refugees, however, are being granted asylum because the State Department officially recognizes their flight from the communist rule of Fidel Castro.

To draw this distinction is ridiculous. Both countries are characterized by extreme poverty; it's just worse in Haiti, the poorest country in the Caribbean.

Both countries also are characterized by political persecution. While the Cubans are fleeing the harsh rule of Castro, the Haitians are fleeing the repressive regime of right-wing dictator Jean-Claude "Baby Doc" Duvalier.

Who is to say whether a particular Cuban or Haitian refugee is escaping poverty, persecution or both? No one can really make that judgment fairly.

The only telling difference is that most of the Cuban refugees are white, while most of the Haitian refugees are black. That's what makes it so difficult to refute charges of racial bias and to swallow the State Department's official justification for discriminating against the Haitians.

Crossing the treacherous sea in tiny sailboats, the Haitians have been entering South Florida illegally for the past eight years. The recent arrival of Cuban refugees, who are being received warmly, makes the State Department's anti-Haitian policy stick out like a sore thumb.

FORTUNATELY the Haitians are not being deported now because a legal challenge to their status is pending in Miami. But life in the United States is so dreary for the Haitians, their leaders claim that they often return to their homeland only to be routinely jailed, tortured or killed — a sure sign of political persecution.

In the long run, whether the United States should welcome people who are escaping economic hardship must be resolved with an immigration policy that treats all refugees fairly, compassionately and equally.

In the short run, the discriminatory treatment of the Haitian refugees strains the credibility of the United States' commitment to human rights.

President Carter has until May 15 to use emergency powers and grant political asylum to the Haitians on a group basis.

Yet Carter's interest in their plight is called into question by human rights activists and several members of Congress, including Sen. Richard Stone, who asked for a meeting with Carter before April 21 to discuss the problem. The meeting has not been scheduled yet.

In contrast, Carter declared Monday that the United States will accept tens of thousands of Cuban refugees with "an open heart and open arms." It would be fitting for Carter to offer the same warm, albeit belated welcome to the Haitian refugees.

THE PLAIN DEALER
Cleveland, Ohio, May 7, 1980

In assessing the stream of refugees from Cuba to America, Rep. L. A. Bafalis, R-Fla., said: "We need to stop the boats from going to Cuba. If we are going to accept these people, we have to do it on the basis of a rational plan."

He is right. The sea lift of Cuban refugees has gotten way out of hand. Already almost 18,000 Cuban immigrants have arrived and hundreds of boats continue to shuttle between Cuba and Florida.

Processing centers are strained beyond their ability to perform. Reportedly, immigration regulations are being bent and ignored.

There have been warnings that Cuban President Fidel Castro is slipping his less desirable citizens, including criminals, into the refugee flow. While we are aware that what is a crime in Cuba might be considered a patriotic act in this country, we think federal officials need to take the warnings seriously and not just ignore them.

There have been legitimate protests from many people that letting Cubans into the United States willy-nilly will aggravate the nation's already deep problems of unemployment in a recession.

This could become a frightening development if there is any substance to estimates that the eventual alien influx could reach 250,000. We have seen no evidence as basis for that prediction, however.

The United States is a nation of immigrants. Americans have found ways to accommodate economic refugees. But times change and the needs of the nation change. What was good for America in 1890 may be harmful today. Who is going to pay for all this generosity, including jobs?

How can the nation welcome large numbers of Cubans while denying equal access, for example, to Mexicans, Haitians or refugees from any other nation?

President Carter has said he will open the country's door to all Cubans who wish to come here. He should thoroughly examine with members of Congress the consequences of that act and temper his policy accordingly. So far, his policy appears to be a mess to take care of chaos.

The Birmingham News
Birmingham, Ala., May 10, 1980

AFTER 21 YEARS UNDER the ministrations of the champion of the proletariat, apparently half the population of Cuba has found that workers' paradise beyond redemption. And while Comrade Fidel Castro wanders the halls of the presidential palace in Havana, pausing from time to time to deliver 90-minute tirades against Yankee imperialism, hordes of distraught traitors to the planned poverty of socialism have voted for freedom with their feet, waterwings and swampy boats.

(Will the *The New York Times*, Barbara Walters and embattled Sen. George McGovern please note before the mirage vanishes?)

Not to miss out on the re-election potential, the lugubrious President Jimmy has — after blundering about a bit — welcomed the refugees with open arms; welcomed them to Florida, that is. Stout-hearted Floridians, however, need more than a welcoming speech and a reminder that they are now pawns in international politics. What they want — and need — is money and not peanuts.

THE BLADE
Toledo, Ohio, May 4, 1980

ONE cannot help but sympathize with the plight of refugees who have been streaming into the country, most lately from Cuba across the Florida Strait. But there are indications that the Carter administration is trying to make political capital of the issue, and the time has come to call a halt to the illegal immigration.

Instead of sending U.S. naval units to help the coast guard aid the Cuban refugees land in this country, President Carter should be upholding American immigration statutes.

There was a time when the United States was able to welcome the tides of immigrants who washed up on its shores. But with all the best will possible this country cannot go on being a dumping ground for the poor and dispossessed of the entire world.

The Administration bears a large share of the blame for the grim state of affairs which has caused two Florida counties to declare a state of emergency. They simply cannot handle the flood of aliens from Cuba and, to a lesser extent, Haiti. Only belatedly did Washington move to set up a temporary camp in northern Florida to relieve the pressure.

Mr. Carter is playing politics with the issue by winking at illegal immigration in the hope that some votes in Texas or California or Florida might be gained by doing so. If the leader of the nation refuses to respect the law, how can anyone else be expected to do so?

In addition to ignoring the law, the Administration is indirectly contributing to the growing welfare burden that the taxpayers of the nation must shoulder in order to accommodate illegal aliens who manage to reach U.S. shores. It should be remembered that annual quotas for immigrants and refugees are set by Congress; these should be enforced by whatever means are required, not ignored.

Simply because Cuban President Castro is ready to let some of his own people flee their homeland is no reason that the United States should flout its own laws to accept them. If it means that the coast guard has to turn back or seize boats — many of which are being operated by American owners eager to make a killing by charging exorbitant rates to ferry the refugees across the strait from Cuba — then that should be done.

The United States has leaned over backward in the past to absorb thousands of Cubans who fled from the repressive Castro regime. So it comes with particularly poor grace from the Cuban establishment in Florida — which has taken advantage of U.S. hospitality in the past — to summarily reject appeals to help stem the flow of refugees in the unlawful boatlift from Cuba.

So far, the Government obviously has been playing games by issuing warning after warning but shrinking from upholding the law. It is time for an effective crackdown on the illegal immigrant traffic, action which might generate a little respect for the laws of the United States for a change.

DAILY NEWS
New York, N.Y., May 7, 1980

THE MASSIVE EXODUS from Cuba has turned into a seagoing stampede to U.S. shores, and President Carter must do more to control and channel this tide.

Swift and decisive action is needed on two fronts. The U.S. must devise a safer and more orderly system for transporting the refugees from Cuba—by sea or air or both. Evacuating them with a motley armada of small craft operating under no central direction is not only dangerous, but also makes it difficult for the U.S. to screen out undesirables.

Sen. Stone

In addition, the administration has to work out a firm plan for distributing the latest wave of anti-Castro Cubans.

Latin American leaders are meeting tomorrow to discuss the problem and, as Sen. Richard Stone (D-Fla.) observes, that's where the solution lies.

Not all of it, of course. Many of the refugees have close relatives in the U.S. It would be heartless to prevent their reunion with loved ones.

All the same, Stone is basically right. More than 18,000 refugees already have made their way to the U.S. and thousands more are waiting to leave Cuba. The U.S. would have a tough time processing such a throng, even with the additional $10 million Carter is providing Florida for the task. Accommodating all of them is a task for all of the Americas, North and South.

Latin American countries were willing to accept a share of the refugees when it appeared there would be only 10,000 or so. The number has swelled, but Carter should make it clear to our neighbors that we still expect them to live up to their earlier commitment.

Detroit Free Press
Detroit, Mich., May 9, 1980

IN THE WAKE of the human flood from Cuba, President Carter had little choice but to agree to accept the refugees with "open arms and open heart." The influx, however, raises serious questions that will linger long after the flow has ebbed. The president would be wise to take those questions as a signal for the United States to formulate clear answers on how future refugees are to be treated.

Milton Morris, an expert on immigration policy and director of research at the Washington-based Joint Center for Political Studies, thinks it critical that the United States develop a policy that defines refugees, that establishes procedures for dealing with them (including adequate provision for their resettlement) and that establishes reasonable limits on the numbers allowed into the United States.

Otherwise, as he points out, there is no real argument for why thousands of Chicanos in California or Colorado should not take trucks across the Mexican border and bring their relatives into this country.

There is, too, no real rationale for treating Cubans one way, Haitians another, and Laotians yet another — or for treating any of those groups differently from thousands of other immigrants who have waited for years to be legally allowed into the United States.

Our present approach is not only unfair to refugee groups and to Americans in general, but it at least temporarily damages the economies of states forced to take the refugees. Clearly, Florida should not have to take major responsibility for the consequences of Fidel Castro's decision to let his people go.

For years now Congress has managed to avoid formulating a reasonable refugee policy by relying on the executive branch to make special exceptions to U.S. immigrations laws as one group after another has knocked on our doors. But with widespread resentment developing against such an arbitrary approach — and to some extent, against refugees in general — and with the American economy being pummeled from all sides, neither the president nor the Congress can take much comfort in our current non-policies.

If we don't reform our refugee policies, Mr. Castro and his likes will do that for us. And in the process they will give us a host of headaches our common sense could have helped us avoid.

THE DENVER POST

Denver, Colo., May 13, 1980

GOV. DICK LAMM misfired in his recent comments about the Cuban refugees now entering the United States. But he's right on the basic point: We need better planning to accommodate this latest influx of victims of communism than we've displayed in the past.

Lamm's reply to federal authorities asking what Colorado could do to help was that resettlement of large numbers "would work against our existing commitments (to refugees.) The only resettlement we think realistic for Colorado at this time is welcoming families who have direct private sponsorship and support from the existing Cuban-American community."

Lamm also worried that Fidel Castro may be using the opportunity for "emptying his prisons and mental hospitals."

In return, Ruben Bonilla Jr., president of the National League of United Latin American Citizens, claimed the governor's comments "border on racism."

That's a bum rap, albeit one which Lamm invited by his own awkward statements. Actually, his record is good on refugee issues: He's worked hard to help resettle the Indochinese arrivals and ease the tensions between them and the native Hispanic population. For that matter, one of his top staff members is Maria Garcia, herself a *refugiada de Cuba*.

Without challenging his intentions, we think the governor underestimated Colorado's absorptive capacity. It is a fact, learned in the Indochinese experience, that direct sponsorship greatly eases the integration of refugees into the community. But sponsors needn't be limited to the relatively small (perhaps 600 strong) Cuban-American community in Colorado.

We are, after all, a state with a strong Hispanic heritage. The *Cubanos* share the same language, religion and much cultural background with our large Mexican-American population, many of whom are eager to help in the resettlement.

Finally, the initial fear that Castro was just cleaning his prisons of criminals turns out to be crude communist propaganda. Initial screening in Key West, Fla., has turned up only about 300 suspected felons and a handful of psychiatric patients among the first 30,000 arrivals. That's not to say we shouldn't be on guard: as Antonio Aguacio, a Cuban-American himself, said, "The American government should screen out the misfits, and send them back."

But most of the refugees are guilty of nothing more than "peligrosidad," or "dangerousness." According to Raymond Morris, chief of the Florida center of the Immigration and Naturalization Service, that "may be anything from not being a wholehearted supporter of the system to criticizing the block leader."

Intolerable in a dictatorship, such behavior is no offense in a free society. If the test is criticizing the top leadership, U.S. *Peligrosidados* include Ted Kennedy, John Anderson and Ronald Reagan.

There is, however, evidence that this latest wave of refugees is weighted more toward the bottom of the economic ladder than the initial middle-class Cubans who made such a rapid and successful adjustment. Lamm is right that we should plan carefully to see that they get such training or other assistance as they need to enter our economy as contributing members. That means close cooperation among federal, state, local and private agencies.

When freedom returns to Cuba, these brave people may return to their homeland. But in the meantime, Coloradans shouldn't hesitate to say "bienvenidos, Cubanos." Colorado welcomes you.

The Washington Star
and Daily News

Washington, D.C., May 9, 1980

President Carter's warm, if belated, welcome to the Cuban refugees who continue to pour into Florida ports at the rate of 3,000 a day is a welcome reaffirmation of what the word "America" is supposed to stand for. This *is* the immigrant's country, the freedom-seeker's country, the country where there's no ceiling on what can come of a new start in life.

At a time when the United States is widely vilified, it is useful to have the world — and ourselves — reminded of how well American society does on the compared-to-what test. At any time, it is agreeable to be able to help desperately unhappy people.

But the justifiable good feeling that goes with these realizations cannot hide the problems that are washing up on our shores with the human tide. Our hope is that it may give us the patience and balance it will take to solve them.

Meanwhile, predictably enough, Fidel Castro has been doing his best to make the situation as hard as possible for the United States. The man whose name should surely be considered the Spanish word for *chutzpah* has even been trying to turn his own natural disadvantage into a lever for forcing concessions from us.

His first strategy has been to catch us by surprise. After many years of keeping Cuban nationals in Cuba by force, he suddenly announced that everybody who wanted to leave could leave and it would be up to the United States to provide for them. It is suspected that, while releasing the politically disaffected, he also speeded the departure of a certain number who were in jail for non-political crimes.

He knows, of course, that even if only the most upright, hardworking and heroic of Cubans were to come to the United States there would be problems. The numbers guarantee it; you can't dump 20,000 homeless refugees on a conventional community without upsetting the earlier settlers, however hospitable their first impulses.

There are logistical problems in getting the Cuban boat people emergency food, clothing and shelter. There are farther-reaching economic problems — will there be enough jobs to go round with them in the competition? And there are cultural problems. Predominantly Anglo-Saxon neighborhoods don't always like it when their streets are perpetually crowded with strangers and the local shopkeepers no longer speak English.

There is the long-range problem of how long we can go on accepting such an influx. There seems to be no limit to the number of people who want to come to the United States. Is there a limit to how many we can admit without putting intolerable strains on our institutions and resources?

The present criteria for asylum have to do with justified fears of persecution. This lets in the Cubans, the Cambodians and the Vietnamese. What about the Haitians? These are the people who are currently raising murmurs of racism because American officialdom has been less receptive to their cries of oppression by the Duvalier government.

It has been said that the Haitians are merely economic refugees — people who want to come here because they are so poor at home. Quite a few Mexicans who are now disadvantaged as aliens qualify to come in and stay under that rule.

Once such people are admitted *en masse,* there are equally troublesome questions about the minimum wage and access to the publicly funded benefits full-fledged Americans get. In spite of all that has been said about how aliens in this country do the jobs citizens won't take and don't take the social services, there's always a policy frontier that's a minefield of moral, political and social dilemmas.

At the same time, the United States has reason to be optimistic about coping with them. The last decade's influx has been an influx of productive energy. The Cuban community in Florida, the other Hispanic enclaves elsewhere around the country and the Asians to be seen north, south, east and west, all testify to the vigor and adaptability of the people who take refuge here.

There are plenty of personal tragedies and civic abrasions in the picture too. And there is undoubtedly a limit to how many new people we can take in. But, clearly, the open arms and open hearts response is still the right one.

The Boston Herald American

Boston, Mass., May 15, 1980

The last thing the Carter administration needs just now is another crisis, either foreign or domestic. But it is getting both in the waves of Cuban refugees washing ashore in Florida.

These refugees have already overwhelmed local and state agencies there and are fast presenting Washington with the necessity of hard choices affecting the domestic economy, the federal budget, and the conduct of American foreign policy.

Nor is the building refugee crisis confined to those fleeing Fidel Castro. As many as 40,000 Haitian boat people have landed illegally in the Florida Keys within the last year. Meanwhile, the administration is admitting 14,000 Indo-Chinese refugees each month for permanent resettlement in the United States. And, while undocumented workers from Mexico and Central America are not considered refugees, the thousands who cross the border each month add that much more to the flow of desperate foreigners entering this country.

Given present circumstances in Asia, Latin America and the Caribbean, this flow is likely to continue. Indeed, it may well increase.

Castro is said to be willing to permit the departure of 250,000 Cubans or perhaps twice that number disillusioned with the barren results of his revolution.

Haiti's economy, hardscrabble in the best of times, is slumping ominously — a process sure to drive many more thousands of Haitians to seek opportunity in the United States.

The refugee flow from communist Indochina is certain to continue for years to come.

Political turmoil and deteriorating economies in Central America promise new migrants and refugees even as economic conditions in Mexico guarantee that our southern border will remain more a way station than a barrier.

Typically, the Carter administration seems adrift in its efforts to shape policies appropriate to both the refugee crisis and the question of undocumented aliens.

The obvious starting point in defining such policies is a recognition, however reluctant, that the United States cannot afford to admit all of the untold millions of persecuted and dispossessed who would like to settle here. So, distinctions must be made and priorities must be established.

For decades, U.S. law has differentiated between economic and political refugees, a distinction recognized as well by the United Nations. Yet, Mr. Carter has blurred this distinction by implying, for example, that the United States will accept Haitian boat people despite the State Department's official determination that none would suffer persecution or retribution if returned to Haiti.

And, of course, the administration has simply refused to confront the necessity for a rational, workable policy to cope with undocumented aliens entering the United States from Mexico and Central America.

All this inevitably complicates the traditional task of granting sanctuary and providing for legitimate political refugees, particularly those — like the Vietnamese — for whom the United States bears a special responsibility. Nowhere are the resulting difficulties more evident at the moment than in southern Florida. Resolving the crisis there will require more than federal funds for tent cities and emergency rations. Mr. Carter needs to define clear policies that make both practical and moral sense in light of even this country's finite resources.

Richmond Times-Dispatch

Richmond, Va., May 9, 1980

America was founded as and has always been a haven for persons fleeing political oppression in their native countries. That is a principle to keep uppermost in mind as the United States struggles to accommodate the latest stream of refugees from Fidel Castro's communist tyranny in Cuba.

For two decades, Miami's expatriate Cubans have been so close—and yet so far from—the loved ones they had to leave behind when they escaped from Castro's Caribbean hellhole. The Cuban commander's temporary lifting of the prison bars—for that is what Cuba is under his direction, one huge prison—has permitted Cuban-Americans to risk the treacherous seas in hopes of reuniting their families as free people in America. What American can fail to have compassion for those families?

Additionally, the talk of Castro "emptying his prisons" and dumping the inmates on the U. S. masks the reality that many of these refugees have been *political* prisoners who were incarcerated for no other reason than daring to oppose the Castro regime. More than 4,000 former political prisoners had been waiting for more than a year, many of them jobless and lacking ration cards used to obtain necessities in Cuba, to obtain entry visas to the U.S. Certainly, the American tradition as a haven for the oppressed ought to apply to such prisoners of conscience as these.

All this does not mean, however, that the floodtide of people landing on southern Florida shores presents no problem or that the U. S. should accept automatically every immigrant as an equally legitimate refugee from political tyranny. Reports indicate that dozens of the Cuban boat people are Castro intelligence operatives. Federal agents should carefully screen out these ringers and see that they are expelled. There may be other undesirables—persons who have committed violent crimes, such as murder or rape—in the refugee masses and efforts should be made to identify them.

The Carter administration's initial reaction to the boat people verged on the callous as the State Department threatened to fine and throw in the slammer those skippers who hauled "undocumented aliens" back to these shores. But this week, President Carter has been playing some catch-up by issuing a general welcome to the Cuban refugees and extending a federal helping hand to Florida's heroic efforts to accommodate the sudden influx.

Still, the situation appears to be rather chaotic and with some ominous overtones. Marines have been dispatched to keep order at makeshift refugee camps. And some Miami area residents are fearful of being swamped by huge numbers of new arrivals. Approximately 25,000 Cubans have arrived so far, but some authorities have guessed that as many as 250,000 may eventually come. And meanwhile, thousands of poverty-stricken Haitians also are seeking entry in roughly the same proportion as the Cubans.

The Carter administration and Congress ought to develop a coordinated policy on this growing immigration crisis. Clearly, Miami and Dade County, Fla., ought not to be expected to bear the entire brunt. Already the character of that area has been substantially altered by past waves of immigration: Miami has a 55 percent Latin population, and Dade is 40 percent Hispanic. What's needed is something that presidential assistant Jack Watson has promised there will be, without offering any specifics—a national program to resettle the refugees in other parts of the country than Florida. And our Latin neighbors also should be asked to accept their share of persons seeking to make a new life for themselves in freedom.

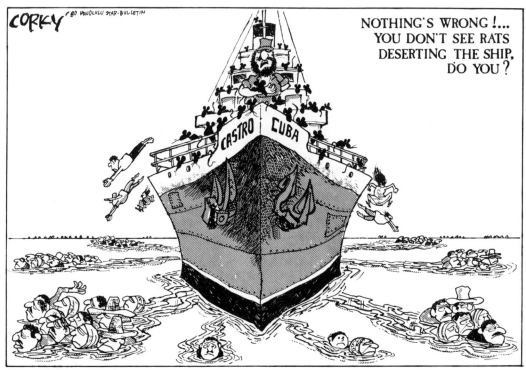

CORKY '80 HONOLULU STAR-BULLETIN

NOTHING'S WRONG!...
YOU DON'T SEE RATS
DESERTING THE SHIP,
DO YOU?

CASTRO CUBA

The Dispatch

Columbus, Ohio, May 7, 1980

THOSE THOUSANDS of Cubans pouring into Florida have created a nettlesome dilemma. Either the U.S. Congress will have to find some after-the-fact way to legalize their status or this nation may be required to — perhaps savagely — slam the door against refugees.

Truth of the refugee matter is that the Cubans represent only a small portion of the refugee-handling process this nation has established.

There are thousands of Haitians already in Florida and more are on the way. All are illegal immigrants. The U.S.-Mexican border, a veritable sieve, constantly is being violated by illegal Mexican entrants.

And do not forget those other "boat people," the ones from China, Cambodia and Vietnam who languish in holding camps throughout the Orient just waiting for a chance to call America home.

President Carter has said this country will welcome the Cuban refugees with "an open heart and open arms." But its response to an obvious human need must be backed up by new procedures and new regulations, all woefully lacking. Declaring a state of emergency to speed federal aid is merely a stopgap.

What is not covered is Cuba's "deportation" strategy. Cuban authorities hand-pick four refugees (many of them criminals and some who do not even want to go) for every two legitimate refugees.

The Philadelphia Inquirer

Philadelphia, Pa., May 4, 1980

Why should the United States feel embarrassed over the flood of Cubans fleeing Castro's Communist paradise? If anyone should feel embarrassed, it is Castro. Twenty years after his revolution, Castro presides over an economy in such dire straits, in a country where freedom is in even worst straits, that thousands of its citizens want nothing more than to leave for a better, freer life elsewhere.

Still, the influx of Cubans, which began when some 10,000 of them poured into the grounds of the Peruvian embassy in Havana early in April, as well as thousands of Haitians fleeing impossible conditions in their country, poses a quandary for the U.S. This nation cannot accept everyone anywhere who wants to settle here. It has economic problems of its own, including a growing number of citizens who want jobs that are not there for the having. Yet the United States, if it be true to its traditions, cannot close its doors to the oppressed from other lands.

The Carter administration has faced up to the question in a characteristically ambivalent way. On April 14, President Carter used his emergency powers under the new Refugee Act to admit another 3,500 Cubans over the 15,000 who had been admitted in the previous 18 months. And the thousands of Cubans and Haitians who risked the high seas to come illegally to this country are not, for the time being at least, being sent back.

The State Department has sought to discourage the massive exodus of Cubans and Haitians to our shores. It has deplored, not without justification, the "commercial element" in the transport of Cubans to the U.S. and it has served notice on boat owners that they may be fined and imprisoned and their boats seized if they persist.

The refugee problem, though, is not limited to Cubans and Haitians. There are the Vietnamese, Cambodians and Laotians fleeing persecution and even starvation. There have been other refugees from Latin America, Africa, Eastern Europe and the Soviet Union.

There may be 12 or 13 million refugees in the world today. Looking to the future, a Library of Congress study predicted last August — quite accurately, as it turned out — that "the crisis shows no sign of abating, and the number of refugees will probably rise markedly over the next few years."

So the refugee problem is not a problem solely for the U.S. It is a problem for the nations of the world. Unhapily, most of them (with some honorable exceptions) have turned their backs on it. Twenty-six months ago, a 92-nation conference called by the United Nations to produce a treaty on refugee rights ended in failure. Last July, another U.N. conference to deal with the Southeast Asia exodus produced only palliatives.

What, then, should be done? The U.S. should accept as many Cubans and Hatians as the law allows, and should grant temporary asylum to others. The U.S. also should take the lead in calling on other nations to share the responsibility. That a tiny country like Costa Rica should offer to take in 10,000 Cubans ought to shame its Latin American neighbors who have done so little beyond making sympathetic sounds. Most nations have subscribed to the U.N. Declaration of Human Rights, which guarantees people's right to freedom of movement and residence. Yet what a mockery that is if, deprived of their human rights in their own countries, people have nowhere else to go.

Impatient Refugees Riot in Arkansas over Delay in Resettlement

About 200 Cuban refugees went on a rampage June 1 at Fort Chaffee in Arkansas, where they were awaiting processing for resettlement in the U.S. Angry at the delay, they burst through the compound's front gate but were forced back by police officers and soldiers. The mob then smashed furniture in the army barracks and set fire to buildings and debris on the streets. Earlier in the day, 300 refugees had escaped from the fort after throwing rocks and bottles at military police. Almost all were rounded up and returned to the base. Tension had built up in the crowded fort during the past week as the 18,000 refugees waited for U.S. sponsors. The slow pace of resettlement was attributed to security checks on the refugees. As a result of the June 1 rampage, Army troops and National Guardsmen were brought in to patrol the base. In all, 40 people were injured, 35 Cubans were arrested and four buildings in the compound were destroyed.

Rocky Mountain News

Denver, Colo., June 5, 1980

THERE is cause for concern but hardly for alarm over the riotous behavior of some Cuban refugees at Fort Chaffee.

The disturbance involved only about 300 of 19,000 refugees at the Arkansas military installation. The ringleaders are reported to have been isolated and ought to be dealt with severely; there certainly is no reason this country should allow such persons the privileges of U.S. residency.

Slow processing of refugees was said to be a major cause of the commotion. But government authorities shouldn't be stampeded into an undue speeding up of the processing.

The United States didn't ask for the flood of refugees. They can darn well be patient while we sort them out.

The Dallas Morning News

Dallas, Texas, June 14, 1980

It's difficult to be patient when someone abuses your generosity, like the child who carelessly breaks and disregards a gift you had hoped would be a cherished possession.

One can understand why so many residents were outraged when Cuban refugees rioted last weekend in Fort Chaffee, Ark. When the Cubans protested about the delays in their resettlement, it must have seemed like colossal ingratitude to the residents who must cope with the swell of unexpected visitors.

But the last thing we need is the kind of vicious reprisals sought by crowds of residents who armed themselves with the intention of "bashing heads."

Such outbursts only make a bad situation worse. Now is the time for talking in measured tones, to keep a difficult situation from turning into a free-for-all. Efforts should be redoubled to speed up the process of resettling the refugees, some of whom believe they have escaped from the confinement of Communist Cuba to a different kind of prison in the United States.

In turn, the Cuban refugees should be counseled that if they wish to remain in this country, violent displays that threaten the lives of innocent bystanders and destroy government property will not be tolerated.

The refugees need to know: Putting up with red tape is an unfortunate but apparently unavoidable part of life in these United States — whether you've been here three days or three generations.

THE EMPORIA GAZETTE

Emporia, Kans., June 3, 1980

THE rioting by Cuban refugees at Fort Chaffee, Ark., raises one large, disturbing question — Why?

Why should people who were willing to brave so much in order to leave Cuba react so violently to the prospect of spending a few weeks (or even a few months) in a relocation center while the U.S. government is preparing them for life in this country? The situation does not make a great deal of sense.

The governor of Arkansas claims that Castro's agents among the refugees are stirring them up in order to embarrass this country and make President Carter appear to be hypocritical in his human rights policy. That allegation has a tinge of red-baiting about it, but it does make some sense. If Castro did not think of it, he probably wishes he had.

A resident of a town near Fort Chaffee spoke for many Americans when he said "Everybody knows we're getting Cuba's trash." Well, everybody doesn't know that, but a great many are willing to accept it without question. Because most of Cuba's best educators, businessmen, doctors and dentists came to the U.S. years ago, Castro is understandably short of educated people to send us. All he has left are the ordinary people who don't like him. He has also sent us some people from his prisons, because the opportunity was too good to pass up.

Imagine that you are a common criminal, and that you have been sprung from prison in a poverty-stricken country and told that, since you are not a nice person, you are being forced to go to a rich country where there are no charges against you, and where your new government is going to spend a couple of thousand dollars getting you squared away with food, housing and a job. Would you riot in a relocation camp?

It just does not make sense.

Now I don't think this calls for a new Warren Commission, or anything nearly as fancy, but when it gets to the point that Arkansas State Police officers feel they have no choice but to shoot at rioting political refugees, it is time to admit that something is drastically wrong, either among the refugees themselves or in the administration of the camps. Let's find out what it is. — P.K.

Sentinel Star

Orlando, Fla., June 3, 1980

CUBAN refugees rioting at relocation camps present President Carter with an opportunity to gain control of a situation that has been careening around the United States like a loose cannon on a storm-tossed deck

For the first time since the episode began — at the initiative of Cuban President Fidel Castro — the refugees are in a clearly defined, manageable area where they are, theoretically at least, under the control of the U.S. government.

That government should utilize this advantage to the fullest in reaction to the riots. Full attention should be directed toward indentifying those responsible for the assaults and arson. Once those behind the outrage are isolated, they should be promptly and forcefully ejected from the United States.

There is simply no alternative to immediate identification and expulsion of those responsible for the riots at Fort Chaffee. It is needed as much for those Cuban refugees who did not participate in the disorders as for anyone else. It is significant that some of those most seriously injured in the rioting were refugees trying to assist American police and military units working to restore order.

It would seem that they would be of great assistance in identifying the troublemakers.

And spare us the predictable hue and cry of self-appointed guardians of due process who will rush to the well-publicized defense of those about to be bounced from this country. The courts have already addressed the probity of special immigration law treatment for specific nationalities posing specific problems for the United States.

Welcome those who came seeking honest sanctuary and an opportunity to prosper through individual labor — but throw the bums out.

THE ATLANTA CONSTITUTION

Atlanta, Ga., June 3, 1980

In the aftermath of what happened over the weekend people across this nation are saying, "Send the Cubans back where they came from; if they don't like it here let them contend with Fidel Castro." Since it is costing the taxpayers about $1 million a day to keep the refugees at Fort Chaffee, Ark., that kind of gut reaction is understandable.

However, consider that there are 18,000 refugees being held at the fort and the number that ran through the gate at Chaffee is set at 1,000. Consider that while some tried to burn down buildings, other Cubans were trying to stop them and entinguish the blaze.

It gets pretty hot in the Arkansas sun and frustrating when government drags its feet on immigration-processing. Consider what these people have been going through — forced to risk their lives to leave their homeland, a place they may never see again. Also consider that Castro probably succeeded in smuggling out a few professional troublemakers with the legitimate refugees and these Castro lieutenants are out for one thing, to make the U.S. look bad.

None of this, of course, justifies damaging property or hurting law enforcement officers trying to do their jobs. The ring leaders should be identified and brought before justice and maybe deported. This is a good time to demonstrate to our new residents that we are a nation of laws and that's what made us great.

As for the frustrations of the slow-moving refugee processing, this is as good a time as any for the Cubans to find out what the rest of us know already — when dealing with the governmental bureaucracy, it's the name of the game.

The Des Moines Register

Des Moines, Iowa, June 4, 1980

"Why are they so impatient and ungrateful?" That's a reasonable question for Americans to ask about the Cubans who went on a rampage at Fort Chafee, Ark.

A reasonable answer is that refugees are a special breed. People who pull up stakes tend to be independent spirits. You don't trade the familiar surroundings of a lifetime for the unknown if you're a docile, accepting type. The Cubans who clambered aboard small boats for a risky ocean crossing are likely to be an especially determined, strong-willed group.

They expected freedom. They got confinement in a military camp. The confinement is temporary, to be sure, but it's understandable how a person who escaped from tyranny would be impatient about being denied freedom.

The confined Cubans are anxious to begin new lives, to begin earning their way. There's nothing unreasonable about that.

Richmond Times-Dispatch

Richmond, Va., June 7, 1980

It would be wrong to conclude that recent outbursts of hostility toward Cubans pouring into this country from Castro's oppressed island indicate a fundamental change in the American people's tradition of compassionately welcoming refugees from foreign tyrannies. On the contrary, such displays constitute understandable reactions to certain troubling characteristics of the Cuban influx.

Coloring the American attitude toward the Cuban refugees is the nagging suspicion, partly substantiated by evidence, that the United States is being "had." It is now generally believed that Castro has used the desire of many political protesters to flee to rid his nation of common criminals, prostitutes and mental defectives. Many such people have been found among the refugees. Moreover, it is widely believed that some Castro sympathizers, and perhaps some Cuban intelligence agents, have sneaked in with the others.

Events like the recent rampage of some of the refugees confined at Fort Chaffee, Arkansas, for processing purposes tend to justify and accentuate these fears. And they naturally arouse bitterness. Already convinced that their hospitality has been abused, many Americans were quick to respond angrily to the Fort Chaffee riot. Some residents of the area around the base armed themselves and threatened to shoot any Cuban who might enter their neighborhoods. Many people called their congressmen and other authorities and demanded that the United States return the refugees to Cuba.

All of which shows an urgent need for the federal government to improve its approach to the Cuban refugee problem. It should, first, intensify its efforts to identify hardened criminals and pro-Castro agitators and send them back to their homeland. And while the government should endeavor to expedite the processing procedure, it should clearly and emphatically inform the refugees that they have no choice but to endure whatever procedure is followed, no matter how tiring and frustrating it might be. Those who persist in violently expressing their impatience, as Fort Chaffee's rioters did, should also be deported. Finally, the federal government has an obligation to provide special financial assistance to those localities and states that bear the brunt of the refugee problem.

Eventually, the American people will generously accept those Cuban refugees who genuinely desire to become constructive members of society, as most of them no doubt do. But it is difficult to be warm and generous toward a group whose violent members make it appear to consist mostly of ungrateful troublemakers.

ALBUQUERQUE JOURNAL

Albuquerque, N.M., June 3, 1980

The United States has no choice but to continue carefully screening thousands of Cuban refugees who have fled their homeland.

Rioting, burning buildings and battling soldiers will only slow the screening. The destructive action of 1,000 Cubans at Fort Chaffee, Ark., on Sunday was counterproductive. It aroused the ire of hundreds of area residents, some of whom were prepared to harm the refugees.

The refugees, some of whom might be disruptive Castro agents, are angered because they feel the processing is taking longer than it should. They ignore the weight of their numbers and the strain it has placed upon U.S. officials and U.S. facilities.

If the Cubans want to remain in this country, they first must be patient. Among those who left Cuba are a number of criminals and others that are not particularly welcome in the United States. They must be identified and authorities must then decide what will be done with them.

The knee-jerk reaction of many Americans is to kick the troublesome Cubans out. That would not solve the problem since there is little place else where they can go. The federal government has decided that it will use whatever non-lethal force is necessary to keep the refugees under control and on the grounds where they are being processed. The screening is being expedited but it still will take time. Somehow, both the refugees and Americans must be patient.

THE LOUISVILLE TIMES

Louisville, Ky., June 6, 1980

The rumpus at the Ft. Chaffee, Ark., refugee resettlement center may possibly have been started by Castroite agitators, as Gov. Bill Clinton and others have speculated.

But even if there wasn't an agitator within 50 miles of the place, it's easy to understand why a few of the 18,000 Cuban refugees quartered there were restless, angry and, for a time, out of control.

Whether they fled Cuba because of political repression or economic distress, most of them came here expecting a far greater measure of freedom and opportunity than they had previously known.

And what happened to them? They ended up behind a fence at Ft. Chaffee, where the U.S. Immigration and Naturalization Service appears to have adopted that time-honored Army slogan: Hurry up and wait.

More than 18,000 refugees have come to the base since it was opened to refugees in early May. As of the middle of the week, fewer than 800 had been processed out, even though, according to the U.S. Catholic Conference, plenty of private sponsors have volunteered to help refugees find housing and jobs.

The task of interviewing refugees, weeding out criminals, and completing the paperwork involved in helping newly-arrived residents get themselves established is admittedly time-consuming. It's important to remember, too, that nearly half the 100,000 Cubans who have come here by way of the Freedom Flotilla have already been able to join their families in south Florida.

But those who were delivered to Ft. Chaffee, many of them single men, may understandably wonder if they escaped one concentration camp only to be trapped in another. While their dissatisfaction doesn't excuse the riots that caused serious injuries and riled up local residents, it does suggest that immigration authorities are still not very sensitive to the newcomers' anxieties.

A month at Ft. Chaffee will impress upon refugees the sad truth that a capitalist bureaucracy can be as slow and ponderous as one in a Marxist "paradise." That lesson will be reinforced when some hapless Cuban experiences the hassle involved in obtaining Kentucky license plates.

But with a minimum of thought and planning, a nation settled by refugees, heretics, draft dodgers and, yes, criminals wouldn't have to welcome the latest wave of immigrants with excessive red tape, armed troops and handcuffs.

The Morning News

Wilmington, Del., June 4, 1980

The legend affixed to that enormous metal lady in New York harbor says, in part, "Give me your tired, your poor, your huddled masses yearning to breathe free." There is nothing there, like the sign in the window of a five-chair barber shop, that promises, "No waiting."

It is not difficult to understand that refugees who have finally escaped Cuba are impatient to be relocated and to begin their new lives in the United States. It is very difficult to believe that the disorders of the past week at Fort Chaffee, Ark., are spontaneous eruptions of violence triggered solely by the frustration and despair of refugees who think they are getting a bureaucratic runaround.

Gov. Bill Clinton of Arkansas lays the troubles to agents of Fidel Castro, who he thinks may have been mixed among the refugees to embarrass the United States. There may be an element of that. Certainly the fights between Cubans seeking to help quell disturbances and put out fires and others seeking to thwart those efforts make the suspicion credible.

Also contributing to the difficulties at Fort Chaffee is the reported failure of authorities to use refugee policies there consistent with those being used at other relocation camps. The representatives sent by President Carter to investigate the Fort Chaffee incidents say that will be corrected.

More important, they promise that any refugees identified as agitators will be isolated at a federal detention center. Whether such persons turn out to be assigned agents of Fidel Castro or simply some of the criminal and antisocial elements reported to have been forced as passengers on many of the boats leaving Cuba, their destructive influence is the same.

The unfortunate result of this violence is to force officials to turn Fort Chaffee and its environs into a heavily armed camp. Soldiers and policemen not only find it necessary to protect the refugees and apprehensive Arkansans from each other but also to protect the Cubans from themselves.

It has turned what should have been an exercise in humanity and liberation into an embarrassing echo of what the refugees were fleeing in Cuba. The circumstances allow no other approach, however.

The heavy tide of Cubans in the past few weeks has tried the patience of those who feel particularly threatened by their arrival, minorities who fear even greater unemployment and communities of Americans who are disturbed and made apprehensive by any strangers, particularly those whose language they do not speak.

President Carter has pledged open arms and open hearts to those who have fled Castro's Cuba. Many of them accommodated themselves to the discomfort and rigors of Cuba for nearly two decades. It hardly seems unreasonable to ask people who have shown such forebearance to accept with patience the necessary red tape and bureaucratic procedures required for their orderly relocation.

DAYTON DAILY NEWS
Dayton, Ohio, June 3, 1980

The Oregonian
Portland, Ore., June 4, 1980

Dissidents waited two decades before Fidel Castro allowed them to leave. Then they came to the United States 100,000 strong in just six weeks. Now, at the very least, they owe their American hosts the courtesy, patience and restraint to behave themselves in U.S. processing centers.

Of course, the procedure is frustratingly slow. The asylum portion (Section 208) of U.S. immigration law was not drafted by lawmakers who contemplated a mass immigration. Fewer than 2,500 people have been handled under its provisions since 1958, Jack Watson, President Carter's assistant for intergovernmental affairs, said in a recent White House interview with editors from Newhouse Newspapers. Forty times that 22-year total now has to be dealt with, case by individual case, in a compressed period, and it simply cannot be accomplished instantly.

Certainly, those who abuse U.S. hospitality with rioting and arson in the processing centers should be denied refugee status, a substantial improvement over asylum status. And if they can be deported, they should be.

American ingenuity. The good yeomen of Arkansas have found a way the make the Cuban refugees who rioted at Fort Chaffee look good. They have managed this by looking worse themselves.

The relative few Cubans who rioted at least had an excuse of sorts. Conditions in the relocation center are frustrating. The process is moving slowly. Many there are keen to join relatives or otherwise get on with being Americans.

None of that justifies the breakout some of the refugees attempted. A nation that is trying to like the devil accommodate them deserves the refugees' patience and understanding, even in its ineptitude.

The reaction of many nearby residents, however, is an even more wretched excess. Many are swanking around with rifles, shotguns and pistols. Local gun stores have sold out of weapons and ammunition. The air is blue with the names the Arkansas citizens are calling the Cubans and electric with their threats to kill, on the slightest excuse, any Cuban who comes their way.

And all this, mind you, without any real provocation. The few Cubans who bolted the center did not personally menace residents of the area. It clearly is their fondest hope not to stay and cause trouble, but to get away quickly. Rape and pillage are not what they have in mind. The exaggerated fears that the locals are citing apparently are meant to put the best face on attitudes that they must realize, in some dim recess of their minds, are horribly unbecoming to them.

Some of that exaggeration comes from the vivid and, it turns out, over-wrought reports a while back that Cuba was dumping its criminals on the United States. Screening has shown that only a very small percentage of the new refugees are criminals. The general impression, however, remains and is much larger than the numbers can support.

It looks as though Washington had better undertake a major effort to put across to the American people a full picture of this latest wave of Cuban refugees. We probably are not generally as thuggish as the gonna-shoot-me-a-Cuban patriots of Arkansas, but it would be best, as matter of policy, if the feds did not count on that assumption.

MANCHESTER NEW HAMPSHIRE UNION LEADER
Manchester, N.H., June 5, 1980

Cuban refugees by the thousands have landed on our shores in recent weeks seeking the "Pot of Gold" across the Florida Straits which separate Castro's communism from the Free World.

Government officials trip all over themselves while trying to justify this incredible infiltration of refugees — more than 100,000 to date!

And what thanks do we get for the millions of dollars it is costing you and me every day to settle them into the American Way?

Soldiers are beaten, stoned and shot at during a wild insurrection at a settlement camp in Arkansas. Barracks, probably far better than any living conditions they may have had in Cuba, are destroyed. Americans living near the camp fear for their lives and the safety of their families and property.

And, now, the coup de grace, as reported by our Veterans Editor, Maurice McQuillen, in a story elsewhere on Page One today.

CUBAN REFUGEES ARE BEING PLACED IN VETERANS ADMINISTRATION HOSPITALS in Florida while American citizens — brave men who went to war for their convictions and to keep this country safe and free — **ARE BEING TURNED DOWN FOR ADMISSION!**

It could happen only in the United States of America.

The shocking revelations in today's story are but another niche in the insane proclamations that have marked the Carter Administration almost from Day One.

While the printed accounts of this latest scar on the President refer to a "White House Directive," there can be no mistaking the fact the Rose Garden Rodent has placed his personal approval on such a disgraceful slap against every man and woman who ever put on a uniform.

It's almost as if every time The President gets his nose fixed up, his mouth goes awry.

Around the world, friends and foes alike must be enjoying a hearty laugh at our expense. When are we ever going to learn that we must take better care of our own before we can play nursemaid to everyone else.

Millions, billions throughout the world, go to bed each and every night praying, dreaming that, someday, they will be able to come to the United States to live.

THAT WE ARE HAVING A TOUGH ENOUGH TIME AT HOME TO TAKE CARE OF OUR OWN IS OBVIOUS. Yet, more than 100,000 refugees from Cuba are allowed in to this country without nary a whimper.

What is this anyway? If the troublesome dissidents who have successfully infiltrated this country from Cuba aren't happy with the Democratic process that is allowing them to stay here, they should leave.

THROW THEM OUT!

The door swings both ways!

After gorging of United States hospitality at Fort Chaffee the other day, one of our country's leading liberal leaders suddenly sprang to life. Observed Democrat Robert Byrd, "The United States must not be allowed to become a dumping grounds for criminals."

Too bad he didn't have the foresight to make that statement prior to April 21, when all this began.

Hot on Byrd's wing was the President, himself, with a resounding: " . . . we will deal firmly with the Cubans who have violated the laws . . . "

Let's see now, in the 215 days hooligans have held American hostages in Iran, "Give-'Em-Hell" Jimmy has promised to deal firmly more times than we can count.

Assaults on Federal troops, disregard for the constitutional laws of this free country, destruction of properties cannot be tolerated for one day, one hour, one minute by the agencies of our government responsible for permitting these aliens to enter our country in the first place.

It must be made crystal clear, purely simple for all to understand, there can be no deviations from the application of every law that applies to you and I, and every citizen of these United States.

Failure to adhere to the restrictions placed on the Cubans being resettled in this country **CAN AND SHOULD BE HANDLED IN ONLY ONE SWIFT, EFFICIENT MANNER:**

SHIP THEM BACK FROM WHENCE THEY CAME.

The sooner the United States begins to take more affirmative action in dealing with its troubles at home, the quicker we will have some hope of restoring our credibility around the globe.

There should be a **MESSAGE** to every man, woman and child in the United States in how we deal with this Cuban crisis:

THE DOOR SWINGS BOTH WAYS!

Rockford Register Star

A Gannett Newspaper
Rockford, Ill., June 6, 1980

We have compassion for those 109,000 Cubans who braved hostile waters and our untried shores to escape the tyranny of Fidel Castro's dictatorship.

But that riot launched by a handful of refugee Cubans at Fort Chaffee, Ark., is beyond understanding.

To be sure, there are delays before these immigrants can begin their new life in the United States. There are immigration laws which apply to everyone. There is red tape to be satisfied for the general good, even in a democracy.

These delays gnaw at the patience of some. But this country simply was not ready to receive 109,000 political refugees. Why should it have been ready?

If these were ordinary times, all the exacting process of immigration controls would apply and they would pre-empt months, even years. Today's frustrations boil down to a mere few days.

On an emergency basis the U.S. said what no other country has said, and in a gesture unmatched anywhere. We have said, "Welcome."

We have demonstrated generosity and charity at a time when 8 per cent of this country's work force can't find jobs.

To provide sanctuary, we have waived the very laws that distinguish this country as "the land of the free and the home of the brave." We have done all this without regard for the ingredient making it possible: American sacrifice.

It may be, as some at Fort Chaffee claim, that resentment built because some Cubans with sponsoring relatives left camp ahead of others not fortunate enough to have sponsoring relatives.

It may also be that among those protesting were Cuban troublemakers no more fit for democracy than for communism.

In the name of fairness, however, let us not belabor the point.

Those Cubans who lobbed stones at police and military officers and who burnt four government buildings to the ground have exceeded their welcome.

Let the troublemakers find their haven and their exile elsewhere if they are proved to have been involved.

And, as they are leaving our country, which should be rapidly arranged, let them be chastened by the vast majority of Cubans who are biding their time in return for the gift of liberty.

Said one of those patient Cubans as he examined the wreckage, "I feel very sad and very ashamed."

His sentiment is well placed.

The Hartford Courant

Hartford, Conn., June 3, 1980

It's easy to understand why Americans would feel annoyance, even outrage, at the rioting among Cuban refugees at Fort Chaffee in Arkansas.

Surely, it could be said, those who have been offered a refuge from life under a totalitarian regime at least owe this country a little patience while they are being processed by immigration officials. No one invited them. If they don't like it, they can just go home.

Some Cubans are guilty of ingratitude, no doubt, but there's more to the story than that, and the rest of it argues for our forebearance.

In the first place, a very small percentage of Cubans isolated in one processing center have participated in the rioting. Of the 18,000 Cubans at Fort Chaffee, only about 300 took part in the disturbance. That's an even smaller percentage — something like .003 percent — of the total 95,000 Cubans who have arrived in the United States so far.

Not to be discounted, either, is the possibility that the protests are in part being organized by Castro agents to take the focus off the massive exodus from Mr. Castro's island empire. But one needn't resort to a conspiracy theory to understand the conditions that might lead to protest.

These people have gone through difficult times. Many of those who left Cuba — and their families — were badly mistreated at home by other Cubans, both officials and ordinary citizens.

Many underwent a harrowing trip, jammed into tiny boats, to get to our shores. And when they arrived, they were locked into compounds, sometimes for weeks, before being released to join friends and families already in this country.

From the point of view of immigration officials, this period of detention is necessary in part to weed out criminals and other undesirables. But from the point of view of many immigrants, the official detention is just one more frustrating impediment to freedom.

They may have a point, too, when they argue that the resettlement procedure is cumbersome and slow. Little was done to prepare for the vast influx of Cubans in spite of a report from the Central Intelligence Agency in January that the Castro regime "may again resort to large-scale emigration to reduce discontent caused by Cuba's deteriorating economic condition."

None of this justifies the Cuban rioting at Fort Chaffee. But Americans — including those Americans who live around the fort and were ready to bust Cuban heads during the protests — should bear in mind the difficult conditions under which the immigrants have suffered and are suffering.

And above all, let's not allow the rash actions of a tiny minority to color our view of this latest wave of immigrants to America.

The Philadelphia Inquirer

Philadelphia, Pa., June 4, 1980

The riot by Cuban refugees at Fort Chaffee, Ark., on Sunday has placed a special burden on the Carter administration to determine the cause of the incident and make a full report public as soon as possible.

The first news reports said the Cubans went on a rampage in protest against delays in processing refugees for resettlement. Then there were reports blaming a small group of agitators for the violence, which inevitably gave rise to speculation that they might be agents of Cuban President Fidel Castro who had infiltrated the ranks of the refugees. Whatever the cause, the outbreak of violence, though quickly contained, has inflamed public opinion and thus has the possibility of consequences far worse than the damage to property and the injuries suffered by 40 persons.

Thus, it is everyone's duty not to jump to conclusions. More than 100,000 Cubans have reached the United States since the boatlift began 45 days ago. Nearly 18,500 have been housed at Fort Chaffee for processing. Of that number only about 300 were involved in the riot. President Carter's press secretary, Jody Powell, noted that "the vast majority of the Cubans there were not involved and many of them were actively engaged, while this disturbance was going on, in persuading their fellow Cubans not to participate and seeking to persuade those who were involved in illegal acts to stop." An FBI spokesman added that "we have no indication that a group of people were sent over here to foment trouble."

The arrival of so many refugees, coming as they do without visas, has strained U.S. capabilities to receive and resettle them, but, by and large, federal, state and local officials are meeting the challenge well. It should be a time of national pride, not recrimination, but the FBI, which is questioning the Cubans who rioted, and other federal authorities must move quickly to dispel the ugly overtones to what happened at Fort Chaffee.

ARKANSAS DEMOCRAT

Little Rock, Ark., June 1, 1980

What's the status of the 1.900 Cuban refugees at Fort Chaffee - 300 of whom fled the base last week only to be reapprehended? Are the refugees prospective American citizens like any other lawfully admitted immigrants - or are they aliens under indefinite detention until resettled through sponsors?

Maybe the Civil Liberties Union has an opinion at variance with Governor Clinton's. No need to ask Clinton the status of the refugees. When the 300 ran off, he instantly put them down as lawbreakers - rioters - and angrily declared that President Carter should make them "obey the law" or deport them.

Well, we know that many Arkansans don't welcome the Cubans' presence and that many or most people living around the fort (including local law enforcement) fear what the rumored criminals among the Cubans might do if allowed to run around outside it. But we hadn't realized that the refugees as a group are prisoners of any description. We thought that Mr. Carter sent them to Chaffee as the quickest way of resettling them.

The federal Emergency Management Commission declares that the 300 who fled didn't riot and didn't injure anybody or damage anything in their flight. We'd be surprised if they broke any laws at all and doubt, in fact, that they legally have to go through the resettlement process - and that's the trouble. Their status should have been made clear to them from the start at the federal level. The failure was there, but Clinton exacerbated it.

The refugees are liable, of course, for any breach of state law - and those discovered to have been criminals back in Cuba (not political criminals) should be detained for later handling. But the notion, helped along by Clinton (and Sen. Dale Bumpers, who might better have called for adoption of emergency laws and policies of restraint) that the refugees are dangerous prisoners until resettled is ridiculous.

Now that they're moving out in numbers, their understandable restlessness and confusion will probably subside. But the governor's election-eve "yellow peril" performance isn't anything for him or us to be proud of. Playing demagogue in a situation that called for an appeal for emergency laws to contain the refugees was no exercise in leadership.

Arkansas Gazette.

Little Rock, Ark., June 3, 1980

A week of skirmishes between Cuban refugees and authorities at and near Fort Chaffee exploded into full-scale rioting over the week end by 2,000 or so of the refugees. The disorder, which was reported under control yesterday, seems finally to have engaged the measure of attention by the White House that Governor Bill Clinton and others have been trying to impress upon Washington for days.

In any event, President Carter, according to Press Secretary Jody Powell, has now "taken steps to increase security" at the military installation near Fort Smith. Powell has not elaborated, but adds that "we are watching the situation carefully." The President, says Powell, sympathizes with the refugees' problems, "but it does not extend to condoning that sort of thing [riots]."

Indeed it doesn't. There is no way to condone such conduct, for injuries, some of them serious, were suffered by refugees, policemen and soldiers alike. Nor is there any way to condone the conduct of some local residents who for a time were threatening military policemen and talking of storming the fort.

Firm order must be established, and from all appearances yesterday this was the case. Governor Clinton says the security force is to be increased from 650 to 2,000. Federal workers skipped processing for the day in order to clean up the mess from the week end disorders.

The principal Cuban complaint — most of the 18,000 refugees, it should be noted, have been waiting patiently — is that it is taking federal workers too long to process their entry into United States society. There is some justification for this view, we must say, in the realization that since refugees began arriving at Fort Chaffee on May 7, only about 250 have been released to relatives or sponsors. About 2,400 more have been cleared, but their departure has been delayed by various factors, some of them transportation problems.

As the bureaucracy seems to grind slowly for those who have been on a desperate journey to freedom, it must be said that some of the Cubans themselves have added to the delays by their disorderly conduct. It is not easy to manage an orderly immigration in the midst of great confusion that has accompanied the massive influx of refugees from the oppression of Fidel Castro, and those engaged in the task should be accorded their own measure of understanding. Mr. Clinton has even suggested that the disturbances could have been provoked by Castro's agents, although we have seen no evidence that this is the case. The Fort Chaffee center does have a higher rate of single males with no family than do the other refugee centers, and a good many of the rioters appear to fall in this category.

Resettling tens of thousands of Cuban refugees is an enormous undertaking. The impression we have had is that not enough federal manpower, either for security or for processing, has been made available until now to smooth the way. President Carter, who sent a White House aide for a first-hand report on Sunday, seems now to be assuring all hands that the painful process will, at the same time, be speeded up and eased.

The Idaho STATESMAN
Boise, Idaho, June 4, 1980

Rioting by Cuban refugees at Fort Chaffee, Ark., is bound to engender spiteful feelings on the part of many Americans, especially those who already feel put upon by the arrival of throngs of Cubans in the 6-week-old "boatlift" to Florida. Some Americans will empathize with the Arkansans who showed up at the refugee camp Sunday with clubs and shotguns, demanding to go in and "bash heads." Such a response, though predictable, is neither mature nor effective in dealing with the problem.

The 19,000 Cubans housed at Fort Chaffee are, for the most part, victims of politics, history and geography. They have been expelled from their homeland by a brutal regime. Consequently, it is not fair to tell them, "If you don't like it here, go back where you came from!" House Majority Leader Jim Wright's suggestion that refugees who participated in the rioting be issued "one-way tickets" back to Cuba is grandstanding.

The acceptance of the Cuban refugees by the U.S. government was, under the circumstances, the only humanitarian, civilized thing to do. Fort Chaffee was one of the places readily available for their temporary residence. With 19,000 people quartered there — people who have just survived traumatic experiences — conditions are no doubt difficult, and emotions are running high. That disturbances occurred in the camps is not surprising.

Because of the special character of this wave of 100,000 immigrants, many of whom have come from hospitals and prisons, the problems of processing them and getting them settled are especially complicated. Government spokesmen say nearly half the refugees already have been settled. For those who remain, the wheels of government are turning slowly. But they are turning, and President Carter has ordered a speedup. If the process of screening and settlement isn't allowed to take its course, the likely result is new oppression of these hapless people.

THE MILWAUKEE JOURNAL
Milwaukee, Wisc., June 6, 1980

The exact reasons for the rioting by a minority of Cuban refugees housed at Fort Chaffee, Ark., are unclear, but the lawlessness itself is intolerable. Quite properly, alleged troublemakers are now in temporary detention — and sterner measures would be in order for any unrepentant rioters.

Generally, it is believed that frustration among the refugees over processing delays prompted the outbreak. This frustration, some government officials say, was accentuated by some Cuban Americans who planted the idea in the heads of their refugee relatives that the delay was unreasonably long. If so, the Cuban Americans should know better. They are only making a tough situation worse.

After all, these new Cuban arrivals are not casual tourists in the US traveling on routinely issued visas. These Cubans intend to stay in the US for long periods, if not indefinitely. Hence, the US has a perfect right to make a reasonably extensive check on who it is accepting. Indeed, such an investigation of each refugee is mandatory under the law. And even an expedited background check takes time.

Furthermore, for those Cuban refugees who do not have relatives here, it is necessary to find sponsors who will take initial responsibility for them until they can get established. That also takes time. In the case of Vietnamese refugees, it sometimes took months — not weeks or days.

America is officially ready to accept the new Cubans. Their predecessors have proved that they can be a positive addition to the cultural melting pot of American life. But the refugees must show patience and respect for law. The patience is a small price to pay for their exit from Castro's Cuba. The respect is a necessity if they are eventually to become solid American citizens.

The Detroit News
Detroit, Mich., June 6, 1980

Last weekend's rioting by 300 Cuban refugees at Arkansas' Fort Chaffee Relocation Center is likely to baffle and anger Americans.

Here are political refugees who have been offered asylum, who are being processed at a pace that any ordinary immigrant would envy, and at a time when the country is facing serious unemployment problems of its own — and they react to American generosity by escaping over fences, assaulting U.S. soldiers, and burning their taxpayer-built shelters.

We deplore the incident, but we would remind outraged citizens that it was only 300 out of the 19,000 at the camp who took part in the violence. To brand all the Cuban immigrants as dangerous ingrates will only exacerbate an already difficult transition from refugee to resident.

Nor is the solution, as House Majority Leader James Wright declares, to deport "every person who is clearly known to have participated" in the riot. Such a move would play right into the hands of Fidel Castro, who has indicated he would refuse to take refugees back and might gleefully use their deportation for anti-U.S. propaganda.

Instead, those suspected of provoking the Fort Chaffee riot should face prosecution in the United States. Security at the relocation camps should be tightened. Most of all, the pace of resettlement should be increased.

President Carter's order to speed up processing does not really solve the resettlement problem. The worst delay is not caused by background checks, medical exams, and other paperwork but by a lack of sponsors for the large number of refugees who do not have relatives in the United States.

At the four relocation centers, 24,500 Cubans have been processed, but only 3,757 have left for new homes. The availability of sponsors is reduced by the Cubans' indeterminate immigration status and ineligibility for medicaid and welfare benefits.

The President and Congress must face the challenge of offering financial incentives to church and charity groups to ease the relocation burden.

It also must be realized that, while earlier Cuban refugees have tended to be white, fairly well educated, and aided by previously settled relatives, this group contains larger numbers of blacks and uneducated, unskilled young males, who may have to be federally subsidized in order to be absorbed into the community. The process is apt to be slow and expensive, especially since the refugees have arrived during a recession. Better lines of communication must be developed within the refugee groups so that ignorance and frustration are not easily transformed into violence.

But the United States has made the difficult decision to welcome the Cuban boat people in the name of humanity and freedom. It cannot now spurn them because of the violent actions of a few or a sudden realization that generosity will not be cheap.

TULSA WORLD
Tulsa, Okla., June 3, 1980

IN RETROSPECT, the rioting that has broken out at Fort Chaffee, Ark., where 20,000 Cuban refugees are being processed before release into U. S. society, could have been predicted.

Putting that many people from any country into confinement, not to mention the obvious criminal element and perhaps dedicated provocateurs, guaranteed unrest.

But now we learn President Carter was warned by the Central Intelligence Agency as early as January that Fidel Castro might seize the opportunity to dump thousands of Cubans on the U. S. to ease the dreadful economic conditions in Cuba.

The Carter Administration, according to Rep. Les Aspin, D-Wis., ignored the CIA warning, hoping instead that Castro would cooperate with a Carter plan to accept a limited number of refugees.

The President at first was talking of 3,500 refugees. Instead, the number is approaching 100,000. There is evidence to believe that Castro operatives were sent out with the refugees to stir the kind of rioting we have seen at Fort Chaffee.

The idea is to compel U. S. security agents to put down the uprisings with force and turn the whole episode into an embarrassment for the U. S.

The chances of that happening remain very good. Despite the combined efforts of Federal and State lawmen and military personnel, it is doubtful that recurrences of the uprisings can be prevented.

The Administration has missed its chance to control the situation. Having lost the initiative, it is now simply reacting, a position that has become a hallmark of the Carter Administration.

It would have been embarrassment enough for the President — and the country — if its inept handling of the refugees was the result of a complete surprise.

But the fact the CIA warned the Administration at least five times, the last time in January, leaves the President with, in Aspin's words, "not one excuse for the amateur and fumbling policy" that has resulted in the Fort Chaffee riots.

The Boston Globe
Boston, Mass., June 4, 1980

The rioting by a relative handful of the Cuban refugees camped at Fort Chaffee, Ark., has hardly aided the complex task of assisting in their orderly resettlement. The rioting did not and could not serve the interests of the Cubans themselves. Fortunately a very small minority of the refugees encamped there were involved, and it should not be forgotten that the 19,000 Cubans in Arkansas are only about 20 percent of the recent refugee influx.

Underlying the violence at Fort Chaffee, according to most accounts, was frustration at the perceived slowness of processing. That has resulted in some back-and-forth between government officials and the voluntary agencies who have the prime resettlement responsibilities. Each has blamed the other.

If those Cubans who are to be admitted — and eventually most of them will be — were given permanent refugee status, it would ease the situation. Legislation enacted earlier this year would then allow the release of government funds to assist the voluntary agencies with resettlement costs and to guarantee local governments federal aid to offset any resulting social service costs. That, more than anything, would speed the relocation of thousands of Cubans in American society, and reduce the cabin fever at Fort Chaffee.

The Evening Gazette
Worcester, Mass., June 7, 1980

The thousands of Hispanic refugees waiting in U.S. camps to be processed have already learned that, dictatorship or democracy, there's always red tape.

Those Cubans at Fort Chaffee, Ark. are also learning that in America one of the freedoms is "passing the buck." The private relief agencies say they have sponsors for many of the Cubans now in exile from their homeland but that the Immigration and Naturalization Service procedures are too involved and slow.

The Immigration officials say they are processing refugees as fast as there are sponsors available and the agencies are way behind in providing them.

The United States Catholic Conference claims it has 4,500 sponsors waiting for Immigration to clear the refugees. The Immigration Service says it has already processed many Cubans who have no sponsors and can't be turned loose.

And as if there weren't enough confusion, some of the Cuban sponsors have managed to get congressmen and other officials to intercede and jump their relatives to the head of the line.

Welcome to America.

The Salt Lake Tribune
Salt Lake City, Utah, June 3, 1980

Rioting by some 200 Cubans at the Fort Chaffee, Ark. relocation center is the latest sorry episode in a botched refugee operation that exposed the many shortcomings of U.S. immigration policy.

Much blame can be placed on the Carter administration which, though reportedly warned several times by the Central Intelligence Agency of an impending mass exodus from Cuba, did little to prepare for the human onslaught.

Not only was there minimal preparation, mixed signals from Washington added to confusion as the refugee boats unloaded their human cargoes in Florida and returned to Cuba for more.

The same indecision, red tape and lack of vision is keeping thousands of refugees detained in relocation camps while final processing moves at a hopeless pace.

According to a House intelligence subcommittee report, the CIA warned the administration five times between late January and March of hints that the Castro government might be considering the large-scale exodus of dissidents. Frank E. Loy, deputy coordinator for refugee affairs, acknowledged seeing the reports but told the New York Times that the warning about emigration from Cuba did not necessarily mean there would be a large, disorderly exodus.

Once the movement was underway, the administration first reacted by insisting that boat captains bringing the refugees to the United States would be fined. Days later President Carter welcomed the Cubans with "open heart and open arms." A short while after that the administration clamped down again and warned boat captains to stop ferrying the Cubans to the United States.

Meanwhile, at the hastily designated relocation centers, the old rules for processing ordinary, business as usual, new arrivals are being observed by over-worked immigration officials. A mere few hundred individuals are moved out of Fort Chafee or Eglin Air Force Base centers each day while thousands sit and wait, grow frantic and maybe try to break out.

The initial reaction of many Americans, to "ship them back to Cuba," is natural enough. But a better solution to the mounting tension would be to eliminate much of the paper work and other restrictions that are holding up quick resettlement of the refugees.

These hapless people were allowed, even encouraged to come to this country under extraordinary circumstances. The same sense of emergency should continue through the processing stage now that they are here.

Puerto Rico Opposes Refugee Camp for Cubans

A U.S. plan to turn an old Army base near Ponce, Puerto Rico into a temporary shelter for 4,500-5,000 Cuban and Haitian refugees aroused heated ire from the Puerto Rican government. The White House announced in September that the Fort Allen base would open in October to relieve refugee congestion in the Miami area. Puerto Rican Gov. Carlos Romero Barcelo filed suit to block the transfer, saying the camp would never be ready within a month and would be able to hold only 800 persons. The suit alleged that the U.S. Administration had misled Puerto Rico into believing that only Cubans would be sent to the site. Most Puerto Ricans objected to the Fort Allen plan, fearing that the influx of refugees would intensify economic hardships and add to the island's 18% unemployment rate.

The refugee transfer was blocked by a federal judge in San Juan in October, then overturned two weeks later by a Boston appeals court. It was briefly blocked again two days later by Supreme Court Justice William Brennan but was allowed to resume by the full Court in November. However, an injunction against the camp was issued in December and upheld in a federal appeal courts one week afterward, leaving the plan still up in the air.

The Miami Herald

Miami, Fla., November 7, 1980

THE U.S. Supreme Court was correct to affirm the right of the Federal Government to place homeless refugees temporarily in Federal facilities, including those in Puerto Rico.

The High Court's decision displeased many Puerto Ricans, but it was necessary nevertheless. It enables the Carter Administration to house up to 2,000 refugees temporarily in Fort Allen in Puerto Rico.

Many Puerto Ricans fear the impact on their society that a mass infusion of refugees might have. They worry that the new arrivals will compete with native Puerto Ricans for the few jobs available in an economy already burdened with high unemployment. Perhaps most troubling of all, many see the Administration's Fort Allen plan as a cynical political calculation to turn Puerto Rico into a colonial dumping ground for unwanted refugees because Puerto Rico has no electoral votes.

Those fears and suspicions, while understandable, are ill-founded. The Fort Allen plan admittedly is a temporary expedient at best; it cures no fundamental problems; and it probably was conceived with some political calculation in mind. Yet it is a reasonable means of alleviating a wrenching short-term crisis while being fair to Puerto Rico as well.

The Carter Administration has stated in court that refugees sent to Fort Allen will never be resettled permanently in Puerto Rico. They will be sent there to a temporary holding facility, removed from society. The Administration also has pledged to hold refugees there no longer than eight months, and that Fort Allen's capacity of 2,000 won't be exceeded.

The refugees have to go somewhere. Many of course remain in South Florida; others are at Federal military bases in Arkansas and elsewhere. There is no good reason to exempt Puerto Rico from sharing the burden.

No one suggests that holding refugees in military bases anywhere represents a ~~permanent solution to America's refugee~~ problems. Permanent solutions will require eliminating the conditions in underdeveloped nations that drive their people into becoming refugees. Permanent solutions will require much more generous aid from the United States and other prosperous societies, and many years to achieve.

Meanwhile, however, there is the urgent problem of what to do with the thousands of homeless, helpless people arriving on South Florida's shores daily with nowhere to turn.

The Supreme Court only affirmed the right of the Federal Government to deal expeditiously with that problem, and it did so not a moment too soon.

The Wichita Eagle-Beacon

Wichita, Kans., September 27, 1980

This week's announcement that all new refugees arriving from Cuba and Haiti would be sent to Fort Allen naval base in Puerto Rico has caused a great deal of justified concern among the residents of the island commonwealth.

With unemployment ranging from 17 to 40 percent, substandard housing, a high crime rate, inadequate health care facilities and 50 percent of the population on federal assistance, the influx of thousands of additional poor people hardly was cause for the Puerto Ricans to stand up and cheer.

Along with new arrivals, many refugees currently in the continental United States also will be sent to Puerto Rico. Included in that number will be criminals, mental patients and other refugees considered to be undesirable. Many Puerto Rican leaders understandably have charged that U.S. problems were being dumped on them.

President Carter was pressed into taking some action by the ongoing displeasure expressed by the people of Florida with the overload of refugees in their state. There is an unsettling feeling that one of Mr. Carter's primary concerns in addressing that displeasure was Florida's 17 electoral votes that he will need in the November election. Puerto Rico has no electoral votes.

Similar motivations may have prompted the decision to move to Fort Chaffee, Ark., all remaining refugees in Florida who will not be sent to Puerto Rico and do not have sponsors. Fort Chaffee also will receive Cubans and Haitians from military installations in Wisconsin, which has 11 electoral votes, and Pennsylvania, which has 27 electoral votes. Arkansas has six.

Little faith can be placed in governmental assurances about the temporary nature of these placements or that all remaining refugees will be placed with sponsors by the first of the year. Such timetables have proved to be unreliable since the flotillas began to deposit more than 100,000 people on these shores.

Admittedly, the problem is a difficult one. There are no simple solutions to finding homes for thousands of people, many of whom are unskilled and do not understand the language and customs of this country. That difficulty is compounded by current economic conditions within the United States.

But treating the refugees like pawns in a political chess match certainly is not the answer. There still is a need for a comprehensive U.S. refugee policy. A greater marshalling of civic, social and religious organizations to find homes for the refugees is also in order.

Continuation of the current erratic approach to the situation only will lead to additional problems. The issue can't be swept under a Puerto Rican rug. It must be addressed with concern for the best interests of everyone involved, rather than deferring to what is most politically expedient.

The Cleveland Press
Cleveland, Ohio, October 11, 1980

A federal judge did the sensible thing the other day in blocking, at least temporarily, an ill-advised Carter administration plan to send several thousand Cuban and Haitian refugees to Puerto Rico.

When the plan leaked out last month, it was estimated that as many as 19,000 might be transferred from refugee camps on the mainland. The estimate has grown steadily smaller as resistance in Puerto Rico has grown fiercer; it came down to 5,000 and now the administration is talking about 2,000.

Whatever the number, it doesn't make much sense to dump Cuban and Haitian refugees on a densely populated island that already is up to its ears in economic problems.

The unemployment rate in Puerto Rico is nearly 18%, and almost two-thirds of the 3.3 million residents receive food stamps.

Furthermore, the former naval communications station where the refugee camp was to be established is rundown. According to Puerto Rican officials, it could not accommodate more than 1,500 persons without overloading medical and sanitation facilities.

To top it off, the Carter administration apparently didn't consult ahead of time with Puerto Rican officials. The island's Gov. Romero Barcelo, a political ally of Carter said he was not informed of the plan until Sept. 19 and was never consulted by the White House.

It smacks of a move by the White House to relieve pressure in several states where the influx of Cuban and Haitian refugees has created political problems for the administration. Puerto Rico doesn't vote in the Nov. 4 presidential election. Florida, Pennsylvania, Wisconsin and Arkansas do.

THE SACRAMENTO BEE
Sacramento, Calif., November 21, 1980

Now that the U.S. Supreme Court has cleared the way for the government to establish a camp in Puerto Rico for Cuban and Haitian refugees, the move must be watched carefully lest the Puerto Rico site become a long-term internment camp for the refugees.

The government has resettled all but 7,000 of the 125,000 people who came to America fleeing Castro's Cuba six months ago, and all but 300 of the 10,000 Haitians — a good record. As of Oct. 31, the refugee camps at Fort McCoy, Wis., and Fort Indiantown Gap, Pa., had been closed and the 7,000 remaining Cuban refugees were in Fort Chaffee, Ark. A spokesman for the federal Cuban-Haitian Task Force says that only new arrivals from Cuba and Haiti will be sent to Fort Allen in Puerto Rico.

The camp was established in Puerto Rico for newcomers, the government says, because it is easier to house the refugees in a warm climate, and because Arkansas officials were promised that no more refugees, Haitians or Cubans, would be sent to Fort Chaffee.

Nonetheless, there are dangers in this shift to a camp outside the United States because there is a temptation to sweep the politically sensitive refugee problem under the rug, and because the Puerto Rico camp could easily become a long-term internment center for Haitians, who are coming to the United States at the rate of about 100 a day.

Once the refugees are here, they must be helped. And the help they want and need is help to get out of the camps. The morale in the compound, whether it is in Arkansas or Puerto Rico, will depend on how many persons are resettled and leave the camp for good. If setting up a staging area in Puerto Rico for new arrivals will achieve that, then no one can quarrel with the move. But that makes it all the more necessary that a renewed effort by government agencies and religious organizations is made to find sponsors for the new arrivals so that the Puerto Rico camp does not become a permanent holding tank for unwanted or forgotten refugees.

Wisconsin ⬥ State Journal
Madison, Wisc., October 14, 1980

As the operation of the Refugee Processing Center at Fort McCoy winds down, it is intersting to note what has been happening to the 5,000 refugees who remained there until late last month.

First, President Carter proposed to consolidate the refugees at McCoy and Fort Indiantown Gap, Pa., at Fort Chaffee, Ark. That made sense, since Wisconsin and Pennsylvania have cold climates. The Cubans are not used to cold weather, and Forts McCoy and Indiantown Gap are ill-suited to house refugees because of lack of insulation in their buildings.

However, Arkansas Gov. William Clinton, a Democrat, vehemently objected and set a number of restrictive conditions on expanding the trouble-plagued Fort Chaffee's refugee center. He also demanded a ceiling on the number of refugees to be housed there. Carter quickly agreed. He needs to carry Arkansas in the election.

So, what to do with the rest of the refugees?

Some Democratic political leaders suggested sending them to an Army post in a western state Carter was sure to lose anyway. Maybe Kansas, Wyoming, or the like.

Carter turned that down, which spawned the idea of sending them to Puerto Rico. Superficially, that made sense, except that the likelihood of resettling many refugees there is virtually non-existent. Puerto Rico has a poor economy and chronically high unemployment. It is singularly poorly equipped to absorb a big influx of refugees, even through Spanish is the official language there. Puerto Ricans are loudly protesting the move.

The key to the decision, it appears, is that Puerto Ricans don't vote in the presidential election.

St. Louis Globe-Democrat
St. Louis, Mo., October 11, 1980

Without a single electoral vote to its name, Puerto Rico ranked high as a near-perfect political solution to the remaining remnants of unsponsored Cuban and Haitian refugees.

A temporary federal court order is the lone hurdle blocking the White House plan to whisk 5,000 refugees out of the U.S. beginning in mid-October just in time to beat the Nov. 4 election. Puerto Ricans are opposed to the plan to temporarily house the refugees, including hundreds with mental and behavioral problems and criminal records, at Fort Allen Naval Base on the island.

President Carter stretched considerably to find a law to pull off the scheme. The court held the Carter executive order for the move had not proved a disaster would result if the refugees were not transferred to the island. The court also ruled the president had no right to waive local environmental laws regarding sanitation and crowding at the proposed refugee camp.

Dropping another big problem in the island's lap is unconscionable. Puerto Rico can barely hold its head above water now. Large numbers of refugees, including more than 70,000 Cubans, settled there in recent years. Life is not easy for the three million who inhabit the 3,500 square-mile commonwealth.

Unemployment is officially put at 17 percent, although some estimates are more than double that figure. About 80 percent of the population is eligible for food stamps and more than half receive some sort of federal aid.

Gov. Carlos Romero still is expected to win re-election but the refugee issue is likely to ultimately bring about his political demise. The Carter action also has enraged the previously fragmented leaders opposing statehood into a unified front. Most Puerto Ricans, noted for their political divisions, are united against the Carter refugee plan. The Socialist Party, a pro-Cuba faction of the independence movement, has been handed an issue with which to seek to expand its ranks.

The worldwide refugee problem calls for genuine compassion and understanding. Turning it into a political football is a ruthless act. The danger of heading in that wrong direction is displayed by the discord that is rocking Puerto Rico.

From its beginning the entire illegal entry of Haitians and Cubans has been grossly mishandled. The Carter administration bungled on all sides and gave Castro an opportunity to dump Cuba's undesirables, along with the huge influx of deserving refugees, on Uncle Sam. The White House flouted U.S. laws covering the acceptance of refugees.

The Carter administration still follows a disgraceful approach to the very end. Instead of pursuing the dictates of decency, the president decided to follow in the footsteps of Castro by atttempting to dump the undesirables onto Puerto Rico.

That sort of despicable action can be expected from a Communist dictator but not from a U.S. president. The unfortunate Carter course has triggered an outpouring of catcalls accusing this country of imperialism and colonialism. The once placid Caribbean has been growing choppy. For the United States to intensify the existing turbulence is an invitation for more troublesome times.

The Providence Journal

Providence, R. I., September 26, 1980

It may be uncharitable to suspect the White House of trying to engineer a quick political fix in its proposal to ship as many as 5,000 Cuban refugees to Puerto Rico. Even if that is not the case, however, the plan promises to exchange one problem for a potentially far greater set of problems down the road.

Suspicions that campaign politics are involved arise from the discontent of citizens and officials in states where the federal government has herded thousands of refugees into former military bases to await permanent relocation. Florida and Arkansas are particularly aroused by the situation. Their concern has not been diminished by riots among the refugees who came looking for the Promised Land and find themselves instead in limbo.

Enemies of the White House lost no time in charging that the President was trying to stave off anti-Carter sentiment in those states by removing the offensive problem to the island commonwealth, where the people have no vote in a presidential campaign.

To shuffle helpless human beings around in such cavalier fashion in order to garner votes would be unconscionable under the best of circumstances. But with Puerto Rico rapidly evolving into what could be a dangerous political hotspot, the circumstances surrounding such a move are poor indeed.

That island is currently in ferment, with a 20 percent unemployment rate causing considerable social and political tension. A tiny fringe minority of *independentistas* is stirring up trouble — terrorist bombs have claimed numerous lives this year — and even the existent Cuban refugee community, numbering some 25,000, resents the proposal to send yet more refugees to compete for nonexistent jobs.

To further confuse the situation, Governor Carlos Romero Barcelo is trying to persuade the people to vote for statehood. This would be perfectly all right were Mr. Romero not risking a backlash of unfulfilled expectations by promising them all sorts of things, including continuation of

> *Shuffling human beings around in such cavalier fashion is unconscionable under the best of circumstances*

the tax-free status they now enjoy as a commonwealth and double the present $3 billion handout from Washington. Congress is as likely to deliver on those promises as it is to annex Cuba as the 52d state.

The political climate in Puerto Rico is so volatile today that for Washington to dump 4,000 or 5,000 homeless and jobless refugees there — including more than 400 mentally ill or severely retarded persons — is to court future problems far worse than the conditions that move would allegedly correct. The danger signals are clear, and the White House will ignore them at its own peril.

ARKANSAS DEMOCRAT

Little Rock, Ark., October 5, 1980

The people of Arkansas didn't like it either, but they had to take the Cubans, and he's certainly not going to treat Puerto Rico any different from Arkansas! That's President Carter talking — letting Puerto Ricans know that they have to take 5,000 Cuban and Haitian refugees whether they like it or not.

They don't like it. The Puerto Rican government is vainly filing suit to stop it — not so much because the island has already absorbed scores of thousands of Cuban refugees over the years of Castro's rule, but because they think Carter is taking political heat off himself at the expense of a U.S. possession that has no voice in the presidential election.

Puerto Rico casts no presidential vote — has no electoral votes to deliver. It sends delegates to both presidential conventions and even has a presidential primary, but its status denies it any electoral say.

So Puerto Ricans see the refugee dump as sort of a taxation without representation. Unlike Arkansans, they can't voice their resentment in November, but they're being forcefully reminded that they aren't really part of the United States — just a commonwealth, a colony.

That realization might swing them more toward the idea of statehood, one of the options — the other being independence — that they could trade their commonwealth status for. They haven't done so because they have free immigration to the U.S., but they could change their minds.

We don't need a 51st state of any kind. And seeing now how Puerto Rico can serve as a political dumping ground for presidents, we don't imagine that Carter does either. It's mighty handy having a sort of political Devil's Island.

ST. LOUIS POST-DISPATCH

St. Louis, Mo., October 4, 1980

Now that the Cuban refugee sealift seems to be over, calmer consideration can be given to the 125,000 who have recently arrived and the thousands of Haitians who continue to trickle in. One thing the administration ought to reconsider is its decision to send 2,000 refugees who have no family ties in the U.S. to Puerto Rico.

One immediate reason for this reconsideration is a report from the island that Fort Allen is unlikely to be ready for the refugees by the set date of Oct. 15. Of a more general nature are the facts of the Puerto Rican economy. Just last week Puerto Rico's Department of Labor and Human Resources announced that unemployment had reached 17.7 percent; but that figure may be too low, as other statistics indicate that a little more than 1 million of the 3.1 million population are working. Puerto Rico also suffers from substandard housing and a high crime rate.

A recent study has shown that immigrants have been more of an economic asset to the U.S. than a liability. So the concern apparent on the island may be unfounded. But how can the refugees be expected to help an economy when the jobs are not there, as is the case in Puerto Rico? And if special jobs were to be created for them, the suspicions of those who believe that the U.S. treats its commonwealth neighbor as a second-class citizen would naturally deepen.

Puerto Ricans ought to be encouraged to sponsor some of the Spanish-speaking refugees. But to use the island as a staging ground from which the refugees are to find homes and employment could well slow their settlement. Those who have been allowed into the U.S. to start a new life ought to have the best possible chance to make a success of it, and there simply are more options for the refugees in the states.

Criminals Found Among Refugees of 'Freedom Flotilla'

Relieving Cuban jails of political prisoners created no problems of conscience for most Americans. However, President Fidel Castro was widely believed to have emptied his jails of everyone, common criminals and dissidents, and packed them off to waiting boats at Mariel harbor. Rumors of a flood of hardened Cuban felons were not put to rest by the uprisings at Fort Chaffee, Ark. where impatient refugees went on a rampage. The figures, however, presented grounds for optimism. The criminal element was estimated to be less than 1% of the 115,000 Cubans in the refugee flood. The Justice Department reported in June that 1,395 Cubans had been transferred to U.S. prisons after investigations determined that they had committed serious crimes in Cuba. The rest of those with Cuban criminal records were found to be guilty of only petty offenses or economic crimes, such as speculating, that were outlawed in communist countries. Meanwhile, Cuba made no reply to repeated U.S. requests to accept the return of hardened criminals who qualified for deportation.

St. Petersburg Times
St. Petersburg, Fla., December 10, 1980

After months, and despite massive efforts to find them new homes, hundreds of Cuban boat people continue to roam the streets of Miami, scrounging for food and sleeping in parks. This is ridiculous. It isn't fair either to them or Dade County, which has suffered more than its share of headaches in the "freedom flotilla" that landed 125,000 Cuban refugees on South Florida shores.

BUT THAT ISN'T the most shameful news about the government's attempt to wrap up and wind down the Cuban immigrant crisis. Some of the refugees, and not just hardened criminals either, have been stuffed into prison where they languish under what amounts to an indeterminate sentence.

A *New York Times* reporter recently found 800 men, many of them packed 8 to a 4-man cell, locked behind the grim walls and iron bars of Atlanta's "hard time" federal penitentiary. More than 900 others remain incarcerated in 17 other prisons, he learned.

Many among them are admitted killers and rapists, of course. Fidel Castro announced he was getting rid of his "scum," and he unquestionably did use the boatlift to lighten the load in his own notorious prisons.

BUT MANY had been jailed for minor offenses (smoking marijuana among them), and others for what would have to be called political crimes. Attempted escape from Cuba, for instance, can hardly be considered an inexcusable breach in view of the welcome extended the refugees by President Carter.

And *New York Times* reporter Paul Montgomery said some of those jailed appear to be innocent even of minor offense, the unfortunate victims of misunderstanding, bureaucratic mixups and sheer bad luck in the vast resettlement shuffle.

The lawbreaking, real or not, was committed in Cuba, of course, and as evidence the government relies on the confessions of the persons involved. The jailed refugees aren't Americans, officials point out. And since they haven't been "admitted" as prospective citizens they don't enjoy traditional American rights.

EVENTUALLY, they all are supposed to get hearings, and some will be cleared for release, provided sponsors have been found to receive them. But in this land of the free they have been been waiting in prison for as long as seven months, with no sign they are about to get out.

The lingering disgrace in the streets of Miami, involving as it does individual transients who can't be dealt with as a group, defies any easy solution, even granting the compassion of involved officials and their earnest desire to find one. But the plight of those now wasting in prison could be resolved by the bureaucrats in a hurry.

They could free the seemingly innocent and the good risks among the petty offenders, without further delay and subject only to the usual immigration restraints.

AS FOR THE real criminals — who quite possibly make up most of the group — order them deported and give Castro one more chance to receive them. If he turns this down, as he has rejected previous offers, fly his convicts to Guantanamo Bay. And let U.S. Marines there hoist them over the fence.

The Cleveland Press
Cleveland, Ohio, September 5, 1980

When Cuba's Fidel Castro dumped thousands of criminals and mental defectives on a paralyzed, hand-wringing Carter administration, it was clear deep trouble was in store for this country.

That trouble is here now, and the administration characteristically is unable to deal with it.

Most of the 120,000 Cuban refugees who came since April have been resettled, with relatives or friends as sponsors. These decent people, who fled Cuba for freedom or economic opportunity, will make a valuable contribution to America, as did the Cubans who arrived earlier.

But the 14,000 remaining in military camps here are mostly single men lacking relatives, useful skills and knowledge of English. Most of them have prison records and comprise Castro's poisoned gift to this nation.

In Fort McCoy, Wis., for example, the sweepings of Cuba's prisons are terrorizing and robbing other refugees, gang-raping girls and homosexually attacking boys. Wisconsin's Gov. Lee Dreyfus had to ask the White House for military police to retake control of the camp from the criminals.

No other nation would supinely allow a hostile dictator to handicap it with the dregs of his jails and asylums. But our White House, straitjacketed by legalisms and feckless when challenged, tamely submits.

Listen to Art Brill, spokesman for the State Department's Cuban-Haitian Resettlement Task Force, on the problem of Cuba's criminals among us:

"We have to blame Mr. Castro for sending them to us. It was kind of a gross thing to do. As to what we have left (in the camps), we're getting down to the hard core. We cannot send those that are here back, because Castro won't take them back."

Those are the words of weak-kneed defeatism, which runs from Brill through the secretary of state to the Oval Office.

A self-respecting country would collect Castro's thugs and perverts, put them aboard a ship to our naval base at Guantanamo Bay, open the gate and shove them back into communism's Caribbean paradise.

Instead, the administration's position toward Castro is to crouch on all fours, raise its posterior into the air and await the next kick.

The Miami Herald

Miami, Fla., August 9, 1980

CITIZENS of foreign countries who are convicted of a serious crime in the United States can be deported. Those who have criminal records in their native land can be denied entrance to the United States. That's what Federal immigration law clearly says.

But officials of the U.S. Immigration and Naturalization Service (INS) report a reality very different from the law's ideal. They report that the U.S. Government has had no success in deporting criminals from Cuba and other Communist-bloc countries. And there is no procedure for shifting responsibility for such foreigners onto Federal agencies and off of local criminal-justice systems.

Even before the Mariel sealift, several hundred Cuban nationals were under deportation orders for drug-dealing and other criminal convictions. They're still here. After they serve their state-prison sentence, they go back on the street just as an American citizen would.

Unless there's a dramatic shift in policy in Washington, the same official helplessness will prevail with regard to the new refugees. Some of them were loaded onto the boats directly from Castro's prisons.

South Florida cannot tolerate any more of that Federal indifference. One local INS officer commented that his agency is "waiting for divine guidance" — not from Heaven, but from Washington. No one at the White House or on Capitol Hill knows what to do. Whether anyone even cares is questionable.

But South Floridians care. Miami Beach Police Chief Peter Corso on Wednesday told city commissioners that more rapes were reported in his city last month than during all of last year. "Almost all of it ... is directly attributable to the Cuban prisoners Fidel Castro unleashed upon us," the chief said. He estimates that of the 2,000 newly arrived Cuban refugees living in Miami Beach, 200 to 300 are suspected criminals. The problems are only beginning.

Federal officials must be made to understand how the breakdown of U.S. immigration law at Mariel translates into specific, serious, local problems. City, county, and state officials — including delegates to next week's Democratic Convention — should press persistently for a Federal response that is in proportion to the size of the Federally created local problem.

If the Administration cannot deport foreign criminals from the United States, then it should at least find a way to remove them from the streets of American cities. The pressure to release all the refugees still being held in Federal camps should be resisted and then reversed. Many who were released too hastily should be sent back to await deportation or a long-range, carefully supervised resettlement program.

Criminals who enter the United States without permission and who have not earned the status of permanent resident or naturalized citizen are a responsibility of the Federal Government. City, county, and state officials should use every ounce of political clout they possess to force Washington to take that responsibility.

Miami, Fla., November 26, 1980

NO ONE KNOWS how many criminals came into the United States on the Mariel sealift. Certainly it is a minority of the 124,000-plus persons who came, yet just as certainly the U.S. Government has made no visible progress toward doing what must be done: sending back to Cuba the people who never, ever should have been allowed to come.

About 1,700 persons who came from Mariel were identified immediately as felons and imprisoned. They continue in legal limbo — too dangerous to be released, patently unacceptable as immigrants, but convicted of no crime in the United States.

Those are not the people spreading fear in the streets of Miami, especially in areas such as Little Havana and Miami Beach, where residents, many of them elderly, are accustomed to feeling relatively safe while walking in their neighborhoods.

Some knowledgeable observers believe that as many as 20,000 of the *marielitos* lived in Cuba by skirting the law: stealing an orange here, a fish there. Many of them are young, too young to remember when the Cuban state did not claim to apportion resources according to need, that never-attained goal of communism.

They came of age, streetwise, in a society that suppresses individual initiative. The presumption is that it is persons of that formative background who are having so much trouble adapting to this complex free-enterprise society.

Some of them did not want to come to America and now want to go back to Cuba. They rarely have worked and don't want to start now. What some seem to be finding in the streets of Miami is not gold, but little old ladies with purses.

There is the suspicion — unproven but indicated — that some Mariel refugees are more violent and dangerous than any other segment of this community except the big-time drug dealers. The public has the sense of hearing incessantly about another Mariel refugee who has killed someone in a petty dispute, or murdered or raped or mugged an innocent victim.

The continued inaction of the U.S. Government is reprehensible. Local communities, and especially Dade, feel they must await an atrocity to get some person unacceptable by any standard of immigration policy off the streets. The tainting brush of that violent minority has hobbled the process of this nation assimilating the majority of newcomers from an island that has contributed so much to this community.

One cannot help but wonder what passes for thinking in Washington when Haitians who want to work are left to sit for weeks on a Cayo Lobos, while no attempt is made to identify and deport those Mariel refugees who no one thinks should be in the United States, including themselves. Action is long overdue and becomes more pressing each day.

San Francisco Chronicle

San Francisco, Calif., July 3, 1980

THE AMERICAN PUBLIC is outraged to learn that 1395 of the 115,000 Cuban refugees lately allowed by Fidel Castro to leave Cuba for Key West, Florida, are common criminals, most of whom have committed such felonies as murder, homicide, robbery, theft, narcotics violations, assault and rape.

Castro has taken advantage of the outrush of dissident Cubans from their island prison to empty some of his notorious internal prisons and rid his society (he hopes) of these hard core criminals, plus about ten times as many petty offenders and political criminals. (The U. S. government is accepting the latter two groups.)

If the leaders of Congress are speaking for public opinion — and we believe they are —, Castro will not get away with foisting his underworld elements on this country.

"THE UNITED STATES must not be allowed to become a dumping ground for criminals," said Democratic leader Robert Byrd in the Senate last month. Along with the House Democratic leader, Jim Wright, he called for their deportation. Secretary of State Muskie later warned that if Castro did not respond to a strong U. S. note of protest over the criminals' entry, the United States would find means for "excluding" them. This is the term used for sending home aliens trying to enter the country, as opposed to "deportation", which is used for aliens already here.

How to exclude the Cuban jailbirds is the question. Muskie pointed out you can't just drop them off in Guantanamo, for the gates of that base "swing both ways," and if we pushed criminals out through the gates, Castro might turn around and push another crowd right back in.

SOME WAY HAS to be found — possibly by putting the unwanted back on board those impounded fishing boats that the "tired, huddled masses" came in. Let the Coast Guard escort these vessels back to Mariel where the refugees embarked and invite the returnees to go back ashore to their Marxist-Leninist homeland.

DESERET NEWS

Salt Lake City, Utah, May 9, 1980

When some 10,000 Cubans crowded into the Peruvian Embassy compound in Havan, in hope of escaping their homeland, the United States agreed to accept 3,500 of them as refugees.

What began as a trickle has now become a deluge, with about 27,000 Cubans ferried to the United States. The Cuban exodus has been aided by President Carter's consequent promise to accept all those who wanted to leave their island nation.

One worrisome aspect of the sealift is the apparent ploy by Fidel Castro to relieve his overcrowded jails by exporting felons to the United States. Boat captains have reported that Cuban officials have forced them to ferry one boatload of persons selected by Cuban authorities before a boatload of relatives could be taken off.

Government officials in Florida have detained at least 112 of the refugees on suspicion of criminal activities in Cuba for which they were jailed. Crimes range from petty theft to assault and possibly murder. No one knows how many other criminals hve gone undetected.

The United States should not continue to help Castro clean out his jailed undesirables. The administration must find a way to screen the refugees and send the common criminals right back to Cuba.

Los Angeles Times

Los Angeles, Calif., June 10, 1980

Something less than one-half of 1% of the more than 112,000 Cubans who have made up the latest wave of immigration to the United States have been identified as "hardened" criminals, convicted and imprisoned in their homeland and then, when the opportunity presented itself, infiltrated by their government into the ranks of ordinary refugees. Secretary of State Edmund S. Muskie has denounced this exporting of felons as a violation of international law, as no doubt it is, and President Carter has ordered steps to expel these undesirables. That should be done, but the question is how.

The first approach will be to try to get Cuba to take back the criminals, though the chance of this effort working seems slight. The outpouring of Cubans fleeing political repression and economic hardship has been eloquent testimony to the failures of the Fidel Castro regime, but quite clearly Castro has sought to salvage some small advantage from this embarrassment. He has fed into the stream of refugees some Cubans suffering from mental illnesses, some with terminal diseases and something under 500 identifiable criminals. He has, in short, sought to rid Cuba of some of its economically unproductive population. The deliberateness of that act does not indicate that he will be very receptive to having them returned.

If Cuba refuses to readmit the criminals, Muskie has suggested that help might be sought from the United Nations or the Organization of American States. But here, too, the prospects are not encouraging. At best, the international organizations can ask Castro to resume custody of the exiled convicts; they can't force him to do so, and it is problematical whether they would even try. Neither is the proposal feasible that the United States simply push the criminals back into Cuba through the gate of the U.S. naval base at Guantanamo. As Muskie warned, that would give Castro the excuse for putting new pressures on the base.

On an interim basis, the identified criminals will be kept in detention in the United States while an answer to the problem that they pose is being sought. The legal issues are complex. Under U.S. law, the Cubans are entitled to due process. They can contest efforts to return them to Cuba and, if Castro won't take them back, they can contest efforts to keep them under detention here.

The White House promises that known Cuban criminals won't be set loose in U.S. communities. What will ultimately happen to these people, though, is by no means clear. The mass flight of Cubans that began in April has been a humiliation for Castro. The small criminal element included in this exodus has become a burden for the United States.

Chicago Tribune

Chicago, Ill., June 10, 1980

President Carter, we're afraid, is dealing with the problem of undesirables among the Cuban refugees just as he has dealt with many controversies in the past. That is, he has issued a stern statement about it in response to popular feeling, evidently hoping that this will settle the matter. If it doesn't, of course, he can make an equally resolute statement in a week or two saying something different.

On Saturday, Mr. Carter ordered some 900 refugees sent back to Cuba. They included people with criminal pasts, plus 100 or so who staged a destructive riot at Ft. Chaffee, Ark., last week to protest delays in finding homes for them. That seemed a firm and welcome action; even Americans who welcomed the refugees were furious at the way they abused their hospitality.

Mr. Carter's ringing words, however, have not been followed by a plan of action; in fact he himself does not seem quite sure what he meant by them. In practice, they seem to mean that the unwanted refugees will be detained somewhere until the Castro government can be persuaded to let them come back, however long that may take.

That is a feeble hope. The desperate, months-long exodus of some 112,000 Cubans from their homeland has disgraced Fidel Castro and his shoddy government; about the only advantage he could get out of it was to palm off on the United States a number of criminals and misfits unwanted in Cuba or anywhere else. Since he has absolutely nothing else to boast about, this cheap little triumph will have to be ballyhooed as a real achievement, and Mr. Castro won't want to be deprived of it.

The question Mr. Carter has avoided will not go away: What exactly is to be done with the unwanted refugees [who undoubtedly include Castro provocateurs]? The rioters can at least be charged under U. S. law, but what about those whose crimes were committed in Cuba, and are known to U. S. authorities only by hearsay? Can they be imprisoned indefinitely just because we don't know what else to do with them? A good defense lawyer would blow any such plan out of the water.

Since the administration doesn't seem to have any ideas, we'll suggest one: Send these people to the U. S. base at Guantanamo and confine them, preferably near the border fence. They would then at least be on Cuban soil, and we wouldn't have to worry much about their escaping [in fact, escapes over the fence might be tacitly encouraged].

There is a certain offbeat logic to this. After all, the usual punishment for an escaped criminal is to send him back to prison with a lengthened term, and Cuba qualifies admirably for that purpose. [The danger, we suppose, is that "free" Cubans watching through the fence while the detainees got three meals a day might break into the Guantanamo base and join them.]

The plan is not, let us say, perfect. But until the Carter administration can come up with a better way of getting unwanted Cubans back to Cuba, it is something to think about.

St. Louis Globe-Democrat
St. Louis, Mo., June 11, 1980

President Carter, belatedly recognizing that he let the Cuban refugee influx get totally out of hand, now has made a great show of ordering the Justice Department to return to Cuba any refugees known to have serious criminal backgrounds or who have violated U.S. laws since their arrival.

"What concerns most Americans," said White House press secretary Jody Powell, **"is the prospect that some of the people who have committed crimes might be relocated in American communities. That will not happen."**

Oh, no?

How does President Carter propose to get these criminals, mental cases et al back to Cuba? "Friendly" Fidel, after having dumped these undesirables on the United States, certainly hasn't indicated he would take them back.

After making this grandiose pledge, Powell said the administration would attempt to return about 700 Cubans that have criminal backgrounds and another 100 who committed crimes after their arrival, through such international organizations as the United Nations and the Organization of American States, but he would not predict the likelihood of success.

"The president has directed the secretary of state to press this issue urgently through diplomatic channels and in the appropriate international forum," said Powell.

This sounds like a lot of hot air. The Carter administration allowed Fidel Castro to take charge of our immigration policy when it stood by and let an armada of boats go to Cuba and pick up more than 100,000 Cubans in a totally disorganized mass emigration from Castro's giant slave camp. Castro took advantage of this opportunity and forced a number of boat captains to take large numbers of criminals along with their other passengers.

Anyone who knows how unprincipled Castro is recognizes that he won't take these criminals back. The U.S., thanks to another example of bad administration by President Carter, seems certain to be stuck with these dregs.

The Pittsburgh Press
Pittsburgh, Pa., June 11, 1980

The flow of Cuban refugees has finally been reduced to a trickle. But the question of what to do with all of them remains to be resolved.

More than 110,000 men, women and children have left Fidel Castro's paradise to seek a better life elsewhere, preferably in the United States. But neither the United States nor any other country should be expected to absorb them all.

The human tragedy involving the Cuban refugees is an international tragedy. Yet the Carter administration is doing virtually nothing to help resettle any of them in other countries.

★ ★ ★

Moreover, the Carter administration doesn't even know what to do with the undesirable Cubans who sneaked into the United States along with the truly downtrodden and persecuted.

Obviously, most of the refugees out of Cuba are not criminals. But the White House says at least 700 are suspected of being hardened criminals. These are troublemakers whom Castro has been able to get off his own hands, and we should not let him get away with such a miserable trick.

Sen. Robert Byrd of West Virginia, the Democratic leader in the U.S. Senate, has suggested that "we should take them to Guantanamo," the American naval base that sits inside Cuba, "and push them through the gates" back into Castroland.

But Secretary of State Edmund Muskie, echoing the State Department's usual policy of timidity, handwringing and impotence, has responded feebly to Castro's contemptuous provocation.

Mr. Muskie says Sen. Byrd's proposal would violate the U.S. lease for Guantanamo.

Only a State Department lawyer could say that with a straight face. It isn't any lease but the U.S. Marine presence that has stopped Castro from taking Guantanamo long ago.

The secretary also says that if we dumped Castro's criminals back into his own yard Castro might decide the gate at Guantanamo swings both ways and use it for a further exodus of Cubans to America.

That's a lame excuse for inaction. The gate at Guantanamo opens in only if we allow it.

★ ★ ★

So what action has the United States taken on this?

Mr. Muskie says he has sent a "strong protest note" to Castro demanding that he take his criminals back! Ole!

Come to think of it, this may not be as feckless as it seems. Maybe it's a subtle plan to cause Castro to roll on the floor and die from laughter.

Pittsburgh Post-Gazette
Pittsburgh, Pa., June 10, 1980

In principle, it is hard to challenge the view that U.S. hospitality for refugees from Cuba should not extend to hardened criminals, violent troublemakers and those unfortunate "undesirables" who were forced to join the exodus against their will or their best interests.

But from the beginning of the Cuban exodus, there has been a wide gap between principle and practicality. And given the obstinate opposition of President Fidel Castro to any rational accommodation on the refugee issue, that gap will prove difficult to bridge. If that fact is not kept clearly in view, too much is likely to be expected of promises by the administration to deal decisively with "problem" Cuban refugees.

The latest enunciation of that goal came over the weekend from Secretary of State Edmund Muskie. Mr. Muskie told a television audience that exiles who are criminals or mentally ill will be put in detention centers and then, unless Fidel Castro responds to a strong U.S. protest note, sent home. The Muskie comment followed a statement by presidential news secretary Jody Powell that Cubans who took part in violent disturbances at Fort Chaffee, Ark., would not be allowed to settle here.

Even though the secretary of state was careful to note that fewer than 1,000 of the 111,000-plus Cuban exiles could be called serious criminals, he warned that those undesirables will be returned to "whence they came."

That pledge could raise false hopes. The Carter administration may find it impossible, for constitutional or logistical reasons or both, to deport even those 60 Cuban refugees who have been linked to riots at the processing center in Arkansas. Secretary Muskie himself cast doubt on one scenario for repatriating the troublemakers: flying them to the U.S. base at Guantanamo and pushing them through the base's gates onto Cuban territory. "The gates swing both ways," Secretary Muskie noted pregnantly.

But if the administration ought to be careful about over-sanguine speculation about returning the refugees to a Cuba where they will not be admitted, let alone welcomed, a different sort of caution should be urged on civil libertarians and others who are inclined to rise to those refugees' defense.

Moral as well as practical reasons can be adduced for not even trying to return Cuban criminals to their homeland, but it does not follow that American officials can simply disregard evidence that some of the refugees have histories of criminal and dangerous behavior.

The term "detention camp" has a distinctly un-American ring to it, but faced with refugees who have committed crimes either in Cuba or in this country, federal officials have little choice but to keep them confined pending some resolution of their ultimate status.

So far both officials and private individuals have responded with characteristically American compassion to the unique challenge posed by the Cuban boatlift. That generosity is unlikely to survive any perception that the federal government has allowed the migration to create a danger to public safety.

The Seattle Times
Seattle, Wash., June 10, 1980

AFTER days of delay and apparent indecision, the White House over the weekend announced a clear-cut policy regarding Fidel Castro's practice of dumping criminals and other undesirables on the United States.

President Carter ordered the Justice Department to try to return to Cuba any refugees known to have serious criminal backgrounds or who have violated American laws since their arrival.

Immigration officials estimate that some 9,000 of the 112,000 "boatlift" refugees have criminal records. In addition, some 60 are accused of having been agitators in the riots at Fort Chaffee, Ark.

Castro tried to make a sucker out of Uncle Sam. And the Carter administration's slowness to respond made it appear, for a while, that he was succeeding.

But what the Western Hemisphere's No. 1 Communist really accomplished was to further expose his own cynicism and inhumanity.

Castro put himself in the same category as the East German Communist leaders who sell political prisoners for hard currency in the West, and who encourage old-age pensioners, but not productive workers, to emigrate westward.

Secretary of State Muskie accurately described Castro's policy of shipping hardened criminals and mental cases to the U.S. as "in violation of international law," and sent a protest note to Havana.

If Castro does not respond, Muskie said, this country can pursue the question through the United Nations, the Organization of American States, and its own laws, while holding the undesirable aliens in detention camps.

Whatever else happens, the American people have a right to expect that their own government's screening procedures at the refugee centers will be such as to enable the administration to fully honor its promise that Cuban outlaws will not be relocated in American communities.

Homesick Cuban Refugees Hijack Planes Back to Cuba

Not all immigrants find U.S. life to their liking, but refugees from a repressive government do not have the option of going back. Nevertheless, a number of Cubans decided to return home by force, and a rash of hijackings broke out in 1980, reminiscent of earlier times. Six took place in August alone, involving 20 Cubans who were part of the original "freedom flotilla." A hasty reintroduction of increased security measures at U.S. airports thwarted several hijackings, but the incidents continued to try the patience of Havana as well as Washington. The Cuban government warned its former citizens that their sea journeys had been a "one-way trip," and Havana followed up the warnings by immediately returning two Cubans who had hijacked a jet to Havana from Atlanta in September. The hijacking wave then appeared to subside.

Des Moines Tribune
Des Moines, Iowa, September 2, 1980

Another hijacking last week, again by Cubans apparently disenchanted with what they found in the United States after fleeing Fidel Castro. Some of the disenchantment probably is due to homesickness, but a lot unquestionably has to do with unemployment and their welcome here.

Local governments may be as disenchanted as the unhappy Cubans. The federal government's refusal to shoulder full responsibility for the Cuban and Haitian refugees has put a big financial burden on local taxpayers. Federal law requires Washington to pay all costs for refugees, but the Carter administration has refused to classify the Cubans and Haitians as refugees. Instead, they are called "Cuban-Haitian Entrants/Status Pending."

Victor Palmieri, the administration's top refugee official, explained: "Giving refugee benefits to a disorderly mass was seen as an invitation for more of the same. We didn't want to give a message to the rest of the world that people could become refugees simply by landing on our shores."

So local communities are getting no special federal help with the influx of Cubans and Haitians in schools and with the need to provide extra social services. Legislation proposed by the administration would have the federal government pick up 75 percent of the cost of social and related services, but this would still leave local governments with a heavy burden.

It's embarrassing to have Cubans so unhappy with their reception here that they are willing to risk long prison terms to escape. It's equally embarrassing to have the national government shirk its responsibility to avoid encouraging people to seek freedom in the United States.

The refugee problem is national in scope. The Cubans and Haitians obviously are refugees. The country is asking for more embarrassing incidents by its pretense that Cubans and Haitians are not entitled to all of the benefits accorded refugees.

The Star-Ledger
Newark, N. J., August 19, 1980

Disillusioned and despairing, they left Cuba by the thousands, many risking their lives in unseaworthy craft. But they were going to the Promised Land — the land of freedom and plenty, a mere 90 miles distant by water.

For many, the 90 miles was a forbidding gulf of cultural differences so unsettling that even the sanctuary of expatriate relatives could not provide sufficient solace.

The disillusion of their homeland had followed a number of fleeing Cubans to a political and economic refuge in the United States. The early symptoms were evident in the disorders that broke out in processing centers, although these incidents were mainly attributed to impatience over the lengthy reviews of refugees' backgrounds.

While most expatriate Cubans who arrived in this country in the Freedom Flotilla no doubt will remain, a small group has been stricken with homesickness. And some, in desperation, have resorted to skyjacking to return to Cuba.

The unfortunate result has been a resurgence of hijacking of commercial airliners — several within a week — by Cuban refugees who cannot acclimate themselves to the customs of a strange new country.

While their illegal entry into the United States was understandable in human and political terms, the forcible takeover of aircraft cannot be condoned. Air piracy constitutes a criminal transgression that imperils the lives of innocent persons.

There should be a stern enforcement crackdown on this intolerable rash of hijackings by Cuban refugees. Security has been tightened at airports in Florida, an obvious jumping off area for expatriates who want to go back to Cuba. The experience of dealing with aviation piracies should provide an effective means of discouraging the latest incidence of skyjackings.

For refugees who want to return to the homeland they recently fled, there are legal means of repatriation that the U.S. government no doubt is prepared to make available. Skyjacking only further invites more problems for emotionally troubled refugees.

The TENNESSEAN
Nashville, Tenn., August 23, 1980

INCREASED security measures appear to have stopped the wave of airplane hijackings from the United States to Cuba, but it is doubtful that the problem has really been solved.

The problem is homesickness. Six planes were hijacked to Cuba last week, three of them on Saturday alone. In four of the incidents, the hijackers appeared to be Cubans and it is believed that they came to the U.S. in last spring's "Freedom Flotilla."

Also on Saturday, FBI agents arrested two Cuban men as they were about to board a plane. They were carrying bottles filled with gasoline. An agent said they explained themselves by saying, "they missed their families."

U.S. officials said they have tried to negotiate with Cuba for a process whereby refugees could return to their homeland if they wished. "Thus far, we have had nothing from the Cubans but rebuffs on the issue," said a State Department spokeswoman.

This attitude is not surprising. Cuban President Fidel Castro used the refugee exodus last spring for his own purposes. His government did not show any concern for the people.

Until the Cuban government sees some reason for it to change its stance on the issue of allowing refugees to return in an orderly fashion, things are unlikely to change.

That means the only way to safeguard the airways will be the continued presence of federal marshals on various flights and tight screening procedures at airports. But these are only stopgap measures.

The administration should continue to press Cuba for an arrangement to let any refugees, wishing to do so, to return to their homeland.

Newsday

Long Island, N. Y., August 19, 1980

Two unenviable records were set last week: the most airplane hijackings in one week (six), and the most in one day (three).

All the planes were hijacked to Havana, apparently by Cubans who had fled their country and wanted to go home. All the hijackers were armed, or claimed they were, with flammable liquids that could turn an airplane into a flying incinerator.

Airports are now increasing surveillance of boarding passengers, and air marshals have been assigned to some flights. That can help.

But the only person who can surely end this wave of hijackings is Fidel Castro. And so far he has refused to do so.

Cubans who fled their country last spring are barred by the Castro government from returning by legitimate routes. And Cuban authorities have been unwilling even to discuss repatriating Cubans who have simply changed their minds.

Since the Castro government did a good deal to foment last spring's exodus, in hopes of ridding the country of "socially undesirable" people, that's not surprising.

But that doesn't make it any less unconscionable. Some of the 100,000 or so Cubans who came here, after President Carter liberalized the immigration requirements for Cuban refugees, have had second thoughts. Many left Cuba with government permission and are still Cuban citizens; there's no good reason why they shouldn't be allowed to return.

Persuading Castro to accept that view isn't going to be easy. But the United States should still keep up the pressure, through the United Nations and the Organization of American States.

If some Cubans are so eager to go home, they should be able to—without winding up in a Havana jail on hijacking charges.

The Salt Lake Tribune

Salt Lake City, Utah, August 20, 1980

Many of the recent Cuban emigres are apparently finding out what all Americans already know — The streets aren't paved with gold. The result has been a spectacular surge in aerial hijackings; six in a week.

The hijackings have all been the work, this is what the FBI and other law enforcement agencies speculate, of homesick Cuban refugees who arrived earlier this spring during the mass exodus from Cuba by hordes of their fellow countrymen.

It has been estimated some 60,000 Cubans sought haven in the United States when Fidel Castro opened the floodgates. The Cuban dictator couldn't have picked a worse time to grant wholesale exit permits to dissident countrymen. It was from frying pan to fire for these immigrants.

It has been decades since the U.S. economic situation has been in such disarray; unemployment has been 8 percent and climbing while other economic indicators were just as depressing, or depressed.

It was not the time for 60,000-plus new job seekers, who weren't familiar with the language and who frequently didn't have any marketable skills, to be suddenly dumped on the job market in a land where they didn't know the customs. Add to that the fact that many of them had been abruptly separated from family and friends; jumping impulsively on the first dilapitated boat that would take them 90 miles to "paradise."

What they experienced, for many of them, was anything but paradise. Instead it was a dismal period of endless waiting in crowded and hastily tacked together refugee centers while an overworked, understaffed and often bungling bureaucracy paper shuffled its way out of confusion that had turned chaotic.

It is not surprising that some desperate people decided to "get home" by the fastest means possible; hijacking the next airplane leaving town.

For some weeks now the U.S. State Department has recognized that many of the Cuban emigrants are unhappy in this country; wishing they had thought twice before leaving Cuba. State officials have been trying to arrange with Castro a system for returning these people to their homeland. Sunday, the State Department's Sue Pittman said, "The approaches (to Castro) began in May and many notes have been delivered to the Cubans, including the most recent today. Thus far, we have had nothing from the Cubans but rebuffs on this issue."

This is not surprising. Castro, after all, has said, in essence, "good riddance" to the refugees, branding them variously as traitors, criminals, sexual deviants and other less complimentary characteristics. It would be difficult for him now to do an about face and permit the unfettered return of what he has characterized as riff-raff.

The United States is, thus, left with no recourse except to move quickly to assimilate these refugees; a not too easy task normally, but one made much more difficult because of the recession.

Simultaneously, it must be made emphatically clear to these 60,000 or so Cuban exiles that while they will enjoy the privileges and protections of American law, they will be expressly expected to obey those laws including the ones against hijacking airplanes; homesick or not.

Last week's rash of hijackings underscores the fact that Castro's refugees are now America's worry and it is up to this country to cope with the headache because it can't be sent back to Cuba. Not even a little bit of it.

The Kansas City Times

Kansas City, Mo., September 18, 1980

From all evidence, authorities in Cuba are doing what they can to give the current wave of hijacking a bad name. Havana has announced that hijackers will be punished severely or returned to the United States, presumably for trial — not out of any regard for the U.S., but because "no one abandons the fatherland."

Thus the primary responsibility, as always, rests with the airlines and American law enforcement. It's extremely difficult and expensive. Yet for every passenger who might complain about the bother, we would guess that 100 are grateful for special precautions even if they mean delay.

X-ray machines aren't going to detect a pint of liquid that someone says is gasoline. There will have to be more careful hand luggage inspections, more frisking. That may be the only alternative to an unscheduled flight to Havana or the tragedy that could come as the number of incidents mounts.

Hijackings are the price we pay for the social dislocations such as the exodus from Cuba and the inevitable disappointments of a few that occur in a free land of high technology. But greater care can reduce the risks of calamity.

The Morning News

Wilmington, Del., August 19, 1980

A number of Cuban refugees who risked their lives to reach the United States have discovered to their disappointment that the streets here are not paved with gold.

The freedom that looked so attractive from 90 miles away turns out to be less than they expected.

Angry and frustrated at their failure to begin immediately to enjoy the good life, some of these refugees are now prepared to risk the lives of hundreds of American airline passengers in desperate attempts to hijack their way back to Cuba.

Their methods are frightening and outrageous. Bombs and firearms are too easily spotted these days in airport terminals, so they resort to carrying containers of gasoline with which they intimidate airborne flight crews. It's "turn the plane toward Havana or I'll blow all of us up."

Suddenly, airline hijackings, which had become a rarity, are epidemic in the southeastern United States. Trained sky marshals are being assigned to the most susceptible flights. Personality profiles, by which potential hijackers can be tentatively identified, are back in use.

Why all the fuss, you might ask. We Americans, with all good will, would say, "Let them go." Indeed, we are prepared to urge the federal government to help in every way possible to speed their return. Unfortunately, Fidel Castro, gatekeeper of the island paradise to which they wish to return, is as petulant as a jilted suitor. He doesn't want them back.

Under the circumstances, who can blame him? The lawless behavior of these extortionists makes it easier to understand why Premier Castro helped many of them to "escape" to the United States. Persuading him to welcome them back might be difficult, but it needn't be impossible.

The U.S. State Department says its formal and informal urgings to let the refugees return home have been rebuffed by Cuba. Perhaps they have been too direct. Why not point out to Fidel Castro that he is overlooking a golden opportunity for international embarrassment of the United States?

If there is no hope of that, these disenchanted desperadoes must be dealt with swiftly and sternly. They must be given the kind of enforced U.S. hospitality that will convince them and their compatriots that refugee life in these United States was not as uncomfortable as the legal alternative.

OKLAHOMA CITY TIMES

Oklahoma City, Okla., August 20, 1980

THE rash of airline piracies, mostly from Miami, has been laid to disillusioned Cubans who fled Castro's regime, only to find that their dreams of instant prosperity in this country were running afoul of Miami's worst unemployment in a decade.

Another — and perhaps more likely — explanation offered by an official of the U.S. Immigration and Naturalization Service is that when the screening for Castro agents was dropped at Washington's orders, many of those agents got through to resettlement camps. Those are the ones now leaving this country, because they know they will be returning to official rewards, according to the INS official.

If this is so, it is logical, by their standards, for them to choose a way that will embarrass the U.S. government. Airliner hijackings certainly do that.

But for the traveling public, flights from Miami — and even to Miami — have suddenly become frightening prospects. Some of the passengers report the Cuban airport officials were glad to have them buy rum, cigars and other souvenirs at the airport stands and were quite cordial. But there is never any assurance that the Castro regime will even release the helpless passengers within a week, or a month. The history of impromptu side trips to Havana is not encouraging.

Thus, the return of sky marshals to the flights most likely to be affected is welcome. So is the instruction of airport ticket and gate personnel in the "suspicious profile" of a would-be hijacker. This was in common use some years back, but as the threat waned and personnel changed, it became unfamiliar to many present employees.

If Castro really wanted only to let those who oppose his regime emigrate, he would long since have permitted the departure of the 200 still inside the Swiss Embassy's U.S. interests section. His manipulation of the exodus hs been cynical and brutal.

But for those who want to go back to life under Castro, there must be an easier way. The U.S. government, Miami officials and the airlines have a common interest in providing a "reverse sealift" for such Cubans, whether they genuinely have changed their minds or are Castro agents. There is no worse punishment available than to send such agents home.

The return of air piracy must be made unnecessary.

Richmond Times-Dispatch

Richmond, Va., August 19, 1980

It all seems like a grotesque replay of happenings a decade ago: American commercial airplanes being pirated to communist Cuba; and "behavorial profile" scans at airports and armed federal air marshals aboard selected flights in an effort to deter skyjackers. But of course this time there is a difference: These are recent Cuban refugees who claim they are homesick or fed up with their life in the United States and who have chosen this drastic action as their only available return ticket.

This development presents Cuba's Maximum Leader, Fidel Castro, with a splendid opportunity to make propaganda hay at the expense of the U. S., a favorite pastime of his. Having tasted life under decadent capitalism, Cubans are desperate to return to the communist workers' paradise, Castroites may now boast. But that would be a woefully distorted impression for anyone to gain, whether from communist propaganda or otherwise.

While a handful of apparently disaffected Cuban refugees have hijacked airliners or tried to, hundreds more have quietly continued to arrive in small boats in Florida, late arrivals in the "Freedom Flotilla" that brought more than 100,000 to these shores earlier this year. And thousands of these refugees have been resettled throughout the United States, including the Richmond area, where they are becoming productive citizens.

Plausibly, some refugees still in the dispiriting "tent cities" have despaired of delays in being relocated and have concluded that a return to Castro-style austerity would be preferable to endless limbo. Some may long for relatives and friends left behind. But it is also plausible that the sudden rash of skyjacking has been promoted by Castro himself as another way to embarrass the U. S. It is known, after all, that a small portion of the refugee stream contained agents of the Castro regime. Despite the fact that the root cause of the exodus from the Caribbean island is the economic and political blight of 20 years of Castroism, Castro has sought cynically to use the refugees to his advantage: For example, he has emptied some of his prisons and mental hospitals into the refugee stream.

No Cuban refugee is being forced to stay in America. There are regularly scheduled flights to Havana, and U. S. authorities no doubt would be happy to help those who might want to leave. The problem, of course, is that Castro refuses to accept refugees that the U. S. seeks to repatriate. It would be useless to appeal to him on humanitarian grounds to do so, but perhaps Washington could find ways to pressure him into handling the flow of people between these two nations on a more civilized basis.

As for the emergency measures the Federal Aviation Administration has reinstituted to discourage skyjackers, they are probably necessary. But great caution should be exercised by the airborne marshals. There would be less chance of tragedy in allowing a plane to proceed to Havana than in engaging in a shootout in flight. Closer surveillance of passengers and their baggage at airports appears to be the most realistic hope of stopping this new outbreak of the 20th century disease known as skyjacking.

Haitian Drownings Highlight Illegal Immigration

U.S. attention was first focused on illegal immigration from Haiti in August 1979 when a mother and five children drowned off the coast of Florida as they tried to enter the country. They were part of a group of 16 Haitians on board a smuggler's boat headed towards Palm Beach when they were discovered by a police patrol on shore. The smugglers forced all the Haitians off the boat at gunpoint into heavy seas, but nine of the Haitians were rescued. Another Haitian was believed to have drowned. Three men, including the owner of the boat, were arrested and charged with first-degree murder.

About 9,000 Haitians were believed to be living illegally in the southern Florida area. They had escaped from the poorest country in the Western Hemisphere to find work and relief from government repression. Haiti's six million people were estimated to have a per-capita income of less than $90 a year.

DESERET NEWS
Salt Lake City, Utah, December 6, 1979

"Small Hope Bay" in the Bahamas seems aptly named — at least for the boatload of Haitian refugees that floundered there in heavy seas this week on their way to the United States.

Luckily, 92 survived, many with cuts and bruises from several hours of battering against a reef a mile offshore. At least two refugees, and perhaps several more, died.

But the survivors' luck is lamentably short-lived; they're due to be deported to Haiti as soon as Bahamian officials can process them. There they face at best a harsh future in a nation that's clearly the poorest country in the hemisphere, that has been charged with selling thousands of Haitians as slaves to the Dominican Republic for $11 each.

The boat mishap is another chapter in a long battle over Haitian refugees. U.S. law provides sanctuary for victims of political persecution. But there is a question among U.S. authorities whether the refugees are political or economic refugees. They're ineligible to stay if they flee because of poverty alone.

The rulers of Haiti are, however, considered among the most repressive in the Western Hemisphere, backed by a dreaded and arbitrary secret police.

The U.S. has deported no Haitians for almost a year now. Last January the National Council of Churches sued the Immigration and Naturalization Service, which stopped the practice at least temporarily. Must we really resume it?

The Miami Herald
Miami, Fla., August 15, 1979

AN UNDERGROUND railroad to hell took a young Haitian mother and five children to their death in the Atlantic Ocean just south of Palm Beach Monday. The smugglers who had promised the family safe passage to Florida from Freeport, Bahamas, panicked, forced the passengers overboard, and left them to drown.

Until the searchlight of a police patrol car spooked the boat's crew into dumping the human evidence like so many bales of dope, the story was reminiscent of those found in family albums in millions of American homes. Weary of the squalid, grinding poverty of their homeland, a married couple had decided to make a better life in a place where their children could grow up without the constant hunger. The husband and older children emigrated first, leaving the wife and younger children alone in order to try to save enough money to bring them along later.

And after a year of hard, menial labor, the money had been accumulated — $1,500, enough to pay passage for the remainder of the family. And so these hopeful travelers became the first *documented* cases of Haitian refugees being dumped in the ocean to die.

There is one main difference between this doomed group and the millions of Italians, Irish, and others who came to the land of opportunity before them. Those earlier immigrants were legal. The Haitians in the 28-foot Chris-Craft were not. And because their flight to freedom and opportunity is against the laws of the sanctuary they are trying to reach, Haitians are easy prey for the human scavengers who take their money and then may — or may not — deliver them safely to Florida.

The same scenario also plays out day after day along the Texas border, with Mexicans instead of Haitians. There, too, the work-starved illegal immigrants often are mistreated by those who promise to transport them. But at least the Mexicans don't face a potential ocean grave as do the Haitians, who have become the boat people of the Western Hemisphere.

So what can Americans do? They cannot absorb the entire four-million-plus population of Haiti, but neither can they tolerate the murder of would-be immigrants by smugglers. Investigation and prosecution should be thorough and swift.

But beyond merely treating this awful symptom, the United States Government must address the disease itself — the massive pressure created by dire poverty and cruel unemployment in our neighbor nations. It makes no moral sense to send the U.S. Navy to rescue Vietnamese boat people and bring them to certain sanctuary in the United States while turning back Haitians who also drown at sea.

Granted that the element of political, rather than economic, repression is more clear in Southeast Asia than in Haiti. But how long can Americans cling to the distinction between starving to death in a concentration camp and starving to death in one's own hovel?

The Carter Administration earlier made a promising start toward developing a coherent approach to immigration and human rights that would erase many of the contradictions in U.S. policy. Unfortunately, that effort stalled in a Congress immobilized by parochial concerns and special interests.

Clearly the effort should be renewed. The United States needs a consistent policy that will deal even-handedly with all suffering peoples everywhere. And if that requires a creative array of new categories for temporary workers, long-time undocumented residents, or relatives of American citizens, then perhaps some new categories should be considered. At the very least, new emphasis on foreign aid for this nation's nearest neighbors is in order.

The American conscience simply cannot tolerate such tragedies as the one that occurred off Palm Beach on Monday.

The Providence Journal

Providence, R. I., November 19, 1979

Things are changing in Haiti, and not for the better. When Jean-Claude Duvalier took over as President-for-Life from his father, "Papa Doc," there was some initial hope that the old tyrannical ways had died with the elder Duvalier.

And indeed, for a while, that seemed to have been the case. The Ton Ton Macoutes, Papa Doc's hated and feared secret police, were muzzled. Press censorship was lifted. Life for the Haitian people became at least somewhat less threatening.

Now the pendulum appears to be swinging back. The Ton Ton Macoutes are back swaggering on the streets of Port au Prince. They go under a new title — Volunteers for National Security — but this particular bunch of roses by whatever name has the lingering smell of blood and death about it. An authoritarian press law has been promulgated and criticism of the regime is confined to discreet whispers.

Human evidence that the evil ways of Papa Doc have been revived by "Baby Doc" can be seen firsthand in this country. It takes the form of thousands of Haitian "boat people" who head for Florida's beaches. Many are ferried by unscrupulous bandits who are prepared to jettison their human cargoes into the sea if apprehended by U.S. authorities. For reasons understood best by officialdom, the Justice Department and the Immigration and Naturalization Service review Haitian boat people as "economic refugees" and not legitimate seekers of political asylum. U.S. authorities have rounded up some 8,000 Haitians. Some are being held in prison, and the others are under restraints. The Department of Immigration and Naturalization policy is to ship all Haitians back and to this end instituted a program of "voluntary return" that is hardly what such a euphemism suggests. As the Haitians were picked up, they were interviewed by Creole-speaking interpreters and warned that if they did not agree to return to Haiti they would be jailed, denied work permits and ultimately deported.

Before a federal court, on the appeal of civil and humanitarian groups, ordered a stay of such deportations, 600 Haitian refugees were repatriated in this way. Unauthorized departures are a political offense in Haiti, and returnees are either jailed or placed under surveillance.

While U.S. authorities have treated illegal Haitian immigrants much as they have treated their Mexican counterparts, the circumstances are hardly similar. The Mexicans are indeed "economic refugees" who cross over the border in search of better economic conditions. Unlike the Haitians, they are encouraged to do so by the Mexican government, tacitly if not overtly. And they are free to return at any time without prejudice.

No such option exists for the hapless Haitians. Now that a federal court has recognized this distinction and rightly called the Haitian refugee problem a political issue, it would grace the Carter administration to recognize that fact and to come up with a political solution. Given the latest turn of the screw in Haiti, amnesty for the 8,000 Haitians now in this country seems to be called for, along with a humane policy for handling what may well be an increased inflow of escapees from increasing oppression.

Chicago Defender

Chicago, Ill., August 30, 1979

Elaine Forfils and five of her children were forced from a smuggler's boat at gunpoint a half mile off the Palm Beach, Florida shore two weeks ago. All six of them drowned. There afternoon funeral is still fresh in the minds of the thousands of Haitians still in South Florida, outraged at the way these refugees and those still alive seeking political freedom here, are being treated by this country.

The assistance given to the Cuban refugees who began fleeing their country some 20 years ago because of the overt oppression of Fidel Castro's regime, stands out as a glowing example of how America has traditionally received refugees seeking asylum in this country.

The privileges afforded Cubans in the late 50s and early 60s are still being extended today. And more recently, the position Carter has taken on the Vietnamese boat people only adds fuel to the fire of disenchantment of those who can't understand this country's policy.

The double standard employed by the U. S. in its treatment toward refugees has been all the more highlighted with the recent announcement that certain regulations, which supposedly few, if any Haitians can meet, have been waived by the State Department so that Nicaraguan refugees can be issued work permits, receive free food stamps, free medical services and free governmental social services. Those who will be shocked at this news in the wake of the present plight of the Haitians, must be reminded of what the Nicaraguans have in common with the Cubans — the color of their skin.

Thousands of Haitians abandoned their country because of what they considered a dictatorial government, one which fails to recognize the Democratic process. However, Haiti represents no problem to the United States government.

Last week U.S. Senator Richard Stone accused the U.S. of employing a double standard in regards to the Haitians and stated that they (the Haitians) were suffering in this country because they were black. A belated observation, but yet, perceptive. Haitian refugees who have sought political assylum here are not welcome and have not been treated in a manner other refugees are afforded.

Haitians are even denied work permits to care for their families and are thus forced to live off handouts while the government decides just what to do with them. Many of them have been incarcerated and many more face possible deportation, back to a country they feel, now, has even less regard for them.

But the picture won't change, according to many Haitian refugees. Others will come and be faced with disappointment because of this country's lack of hospitality, and others will die like Elaine Forfils and her five children. But the Haitians say, whatever happens, its far better than what they've had in Haiti.

The Sun  Reporter

San Francisco, Calif., October 4, 1979

The Congressional Black Caucus and the California Legislative Black Caucus have joined the growing struggle to urge the U.S. State Department to treat Haitian refugees with justice and dignity. This is a righteous cause that deserves enthusiastic support from Black America.

Throughout its history, the United States has opened its doors to refugees from all over the world. Since our nation was founded by people fleeing from religious and political persecution, we have always had a soft spot in our national heart for people who seek to escape harsh conditions in their homelands. We held to this open door policy enthusiastically when we were a growing nation with few people and thousands of square miles of vacant land and untapped resources, and we still held to it today, in spite of the pressures of overpopulation and rapidly depleting resources. We give haven to the "boat people" from southeast Asia, and our doors always remain open to those who seek to flee from totalitarian oppression, particularly from Communist nations.

But for the past several years, our country has cruelly withdrawn its welcome mat when faced with attempted immigration by another group of wretched "boat people," those who have journeyed across the Caribbean seeking refuge from the economic disaster and political repression that was their lot in their native Haiti. These Black refugees have been denied asylum in our country, have not been granted work visas, and have been jailed and put through a dehumanizing maze of hearings and screenings such as only the immigration service could have devised. The excuse most often given for this double standard is that the Haitians are "economic" and not "political" refugees. That's not true, and even if it were, why should it matter? They are fleeing the same kind of harsh lives that the ancestors of millions of people who now call themselves Americans fled in their time.

We agree with Assemblyman Willie Brown that the harassment accorded to Haitian refugees "demonstrates this government's absurd policy that certain categories of oppressed people are less deserving of equal treatment than others," and we join in the call for fair treatment and a traditional American welcome for these unfortunates.

Haitians in Florida Called Economic, Not Political, Refugees

Swept in in the wake of the Cuban boatlift were several thousand Haitians, who had already been trickling into Florida long before the Cuban exodus. In 1980 alone, 15,000 were estimated to have arrived on Florida's shores. The total number of Haitians in the area depended on which agency was counting: 12,000 according to the Immigration and Naturalization Service, 23,000 according to Dade County authorities, and 30,000 according to Haitian community leaders.

Unflattering comparisons were drawn between the Administration's treatment of the Cubans and the Haitian refugees, who were classified as illegal aliens. The Justice Department said the Haitians were fleeing economic deprivation and thus could not be classified as political refugees like the Cubans. Under U.S. law, a person could be classified as a political refugee only if he had a "well-founded fear" of returning to his homeland because of persecution. This prompted the public to speculate whether the Administration attributed repression only to leftist governments. Rep. Shirley Chisholm told a House Judiciary subcommittee in June that, "You cannot separate the economic factors from socio-political factors" in dealing with Haitian refugees. Other black congressmen and community leaders charged that the Administration's policy amounted to racism, since the Haitians were black and the Cubans were white or mixed. To compound their difficulties, Haitians had few relatives in the U.S. and no organized community to lobby for them. They also were less skilled and less educated than the Cubans.

In June, the Administration finally granted permission for both the Cubans and Haitians to remain legally in the U.S. for six months while their status was examined, and they were made eligible for government and local welfare services.

Portland Press Herald
Portland, Maine, May 17, 1980

Our open-arms policy toward Cuban refugees is an inspiration: America remains the hope of oppressed people everywhere.

But the success stories of industrious, freedom-loving new Americans may allow us to forget our arms open wider for some than others.

For years, desperate Haitians have packed themselves into small boats to escape the fascist terror of Jean Claude "Little Doc" Duvalier. Most are turned back or jailed and eventually, deported.

The U.S. has only paid lip service to the idea of better treatment for Haitians who fled heart-rending poverty and politcal oppression. Our policy suggests Haitians merely want jobs whereas Cubans are legitimate political refugees.

The only differences are the U.S. has diplomatic relations with Haiti's dictatorship because it isn't Marxist; its refugees are black, uneducated, and speak a French-Carib dialect few understand; and most important, while Cuban defectors embarrass Castro, the Haitians have no propaganda value.

Justice demands the Carter administration grant the black boat people refugee status.

THE INDIANAPOLIS NEWS
Indianapolis, Ind., April 17, 1980

The U.S. State Department said this week that, while the U.S. will do its part, Latin American countries must take the lead in resettling the 10,000 Cubans who rushed the Peruvian embassy in an effort to get out of Cuba.

If these were strictly political refugees, the U.S. attitude might be different. But indications are that Cuba's unsolved economic problems are as much, or more, a reason for the exodus as politics.

A similar situation is developing in Haiti. Boatloads of Haitian refugees have been putting ashore on the Florida coast. Although some of them claim their lives would be in danger if they returned to Haiti, most of them are economic refugees, fleeing the poverty and hopelessness of their native land.

An awareness, fortunately, is growing in government that the U.S. cannot take refugees on this basis without setting a dangerous precedent. The Caribbean is a region of undeveloped but overpopulated countries, and some parts of the U.S. could be flooded by their economic refugees. Instead of exporting their excess population, these nations must be encouraged to solve their economic and social problems.

U.S. policy on refugees must continue to be humane and understanding. But the U.S. cannot allow it to be used by other nations to duck their responsibilities to their own people.

The Wichita Eagle
Wichita, Kans., April 28, 1980

If ever there was a time for America to show that it is a country with a heart, it is now, with thousands of Cuban and Haitian refugees pouring from small boats onto Florida shores.

It is not the time for State Department bluster and threats of fines and imprisonment for those who, despite knowledge that what they do is illegal, are compelled by love and concern for their countrymen to do it. The United States simply cannot turn these people away.

The Cubans are fleeing political oppression, and their flight by boat to Florida because the Cubans cancelled refugee flights to Costa Rica and other countries, may play into the hands of the Cuban government. But they already have endured hardship during their weeks on the Peruvian Embassy grounds and during the years they lived in Cuba while relatives tried to get them out.

The Haitians have suffered even greater hardships. They have endured destitution and political repression under President Jean-Claude (Baby Doc) Duvalier, after having suffered previously under his father. Their country is the poorest nation in the Western Hemisphere. Those lucky enough to have jobs earn as little as the equivalent of 20 cents a day.

It is no wonder that many try to flee, often in leaky boats that shouldn't be allowed on the water. About 2,500 Haitians landed in Florida last year, and another 9,000 are expected by the end of 1980.

Clearly, the United States should extend political asulum both to the Haitians and the Cubans. But the state of Florida should not be expected to shoulder the whole load. The state's social resources already are stretched to the limit, and the people of Florida have been generous despite some grumbling.

First, the U.S. government ought to do everything possible to convince the Cubans that it would be in the best interests of the refugees and the Cuban government to resume the flights to Costa Rica. Then plans should be made to disperse as many refugees already landed in Florida as can be to other states.

Meanwhile, urgent new efforts should get under way to help Haitians out of their poverty. Added pressure ought to be exerted on the Duvalier regime to bring about social reforms and to use U.S. aid in ways that will reduce illiteracy and improve the Haitian economy.

There are those who oppose granting sanctuary to more refugees. The United States has economic problems of its own, they say. That is true, but America is strong and its people are generous. America has a heart, and it is right to open it to these unfortunate people.

Sentinel Star

Orlando, Fla.. April 17, 1980

THEY all come claiming the crucial need for political asylum. They all come with tales of brutal government repression and a future without hope for those they left behind. Their surging numbers have literally changed the complexion of the communities they enter. And the prospect of an increase in their numbers has officials and citizens alike wringing their hands.

They are the Cuban and Haitian refugees swarming into South Florida.

Thus far, the Cubans have been accepted far more readily than their Haitian counterparts. On the surface, this is because of the official enmity existing between Cuba and the United States and Washington's willingness to accept Cuban expatriates as proof of Mr. Castro's failure.

The Haitians, on the other hand, have fared less well. They are auto-matically viewed with suspicion by immigration authorities skeptical of their tales of political repression at the hands of the Duvalier family fiefdom. The Haitians constitute an enormous strain on the social welfare and health agencies of South Florida since most arrive with severe medical problems, no money, no skills and no personal connections.

The Cubans' situation and the official assistance rendered to them is similar to that accorded to the Indochinese refugees while the official welcome extended to Haitians most closely resembles that given to Mexican wetbacks. Refugees from communist countries get automatic asylum while those from anywhere else have their claims weighed on an individual basis.

The rising tide of refugees washing onto Florida shores is a huge problem for the state that is getting bigger and bigger.

Florida's refugee problems are a national not a state or local issue. As such, they should be addressed in their entirety by Washington, not Miami or Tallahassee. Floridians alone cannot be expected to shoulder the economic burden the refugees represent.

In the short term, it is essential for Washington to get the situation under control by assisting the Haitian government to stem the tide of boat people. Once an emergency tourniquet is in place on this human hemorrhage, further talks, preferably under the aegis of the Organization of American States, should be held with an eye to long-term solutions to both improve the Haitian economy and put some order into Haitian emigration.

Most of that long-term work will be enormously difficult because poverty and corruption are so endemic that they almost defy efforts to dislodge them from that miserable island.

However until some economic progress is made Haiti will continue to export its largest product; unskilled labor desperate for work, for hope.

And Florida will have to bear the brunt of that cynical export policy to the ultimate detriment of all Floridians.

THE COMMERCIAL APPEAL

Memphis, Tenn., April 25, 1980

IF ANYONE IS playing into the hands of Cuban authorities on the Caribbean "boat people," it is the United States government.

Fidel Castro didn't renege on allowing the Cuban Ten Thousand who sought sanctuary at the Peruvian embassy to be airlifted via Costa Rica without a reason. It is no coincidence that he's stalled negotiations to resettle these refugees in the countries offering them asylum. And it was no accident that his government made it known that anyone wanting to leave Cuba could go to Mariel, a mere 90 miles off the U.S. mainland.

Those people were lured there deliberately, and the reason is plain. It was a bald attempt to turn this from a hemispheric problem into a Cuban-American one in the hope that the *Yanquis* would get snagged on their immigration laws and embarrass themselves.

The United States has taken the bait, and not only by seeming to stop Cubans hoping to resettle in a land of freedom and opportunity. Granma, the daily newspaper published by Cuba's communist party, has tried to capitalize on our unwillingness to grant asylum to Haiti's "boat people," who are risking their lives on a two-week, 700-mile voyage to escape the repressive political and economic climate of their steamy island nation. How would it seem if this nation also appeared unwilling to accept more Cubans?

Consider the official U.S. response on Cuba. The State Department has fired verbal volleys at the armada of fishing boats and pleasure craft staging the rescue. It warned that "violators may be arrested and vessels seized," and that anyone caught transporting undocumented aliens into this country could be subject to a $2,000 fine and five years in jail for each person brought in without a valid visa. That the Coast Guard backed off from stopping the vessels and making arrests hasn't made matters better.

And then, there are the Haitians. A thousand more "boat people" have made it to South Florida in the past 10 days. Now, they must wait with 8,000 other Haitians until a U.S. district court determines their status. If it finds they fled for political reasons, they would get a rehearing before the Immigration and Naturalization Serivce. If the court decides they came for financial gain, they will face deportation.

A temporary injunction has stopped the INS from sending the Haitians back, but that hasn't stopped the Inter-American Commission on Human Rights, a branch of the Organization of American States. The commission has taken the unusual step of asking U.S. Secretary of State Cyrus R. Vance to suspend deportation until it completes its own investigation of the Haitian problem.

WE HAVE SAID before that the Haitians are political refugees and deserving of asylum. It is likewise apparent that the Cubans are searching for political freedom they don't find under the Castro regime.

Castro has used the refugee situation to score propaganda points against the United States, but this country should be smart enough to rise above his game. When it comes to refugees, Americans cannot focus solely on Fidel Castro or on how we appear in the eyes of the world.

What is most important here is how we look to ourselves and to those who look to us for hope. How can a nation which professes its commitment to human rights around the world refuse to admit these refugees?

President Carter recently signed into law the Refugee Act of 1980. It is enlightened legislation which triples the number of refugees regularly allowed to enter each year, and it also defines refugees not by where they come from but by the reasons they came.

That should be sufficiently broad to embrace the Cubans and the Haitians. Offering refugees shelter doesn't preclude international cooperation to help solve their problems. But if U.S. law is blind to the Caribbean "boat people" and their plight, it isn't broad enough.

Detroit Free Press

Detroit, Mich., April 25, 1980

THEY ARE the new "boat people," hard-pressed farmers from the West Indian nation of Haiti, among the poorest of the poor. They are flooding Miami, wave after wave of them washing up onto its shores. Are they mere illegal aliens? Or have they, like the Indochinese, taken to their boats to escape stark repression?

It is a debate that will gain steam. The Haitians do not prick our consciences as did the Cambodians and Vietnamese. We never bombed their soil. Nor will they help us to prove a political point, as did the Cubans seeking refuge in the Peruvian Embassy in Havana. They are only a desperately poor people running out of options.

Haiti is one of the least developed countries in the hemisphere. Farmers raise barely enough food to keep their families alive. In some parts of the country, they must anchor themselves with ropes to keep from sliding down hills. The life span in Haiti is about 33 years.

Their political regimen has been just as harsh. Francois "Papa Doc" Duvalier, the country doctor who declared himself president for life in 1964, ruled as a dictator until his death in 1971. His son's administration has been little better.

Participants in a massive human rights rally in Port-au-Prince last year were beaten, reportedly by the secret police. The founder of a fledgling opposition party was arrested. Refugees report having spent years in jail merely for knowing someone suspected of anti-government sentiments. Haitian exile Patrick Lemoine, writing in the March issue of Inquiry magazine, claims he was thrown into Haiti's Dessalines prison after the wife of an arrested friend told officials he must have been implicated in any plot of her husband's. Six years later, Lemoine says, he was released following American officials' criticism of the Haitian regime. He and other exiles were put on a round-trip flight that was meant to bring them back to Haiti and imprisonment again. He managed to immigrate to New York instead.

Yet the State Department says the Haitian migrants do not deserve asylum, as did the Cubans, because they are only seeking economic opportunity. That is specious reasoning at best.

President Carter used new emergency powers to admit 3,500 Cubans fleeing the Castro regime. He must be willing to take similar action on behalf of the Haitians. In the hard-bitten world of refugees, political and economic hardships often go hand in hand. The Cubans resent their government because it has mismanaged the economy — and their lives. The Haitians face political reprisals for objecting to economic conditions. Two sides of the same coin. The Haitians are a people in grave circumstances. They need our help.

The Salt Lake Tribune

Salt Lake City, Utah, April 24, 1980

Those 8,000 or so "boat people" from Haiti now ashore in the Miami area are forcing a poignant question:

Is a person who flees political persecution entitled to asylum while an individual who leaves a country for economic reasons is denied a safe haven?

Put another way, is hunger and grim privation as legitimate a motive force for fleeing as the threat of political persecution?

For the Haiti boat people the question is starkly real. Most of them are claiming they left their impoverished island homeland because they were targeted for mistreatment as foes of the repressive Duvalier regime. But there is ample evidence that the constant press of abject poverty at home was also a force in their decision to risk death and sail for the United States.

As victims of political persecution the Haiti exiles stand a good chance of being allowed to stay in the United States. As victims of an impoverished land, they stand a good chance of being sent back to Haiti.

The United States cannot go on accepting every pitiful soul who reaches its shores. That means a fair standard for judging who will stay and who will return should be fashioned while the influx is still relatively small. Present policy of favoring political refugees over those who fled for other valid reasons is increasingly difficult to defend.

When Thailand and other Southeast Asia countries forced some Vietnamese and Cambodian boat people back out to sea, the world recoiled at the heartless spectacle. The United States has not come to that sorry point yet but the refugee invasion from the Caribbean is increasingly menacing.

In addition to shaping better guidelines for dealing with those now reaching the Florida beaches, the United States must address root causes of the influx and try to improve political and economic conditions in such distressed places as Haiti.

Failure to deflate pressures causing the Caribbean exodus could someday mean having to face a more serious refugee delemma as the hopeless hordes are coming out of the water.

The Courier-Journal

Louisville, Ky., April 23, 1980

THE TWO BIG refugee dramas in the Caribbean, involving socialist Cuba and voodoo-feudal Haiti, have brought out the best and worst among neighboring nations. The most encouraging example of generosity has been Costa Rica's offer, not yet accepted by Fidel Castro, to grant permanent asylum to all of the up to 10,000 Cubans who poured into the Peruvian embassy in Havana in a desperate attempt to escape their homeland.

Meanwhile, the United States, which has agreed to resettle 3,500 Cubans, is taking a very different and much harsher position toward the hundreds of Haitians who have been arriving by leaky boats in Florida in recent weeks. The State Department, perhaps reflecting the general ambiguities of American immigration policy, has decided generally that fleeing Cubans are political refugees and therefore qualify for asylum in this country. But the Haitians are deemed economic refugees and therefore must be sent back.

A court challenge on behalf of the Haitians has temporarily blocked implementation of this policy. But while the deportations have ended, the policy remains intact. The State Department still views arriving Haitians as illegal aliens who are seeking merely — merely? — to escape extreme poverty and possible starvation in their drought-stricken homeland.

It makes no difference that the regime of Haiti's "president-for-life," Jean-Claude Duvalier, is every bit as bloody and repressive as Castro's in Cuba. As far as the State Department is concerned, two or three dangerous weeks at sea to escape the hell that is Haiti don't qualify these new arrivals as political victims.

Two facts make this official position especially hard to swallow. The first is the State Department's apparent willingness to treat fleeing Cubans as political refugees, even though many of them, like the Haitians, obviously are seeking the opportunity for economic betterment. The other is the embarrassing fact that almost all the Haitians are black, while only a portion of the Cubans are.

Together, these facts suggest — though they certainly don't prove — that the Haitians are victims of an official double standard. And even if this impression is unfair, one wonders why, aside from obvious propaganda value, the U.S. is so ready to help resettle refugees from Castro's Cuba — while trying to keep equally desperate Haitians from our shores.

The Miami Herald

Miami, Fla., April 17, 1980

HAITIAN refugees who are already in the United States must be granted sanctuary by the Government of the United States. Humanity and what the Declaration of Independence calls "a decent respect to the opinions of mankind" demand no less.

The world's richest nation simply cannot hide its eyes and ears in cold legalities when poor, courageous refugees from one of the poorest nations literally throw themselves at the doorstep of freedom and opportunity and beg for mercy.

Rumors abound these days of an imminent decision by the Carter Administration to exercise its parole authority to grant sanctuary to the undocumented Haitians already in the United States, estimated to number between 12,000 and 25,000. That authority should be exercised before it expires a month from now. This nation simply cannot avoid the irony of accepting 20,000 to 30,000 additional Cubans this year while rejecting the smaller number of Haitians who are here already.

For many months now, an unending stream of boats has dumped load after load of desperate Haitians on South Florida's shores. More than 3,100 Haitians have arrived that way so far this year, nearly 900 in a single long weekend. Some appear to have risked their lives to come 700 miles from Haiti in questionable old sailboats. Others, crisply clean and neat, obviously debarked from the nearby Bahamas or from a smuggler's mother ship.

Whatever the course, it is dangerous at worst and exploitive at best. Often it is financed by the meager savings of husbands and fathers who already have made it to Florida and then sent back money to buy passage for wives and children. The strength of family that shines in such histories bodes well for the future success of these new immigrants in the United States.

If asylum were granted the Haitians already here, the status of any who arrived illegally afterward would not be resolvable easily. Certainly the immediate families of those already here would be eligible to apply for visas and enter the United States through normal channels. They would not need to take to the sea or pay smugglers' exorbitant fees.

Those smugglers should be put out of business, and realistic consultations toward that end should be organized among Washington, Nassau, and Port-au-Prince. The scope and nature of the exodus from Haiti must be identified and plans made to encourage a long-range stability that will make fleeing unnecessary.

The United States took in more than a quarter-million refugees last year, including 190,000 from Indochina, 20,000 Russian Jews, and 11,000 Cubans. The 12,000 to 25,000 Haitians who have made it to America in the last 10 years deserve to be included in those ranks. The Administration should act now, while it has both the legal authority and the popular support of compassionate Americans who remember their own immigrant origins.

Roanoke Times & World-News
Roanoke, Va., April 17, 1980

While attention focuses on the 10,-000 Cubans who jammed into the Peruvian Embassy in Havana seeking asylum, a steady stream of refugees continues from elsewhere in the Caribbean. In the past several months, thousands of "boat people" from Haiti have landed in Florida, presenting authorities with a legal and humanitarian dilemma.

No question, these are desperate people. Scores of them crowd into boats built for a fraction of their numbers; sometimes the craft are swamped and sink.

Still they make the 700-mile journey. An estimated 12,000 Haitians are believed to be in south Florida, and more arrive daily, now that spring is here and the waters relatively calm.

Why do they flee? Usually they claim to be political refugees; under U.S. laws, this gives them a better chance of staying. Immigration officials say it's more likely they are trying to escape Haiti's abject poverty.

Either explanation is tenable. Haiti is the poorest, most densely populated nation in the hemisphere: Its 6 million people had a per capita income in 1978 of $90. Most of them scratch out a subsistence from the small area of arable land. Some hold factory jobs imported from other countries (Haitians sew covers on the baseballs swatted by millionaire U.S. athletes). Illiteracy and debilitating diseases are rife.

Politically, Haiti isn't the dungeon it was under the late Francois (Papa Doc) Duvalier, a devotee of voodoo who maintained a retinue of brutal enforcers called Tontons Macoutes. His son Jean-Claude (Baby Doc), who succeeded him in 1971, has been less oppressive. But there still are no political parties in Haiti, and government-paid toughs make short work of events such as the human rights meeting attended by 6,000 people in Port-au-Prince last autumn.

Under the circumstances, immigration authorities prefer to turn the refugees around and reboard them for Haiti. "Baby Doc" told *The Miami News* last year that he would welcome refugees home with "all possible guarantees" against reprisal, and the U.S. Embassy in Haiti says it has no firm evidence contradicting that. But efforts to deport them have been halted by suits charging that they haven't been given due process here. In one suit in federal court in Miami, a witness — identified as an ex-member of Haiti's secret police — said returning refugees face severe punishment.

While the courts hear evidence, immigration officials in south Florida struggle to cope with the influx of Haitians (nearly 900 in a four-day period this week). There's no place, like Ellis Island, to confine so many; they are processed and then released into the community, if there are friends, relatives or sponsors for them.

If the federal government gets its way in court, it will be able to round up most of these thousands of Haitians and ship them back home. The word then will spread on the island that Uncle Sam is less receptive than hoped, and the northward tide may be stemmed.

It is not a solution to gladden any but the hard-hearted. Perhaps immigration quotas for some poverty-stricken neighbors should be increased; aid programs and encouragement for capital investment in those countries are among appropriate relief measures. But the United States cannot, in the end, take care of other countries' economic problems merely by throwing open its doors to their jobless. This nation's capacity as a relief valve is limited, and there will be no solution to those problems if they aren't solved where they originate.

The Hartford Courant
Hartford, Conn., April 28, 1980

South Florida has been a refuge from the storm, both literally and figuratively, for thousands of people who fled Haiti.

They braved — many are still braving — a trip of some 600 miles on leaky boats to escape their West Indian homeland, set to sea by extreme poverty and autocratic government. But America has not exactly welcomed the refugees with open arms.

In fact, the Immigration and Naturalization Service has established a program of questionable legality to send only Haitians home — and posthaste. That program is being held up in court for now.

The government has been quibbling about whether the Haitians are really "political" or "economic" refugees; the INS says the refugees are economic and must be deported. But the distinction may be academic since those Haitians sent home face the possiblity of torture and imprisonment under the authoritarian regime of Jean-Claude "Baby Doc" Duvalier. Surely, the INS would have no trouble categorizing the refugees as "political" if they managed to escape Haiti twice.

Singling out Haitians for deportation also exposes the government to charges of racism, since the Haitians are black, and calls into question the depth of the administration's concern for human rights when violations occur under a friendly, right-wing dictatorship.

Human rights should not be invoked only when that invocation can be used to chalk up political points for our side. The government hastens to accept refugees from Castro's Cuba and scientists and ballet stars from Eastern Europe. Surely the people of Haiti are no less acquainted with oppression.

The Boston Globe
Boston, Mass., April 16, 1980

For those of us who live in relative peace and comfort, there is no good way to evaluate the motives that drive people to forsake their homelands to throw themselves as refugees on the mercy of others.

Whether it is the fear of hunger or beatings or imprisonment or being deprived of freedom in more subtle ways, it is terror that drives people to barter with death to escape.

Ten days ago thousands of Cubans stormed onto the grounds of the Peruvian Embassy in Havana when President Fidel Castro said that any who could get Peruvian visas would be able to leave Cuba. Castro apparently thought a couple of hundred Cubans would rush to the embassy, just enough to complicate the Peruvian embassy's routine with requests for asylum. Instead, the small compound was besieged by more than 10,800 Cubans who want out. Sanitation is nonexistent. Food and other supplies are meager. And the Cuban government, embarrassed by the reaction, is no longer quite so willing to let all those people go.

It has become, as the Carter Administration puts it, "a humanitarian crisis." The United States has agreed to take 3500 refugees, Peru 1000 and other nations a few hundred each, but many still have not been spoken for. In the end, the United States may feel compelled to take more.

Meanwhile, there is another humanitarian crisis swirling in the Caribbean. Last weekend 871 black Haitian boat people stumbled ashore from leaky boats in southern Florida, fleeing the oppressive poverty and politics of President-for-Life Jean-Claude "Baby Doc" Duvalier. Some came directly, others from the Bahamas, pressed northward because they are unwelcome there. Fourteen hundred have arrived in the last month, 3000 since January. An estimated 25,000 have made the journey over the last few years and more are undoubtedly on the way. The latest wave of Haitian boat people is filling up the prisons of southern Florida and spilling over to armories, hospitals and other facilities that are serving as holding areas while immigration officials deal with them.

There is a great difference between the handling of the Cubans and the Haitians. The 3500 Cuban refugees we accept will be considered political exiles from a Communist regime. Immigration authorities will be empowered to process them quickly and efficiently when they arrive. They will be eligible for special services to help them become settled.

The Haitians are considered to be illegal aliens, sneaking in to steal American jobs. The United States does not consider Duvalier's right-wing dictatorship politically hostile, and under the old immigration laws, the Haitians could not be considered political exiles. Because of their status, the Haitians will not be eligible immediately for settlement help nor can they legally hold jobs while officials and the courts decide what should be done with them.

At least part of the reason the Haitian boat people are risking their lives to get to the United States are rumors filtering through the Caribbean about a new law which may make them eligible for political asylum. Unfortunately the law, which redefines who may be considered a refugee, is so new that the National Immigration Service has not had time to produce the regulations to implement it.

The people spilling out of those boats onto the crystal white strands of West Palm Beach and the Florida Keys are no less refugees than those desperate souls jammed into the Peruvian embassy in Havana. Their actions have made them political refugees regardless of their personal motives.

Over the years, we have opened our doors to more than 800,000 Cubans, 200,000 Southeast Asians and numberless East Europeans. It is hoped we will not now turn away the 25,000 Haitians who have made their way to Florida at such risk.

The News American

Baltimore, Md., April 22, 1980

In the past week or so, a thousand Haitians have reached Florida after 12 or more days jam-packed in rickety boats, bringing to more than 8,000 the desperate number to flee the not-so-benign dictatorship of President-for-Life Jean-Claude "Baby Doc" Duvalier.

All are poor — Haiti is one of the world's poorest nations anyway (as columnist Colman McCarthy points out on this page) — and right now a drought has made farming in many areas impossible. And all are terrified — they say that refugees returned by the United States have been imprisoned or executed, and although they are finding scant succor in Florida, being sent back is their greatest fear.

Ah, but hasn't this country traditionally helped refugees from such places as Vietnam and Cambodia and Laos and Nicaragua get a new start? Yes, but the Carter administration says the Haitians aren't political refugees; they're refugees from economic hardship, and that's different. Until recently, the administration had been sending some of the Haitians home. Now, while reconsidering whether these people should be regarded as exiles from political oppression, it's letting them stay as sort of non-persons; save for opening some reception centers, it's providing virtually no help.

As a result, the black boat people have become the problem of Florida's local governments and of such private groups as Catholic Charities. But both money and places to put the Haitians has run out. Dade County is pleading with the feds to help.

The refugees have gone to federal court to get the government to accept them as political refugees so they can get federal help. As for the administration, it has refused to make up its mind. The president has until May 15 to use his special powers to grant the Haitians political asylum. If he doesn't, their future will be up to Congress, whose duty it will be to set quotas under a ceiling of 50,000 immigrants a year.

Evidence given in federal court makes it plain that a grim fate awaits them should they be returned. It seems to us that a humanitarian nation shouldn't have to think twice in this matter. We especially like the way our colleagues at the *Miami Herald* put it: "The world's richest nation simply cannot hide its eyes and ears in cold legalities when poor, courageous refugees ... literally throw themselves at the doorstep of freedom and opportunity and beg for mercy."

Los ANGELES HERALD EXAMINER

Los Angeles, Calif., April 24, 1980

It is no coincidence that some 3,500 Cuban refugees, and an unknown number of Haitians, are coming to the United States just as fast as they can get in. The fact of the matter is that Cuba is an island dictatorship of the left and Haiti is an island dictatorship of the right. The fact of the matter is that the Castro regime wouldn't last another 30 days without its extensive secret police

Duvalier

network, and the Baby Doc Duvalier regime probably wouldn't last another 10 hours without its own political police (for some astonishing insights into the current situation in Cuba, you might want to take a look at our lead article in this Sunday's Comment section).

And an additional fact of the matter is that for all its problems, the United States is not a secret police state and, by the exceedingly repressive standards of Cuba and Haiti, does not come even close to being one. It is also, for many of these Haitians and Cubans, a land of economic opportunity, despite the problems of inflation and recession that we here are so aware of. All these are facts and truths. What is not truthful is the proposition that the U.S. has had a clear-cut and well-thought-out refugee policy, until perhaps recently. For under the just-passed Refugee Act of 1980, the U.S. now officially understands that not only *Communist* dictatorships have repressive secret police. The working assumption has been that refugees from places like Haiti come here solely out of economic

Castro

misery. Well, that just is not always the case. Haiti is a place of political as well as economic misery (much like Cuba), and for the U.S. to ignore that reality solely because the political misery there isn't Communist political misery is hypocritical, self-serving, short-sighted, dumb, anti-humanitarian and anti-American.

THE ARIZONA REPUBLIC

Phoenix, Ariz., April 23, 1980

HAVING agreed to take in at least 3,500 of those 10,000 Cubans claiming political asylum in the Peruvian Embassy in Havana, the United States once again has shown its compassion.

But the Cuban refugee problem is the least of the refugee problems facing the United States right now.

Worse, by far, is what's happening with Haitians, who are fleeing that impoverished Caribbean land by the hundreds.

Since the first of the year, more than 3,000 Haitians are known to have landed illegally in Florida. Some came directly from Haiti by leaky boats, others from the nearby Bahamas where they went originally, then were put back to sea by Bahamian immigration officers.

So far, American immigration authorities simply have been unable to handle this new flotilla of "boat people" streaming across the Florida Straits.

They are penniless, often in poor health, do not speak anything but creole, and generally are unskilled field hands.

Florida lacks the housing or the welfare resources to absorb them.

The 3,000-plus who've fled to Florida exceed the quota observed by the Immigration and Naturalization Service.

And, yet, what can the United States do when refugees — hungry, and in danger of dying at sea — come banging on the door for haven?

Haiti is a depressing country. Its scenic grandeur and romantic history are overshadowed by the political tyranny and economic devastation that have kept the people in illiteracy, sickness and poverty.

The hundreds who are fleeing come mostly from northwestern Haiti, where prolonged drought has turned farmlands into veritable deserts, and where a typhoon last August left widespread ruin.

They're selling off land that has been in their families for generations, to pay the reported $1,000 being demanded by boat captains for illegal trips to Florida.

Some of the leaky vessels arrive with 100 or more aboard, which indicates the fortunes being made from human misery.

The United States sends about $32 million to Haiti in aid.

But this has made no measurable improvement in the lot of Haitians, whose average daily wage can be counted in pennies.

If, as the State Department predicts, Cuba's Fidel Castro exports his brand of Marxism throughout the region, the United States can look forward to a future of receiving more refugees fleeing tyranny in the Caribbean.

San Francisco Chronicle

San Francisco, Calif., April 17, 1980

BOATLOADS OF HAITIANS are now turning up on the expensive sands of South Florida — an area already feeling deep strains because of the turmoil over Cuban refugees. Sunbathers at Key Biscayne and Pompano Beach look up and see sick and hungry people clamber out of small, open craft.

Such a large number — a record 736 — arrived up and down the Florida coast over last weekend that immigration officials had to accommodate them at a National Guard armory. This influx of Haitians is not new; thousands have fled repressive regimes on that island over the past 20 years. But it is increasing, and, combined with turmoil over those who wish to leave Cuba, serves to accentuate the problems that face the U.S. in the refugee crisis.

MIAMI HAS ALREADY taken in 500,000 Cubans and other thousands from Nicaragua and Indochina. There is a strain on all involved — on the long-time Florida resident and on the bewildered new arrival. It is a situation that lends considerable validity to President Carter's statement that while the U.S. will accept 3500 of the Cubans who have jammed the Peruvian embassy in Havana, other nations must make their contributions as well.

More than half of the Cubans seeking exit have been spoken for: in addition to those accepted by the U.S., 1000 will be taken by Peru, 500 by Spain, 200 by Ecuador, 300 by Costa Rica and undetermined numbers by Argentina, Brazil, Canada, Belgium, West Germany and Sweden. As President Carter says, the refugee problem is one for "all the Americas, as well as the world."

The Cincinnati Post

Cincinnati, Ohio, April 28, 1980

The United States accepts several thousand refugees every month from Indochina.

It has taken some 800,000 Cubans who have fled Fidel Castro over the years. The current exodus of refugees from Cuba no doubt will result in thousands more becoming U.S. residents.

This country takes Jews from Russia and persons escaping tyranny elsewhere around the world.

Mexicans illegally cross the border in droves.

But officials have taken an uncharacteristic hard-nosed attitude toward Haitian blacks fleeing a woeful existence on their Caribbean island.

Estimates on how many Haitians have fled their homeland in the last decade range up to 25,000.

The Immigration and Naturalization Service is trying to deport the Haitians on the ground that they are not trying to escape political persecution but are fleeing economic conditions at home.

Certainly Haiti is among the most impoverished places of the world. But it is equally certain that the Duvaliers, who have ruled Haiti for more than 22 years, are among the world's less enlightened rulers.

It is highly incongruous for the United States to accept refugees by the tens of thousands from around the globe but to close its heart to a few thousand Haitians seeking sanctuary at great personal risk.

THE PLAIN DEALER

Cleveland, Ohio, April 28, 1980

The Carter administration has been treating the Cuban and Haitian refugee problems with such an uneven hand that average Americans can only wonder whether racial prejudice is subtly at work.

In addition to the human misery involved, there are the conflicting policy signals and vacillations of administration officials which typically confuse our allies in foreign affairs and the public in domestic affairs.

For example, State Department spokesmen have repeatedly said refugee and immigration laws would be enforced, that captains of boats hauling Cubans face stiff fines and that the boats would be seized by the Coast Guard.

But neither the Coast Guard nor the Navy nor local police boats were making any attempt to stop the Cuban refugee traffic.

Furthermore, immigration officials have been quoted as saying that the Cuban refugees now entering the country are being allowed in under the parole power of the president and that they could file for political asylum within 60 days. They said the refugee law is not being followed.

Last month Congress passed a new refugee law that allows up to 50,000 refugees total a year to enter the country, with an additional 50,000 permitted in by the president in consultation with Congress. An old Cuban refugee resettlement program, which is still alive, is being phased out over several years. Under it, 18,000 Cuban refugees could enter this country this year.

But the armada of small boats could bring more than the limit into the country. With Carter officials working at cross purposes, there is no telling how many may enter. There is no real effort to keep them out.

The Cuban refugee issue developed several weeks ago when more than 10,000 refugees crowded into the Peruvian embassy grounds in Havana. Cuban President Fidel Castro decided to let Cubans who wish to emigrate do so — thus the armada.

But bad economic times in Cuba have led to social pressure for Castro that is being relieved somewhat by emigration. Thus to some extent, the Cuban refugees are seeking emigration for a better life economically, as some have said, rather than only fleeing repression.

But to the Carter administration, the Haitian refugees apparently are being viewed with less leniency. Those boat owners carrying Haitians for money are afraid of being caught and prosecuted to the extent that they frequently force Haitian refugees into the open seas. For several years there have been repeated reports of Haitian bodies washing ashore in Florida and in the Bahamas.

Unlike the Cubans, Haitians arriving in the United States have been arrested. They faced deportation until recently when a suit was filed to have them treated as political refugees. An estimated 10,000 Haitians are awaiting a court clarification of their status.

A dictatorship on the right is just as much a repressive government as a dictatorship on the left. But the Carter administration sees the Haitians fleeing only for economic opportunity and the Cubans fleeing only from repression.

The real difference is that there are an estimated 500,000 Cuban emigres here to welcome arriving friends and relatives — a potent political force — and no more than an estimated 30,000 Haitians — a minor political voice.

Newsday

Long Island, N. Y., April 16, 1980

The United States, to its credit, always seems ready to make room for a few thousand more Cubans who want to get away from Fidel Castro. But it's been a different story with refugees from right-wing dictatorships—even if they're as oppressive as Castro's communism.

Haiti, for instance.

Day in and day out, boatloads of weary but determined Haitians land in Florida. They've escaped from one of the world's poorest countries, ruled for two generations by the Duvalier family and the brutal security forces called Ton Ton Macoutes.

If these boat people were Cubans, they would routinely be welcomed as political refugees from communism. But as Haitians they're considered merely refugees from unemployment and poverty. While Washington claims it would willingly grant them asylum if they were fleeing persecution, apparently it's not enough if they're simply trying to avoid starvation.

About 800,000 Cubans have been admitted to this country legally since Castro came to power in 1959. Now President Carter proposes to take in 3,500 more—approximately one-third of the 10,000 would-be emigrants encamped at the Peruvian embassy in Havana. By doing this, Washington can underline Castro's unpopularity and tweak the nose he's been thumbing at the United States for years.

Coincidentally, however, the number of Haitians who have applied for asylum in Florida is also somewhere around 10,000. In theory, their applications have been dealt with individually by the Immigration and Naturalization Service; in practice, they've been denied in droves.

Until next month, the President has the authority to grant refugee status to these Haitians. That would serve notice on Baby Doc Duvalier that the United States will no longer ignore his regime's offenses against human rights. If Washington can take in still more Cuban refugees, surely it's time to welcome the beleaguered Haitians who are already here.

Los Angeles Times

Los Angeles, Calif., May 7, 1980

The wave of thousands of Cuban refugees and, to a lesser extent, Haitians, is overwhelming authorities in Florida. But the emigrants must be admitted, welcomed and assisted; there is no other acceptable response at this time from this government.

The United States cannot be a nation that says no to refugees. Sometimes the cost is high—up to 3,600 Cubans are arriving daily after the 130-mile crossing. The scenes of jubilation on arrival in Florida recall those of other days when other emigrants from other lands came to these shores.

The image of the Castro regime has probably been tarnished more than ever before by the fleeing Cubans who have chosen to vote by boat. The political and economic disaster that is Haiti has been underscored. As for this country, however, the way the Carter Administration is now approaching the whole problem is very much to its credit.

President Carter's decision this week to proclaim an "open heart and open arms" policy for the Cubans, to make $10 million available to Florida immediately and to declare a state of emergency in affected areas there came after some hesitancy over just what to do. Fines on boat owners carrying the refugees now have virtually stopped. And the Administration is trying to speed processing of the newcomers.

Haitians fall officially into a different category than the Cubans—regarded as economic rather than as political refugees. That is too fine a line to draw. The Haitians are still refugees, desperate ones who travel some 800 miles on the seas to reach this country. Can they be turned around and sent back while Cubans are welcomed?

Obviously, this country's policies may have to be reconsidered once again if the flood of Cubans, Haitians and others continues unabated. But, in the meantime, Washington must do all possible to aid Florida financially and to encourage other nations in Latin America and elsewhere to open their doors as well. In the case of Haiti, the United States should examine ways to bolster its economy to provide at least some encouragement to Haitians to remain at home.

It would be so much better if Cuba and Haiti would cooperate in establishing a more orderly procedure for the exodus. That is not happening; refugees are coming any way they can. And the United States is right to help in any way it can.

The Des Moines Register

Des Moines, Iowa, May 24, 1980

The Cubans are not the only foreigners who have been arriving on the coast of Florida in small boats seeking refuge. In recent years, thousands of Haitians have landed on U.S. shores.

On May 14, President Carter said: "I continue to be greatly concerned about the treatment of the Haitians. . . . I've instructed all appropriate federal agencies to treat the Haitians now here in the same exact humane manner as we treat Cubans and others who seek asylum in this country."

The president's statement bore almost no relationship to reality. The Haitians have received neither equal nor humane treatment.

A 1979 Library of Congress study concluded that there are between 200,000 and 300,000 Haitians in New York City, up to 25,000 in Florida and 15,000 in other cities. The majority are here illegally. A State Department official said that most of them hope to remain in this country by avoiding the federal immigration authorities. But in Florida, some 15,000 Haitians have applied for political asylum. If it is granted, they will be allowed to remain here permanently.

The federal government has provided little aid. Many Haitians live under desperate conditions. Even those who have applied for political asylum must live with the fear that they will be deported. Political asylum generally is granted only to those who have a legitimate fear that they face political prosecution if they return to their native country.

So far, only 250 Haitians have met this test. The fate of the remaining 15,000 rests with a court in Florida, which is expected to rule shortly.

The State Department generally has taken a skeptical view of the Haitians' claim that they have a legitimate fear of political persecution. The department has argued that the Haitians are fleeing the poverty of their island to find a better life in the United States.

The State Department's 1980 report on human rights conditions around the world sharply indicted Haiti. The report concluded: "Haiti has a long history of authoritarian rule with many periods of instability and the most serious types of human rights abuses."

The study found that Haitians have almost no ability to participate in the political process. Freedom of the press has been curtailed sharply. Freedom of association is limited by the government's ban on anti-government groups. There have been reports of beatings and torture of political prisoners.

Most Cubans are expected to be granted political asylum here. Why should people who live under Haiti's nightmarish conditions be denied similar treatment?

Until recently, the reason for this discrepancy was the Refugee Act — which basically defined a refugee as someone fleeing Communism. The Cubans met this definition; the Haitians did not. The new refugee law, which was signed on March 17, eliminates this unjustified distinction. It is time to bring U.S. policy into line with the law.

The Evening Bulletin

Philadelphia, Pa., April 25, 1980

What's the difference between a person who comes to the United States on a plane or boat from Castro's Cuba — and one who arrives on a boat from Haiti that washes ashore in Florida?

To some, the only difference is that the U.S. State Department considers the first to be a political refugee. The second, however, is an illegal alien, a target for deportation to Haiti.

The real differences between the two men could be quite complex, of course — as complex as the decisions facing the State Department regarding its handling of refugees from the Caribbean. But recent actions have brought accusations that the Federal Government is guilty of a double standard regarding the Cuban and Haitian refugees.

The plight of the Cubans is well known here. Recently 10,000 jammed the Peruvian Embassy in Havana, seeking exile. Some 3,500 of them are due to be admitted into the U.S. soon. The Haitians have not been as visible, but thousands have left their impoverished, dictator-ruled island in barely seaworthy vessels, drifting onto Florida beaches.

The Cuban and the Haitian refugees hold many goals in common: to escape from an authoritarian government, to build a better life in a free country. Yet the Cubans are granted political asylum and given the help our government affords those fleeing communism. The Haitians, however, are required to prove they suffered directly under dictator-president Jean Claude Duvalier. If they can't, the Immigration Service assumes they came here only to escape poverty, and initiates deportation.

It's probably fair to assume that a *mixture* of economic and political reasons motivated many Cubans as well as Haitians. Is it right, then, to accept one group with open arms while requiring the other to make a case for staying? The State Department's position is a difficult one. Its policies toward Communist governments are sharply defined. However, the Haitian government of "Baby Doc" Duvalier is pro-American, and for the U.S. to admit Haitians as refugees from repression would be an acknowledgement that all is not well in that "friendly" Caribbean country.

Clearly, the U.S. has not yet formulated a fully equitable policy regarding its acceptance of refugees — one that acknowledges the concerns and needs of the Haitian farmhand as well as the Indochinese scholar, the Cuban shopkeeper or the Mexican factory worker. As long as refugees exist — and they always will — and as long as the United States upholds its tradition as a homeland for all who seek freedom, the need for such a policy will remain.

Haitians Win Suit To Be Political Refugees

A federal judge in Miami ruled July 2 that Haitians should be classified as political refugees and given the right of asylum in the U.S. In response to a class-action suit by Haitian leaders, Judge James L. King said the Immigration and Naturalization Service had knowingly violated the "constitutional, statutory, treaty and administrative rights" of the Haitians by classifying them as economic refugees. Denying the political nature of their request for asylum, King wrote, showed "a profound ignorance, if not an intentional disregard, of the conditions in Haiti." Witnesses had testified to detentions, torture and other abuses they had suffered under President Jean-Claude Duvalier. King said a 1979 State Department report denying a pattern of repression against would-be emigres in Haiti was "unworthy of belief." He added that "much of Haiti's poverty is a result of Duvalier's efforts to maintain power." Most damaging of all, King said, the Haitians "faced a transparent discriminatory program designed to deport Haitian nationals and no one else." Therefore, he ruled, the INS must halt its efforts to return Haitians to their homeland.

The Miami Herald
Miami, Fla., July 5, 1980

MEN were imprisoned who had committed no crime, who were not even accused of committing crimes. Some were moved from one jail to another under cover of darkness. Women and children, destitute, were left to the charity of strangers. Families were separated. Sworn evidence was ignored and answered only by printed form letter. Attorneys were denied an honest opportunity to defend their clients' interests.

All that and more has happened to thousands of Haitians who fled their poverty-stricken, repressive homeland to seek freedom and opportunity in America. When the injustices were perpetrated in Haiti, at least they were beyond the reach of Americans who care about human rights.

But those wrongs all took place here, in Miami, under the name and jurisdiction of the U.S. Immigration and Naturalization Service (INS). Federal Judge James Lawrence King found this week that the INS had violated "the Constitution, the immigration statutes, international agreements, INS regulations, and INS operating procedures" in harassing Haitian applicants for asylum. Correctly he also ruled, "It must stop."

The immediate result of Judge King's eloquent, 164-page order is that deportation orders against the 5,000 Haitians at issue cannot be carried out. The cases will have to be reprocessed, very likely, after lengthy appeals through the Federal courts.

For now, at least, this group of Haitians will be allowed to stay. That conclusion overlaps and is compatible with the Carter Administration's designation of all Haitians and Cubans who entered the country without documents before June 19 as special entrants entitled to a minimum of six months' parole status and accompanying benefits.

Perhaps the most damning finding in Judge King's order is that "much of the evidence is not brutal but simply callous — evidence that INS officials decided to ship all Haitians back to Haiti simply because their continued presence in the United States had become a problem."

That suggests that those who saw racism in the INS's attitude toward Haitians were close to the mark. Judge King concluded that the INS essentially made its decision regarding brutality in Haiti first, basing it on the desire to get rid of these poor — and black — refugees. Then the INS merely went through the motions of hearing evidence. That is an intolerable attitude for any Federal agency.

If upheld, Judge King's ruling will force Congress and the Administration to start over with a consistent, nondiscriminatory policy on applicants for political asylum. Almost certainly the result of that reassessment will be an amnesty for those Haitians, Cubans, and others who entered during the period of bureaucratic bumbling. With that probably will come a tight enforcement of the new rules with respect to subsequent arrivals. That is a proper resolution of a hopelessly tangled controversy.

Many undocumented aliens who arrive in South Florida in the future — from Haiti and elsewhere — may not merit political asylum. Most may be turned away. Yet Judge King's ruling properly has made clear that everyone who reaches American soil *is* entitled to the Constitution's guarantees of due process and equal protection of law.

San Francisco Chronicle
San Francisco, Calif., July 8, 1980

ALMOST NIGHTLY, at some point along the Florida coast, often near its wealthy estates, small and frail boats arrive with the incoming tides, their cargoes emaciated Haitians who sometimes die near the house and street lights that spelled hope to them.

No one knows how many have disappeared; no one knows specifically how many have succeeded. There are at least 15,000 of these black refugees in Florida, more are certain to be on the way for the number is apparently limited only by ability to obtain a boat, any kind of boat, for the dangerous 900 mile voyage to the United States from the poorest nation in the entire Caribbean.

The plight of the recent flood of Cuban refugees is well known, and resulted in an ambivalent federal policy. President Carter's "open hearts, open arms" policy was followed by a crackdown on boat operators sailing the 90 miles between Cuba and Florida; the president expressed his concern that the Cuban flight be orderly and safe. The Cubans were accepted, in large part, and most will receive not only governmental assistance but help from relatives already resettled in new homes.

THERE WAS no such expression of concern over the safety of the voyages of the Haitians and, until recently, not much expression of federal concern. And a Miami federal court has heard testimony that official policy was, in fact, discriminatory to the extent that it may have caused loss of life. The Immigration and Naturalization Service deported some 700 Haitians back to Haiti between 1977 and early 1979; witnesses testified in the Miami court that some of these deportees were immediately confined to prison under conditions almost indescribably inhumane.

President Carter's "interim assistance order" dealing with Cuban and Haitian refugees announced June 20 made a start toward correcting the discrepancies between what amounted to a welcome for refugees from a left-wing country and refusal to recognize that refugees from a right-wing dictatorship had a problem. Both Haitian and Cuban refugees were granted a six-month "entrant" status, not further defined until Congress acts, and some limited aid programs have been set up for the Haitians.

And now U. S. District Judge James L. King has found that the government flatly discriminated against Haitians by holding that they were "economic" and not "political" refugees and thus subject to expulsion. His ruling said that politics and economics were inseparable in the Haitian dynasty now controlled by Jean-Claude (Baby Doc) Duvalier. The judge ruled that conditions in Haiti were "stark, brutal and bloody," and that the Immigration and Naturalization Service had wronged Haitians when it refused to consider their pleas for political asylum on a case-by-case basis. He also accused the INS of racial discrimination.

His ruling does much to restore equity and sanity in the present complicated refugee situation, and we believe he has acted most humanely. The United States can not possibly accept all refugees who wish to come to these shores; it can, at least, guarantee equal treatment to those which do arrive and not discriminate by either right or left-wing place of origin or race.

THE COMMERCIAL APPEAL

Memphis, Tenn., April 16, 1980

WHY HAVE HAITI'S "boat people" risked their lives on the two-week, 700-mile voyage from their island homeland to the United States? Have 5,000 Haitians set sail in search of political asylum, or is it economic gain they seek?

That is the question before a federal court in Miami. If it rules they fled for political reasons, the refugees would get a rehearing before the Immigration and Naturalization Service. They would be deported if the court finds they came for financial reward.

However the court decides, the answer is evident. Haiti's history of repression under the Duvalier family, *pere et fil*, is well-known and well-documented. Life may be less bloody under 'Baby Doc' than under his Papa; some Haitians may be speaking out to challenge the dynasty, and Duvalier Jr. may not have rejected demands for reform as entirely out of hand. Still, the country remains an absolute dictatorship with an unenviable record on human rights — present as well as past, according to the U.S. State Department.

Things would have been bad enough for the Haitian people if this had been 'Baby Doc's' only legacy, but along with it and with the family's wealth (which is sufficient to maintain homes in Europe and Haiti as well as a yacht), he also was left a country drained of its one-time prosperity. Haiti is the poorest nation in the Western Hemisphere and one of the poorest in the world.

Education, health care and jobs aren't the only things in short supply. An island whose agricultural abundance made it an anchor for world trade in the 18th Century has "been ravaged nearly to exhaustion," according to the Conservation Foundation. Inheritance laws dating back to the Napoleonic Code have forced the land to be split into smaller and smaller plots, which could not be farmed efficiently even if owners had modern production methods available to them. Whereas Haiti used to grow such crops as coffee, cocoa and sugar for export, it has had to switch to corn, sorghum and beans for consumption at home to avoid starvation. Even sugar, the basis of Haiti's former wealth, now must be imported.

The international community has recognized these problems and has come forth with help. The United States, for instance, has provided $93 million in aid, more than half of it emergency food supplies. Increasingly, however, assistance is being linked to 'Baby Doc's' performance on human rights.

UNTIL HIS ACT improves, however, it makes little sense for the United States and its courts to quibble over whether it's freedom from want or freedom from fear Haiti's refugees seek. These Caribbean "boat people" have risked their lives to break free of a cycle of repression and deprivation, and freedom should not be denied them.

St. Petersburg Times

St. Petersburg, Fla., April 11, 1980

In one South Florida court this week a boat captain is being tried for throwing overboard to their deaths a mother and five children, refugees from Haiti, within sight of the shore where they had hoped to build a new life.

In another, the United States government stands accused of an offense less heinous but far broader in scope: condemning thousands of other Haitian boat people — the lucky ones who managed to make it to shore — to persecution and torture, by arbitrarily sending them home.

IN THE West Palm Beach murder case, the prosecutor cried as he detailed the state's allegations.

He said the doomed mother and children, aged 3 to 10, were among 17 Haitians who paid a smuggler for passage to Florida on a 23-foot boat from Freeport in the Bahamas. He said the captain and mate dumped the passengers into the ocean a few hundred yards off the beach when they thought police had detected their mission.

IN A class-action suit in federal court in Miami, against immigration officials, witnesses described dictatorial abuse in Haiti that in the past few years has prompted poor Haitians to flee by the thousands, most of them to the United States.

The Immigration and Naturalization Service generally has rejected their pleas for asylum, contending they came for jobs, not for political freedom. When caught, they have been ordered deported. The testimony was that when they got home they often were imprisoned and tortured.

Last year Judge James Lawrence King ordered a halt to further deportations to Haiti pending this hearing on claims by the Haitian Refugee Center that the Haitian boat people deserve better treatment.

Immigration officials contend they have merely followed the law as to which boat people qualify for admission. Cubans, for instance, may be granted automatic asylum, because they have fled a communist nation. Haiti's dictatorship is right-wing rather than left. So Haitians don't get the same deal.

IF THE law says that, to quote Mr. Bumble in *Oliver Twist*, the law "is a ass" and ought to be changed. In the absence of that, however, it can be administered with less regard for its letter and more for its spirit.

Despite the noble invitation graven on the Statue of Liberty, it is an obvious truth that the United States no longer can open its arms to all the world's poor huddled masses. Nowadays there are too many of them and of us. In today's world there have to be limits. But now, more than ever, there also is urgent need for compassion.

MOST OF the Haitian boat people wouldn't know one dictatorship from another. They voice no eloquent thoughts on the concept of political freedom. But they have had it at home, with oppression and poverty, too. Driven by desperation, of whatever nature, they have entrusted their lives to small leaky boats on the slim chance they can reach the United States.

President Carter could, and according to Rep. Dan Mica, D-Fla., still may grant amnesty to all the estimated 12,000 Haitians who are already here. Failing that, let each hearing on a plea for asylum be conducted on its individual merits. Toward a passing score of 100, desperation should count at least 50.

The Washington Star

Washington, D. C., July 7, 1980

Judge Lawrence King may have been guilty of a bit of rhetorical extravagance when he denounced the federal government's treatment of the Haitians now claiming asylum in this country as political refugees. History being the sad story it is, it's always dubious wisdom to call any one questionable course of action the worst on record. Still, the turn toward a more generous — and more realistic — Haitian policy is a welcome one.

The judge's ruling does not automatically end the threat of deportation for the 5,000 Haitians who have been trying through the courts to get into the political refugee category under which so many Cubans have won the right to stay in this country. It merely calls upon the Immigration and Naturalization Service to rethink its position that economic hardships present the only reasons for wanting to get out of Haiti.

Everything that is known about the Duvalier dynasty's way of running things — and a good deal *is* reasonably well documented — argues to the contrary. It is not only in economic squalor that Haiti resembles Cuba; the prisons and goon squads of Port-au-Prince may rival those of Havana.

Fairness demands that the American government recognize the physical and moral parallels. So does political pragmatism. The Carter administration's championship of human rights has too long been flawed by selectivity. Chile yes, China no. South Africa yes, Angola no.

The double standard that labels Cuban immigrants political refugees and fails to recognize Haitian claims to comparable status has understandably heightened the indignation of Florida blacks already aggrieved over their sense of being displaced by Cubans. A change in official standards for processing Haitian immigration applications should help to ease the tensions that brought last month's riots.

This in no way obviates the need for controlling the flow of immigration to the United States. We are still up against the brute fact that millions of people would like to trade their poverty and constraint for a chance to share our opulence and freedom. We are still up against the brute fact that any mass influx of newcomers is going to be hard on the people already here, disrupting social patterns and competing for finite resources.

What must be accepted is the need for trade-offs and compromises that will balance need against need, right against right. Adopting a more liberal policy toward the Haitians will create problems as well as ameliorating them. But it is as distinctly in line with the broader interests of the nation as of the fleeing Haitians themselves.

Haitians Deported from Island in the Bahamas

Bahamian police wielding clubs Nov. 13 forced 102 Haitians, including several pregnant women, off the island of Cayo Lobos and onto a Haiti-bound ship. The Haitians had been discovered on Cayo Lobos by a U.S. patrol plane Oct. 9, but the Bahamian government had waited more than a month before taking action. Five persons died of starvation in the interim, and the rest were suffering from malnutrition. They had started out for the U.S. in a sailboat but were blown off course to Cayo Lobos, 20 miles north of Cuba. They were stranded on the island when their boat drifted away. (ABC and NBC newsmen covering their eviction were killed when their helicopter crashed into the Caribbean Nov. 13.) Haitian President Jean-Claude Duvalier said the returning Haitians would not suffer "discrimination."

ST. LOUIS POST-DISPATCH
St. Louis, Mo., November 16, 1980

The specter of persons who are fleeing poverty being clubbed into submission to be sent back to the country they left is a depressing one. But aside from deploring the recent forced repatriation of Haitians by Bahamanian police, what should other governments, including the U.S., do?

The U.S. has accepted thousands of Haitians, giving them special status — but not as refugees or as immigrants. And in the strict sense of the word, they are not refugees. International declarations, including the American Convention on Human Rights, state that all persons have a right "to seek" asylum when they are fleeing persecution. But that persecution is political, not the threat of hunger or despair that prompts many to leave Haiti.

If individuals can make a case for political asylum they deserve to be heard; and as those shipped back to Haiti under duress were denied the chance to make that case, the Bahamanian government erred. President Duvalier has said that none of the returnees is in danger, and it can only be hoped that is the case. Perhaps a regional monitoring force could be set up to help ensure the safety of those who are returned.

The Organization of American States will begin its annual session this week and emphasis is to be placed on human rights. Surely the situation in Haiti merits attention. The long-term U.S. response to the problems in Haiti has been to provide aid to try to alleviate some of the economic suffering; but not all of that aid is reaching those in need. Still, poverty is the basic villain that fosters totalitarian rule, and the U.S. should continue to work to improve aid and the system for getting it to the people.

The Charlotte Observer
Charlotte, N. C., November 11, 1980

One hundred Haitians marooned on an uninhabited Caribbean island for the last month are a stark reminder of an intractable problem for the United States: illegal migration.

More than 25,000 Haitians have fled their country — considered among the world's most impoverished — for jobs and refuge in South Florida in recent years. Several thousand more have taken refuge in the Bahamas, but late last month the Bahamian government said it will deport illegal Haitian immigrants by Jan. 18. Within hours of the announcement, scores of Haitians left the Bahamas by boat, heading for Florida.

It's unclear whether the marooned Haitians were among those escaping arrest in the Bahamas, but they symbolize Americans' concern about such headlong migrations here. Members of Congress and other government officials are asking whether U.S. immigration laws ought to be changed to shut off the huge flow of illegal immigrants into this country not only from Haiti but also from Mexico, Cuba and other Caribbean nations.

Such migrants are motivated by poverty and the lack of job opportunities at home. They are symptoms of their own governments' failures in economic planning and population policy. Those are the problems U.S. officials must address if they want to stop illegal migration rather than paper it over with new immigration quotas and draconian measures to guard U.S. coastlines.

It's a hopeful sign that U.S. officials, who met last month with foreign ministers of Haiti and the Bahamas to discuss how to shut off the illegal immigration, came away agreeing that the root of Haiti's migration problem is poverty and that more foreign assistance might help curtail the migration.

There's no agreement yet on specifics. Even if measures are taken to attack Haitian poverty — such as training unskilled people and providing more jobs by labor-intensive expansion of Haiti's agricultural sector — the effects won't be felt for some time. No doubt, illegal migration will trouble us for decades.

The Boston Globe

Boston, Mass., November 30, 1980

It might be difficult to find a more graphic plea for help. The man's arms are outstretched in a universally-understood gesture; his surroundings, the baking sand and the scrubby bushes, dramatize his plea. He was one of the 102 Haitians, castaway on a deserted Bahamian island when the boat in which they were trying to reach Florida and political asylum was driven ashore in a storm. They suffered there for 47 days, some dying while the others lived off fish and airlifted emergency rations, while state departments and foreign ministries wrangled over their "status." In the end, it was a story of help refused, of a plea unanswered. Bahamian police rounded up the survivors and shipped them back to Haiti; it is unlikely we will ever learn the dismal end of this story.

The case appears to be one in which humanitarian concerns lost out to political concerns, in which policies geared to case-by-case reviews of *individual* applicants for asylum got morally tangled up because more than one person was involved. It is the kind of incident that provides an opportunity to air all the comments that start off "we can't take in everyone"; but more important, it supports the notion that moral decisions that involve *groups* of people sould be made on the basis of the interests of each *individual* involved.

The notion creates a minimal principle of equality. It is not a guarantee of equal treatment, but merely a recognition that one person's interests cannot count for any more than someone else's, and that one must take account of the interests of all those who may be affected by a decision.

In the case of the refugees on Cayo Lobos, we might start by weighing the interests of that man kneeling on the sand, the one with his arms outstretched, against the interests of the society he wishes to join; and having (let us assume) determined a duty to admit him, repeat the process with the woman behind him, and so on. This weighing of interests, however, will not automatically grant asylum to the entire *boatload*. At some point, as the conflicting interests are being weighed, those of the society as a whole may very well come to outweigh those of a specific individual.

Perhaps, but it may take a while for that point to be reached. There is a hidden factor in the "equal consideration of interests" principle that has to be taken into account in making these determinations. Once the notion of *equal* right to consideration of interests is acknowledged, a question of *unequal* benefits has to be considered.

Princeton philosopher Gregory Vlastos describes the process in terms of a person who receives a very serious threat of harm to himself or his family, serious enough for the police to station an officer on guard at his home and provide him with police escort during the day. This security for one man costs several times more than the per capita cost of police services for everyone else in the city. "The greater allocation of community resources in X's favor," Vlastos explains, "is made precisely because X's security rights are equal to those of other people (in the city)." In the special circumstances of the threat he has received, his "security level" would fall below that of everyone else unless he is given the extra resources of the guard and escort.

Although there will be a temptation to assume that these extra resources are something that should be provided more readily to some important politician, businessman or community leader — and perhaps that is exactly what happens in the real world — Vlastos makes the point that neither "merit" nor "worth" are factors that can be considered in this process of giving equal consideration to the interests of an individual. We do not require "merit" as a qualification for voting, he argues, and a person going to rescue a drowning man is unlikely to inquire about his "worth" before jumping into the water.

We really cannot even take a person's *relative* merit or worth into account. An agency official involved in the case of the Haitian refugees and one of the refugees might require relief from some terrible pain. The official, given relief, might be able to accomplish more for humanity than the refugee, but the intrinsic value of pain, and of relief from it, is the same for both men. Thus, in the police protection case, security has the same intrinsic value to the important politician, an average citizen or even an unattractive criminal, and any of them can demand the services necessary to ensure it.

The important point, Vlastos writes, is "that it is benefits to persons, not allocations of resources as such, that are meant to be made equal," even if that means an *unequal* allocation of resources is needed to achieve the goal of *equal* benefits.

On one level, this notion that one man's wellbeing is as valuable as another's leads to a notion that each man has an equal right to well-being, and from that follows the basis for our social welfare rights: education, housing, medical care, recreation, and so forth.

But there is a personal dimension to this argument, one not directed at the makers of public policy, the officials with the power to grant asylum to a boatload of refugees, or to determine the level of social welfare funding. There are personal decisions that we make daily which determine the well-being — the happiness, comfort, security — of others, and they are decisions, it now seems clear, that are best made with regard to one person at a time, without regard to the merit or worth of that person.

The Evening Gazette

Worcester, Mass., November 18, 1980

The Haitian Red Cross was there to welcome the 206 arrivals from the Bahamanian island of Cayo Lobos. The media, too, were interested in the return. And the presence of the newsmen and cameras brought out smiling representatives of the Haitian government who handed each arrival $40 for a new start.

But most of the arrivals — gaunt, hollow-eyed, shuffling, tired and hungry — hadn't asked for the welcome or the $40. They wanted to leave Haiti for good.

The Bahamas, concerned for its resort business, dumped the Haitians back on Haiti, from which they fled months ago. Haiti, concerned about international reaction to the plight of these people, appeared to welcome them back in forgiveness, at least for a moment.

But the future is bleak for them. "The horizon is low. We see nothing. We don't know what is going to come, but we are walking toward a catastrophe," is the description given by one Haitian. "Everyone wants to leave," he added, because "there are people who can't eat here every day."

Still, the Haitian government threw a cocktail party Friday night for the press. The reporters were awaiting the arrival of a Bahamian boat transporting 106 refugees who had been shipwrecked while trying to escape and another 100 picked up by Bahamian authorities after fleeing Haiti.

The U.S. Coast Guard had spotted the refugees on uninhabited Cayo Lobos Island on Oct. 9. Food was dropped to them four times while the Bahamians asked the United Nations or the United States to do something. The Bahamians are also returning 150 refugees a month to Port Au Prince.

The plight of the Haitians is a reflection of the plight of millions of people all over the globe — in Africa, Southeast Asia, the Middle East, in the huge dark empire run by Moscow.

But Haiti is in our own backyard. It is a constant reproach to the conscience of the world.

The Miami Herald

Miami, Fla., November 15, 1980

HORROR heaps upon horror in the saga of Cayo Lobos. Pitiful Haitian refugees flee their barren homes under gunfire from Haitian authorities. Storm tossed, they land in Cuba, only to be turned back to the sea by force.

After several suicides and other deaths, more than 100 survivors land on a tiny Bahamian islet just north of Cuba. They huddle there, starving, while three governments quibble over jurisdiction and responsibility. The United States has ready means to evacuate the survivors of the *Vivant Dieu* to Florida for processing along with thousands of their countrymen. But the world's richest nation lacks the will to effect a rescue.

When rescue finally comes, seven weeks after the shipwreck, it is in the form of a Bahamian ship laden with khaki-clad, club-wielding soldiers determined to return the Haitians to an uncertain fate at the hands of the dictator who rules their country. These were not the white-gloved Royal Police who so charm tourists in Nassau. These were men with clubs who unmercifully beat weak, helpless victims who fear their homeland even more than they fear the sea.

The world watched those beatings on television in shock. Despite the characteristically civil pronouncements from Nassau, there was no misinterpreting the event. Haitians long have complained of abuse at the hands of Bahamian authorities. Now that treatment is confirmed.

Americans sitting in the comfort of their secure homes cannot afford to be smug, however, about the inhumanity of Bahamian "rescuers." The U.S. Coast Guard had landed earlier at Cayo Lobos. The emergency was well known to American authorities, who have much greater resources at their disposal than does the struggling Bahamian government.

Bahamians must wrestle with their conscience about the brutality of their police and the lack of due process in summarily returning the survivors to Haiti without hearings. But Americans cannot shrug off their responsibility for the fact that more than 100 poor, suffering people were left to an unpredictable fate *after* Federal authorities became aware of their plight.

Civilized peoples simply cannot conduct their affairs with so callous a disregard for human life. The nations of the Caribbean *must* join in concerted effort, possibly under the auspices of the United Nations commission on refugees, to resolve the issue of the boat people from Haiti. Conscience will permit no less.

Miami, Fla., November 18, 1980

SO LONG as American reporters are standing by, the Haitians of Cayo Lobos have nothing to fear from their repressive government. What will happen to them, and to others like them, when the press leaves can only be inferred from the heavy-handed tactics that Haitian police used to control the crowds gathered to greet the returners at Port-au-Prince.

The accusations of beatings, torture, and arbitrary imprisonment by Haitian authorities are legion. Whether a particular act of cruelty is inspired by political differences, by sadism, or by financial motives hardly seems relevant to the thousands of people who each year flee the Western Hemisphere's poorest country. The fear is real. The poverty is verified. The desperation is etched into the faces of men and women who risk their lives and those of their children in a frantic gamble for survival.

People of goodwill in the United States and elsewhere should not waste the leverage that was created by the spotlight of Cayo Lobos. The plight of more than 100 castaways — marooned on a barren islet, ignored by three governments, driven by force away from the Cuban shore, then beaten by their Bahamian rescuers — focused unprecedented attention on the boat people of the Caribbean.

That attention now should be transformed into multilateral action to ease the stranglehold with which the Duvalier family grips Haiti and to provide some hope for the people of that woe-begotten island-nation.

The United Nations High Commission on Refugees tried unsuccessfully to intervene in the return of the Cayo Lobos survivors to Haiti. Bahamian authorities rebuffed the effort, testily citing an estimated 20,000 to 40,000 other Haitians who also are in the Bahamas without legal immigration status. That presence is a major burden to a country plagued by unemployment whose native-born population is about 250,000.

The Dominican Republic, which shares the island of Hispaniola with Haiti, also feels the weight of that country's grinding poverty. Ethnic Haitians compose nearly one-third of the population of the Dominican Republic.

Clearly the Haitian people need more help than their struggling next-door neighbors can provide. Economic resources will have to come from the United States if Haiti ever is to become a nation that its people can love, instead of fear. That aid must go directly to the Haitian people, not to the corrupt dynasty that has bled them for two generations.

The United Nations High Commission on Refugees was correct in trying to help the unfortunates of Cayo Lobos. Now Washington should urge the commission to sustain that effort by establishing a permanent multilateral task force to address the Haitian problem at its source: Haiti.

Refugee Reform Law Passed in 1980

One year after its introduction, the Refugee Act was signed into law by President Jimmy Carter March 17, 1980. It was the first major revision of U.S. refugee legislation since 1965. The new law raised the ceiling on refugee and immigrant admission to 320,000 from 290,000 a year and set no limit on country of origin. The limit on refugees alone was to be 50,000 instead of 17,400 a year, and the president could decide to admit more refugees after consulting with Congress. The president also could grant refugees permission to stay in the U.S. for up to one year in cases of "grave humanitarian concern." The bill had the practical effect of replacing the attorney general's parole authority, which had been granted to him by the 1952 Immigration and Nationality Act and allowed him to admit more refugees than the annual quota. The Justice Department had objected to parole authority because, as Associate Attorney General Michael Egan told Congress in 1979, it "has the practical effect of giving to the attorney general more power than the Congress in determining limits on the entry of refugees into the country."

The 1980 Refugee Act rewrote the definition of refugee to include anyone fleeing from persecution anywhere in the world, instead of just communist countries. It excluded anyone who had aided in persecuting anyone else because of race, religion or politics. (A number of Nazi war criminals had been allowed into the U.S. as refugees after World War II.)

ST. LOUIS POST-DISPATCH

St. Louis, Mo., June 9, 1979

The tired, the poor, the huddled masses yearning to breathe free are queued up en masse in Indochina and in long lines in the Soviet Union, but America's golden door is only open a crack. And, although the Carter administration is pushing for legislation that would ease the way into the country for thousands of additional refugees, it is unlikely that Congress will act quickly or that the U.S. could handle the enormous world refugee problem alone.

The immediate need is for passage of nearly $105 million in supplemental appropriations for this year's refugee program. Soviet Jews and Indochinese, at a lower-than-planned level, are still getting government aid to enable them to come here, but to allow this the State Department has had to borrow from other funds. The administration's emergency funds for refugees have been exhausted, contributions to the U.N. High Commissioner for Refugees and the Red Cross have been deferred and payment may be delayed to the United Israel Appeal. The U.S. needs to maintain the refugee pipelines, for money that could help people would be wasted if it had to be spent to restart the machinery. So the intergovernmental borrowing makes good sense, but the funds have to be repaid and that lends even more urgency to the need for congressional approval of the funds.

For the long term, Congress needs to change the laws that cover refugee admissions. Currently 17,400 refugees from communist countries or the Middle East are permitted in annually through normal channels. This figure is unrealistically low, so the attorney general has used his emergency parole authority to admit many more. From March 1975 to the end of April, 1979, the U.S. had admitted approximately 250,000 Indochina refugees. The administration would raise the "normal flow" limitation to 50,000 and drop the restriction on country of origin — in its stead would be a requirement that the refugees be of "special concern" to the U.S. The 50,000 figure might be raised after consultation with Congress. Also after congressional consultation, the president could use a new emergency admissions program to admit more refugees conditionally. And in individual and unique refugee cases, the attorney general could use his parole authority.

Congress ought to look favorably on these changes since they would be a definite improvement over existing law. One problem area, however, could be the "special concern" requirement. The U.S. involvement in Indochina and our current relations with the Soviet Union and Israel fulfill that demand in regard to the bulk of the refugees that are now being admitted. But there are hundreds of thousands of refugees in Africa and elsewhere who have not asked to immigrate here; neither can they claim that the U.S. contributed to their plight. Still, they deserve help from the world.

In this connection special ambassador Dick Clark will need to redouble efforts to get other countries to open their doors and their coffers to the victims of war, racism or political persecution in Indochina and elsewhere. The U.S. must increase its efforts, but it cannot carry the entire burden.

The Boston Globe

Boston, Mass., July 11, 1979

The Senate Judiciary Committee has unanimously approved the first comprehensive reform of the nation's immigration laws since 1965, a reform that enables the nation better to meet its historic commitment to providing a home for refugees who have no other. The Senate committee's lead should be followed by the House Judiciary Committee and the full Congress should move quickly to enact the legislation.

The plight of refugees in the world has been dramatized by the continuing tragedy in Indochina, where thousands have died in their struggle to reach a new homeland and 300,000 are now subsisting in makeshift, temporary refugee camps. But the refugee legislation approved by the Judiciary Committee goes beyond the Indochinese situation and attempts to improve this country's overall refugee policies.

Maybe most important, it redefines refugees to conform with the United Nations protocol on the subject. At present, refugee status is available only to those fleeing communist countries and certain nations of the Mideast. The new definition would grant refugee status to all victims of persecution or those with well-founded fears of persecution because of race, religion, nationality, membership in a particular social group or political opinion. That change means refugees from dictatorships around the world could now gain routine entry into the country.

The new legislation, whose chief sponsor is Sen. Kennedy, would raise from 17,400 to 50,000 annually the number of refugees routinely admitted into the country. In recent years we have, in fact, admitted up 50,000 annually but only through the use of waivers. The legislation would set up more sensible procedures to allow the President, after consultation with Congress, to exceed the 50,000 figure. It would grant refugees permanent resident status rather than "conditional entry" status. It would for the first time legalize the granting of asylum to foreigners who come to the United States and decline to return home. And it would establish a federal commitment to provide financial assistance for the resettlement of refugees in the United States.

The country takes pride in its frequent self-description as a "nation of immigrants." Passage of the refugee legislation will better assure that for those most in need, that tradition is more faithfully and efficiently followed in the years ahead.

DAYTON DAILY NEWS

Dayton, Ohio, June 23, 1979

The Carter Administration and the Congress are trying to rewrite the laws under which refugees enter the country, starting from plans submitted by the Departments of Justice, State and Health, Education and Welfare. No conflict exists on the need to update the laws, but conservatives and liberals have both raised sharp questions.

The law now permits refugees in two ways. There are "normal flow" refugees, up to 17,400 annually, mostly from Communist countries. That's a chilling phrase, as if this world must always face, as normal, a river of refugees. It also gives the attorney general authority for individual hardship cases.

But for more than 20 years, that authority has been used in large-scale emergencies, admitting thousands of Hungarians, Cubans, Soviet and Eastern European refugees, and now those from Indochina. Attorney General Griffin Bell thinks the authority puts too much power and responsibility on one man. Some conservatives think it's been used to admit far more refugees than Congress intended.

The new law would increase the "normal flow" refugees to 50,000 from anywhere in the world but especially persons of "special concern" to the United States. The number could fall, if need were less, or rise in emergencies after the President consulted with Congress. And the attorney general would use his parole authority only for individual hardship cases.

Conservatives think the plan still gives the President too much leeway. Amnesty International and civil liberty groups say the phrase "of special concern" make political what should be humanitarian.

So the debate will go on, in Congress and among U.S. citizens, many the children and grandchildren of refugees. How many more of the poor, the tired, the huddled masses yearning to be free will, or can, this nation receive?

It is an important debate, and how we conduct and resolve it will say some things about us as people. Let's work to make them the good things.

OKLAHOMA CITY TIMES

Oklahoma City, Okla., May 30, 1979

REFUGEE programs of the United States government have been remarkably disorganized affairs for the past 40 years, despite the history of this nation. Now formal reorganization has created a federal "coordinator of refugee affairs" whose task it is to bring order out of the chaos. It is one of the most promising achievements of the Carter administration.

The federal government sees three major areas of refugee problems as threats to the peace and prosperity of the world. Each involves incredibly large numbers of people. The costs of dealing with them in their new or temporary locations are climbing daily, and no budget can contemplate next year's probable price with any degree of certainty.

The three major migrations now taking place involve the Southeast Asians, Soviet Jews and Africans of many nationalities and tribal groupings.

It seems unlikely that this country will be able to do much right away about the 2 million African refugees, except through international aid plans. The United Nations high commissioner for refugees now aids 1 million people, and this country pays one-third of the cost.

In Southeast Asia and in dealing with emigrating Soviet Jews, the U.S. programs are taking on more distinct forms.

As of May 1 there are an estimated 250,000 Indochinese refugees in camps. Of these, 150,000 are those known as "land refugees" — because of the way they have fled their homelands — and 100,000 are the "boat people." Most of the land refugees are now in Thailand. The boat people, who have had more international publicity, are found in Hong Kong, Indonesia, Malaysia and Thailand. The UNHCR estimates that their number, in all, will reach 500,000 by May 1980.

The Vietnamese have proved adaptable and willing workers. Some 94 percent of those in this country now are employed, although many are seriously underemployed in relation to their skills and education. Yet 30 percent still receive some form of federal or state aid, such as food stamps, to help them make ends meet.

The number of Soviet emigres, mostly Jews, who secure visas to go to Israel, has doubled in the past year alone. They go to Vienna by train and there 70 percent of them opt to go to America instead of to Israel. New York has received most of them so far.

The new coordinator will take on the jobs done in the past by the State Department, HEW, Justice, AID and other agencies. And he is having trouble telling Congress what to expect.

His proposed legislative package calls for 120,000 admissions a year of refugees above the normal immigration quota of 290,000. He expects 36,000 a year from the Soviet Union and East Europe, and 7,000 a month from Southeast Asia in this and next fiscal years. But that may not make a dent in the lists of waiting families, many of whom had to flee because of their support of the U.S. position during the Indochinese war. Yet 84,000 out of 120,000 total per year is a high quota for Southeast Asia.

Whether former Sen. Dick Clark, now the coordinator, can bring the loose ends together, meet the human needs of the dispossessed in a way that is fair to Americans as well as to the refugees and convince Congress that a rational program is the most effective way to go remains to be seen. But the effort seems a great improvement over the improvised programs of the recent past.

THE PLAIN DEALER

Cleveland, Ohio, June 25, 1979

The plight of refugees as portrayed in newspapers and on television has been an assault on the conscience of many Americans living in relative comfort.

Some believe more refugees should be admitted to this country. Others believe there is a limit, or relatively low threshold, on the capacity of the country to absorb large numbers of refugees.

The Refugee Act of 1979 proposed to Congress by the Carter administration attempts to increase the number, yet provide limitations; to set a limit, yet provide for emergencies that would require that more than the normal limit of refugees be admitted.

Despite attacks that the bill's emergency provisions are too open-ended, the bill is a good one and deserves support. The problems of the current refugee law stem in large part from it being too rigid.

The bill would eliminate some of the confusion surrounding the admission of refugees. It provides a systematic procedure for admission. And it eliminates some restrictions such as the ideological and geographical limitations in defining a refugee.

Currently, the law provides that the country yearly may admit 17,-400 refugees, a total of 290,000 immigrants and an additional number of refugees under the attorney general's authority to grant paroles. The 17,400 were limited to those fleeing a Communist or Middle East country. The parole authority was used to dodge such restrictions.

As a result of the parole authority of the attorney general, 133,000 Indochinese were admitted to the United States in 1975. For 1978 and 1979, a total of close to 50,000 will be admitted on parole. Previously refugees from Cuba, Hungary, the Soviet Union and other Eastern European countries entered under parole rather than in the refugee category.

The proposed law would push the refugee category limit from 17,400 to 50,000 a year and be called the normal flow of refugees. But, as before, this would be a technical limit. The total number of immigrants allowed in would be 320,000, including normal flow refugees.

More refugees could be admitted as part of the normal flow if prior to each fiscal year the president consults with Congress, notifying it that humanitarian concern or the national interest requires more refugees to be admitted.

If an unforeseen emergency develops, the president would not have to wait for a new fiscal year. He could notify Congress and specify the number to be admitted, again in excess of the 50,000 limit.

The attorney general's parole authority would remain, but would be limited to dealing with individual and unique refugee cases as originally planned.

The admission of refugees would continue to be a political as well as a moral act under the proposal. For example, the administration already has said the 50,000 limit is too low for the next three fiscal years and expects 120,000 refugees in the next fiscal year. Sen. Strom Thurmond, R-S.C., last month objected to more than 50,000.

The judiciary committees of both houses of Congress should approve the proposed bill. The Statue of Liberty's inscription includes, "I lift my lamp beside the golden door!" The bill would shed the light.

The State

Columbia, S. C., June 9, 1979

Give me your tired, your poor
Your huddled masses yearning
to breathe free,
The wretched refuse of your
teeming shore,
Send these, the homeless, tem-
pest-tost to me.
— *The New Colossus*
By Emma Lazarus

THOSE immortal lines, inscribed on a tablet within the pedestal of the Statue of Liberty in New York harbor, have characterized the traditional American attitude toward immigrants.

Emma Lazarus' ideal, however, has not always been the reality, and today the United States finds itself with a dilemma created by that reality. The tide of refugees and immigrants is rising beyond numbers ever dreamed of in 1886 when the monument to liberty was dedicated.

This nation's immigration and visa laws are complicated, but also have been made flexible in an effort to meet the problems. But the system and laws are not adequate for these times. Recognizing that fact, President Carter has created a Select Commission on Immigration and Refugee Policy, but it will take two years to do its work.

While most public attention focuses on the tragedy of the Vietnamese "boat people" who are fleeing their homeland by the thousands every week, there are other immigration troubles.

The so-called "undocumented aliens" from Mexico are said to number as many as 3 million, and the traffic back-and-forth across the border is unremitting. Until Mexico can offer its masses an alternative to their economic misery, the United States will have to deal with the "wet-back" problem and its ramifications on Mexican-American relations.

There is a new rush of Haitians, mostly from Florida. They are asking for political asylum. Of course, there is a steady flow of Jews from the Soviet Union as well as many immigrants from the East European countries. And there are large numbers of Cambodian and Laotian refugees still in Indochina.

For the moment, however, the problem crying most for attention is that of the Vietnamese. It is one that the Hanoi regime has created for the rest of the world while making money on the human refugee traffic. The thousands of fleeing refugees are paying in gold for the freedom to escape.

The United States is not alone in its concern for the Vietnamese refugees. The British colony of Hong Kong is nearly overrun with 40,000 awaiting resettlement. The French and Australians have taken large numbers into their countries. Japan has taken several hundred.

The United States needs new and workable immigration policy and laws. There must be some reasonable idea, however, of how many immigrants and refugees this country can and should eventually accept from throughout the world.

In the meantime, the United States should join with Great Britain in calling for a special conference of the United Nations to deal with resettlement of the Indochinese refugees. The United Nations already has a High Commission on Refugees — and that is an acknowledgement of the problems. The United Nations members now should be confronted with their responsibilities for others.

Houston Chronicle

Houston, Texas, June 17, 1979

The number of refugees in the world today is estimated at from 10 million to 13 million. Given their choice, a hefty percentage would be only too glad to make the United States their home.

In addition, there are other millions who, though not refugees, would like to better their lot by coming to this country. Some seek freedom from persecution. Some seek a chance to work. A Texas example: The Immigration and Naturalization Service facility at Port Isabel has so far this year arranged for flights to return illegal immigrants to Pakistan, Lebanon, Nigeria, South Africa, West Germany and Spain. The cost for such flights from Texas and California annually is $11 million. And that doesn't include the return home of nearly 1 million Mexicans a year.

The size of this problem requires that this country revise its total immigration policies. Some steps have been taken along that line. Congress has created a commission to review the laws. The White House has named a coordinator for refugee affairs. And legislation has been jointly proposed by the Departments of State, Justice and Health, Education and Welfare.

The commission has met only once and the coordinator is trying to form a policy. Attention, therefore, is focused on the pending legislation. Hearings have been held and debate has begun. Changes in the legislation to set firmer limits are needed. Federal law now sets a quota of 17,400 refugees, a figure quickly filled. In addition, the attorney general has parole authority to deal with individual hardship cases. In practice, attorneys general have been using that authority to grant admission to large groups instead of just individuals. That authority has been used to admit Hungarian refugees in the 1950s, Cuban refugees in the 1960s and thousands of Soviet and East German refugees in the last decade. In the last four years, about 250,000 Indochinese have been admitted under this parole authority. Attorney General Griffin Bell himself says the parole authority gives too much power to one man.

The pending legislation would raise the refugee quota from 17,400 to 50,000 and they would have to be persons of "special concern" to the United States. This is a more realistic figure, and would be justified if at the same time the parole authority is drastically restricted. The total immigration figure for the United States worldwide would increase to 320,000 annually, an indication that this nation is maintaining its tradition of accepting large numbers of people seeking new homelands.

A weak part of the pending legislation is that the president is given the power to specify a higher number of refugees that could be admitted conditionally. As Rep. Sam B. Hall Jr., D-Texas, pointed out, this is "very openended." The president would be required to "consult" with Congress before acting, but consultation might mean a couple of phone calls. A vote by Congress on increased quotas would be more appropriate.

A stronger U.S. law on refugees could result in other countries accepting more of them. In addition to the United States, only France, Australia and Canada have admitted Southeast Asian refugees in any numbers. Once there is a firm U.S. limit, more pressure would be put on those other nations that have been expressing themselves so loudly about the problems of that area of the world but have not assumed any portion of the burden.

DESERET NEWS
Salt Lake City, Utah, June 4, 1980

The Carter administration has blown hot and cold on the Cuban refugee dilemma: first threatening boat captains with arrest, then welcoming the horde of Cubans, then seeking to screen those who leave, and now, again, warning of arrests.

Such vacillation is largely the product of the lack of a firm policy on refugees. Ironically, that's the very problem that was supposed to have been solved by passage of the 1980 Refugee Act in Congress shortly before the Cuban exodus began.

Early in May, President Carter set the 1980 quota for Cuban refugee admissions at 19,500. But four times that number had arrived by late May. This week, the count reached 100,000 in the 43-day-old Cuban sealift.

At the same time, Haitian refugees have been pouring in — as many as 1,000 in a single weekend. The influx is straining the ability of Florida and the U.S. government to care for them

That has brought tension and even violence among some refugees, including this week's riots at Camp Chaffee, Arkansas. At least 200 Cubans broke out of camp and had to be rounded up by policemen and troops.

There can be no quarrel with the idea that this country must maintain an open door, as far as possible, to political refugees. But some line has to be drawn between those who are fleeing political oppression and those fleeing poverty and seeking a richer life.

Already there are an estimated six million illegal immigrants in the country, and 750,000 more arriving each year. If all the Cubans in the current sealift are permitted to stay, what about Mexican and other illegal aliens? How much of a drain should these aliens be allowed to exert on welfare and other benefits? The U.S. isn't going to let these people starve.

In the 1980 act, Congress set an annual limit of 50,000 for the "normal flow" of refugees. But it also recognized that international emergencies may require admitting far more refugees than the statutory number. Persons admitted as refugees would qualify for cash and medical benefits for two years, and for even longer periods of education and training.

A law as loose as the new one provides little or no guidance, particularly in unusual circumstances like the current Cuban exodus. Clearly, another look at the 1980 Refugee Act is in order.

The Miami Herald
Miami, Fla., May 26, 1980

WHEN Congress wrote the Refugee Act of 1980, it envisioned an immigration policy of controlled compassion. Persons fleeing repression first would go to another country, say from Cuba to Costa Rica. From there they would apply for permission to enter the United States as refugees. The United States in turn would consider their applications one by one, subtracting each person admitted from a predetermined quota.

On paper it sounded fine. In practice, as the exodus of Cubans from Mariel has proved, the act is fatally flawed. It did not anticipate the United States becoming the first nation of refuge. Its contingency provisions did not count on that most devious contingency of all, Fidel Castro.

Exodus '80 is palpable proof that the Administration and Congress must rethink and re-articulate U.S. immigration policy. The first-refuge loophole in the new law must be closed. Funds to help local governments cope with an unanticipated horde of statusless immigrants must be authorized.

These imperatives go quite beyond the present illegal flotilla that is bringing to Key West thousands of Cubans who don't meet U.S. admissions standards and leaving behind thousands who do. Exodus '80 is symptomatic of more than the desire of Cubans to flee Castro's brand of enlightenment. It is a warning that, in a hemisphere speckled with marginally viable nations, the United States is an irresistible lure. To fail to heed that warning is to invite peril.

No nation can be a lifeboat to all who want to climb aboard. Allow too many aboard, with needs that cannot be met, and the lifeboat will sink, taking all hands with it. But limit the number of passengers, and enforce that limit, and the lifeboat will stay afloat.

This nation must weigh the needs of its own citizens against the desperation of the non-Americans floating by. Immigration quotas predicated upon that balance should be set by Congress *and then enforced.* If Congress wants to violate the quota for Cubans, say, then it should have to reduce the number of immigrants from other nations proportionately.

Besides setting and enforcing quotas, Congress must insist that every Administration enforce immigration laws. Which is more heartless: to deport an illegal alien who reaches Florida by boat, or to let him take the place of a qualified applicant who has been waiting, perhaps for years, to enter the United States legally?

Finally, the United States must redouble its efforts to address the refugee problem hemispherically. To that end it is proper that U.S. authorities now are asking refugees whether they'd be willing to go to another country.

No nation can absorb all the impoverished or oppressed millions who want to start life anew in a new land. But all nations in the hemisphere must be made willing to absorb some of them. For if they overload the American lifeboat, their own will not long stay seaworthy.

Des Moines Tribune
Des Moines, Iowa, May 9, 1980

The sudden arrival of thousands of Cuban refugees seems to have left the Carter administration confused about this nation's policy toward refugees.

The confusion was unnecessary. Congress two months ago rewrote the laws governing refugees. As former Secretary of State Cyrus Vance told the Senate Judiciary Committee in April, the purpose of the Refugee Act of 1980 is to "establish the legal framework" for a "uniform, coherent and manageable policy governing refugee admissions to this country."

From 1952 until President Carter signed the Refugee Act on March 17, a refugee was defined as someone fleeing communism or certain areas of the Middle East. A refugee now is defined as a person who has left his native country because of persecution, or a well-founded fear of persecution, based on the person's race, religion, nationality, membership in a particular social group, or because of his political opinions.

Most of the Mexicans who enter this country illegally are immigrants, rather than refugees. They are coming to the United States not because they are afraid of being persecuted in Mexico, but out of a desire to seek a better life.

Once a person has been defined as a refugee, the United States is still faced with a decision of whether the person should be allowed to settle here. In his April testimony, Vance laid down several principles for deciding which refugees should be admitted:

● "We must . . . be sensitive to the needs of refugees with close ties to the United States." This includes refugees who have relatives here.

● "Where the United States has stood uniquely as a symbol of freedom from oppression for a particular group, we must respond to their understandable aspiration for a safe haven in our country."

● When international efforts are needed in emergencies to help absorb a large number of refugees.

● A special responsibility exists to provide a temporary safe haven when the United States is the country of first asylum.

● Refugee admissions must be limited by the "practical limits on U.S. resources."

The Refugee Act tripled the number of refugees that would normally be admitted to the United States every year, from 17,400 to 50,000. It provided that this number could be increased in special circumstances, as long as the president consulted with Congress.

On April 17, Vance proposed that the United States accept 231,700 refugees in fiscal 1980. This total includes 19,500 refugees from Cuba.

The flood of Cubans to Florida since April 17 has outdated Vance's testimony. As of May 9, more than 26,000 Cubans had arrived in Florida. This was in addition to the 9,000 Cubans who were admitted in the first half of fiscal 1980. Thousands more are on the way.

The sudden flood of refugees from Cuba doesn't undermine the new Refugee Act. The act provides a definition of refugees that the Cubans clearly seem to meet. It provides that the president may increase the quota for refugee admissions from a given country — as long as he consults with Congress. Finally, it provides for additional federal spending to help resettle the extra flow of refugees.

In short, the Refugee Act provides an orderly process for handling unexpected and sudden flows of refugees.

It's too bad that the Carter administration didn't rely more heavily on this act in the early stages of the Cuban refugee crisis.

America's Dilemma: To Close the Golden Door?

The U.S. is justly proud of its reputation as a haven for refugees. From all over the world, people fleeing oppression have found in America a chance to rebuild their lives. Providing refuge for the "homeless, tempest-tossed" is as firmly stamped into our national consciousness as respecting freedom of speech. Yet there is a deep-rooted ambivalence toward this aspect of our heritage. Refugees have been received grudgingly at best, and they have had to struggle to be accepted.

The problem of taking in refugees is more acute in the second half of the 20th century than at any other time in American history. War, mass murder and political repression have created refugees faster than ever before. Voices that used to cry out against admitting "inferior" peoples now say that America has no more room or resources to cope with new waves of refugees. These arguments fail to prevent refugees from coming, however, and their pleas for asylum weigh on our consciences. The arguments change with circumstances, but the central question remains: shall we close the door?

The Providence Journal

Providence, R. I., November 12, 1978

Giving aid and asylum to refugees from Indochina, Lebanon or Cuba is a concrete way in which the United States can show its dedication to human rights. The promise of rescue for these unfortunate victims of oppression and war around the world was an appropriate way for President Carter to observe the 30th anniversary of the Universal Declaration of Human Rights.

That document has been ignored so much of the time since it was adopted by the United Nations in 1948 that the Carter administration's stress on human rights has been a welcome breath of fresh air in international affairs. The American commitment to helping refugees is particularly pertinent in these times, when men, women and children have been fleeing by the thousands from Vietnam and Cambodia, when hundreds have been driven from their homes by civil war in Lebanon, and when political prisoners are being freed by the Communist regime in Cuba.

The flood of refugees in Indochina is so great that the United States alone cannot handle it. Indeed, the neighboring countries cannot, either, and they have balked at accepting shiploads, with agonizing results for everyone involved. Aid and resettlement for all the victims is an international problem and must be handled by international agencies, with cooperation from many countries.

"I hope we will always stand ready to welcome more than our fair share of those who flee their homelands because of racial, religious or political oppression," President Carter said. But he also went on to denounce those countries that have persecuted their own citizens, in violation of the human rights declaration.

U. S. observance of the declaration has not been perfect. We have overlooked oppression by nations with which we are allied, because we needed the cooperation of their governments for our own protection or that of the non-Communist world. We have failed at times to denounce violations of the rights that we accord our own people as a matter of course. But the United States has worked to improve conditions in many countries. It has criticized friends and foes alike. It has applied sanctions against some of the worst offenders. It has given refuge to victims from other lands.

Human rights, said Zbigniew Brzezinski, the President's national security adviser, are "the central facet of America's relevance to this changing world." America is still the beacon of freedom for the oppressed everywhere. The promise of America is that it always will be such a beacon and that it will strive to assure the human rights of its own citizens and those from abroad who turn to us for help.

THE SUN

Baltimore, Md., December 1, 1978

The Statue of Liberty should be standing a little taller now in New York Harbor. The United States showed compassion and leadership when Attorney General Griffin B. Bell told Congress that he is using his "parole" authority to allow in about 25,000 refugees more than quotas allow.

Most of these—tired, poor, huddled masses yearning to breathe free, wretched refuse of teeming shores, homeless, tempest-tossed—are Vietnamese "boat people." Some are the Cuban political prisoners that dictator Fidel Castro promised to free if the United States would take them all. (The number is somewhat lower than he specified and involves slow case-by-case screening.) And a small number are Lebanese, already fled from their native land.

Of these, only the Cubans can be said by the strictest of standards to be the particular responsibility of the United States because of past American policies, in their case the encouragement from 1960 to 1962 of insurrection in Cuba.

The "boat people" are not those Vietnamese who suffered from the American pull-out and Communist takeover because of association with the United States. They are mostly ethnic Chinese resident in the country for generations and persecuted as a group by the government because of who and what they are as a group, and not because of individual actions on their part. Afloat at sea, extorted of material wealth by the government evicting them, denied status as political refugees by some because of that extortion, talented contributors to the society that turned on them, rejected on all sides, these people resemble in those respects the Jews driven from Germany by Hitler before the Holocaust.

The Lebanese are a small number of those who could no longer take the complex communal and inter-Arab warfare that engulfs their people. In large part they are Christian and their departure helps those in Lebanon and Syria who wish to make Lebanon a Muslim country by any means.

The world of the '70s creates political refugees in increasing numbers. But the places for them to go are disappearing. Countries historically hospitable to immigration are shutting their gates. Britain refuses to take even holders of British passports. Canada, New Zealand and Australia are reluctant. The Canadian province of Quebec wants some who will add to its French-speaking majority.

For all the poetry of Emma Lazarus on the Statue of Liberty, the United States is not going to be big enough in land or heart to take in all the people who want to come and who cannot safely stay any longer where they have always lived. But by setting an example of decency it can better influence other countries to do the same.

The News and Courier
CHARLESTON EVENING POST
Charleston, S. C., May 3, 1980

'Keep ancient lands, your storied pomp!' cries she
With silent lips. 'Give me your tired, your poor,
Your huddled masses yearning to breathe free,
The wretched refuse of your teeming shore.
Send these, the homeless, tempest-tost to me,
I lift my lamp beside the golden door!'

Throughout most, but not all of American history, the above words by Emma Lazarus, which are engraved in the pedestal of the Statue of Liberty, have stated this country's immigration policy. The "golden door" has opened wide to admit a flood tide of refugees from war, political tyranny and economic hardship. America has been the better for it; immigrants have tilled the waiting land, built the great factories and manned them, made this the strongest economic and military power on earth.

The American "melting pot," while it ensured a common language and culture, preserved the ethnic diversity that is at once America's treasure and, in an era of civil "rights" run wild, its cross.

Today the melting pot no longer works very well. The public school system in many parts of the country is becoming bilingual at best and non-English at worst. Abandoning the requirement for immigrant children (and in some cases the children of American ghettos) to read and write English is a well-intentioned cruelty, the effects of which we will suffer as a nation in ways as yet dimly understood.

Large cities and parts of states are undergoing immense demographic and cultural change. Miami is virtually a Cuban city. Spanish Harlem rivals Black Harlem in size and social isolation. The southwestern tier — Texas, New Mexico, Arizona and Southern California — have huge and growing immigrant populations that show every evidence of *assimilating rather than being assimilated*.

An estimated 234,000 immigrants will settle here legally this year. No one knows how many hundreds of thousands more will enter illegally as Castro empties his jails and struggling countries around the world export their poverty, their political dissidents, their insolvable social problems to the United States.

As new waves of immigrants storm ashore in Florida and elsewhere into a land no longer vacant, America is changing in ways hardly dreamed of by those who, generations past, swung wide the golden door to welcome the Old World to the New.

A new reasoned policy on immigration cries for attention and ranks high on our list of urgent national priorities. If we don't reach and implement a decision shortly, the influx of poor and starving will make the decision for us. Then, in the not distant future, America will replace India as the world's largest and most ill-fed democracy

The Houston Post
Houston, Texas, April 26, 1980

In open boats, hungry and penniless, more than 900 Haitians landed in Florida in one recent week, not so much fleeing oppression as seeking a better life. West Germany received 50,000 people from the Third World last year, expects some 100,000 this year. Since Portugal gave up its colonial possessions, it has taken in over 2 million European, African and Asian refugees from Cape Verde, Mozambique, Angola, Goa and Timor. More than 17,000 Timoreans are waiting for passage to Portugal.

Historically the United States has accepted immigrants who came hoping for opportunity. We thought of them as seeking freedom, but we understood that they were seeking freedom from want as well as freedom from oppression. "Give me your tired, your poor . . ." But the world is filling up. The spare room, the open space, the unused land — all are shrinking. Every industrialized country has more people coming in than it can comfortably handle.

The United States will accept 3,500 of the Cubans who fled their country through Havana's Peruvian Embassy. They would face persecution if they stayed in Cuba. It was moving to see the almost painful gratitude they showed when they felt themselves free at last. The State Department recognizes their right to asylum. But what of the Haitians? They came because of inescapable poverty at home. The State Department considers them migrants hunting economic opportunity. But by leaving their country, they protested the regime in power. Forced to go back, they, too, can expect punishment for their protest.

When the West Germans wrote their constitution 30 years ago, they remembered the thousands that Hitler had forced upon the world as refugees. In return, they felt Germany should become a haven for the politically oppressed, and wrote a guarantee of asylum into the constitution. Nobody could foresee that West Germany's economic boom would act as a magnet on the poor of other countries.

By the thousands they spend all their savings to get to West Germany, arriving destitute. Those who would face reprisals for political views if they went home are given a work permit, welfare payments and an unlimited stay. But what of the others? They come from Turkey, 35 percent; Pakistan and India, 15 percent; Eritrea, Zaire and other impoverished countries. Any who say they only came to hunt work are promptly sent home. Those who know enough to ask for political asylum get a provisional certificate to live for two months, plus money for food and lodging. They may stay more than six years in West Germany, simply by fighting deportation through the courts. West Germany has survived the tide so far. But if the numbers continue to double annually, as they have been doing, the life raft may sink under the burden.

All over the world prosperous nations face this new problem — a philosophical question. Where do you draw the line that lets some stay, sends some home to poverty, disease, early death? Where do you draw it, and *how?*

The Charlotte Observer
Charlotte, N. C., June 9, 1980

They came in waves, 100,000 immigrants. As they poured in, the nation was jolted by a depression and then by fear of those "inferior" peoples. Thus, in 1882, two years before France presented the Statue of Liberty, the United States passed its first racist immigration law, the Chinese Exclusion Act.

Nearly 100 years later, 100,000 impatient Cubans are packed into refugee camps around the nation. The American economy is sliding into a major recession. And some Americans are caught up in old, familiar fears.

Severe problems plague the current effort to process and resettle the enormous number of Cuban refugees who flowed into this country in a matter of weeks, apparently before government agencies got organized to handle them efficiently. The processing delays and the riots and attempted breakouts at places such as Fort Chaffee, Ark., are disturbing.

But some Americans have a deeper concern: They fear large numbers of Cuban immigrants will somehow change or subvert this nation.

Such fears are not new. They are part of America's history, as much a part as the undeniable contributions made by previous immigrants.

Those fears, today as in the past, stem mostly from prejudice about which cultures are "superior." The first census, in 1790, showed a nation of about 3 million — 75 percent of British origin, 8 percent German and the rest Dutch, French or Spanish in origin. In 1882, when the Chinese Exclusion Act passed, 95 percent of America's immigrants had come from northern and western Europe. Their cultures and physical features were similar to the English colonizers. So, although many of the immigrants were poverty-stricken and illiterate, they melted into the nation.

That wasn't true in every case. One batch of British subjects, the Scotch-Irish, ancestors of so many Carolinians, were looked down upon as ill-mannered, poor upstarts who threatened America's "better class." Some of the "better class" unsuccessfully proposed during the 1820s a *21-year* waiting period before immigrants could become citizens.

During the 19th century, Americans worried at different times whether Irish Catholics, Asians, Jews, Italians, Poles and Slavs could ever become "100 percent Americans". Indeed, the debate was raging when Emma Lazarus's poem about "huddled masses yearning to breathe free" was placed on the pedestal of the Statue of Liberty in 1903.

A joint congressional-presidential study commission agreed in 1911 that the United States should restrict immigration to keep out so-called "inferior peoples." The nation lived with a policy of racist "quotas" until 1965, when Congress began amending immigration laws to set equal limits for immigrants from every nation.

Yet many Americans remain fearful of cultures different from their own. They should examine their concerns about Indochinese or Cubans or Haitians, compare them with past predictions about the trouble Italians, Irish Catholics and Polish immigrants would bring. Those fears, as it turns out, were groundless. So, we think, are concerns about most Cubans.

The Des Moines Register

Des Moines, Iowa, November 19, 1980

"Give me your tired, your poor,
Your huddled masses yearning to breathe free,
The wretched refuse of your teeming shore,
Send these, the homeless, tempest-tossed, to me:
I lift my lamp beside the golden door."

This poem, inscribed on the Statue of Liberty, eloquently describes the immigration policy of the United States during the 19th century and first years of the 20th. A new report from the Population Reference Bureau Inc. questions whether this is an appropriate policy for the years ahead.

About 700,000 immigrants and refugees enter the United States legally every year, plus an estimated 100,000 to 500,000 who enter illegally. These immigrants and their children now account for about half of the U.S. population growth, according to the Population Reference Bureau, and are likely to account for more in the future.

Assuming the present number of about 1 million immigrants a year and a continuation of the present U.S. birth rate of 1.8 children per woman, in 50 years the population would be 310 million (it now is 226 million). If there were no immigration for 50 years, the population in the year 2030 would be 245 million. or 65 million less.

The level of immigration clearly will have a major impact on the nation's ability to surmount energy shortages, to export grain, to provide education for its children and to manage a variety of problems.

Whether this country should — or even could — build an impregnable wall around its disproportionate share of the world's bounty is part of the question, too. How many immigrants to plan on admitting is too important a question to ignore.

THE ATLANTA CONSTITUTION

Atlanta, Ga., April 28, 1980

By day and by night they come, by land and by sea, bringing new ways, strange tongues and a sometimes-fearful, sometimes-hopeful sense of what they might expect from a nation that throughout its history has been a haven for the poor, the homeless and the politically alienated.

Some the fugitives of Mexican canefields — come illegally, splashing across the Rio Grande under cover of dark, appearing furtively by day on the streets of Tucson, El Paso and San Antonio. Others — the Vietnamese and the Cuban refugees — come with the full and unwavering consent of the American government.

To refuse admittance even to the illegal aliens seems to some in the higher circles of government an unseemly violation of America's liberal immigration tradition. Perhaps that is why the government has not put up a kind of Berlin Wall along vast stretches of the Rio Grande — why there is no barbed wire and police dogs and slavering guards anxious for a chance to bust the heads of Mexican "wetbacks." Certainly that is why this nation has agreed to accept almost twice as many Cuban refugees as Costa Rica, Spain, Ecuador, Argentina, Canada, Belgium and West Germany all put together.

But even in this most humanitarian of endeavors there is a question of competing values. Can we continue to accept unlimited thousands of immigrants without further jeopardizing the unemployment problems of our own citizens?

This pluralistic nation is already dangerously divided along both racial and class lines, and inevitably there will come a time when the clamor for a more restrictive immigration policy will become irresistable. Should we hasten that time by refusing to set more reasonable quotas or — worse — by refusing to enforce existing laws against illegal entry?

The Salt Lake Tribune

Salt Lake City, Utah, June 12, 1980

Arrival of more than 100,000 Cuban refugees in the past few months is directing increased attention to United States immigration problems. In a period of economic downturn the influx of foreigners is receiving less than whole-hearted welcome.

That might be a short-sighted reaction.

The American population is getting older. As the post World War II baby boom reaches retirement age about 30 years from now it will be like the classroom "explosion" of the 1950s in reverse. The same people who swelled student ranks a few years ago will be expecting Social Security and pension checks a few decades hence. Because of the post-Vietnam war baby "bust" there will be fewer working age Americans to pay the retirement bills.

That is where immigration policy comes in.

Kevin F. McCarthy, a Rand Corporation senior researcher who is studying problems associated with the greying of America, predicts that if the U.S. birthrate remains at the 2.1 replacement level— and he thinks it will—the country will face a potentially-severe labor shortage by the year 2010. That is when the senior citizen population will begin soaring from 34 million to an estimated 55 million by 2030.

William J. Serow, research director of the Tayloe Murphy Institute of Population Studies at the University of Virginia, predicts a labor shortage of 10 percent in the first quarter of the 21st century. In an article in the Du Pont company publication "Context," Mr. Serow predicts "a change in the immigration laws to rebuild the labor supply."

Present immigration policy is tilted in favor of foreigners who have relatives in the United States. This has been evident in the latest Cuban invasion. While the policy can be justified on humanitarian grounds, it is not the best way to lay a good foundation for enriching the labor force, now or in the future.

One way to begin preparing for the labor pinch in the early part of the next century — now only some 20 years away — is to favor those who bring needed skills with them.

Des Moines Tribune

Des Moines, Iowa, June 3, 1980

The Cuban refugees are restless about the slowness of American officials in helping them begin new lives. For many Americans, this is one more bit of evidence that refugees from Cuba and other Third World countries should stay home.

Before that attitude prevails, it would be well to think about refugees as something other than a threat to American jobs or American ideals.

The United States needs a population diverse enough to understand the forces of nationalism, poverty and revolution that are loose in much of the world. Throughout the 18th and 19th centuries, America was a land of opportunity for the oppressed of Europe. Waves of immigrants from troubled societies came to the United States, not always getting along with one another but giving this nation a sensitivity to the problems and hopes of other societies.

In recent decades, the U.S. population has not changed as rapidly as have the politics of Asia, Africa, Latin America and the Middle East. The homogeneous American population has helped this nation avoid some disruptions, but it has put the national dialogue out of touch with perspectives other than those of the now-assimilated children of earlier generations of European immigrants.

It is all too easy to forget that American living standards and may be the envy of some societies that, at the same time, despise the United States.

From the fiasco of the Bay of Pigs to the amazement at what happened in Iran, punctuated in between by the debacle of Vietnam, Americans find that they have stumbled in their policies throughout the world, because the world wasn't what they thought it was — especially the Third World.

In that sense, for its own good, America needs more refugees from the Third World, people who can show Americans that they still live in a world full of revolutionary forces, despair and hope of the kind that earlier generations of Americans understood in their bones.

The melting pot may have done its work of assimilation too well. American democracy needs new ingredients to retain its vitality in a world where most people live differently than most Americans.

Part III: Policy & Legislation

It is much easier to recognize a problem than to solve it. This bit of obvious wisdom is especially true in relation to U.S. immigration policy. Since World War II, there have been only two major pieces of immigration legislation, the 1952 McCarran-Walter Act and the 1965 Immigration and Nationality Act. One could argue with some justification that McCarran-Walter was the only major piece of immigration legislation, because the 1965 act was merely a modification, not a new law. It kept intact McCarran-Walter's immigration ceilings but made them hemispherical instead of national. McCarran-Walter had set the ceiling at 20,000 per country; the 1965 act set a quota of 170,000 for the Eastern Hemisphere and 120,000 for the Western Hemisphere. Both totals were roughly the same. Subsequent bills in 1976 and 1978 adjusted the figures slightly but did not address the central issues of U.S. immigration: how many immigrants should be admitted, from where and by what criteria should they be selected and what steps should be taken to control illegal entry?

These were the questions tackled by the Select Commission on Immigration and Refugee Policy, which was created in 1978 and delivered its final report to the President and Congress in 1981. The 16 members were selected from Congress, the Cabinet, labor, law and the academic community. The commission was organized by a Democratic administration under former President Jimmy Carter, but it presented its conclusions to a very different government under Republican President Ronald Reagan and a newly conservative Congress.

For now, the most controversial issue is illegal aliens, not annual immigration and refugee ceilings. An annual quota by itself is useless when millions of people evade it with ease. In a country that prides itself on having a minimum of personal restrictions, illegal alien control seems impossible without placing controls on legal residents. Creating an effective policy will require careful consideration of long-term effects, not quick answers that have immediate political advantage.

Pleas for Immigration Reform Mount in Number and Urgency

The flood of refugees and illegal aliens in the late 1970s brought home the woeful state of U.S. immigration policy. The last major piece of immigration legislation had been the 1965 Immigration and Nationality Act, which set annual quotas of 120,000 for immigrants from the Western Hemisphere and 170,000 for immigrants from the Eastern Hemisphere. The act eliminated the separate national quotas that had prompted former President Harry S Truman to veto the 1952 Immigration and Nationality Act (the McCarran-Walter Act), although the act was passed over his veto. In the 1965 law, priority was given to immigrants who had relatives in the U.S. or special skills. Refugees were granted conditional entry for two years, with the option of applying for permanent status afterward. They were limited to persons fleeing persecution in communist or Middle Eastern countries or a "natural catastrophic calamity" in the Eastern Hemisphere.

Illegal immigration had been a problem throughout the late 19th and early 20th centuries, but it took on serious proportions in the late 1940s and early 1950s. Then as now, the Immigration and Naturalization Service complained that it did not have enough manpower to control the flow, but little was done about the problem. Then as now, most of the illegals were from Mexico, and their entry was facilitated by the "bracero" program, which allowed several thousand Mexicans to work legally in the U.S. on a temporary basis. In addition, a presidential commission on immigration had concluded that the U.S. faced a growing demand for manpower. All these factors combined to reduce the incentive to check the flow of illegal Mexicans. After the "bracero" program was terminated in 1964 and the immigration reform bill was passed in 1965, the INS began actively to search for illegal aliens.

St. Louis Globe-Democrat

St. Louis, Mo., May 10-11, 1980

In Missouri, where both legitimate refugees and illegal aliens are relatively few and far between, the current immigration problems may seem to be a distant issue.

Haitians fly to Canada, then sneak into the United States. Cuban refugees, fleeing Castro's tyranny, are flooding southern Florida as confusion created by the bungling Carter administration compounds matters. The U.S.-Mexican border is an old festering sore.

The foregoing is true but deceptive. The federal Immigration and Naturalization Service reports 1,000 or more illegal aliens a month are apprehended in Illinois. Most of them come from Mexico; however, only a few ethnic groups are not found in the sizable illegal labor market in the state.

The strain of soaring inflation and rising unemployment is beginning to show on the citizenry around the country. Buffeted by their own economic plight, Americans are complaining that aid to the less fortunate of other lands is not limitless and that charity should begin at home.

Legislation to curb this flood of illegal immigrants is pending in the Illinois General Assembly. It would provide fines against employers who knowingly hire illegal aliens and against suppliers of such workers. Fines up to $10,000 could be levied.

Similar legislation has failed to move ahead in Congress. Refusal to deal realistically with the issue has prevented a solution to the vexing problem. Other countries in need of workers legally bring in documented immigrants to perform various jobs. Such an approach could legally provide laborers for agricultural and other low-paying jobs shunned by Americans.

The belief that all jobs held by the illegals aliens are low paying is not true. Many of those apprehended in Illinois had been receiving $8 to $12 an hour. This fact has made Illinois a fertile field for illegal immigrants seeking employment. An unscrupulous employer still can make a savings by avoiding such payments as Social Security, unemployment benefits and workmen's compensation.

Most immigrants who enter this country through legal channels prove themselves to be good workers. Hispanics and refugees from Southeast Asia illustrate this point. U.S. Rep. Paul Findley, R-Ill., has proposed that Cuban and other political refugees be required to work for any public aid they receive. This workfare principle could help to mute some of the criticism that is likely to intensify if the recession worsens. It would also keep the parties occupied until other work becomes available.

The status quo is intolerable. As matters stand now an illegal worker can either deprive a deserving citizen of a job or be exploited unmercifully by an unscrupulous employer who can hold an alien's illicit status as an effective threat.

A humane approach will be vital in attempting to resolve the issue, but if the problem continues to be ignored, the situation will go from bad to worse.

OKLAHOMA CITY TIMES

Oklahoma City, Okla., June 11, 1980

WHILE the Carter administration struggles with the complexities of the Cuban refugee problem, a question arises as to its effect on the immigration quotas available to other nationalities.

High administration officials contend the new Refugee Act of 1980, signed into law less than three months ago, already has proved inadequate to deal with the kind of crisis brought on by the arrival of 112,000 Cubans. On top of that are an estimated 35,000 Haitians who have come here to escape abject poverty in their homeland.

The new refugee act was designed to replace a number of existing relief programs enacted sporadically over the years to meet international crises. It also redefined "refugee" by eliminating preferences for those fleeing a communist country and certain Middle East countries. The focus now is on whether a person is leaving his country because of race, religion, nationality, membership in a particular social group or political opinion.

The law boosted from 290,000 to 320,000 the total number of refugees and immigrants allowed into the United States each year. An immigrant, of course, is one who leaves his homeland voluntarily. The overall total was to include 50,000 refugees "under normal circumstances."

The flood of refugees from Cuba and Haiti means already the new law's quota has been breached. But the president is allowed under the act to fix a number above the normal 50,000 refugees in consultation with Congress.

With the refugee influx already more than twice that figure, the question is whether the excess will cut into the immigration quotas for other nationalities. Because of the worldwide demand for immigration to the United States, there is a backlog in accepting applications for visas; right now the only ones eligible are those whose petitions were filed in 1979. However, a Norman man says his brother in Hong Kong has been on the waiting list since 1977.

Compassion for the Cuban and Haitian refugees, and the Vietnamese before them, is fine. But it seems unfair and discriminatory to restrict regular quotas for immigrants from other lands who have sponsors and jobs and prospects for becoming constructive citizens.

The Miami Herald

Miami, Fla., August 5, 1980

THERE'S no immediate solution to the problem of excessive and illegal immigration to the United States. But there are numerous short-range steps that can help stem the flood while a long-range program of economic development is implemented throughout the hemisphere. Congress should hurry to enact such measures.

Immigration reformers who advocate a national identification card for all workers, citizen and noncitizen alike, ought to forget that dangerous notion and concentrate their energies on steps that really can work. Americans simply aren't going to stand for such regimentation, nor should they. American democracy cannot be defended by infringing on the rights of citizens.

Tight policing of Social Security numbers, on the other hand, is a worthwhile effort. Washington's computers should be able to spot counterfeit numbers or forged duplicates. And employers can be held responsible for ascertaining the legal status of workers. The truth is that American employers have created the bulk of the illegal immigration by hiring, and often soliciting undocumented aliens.

The Immigration and Naturalization Service (INS) has been in shambles for several years. While its agents in South Florida shamefully harassed poor, black Haitian refugees who openly presented themselves to authorities, tens of thousands of more-sophisticated foreigners simply overstayed visitors' visas that had been issued in good faith by American consulates.

These visa-jumpers are by far the largest single category of undocumented aliens from the Caribbean, but the INS doesn't even have a system for keeping track of them. That dismal fact was demonstrated last year when the Federal Government found itself unable to make good its threat to deport Iranian students. The INS must police visas, and Congress must provide the money and personnel necessary to do the job.

Along with the crisis in *illegal* immigration, Congress must reassess its policies on *legal* applicants. There should be a fixed immigration quota each year, and conflicting claims should be resolved within that overall quota. An individual wealthy enough to call himself an investor shouldn't automatically take precedence over an applicant who has waited many years, or who is closely related to an American resident.

But the notion of familial ties itself needs re-examination. Certainly spouses and dependent children of legal immigrants should have priority. But there must be an end to the widening circle of family ties through which a single legal entrant becomes the gateway for dozens of other nondependent, adult relatives who can and should apply in their own right.

None of these is a complete or satisfying solution. There will be no end to the immigration pressure until economic opportunity throughout the hemisphere is substantially more equal than it is now. But each of these proposals could cut the uncontrolled influx by several percentage points.

That's the best that can be accomplished for the near future, and it should be achieved quickly. The inability to solve the problem completely is no excuse for failure to take the reasonable steps that are immediately possible.

Houston Chronicle

Houston, Texas, May 14, 1980

U.S. immigration policy is in disarray. The doors have been swung wide open to Cubans, with overwhelming numbers pouring into Florida. The Immigration and Naturalization Service could not cope with its problems before the Cuban influx and is in worse shape now.

There are both short- and long-range problems facing the nation on this issue. On the short range, President Carter offered to admit 3,500 of the 10,000 Cubans who had taken refuge in the Peruvian Embasssy in Havana. Many of them had families in this country. The 3,500 has turned into 35,000. And while reuniting families is one thing, receiving shiploads of people reported to be either criminals or mentally ill is something else entirely. One boat skipper who arrived in Key West with 600 refugees aboard described them himself as "the worst element" in Cuba. He said his life was threatened if he didn't take them aboard.

Obviously, what started out as an attempt to extricate family members and friends from communist domination is turning, at least to some extent, into a parade of boats carrying whatever Castro chooses to discard. This country is under no obligation, even with our tradition of being a haven for refugees, to become a penal colony for Fidel Castro. This country can welcome the oppressed without taking in all who would like to crash the gates of liberty.

The U.S. government has an obligation to the rest of its citizens to establish reasonable standards on who is admitted to this country. That is also a tradition, one applied even during the early waves of migration. A complete screening process for the new Cuban arrivals is necessary, and other countries should be called upon to share this burden.

As to the long-range problem, changes are obviously needed in the U.S. immigration laws. The proposals now being considered along that line are lax, as the Cuban influx is proving. A federal study commission is considering a restructuring of the program into three categories. The first category would be those admitted for family reunification purposes, an estimated 350,000 to 400,000 a year. A second category would include refugees, estimated at 50,000 a year but allowing apparently unrestricted additional admissions on an emergency basis. A third category, called "independents," would admit 300,000 or 350,000 not covered by the other two categories. Those totals could mean 800,000 or more immigrants a year, a considerable increase over the 373,000 in 1970.

Is this country certain it can process, with reasonable screening, that many immigrants? What would be the additional cost in the federal budget? Would the welfare burden rise? Are we certain what the economic impact would be? Would competition for jobs create local frictions?

This is a difficult issue, for this nation has prided itself on taking in those seeking a new life. But it is not an issue that can drift along unresolved indefinitely without damaging U.S. citizens.

The Pittsburgh Press

Pittsburgh, Pa., July 10, 1980

Sometime after the November election, when calm can return to political discussion, this country should give priority to repairing its flawed immigration policy. Or, more accurately, its immigration non-policy.

As matters now stand, the United States is acting as a population safety valve for unsavory or unprincipled regimes — some of them Communist and others either inept, like Mexico's, or corrupt, like Haiti's.

The Communist vanquishers of South Vietnam, for example, have trouble absorbing its people, so they force hundreds of thousands to sea in flimsy boats. As a result, Indochinese come here at the rate of 14,000 a month.

After two decades of economic bungling, Fidel Castro cannot provide jobs or food for his subjects. So he proceeds to unload 117,000 Cubans, including some undesirables, on us.

Mexico, despite all of its potential resources in an oil-crisis age, can't create enough jobs for its burgeoning population. So it encourages its citizens to head north across the border by the hundreds of thousands.

Meanwhile, thousands of Haitians are forced to flee their country in destitution and desperation because of the abominable conditions in that country. And most of them struggle and straggle their way here.

All of this adds up.

About 700,000 immigrants will come legally to the United States this year. But the illegals will lift the total to more than a million, which could be a yearly record.

★ ★ ★

To question the wisdom of mass immigration is to run the risk of being branded illiberal. But unrestricted immigration was a 19th Century policy. It made sense when a continent had to be tamed and peopled. It does not make sense in an era of slow economic growth and nagging unemployment.

As the richest country on earth — still — the United States should take in its fair share of refugees from the troubled spots of the world. But no country, not even the United States, can embrace them all.

We have our own problems. And to be fair to our own citizens we must tend to them first.

That's why it is imperative that we do something about our unplanned, out-of-control immigration non-policy.

THE DENVER POST
Denver, Colo., December 9, 1980

A RECENT OFFSHOOT of the environmental movement has brought its campaign to Denver.

The group is called the Federation for American Immigration Reform (its acronym, FAIR, is not being used locally because of the unpopularity of a recent ballot issue by the same name). Its goals are to limit legal immigration and to end illegal immigration. It has found an ally in Colorado Gov. Dick Lamm.

Those goals easily could be interpreted as elitist, or worse, racist. But Roger Conner, the earnest young executive director of the Washington-based organization, insists they are neither. Rather, he says, they should have broad appeal to the moderate liberals, who want to limit the excesses caused by uncontrolled population growth, and the moderate conservatives, who want to create a healthy economic climate.

Lamm, the first prominent politician who has been willing to align himself publicly with such a touchy issue, said at a press conference last week, "The United States cannot continue to accept twice as many immigrants as the rest of the world combined. With 8 percent unemployed already in the United States, we have more than enough of our problems without uncontrolled immigration."

The organization's roots are in the Zero Population Growth movement. FAIR's founder, John Tanton, was ZPG's national president after Dick Lamm was. And the rationale behind the organization's concern is that the benefits of declining U.S. fertility rates are being negatively offset by immigration. With the Age of Shortages upon us, this reasoning goes, the United States no longer may be able to share its diminishing bounty so freely.

A 16-member Select Commission on Immigration and Refugee Policy has been working for more than two years to bring some order out of years of haphazard and reflexive U.S. immigration laws. Its final report is due in March, and FAIR has some suggested recommendations.

The organization wants to cut immigration back to the old limit of 290,000 a year, or 30,000 less than the current "temporary" limit which was designed to accommodate political refugees. The Select Commission, on the other hand, has considered raising the cap to 750,000 a year.

To discourage illegal immigration — which FAIR figures, conservatively, is 750,000 a year — the organization proposes making it unlawful for employers to hire illegals. Current law makes it a crime for illegal aliens to take U.S. jobs, but not for U.S. employers to hire them. And aliens still could be hired when U.S. employers can't find Americans willing or qualified to do the work.

Conner acknowledges that the limit-immigration movement has attracted some less-than-desirable supporters. "There is hardly a pure heart in the house when it comes to immigration policy," he said, and some people support FAIR for reasons the organization doesn't like. But that is true of every reform issue in history, he said, and once the issues are explained fully, the bigots seem to lose their enthusiasm.

We won't impugn FAIR's motives. It has pinpointed some serious problems with immigration, particularly the weakness of a policy that accepts the inevitability of a high number of illegal aliens in the work force. FAIR sensibly supports encouraging other countries — even with U.S. aid — to limit their population growth and improve their economies. That certainly would reduce the pressure to emigrate to the United States.

But that sort of change in the less-developed nations won't come quickly enough to ease the tremendous immigration pressure now facing this country. And we aren't convinced the United States should retreat, as FAIR suggests, to a limit that probably was unrealistically low the day it was established.

Before making it illegal to hire illegal aliens — or, in more current parlance, undocumented workers — those responsible for U.S. immigration policy should take another close look at institutionalizing temporary worker programs. It's true that "guest worker" plans have created problems in Europe, with "guests" frequently becoming committed residents, but perhaps the United States can learn from that experience — as well as from its own experience with the bracero program.

Those of us who got here first are fortunate to live in a nation that is so attractive to the world's poor, oppressed and dissatisfied. But we wouldn't want to live in a nation that sets unnecessarily strict limits on how many new citizens it is willing to admit.

THE PLAIN DEALER
Cleveland, Ohio, July 13, 1980

Since Good Friday, 114,000 Cubans have escaped from Fidel Castro's communist island paradise and made it to the United States. Their mass boatlift choked America's refugee machinery and showed it is inadequate in such an emergency.

The refugees' dream became a nightmare, as Plain Dealer staff writer Richard G. Zimmerman described it in a series of articles.

President Carter offered these newcomers "an open heart and open arms" but they got only "a temporary, twilight legal status," a six-month parole that may end in a trail of lost files and unreturned phone calls in bureaucracy's jungle.

The United States needs a definite, enforceable immigration policy. It needs to control the influx of aliens. It should offer asylum and not expel refugees to where their lives and freedom are endangered, but it must put limits on admissions.

While the 114,000 Cubans were flooding in, 35,000 Haitians also arrived illegally. Three million illegals a year try to sneak into the United States and two-thirds of them succeed, the Immigration and Naturalization Service (INS) estimates.

Aliens add to the burden on U.S. resources, on social services, schools, health and the like. Those costs and population trends and manpower needs must be taken into account when figuring which and how many aliens to accept.

Waves of aliens are overpowering the INS, which cannot keep track of its legal-status aliens, much less the border-hopping illegals.

One solution is to increase INS manpower. The INS has a budget of $336.5 million. It would need more money and more staff and power to prosecute employers of no-status aliens and to carry through deportation proceedings.

Another proposal is simply to document each entering alien at the border, giving him or her a Social Security card and granting most U.S. citizen benefits. Hong Kong has a similar system. It gives Hong Kong cheap labor which keeps its products competitive in the world market.

But right now is a poor time to allow a flood of aliens into the United States, with unemployment at 7.7%. Most illegal aliens here work at jobs at which U.S. citizens turn up their noses. But in hard times they are unwanted intruders.

Some system of identity cards, renewable at intervals variable according to the economy and population curves, should be started. From there the federal authorities should be able to work flexibly, screening out undesirables, letting in the most useful and those with genuine family ties to residents here, doing a selective job case by case so far as it is possible.

America should continue to shield refugees from the persecution they fear. It should be a haven for the oppressed. But it has to guard first the well-being of all who live here: their jobs, their taxes, their services, their social fabric and way of life.

That means America should use its absolute sovereign right to determine who shall be admitted to its territory. It should be governed by what is best for this nation.

The Providence Journal

Providence, R. I., September 19, 1980

Under the impetus of the Cuban and Haitian flotillas, the boat people of Vietnam and Cambodia, the flood of immigrants from Mexico and in general America's position as the world's principal haven for refugees from other lands, the issue of what to do about U.S. immigration policy and laws is swiftly coming to a head.

Public dissatisfaction is growing. Rioting in the Cuban refugee camps is only one cause. More important is the public's perception of the economic impact of nearly a million legal and illegal aliens each year. "Immigration and refugee issues," writes Michael S. Teitelbaum, program officer at the Ford Foundation, in the current issue of *Foreign Affairs* magazine, "may prove to be among the most important and troubling world problems of the next decade."

Early next year the Select Commission on Immigration and Refugee Policy is scheduled to report its findings and recommendations. This week the U.S. Commission on Civil Rights called for sweeping reforms, including the adoption of a single worldwide limit of 270,000 immigrants a year on a first come, first served basis. And as Matt W. Garcia prepares to take over as commissioner of the demoralized, understaffed and underfunded Immigration and Naturalization Service, there is mounting pressure for employee identity cards and legal penalties for employers who hire illegal aliens.

The answers are not likely to come easily. Sentiment ranges widely from those who would like this country to adopt a closed-door policy in sharp contrast to historical precedent and those who favor virtually unlimited entry. Clearly, responsible public policy should lie somewhere between. As Mr. Teitelbaum points out in his article, the United States has progressed steadily from discriminatory immigration policies of the late 1800's and early 1900's to the present system of allocating a maximum of 20,000 visas per year to every country. To break that progression could have unwelcome international consequences.

In this controversy several points stand out:

● The United States cannot continue to admit the 700,000 to 800,000 legal aliens expected to enter this year. That number, according to Mr. Teitelbaum, is "at or near the highest levels ever experienced in American history."

● The federal effort to stem the tide of illegal aliens must be strengthened. On an average day, only 350 INS patrolmen are assigned to monitor the 2,000-mile U.S.-Mexican border. That is the equivalent,

Mr. Teitelbaum notes, of the forces assigned to guard the U.S. Capitol and office buildings located on only 103 acres.

● Because jobs are the principal attraction for most illegal aliens and the lure of less costly labor willing to accept lower level work is an inducement for industry to hire them, something must be done to break this linkage if enforcement of immigration laws is to become a realistic goal.

● Some means must be adopted to identify those aliens who are in this country legally and those who are not.

● Amnesty for illegal aliens, at least those who have lived here a number of years, ought to be considered seriously.

● And finally a point Mr. Teitelbaum emphasizes in his *Foreign Affairs* article, "In the long term, it will be important to ensure that no single national, ethnic, religious, racial or linguistic group comes permanently to dominate American immigration — in short, we shall have to find fair-minded ways to assure the true diversity among immigrants to the United States that has been the intention, if not the effect, of much of the legal reform realized over the past two decades."

That tall order faces whomever is elected president for the next four years and a Congress that has an obligation to exercise supreme statemanship in an area that goes to the heart of the American philosophy.

The Times-Picayune
The States-Item

New Orleans, La., September 17, 1980

The nation's immigration laws and policies clearly are in need of reform to bring them in line with modern realities, the most salient of which is that the United States no longer can afford to be as receptive as it once was to virtually anyone wanting to join us in enjoying and building the American way of life. The confusion and ambiguities associated with the Carter administration's policies toward Cuban and Haitian refugees, and the controversies and social tensions created by the refugees in this country, have lent new urgency to the subject.

A look at one of the major problems demonstrates that practical remedies will not be easy. The problem is how to fix equitable immigration quotas while allowing for emergency situations such as this summer's exodus of Cubans and Haitians.

Under existing statutes, the State Department can issue 20,000 visas per country each year, more than enough to take care of immigrants from such stable countries as Britain and Sweden, but far too few to cover would-be immigrants from such nations as Mexico and the Philippines. The quota was obviously disregarded in efforts to accommodate the more than 100,000 Cuban refugees who flocked to the United States this summer.

At the same time, the administration has been considerably less friendly toward Haitians, where the distinction between political oppression, traditionally a reason for accepting immigrants, and economic hardship, which does not except prospective immigrants from the normal requirements for entrance, is somewhat blurred. In both cases, the refugees have not entered through normal immigration channels, but simply showed up like hungry uninvited relatives to be dealt with as discreetly as possible.

For obvious political and propaganda purposes, the Carter administration has been disposed to favor the Cubans while attempting to discourage the Haitians. The conspicuous discrimination has raised the question of proper criteria for emergency immigration. That is one more sticky dilemma to be considered in any proposed reforms.

The U.S. Civil Rights Commission now recommends a total limit of 270,000 immigrants annually, worldwide, first-come, first-served. While this would offer absolutely equitable access, it ignores valid criteria for selection such as uniting families and favoring those with professional qualifications useful to the nation. Another valid criterion for selection, which is vulnerable to attack as racial or ethnic discrimination, is population balance. Conceivably only Latins and Asians might be admitted over an extended period, which might have a significant impact on U.S. demographics without any preparatory study and decision on the consequences.

The other half of the immigration problem is how to deal with the immigrants and/or refugees after they have arrived. The recent influx of Cubans and Vietnamese has created tensions over jobs, as has the steady flow of illegal immigrants, principally from Mexico. Recent proposals in Congress would make national identity cards compulsory and apply sanctions against U.S. employers who hire illegal aliens. Although the Civil Rights Commission opposes these measures, they are worth further discussion. Ideally, agreements should be reached between the United States and foreign governments to limit the influx of illegal immigrants; but accords, most conspicuously in the case of Mexico, have been hard to achieve, since emigration provides troubled countries a useful safety valve.

Few U.S. government policies and practices are as tangled as those involving immigrants. It is a problem that the Executive Branch and Congress should tackle jointly and comprehensively without further delay.

THE CHRISTIAN SCIENCE MONITOR

Boston, Mass., September 17, 1980

One of the thorniest problems Congress and the White House will face when they eventually get around to overhauling the nation's outdated immigration laws and policies will be how to eliminate discrimination from the statutes themselves and from the federal government's enforcement of them. If there were any lingering doubts in Washington as to the unfairness of current immigration practices, they should have been dispelled by the findings of a just released two-year study by the US Civil Rights Commission.

Among other things, the commission found that the 30-year-old Immigration and Nationality Act still contains numerous discriminatory provisions that "result in the denial of rights to American citizens" as well as to documented and undocumented aliens. For instance, the commission faulted federal agents and local police departments for conducting unconstitutional "searches and seizures" in their neighborhood sweeps for illegal aliens. In another area, it found that some would-be immigrants to the US wait up to ten years to gain entry while applicants from other countries, supposedly no more eligible to be admitted, get immediate attention.

The Civil Rights Commission has focused on only one small, albeit important, aspect of the much broader immigration issue that must be faced up to by Americans. Justifiably proud of its oft-proclaimed label as a "nation of immigrants," the US now is being forced to come to grips with the uncomfortable question of how to cope with the social, economic, and population strains of providing a home for an ever larger number of legal and illegal immigrants. A separate group — the President's Select Commission on Immigration Policy — is currently studying the overall problem. Among some of the key recommendations expected to be put forward by the select commission in its report to Congress next year: a bigger, better-trained Immigration and Naturalization Service (INS), stiffer laws against smuggling aliens into the US, and a worldwide quota of fewer than 1 million immigrants to the US (about the number of legal and illegal aliens believed to be entering the country this year.)

Along this line the Civil Rights Commission urges that the current limits on the number of immigrants from each country be eliminated and that they be admitted on a first-come, first-served basis in accordance with the six preference categories already in use (i.e., with priority given to relatives of US residents, professionals, scientists, etc.). However, the civil rights report has words of caution about some of the presidential commission's widely discussed proposals, such as the issuance of national identification cards which the civil rights group warns "could be used to violate the right to privacy of the individual." Three of the five members of the commission also cautioned against the use of compulsory work permits or enactment of a law to penalize employers who hire illegal aliens.

The split among the commission members on such controversial issues is no doubt indicative of the difficulties Congress and the President will encounter later on in trying to hammer out an equitable and effective immigration policy. In their zeal to defuse the potentially explosive immigration problem, the lawmakers ought not to lose sight of the importance of ensuring that the individual rights of every person within the US borders are respected and protected.

Los Angeles Times

Los Angeles, Calif., July 29, 1980

Sometimes it helps to hear the obvious stated, especially when "the obvious" is plainer to one segment of the community than to another

Such is the case with a report released last week by the California Advisory Committee to the U.S. Commission on Civil Rights. The advisory committee concluded, after 18 months of study, that efforts to enforce immigration laws in California are applied unequally, with persons of Latin American extraction bearing the brunt of them. The worst effect of this, from a civil-rights perspective, is to adversely affect the rights of U.S. citizens and legal resident aliens who are sometimes caught up in drives to track down illegal immigrants.

The committee report says flatly that "the federal government's enforcement effort is not applied equally to every racial and ethnic group. Despite evidence that many undocumented aliens from countries other than Mexico live in the United States . . . enforcement efforts focus on Mexican nationals." The report goes on to say that, although immigration-law proceedings are civil in nature, the practices and policies followed by the U.S. Immigration and Naturalization Service "often had the effect of treating persons as harshly as criminals or worse."

Latino civil-rights groups have been saying this for generations—as far back as the 1930s, when U.S. citizens of Mexican descent were deported during a campaign by Los Angeles County welfare officials to get noncitizens off Depression-era relief rolls. Latino complaints about the enforcement of immigration laws have grown louder recently, as national concern about the flow of refugees and immigrant workers into this country has increased.

The California Advisory Committee's report is one part of a larger study by the U.S. Commission on Civil Rights into the immigration controversy, so it is not the last report that will be issued on this complex and troubling issue.

But the California report can serve as a useful reminder that, while the pros and cons of mass migrations and their social and economic effects are often discussed in coldly academic terms, there is also a human element to the equation. The advisory committee's 61-page report is filled with anecdotes that emerged during the panel's hearings into Immigration Service practices. Many witnesses came forward to allege harsh or improper treatment of both citizens and noncitizens by immigration officers and other employees of the service. But this testimony is balanced by the protestations of several immigration officials who repeatedly assured the committee that employees of the service are trained not to violate or diminish the rights of people who come into contact with their agency.

Reading the report is not unlike watching a long rally at a tennis match, with players hitting charges back and forth like tennis balls.

The many reports prepared by Times reporters on this issue have convinced us that there is merit on both sides of the argument between immigration officials and Latino advocates. There have been unnecessary violations of individual rights by immigration officers. A handful have even been convicted in courts of law for improper activities. But there are also many good immigration officers who are trying their best to honestly and competently do an impossible job—impossible given the disarray of the country's immigration laws and the reality of life along the U.S.-Mexico border.

The California Advisory Committee reached several other notable conclusions in its report, among them:

—That, because there are inadequate data about illegal immigration, many government policies to deal with it are based on speculation and myths.

—That local police have been given inadequate guidelines by the federal government and California's attorney general as to their authority to enforce immigration laws.

—That the Immigration Service has placed too much emphasis on its law-enforcement activities, to the detriment of its other major responsibility—helping to legalize the status of immigrants who are eligible to remain in this country.

Again, many of these conclusions have been reached before, by other study groups and by experts on immigration. But this should not diminish their importance. The study conducted by the California Advisory Committee deserves the consideration of the Select Commission on Immigration and Refugee Policy. Of all the government bodies now studying the immigration issue, it is the most important, for it has been charged by Congress to recommend specific reforms in the country's immigration laws, and to suggest policies for dealing with the migration of people to this country from outside its borders.

Reforming the INS, The First Step

The U.S. Immigration Bureau was created in 1891 and for the first time brought responsibility for immigration under the sole control of the federal government. Prior to that date, the states had primary responsibility for immigration, subject to federal guidelines for eligibility. In 1906, another bureau was created to be in charge of naturalization, the process by which immigrants become legal American citizens. The two bureaus were consolidated as the Immigration and Naturalization Service in 1933, and transferred from the control of the Department of Labor to the Department of Justice in 1940. The INS examines applications for immigration, determines whether a resident alien may become a citizen or whether he must be deported and keeps track (theoretically) of all aliens in the U.S.

In recent times, criticism of the INS has centered on its inefficiency and duplication of responsibility. For example, the INS is required to inspect travel documents at U.S. ports of entry, while the Treasury Department is in charge of customs inspection. Beside inefficiency, the INS has been charged with corruption, but a 1972 Justice Department investigation of INS activities in the Southwest resulted in 1975 in only a few indictments and much ill-feeling between the agency and its boss. Congressional studies of the INS have blamed the agency for faulty record-keeping, waste, poor service, low employee morale and ineffectuality in controlling illegal immigration. In 1979, INS head Leonel J. Castillo resigned, acknowledging that he was "still disappointed in the lack of change in national immigration policy, which has serious and glaring deficiencies." The first Mexican-American to hold the post, Castillo had called for amnesty for illegal aliens and had attempted to computerize the agency's records.

THE MILWAUKEE JOURNAL
Milwaukee, Wisc., September 15, 1979

Leonel Castillo, the first person of Latin extraction ever to head the US Immigration and Naturalization Service, is leaving after two years on the job. We don't blame him. For a person of Latin background with political ambitions, he was in a no-win situation.

Castillo alienated portions of his own Latin constituency by refusing to advocate an open border with Mexico — the major source of the millions of illegal immigrants who enter the US annually. Instead, Castillo tried humanely to enforce the border laws, thereby angering segments of the Immigration and Naturalization bureaucracy that saw him as not tough enough with undocumented aliens. Castillo was being eaten alive.

In many ways, Castillo was the victim of US ambivalence toward immigrants. The nation cannot forget its immigrant roots, yet it also has unfortunate nativist tendencies that today seek to keep the "foreigner" out. That ambivalence is typified by a Carter administration that proposes to legitimize many of the illegal immigrants now residing in the US and by a Congress that has said neither "yes" nor "no"; it has just stalled.

Castillo looked at the present wave of Latin immigrants in historical terms. The Latin today is an outsider who must cope with a new language, customs and job requirements to assimilate — just as all other immigrant groups did in the past.

We agree with Castillo that immigration has been a national strength in the past and remains so today. The Mexican immigrant, performing work that most Americans shun, is much more of a boon than a burden. These immigrants are not a drain on the economy. And though many of the new wave of Latin immigrants may enter the US illegally, they are hardly criminals. They mainly are industrious people seeking US employment and support for their families because it is denied them by economic conditions in their own countries.

These people deserve to be treated as the human beings they are. They need legal protections to spare them the exploitation that now occurs. They need a regularized way of entering the US temporarily so that necessary protection can be granted them and the flow of people can be better controlled.

So far, America has fallen sadly short of meeting those needs. Castillo is leaving with a sense of frustration. He has good reason to feel that way.

DESERET NEWS
Salt Lake City, Utah, June 9, 1979

With illegal aliens filtering through the immigration barriers erected by the United States in a steady stream, the nation's select Commission on Immigration and Refugee Policy held its first meeting this month.

The 16-member commission, chaired by former Gov. Reubin O. Askew of Florida, was created last year by Congress to review the immigration laws.

Just how many illegal aliens are living and working in this country is a matter of conjecture. Estimates range from two million to as high as 12 million. Approximately 400,000 legal immigrants come to the United States each year.

Studies show that both legal and illegal aliens fare well here, compared with native sons of similar education, age and place of residence. The children of immigrant aliens attain higher earnings than those of comparable native-born offspring.

Such studies have led University of Illinois economics professor Barry R. Chiswick to the conclusion that the country has benefitted whenever it has liberalized its immigration policies.

On the other side of the coin are labor groups who see the influx of immigrants as a depressant on wages and working conditions. Similarly, zero population growth forces that consider immigration a major factor in population growth in this country want to hold the number of persons coming to live here at the same level as our out-migration. Emigration from the United States is minimal.

Traditionally, the nation's immigration restrictions have been weighted in favor of the nations of northern Europe. Even the 1965 legislation which abolished national quotas maintained the balance in favor of northern Europe, which has provided the majority of the immigrants to the United States since the beginning.

The United States has amply demonstrated its ability to absorb all national and racial groups as long as they come at a moderate rate. The moderate rate of immigrant flow must be maintained, but standards of admittance should be based on criteria other than race, color or place of birt

The Providence Journal

Providence, R. I., November 5, 1980

Horror stories about the problems in the Immigration and Naturalization Service have become commonplace in the past year, as the influx of refugees has swamped the agency.

But a new report from the House Committee on Government Operations provides fresh examples showing why the troubled agency needs reform and assistance now.

Investigators found mail goes unattended for weeks because of staff shortages and a flood of applications. Four milk crates full of unopened mail were found in the INS district office in Washington, D.C.

Records are in disarray, so the aliens who show up for required interviews are told their records cannot be found. They must return a second and third time and wait in crowded waiting rooms with dozens of others who have not been able to get action by telephone or mail or in person.

The House committee concluded the confusion is causing unnecessary hardship on immigrants who would make good citizens. And it often has stymied efforts to expel troublemakers. According to *U.S. News & World Report,* when the Carter administration sought to crack down on Iranian student demonstrators, the beleaguered INS had to call college campuses to find out how many there are.

The INS was not a major issue in the recent campaign, but should have been. It's time to streamline our procedures for admitting foreigners to our country as well as procedures for asking them to leave.

Roanoke Times & World-News

Roanoke, Va., April 22, 1979

Illegal aliens are one of America's least tractable problems. There are millions (estimates range from 2 to 12) in the United States. They compete for jobs — often, high-paying jobs — with citizens and legal aliens. They require services that they may not pay taxes for. They are pursued and some of them periodically rounded up at considerable expense.

They even constitute a foreign-relations problem, since most of them come from Mexico. But whatever their origin, in trying to deal with illegal aliens the United States often comes off looking like a selfish bully. For now, it is a no-win situation.

Since his assignment to House Judiciary's subcommittee on Immigration, Refugees and International Law, Sixth District Rep. M. Caldwell Butler has been educating himself and his constituents on this issue. In a recent weekly report, he said that the subcommittee had reviewed the proposed 1980 budget for the Immigration and Naturalization Service (INS) as well as the agency's operations. Both were disturbing.

INS, said Congressman Butler, is poorly organized and inefficient. It can barely keep up with its daily responsibilities, which include dealing with legal and illegal aliens. Record-keeping is antiquated. INS' Border Patrol can stop only one of every two or three people who try to enter the United States illicitly

The 1979-80 budget priorities would, if anything, make matters worse. The number of authorized INS positions would be cut 5 percent, including 624 positions from policing along the U.S.-Mexican border. Places would be added in record-keeping and processing, but no funds are asked for additional automating of INS' primitive methods. Mr. Butler concludes:

"The problems faced by the INS are staggering. Our oversight hearings indicate the need for a major update of the internal organization and procedures of the INS itself before we can think seriously about a policy to solve our illegal alien problem."

The INS is a once-obscure agency thrust into prominence by changing social and economic conditions. It is not equipped to cope with its new role, and Mr. Butler is correct in that it is time for overhaul. It's not strange that the government can't yet make up its mind what to do about illegal aliens, but that shouldn't preclude efforts meanwhile to redeem INS, which has long been treated like an alien within the Justice Department.

The Honolulu Advertiser

Honolulu, Ha., August 27, 1979

"We have greeted each immigrant group by expressing our worst feelings, and yet we have always managed to get past our worst feelings and have ended up with a new group that has contributed a great deal to the country."

Those are the words of Leonel J. Castillo, outgoing commissioner of the U.S. Immigration and Naturalization Service. In a recent interview with the Los Angeles Times, the controversial commissioner talked about some of the myths of immigration, and many of his comments have particular relevance to Hawaii.

THE BIGGEST fear many Americans have is that immigrant groups take jobs away from others.

Not so, says Castillo: "I'm very well convinced that overall, immigrants contribute to the economic well-being of the country and that they create jobs in effect because they add to productivity"

In the southwest, the problem of illegal aliens is particularly difficult. But even they do not burden our economic system, Castillo contends. Few illegal aliens go on welfare for fear of being caught and deported, and they would not enter the country in the first place if there were not jobs available.

Most of the jobs are menial positions Americans do not take.

PROBLEMS OFTEN stem from our immigration policies. Restrictive quotas are established, but employers can offer more jobs (often at low wages) and the result is "to have a half-open door and a half-open wallet."

"I would rather have people come to this country in broad daylight, walking straight across the border with their rights fully protected — at home and here — and then returning to their country with some money in their pockets and with a way to help their own country and not have to sneak in at night and put themselves in the trunks of cars and backs of pickups and go through all the degrading stuff that they have to go through."

Castillo summarizes the dilemma by noting that for generations, the popularly accepted belief that the United States was a haven for the world's dispossessed attracted many talented people to the country. But now the country is preaching a different tune. He says:

"We have opened the gates in such a way that we legally let in the people who are the exact opposite of what is said on the Statue of Liberty We let in the rich, we let in the oppressors in some cases, if they have money. Our foreign policy as expressed through immigration is to receive foreign aid from the poor countries, except in the dramatic occasional cases of refugees from Communist countries."

FOR A STATE which draws its strength from the diversity of its many ethnic groups — all of which, with the exception of native Hawaiians, are immigrants — we should be particularly sensitive to the problem.

Yet we have our own difficulties between established groups and more recent immigrants. It is the old story with some different faces.

There are no easy answers, especially since our island environment makes it difficult to physically absorb more and more people. But we should not forget that most of our families started out in this country as immigrants. By saying, "We've made it, let's close the doors," we forget that heritage.

The San Diego Union

San Diego, Calif., April 6, 1979

For many years the U.S. commissioner of immigration was a relatively low-profile official in Washington. Not so for Leonel J. Castillo, who took the post two years ago at a moment of rising concern about the complex of immigration and labor problems summed up as the "illegal alien" issue.

Mr. Castillo visits San Diego today to speak at an "Hour in the Barrio" luncheon, a monthly event dedicated to building bridges between the Anglo and Hispanic communities here. He and his office have become a bridge on which conflicting views on the alien problem often collide.

On the one hand, Mr. Castillo is charged with enforcing U.S. immigration laws which are being violated wholesale in the flow of undocumented workers north from Mexico. On the other hand, that enforcement effort must respect the human rights of alien workers and be attuned to the sensitivities of Spanish-speaking U.S. citizens who see their own interests at stake.

Mr. Castillo cannot rewrite our immigration laws, and it now appears Congress will make no effort to pass new legislation affecting the alien problem at least until 1981. This leaves the Justice Department and the Immigration and Naturalization Service to cope with the problem with the tools at hand.

Mr. Castillo has an arduous task, and speaks as a representative of an agency responsible for enforcing federal laws and as a member of the ethnic group which has a keen interest in the direction that enforcement takes. That is a fortunate combination, and should lend weight to his words at today's "Hour in the Barrio."

The Miami Herald

Miami, Fla., January 12, 1981

ONCE, the Immigration and Naturalization Service (INS) was a proud representative of American efficiency. Would-be U.S. citizens scrupulously obeyed the letter of the rules and laws that would determine their acceptance or rejection. Resident aliens meticulously complied with the Post Office signs that warned, "Aliens must register."

Not any longer. A noble and essential Federal agency has been humiliated beyond reason and reduced to shambles. The INS office in Miami today looks more like the county welfare offices of old, with hundreds of supplicants standing in line for hours and often leaving empty-handed in spite of the wait.

Most Americans got their first inkling of the current sham that is the INS in late 1979, when President Carter announced his intention to deport any Iranian students whose papers were not in perfect order. The agency, it turned out, was simply incapable of carrying out that threat. It couldn't even document the total number of Iranian students who were living in the United States, much less identify those who were in violation.

Last January, it is estimated, as many as half of the foreign nationals living in Florida may have ignored the requirement that they register their address and status with INS. This year, the post cards on which aliens are required by law to register haven't even arrived in the state yet from Washington. Obviously they will not be completed and returned as Congress intended. What will be posted is another dismal failure by the INS to measure up to the awesome responsibility with which it is charged.

In the national zeal to reform the Federal bureaucracy this year there should be no higher priority than to restore the immigration service to its rightful position of respect. Congress should review the agency's responsibilities, redefine them if necessary, and then appropriate whatever money is necessary to do the job right.

The manpower cuts that President Carter's budget proposal are expected to contain this week should be rejected. The INS needs much more staff, not less. It also needs a strong, permanent boss instead of an acting commissioner who lacks the mandate for serious change.

When Congress or the President undertakes to make policy regarding immigration and refugees, it is the INS upon which they must rely for the raw information on which to base their decisions. Now, and for several years past, those data have been inadequate to the point of being meaningless. Little wonder that policymakers have been unable to frame coherent guidelines.

Any nation, but especially a nation of immigrants, must have an immigration service upon which it can depend and of which its people can be justifiably proud. Restoring the stature of the INS is a critical priority for 1981.

Miami, Fla., March 29, 1981

SOME Senate Democrats, including Florida's Lawton Chiles, this week presented a comprehensive package of reforms for the nation's chaotic immigration policy. The proposals should be reviewed and in large measure adopted promptly.

The most important element of the plan is a dramatic increase in the agents and equipment of the Immigration and Naturalization Service (INS). That proposal could trigger a confrontation with the Reagan Administration.

The senators want the number of border agents raised to about 6,000. Now the number of agents on duty along the 2,000-mile Mexican border at any time averages 350 — less than the number of police officers guarding the U.S. Capitol and its surrounding office buildings and less than the number of transit police in New York City. The Reagan budget cuts would gut the minuscule team of investigators and inspectors even further. Senator Chiles and his colleagues rightly seek to cap the number of legal immigrants at 350,000 per year. The current chaos, which operates more like an entitlement program than a quota system, is estimated to have admitted 1.4 million legal immigrants in the past two years.

Penalties for employers who knowingly hire undocumented aliens are critical. Jobs are the magnet for most immigration, legal and illegal. Employers who exploit the lure of comparative U.S. prosperity should be punished.

That punishment must be preceded by a practical and efficient method for employers to distinguish between undocumented aliens and American citizens or legal residents. The integrity of the Social Security card should be improved dramatically by making it harder to get and more difficult to counterfeit. Computers should routinely verify the validity of numbers presented by new employes. Those measures should be tried before the Draconian step of a universal identification card is considered.

No reform can succeed without an effective INS to administer and enforce it. Yet that critical agency, neglected by two Presidents, has lacked even a permanent commissioner since Leonel Castillo resigned in September 1979.

Several names have surfaced recently as potential commissioners. Those names have been conspicuous for their political connections and their Hispanic origin. They lack identification with the needed combination of management experience, unquestioned integrity, and determination to enforce the laws that Congress adopts. The President should look again — for a tough, fair administrator who can lead the INS back to its once-proud role in maintaining the U.S. reputation for rule by law, not men.

Senator Chiles and his group have addressed the immigration dilemma squarely. Now it's up to their Republican colleagues in Congress and in the Administration.

The Dallas Morning News

Dallas, Texas, February 7, 1981

Sen. Lloyd Bentsen is calling on the new Reagan administration to overhaul the floundering Immigration and Naturalization Service, which has been overwhelmed by the task of keeping up with the new waves of foreigners in our country.

In a letter to Atty. Gen. William French Smith, Bentsen has singled out the poor INS record in deporting Iranians who are in the United States illegally. According to Bentsen, some 6,500 Iranians have remained here despite expired visas or other valid reasons to deport them. Reason: The beleaguered INS simply can't keep track of them.

What the INS needs is strong leadership, better organization, more personnel and more sophisticated record-keeping systems. A House Committee on Government Operations recently reported that the INS has been so overburdened by the numbers of immigrants seeking admission to this country — including "boat people" from Southeast Asia, Cuba and Haiti — that mail often went unattended for weeks because of staff shortages. Crates full of unopened mail were found in the district INS offices in Washington, D.C.

Bentsen is right. The current situation is intolerable and should not be permitted to continue. We must streamline the procedures for admitting foreigners to our country and tighten supervision of those who are here illegally. The INS has been crippled by neglect for too long.

THE SACRAMENTO BEE

Sacramento, Calif., March 19, 1981

Attorney General William French Smith astonished the House Judiciary Committee the other day when he revealed his budget reductions for the Justice Department. The hapless Immigration and Naturalization Service accounts for 44 percent of the department's cuts. The Reagan administration wants to slash the INS-proposed $385 million budget by $21.6 million and reduce the 10,281-member work force by 750. For an agency already suffering the effects of meager resources in its attempt to perform a monumental task, this proposal doesn't cut fat; it cuts bone.

The archaic INS administrative system — which one congressman described as a "shoebox" operation — has for years been ignored and remains understaffed and underbudgeted. It must make do with a non-automated record system to keep track and assure the departure of millions of tourists and others admitted annually for temporary visits. INS is also expected to patrol 6,000 miles of border with a few helicopters and small planes and a few hundred U.S. Border Patrol agents.

It's hardly surprising then that INS enforcement of laws on those entering the country legally on temporary visas has been deplorable. Of the 8 million who entered the United States on temporary visas in 1977, for instance, INS officials could not account for 15 percent, or more than 1.2 million persons. One congressman reminded Smith during the hearing that INS last year couldn't even locate Iranian students and diplomats in this country

The 2,000-mile Mexico-U.S. border and the 4,000-mile Canada-U.S. border have become so porous that virtually anyone entering this country with a temporary visa can stay permanently and even get a job. If INS can't keep track of legal visitors, what does that say about the millions of aliens living here illegally? To make matters worse, INS has been without a commissioner since Oct. 1, 1979, when Leonel Castillo resigned.

INS has become the convenient whipping boy of politicians and a public angry about poor border enforcement, out-of-control immigration policies, and inhumane treatment of aliens. The fault, however, lies not with INS; it lies with Congress and the White House, which for years have dodged tough decisions and refused to offer any leadership. The Select Commission on Immigration and Refugee Policy recently issued its recommendations to address those problems. They weren't clean-cut solutions, only messy and unpopular compromises, but they did represent a direction in which to go. Congress has yet to come up with anything better.

Smith reassured the committee that the proposed cuts will not damage the "operational capability" of the immigration service. That's little comfort; this agency hasn't much capability left to damage. If Smith wants to trim bureaucratic waste from the Justice Department, he won't find it here. If he seriously wants to come to grips with the immigration problem, he's going about it all wrong.

ST. LOUIS POST-DISPATCH

St. Louis, Mo., March 29, 1981

Congress and the Reagan administration are diverging on immigration policy. The administration has proposed a budget of only $363 million in the next fiscal year for the Immigration and Naturalization Service, reducing the number of employees Congress authorized for the current year. But bipartisan legislation has been introduced in Congress to give the INS an additional $200 million a year and to increase the number of Border Patrol officers from 2,100 to 6,000.

Congressmen say the public is thoroughly resentful at the huge and almost unchecked inflow of illegal immigrants. Members from both parties told House Judiciary Committee hearings on the Justice Department budget that INS funds were their main concern and that the agency does not have enough funds to do its job now. Certainly it does not, especially on the lengthy border with Mexico. In 1977 the INS turned back more than 1 million deportable aliens, but an equal number probably slipped into the country.

Earlier this month a special presidential commission recommended that amnesty be given to several million illegal aliens now in the U.S. But it also proposed to close the "back door" to immigration by strengthening the Border Patrol and by punishing employers who hire illegal entrants. Sen. Huddleston of Kentucky and Rep. Beard of Tennessee have offered legislation to base employer identification of job applicants on Social Security numbers, and otherwise to support the commission's findings. The Reagan administration's budget cuts, to the contrary, fly in the other direction from the commission's report.

Houston Chronicle

Houston, Texas,
March 21, 1981

Let's examine the plight of the Immigration and Naturalization Service.

The agency doesn't have a permanent director, and hasn't had one for more than a year.

The attorney general acknowledged to Congress: "We don't have (an alien) policy and we don't have organization."

The acting commissioner told a congressional panel the INS "has a serious corruption problem."

The new budget would eliminate 1,366 jobs in the service, including 240 from the unit that seeks illegal aliens in the interior of the United States, meaning that once past the border area any alien would be "home free."

The INS lines at international airports are causing so many delays some foreign airlines are threatening to cut back on their scheduled arrivals.

The INS employees' union says illegal immigration is out of control and that if the new budget is approved "there will be, in reality, no border at all."

One congressman, after hearing all of this, declared: "INS is literally the pits." He'll get no argument for us on that point.

The Boston Herald American

Boston, Mass., January 5, 1981

It is not surprising that the nation is uncertain as to the number of illegal aliens living and working in many urban centers.

The Immigration and Naturalization Service, which is supposed to keep track of foreigners in the United States, has little knowledge of even those who are in the country lawfully.

The House Committee on Government Operations has reported that INS offices are unable to cope with the flood of refugees and that records are in a hopeless mess. Mail is unanswered for weeks. Telephones ring unanswered. Offices are jammed with long lines of immigrants, many seeking citizenship, unable to get answers for their questions.

When President Carter wanted to penalize Iranian students for provocative actions, the INS was unable to say how many were in the United States or where they were located.

INS personnel have long complained that manpower is inadequate to deal with the stream of Latin Americans crossing the Mexican border illegally.

Administrative and housekeeping chores seem similarly understaffed. The clerical collapse is a hardship for everyone. Now that Congress has had the problem defined, it should act to provide a remedy — better funding and more manpower for the agency.

Hesburgh Commission Begins Immigration Policy Review

The Select Commission on Immigration and Refugee Policy, created in October 1978, was the nation's first joint presidential-congressional examination of immigration and refugee policy. Rev. Theodore M. Hesburgh, president of Notre Dame University, was the chairman, and the 15 other members were: Secretary of State Cyrus Vance, Attorney General Benjamin Civiletti, Labor Secretary F. Ray Marshall, Health, Education and Welfare Secretary Patricia Harris, Senate Judiciary Committee members Edward Kennedy, Dennis DeConcini, Charles Mathias and Alan Simpson, House Judiciary Committee members Peter Rodino, Elizabeth Holtzman, Robert McClory and Hamilton Fish, Los Angeles mayoral assistant Rose Matsui Oshi, railway union vice president Joaquin Francisco Otero and California Appeals Court Judge Cruz Reynoso. The commission heard two years of testimony, including 12 public hearings around the country and 21 private hearings.

Los Angeles Times

Los Angeles, Calif., February 10, 1980

Guadalupe Pule, an illegal immigrant, testified in Los Angeles Municipal Court this week that she was the victim of exploitive labor practices in the garment industry.

Simultaneously, the Select Commission on Immigration and Refugee Policy was hearing testimony at Occidental Center on what should be done with millions of others who have come across the borders to live and work in this country in violation of the immigration laws.

It would have been useful to the commission if it could have heard Pule's story. She is both an expert and a courageous witness. In appearing in court to testify against her former employer, she knew that she was risking deportation by acknowledging her illegal status.

But who was in greater contempt of the law: Pule for entering this country without documentation to support her four small children, or the garment contractor who she says took advantage of her?

Speaking through an interpreter, the Mexican woman told the court that she was paid only $50 for her first 72-hour week, although the minimum wage at that time was $2.90 an hour, with time and a half for overtime after eight hours. She also testified that another of her paychecks was written on a defunct account, and that she was not paid at all for other weeks of work.

In Pule's position, most illegal aliens would have kept their silence for fear that a complaint might prompt their employers to tip off the Immigration and Naturalization Service, which could arrest them and send them back across the border.

Pule was almost a victim of that tactic. The attorney for the garment contractor told INS officials of her illegal status, and where and when she would be testifying against his client. But the attempt to silence her did not succeed, because the INS practice is not to arrest persons involved in court actions.

After her testimony, Pule told reporters that "many people are afraid," and that their fear deters them from coming forth, as she did, to testify to wrongful practices not only in the garment industry but also in many others that employ large numbers of illegals.

At Occidental Center, the Select Commission on Immigration and Refugee Policy was listening to its own witnesses: a college professor of Chicano studies, a member of the governor's cabinet, labor leaders, farmers and others who have a social, political or economic interest in the new immigration policies that the commission will recommend to Congress early next year.

But, in our opinion, the most compelling case for a reasonable and compassionate reform of the immigration laws was made by Guadalupe Pule. She is one of the victims of a policy that acknowledges the presence in this country of vast numbers of illegal workers, but does little or nothing to protect them from substandard wages and working conditions.

No one knows how many have come to this country to escape frustration and poverty in their homelands; the estimates range from 4 million to 12 million. No one knows what their effect is on the unemployment rate among Americans; unions insist that it is considerable, but others say that most of them take menial, low-paying work that no one else wants. No one knows the effect of illegal immigrants on Social Security and health and welfare systems and tax collections, although certain studies indicate that they contribute more in payroll deductions than they take out—again, because they are afraid to contact government agencies.

For ourselves, we believe that this country can absorb those who are already here without status, and we support a generous amnesty that would permit them to remain and become citizens. We also believe that there should be a substantial increase in the quota for legal immigration from Mexico.

But there is agitation to limit the number that the country can accept, and, to reduce illegal immigration, a means must be found to control their employment—the single most powerful incentive that brings them here.

We favor a forgery-proof Social Security card for all residents of this country—one that would be shown only at a time of employment and that would quickly confirm the applicant's legal status. Without such identification, it would be impossible to enforce another necessary element of a rational immigration policy—criminal sanctions against employers who knowingly hire illegal immigrants and, all too often, exploit their vulnerability to deportation.

The Rev. Theodore H. Hesburgh, president of the University of Notre Dame and chairman of the select commission, supports both the concept of an identification card and of extensive clemency. We hope that a commission majority will agree with him and that Congress, after years of cynical neglect, will act affirmatively on recommendations that will insure just and humane treatment to the millions now living in fear and anxiety, among them Guadalupe Pule.

THE ARIZONA REPUBLIC
Phoenix, Ariz., February 7, 1980

THE Select Commission on Immigration and Refugee Policy came out from Washington and held an interesting meeting in Phoenix this week.

It heard:

✔ Gov. Bruce Babbitt oppose any "sealing of the border" to prevent illegal immigration from Mexico.

✔ State Sen. Alfredo Gutierrez say "the removal of (illegal) Mexican immigrants from the American labor market would contribute inordinately to the growth of unemployment. ... "

✔ Suzanne Dandoy, director of the state Department of Health Services, say the cost of health services for undocumented aliens in Arizona probably amounts to $3.5 million annually, and that these costs "should somehow be accepted as costs the government should assume."

What the witnesses did not address is whether Americans would be better off if they decided to allow immigration by any foreigner who can get here, regardless of whether he has been documented by the Immigration and Naturalization Service.

It seems strange that one commission should be appointed to deal with both immigration and refugee policies. The refugees in this country today are political refugees, whose lives were in danger if they had stayed in their own countries.

No such dangers haunt illegal Mexican immigrants. They come to this country without permission because they can earn better wages, get better medical treatment and send their children to better schools.

These immigrants are sometimes spoken of as "economic refugees." The description is not apt. If economic hardship were a valid reason for allowing foreigners to come to this country, 90 percent of the people of the world would be eligible.

Justin Blackwelder, president of the Environmental Fund, who also testified before the commission, said:

"Americans have inherited the best piece of real estate in the world. In the process, we have destroyed a great deal of it.

"If our population continues to grow at present rates," Blackwelder said, "the destruction can become complete within a matter of decades.

"If we had wanted all these additional people, we would not have passed immigration laws. The number of illegals already here is unknown, but ... it is small, however, compared to the number who will come in this decade alone unless something is done about it."

The Select Commission on Immigration and Refugee Policy may come up with suggestions that are economically sound, racially fair, and politically viable.

If it doesn't, and Congress finds no way out of the impasse, the United States will be facing a crisis even more serious than those of energy and Soviet expansionism.

The Des Moines Register

Des Moines, Iowa, April 27, 1980

Thousands of Cubans scurry to the beach, board boats and head for Miami, there to be cheered and welcomed by some of the 500,000 Cubans who have come to Florida since their country's revolution in 1959.

Immigration officials say hundreds of thousands more Cuban citizens may take advantage of Fidel Castro's decision to open the doors to anyone who wants to leave the country and try to make it to the United States.

Cuba is not the only country that is producing refugees. Haitians have been landing boats in Florida. Wars, political unrest and the double-whammy of overpopulation and underdevelopment have produced mass migration from El Salvador, Nicaragua, Colombia and other Central American countries. At least one-third of the population of Jamaica now lives outside that country — in the United States, the United Kingdom or elsewhere.

There are also the more widely publicized refugees produced by wars in Vietnam, Cambodia, Laos, the Middle East and Africa. Iowa has provided homes for thousands of Indochinese boat people. Others may seek asylum here.

Can they all be welcomed? This question constitutes a moral dilemma for Americans accustomed to seeing their country as a safe haven for the victims of political and religious persecution, and for those seeking to earn a more prosperous living for themselves and their children.

As a result of mass immigration, "America is losing control of its own future," according to Roger Conner, executive director of the Federation for American Immigration Reform.

The country, he argues, is moving gradually in the direction of allowing almost unrestricted immigration. "That will obviously inflate the labor supply and slow the upward mobility of America's own disadvantaged workers — those in America's big-city slums, for example, where unemployment among young people sometimes reaches 50 percent."

Conner argues that the United States cannot provide jobs for its own people and at the same time admit hundreds of thousands of new job-seekers. However, the United States cannot turn itself into a kind of fortress and ignore the needs of those seeking refuge. It is unthinkable for this country to turn its back on Cuba's "boat people," as the administration seems to be urging.

Perhaps the country will get a better understanding of its limits and its responsibilities on March 1, 1981, when a presidential Commission on Immigration and Refugee Policy, chaired by the Rev. Theodore M. Hesburgh of the University of Notre Dame, makes its final report. This 16-member panel has been asked to examine all aspects of immigration policy and to make recommendations for change.

The present state of uncertainty is helping no one, least of all those who have left their homelands and hope to create a new life here or in other countries.

THE INDIANAPOLIS STAR

Indianapolis, Ind., May 5, 1980

The federal government's decision to use Navy ships to help safely sealift Cuban refugees is a commendable and humanitarian act, reminiscent of the late President Johnson's "Open Door" airlift in 1965 when a callous Fidel Castro last tried to export his problems to the United States. It is in the best traditions of this nation.

Certainly as the leader of the free world this country cannot be hostile to those who vote against communism "with their feet."

Still when they come — from Cuba and Haiti, the legals and the illegals — washed ashore in Florida by the waves of tyranny or the timeless hunger for a better life, they are a dramatic illustration of a festering problem which the nation must surely face soon.

Stemming the tide is a woefully undermanned and under-funded immigration service that is being forced to bend more to the political whims of headlines than to the law.

It is David against Goliath and not a slingshot in sight.

The Refugee Act of 1980 permits an annual total of 320,000 refugees and legal immigrants from all over the world. But already that new legislation is bogged down in a complicated series of exceptions and addenda.

It is estimated that more than double the stipulated legal quota is admitted each year. But estimates are all that is available. The immigration service has cracked under the weight of new demands and pressures.

To compound the confusion, conflicting policies surface almost daily in response to political pulse-taking. Some departments of the federal government are urging a huge increase in refugee admissions, while other departments seek a reduction in numbers in order to trim rocketing resettlement costs, which have risen to more than $1.3 billion a year.

Beyond the unmanageable legalities is the magnitude of illegal immigration that is estimated as high as 6 million.

The truth is that we have not the slightest idea how many illegal immigrants reside in the United States. Nor are we likely to know any time soon, despite the best efforts of the Census Bureau to get them counted in the 1980 census.

There is no doubt, however, about the economic impact of illegal and legal aliens are having — an impact that is bound to be vividly demonstrated as the economy worsens and unemployment rolls rise. The flood of refugees on top of the escalation of illegal aliens is creating a situation ripe for widespread rancor and resentment.

A presidential commission, chaired by University of Notre Dame President Theodore Hesburgh, is currently studying a complete overhaul of immigration laws. But its recommendations are not expected until sometime next winter.

Father Hesburgh's commission should be pressed for a preliminary report and an earlier deadline or Congress itself should act at least with temporary measures to review and as quickly as possible act to better orchestrate a humanitarian but a clear and realistic policy.

Our ports of entry teem with refugees, not only from Cuba but of all nationalities and our consulates overseas are beseiged. Changing law, conflicting policies and a series of worldwide tragedies have conspired to create a monumental wave of human hope beating against the golden door of America.

The Times-Picayune

New Orleans, La., June 1, 1980

It's a commonplace that we or our forebears were all immigrants, unless we are American Indians. In the old days there was no distinction between "legal" and "illegal" immigrants: it was a vast, underpopulated continent and no questions were asked. It was 1875 before the first restriction occurred — a law barring the entry of prostitutes and convicts.

Later laws created other restrictions, and in 1921 the quota system permitted immigrants according to national origin. That system, reaffirmed by the McCarran-Walter Act of 1952, is openly biased along the lines of ethnological judgments, though its defenders claim it preserves "sociological and cultural balance" in the population.

In the last quarter-century, however, attorneys general have had discretionary power to admit a million refugees from Hungary, Cuba and other countries, and Congress has made other exceptions.

So much for legal immigration. But as everyone realizes, the back door is wide open to illegal and quasi-legal immigration like that from Mexico and in recent weeks from Cuba. More people are pushing and shoving through that door than are coming in legally through the Immigration and Naturalization Service, which is notoriously understaffed and underfunded and unable to check the flow.

Americans want this peculiar system changed. They are not opposed to immigration as such, but they resent the wholesale illegal immigration as it rages out of control. Our own letters to the editor reflect this outrage almost daily.

A Select Commission on Immigration and Refugee Policy, headed by Fr. Theodore M. Hesburgh, president of Notre Dame University, has been working on reform of the law and will render its report next March. It is expected to propose concrete controls on illegal immigration as well as amnesty for illegal aliens already here, and a new visa system that might have a special category for "seed immigrants," persons without relatives here who can nevertheless enrich the nation with their talents.

The lines along which the commission is working are acceptable as a beginning. The immigration-refugee problem will not be solved overnight, but it is a sad yet obvious fact that the United States cannot continue to be a haven for the world's oppressed to the same degree that it was a century ago. The country sorely needs reformed immigration codes that draw the line equitably.

Houston Chronicle

Houston, Texas, June 22, 1980

Some form of mass amnesty for illegal aliens is considered certain to be a major recommendation of the blue-ribbon Select Commission on Immigration.

We believe such an amnesty would be wrong as a matter of national policy and disastrously naive as a matter of practicality.

It would be breaking faith with American citizens and those who enter the country legally to effectively void U.S. immigration laws and reward a huge, and unknown, number of people for their illegality with the rights, privileges and benefits of citizenship.

A mass amnesty would abdicate the right of this country to control who, and how many, become citizens. It would have political, social and economic effects which cannot be accurately foreseen and thus obviously cannot be judged whether they would be in the best interests of the nation and its citizens.

It would be sheer folly to grant an amnesty when there is no knowledge of the number of people involved. This could involve literally millions. Put simply, no one knows what is in that Pandora's box, but they are willing to open it.

These amnesty proposals are all predicated on granting it to people who have a certain length of illegal residence here — two years, four years, whatever. This is attempting to apply the logic and standards of a legal and aboveboard society to an illegal and underground society. There is no reason to suppose that such rules would not be as easily circumvented as is being done now in the presence of illegal aliens. Illegal immigration and residence is being aided and abetted by various groups and individuals in this country, for various reasons. It defies common sense to assume the same would not be the case with an amnesty. In practice it would be as out of control and regulation as the present situation.

Another predicate is that the United States would, after an amnesty, strictly and effectively control future illegal immigration. There is absolutely no indication that Washington is, or will be, prepared to take the steps that would be necessary to do this. The most probable result would be an amnesty for millions and a continuation of the same illegal alien problems.

An amnesty for an unknown and uncontrollable number of people, with unknown effects, would be an abandonment of responsible government and a disservice to the nation.

SAN JOSE NEWS

San Jose, Calif., September 19, 1980

THE Carter administration conceded in 1978 that it didn't have an immigration policy, but it promised to help Congress find one. Now, two years into the effort, it's hard not to wonder whether the administration's right hand knows what the left hand is doing.

Time, in the statutory sense, is running out. The 97th Congress, which convenes next January, is scheduled early on to receive, evaluate and act on the recommendations of the Select Commission on Immigration and Refugee Policy. The commission was created by Congress in 1978 after it refused to buy President Carter's plan for dealing with undocumented immigrants; the president proposed amnesty for most of those here and tighter border controls.

For nearly two years the select commission, made up of private citizens, members of Congress and administration representatives, has been conducting public hearings in various parts of the country. In general, it has learned that the American people are of two minds about illegal immigration. They like the low-priced goods and services cheap labor can provide, but they are uncomfortable with the side effects: exploitation of undocumented aliens, depressed wage scales for all at the bottom of the employment heap, and supposed increases in health and welfare costs.

The select commission is still formulating its policy recommendations, but two approaches to the problem appear to have found favor with a majority of commissioners: legal sanctions against employers who hire the undocumented and the issuance of a national work-identity card. The card would be issued only to citizens and to those in the country legally.

It was over these two points that the select commission ran head-on into the U.S. Civil Rights Commission this week.

The civil rights commission, which has been conducting its own immigration policy study for the past *three* years, sees employer sanctions as racist in effect if not in intent. They would, in the commission's words, work a hardship on citizens and legal resident aliens "who are racially and culturally identifiable with major immigrant groups."

The civil rights commission objects to identity cards as an invasion of privacy and a potential club over everybody's head: If the government can issue "working papers," it can refuse to issue them or threaten to revoke them if the worker behaves in some way the government doesn't like.

The points are well taken on both sides.

The dilemma is real, and Congress is left stranded in the middle. It must draft a policy that meets the nation's economic needs, offers hope for the economically and politically oppressed of other nations and preserves the civil rights and liberties of all. That's a tall order, and the last thing Congress needs is conflicting advice.

Unfortunately, the civil rights commission isn't being too helpful, even setting aside its squabble with the commission on immigration policy.

Take the matter of immigration quotas, for example. Present law limits them to 270,000, split roughly between the eastern and western hemispheres; each nation is allotted 20,000 visas a year from its hemispheric total. The civil rights commission would hand out all 270,000 visas a year on a first-come-first-served basis, pointing out that some nations, Britain for instance, never use their full quota while others, such as Mexico, can never get enough visas for would-be immigrants.

First-come-first-served makes sense, but the civil rights commission failed to deal with a more fundamental problem: Should the United States limit immigration to 270,000 persons a year, exclusive of political refugees? Should the total be higher, or lower? What is the optimum population for the United States? As the national birthrate declines, will the country need more than 270,000 immigrants a year to maintain a stable population?

Similar holes appear in other sections of the civil rights commission's report, titled "The Tarnished Golden Door."

The commission recommends disbanding the Border Patrol, which is part of the Department of Justice, and transferring its responsibilities to a new Border Management Agency within the Treasury Department. But such a shift will have little point, and probably less effect, until and unless Congress decides what kind of border serves the nation best. The present one is porous, letting an estimated 6 million to 8 million undocumented immigrants live and work in the United States on any given day.

Shuffling the Border Patrol from one Cabinet department to another doesn't answer the fundamental question of what kind of border we want.

That's the question Congress must answer to its own and the people's satisfaction before it can deal intelligently with the nuts and bolts of Border Patrol organization. Unfortunately, conflicting advice and proposals that avoid underlying problems don't help Congress find useful answers.

The Miami Herald

Miami, Fla., November 25, 1980

WHAT ON EARTH could have come over the Rev. Theodore M. Hesburgh? He seems to have suffered a grievous lapse in judgment that, left uncorrected, threatens severe damage to the public interest.

Father Hesburgh, president of the University of Notre Dame, is also chairman of a 16-member commission on Federal immigration policy. The commission was created by Congress in 1978 to review American immigration policy and practices, and to recommend changes.

The commission's final work session is scheduled to be held Dec. 5-7 at the Tides Lodge, a secluded resort three hours from the nation's capital in Irvington, Va. Father Hesburgh has decided that 20 of the session's scheduled 23 and one-half hours will be conducted *in private.*

There is no justification for that. The commission is a public body. It is funded with public money. Its mission is critically important to the public interest. And the issues it intends to pronounce recommendations for are properly the objects of significant public controversy. The public has the right to be present.

Consider some of the issues the commission will grapple with: what numerical limits to place on immigration; what selection criteria shall govern admission of immigrants; whether national identity cards should be instituted; what standards to adopt for temporary admission of Mexican workers; where to draw the lines for asylum for political dissidents; how to structure deportation procedures; and more.

Despite the clear and commendable commitment toward opening Government to the public embodied in recent Federal law, Father Hesburgh succeeded in circumventing legal impediments to closed meetings.

He claims that secrecy is necessary because the agenda will include "ticklish questions of national security" affecting relations with Mexico and other countries. However, his fellow commission member Patricia Roberts Harris, the Secretary of Health and Human Services, said through a spokesman that "she knew of no national-security considerations." Mrs. Harris objects to the conference's remote location and secrecy.

Objections also have been voiced by immigration lawyers, civil libertarians, and refugee coordinators, including one group representing Haitian refugees that threatens to sue to gain access to the meeting. Their protests are legitimate. Immigration issues are indeed sensitive, but the Hesburgh Commission should not try to hide them from public view. To the contrary, their controversial nature is an indicator of how very important are the questions being dealt with; matters of that importance cannot be left for resolution in closed rooms with the public shut outside.

Anything the commissioners have to say about who enters the United States, and under what conditions, they should be willing to say and defend in public. There is no justification for the commission to meet behind locked doors. Father Hesburgh should open the meeting.

Newsday

Long Island, N. Y., December 4, 1980

A White House commission meets in a few days to begin the difficult task of forging final recommendations on complex immigration and refugee problems. The task won't be easy. The 16-member panel must wrestle with vexing questions about national identity cards, amnesty for illegal aliens, temporary worker programs and immigration quotas.

Fundamental to any final report, however, must be a policy that calls for adequate control of the borders. By itself, of course, such a policy cannot begin to address the colossal immigration problems. But the utter lack of control at the border dramatically symbolizes for many Americans the nation's chaotic, contradictory immigration policies and laws. Worse, the lax border governance symbolizes Congress' unwillingness to confront those problems.

In that irresolute climate, the Immigration and Naturalization Service (INS) has been left to drift without a commissioner since October 1979 when Leonel Castillo resigned. The INS investigative staff, responsible for apprehending and processing millions of undocumented migrants numbers barely 1,000 nationwide. Its Border Patrol is expected to maintain surveillance of 2,000 miles of border with 350 agents in any given shift. The entire INS aircraft fleet to survey the borders and coastlines consists of three leased helicopters and 28 small planes. Its budget totals $77 million. The Los Angeles Police Department, by contrast, works with a $222 million budget. In short, the Border Patrol is severely understaffed, underpaid, poorly trained and poorly equipped. Is it any surprise then that its ranks are riddled by corruption, brutality and miserable morale?

To complicate matters, Mexico views any American efforts to properly control its borders as a dangerous and unfriendly act. Various groups here view anything less than an open border as a blatant racist move. Other pressure groups, meanwhile, demand that the border be sealed.

And yet, when the issue is shorn of emotional arguments, there is nothing inimical or racist in a government's desire to control its borders. Indeed, it's a basic responsibility of any sovereign nation. Exercising jurisdiction of the border in a firm but equitable and humane manner is certainly a reasonable and realistic alternative. Whatever proposals the commission finally agrees upon, it's clear that any serious immigration policy must begin at the border.

St. Petersburg Times

St. Petersburg, Fla., November 28, 1980

As anyone from Miami might tell you, the United States is in painful need of a coherent and consistent policy on the admission of immigrants and refugees. This has proved easier to wish for than to achieve. Each choice is difficult, and each solution has its own complicated consequence.

SHOULD THE Mexican border be sealed, and are we willing to pay what it would cost to attempt it? But what to do about the millions of illegal Mexican workers on whom U.S. agriculture and industry have come to depend? Should an employer be jailed, as organized labor might like, for hiring undocumented aliens? But wouldn't this require the issuance of a national identity card, and what would that mean to our civil liberties? And what about the refugees: Can we berate Castro and the Kremlin for not letting their people out if we aren't ready to take them in?

Confronted with this welter of dilemmas, a select presidential commission had seemed to be doing a pretty thorough job of research and public discussion. The commission is the same one formerly chaired by Florida's ex-Gov. Reubin Askew. Rev. Theodore M. Hesburgh, president of Notre Dame University, heads it now. Until recently, at least, the commission was doing well at evading the oblivion that is the usual destiny of such commissions — and of inspiring public trust in its sincerity.

BUT WHAT now? To complete its deliberations, the commission is withdrawing from Washington and from access by the public. It is retreating to a secluded resort on the Rapahannock River in rural Virginia for a three-day meeting early next month. The public will be barred from all but the final three-and-a-half hours.

Hesburgh told *The New York Times* that it's because there are "ticklish questions of national security" affecting U.S. relations with Mexico and other nations. Well, so what? Sooner or later they're going to have to come out in public anyhow, unless the commission intends the Congress to simply file and forget its report.

IMMIGRATION lawyers and citizens' groups who have protested the closed meeting have their own ideas why it's happening. It is suggested that some commission members simply didn't study their staff reports and don't want their poor preparation to show. Or perhaps the commission wants to work out a secret political strategy for impressing the incoming Reagan administration; four of the 12 commission members are outgoing Carter Cabinet officers.

Whatever the reason, it's a shame that the Hesburgh commission chose this course. Secret debates at a secluded private resort are not the sort of stuff to inspire confidence in any recommendation that it may present — and confidence is the stuff from which difficult decisions are made.

Amnesty for Illegal Aliens, Other Policy Changes Proposed

In a preliminary report issued Dec. 7, the Select Commission on Immigration and Refugee Policy recommended an amnesty for all illegal aliens in the U.S. as of Jan. 1, 1981 and a 30% increase in the annual immigration quota to 350,000. The commission, headed by Rev. Theodore M. Hesburgh of the University of Notre Dame, had been created by Congress in 1978 to study the prospect of overhauling U.S. immigration laws. The 16-member panel estimated that there were between three million and six million illegal aliens currently in the U.S. The amnesty would permit them to remain legally in the country, while anyone who entered illegally after the beginning of 1981 would be subject to prosecution.

Other recommendations in the preliminary report included: raising the immigration quota each year, reducing the number of close family members admitted, increasing the admission of skilled immigrants, granting exemptions from ceilings on specific countries to spouses and children and continuing the practice of issuing permits for foreign workers to enter the U.S. for temporary or seasonal jobs. The panel added that those temporary foreign workers should be required to pay taxes and unemployment insurance.

One controversial proposal, supported by a majority of the panel but not adopted, was to prosecute employers who hired illegal aliens. Hesburgh noted that the plan would not work unless there was some form of national identification for U.S. workers.

Pittsburgh Post-Gazette
Pittsburgh, Pa., December 15, 1980

"There is no doubt that foreign immigration has been of enormous benefit to this country. It is getting, however, to be a pertinent and pressing question whether this benefit is not impaired by the crime, communism, riots, and official demoralization which foreign immigration has thrust upon us."

A Floridian worried about Cubans and Haitians? A Pennsylvanian or Texan worried about Vietnamese refugees?

No, this statement was made by an editorial writer for the Chicago Times on May 10, 1876. And the immigrants he was worried about were people from Germany and Ireland — the ancestors of some of today's Americans who think present-era immigrants should be kept out.

Look at civil disturbances, the 1876 editorial said, and you'll find that "every name is that of a foreigner . . . the names are all barbarous, guttural, the evident product of other climes and a different national growth." If the reader goes to the state prison at Joliet and "looks over the convicted whisky-men, the Rehms, Hesing Roelles, Junkers, Keeleys, Goldbergs and Rindskopfs are in a majority."

Such an attitude is shocking, considering the contributions then and in the century since that editorial which these and other nationalities have made to the United States. But they should put in perspective some equally shocking, thoughtless remarks made about today's immigrants.

If this parallel isn't thought-provoking enough, a recent study made for the federal government's Select Commission on Immigration and Refugee Policy should. The survey, conducted by Prof. Julian L. Simon of the University of Illinois, found that immigrants as a group from their first sight of the Statue of Liberty to their retirement on Social Security contribute more in taxes than they receive in government services, such as welfare, food stamps, and Medicaid.

Subtracting services used from taxes paid, Mr. Simon found the yearly net contribution ranges from $426 to $1,180 per immigrant family.

On the other side of the equation, Mr. Simon concludes that the average immigrant family earns as much as native Americans between two and six years after entry and, after that, earns more. To be sure, this has caused complaints that extensive immigration, both legal and illegal, deprives native workers of jobs.

If that is true, the answers should be found elsewhere, rather than blaming immigrants for their enterprise and success.

Interestingly, the Select Commission which ordered the Simon survey has just voted to recommend an amnesty for illegal aliens already in the United States and penalties for employers who hire illegal aliens in the future. However, the action was not final, and the stands could be refined or changed before the commission makes its final recommendations to the president and Congress by March 1.

All of this should provide food for thought concerning immigrants, and especially for those all too prone to forget some of the bigoted receptions that met their immigrant ancestors.

The Cincinnati Post
Cincinnati, Ohio, December 13, 1980

A select commission established by Congress two years ago to recommend revisions in immigration policy has voted for a mixed bag of changes—some sound and some utopian.

Headed by the Rev. Theodore Hesburgh, president of the University of Notre Dame, the commission called on Congress to make it a crime for an employer to hire an illegal alien.

This is a sensible suggestion because jobs are the lure that attracts millions of border crossers to this country. Paradoxically, though, the panel opposed any new way of identifying illegal job seekers, such as an identification card or use of data banks.

That or some other foolproof means of identification is much needed to slow the flood of illegal immigrants, whose total is estimated between 3 million and 12 million.

Most of the commission's other stands showed more compassion for foreigners who want to come here than for the interest of legal residents, including 8 million currently unemployed.

For example, the body urged boosting the immigration quota to 450,000 a year for five years from the present ceiling of 270,000. The new figure would not include non-quota immigrants, mostly relatives of residents, and refugees who alone totaled 366,000 this year.

All told the United States is accepting about 800,000 legal immigrants annually, plus an uncounted number of illegal ones. This is a more liberal immigration policy than is conducted by any other nation, and the Hesburgh commission would open the door still wider.

When America was a sparsely populated continent, a wide open immigration made sense. Now with high unemployment and low economic growth, it would force this country's poor and minorities into fierce competition with foreigners for jobs.

Congress should not buy that headache part of the commission's prescription.

THE INDIANAPOLIS STAR
Indianapolis, Ind., December 15, 1980

A recent Gallup poll shows that 76 percent of Americans are opposed to the entry and employment of illegal aliens. The figures reflect a continuing exasperation with present immigration policy or, more precisely, with the disregard of policy and lack of enforcement.

Resentment has grown with unemployment. Minority groups charge illegals are taking jobs from them. Budget-conscious state officials say welfare-related services to illegals are straining resources.

The long-simmering problem came to a boil with the influx of an estimated 125,000 refugees from Cuba last year. But the controversy has been fired for years by the border crashing of Mexican nationals, whose numbers now total anywhere from two to six million.

The disparity in figures is part of the problem. The Department of Immigration and Naturalization has, to all intents and purposes, ceased to function. It has been without an agency chief for more than a year. It is awash in a sea of misdirected or lost files. Its main function, that of guarding the borders, has become a sad joke even among the beleagured border patrol.

Father Theodore M. Hesburgh, president of the University of Notre Dame, said recently that the nation's immigration policy is out of control. He should know. He heads a 16-member commission now studying the policy and preparing recommendations for change.

The crux of the dilemma, in Father Hesburgh's words, is this: "We cannot be the single refuge for all of the people in the world who flee persecution or seek opportunity."

Yet events of recent years have promoted the very development we fear. Lack of a definitive policy, impartially and firmly enforced, has encouraged politically and economically oppressed aliens to presume that — legally or illegally — they will find room behind "the golden door."

President-elect Reagan has made no statements on immigration and refugee policy. Understandably, the economy will be the focus of the first few months of his administration. But the final report of the Hesburgh panel is due in March. We hope recommendations are carefully considered and sifted with both compassion and a healthy self-interest.

The world has entered an era of mass migration, of unprecedented population displacement. We ignore the momentum of history at our peril.

THE DAILY OKLAHOMAN
Oklahoma City, Okla., December 27, 1980

AMNESTY for all aliens now in this country illegally, as proposed by a special commission the other day, is not the best solution to the overall problem. The illegals — or "undocumented aliens" in government parlance — present a whole shelf of differing problems.

Certainly the 120,000 Cubans granted legal entry status during the latest boat lift to Florida present different problems, must make different adjustments and face different opportunities from the estimated million illegal Mexicans who are in the Chicago area alone.

There are thousands of Iranians, educated here, who cannot go home because they would face persecution and possible execution. Their problems are compounded by their countrymen who have overstayed here but support the revolutionary regime in Tehran — in our streets.

A federal report says that a million Mexicans are intercepted and returned to their homeland annually after entering this country illegally. One study says there may be as many as 10 million foreigners who have either entered this country in violation of our laws or have overstayed their legal permits and merely disappeared into the population.

Most of these did not respond to this year's census, and most will not fill out alien registration forms in January.

The big problem, clearly, is the Mexicans. They usually become hard workers, and will tackle almost any kind of work, no matter how unpleasant or menial. Since the old bracero agreements were terminated some years ago, there is no legal way that the typical Mexican can come to this country, earn a stake and go back home. (The number allowed by law is quite small in comparison to the number who want to come.)

Formerly, the pattern was that they usually did just that. The stake may have been used to get married and start a home, to buy tools and become a worker in a trade at home or to buy a piece of farm land. But once the bracero made his stake and took it home, he was no longer a problem either to this country or to his own.

What we need today is a return to common-sense accords with Mexico which would legalize the temporary import of labor, with no restrictions on the worker's right to repatriate his earnings. Since there are seldom real conflicts with organized labor in this country — skilled Mexican workers do not need to emigrate, even temporarily — U.S. craft unions ought to cooperate in formulating such a system.

In the present circumstances, it is not only foolish but could be tragic to offer the hope of free entry, or of freedom from penalty for those who have entered in violation of our immigration laws. It can lead only to new waves of hopefuls heading for our borders and coasts.

The problem of the illegal Mexican must be treated apart from the refugee flights that occur from time to time. Yet since Mexicans comprise the largest component of the illegal alien population, they cannot be ignored, and should not be granted blanket approval to stay just because their illegal entry was successful.

The long-range solution, as far as the Mexicans are concerned, is for Mexico to provide employment for them in Mexico. With the oil wealth expected from the prodigious new fields that stretch from Texas to Tehuantepec, Mexico must undertake more development of its own resources, and the Mexican worker stands high among those resources.

This country can assist in that development, but only Mexico can do the job required.

Sentinel Star
Orlando, Fla., December 15, 1980

A FEDERAL commission studying immigration has recommended amnesty for all illegal aliens.

It is argued that blanket amnesty is the only way to get a handle on the estimated 6 million illegal immigrants already in the country. Immigration officials say there is no way to track down all those people, much less to return them to their native counties.

But once legalized, their families would become eligible for entry under laws which favor relatives of immigrants already accepted. Thus, the effect of amnesty for 6 million could mean opening the doors to 18 million to 24 million.

This would repeat the major mistake of the existing non-policy. It would, in effect, allow people who entered the country illegally to determine the nation's immigration policy. This would be an injustice to those who have complied with the law and are either seeking to bring in their families or are waiting for visas.

Furthermore, amnesty would add the promise of future amnesty and would probably encourage even more people to enter the country illegally.

No law can be made enforceable by rewarding those who violate it.

The Hartford Courant

Hartford, Conn., December 20, 1980

The recommendations of the federal commission studying immigration reflect Americans' basic ambiguity about newcomers: The United States is both a nation of immigrants and a nation which has discriminated against the foreign-born.

Americans traditionally have welcomed newcomers, and the economy needed them. But the distinction between legal and illegal immigrants created the dilemma of what to do about people who came to this country in violation of existing quotas.

How hard should the government move to deport them? How diligent should the government be in keeping illegal aliens out of the country?

The Select Commission on Immigration and Refugee Policy, appointed by President Carter, has tried to balance competing concerns. Aliens already in the country, albeit illegally, would be granted amnesty. But employers in the future would be prohibited from hiring illegal aliens and fined or imprisoned if they did.

Wisely, the commission rejected a proposal which would have required that every legal resident of the United States be issued a permit in order to work. That would have created a United States more like a totalitarian state than a land in which everyone is free to work and move from place to place without carrying some sort of internal passport.

The plan to crack down on employers is the better approach; an employer should know who he is hiring. If employers refused to hire illegal aliens, there would be no illegal immigration because most people come to this country to work.

If the United States is serious about curbing illegal immigration, it would beef up the border patrol and the Immigration and Naturalization Service, both to prevent people from entering the country illegally and to seek them out once they are here.

One reason why government has tolerated illegal immigration is because illegal aliens hold jobs that no one else will perform and at wages lower than those most Americans and legal residents will accept.

That always has been the economic role of immigrants to this country and that is why it is so difficult, practically and politically, to keep them out.

DAYTON DAILY NEWS

Dayton, Ohio, December 12, 1980

It's not difficult to decide what should be done with aliens illegally in this country. The tough nut to crack is how to control the flood of those who may yet come in violation of law and in numbers the social order cannot handle as responsibly as it should.

The federal government has to get some semblance of mastery over the problem. This, in time, probably will require some kind of individual worker identification keyed to a centralized a system for quickly cross-checking emigre citizenship and status. It will require drastic reform of the information system presently maintained by the federal immigration service. It will require a substantial increase in immigration management and law enforcement manpower. And it will require a clear national policy for the immigration department to follow.

President Carter's federal commission studying immigration has released its first tentative recommendations. Those include amnesty for aliens already in this country illegally and penalties on employers who hire them illegally. For the present, the commission rejects proposals for issuing emigres identification cards and work permits and for their registry in a computerized data bank.

Certainly any commission sensitive to its Big-Brother-is-watching-you implications would hestitate to recommend a master-file system for keeping tabs on people; it offends the free spirit of Americans.

On the other hand, laws regulating immigration must have clarity, consistency and teeth if they are to be equitably enforced. Otherwise it is unfair to hold employers of aliens liable for hiring those here illegally while the federal government shirks its own regulatory responsibility.

Further, putting the liability burden on employers without providing back-up information simply invites the unscrupulous to, for instance, exploit or otherwise discriminate against those with strange accents; to accept such forged identification papers as birth certificates or passports — no questions asked. (Indeed, a long-overdue crackdown on forgers also waits on some systematic address to the overall problem.)

In recent years — although not during past waves of anti-alien sentiment — the United States has been at least selectively generous in granting easy entry to large numbers of refugees in flight from homeland persecutions or troubles, oftener than not by special dispensation or act of Congress rather than under any quota.

But the ability to absorb newcomers on an emergency basis is threatened by stresses imposed on the economy and on public and social services by newcomers here in violation of the law. There are already so many millions as to constitute an underworld of noncitizens whose presence is not reflected in the census or the political process.

If amnesty is to be granted illegal aliens already here, a way must be found to deter the further flow of illegal newcomers. Otherwise amnesty invites more difficulties than it resolves.

ST. LOUIS POST-DISPATCH

St. Louis, Mo., December 13, 1980

A federal commission has completed part of a report on what the United States ought to do about immigration, especially illegal immigration. What it has been doing is pretending to enforce immigration laws and not doing it.

As to legal entries, the Select Commission on Immigration, ordered by Congress to report finally in March, simply recommends a bit more generosity in the world's most generous policy. That is, it would increase the permanent immigration quota from the present 270,000 a year to 350,000, with some extra room for five years to clear up a backlog of admissions applications. Most of these additional spaces would be reserved for relatives of U.S. citizens and permanent resident aliens.

Illegal immigration is another — and enormous — matter. Immigration officials estimate the number of illegal aliens in this country at between 3.6 million and 6 million. Most have come from Mexico, looking for jobs. Keeping them out has proved almost impossible; at any one time the undermanned border patrol has no more than 300 officers to guard 1,900 miles of frontier.

The commission headed by the Rev. Theodore M. Hesburgh suggests legalizing the status of aliens who have already been in this country two or three years. "You can't deport 5 million people," a commission officer says, and that is the fact of the matter. President-elect Reagan, who will have to deal with the commission's final report, would go further by allowing temporary visas for many Mexicans who want to earn money in this country and take it home. The commission, however, recommends against an expanded worker program; it would settle for legalizing the present situation and trying to prevent future illegal entries.

But how can the government enforce the laws against those who continue to seek illegal entry? To remove an inducement for such migration, the commission's draft report proposes making it a crime for an employer to hire illegal immigrants, who are too easily exploited for cheap labor. The commission also suggests that workers demonstrate their legal residence through documents such as birth certificates. It rejects the idea of requiring all Americans to carry identity cards to prove their legal status. That would make it easier to enforce the law, and some commission members favor it for that reason. Still, a majority feels that requiring Americans to demonstrate that they are Americans, just to locate those who are not, smacks of totalitarianism.

Most Americans probably would agree with that. At the same time, the commission found a sense of public outrage over an immigration policy that, in the face of domestic unemployment, has for some years been thoroughly out of control. Congress undoubtedly will debate legalizing the illegals as well as the matter of identity cards. Yet the problem is to make the best of a bad situation. Giving many aliens legal status now could make it easier to block an increasing flow of illegal entrants in the future. It is clearly too late for massive deportations.

The Houston Post

Houston, Texas, October 11, 1980

It was a beautiful poem that Emma Lazarus wrote. "Give me your tired, your poor, your huddled masses yearning to breathe free, the wretched refuse of your teeming shore." But it leaves an indelible impression of helplessness, of people needing always to be helped. New federal statistics show that immigrants are not a burden on the resident taxpayers. Once in this country, they prosper.

The average immigrant family starts earning more and paying more taxes than native-born American families within 10 years after arriving in the United States, a federal study commission has found. Although children of immigrants start at a disadvantage, they tend to overtake native-born children in academic performance. They complete more years of school and a higher percentage of them graduate from college. T. Paul Schultz, Yale University demographer and economist, suggests that immigrant children star in school because the immigrants "are selectively drawn from their country of birth" and "are more strongly inclined to invest in their children's school than are native American parents."

The study was made at the request of the Select Commission on Immigration and Refugee Policy created by Congress to recommend changes in immigration laws. Conducted by Schultz and Julian L. Simon, University of Illinois economist, the studies were based on a computer analysis of 1976 Census Bureau data from 150,000 families. They confirm an earlier study made by another University of Illinois economist using 1970 census data. Simon found that immigrants in their first 12 years in the United States use fewer public services. Because they are young, they are less likely to need Social Security than native families. After two to six years, immigrant families pay as much in taxes as natives. After that they pay more.

All this suggests that native-born Americans enjoy what these economists consider a net profit from taxpaying immigrants. Legal and illegal immigrants are similar, differences depending more on the country of origin. Although refugees were among those surveyed, the study did not include more recent refugees. The researchers believe the trends of 1970 and 1976 will continue. This study should help cool the controversy now astir over continued immigration. It should enable Congress to enact laws on the basis of facts and logic rather than sentiment. It is to be hoped that members of Congress will make use of this study they so wisely requested.

BUFFALO EVENING NEWS

Buffalo, N.Y., December 10, 1980

A federal commission has made some useful proposals concerning illegal immigration, although much more will have to be done to solve this nagging problem.

In a report that resembles President Carter's proposals in 1977, the Select Commission on Immigration and Refugees, headed by the Rev. Theodore M. Hesburgh of Notre Dame, proposed an amnesty for illegal aliens already in the U.S. and penalties for employers who hire other illegal aliens in the future. The amnesty is the only practical and humanitarian course for dealing with the millions of present aliens, many of whom have been in this country for many years.

* * *

Illegal migrants, mostly from Mexico, have created complex economic, sociological and diplomatic problems. No one really knows how many such aliens there are, but they have been variously estimated at from 3 million to 12 million.

Perhaps a million filter through the porous U.S.-Mexican border each year, although many eventually go back home. Desperately poor, they often brave great hardships to get to the U.S. in search of a better life. Mexico considers the exodus a means of easing its own population pressures and resents any U.S. efforts to slow down the human tide.

Since almost all the illegal aliens come in search of jobs, the best way of discouraging them is to effectively bar them from employment. The commission staff proposed doing this through the use of work identification cards or computerized data banks to verify the legal right of prospective employees to work in the U.S., but the commission voted 7 to 5 against this proposal.

It urged instead that employers use existing means of identification, such as birth certificates or Social Security cards, to establish whether applicants were legal residents. Unfortunately, the U.S.-Mexican border area carries on a flourishing business in forged documents — birth certificates, Social Security cards, driver's licenses, passports or baptismal certificates. Father Hesburgh noted that the plan to penalize employers would be meaningless without a system of verification.

A great many people have doubts about any system of worker identification. Some of this opposition is largely emotional, stemming from the connotation of identity cards in totalitarian countries. But some of the doubts are justified and are reinforced by the power of computer systems to store and retrieve personal information. Many people rightly fear the formation of national computer dossiers that could reveal one's life history to some unknown bureaucrat at the push of a button.

But it should be remembered that most Americans already have a type of identification card — the Social Security card — and we see little danger in making it counterfeit-resistant. And a computer verification system does not necessarily have to invade one's privacy if its function is strictly limited.

* * *

Mexico's opposition to any immigration curbs raises serious problems, both because Mexico is a neighboring country and because it is now an important oil exporter. But these objections can be eased by assuring Mexico of the continuance of a generous program of legal immigration.

The U.S., with high unemployment and other pressing economic problems, cannot afford to throw open its borders to anyone who wants to come to it. Ways must be sought to check the present massive illegal immigration, which has given the U.S. the highest population growth rate of any developed nation. The challenge to Congress and the Reagan administration is to work out a program that will be generous to Mexico, sympathetic to the impoverished would-be immigrants, fair to prospective employers and free of any threat to privacy or civil rights.

The Washington Post

Washington, D.C., December 16, 1980

THE executive-legislative-public commission that Congress and the president created two years ago to sort out the tangle of immigration and refugee policy is about to issue its final report. It's a good thing, too. The massive flow of illegal aliens across the Mexican border and successive flotillas of "boat people" have produced in the public a sharp sense that the United States has lost control over this vital and sensitive area of its national life. There was some thought that it might help to pause to "Reaganize" the Carter-appointed Select Commission on Immigration and Refugee Policy. But the consensus of the key people, including Sen. Alan Simpson (R-Wyo.), Rep. Romano Mazzoli (D-Ky.) and the chairman, the Rev. Theodore Hesburgh, is that it makes more sense for the commission to wrap up its work of making recommendations so that the process of legislating can begin.

Within the commission there are, as intended, many points of view on the central issue of what to do about illegal immigration. Nonetheless, a consensus has evolved in support of a broad package deal. The millions of illegals already here would be legalized; the numbers and the legal and political difficulties make it virtually impossible to dig them up and deport them anyhow. The American people cannot be expected to accept this step, however, in the consensus view, unless they are assured that another flood of illegals will not then seep in. This will require, among other things, more effective border controls, sanctions to punish employers who hire illegals (who come mostly for the jobs), and some way to identify the illegals. The identification requirement poses vexing issues of civil liberties and administration, and the commission may buck that one to Congress with some of its disagreements intact.

Although President-elect Reagan comes from a part of the country in which illegal immigration is a daily and pervasive phenomenon, he is not identified strongly with a single approach to it. In fact, the whole question of immigration and refugee policy lends itself increasingly poorly to regional or, for that matter, partisan thinking. What the commission has done is to set out a framework in which traditional American values of openness, fairness and ethnic diversity, which don't change, can be reconciled with national economic and social conditions, which do change. Its recommendations should give Congress and the new administration something that the political system has not enjoyed before on this set of issues—a basis for intelligent choice.

THE CHRISTIAN SCIENCE MONITOR
Boston, Mass., December 10, 1980

The US Select Commission on Immigration and Refugee Policy is fundamentally on target, we think, in its approach to the tangled — and politically sensitive — question of controlling illegal immigration. As most Americans now realize, US laws have been consistently violated these past few years (if not redt^ed to a large measure of mockery) by soaring illegal immigration, particularly along the US border with Mexico. But exactly how to control that massive influx has so far defied solution.

At this still exploratory stage of its two-year inquiry, the commission is proposing that amnesty be offered aliens already in the US. It would increase the number of persons allowed to legally immigrate by 180,000 annually for five years. Civil and criminal penalties would be imposed against employers knowingly hiring illegal aliens. The commission, which will not submit its final report to the president and Congress until next year, tentatively rules out use of national worker identification cards.

So far so good. We have great trouble with the concept of national identity cards, involving as it would, numerous constitutional questions. Most Americans have access to a broad range of identity documents, from birth certificates to social security cards and drivers licenses, to name just a few. And "legal" aliens have to carry proper documentation.

The idea of some type of amnesty for current illegals warrants sound consideration by lawmakers. After all, many of these aliens, estimated by analysts as between three million and six million people, are now making a substantial contribution to the US through jobs in plants and on farms. To a great extent, many of the factories throughout the US Southwest are virtually dependent on their skills.

We would hope, however, that the commission (and eventually elected officials) will not let timidity or political pressure block a fair examination of the other side of the whole illegal immigration question — finding ways to directly deal with the massive influx across US borders. Some tough decisions will have to be squarely faced.

For example, what should be the proper role of the US border patrol? Is the size and disposition of the force currently adequate to properly fulfill its assigned task? Some critics allege that the force has been cut back in its enforcement duties by a Carter administration that has been overly sensitive to political considerations from the increasingly large US Latin-American community. What sanctions should be imposed against persons found illegally crossing the US border? What should be asked of other nations to help prevent violations of US immigration laws? Should it not be made clear to all that open US borders do not mean uncontrolled borders?

Finally, while generally supporting the idea of penalizing business firms that hire illegals, we would want to ensure that there are clear safeguards for employers in this day and age when "official documents" can be so easily fabricated. Employers should not have to face the threat of criminal sanctions merely because they unwittingly hired illegals who were carrying what seemed to be perfectly legal documents. Also, sanctions must be devised in such a way that employers do not skittishly turn down qualified job applicants because they believe they might be illegals — such as refusing to hire anyone with an accent.

The commission, however, is asking the right questions at this stage of its inquiry and proposing reasonable solutions. Given the fact that as many as a million people may be entering the US illegally each year, and that an estimated 7.5 million Americans are out of work, resolution of the illegal alien issue is long overdue. We will look forward to the commission's final report next year. Followed, we would hope, by decisive White House and congressional action.

The Boston Herald American
Boston, Mass., December 31, 1980

Public discussion of the problem of illegal immigration has been stimulated by reports of the drafting of recommendations by a federal commission that has been studying the problem for the last two years.

That's good, but the tone of much of the discussion strikes us as utterly unrealistic and irrelevant.

There is a common tendency on the part of well-intentioned people to turn a difficult but solvable problem into one that is so enormous that no solution is possible.

Case in point, the argument that nothing can be done in the war against crime until all poverty and ignorance and inequality are eliminated from our society. This ignores the fact that only a small fraction of those born in poverty and ignorance and inequality turn to crime, and that there are practical and workable disincentives that could be adopted to reduce that fraction even further.

The tide of illegal immigration from abroad is a problem of equally unmanageable proportion when it is demanded that a solution must eliminate poverty and overpopulation and underemployment in Mexico. We cannot solve Mexico's economic problems, and the Mexicans would not want us to. After all, they have always refused any offer of general aid from the U.S. government, accepting assistance only for specific purposes, such as narcotic law enforcement. They are a proud people and believe that their country's independence would be threatened by massive aid from the neighboring superpower.

What we can and must do is to see that our immigration laws are brought into line with economic realities in this country and that the Immigration and Naturalization Service and the Border Patrol are given the tools necessary to enforce the laws. The massive flouting of our laws by millions of aliens and citizens of the United States must not continue. It undermines respect for the law, weakens the morale of law enforcement officers and breeds hypocrisy, injustice and social anarchy.

This intolerable problem is one our own representatives in Washington can solve if they will only address it with the necessary courage and the appropriate sense of urgency.

To inject the domestic problems of foreign nations into the debate is simply to evade the issue.

The Select Commission on Immigration and Refugee Policy will submit its final recommendations to the president and Congress by March 1. Thereafter there should be no further delay. The problem has been studied long enough. The time has come for action.

And that action must be to enforce existing U.S. immigration laws or to change the laws so they can be enforced.

The Providence Journal
Providence, R.I., December 2, 1980

Among the major challenges facing the Reagan administration is the pressing need to alter U.S. immigration policy. Though complex and highly sensitive in terms of international relations, the problem is one on which a public consensus already exists, and continued neglect can only worsen a bad situation.

In April, 1977, a Cabinet-level task force handed President Carter a legislative package. Stiff measures were proposed to deal with illegal aliens. As the 96th Congress prepares to adjourn, little has been done beyond giving the chief executive complete discretion on the question of admitting political exiles. The single most important hope that something will be done in the next four years rests with the Select Commission on Immigration and Refugee Policy created by Congress two years ago. Headed by the Rev. Theodore Hesburgh, president of Notre Dame University, the commission is expected to report its findings in March, 1981.

Meanwhile, public opinion seems rigid. A recent Gallup poll found 76 percent in favor of a law that would prohibit the hiring of illegal aliens. In every region, at every age and education level, among both whites and non-whites and white-collar and blue-collar workers the response was overwhelming. Employing aliens who come into the country without proper papers should be against the law.

Such a law would not represent a panacea, but it would be a beginning. Enforcement could be difficult. Although the poll shows strong support for the mandatory carrying of a universal identification card, that provision smacks too much of police-state tactics to warrant congressional approval. Even without that enforcement tool, the mere existence of a federal prohibition subject to fines or jail terms could act as an important deterrent — first, to the employer who seeks to exploit illegal aliens and second, to foreign nationals attracted to this country for economic reasons.

Should regional weak spots in the labor market occur, imperiling perishable commodities for example, temporary work permits could be issued as they are now in some parts of the West and Southwest. For the most part, however, protection for American workers against job competition from illegal aliens ought to have high priority when Congress seeks to bring U.S. immigration policy into line with realities of the 1980s.

Copley News Service

The Evening Gazette

Worcester, Mass., September 23, 1980

● Most immigrants very soon start contributing more in taxes than they take in public services.

● The average family of new-comers is earning more within 10 years than the the average native-born American family.

● Children of immigrants, after an initial disadvantage, tend to over-take the children of native-born families in academic performance, as measured by years of schooling and percentage of children completing college.

These are three of the more star-tling conclusions drawn in studies done by two economists at the re-quest of the Select Commission on Immigration and Refugee Policy, created by Congress to recommend changes in immigration law. The economists are T. Paul Schultz of Yale University and Julian L. Simon of the University of Illinois.

The research seems to argue that America has little to fear from in-creased immigration. This is likely to be much talked about in view of na-tional concern over the recent influx of Indochinese and Cuban refugees, the continuing flood of illegal immi-grants from Mexico and the question-able effectiveness of bilingual educa-tion programs.

The studies are based on a com-puter analysis of data from a 1976 Census Bureau survey of 150,000 families, so they do not include the more recent Indochinese and Cuban refugee groups.

The researchers note that refu-gees commonly take longer to achieve economic parity with native-born Americans than immigrants who are "self-selected" for innate abilty of work motivation. And they say that Mexican and Filipino immi-grants have had more difficulty im-proving their lot in the U.S. than non-Hispanic whites, Chinese and Japanese. But they say none of these considerations is likely in the long run to alter the validity of their con-clusions about the value of immi-grants to the American economy.

Simon calls the average immi-grant "a remarkably good invest-ment for taxpayers." He says immi-grants are "not heavily on welfare or unemployment compensation rolls, as the popular wisdom has it." And he notes that hardly any immigrants are eligible for Social Security until many years after their arrival.

The Schultz and Simon findings are already being challenged. Roger Conner, executive director of the Federation for American Immigra-tion Reform, a group that wants to end illegal immigration and reduce legal immigration, says such studies are often misleading. He says they commonly fail to count the full costs of government services to immi-grants.

Even those who grant that most immigrants soon pull their own weight in America may raise the question as to whether this country any longer has the space and re-sources to take in newcomers as it did during its years of westward expan-sion and industrialization.

The Schultz and Simon studies seem sure to add fuel to what is rap-idly becoming a hot controversy about immigration in this nation of immigrants.

THE COMMERCIAL APPEAL
Memphis, Tenn.,
December 14, 1980

THE PRESIDENTIAL Commission on Immigration Policy, which is nearing the end of a two-year study of that subject, has made its next-to-final report. It hasn't been much help in setting forth policies to guide future administrations.

The commission, which has been head-ed by Rev. Theodore Hesburgh of Notre Dame University, confirms what most of us had suspected. That is, illegal immigration now exceeds the legal. The report says about 700,000 immigrants a year now arrive in the United States legally, while another million may be entering each year illegally.

Sen. Alan K. Simpson (R-Wyo.), who is one of the 8 congressional members of the 12-member commission, blames the large number of illegal immigrants on "utter cha-os" in parts of the immigration enforcement program. That, too, we knew before this study began.

The real question is what the federal government could and should do about the problem.

On that the commission remains badly divided. It spent many hours debating whether to recommend a program that would require every person in the United States to possess a "worker identification" card. Strangely, the opposition to that pro-posal from commission members seems to have resulted not so much from its similar-ity to programs enforced in totalitarian na-tions, as from the fear that the cards could too easily be counterfeited.

The issue still is being debated by the commission, which must conclude its study by March 1.

So as things stand the commission's po-sition is that amnesty should be granted for most of the estimated 3.5 million to 6 million illegal immigrants already in the United States, but that civil and perhaps criminal penalties be imposed on employers know-ingly hiring illegals. The seeming contra-diction in this appears to have escaped the commission thus far.

The commission also proposes that the number of legal immigrants be increased by 180,000 a year for the next five years.

But as Simpson said, too, that will de-pend upon the reaction of the citizens of the nation who already are believed to be suf-fering from what he calls "compassion fa-tigue." He apparently draws that conclusion from the difficulties encountered in placing the recent wave of Cuban refugees follow-ing the entry and placement of large num-bers of Vietnamese. Reports from the South-west have indicated growing concern about the growing number of illegal immigrants from Mexico.

WHAT THE UNITED States can and will do about the problem will depend upon how Congress balances this nation's compassion against the evidence of limited resources. Immigration limitations have existed for many years because Congresses have feared open gates would result in overburdening the economy and perhaps even forcing the nation to reduce still more the amount of foreign aid it now is giving.

There is no way of knowing for sure what increased immigration would do to this nation. But since nobody seems to have found an acceptable and workable way of preventing the illegal immigration we may sometime in the future test that theory by default.

The Courier-Journal

Louisville, Ky., December 13, 1980

IF YOU LIKE RIDDLES, imagine yourself one of the 16 members of the federal commission on immigration and refugee policy. In trying last weekend to solve the problem of illegal aliens, they proposed the immigration equivalent of a fire department without hoses.

Every day, an average of 1,900 persons legally enter the U.S. to live. But an estimated 2,740 others join those already here illegally — a number estimated by the commission at 3 million to 6½ million. The pressure to do something about this illicit flow, especially with 7½ million citizens out of work and unhappy about supposed added competition for jobs, grows stronger by the day.

The federal commission must submit its final recommendations to the president and Congress by March 1. It evidently had little difficulty, at last weekend's interim meeting, agreeing on two major proposals. One was to boost the nation's permanent immigration quota from 270,000 yearly to 350,000. The other was to grant legal status to all illegal aliens already in the country. But a third question was something else again.

What the commission did on that question was vote to recommend civil and criminal penalties against those who hire illegal aliens — a step proposed three years ago by President Carter and earlier approved twice by the House. But like the President, the commission then refused to endorse the one proposal — national work-identification cards — that many people think would be the only way to make the hiring ban work.

That's because, if employers are to be held responsible, they must be able to separate sheep from goats. The commission staff pushed the old idea of tamper-resistant worker identification (or Social Security) cards to solve this problem.

But that proposal, even if the cards could be legally used only when applying for jobs, offends many Americans concerned about government encroachment on personal privacy.

Two study groups say 'no'

The 1977 report of the federal Privacy Protection Study Commission, in fact, recommended that any consideration of universal identity documents be deferred until laws restricting the collection and disclosure of information about individuals have been proved effective. And the Federal Advisory Committee on False Identification in 1976 rejected the proposal on grounds that imposters or counterfeiters would defeat its purpose.

So there's the dilemma — similar to the one faced by the nine states that forbid hiring legal aliens but have found it impossible to enforce their laws. And the dilemma wouldn't necessarily be eased if the commission later broke its deadlock and endorsed the idea of identification cards. Congress hasn't been hot for the idea either, while recognizing the futility of a ban on hiring illegal aliens without some form of reasonably foolproof identification to protect both employers and qualified applicants.

One alternative to a hiring ban, of course, would be a massive increase in the size of the Immigration and Naturalization Service, and especially the Border Patrol. But there is no way to stop all the illegal aliens from slipping through, and our relations with Mexico are not enhanced by making the border look like a war zone.

The Mexican government, meantime has just released the results of a three-year study that downgrades the magnitude of the problem. It says there are only 480,000 to 1.2 million Mexicans residing illegally in the U.S. at any one time. Most of the traffic, says the study, is in males who enter the U.S., spend a few months working and return to their families. But these figures, while interesting, are unlikely to cool immigration enforcement demands by U.S. unions worried about jobs.

For his part, President-elect Reagan is expected to favor another approach, the "guest worker" program. Under it, workers could stay in the U.S. for up to nine months, earning at least the minimum wage in jobs Americans can't or won't fill. They would have full government protection, unlike the exploitive and discredited *bracero* program of the 1940s and '50s, plus medical and unemployment insurance provided by employers. This idea, while opposed by the staff of the federal commission and by many labor unions, has growing support in Congress and the Southwest border states.

Though only a partial solution, the "guest worker" program also would have the great merit of legalizing something that can't be totally stopped anyway. And it would do much more than present programs to improve our relations with Mexico and to fortify the symbolism of the Statue of Liberty.

Until we can do more to solve the problem of illegal aliens, it will be hard to persuade Congress to grant amnesties or raise quotas for the deprived peoples of Mexico, Haiti and other countries in this hemisphere. But there may be effective ways to address the issue that avoid raising civil liberties questions and putting policing burdens on employers. What's important, in a nation founded by immigrants, is that we find something better than a present policy seemingly founded more on fear than on fact

The Morning News

Wilmington, Del., December 13, 1980

There is nothing much wrong with America's immigration law. What is wrong is inability, or unwillingness, to enforce the law.

There are many legal ways to enter the United States. People can come as tourists, business visitors, students, refugees and as immigrants planning to work and live here. For each of these categories, there are regulations. But not enough is done to ensure their observance.

Tourists and short-term business visitors, for instance, can outstay their visa time. Once they have come in through the passport lines at airports, harbors or on highways, no one checks that they leave again when their visas run out. For persons holding student visas, the controls are not much better, as the difficulty of tracking down Iranian students has made clear.

In addition to having no reliable followup for legal entrants, the immigration service has been unable to stem the flow of persons entering this country illegally, mostly from Mexico. Once these secretive border crossers are within the United States, no good mechanism is in place for identifying and deporting them.

The undocumented aliens (the current euphemism for illegal residents) number in the millions. There is increasing concern over their presence for several reasons. With unemployment high there is fear that illegal residents take work away from Americans. There is worry that these unwanted residents stimulate unrest. There is resentment that public education and other services cannot be denied them.

The immigration law cries for firmer enforcement. The Select Commission on Immigration and Refugee Policy, whose final report is due on March 1, is heading in that direction. On the one hand, its recommendations would widen the legal entry route by increasing the number of persons who can be admitted as immigrants. On the other hand, the commission would make it a crime for employers to hire illegal aliens. So far, the commission has said little about strengthening border patrols — woefully undermanned at present — or of finding ways to ensure that short-time visitors actually do depart.

But if the employment question were firmly settled, these other problems would diminish. Life in the United States without an opportunity to earn money is not an enticing prospect. Strict enforcement of work rules would add credibility to our immigration law. And it would put us on an equal footing with other industrialized nations, all of whom regulate strictly the employment of foreigners.

Chicago Defender
Chicago, Ill., January 14, 1981

The United States, a nation of immigrants — and of the original black population unwillingly brought here as slaves, has always had the problem of how immigration should be handled, and in recent decades it has become more of a problem.

Employers have often wanted workers from other lands who would labor for small pay and compete with established American workers. In recent years, the question of migrants from Latin American countries, especially Mexican farm workers, has become an acute interest to the already established citizenry.

Now the Select Commission on Immigration and Refugee Policy, created two years ago by Congress to thoroughly study the nation's immigration law and practices, has decided, by a narrow margin, to recommend that this country develop a "secure system" that employers could use to verify that persons who apply for jobs are in this country legally. It was approved by 8 to 7, with one abstention.

It isn't known yet what this "secure system" will be. But, apparently, there is in the works some kind of tightening up on who is entitled to stay in the country legally. It is an issue of importance to all who labor.

Roanoke Times & World-News
Roanoke, Va., January 4, 1981

One of the meanest problems facing the United States also is the least-solved problem: immigration. A commission studying the subject is certain to recommend an increase in the annual number allowed legally.

The estimates of "illegal" entries vary widely but none is less than a million a year. Reputable scholars see waves of people, especially from Central and South America, coming into the United States during the decade of the 1980s. Do we want them? Are we able to absorb them? Can we even determine who is a legal immigrant and who is not?

Americans have gotten themselves into a box on the questions: The 1960s' psychology of guilt that absorbed the country has created the logic that the only people who have a right to be in the United States are Indians. That being true, any other immigrants have an equal right to enter a land where everybody's ancestors were immigrants. Why should Americans be so snooty, anyhow? And greedy, to boot!

If there is a respectable past here, if there is a culture and anything that can be praised as "American," the innocent questions invite suicidal answers. The United States produces about 40 percent of the world's gross product; should it, therefore, absorb 40 percent of the world's population?

That would be more than two billion people.

The answer is no more out-of-line than the question. Today's America-haters, escapees from the 1960s, constantly are throwing around figures about American greed that lead to such questions and such answers.

If a national consensus should be reached on the annual immigration increase permitted, there would still be other hard questions. Are we prepared to accept a system wherein everyone would be required to maintain a "work permit," so that the legal immigrants can be distinguished from the illegal ones. But if we are not prepared for such a great departure from tradition, must we not be prepared ineluctably to accept as hopeless any attempt to limit, guide or control immigration?

A Select Commission on Immigration and Refugee Policy is due to report to Congress in March of 1981. It is headed by the Rev. Theodore Hesburgh, president of Notre Dame University; its personnel seems to be of at least average distinction and the staff appears to be well qualified. Its report will be an important document, possibly a landmark appraisal. But it will be truly useful only for those who are willing to follow their opinions to the logical conclusions. Soft thinking on this question will be just as dangerous as narrow thinking, and even less welcome.

THE PLAIN DEALER
Cleveland, Ohio, January 17, 1981

Action by the Select Commission on Immigration and Refugee Policy has moved the United States a step nearer to much-needed clarification and revision of its alien affairs procedures.

The commission is winding up a study of almost two years duration designed to suggest how to deal with problems such as setting quotas for various classes of immigrants, and dealing with undocumented workers — that is, illegal aliens. A final report is to go to Congress in March.

The 16-member commission was almost unanimous in voting to recommend enactment of penalties against employers who knowingly hire illegal aliens. Congress always has avoided the issue before, but the strong 14-2 vote by the blue-ribbon panel for sanctions should convince lawmakers that it is an idea whose time has come. It has been pointed out that enforcement of such a law might be hindered by the difficulty of proving intent, but it also seems reasonable to expect that the prospect of arrest and prosecution could be a deterrent to many employers of illegals.

One of the more controversial issues with which the commission has had to grapple is national identity cards, and it came to no clear-cut decision. Without a secure means of identifying who is or not an illegal alien, employers could not be held responsible for whomever they hire, the argument goes. The counter-argument, which The Plain Dealer has supported, is that a national identity card creates too many civil liberties risks. The commission voted for a "more secure form of identification than now exists," without specifying what it would be — but only by 8-7 with one abstention. By 9-6, with one abstention, it said that "at least some form of identification now in existence, or combination of identification now in existence, should be used." This would seem to be the preferable course, but the subject needs to be fully aired in congressional hearings.

Wide-open discussion also is needed of, among other questions, the commission's conclusion that illegal aliens already living in this country —an average of estimates of their numbers is about eight million — should be given blanket amnesty, and President-elect Ronald Reagan's guest worker plan, which organized labor opposes.

Congress should take up these questions as soon as possible after it has received the commission's report. The result should be a just, coherent reformulation of immigration policy.

Oregon Journal
Portland, Ore., January 19, 1981

Considerable opposition is being roused against the report by the Select Commission on Immigration and Refugee Policy, which is to be presented to Congress and the president on March 1 in final form.

For the past one and one-half years, SCIRP has held public hearings, let contracts for appropriate research and consulted with many who deal with the problems of immigrants. However, no consensus was reached by the commission. Most votes were split, and the commissioners, though attentive to their work, were unable to form an integrated policy to deal with future immigration.

The lack of a clearly defined immigration policy in these sensitive times may cause serious social and economic consequences, according to testimony given at the SCIRP hearings by those who must deal with immigrant and refugee problems on a daily basis.

The chaos of the dumping of Cuban boat people by Fidel Castro is dramatically implanted in the minds of Americans. On the one hand, the dreadful circumstances of the trip could not help but inspire pity, but on the other hand, somber thoughts and misgivings about providing jobs and housing for the crush of helpless humanity.

The commissioners approved sanctions against employers who hire illegal immigrants, increased enforcement of immigration laws and suggested a legalization program for illegal immigrants now in the United States. They ignored the problem of how to find resources to provide implementation.

No wonder there will be criticism of the report.

the Charleston Gazette

Charleston, W. Va., March 21, 1981

IF YOU ASK an American to name the issues that cause him concern, he probably would include the rush of illegal immigrants across our borders.

In the past, it was difficult to discuss illegal immigration. American policy was tied to the invitation on the Statue of Liberty. Now, however, there is general acceptance of an awkward fact: the economy cannot tolerate an endless stream of new citizens ill equipped to support themselves.

Sen. Edward Kennedy says the report on the Select Commission on Immigration and Refugee Policy is "the most significant and thoughtful study" of immigration in three decades. Our reading of an edited version permits us to agree that the study is a thoughful one. Whether it can be of much help to Congress is open to question.

The commission proposes that the ceiling for legal immigration be raised from the present 270,000 a year to 350,000 a year.

It would increase the budget and staff of the Immigration and Naturalization Service.

It recommends, with a narrow vote, penalties against employers who hire illegal migrants, coupling the penalties with "some system of more secure identification."

Each of these major recommendations is calculated, in our view, to keep congressmen awake at night with worry over how their constituents might react.

Increasing the number of immigrants allowed to enter the U.S. legally may strike Americans as a curious way to deal with illegal immigration. It is a farfetched analogy to be sure, but some would surely say that it is like lowering the crime rate by legalizing bank robbery.

Providing more money to the Immigration and Naturalization Service sounds reasonable. But it would take an enormous increase in manpower just to patrol the long border with Mexico, and these are times when constituents are demanding thrift of their representatives.

There's nothing wrong with the proposal to penalize employers who knowingly hire illegal migrants, but that brings up the related recommendation for identification. Since it is unlikely that an illegal immigrant would present himself for an identification card, his illegal status could be determined only by the lack of identification. This means some kind of national identification system, at the mention of which many Americans bristle.

The recommendations are in the hands of a Congress which, conceiveably, could come up with acceptable alternatives. At any rate, the problem remains a sticky one, and we don't envy congressmen who must attempt to solve it.

The Boston Globe

Boston, Mass., March 13, 1981

If Congress follows the recommendation of the special federal commission on immigration and refugees, most of the estimated 5 million illegal aliens now in the United States would become legal immigrants.

It is a sensible recommendation. Coming at a time when there are demands for more restrictive policies, it is also a courageous one. The one-time amnesty would be a good starting point for redrafting the entire Immigration and Naturalization Service codes, which are outdated and ineffective.

The commission, working under the chairmanship of the Rev. Theodore Hesburgh of Notre Dame and the direction of Lawrence Fuchs of Brandeis, studied immigration problems for two years before making its recommendations. It supports a slight increase in immigration quotas for the next five years, combined with better border patrolling and a tightening up of the visa system.

In the past five years, 2.9 million foreign nationals legally immigrated to the United States. Nobody knows how many immigrated illegally during that period. It is known that thousands are being exploited in a subterranean network of sweatshops, migrant farms, back alley factories and middle-class parlors.

The commission said, correctly, that such exploitation is having "pernicious effects," creating an underclass that is beyond the protection of laws and that is depressing US work standards and wages. Hence the idea of bringing them, wholesale, out of the cold.

The report was equivocal about the need for a uniform national identification system that could be used to eliminate uncertainty about citizenship status. Many civil libertarians are queasy about such a system. Without it, however, there can be no effective enforcement of criminal statutes that should be passed to prohibit employers from knowingly hiring illegal aliens. There should be a simple means for identifying legal residents of the United States. Social Security registration may be a useful base for such a system; if it were used, however, its conversion into a national identification program should be specifically noted and mandated by Congress.

President Reagan supports easing the movement of temporary workers between Mexico and the United States. Simply opening the border between the United States and Mexico, an option the President likes, is not the answer. It would eliminate the need for border patrols, but there would then have to be a way to monitor South and Central American nationals who would funnel through Mexico to find temporary work. The Immigration and Naturalization Service is so badly funded that it does not have a tracking system to back up a temporary work permit system. Without being able to determine that cross-border workers returned home at a predetermined time, an open border would not only exacerbate the Southwest's immigrant problems, it would spread them throughout the nation. Currently, the Immigration Service does not even have a workable way to monitor the thousands of people who enter the country on tourist and student visas, many of whom simply overstay their permits and become illegal immigrants.

The development of a new immigration and refugee policy should be a national priority. Needed now is an official Reagan reaction to the report — along with new budget recommendations — so that the congressional subcommittees will know how much maneuvering room they have to revamp the codes.

Houston Chronicle

Houston, Texas, February 19, 1981

We have long maintained that offering amnesty to illegal aliens, aside from being bad policy, would be impractical: There are too many phony documents available and no way to assure the person was in this country before a certain date. Those are practical concerns in a strict sense of the term, but apparently this matter of practicality also takes on an Alice-in-Wonderland atmosphere.

In order for an amnesty program to be successful, according to a respected private authority on immigration matters, the government would have to threaten illegal aliens with adverse consequences if they did not accept the offer. It is a mind-boggling thought, the United States of America trying to coerce people into becoming legal residents.

We do not quarrel with the gentleman's conclusion. He is David S. North, director of the Center for Labor and Migration Studies in Washington, who has studied past amnesty programs offered in various other countries (which had minimal success), and whose research has been used by the Select Commission on Immigration and Refugee Policy in coming to conclusions similar to North's. That presidential commission plans to shortly recommend a sweeping amnesty for illegal aliens. North may be quite correct that if an amnesty program is to succeed, in the sense of getting many to apply, it would have to be an expensive effort in both time and money and would need to include "a meaningful combination of the stick and the carrot." In other words, something unpleasant is threatened if an illegal alien doesn't apply for amnesty.

What shocks us is the very idea of proposing, or embarking on, a program which could lead to such a ridiculous situation as this country trying to force its privileges and rights on someone.

The Washington Star

Washington, D. C., March 4, 1981

As everybody knows by now, the immigration problem is a tangle of logical impasses, ethical paradoxes and practical near-impossibilities. The federal commission that has just completed a two-year study on immigration and refugee policy is considerably clearer about that than about what can be done to make sense of the situation.

The trouble, of course, is that so many people want to come to this country. They are fleeing poverty and/or political oppression. Some of them manage to come in legally but far more slip in unauthorized.

Anybody who has seen the crowded refugee camps of Florida knows that the sheer numbers — and they keep growing — are an important part of the problem. For example, immigration officials caught 11,792 El Salvadoreans trying to get into the United States in the fiscal year ending in September. Four years ago, there were fewer than 8,000. Furthermore, it is estimated that for every person the INS apprehends, four or five get across the border undetected.

Legal or illegal, the newcomers need food, housing, jobs and community services. Optimistic analysts like to point out that the illegals, most of whom quickly become part of the nation's underground economy, give more than they get. Neither social security nor welfare is available to them and they do the menial work nobody else wants to touch.

Even the legal aliens cost the host society less than they contribute to it. Because so many of them are young and single, they have less need of medical care, schools or aid to dependent children than a cross-section of the native population. And their presence creates jobs as well as filling jobs.

As last year's Miami upheavals demonstrated, though, not everybody recognizes this. Whatever the statistics say, the presence of the Cubans in Florida has been seen as a fresh deprivation for blacks.

Besides, there are undeniable injustices to the immigrants themselves. Many pay large sums to illegal groups to get them into the United States. Once they are here, without legal status or unions, they are not protected against exploitation by employers who see them as open to virtual serfdom. The treatment of undocumented migrant farm workers is legendary. Recently, too, there have been ugly stories about little sweatshops cropping up in Manhattan where women who don't speak English sit at sewing machines under conditions recalling the Triangle Shirtwaist factory of long ago.

The commission recommends an amnesty for illegal aliens now in the United States — an estimated 3 to 6 million people. It further recommends expanding the quotas for legal entrants, plus tighter controls to discourage further waves of unlawful immigrants. These controls include vigilance at the borders and penalties against those who hire illegal immigrants.

It's a good try and some of the proposals, if adopted, should help normalize life for many people who have fled to the United States. But, for the American government, all too many dilemmas remain.

Nobody likes the idea of identity cards for workers or armies of federal investigators checking employers' payrolls for suspect labor. Nobody likes the idea of driving away people who ask for political asylum or a chance to escape painful living conditions. And nobody wants to turn the Statue of Liberty into a guard whose message is "Keep out."

Yet some or all of these measures may end up on the national agenda, simply because the alternatives are less desirable still. Among the disturbing aspects of the situation is the fact that, short of putting up some kind of reverse Berlin wall, no one knows how to keep the aliens out.

Cooperation from other governments might help, but, in most cases, it's unlikely to be forthcoming. A larger INS staff might help, too, but at considerable cost in opportunities for real and imagined abuses as well as in money. There are already reports of people pressured into accepting deportation without much attention to either their rights under American law or the dangers and deprivations they will return to.

In the end, there are likely to be more compromises than clean-cut solutions. And on most specific points, the best choice is likely to be the bad against the worse.

THE SACRAMENTO BEE

Sacramento, Calif., March 4, 1981

The Select Commission on Immigration and Refugee Policy issued its final report, a 453-page document, after more than two years of exhaustive study, testimony and debate. The result is a well-balanced, if not perfect, proposal based on a four-pronged policy of better border enforcement, employer sanctions, amnesty for illegal aliens and larger immigrant admission quotas. But no sooner did the commission give birth to the report than members turned around and virtually declared it stillborn.

Twelve of the 16 panelists issued dissenting supplementary opinions. Among them was the chairman, Father Theodore Hesburgh, who criticized the commission for failing to support a counterfeit-proof identity card to prevent the employment of illegal aliens. They also included California Appellate Court Justice Cruz Reynoso and Rose Matsui Ochi, who blasted the document as a "sham." It was no surprise then when President Reagan let it be known he would be unavailable to accept the document.

Expectations of the commission's role were far different in 1978 when Congress created the panel. Its members — drawn from the Cabinet, Congress and the private sector — were to forge a consensus for solving the country's vexing immigration and refugee problems and bring order to archaic and conflicting laws. That difficult task completed, the commission was then expected to shepherd its document through the opposition and win support for it among its constituencies. Instead, the commission fell into the same dissension that divides the nation. In the process, it seriously jeopardized its proposal, which, although it may not please everyone, at least offers an evenhanded, humane policy and the best hope of resolving otherwise intractable immigration problems.

With its two-year effort in disarray, the commission also opened the door for politicians to enter with legislation that returns us to a "guest-worker" program. A Republican-controlled Senate and White House are likely to support such a program, which U.S. businesses have been advocating. Its basic flaw is that it looks only at the economic benefits while ignoring the need for a rational system of legal and fair immigration. There's no evidence to suggest that bringing back a bracero program will even slightly impede the flow of undocumented workers or reduce the growing exploitation of aliens.

Whatever disagreements exist over specific items of the commission's document, its fundamental thrust remains sound. For any immigration policy to be successful, it will have to include the four points the Hesburgh commission set forth in its report: border enforcement, employer sanctions, amnesty and realistic admission quotas. To ignore them is to prolong the problems that surely will sow the seeds of ethnic and economic backlash and even greater immigration problems in the future.

Hesburgh Panel Delivers Final Report

The Select Commission on Immigration and Refugee Policy, chaired by Rev. Theodore M. Hesburgh, delivered its final report Feb. 26 to President Ronald Reagan and Congress. The 16-member committee said in its 453-page report that U.S. immigration policy should focus on "family reunification, economic growth consistent with protection of the United States labor market and cultural diversity consistent with national unity." The commission recommended raising immigration limits to 350,000 a year from 270,000. The panel asserted that a "modest increase" in legal immigration would benefit the U.S., noting that 30% of American Nobel prize winners were immigrants. The commission added that there should be "no total cap or ceiling" on the combined number of immigrants and refugees. [See 1980, pp. 1448-1453]

The panel acknowledged that "some immigrants do compete with United States workers for jobs, particularly in times of high unemployment." It recommended serious steps to stem the flow of illegal immigrants, estimated at 3.5 million to six million. Amnesty for illegal aliens already in the U.S. should be considered only in connection with improvements in controlling future entry into the U.S., the report said. The commission gave qualified approval to a "slight expansion" of the "guest worker" program, in which 30,000 aliens worked in the U.S. each year on a temporary basis.

The commission recommended improving coordination among the Immigration and Naturalization Service and other government agencies to control border movements of people and contraband, particularly narcotics. It also recommended penalizing employers who knowingly hired illegal aliens, but the panel split on the question of a national identification system. By a narrow margin, it recommended "some system of more secure identification" of legal residents, but it made no specific suggestions.

The Star-Ledger

Newark, N.J., March 7, 1981

It is not surprising that the nation is uncertain as to the number of illegal aliens living and working in many urban centers.

The Immigration and Naturalization Service, which is supposed to keep track of foreigners in the United States, has little knowledge of even those who are in the country lawfully.

The House Committee on Government Operations has reported that INS offices are unable to cope with the flood of refugees and that records are in a hopeless mess. Mail is unanswered for weeks. Telephones ring unanswered. Offices are jammed with long lines of immigrants, many seeking citizenship, unable to get answers for their questions.

When President Carter wanted to penalize Iranian students for provocative actions, the INS was unable to say how many were in the United States or where they are located.

INS personnel have long complained that manpower is inadequate to deal with the stream of Latin Americans crossing the Mexican border illegally.

Administrative and housekeeping chores seem similarly understaffed. The clerical collapse is a hardship for everyone. Now that Congress has had the problem defined, it should act to provide a remedy — better funding and more manpower for the agency.

Los Angeles Times

Los Angeles, Calif., March 1, 1981

The most noteworthy feature of the final report of the Select Commission on Immigration and Refugee Policy was the lack of consensus among the commission's 16 members.

The commission was appointed more than two years ago by former President Carter to recommend the reform of immigration laws and practices. Its membership was made up of eight members of Congress, four key Cabinet officers and four distinguished private citizens. The fact that these influential Americans could not reach agreement on many aspects of the complex and emotional immigration issue is not surprising. It is merely a reflection of how difficult immigration reforms will be to legislate and to make effective. But dissension on the select commission is no excuse to put off action any longer, for, even if Congress were to begin acting right away on its recommendations, many of the reforms would not go into effect until 1983.

Like everyone else interested in immigration problems, we agree with some of the commission's recommendations and disagree with others.

The commission recommended an amnesty for illegal immigrants in the country as of January, 1980. This is a generous amnesty, and Congress should not delay adopting it. Every day that passes will make the cutoff date seem less attractive to the illegal immigrants it is designed to bring out of hiding.

The commission recommended that enforcement to limit the continued flow of illegal immigrants into the United States be concentrated at the Mexican and Canadian borders, and at major ports of entry. This would be a more efficient and humane approach than trying to track down illegal immigrants already here by pursuing them into their homes, neighborhoods and places of work.

The commission also recommended sanctions against employers who knowingly hire illegal-alien workers. But only one dissenting member of the commission, the Rev. Theodore Hesburgh, president of Notre Dame University, went a step further and suggested basing the sanctions on the use of a secure, counterfeitproof Social Security card as a universal identifier for all workers. Such a system would be costly to establish, but we are persuaded that only such a card, which would have to be shown by all job applicants, could make employer sanctions workable and nondiscriminatory.

Enforcement of new employer sanctions should be linked to stricter enforcement of the many worker-protection laws already on the books, such as minimum-wage and health-and-safety regulations. Enforcement of these existing laws would not necessarily dry up the jobs that entice many foreign workers to enter the United States illegally, but would at least insure that the exploitation of those workers could be kept to a minimum.

Congress and the Reagan Administration should now proceed with their own deliberations on the immigration issue, using the select commission's findings and recommendations as useful guidelines.

TULSA WORLD

Tulsa, Okla., March 5, 1981

PRESIDENT Reagan says he is considering a rather simple answer to the problem of illegal entry into this country by Mexican aliens: let them in legally.

Critics will find plenty of objections to this idea. But, as far as we know, none has come up with a faultless solution or even a better solution.

For one thing, controlling the illegal immigration has proved to be an impossible task. Given that impossibility, wouldn't it be better to accept reality and settle for immigration controls that can be reasonably enforced?

Reagan also pointed out that emigration from Mexico is a necessary economic pressure valve for our neighbor to the South. Even if we could find a way to stop the flow, it would outrage the Mexican Government and the Mexican people.

Maybe it's time to face facts in the immigration problem, and adopt some kind of program that will work.

Just about anything would be an improvement over the present intolerable, uncontrolled influx of illegals.

Des Moines Tribune

Des Moines, Iowa, March 6, 1981

U.S. immigration policy needs an overhaul. Every year, hundreds of thousands of foreigners enter the country illegally, and there is debate about how many legal immigrants can be accommodated.

The Select Commission on Immigration and Refugee Policy has just provided a 453-page answer to these questions. Its central conclusion, as summarized by Chairman Theodore Hesburgh, is that the United States should move toward "closing the back door to undocumented/illegal migration" while "opening the front door a little more to accommodate legal migration in the interests of this country."

Unfortunately, cracking down on illegal immigration won't be easy, with an estimated 3.5 million to 6 million illegals already in the country and no real estimate of how many more come in every year.

To close this "back door," the commission called for a crackdown on employers who hire illegal aliens (they are not now subject to prosecution) and a strengthening of the Border Patrol.

The most important, yet most controversial, recommendation was for some form of "secure identification." The commission was unable to agree on what form such identification should take: a Social Security card more resistant to counterfeiting than present cards, or a computer system that employers could call to check on job applicants.

There is a proper concern that some identification systems would infringe on the U.S. concept of civil rights, but identification of aliens (and, necessarily, of everyone else) is an issue that must be confronted if the problem of illegal immigration is to be dealt with realistically.

The commission recommended amnesty to most illegal aliens already in this country by the time an identification system went into effect.

As for the "front door" of legal immigration, the commission recommended that the United States admit 650,000 immigrants annually for the next five years, a moderate increase over the average number during the past five years. The commission believes that this country can never again afford to "become a land of unlimited immigration."

The commission's report goes to Congress, which probably won't endorse every detail, but which ought to honor the spirit of the report by trying to place immigration policy on a more rational basis.

Detroit Free Press

Detroit, Mich., March 6, 1981

THE HEAVY flow of illegal immigrants into the United States has left politicians quivering, labor unions resentful, many ordinary citizens concerned and the country without a workable policy. A federal study commission now has offered proposals that, on the whole, are sensible, humane and realistic — if the Reagan administration wants solutions.

The "if" must be acknowledged, principally for two reasons: controlling illegal immigration will cost money, and it will be unpopular among employers who are exploiting the illegals or at least benefiting substantially from the influx.

Permitting massive back-door entry into the United States has heavy social costs. It encourages violation of the minimum wage and occupational health and safety laws, and it generates disrespect for law in general. It depresses wages in some areas and poses public health hazards. And because of the heavy volume of illegal entries, the level of legal immigration must be curtailed.

Who are the illegals? Probably less than half are Mexicans, who cross the border easily without detection. Other large numbers come from Jamaica, the Dominican Republic, Haiti, El Salvador, South America and some Asian countries. Census Bureau researchers estimate the total number at between 3.5 and 5 million.

The new federal report is the most thorough and thoughtful one done on the subject in decades. It was issued by the Select Commission on Immigration and Refugee Policy, headed by the Rev. Theodore Hesburgh, president of the University of Notre Dame.

The commission proposed a moderate increase in the level of legal immigration. Assuming a normal flow of about 50,000 refugees, the total suggested by the commission would be about 650,000 in each of the next five years, compared with about 580,000 in each of the past five years.

It also suggested a temporary amnesty during which illegals already here might come forward without penalty under rules established by Congress that might include a requirement for continuous residency here for a designated period.

The most difficult decisions are related to illegals who find jobs in areas, such as the Southwest and California, that depend heavily upon their work. Those workers now face penalties if they are caught but those who knowingly employ them, except for farm labor contractors, do not. The Hesburgh commission proposed that the employers be subjected to civil and criminal penalties.

That brought the commission to a tough civil liberties question: how to enable employers to identify illegals without resorting to worker identification cards for everyone. Half the commission thought the answer may be to create counterfeit-resistant Social Security cards. Other commission members saw that as smacking of a police-state identification system for all citizens and came up with what seems to us a better idea. They proposed a computerized call-in system that would enable employers who are doubtful about the legality of workers they are hiring to check on them in the same way bearers of credit cards often are checked.

The commission's study should not be set aside because of immediate costs or political timidity and fear of employers who might be affected. The problem of illegal entry is likely to grow. It reflects unhappy conditions in countries not far away: conditions that the United States, in its own self-interest at least, should try to alleviate. Even with that, though, the country simply must find a better way to regulate immigration. The Hesburgh commission has given us significant help in finding the right approaches.

THE  SUN

Baltimore, Md., March 11, 1981

The U.S. does not have an illegal immigrant problem with Canada. Daily, thousands of Canadians and Americans cross the border back and forth to work, visit or conduct business on either side of the border. Is such an arrangement possible with Mexico or other countries south of the border? The question underscores the economic aspects of the problem.

Illegal immigration is a growing concern for the U.S. simply because countries like Mexico, Jamaica, the Dominican Republic, El Salvador, Haiti or South American nations like Colombia cannot provide enough jobs for their people. So the pressure for survival drives their citizens here in search of work. Any attempt by the U.S. to develop a long-range solution for the problem that is not related to economic development throughout the region will again collapse as badly as present immigration policy.

The presence of a common border between Mexico and the U.S. will also require that "illegals" or undocumented workers be given special consideration in the development of new policy. As President Reagan has acknowledged, the most appropriate solution for Mexi-

cans might be creation of a "guest worker" or a two-way visa program.

On the whole, though, the need to overhaul U.S. immigration laws is long overdue. A special panel headed by the Rev. Theodore M. Hesburgh, president of Notre Dame University, performed a valuable service by conducting a comprehensive study of the problem. One of its most pertinent findings is the extent of which illegality compounds itself. Undocumented workers, lacking legal standing, become victimized by employers who hire them at substandard wages and violate occupational safety laws. Smuggling people across borders is also a frequent occurrence.

The commission's three-part program for addressing the problem is a worthy initiative. Better border controls, penalties against employers who hire illegals and the legalization of certain undocumented aliens already in the country could reduce the problem. Increasing the annual numerical immigration limits might help. But until people south of the border are as economically secure as those to the north, the immigration system will always be subject to huge pressures.

The Courier-Journal

Louisville, Ky., March 4, 1981

SHARP DIFFERENCES of opinion in the newly released report of the Hesburgh Commission on immigration have led many to dismiss the group as a failure — a product of exaggerated expectations and blown opportunities. If the report, which President Reagan studiously avoided recognizing, has any value, it's only as an outline of routes for seeking future consensus.

The Select Commission on Immigration and Refugee Policy was created, by an act of Congress, largely to stave off demands for policy decisions. Those demands followed a 1977 White House proposal to grant amnesty to substantial numbers of aliens, then to clamp down border controls and introduce a tough ban on the hiring of "illegals."

One by-product of establishing the commission was political. By asking the commission to file a report by early 1981, Congress assured that neither Edward Kennedy nor Jimmy Carter would be compelled to address the burgeoning problems of migration and refugees in the 1980 campaign.

The combination of a slow approach and too many high-level members, including four members of Congress, filled the final report with evasions.

Commission members *did* agree on the soundness of the basic Carter approach. They approved the idea of granting amnesty to about 4 million of the estimated 6 million resident, undocumented aliens. And they agreed immigration quotas should be liberalized — in effect, to fill a labor-market gap left when border patrols were bolstered and employers' recourse to illegals was outlawed.

But the commission "punted" on two issues: It failed to acknowledge the ineffectiveness of the Immigration and Naturalization Service, Washington's most downtrodden bureaucracy. The Service and its Border Patrol clearly need more money and people.

And the commission reached no consensus on the sensitive issue of giving businesses a way of identifying legal residents, the better to obey the strict ban on employment of illegal aliens. There was vague talk of establishing an official list of possible identifiers, ranging from birth documents to Social Security cards to alien registration papers, but little agreement that this approach would work. Several dissents by commission members made the civil-liberties case against creating a new identity card.

There was one new idea. Former Labor Secretary Ray Marshall suggested giving employers a toll-free number for checking a central registry — the same principle used in checking credit-card purchases. But this, while avoiding the potential police-state abuses of an ID card, would only open another can of worms: centralized memory banks whose Big Brother possibilities are only beginning to be recognized.

In this, as in other aspects of its work, the commission's achievement was limited to calling fresh attention to an international economic and social problem that can't be shelved. Help may be coming from another quarter, now that the Mexican government has said it would like to negotiate a joint approach to migration and border problems. The report could come in handy when President Reagan opens a two-part April meeting with President Lopez Portillo of Mexico.

This is the one slightly positive note of the three-year exercise: the United States has in effect admitted it can't solve the migration problem on its own. It will, presumably, need the help of others. This could make the meetings in Tijuana and San Diego next month a refreshingly honest demonstration of Mexican-American interdependence.

Roanoke Times & World-News

Roanoke, Va., March 6, 1981

For millions of people, the American Dream — upward mobility, economic betterment — lies in tatters today. But for millions of others who live elsewhere, this remains the land of opportunity. If they cannot get past the lady who lifts her lamp beside the golden door, they find entrance elsewhere.

Some 160,000 of them — Cuban and Haitian refugees — flocked to U.S. shores in small boats last year; this country bent its rules and let them in. They were the tip of an iceberg; only heaven knows how many illegal aliens are in the United States. One estimate is from 3.5 to 6 million. We don't know the number; we don't know, either, the effect, good or bad, these people have on the economy. But there's a growing conviction that the nation needs to grapple with the problem they represent.

A 16-member advisory commission, chaired by the Rev. Theodore M. Hesburgh, president of Notre Dame, recently presented a 453-page report with recommendations on the illegal alien situation. In his words, it suggests "closing the back door to undocumented/illegal migration" while "opening the front door a little more to accommodate legal migration in the interests of this country."

Under the commission's plan, 650,000 people would be admitted as legal immigrants in each of the next five years, compared with an average of 580,000 a year for the last five years. It proposes a one-time amnesty for illegal aliens already here; to take advantage of it, they would have to declare themselves.

Under current law, illegal aliens can be arrested and deported; such roundups, putting people back across the border, go on all the time, and some persistent aliens wind up in a shuttle between the United States and Mexico. But except for farm labor contractors, there's no penalty in U.S. law for employers who knowingly hire such illegals. By an 8-7 vote the commission called for penalties, along with an unspecified "system of more secure identification."

There was no immediate reaction from the Reagan administration. Carrying out these recommendations (which include better border and internal controls) would cost money, and the Immigration and Naturalization Service is among agencies under the budget ax. Maybe that's the way it must be. But cutting government spending isn't always the answer; as a means of improving the economy, it seems doubtful strategy if one result will be leaving that back door ajar to thousands who'll enter to compete illegally with American citizens for jobs.

The Pittsburgh Press

Pittsburgh, Pa., March 3, 1981

The Select Commission on Immigration and Refugee Policy, established by former President Jimmy Carter, has made its long-awaited report after two years of study and hearings.

Two of its key recommendations can readily be supported. One should be vigorously opposed, and — at best — the rest are of doubtful merit.

There is no question, for instance, about the need to beef up the Immigration and Naturalization Service's undermanned and underequipped Border Patrol. The commission recommends about $50 million to $60 million a year in additional funds.

Since at least half the estimated four million to six million illegal aliens in this country have slipped across the Mexican border, curbing this inflow must be a first priority.

★ ★ ★

Coupled with that, the commission's call for civil and possibly criminal penalties for employers who knowingly hire illegal aliens deserves support. This would be difficult to enforce, short of some kind of tamperproof identification card for everyone (an idea the commission rejected). But the lack of such a law only encourages the continued recruitment — and exploitation — of illegal workers.

However, the commission also recommends an amnesty for all illegal aliens who had lived in the United States before Jan. 1, 1980, for a period to be determined by Congress. This should be opposed.

It would be a reward for the violation of this country's immigration laws, an insult to would-be immigrants who have patiently waited for legal admittance and an open invitation to a new wave of illegal entries in anticipation of another amnesty one day.

★ ★ ★

In light of the nation's current economic situation, it also seems inadvisable to increase present annual immigration quotas from 270,000 to 350,000, with an additional 100,000 for five years to clear up the backlog of people waiting to join relatives in this country, as the commission recommends.

The United States already admits more immigrants — not including an annual 50,000 political refugees outside the quotas — than the rest of the world combined. The "Golden Door" must never be shut but there is a limit to how far it can be opened.

Conspicuous by its absence in the commission's report is one other idea worthy of support. And that is to work with Mexico and other Latin countries, which are the chief source of illegal aliens, to help them develop economic opportunities for their people so that the United States is no longer such a lure to them.

THE BLADE

Toledo, Ohio, March 6, 1981

IT is premature to assume that the thousands of hours the Commission on Immigration and Refugee Policy spent attacking its subject will go for naught. But it is obvious that many of its proposals to alter the Federal Government's methods of dealing with illegal immigration are going to be discarded or reworked by the Reagan administration.

A few hours after the commission, appointed by former President Carter, unveiled its final report, President Reagan announced he was appointing his own task force, consisting of four cabinet officers, to restudy the problem.

Such a step was to be expected when a commission named by a Democrat submits a report to a Republican president — or vice versa. Nevertheless, there are several recommendations that deserve critical attention from the new Administration.

Most important, the group recommended that penalties imposed on employers who hire illegal aliens should be coupled with "some system of more secure identification." The Blade has supported civil and criminal penalties for those who hire illegal aliens, especially those employers who demonstrate a pattern of such activities. And there is also a need for some kind of universally recognized identity card which would be an improvement over such easily counterfeited forms of identification as birth certificates and high school diplomas.

Under normal circumstances such a mandatory identification system would be repugnant. But with the Census Bureau now estimating between 3.5 million and 6 million aliens residing unlawfully in the United States and with millions of Americans unemployed, more drastic measures are in order.

Within the confines of the Reagan administration's scaled-down budget, firm steps should be taken to curb illegal immigration. It is up to Mr. Reagan's panel to cull the best of the commission's proposals and present its own recommendations to Congress.

THE DENVER POST

Denver, Colo., March 5, 1981

A CHILDREN'S game called "rock, paper, scissors" has players simultaneously show their fists either clenched (rock), flat (paper) or with middle and index fingers extended (scissors.) The rule is paper covers rock, scissors cut paper, rock blunts scissors, so the competitors can spend all day trying to outguess each other.

Well, play prepares children for life, and exceptionally gifted "rock, paper, scissors" players can go on as adults to staff blue-ribbon committees studying U.S. immigration policy. For a decade, such studies have done little but dispute previous studies without resolving the issue.

This time, of course, it was supposed to be different — but then, it's always supposed to be different. The U.S. Select Commission on Immigration and Refugee Policy was created three years ago by Congress as the putative commission to end all commissions. It contained eight Congressmen, four Cabinet members and four presidential appointees.

Well, as usually happens, most of that political firepower was too busy with other duties to pay much attention to the commission, which was dominated by its staff. The staff, alas, was torn by internal dissension. Then, when the big names saw the conclusions, they started squabbling — because of the same political pressures that caused the commission to be created to take the heat off Congress in the first place. Some commissioners couldn't even agree that illegal immigration is a problem for the United States. Others couldn't agree about what to do with illegal aliens already here. In short: Another round of paper covers rock.

But amid the ruins of the commission's study are two points so inescapable that even a blue-ribbon panel couldn't overlook them. First is the fact that most illegal aliens come to this country to get jobs and therefore the way to control illegal immigration is to see that employers don't hire illegal immigrants.

Second, before employers can be penalized for hiring illegal aliens, there must be a simple and effective way for employers to determine citizenship.

By a 14-2 vote, the commission accepted the notion of sanctions against employers of illegal aliens. But it could muster only 8-7 in favor of a more fraud-resistant ID card such as an improved Social Security card. Others favored former Labor Secretary Ray Marshall's plan for a "call-in data bank" where employers could check a would-be worker's status.

The first method is superior since a national ID card could simplify a lot of other things as well. But some nervous liberals foresee it as a precursor to a police state — though European and Asian societies as democratic as our own use national ID cards. If that's really a worry, then the Marshall approach would work also — the key thing is to get off the dime.

Then, with illegal immigration controlled, we need a better system for *legal* aliens — such as the guest worker program in Germany or the old *bracero* plan in the United States. That would protect foreign workers against the kind of exploitation they now endure from some employers who simply report them to the authorities if they resent being cheated — while allowing rational regulation of both our permanent immigration pool and seasonal labor demands.

It's a pity it took three years and all that money to simply underscore the obvious. But the game now moves to Congress where Wyoming Sen. Alan Simpson heads the Senate immigration subcommittee and Romano Mazzoli of Kentucky leads the House counterpart. We've got particular confidence that our neighbor Simpson is in a mood to substitute an equitable order for the present chaos in U.S. immigration policy. But please, no more studies. The rock-scissors-paper game in immigration is getting old.

THE PLAIN DEALER

Cleveland, Ohio, March 6, 1981

Current U.S. immigration policy amounts to this: It works well enough among prospective citizens who play by the rules and wait their turns; it works virtually not at all among aliens who slip illegally across the nation's borders, and who then mainly are harbored by employers who exploit them.

The need for new immigration procedures has been evident for some time, and for two years a Select Commission on Immigration and Refugee Policy studied the problem. The commission sent its final report to Congress and the White House recently.

It is a working document; that is, while making a number of specific recommendations, it discusses but leaves unanswered some sticky questions, chief among them what kind of system might be adopted to allow employers to identify legal workers.

The commission rejected a system of national identity cards, a decision in which we concur. As we have said, such a system poses dangers to civil liberties. We also are not persuaded that such cards could be made counterfeit-proof, as has been claimed. The commission did say that some form of identification should be adopted. But it did not recommend a specific document, such as a driver license.

The commission recommended that employers be prosecuted for hiring illegal aliens. We support the suggestion. While it could be difficult to enforce under current conditions, it should have some deterrent effect.

And it would have more than that if commission recommendations to strengthen the Immigration and Naturalization Service were approved. But such a revitalizing of the stretched-thin INS does not seem likely in today's cost-cutting Washington.

One of the major questions at issue is whether some 4.5 million to 6 million aliens already residing illegally in the United States should be given amnesty as a part of new law. The commission, a bipartisan group, agreed that they should. We will have to be convinced of that by testimony in congressional hearings.

It is less than encouraging that President Reagan, the same day the commission reported its findings, appointed a new task force to go over the same ground. Congress has before it the commission's report, and while it certainly will want administration input, it should not wait any inordinate amount of time for the new presidential review. The timetable for finally coming to grips with immigration problems should be measured in months, not years.

THE INDIANAPOLIS NEWS
Indianapolis, Ind., March 9, 1981

In four preceding editorials *The News* has provided information and illustrations of what many authorities call the third most threatening economic problem — with social ramifications — facing Americans. After inflation and energy, they say, comes illegal aliens.

The subject is so complex that editorials — even five of them — can barely brush the surface; what is even more challenging is to treat a subject objectively about which there is so much disagreement. For two years a Federal commission has grappled with it, with hardly a clean pin-down. And that commission descends from a long line of such think-teams, dating back to President Nixon.

The News has reviewed many of the unused deposits from such groups and found them distinguished mostly by their strident viewing with alarm. We are reluctant to join the shrill chorus, but the evidence becomes more compelling every day. We have tried to do the essential homework;

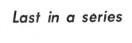

Last in a series

we have visited the front; we have faced all directions and returned to report as fairly as possible. From all sources and from a pile of contradictory evidence and arguments, we feel confident in relaying these conclusions:

• Illegal aliens are displacing American citizens in the work force to an alarming degree. The mythology has it that they perform work that "Americans won't do." There is some truth here, of course, but illegals from around the world are in well-paying positions which Americans would eagerly accept if they had a chance.

• Hundreds of employers are taking advantage of undocumented workers, mostly Mexicans, in order to cut labor costs and to have personnel who "work hard and don't cause trouble." "Causing trouble" often means joining unions.

• Thousands of illegal aliens are drawing welfare and Supplementary Security Income payments, but the majority — above 60 percent — are paying Social Security taxes from which they will never benefit and having state and Federal taxes withheld. In spite of all this, the Immigration and Naturalization Service estimates that illegal aliens constitute at least a $16 billion tax burden on the system.

• Because of the high birth rate of most aliens — epecially Mexicans — the United States is headed toward a bilingual society with all of the attendant problems and costs. The Mexican "invasion" is somewhat different from other immigrant populations because of proximity to its cultural base and the easy movement back and forth across the borders.

There are hundreds of nuances and sidebars, but these four conclusions stand out. Anyone sensitive to such trends will share the concern that fundamental American procedures and principles are vulnerable to these alien penetrations. This is not another case of heating up the "melting pot" again. The pot is boiling over. It can not be cooled down by "requiring" a new counterfeit-proof identfication card or by hiring additional guardians of the border. All such schemes will be as effective as moving the jello with a fork.

What should, then, be done? Again, space constricts the range, but here are two recommendations at the top of the list:

Overhaul both the immigration laws and the service that administers them.

These twin challenges cannot be accomplished overnight or unilaterally. They must be achieved within the framework of bilateral discussions with Mexico. After this investigation, we are convinced that there is nothing the U.S. can do to keep all the Mexicans out. The starting point is that a number of Mexicans will be admitted under controlled conditions and that those admitted will not have to hide in the sewers any more. Approaching the border task in collaboration with Mexico does not preclude the necessity of the U.S. getting its borders under control. Techniques for doing this need not be belabored here.

Mexico must be persuaded of U.S. sincerity and of the mutual benefits accruing from both the U. S. and Mexico restoring order and control to their migrant populations.

Mexico has labor, gas, oil, minerals. The U.S. has capital and technology. It makes sense to collaborate, even at some temporary sacrifice to both sides. The U.S. must cease its paternalistic attitude toward Mexico, and Mexican leaders must be persuaded to stop blaming all their problems on the "colossus to the north." The Mexicans should draft a long-term compact with the U.S. for supplying much of the latter's energy needs in return for capital and technology — and also assistance in rehabilitating the villages and farms from which many of the illegal aliens come.

Against the broad canvas of refugees, aliens — including students — and undocumented workers, Mexico stands out because its wave is overpowering. The Immigration and Naturalization Service cannot handle it; its impotence was illustrated in its handling of a few thousand Iranian students. The first step, then, to be taken by the Reagan administration is to make that agency vigorous and well-staffed backed up by law and technology. At the same time, talks must begin with President Lopez Portillo along the lines we have suggested. This is a high priority issue which can not be postponed much longer.

Democrat and Chronicle
Rochester, N. Y., March 18, 1981

RATHER OVERLOOKED in the nation's concentration on economic concerns has been the final report delivered recently to the president and Congress by the Select Commission on Immigration and Refugee Policy.

Essentially, the commission called for stricter enforcement measures against illegal aliens, a one-time amnesty for most illegals, and a "modest increase" in legal immigration.

If some of these recommendations seem contradictory, they are if they're considered separately. Together, they make some sense.

For example, the commission emphasized that its plan for legalizing the status of illegal aliens is vitally contingent on improvements in the enforcement of immigration laws both at the borders and inside the United States. Without such improvements, it said, the amnesty "could serve as a stimulus to further illegal entry,."

The commission did not question the value of immigration as a force for economic growth and cultural enrichment, pointing out, for example, that 30 percent of the United States' Nobel laureates were immigrants. Although the commission recognizzed that some immigrants do compete with U.S. workers for jobs, particularly in times of high unemployment, it did not make a major issue of this.

THE CRUX of the whole immigration question is the growing number of people who enter the country illegally and who make a shambles of our immigration policies. Although they could not agree on how to do it, commission members were emphatic in saying that some way must be found to identify illegal workers.

It also drew attention to one glaring omission in the law. At present, illegal aliens can be arrested and deported, but the employers who hire them knowingly cannot be punished, excpt under a special law that covers only farm labor contractors.

To end this anomaly, the commission said that employers hiring undocumented workers should be subject to civil and criminal penalties.

If such penalties can be coupled with what the commission described as "some system of more secure identification," runaway illegal immigration can perhaps be brought under control. Until it is, the U.S. has no rational immigration policy at all.

National ID Cards Suggested to Combat Illegal Aliens

When word of the Select Commission's discussion of worker identity cards reached the press in July, a storm of controversy erupted. The panel split sharply over the proposal, which would require that everyone applying for a Social Security number furnish proof of citizenship or legal residence in the country. The applicant then would be given an identity card carrying the bearer's photograph. During 1980, problems such as separating legal from illegal Iranian immigrants in the U.S. and absorbing the influx of Cuban and Haitian refugees gave rise to serious consideration of an identity-card system. However, there was fear that the cards would facilitate government intrusion of privacy and control of individual movement. Opponents argued in addition that no matter how well the cards were designed to thwart forgeries, there would always be the danger that they would be tampered with.

THE COMMERCIAL APPEAL
Memphis, Tenn., December 7, 1980

We oppose a suggestion that the federal government issue national identity cards to U.S. citizens. The potential for abuse of such a system is much greater than any benefit that might be derived.

Cards initially would be issued to the nation's 110 million persons in the labor force, and would function as work authorization permits. But it is obvious to us that they soon would become the primary means of personal identification for all those purposes that driver licenses, for example, now serve. So it would not be long before everyone in the United States — some 120 million more people than are in the work force — would have to have similar identity cards. It could become a cradle-to-grave system with frightening overtones.

The system, of course, along with the information required from individuals to get a card, would be computerized. A bureaucracy would have to be created to manage and administer the system. And with so much personal information available to so many people, the implications for civil liberties are ominous.

All information in other government computers on individuals no doubt would be keyed to their national identity card numbers, for clarity and ease of recognition, of course. That could mean tying in the Internal Revenue Service, Defense Department, Social Security Administration, FBI, passport office or any other of the myriad federal offices that for any reason might have a file on a person.

We all have seen from time to time how easily computer banks can be invaded for information.

As for the cards themselves, they are said to be tamper-proof and counterfeit-resistant. But given their importance, we have absolutely no doubt that ingenuity and greed would combine to put forgeries into the marketplace quickly. Theft of legitimate cards for street sale would become attractively profitable.

That would undermine the primary purpose of the cards, which would be to keep illegal aliens from taking jobs away from American citizens. But the illegal alien question goes far beyond the simplistic answer represented by identity cards. A policy on whether the illegals should be controlled under guest worker laws, or whether more stringent statutes against them should be enacted, needs to be formulated. Whether employers should be prosecuted — and how vigorously — for knowingly hiring illegals needs to be worked out.

The Select Commission on Immigration and Refugee Policy is meeting this weekend to decide what it will report to Congress about national identity cards. It should recommend against them. The potential abuses are too great, the possible damage to civil liberties too risky.

THE PLAIN DEALER
Cleveland, Ohio, December 14, 1980

IF at least one of the recommendations from a commission studying illegal immigration is heeded by Congress and the Reagan administration, some inroads might be made in coping with the flood of illegal aliens entering the United States.

Although the General Accounting Office, for example, recently concluded that prospects were poor for stemming the alien tide, the Select Commission on Immigration and Refugee Policy has proposed specific ways to attack the problem.

Among its proposals are civil and criminal penalties for employers who hire illegal aliens, especially those who demonstrate a "pattern" of such hiring. This would not only discourage Mexicans and other Latin Americans from coming here illegally, it also would limit severely the low-salaried bondage into which many illegal immigrants are thrust.

The commission's recommendations, however, do not go far enough. The federal group failed to endorse a plan to require all U.S. citizens to carry identification cards. In its place it agreed that employers should insist on additional proof of identity, such as birth certificates and high school diplomas. That position ignores the fact that such documents are easily falsified. A universally recognized identity card would be preferable.

The Blade argued earlier this year that under normal circumstances such a mandatory identification system would be repugnant. But with several million illegal aliens living in the United States — neither the Census Bureau nor the Immigration and Naturalization Service can provide anything resembling an accurate estimate — American citizens are losing jobs and federal benefits as a result. If the practice continues unabated, sterner measures will indeed be required.

When the commission issues its final report in March, the opportunity will be at hand for President Reagan to support measures to bring about a crackdown. An employment law and perhaps a national identification-card system would prove more desirable than the costly steps that would need to be taken to physically seal off the nation's borders.

The Houston Post

Houston, Texas, December 11, 1980

The proposal has reared up again — government identification cards for the nation's work force. This time it is recommended by the staff of the Select Commission on Immigration and Refugee Policy. Under the staff plan, as drawn up for consideration by the 16-member commission, all job applicants would be required to present an identification card showing their citizenship or immigration status. The proposal is in response to a national problem that admittedly cries for a solution. But there must be a better way.

Rightly enough, the commission staff was trying to find a way to prevent discrimination against American citizens who may be turned down for a job because they look or sound foreign. Also, the plan was held out as a way to help employers determine whether a job applicant is an illegal alien. Civil and criminal penalties against employers who knowingly hire illegal aliens are provided in the recommendations. As noble as the aims may be in protecting minority citizens and foreigners residing legally in the United States either on a permanent or temporary basis, the suggested system would bruise the rights of the majority.

·The potential for abuse and the consequences of error are too great. When a person enters the work force for the first time, he or she would be required to complete a form, swear to its accuracy and the employer would send a copy to the appropriate government agency and keep a copy in the company files. Some of the information would be stored in government computers. The staff sought to allay possible fears that the information might be made available to other government agencies or private interests for various uses.

It said rules against such a practice should be included in the program. But the ease with which confidential government documents are leaked almost routinely causes one to wonder about the integrity of such a data bank. In addition, a work card system would create a whole new branch of bureaucracy costing an initially estimated $2.7 billion for the first 15 years. It would also add to the paper work burden of business and industry. If Congress thinks draft registration was a sticky issue, just wait until it hears the protests over registering for work permits.

THE DAILY HERALD

Biloxi, Miss., December 9, 1980

The Select Commission on Immigration and Refugee Policy has turned down a staff recommendation to issue work identity cards for every person eligible to work in the United States. The idea behind the worker ID card was to help enforce immigration laws.

We've said before that the idea of enforcing immigration laws is commendable, but the method of issuing worker ID cards to every American worker to help catch some illegal workers smacks too much of the tactics more common to totalitarian governments than of our democratic society. Apparently, the study commission shared that view and tossed out the worker card.

The commission did recommend making it a crime for an employer to hire illegal immigrants. This is a better approach to solving the problem that results from illegal immigrants planting deeper roots through their employment. Nor is it unfair to place responsibility on the employer. We suspect that in the majority of cases of employed illegal aliens, the employers not only know of the illegal status, they often exploit the workers in various ways.

Too many reports of such exploitation have surfaced in recent years, particularly of migrant farm workers, to be ignored. The human misery this exploitation creates should not be allowed to continue.

Another commission recommendation is to legalize the status of one million or more illegal immigrants who were already in the United States before the start of 1980. If that recommendation is implemented, it would be a public admission of past failures to enforce immigration laws. No one argues that the immigration laws have been successful, though there is disagreement on the number of illegal aliens already in the country.

As a matter of policy, the commission wants the permanent immigration quota increased by 80,000 people per year, plus adding 100,000 people to the quota each year for the next five years. The latter quota increases are designed to clear up a backlog of applications.

One-fourth of the 80,000 quota increase would be designated as general worker applicants, a new category that would permit aliens to enter the U. S. temporarily to work at specific tasks when the Secretary of Labor determines their services are needed because of a lack of available Americans. The general workers would return to their homelands when their permits expired. This provision would be an improvement over the current "wetback" practices that have prevailed along the Mexican border areas.

The panel's recommendations now go to the president and to Congress where they may be adopted, rejected or amended.

CHARLESTON EVENING POST

Charleston, S.C., December 5, 1980

In a recent report to the Congress, the General Accounting Office said that prospects for controlling illegal immigration into the United States are poor and the costs of doing so would be formidable. The various agencies cannot even agree on how many illegal aliens are living in this country: the Immigration and Naturalization Service has estimated four million, but some Census Bureau estimates say more than five million.

We agree with the GAO that to try and seal the borders of the United States as a means of controlling illegal immigration would be very expensive. (Though the Russians have succeeded in doing so with their much longer borders.)

Something we think might be helpful is an expanded use of the Social Security identification system. When the cards were first issued, the law was quite restrictive concerning their possible use in a national identification system. Some feared such use. But that's exactly what has happened, gradually, over the years. All bank accounts, investments, etc., are tagged somehow to the individual's Social Security number, so that IRS computers can more readily track the income flow. The military's service numbers were supplanted by the nine digit Social Security number years ago. And the world hasn't come to an end.

It would ease the illegal immigrant problem if applicants for federal and state programs (and perhaps job seekers) were required to produce an identification card. The familiar nine digit Social Security number could also be used for national automobile license plates, bank accounts, charge cards, etc. Instead of remembering or recording dozens of numbers, there would be only one.

Of course there are those who would see this as another encroachment on privacy by Big Brother. But in the long run, the benefits easily should outweigh the costs.

The Des Moines Register

Des Moines, Iowa, August 4, 1980

A determined person can readily evade laws that establish personal identity for legal purposes. The most far-reaching issue involving that consideration is the question of illegal aliens. A special national commission on immigration and refugee policy is studying the question and will make its recommendations to Congress next spring.

The Rev. Theodore Hesburgh, commission chairman, has stirred controversy by advocating that all citizens and legal aliens carry special work identification cards. The idea has split the commission.

The most publicized civil-libertarian concern is that a required universal work ID card could end up as a national police passport of the kind that many other countries have had but Americans always have abhorred. Such a passport could lead to ideological and political harrassments having only the flimsiest connection with controlling illegal aliens.

Less publicized, but also a justified concern, is the matter of what would happen to those illegal aliens who have avoided detection, who have established their homes and families here. Would required ID cards amount to a government-imposed, almost *ex post facto* requirement of self-incrimination? Are they to be uprooted and expelled summarily from the country that has become their home?

But there are civil-libertarian and humanitarian arguments on the other side of the question. In Iowa, immigration officials estimated last December that there were at least 6,000 Mexicans living illegally in the state. Many were smuggled here in demeaning conditions, exploited in dirty jobs and sometimes employed to frustrate legitimate unionization efforts.

Without an effective worker ID system, it is impossible to require better conduct on the part of unscrupulous employers. They can claim they did not know that their employee was an illegal alien. There is no law against employing such persons, anyhow.

Before the worker ID requirement comes anywhere near to enactment, potential abuses should be pondered fully — and so should the possibility that, without such cards, there may be no way to have an effective immigration policy or to protect adequately from degradation and exploitation those who come to America seeking a better life.

The Idaho STATESMAN

Boise, Idaho, December 12, 1980

A truly bad idea has been proposed as a step in dealing with the problem of illegal immigration into the United States. The idea is to issue worker identification cards to U.S. citizens. The rationale is that illegal immigrants would be found out when they failed to produce the cards upon request.

The idea comes from the staff of President Carter's Select Commission on Immigration. Its practical effect would be exactly what San Diego immigration activist Herman Baca claimed after learning of it. "In practice," Baca said, "it will be the Chicano-Latino community whom employers and law enforcement agencies will be asking for ID cards."

To date, undocumented workers have had little trouble obtaining documents. If steps were taken to require workers to carry cards, unscrupulous printers would start cranking out imitations.

Beyond these considerations is the regimentation inherent in the government's issuance of work cards to U.S. citizens. Since when did U.S. citizens have to carry a card from the government in order to obtain work?

The answers to the illegal immigration problem are what they always have been: criminal sanctions against U.S. employers who knowingly hire illegal aliens and a program to allow aliens to work at jobs U.S. citizens won't take. Because of the power of business lobbyists and the AFL-CIO, those steps aren't easy for politicians to take. All the cards in the world won't change that fact.

The Virginian-Pilot

Norfolk, Va., August 9, 1980

The Select Commission on Immigration and Refugee Policy rightly suspects that a work-identification system—probably a forgery-resistant Social Security card—would be the most effective barrier the United States could raise against illegal immigration.

Most aliens illegally in this country come in search of jobs and find them. Most labor at tasks that Americans shun. How many are exploited—underpaid, exposed unlawfully to industrial hazards—is anyone's guess. For the illegals necessarily keep a low profile to frustrate the Immigration and U.S. Naturalization Service.

A tough work-identification program would put employers on the spot, especially if Congress legislated stiff penalties against the hiring of cardless workers. Some civil libertarians denounce such an arrangement as a gratuitous restriction on freedom. They deplore the identity papers customary in European countries and other lands.

But what's new about employers being given employes' names and Social Security numbers? What's menacing about a forgery-resistant card—an innovation that would answer the counterfeiting of cardboard cards?

Social Security numbers are already widely used. They assure correct identification of taxpayers, motor-vehicle operators, military personnel, bank customers, and beneficiaries of medical policies. Many persons mark their property with Social Security numbers as protection against theft and as an aid to the police if it is stolen. Where is the threat to personal freedom in such practices?

Stemming illegal immigration is a national priority. Census Bureau studies put the total of illegals at 3.5 million to 6 million, depending upon U.S. economic conditions. Roughly half of these are from Mexico.

More illegals are the prospect, unless something is done. Half of Mexico's 72 million inhabitants are under the age of 15. Ten million school-age Mexicans are not being educated because of lack of teachers and classrooms. Some 2 million persons enter the Mexican job market annually; that is, in a society that creates but 500,000 new jobs each year. Mexico's jobless rate is 20 percent, the rate of underemployment equally high. Little wonder that many job-hungry men and women stream across the border to the U.S.

A work-identification system could retard that flow. Congress would balk at legalizing the millions of illegals already here absent a credible guarantee that the flood could be contained. Electrified fences and beefed-up border patrols are necessary but clearly inadequate to the challenge.

America is the promised land for much of humankind. But with 8 million U.S. unemployed, the promise obviously cannot be bright for all. We are poorer for lack of immigration and refugee policies that balance the desperate needs of millions beyond America's boundaries against the desperate needs of those inside. The Select Commission on Immigration and Refugee Policy is expected to recommend answers next spring. A work-identification system should be part of the package.

The Courier-Journal

Louisville, Ky., July 4, 1980

THE LINGERING PROBLEM of what do about illegal aliens in the United States is compounded by the current recession and by the latest influx of refugees from Cuba and Haiti. Americans worried about their jobs tend to be cool to "open door" immigration. And they can be downright hostile to proposals that an estimated six million Mexican "wetbacks" and other illegal entrants be granted amnesty and allowed to stay.

A proposal for a limited amnesty for aliens who have found jobs and made homes in the United States was endorsed by the Justice Department in the Ford administration. The idea was taken up by President Carter while campaigning among Hispanic-Americans in 1976.

Once in office, Mr. Carter continued to discuss the idea. But it became entangled in such related questions as border security, the U.S. commitment to refugees everywhere in the world and our tangled economic relations with Mexico.

So a Select Commission on Immigration and Refugee Policy was appointed to study the major hangup, which is how to assure that a continuing flood of illegals wouldn't start the problem all over again after the amnesty took effect.

Meantime, the gulf has widened between stringent border-security efforts and Washington's hands-off policy on border-crossers who successfully enter.

In all this, the economic role of the illegal alien and the Mexican immigrant in particular is disputed. Some economists say they are tolerated, especially in the Southwest, because the illegals take unpopular jobs and pay much more into Social Security than they can risk seeking in benefits. Others say the U.S. will need more immigrants during the next two decades to compensate for a falling domestic birthrate that means fewer workers entering the job market.

Possibly so. The presidential commission has surveyed all these questions. But it considers them secondary to the need, never confronted by Congress, to straighten out our policy on "illegals."

Everyone concedes that it's impossible to solve this problem at the Mexican border; many "wetbacks" slip through for every one caught by the U.S. border patrol. Attention has shifted to attacking the problem from another angle — cracking down on employers who find it profitable to ignore state hiring laws and exploit illegal workers.

The House of Representatives has twice passed a bill outlawing such hiring. But the Senate has not acted, in part because it is unclear how such a crackdown would be enforced.

One solution might be to prohibit hiring any worker who cannot show a government-issued identification card certifying citizenship or status as a legal alien. But this has been attacked as a totalitarian-like threat to civil liberties, an invitation to unending police "sweeps" for illegal workers. Few could look forward with pleasure to life in a *1984* society of constant challenges to produce one's papers.

But the idea of controlling immigration mainly in the workplace is attractive, if the civil liberties objections can be met. That's why a form of work card is now supported by the Rev. Theodore Hesburgh, the noted civil-rights advocate. Father Hesburgh is chairman of the Select Commission, which is to report early in 1981.

He argues that, as a practical matter, Congress would never grant amnesty to illegal immigrants without some foolproof method of identification.

One possibility could be to start with the Social Security card, a document that could be reissued to all current workers in a form extremely difficult to counterfeit. (Those with alternate forms of pension protection, such as state and federal employees, have had to get similar identification numbers in order to submit tax returns. Presumably they would be issued cards, too.)

Such a system would pose the inconvenience of having to produce a card to apply for a job. But it would not have to be carried at other times. And those who fret about the information in Big Brother's computers should be minimally disturbed by a change that merely establishes that the card-holder is a citizen.

One further objection sure to come up in the Hesburgh commission report and in Congress is the efficiency of the Immigration and Naturalization Service, which supervises legal aliens. The service is a nearly unique bureaucracy, so slow-moving that even Griffin Bell attacked it while, as Attorney General, he was technically its boss. A house-cleaning seems overdue.

It's also likely. Refugee and illegal-alien problems have become a growing national issue. So the new Congress could well be ready to make far-reaching changes in policy — including the worker-card solution if it seems likely to ease, at last, the dilemma of unchecked illegal immigration.

America, as we remind ourselves on this Fourth of July, became great in part because it is a melting pot and a haven for the oppressed. We can't afford to change that. But "open doors" cannot mean that anybody, for whatever reason, is automatically entitled to instant admission — no questions asked.

The Evening Gazette

Worcester, Mass., July 9, 1980

"Stop! Show me your papers!" bark the security guards, the police officers, the employers, hospitals, airplane ticket-sellers.

It's an image called to mind when thinking of totalitarian states or doom-and-gloom futurist novels. The internal passports, work cards and identity cards issued in Europe reflect the old continent's sad old tradition of government regimentation.

But not here. Or will it be?

The Select Commission on Immigration and Refugee Policy, a 16-member federal study group, is considering recommending that all American workers be issued identity cards, complete with photograph and some personal information, probably not including address.

The idea is to combat the problem of illegal aliens. Employers would check identity cards before hiring anyone, and it would be illegal to hire undocumented aliens. No card, no job.

Another idea of the commission, in case the identity cards idea runs into too much opposition, would be to have all workers' names entered on a computer system, with employers required to check the list before hiring to see that the applicant is here legally.

It's like shooting a horse because its saddle is on crooked.

Yes, illegal aliens are taking jobs. Yes, illegal aliens work for low wages and poor benefits, afraid to complain lest they be discovered.

But ID cards? No.

American life is already more regimented, controlled and spied on than we like to admit. Social Security numbers are being used more and more often for identification, such as drivers' licenses which are used as ID cards in many circumstances. But identity cards with photographs would be a giant goose step backwards.

In totalitarian states, work cards are taken from those the government doesn't like, and the victim's productive life is ruined. With identity cards, Big Brother can find out quickly and efficiently where each of us is and what we are doing.

The cards don't make a country totalitarian; they just provide the means — and temptingly easy means — to effect more government control than we have now.

Because so many current illegal immigrants are Spanish-speaking, Hispanic-Americans, legal residents, would be subjected to the discriminatory harassment of being asked over and over again to prove they are here legitimately.

The problem of illegal immigrants must be dealt with through proper and relevant laws enforced by sufficient numbers of border guards and investigators. It isn't an easy task and the work probably never will be done perfectly.

But the idea of work cards goes against the American grain. It is a dangerously misguided approach.

THE INDIANAPOLIS STAR

Indianapolis, Ind., July 3, 1980

Even if a strong case can be made out for requiring a national "work card," there is something off-key and chilling about the idea.

Attorney General Benjamin Civiletti said the other day he favors requiring Americans and aliens in this country to carry a "work card" in order to apply for a job.

He noted that the proposal had raised fears among Hispanic and civil rights groups. But he said limited measures should be taken to control the employment of illegal aliens in the United States.

Civiletti said he would recommend "a very simple work card . . . one which contains a limited amount of information," so as to safeguard Americans from unequal enforcement or intrusions into privacy.

"I personally am not concerned about adding another card, similar to my driver's license, to the many which I already carry," he said. "However, I am sensitive to the fact that many Americans are concerned and fearful of what is sometimes erroneously referred to as a national identity card and the privacy implications of such a document."

It is certainly true that a great many Americans carry so many cards — identity, driver's license, membership, credit, courtesy, pass, union, Social Security, birth certificate, voter registration and the like — that their billfolds come to resemble small briefcases and are quite unwieldy.

But the mere fact that they are overcarded is not grounds for burdening them with still another card.

A "work card" might help detect illegal aliens. In many cases, it might not. ID cards are easily counterfeited. In fact, the false ID racket flourishes in *barrios* and other ethnic quarters.

Use of an existing type of card would seem more practical. Persons who do not drive are still eligible in most states to get license-type cards for ID purposes.

The simplest and most efficient method would be the use or modification of the Social Security card that already serves as a "work card" required for regular employment and which is now issued only upon proof of U.S. citizenship or lawful admission as an alien.

Aside from the threat to privacy, the obvious question remains: Is this card really necessary?

The Detroit News

Detroit, Mich., July 16, 1980

Orwellian fears are blocking efforts to use the Social Security card as a means of identifying illegal aliens.

And no wonder. The use of internal identification papers has acquired a certain aroma because it is so highly favored by totalitarian countries.

Still, something has to be done to detect illegal aliens, and the Select Commission on Immigration and Refugee Policy, a federal study group, thinks the Social Security card could be the key.

The commission favors a requirement that applicants for a Social Security card produce citizenship documents, and also favors the adoption of a new tamper-resistant card (similar to the new "green card" issued this year to legal aliens).

Further, the commission is considering a law that would make it a crime to hire illegals.

Nobody knows how many unlawful immigrants are in the country. Some estimates range up to 12 million. The Census Bureau puts the figure between 3.5 million and 5 million. They are, in the words of Labor Secretary Ray Marshall, "a permanent underclass, outside the protection of our laws."

But how can society deny the illegal alien a job without infringing on the liberties of other citizens?

Restraint must prevail, and safeguards against abuses must be written into the law. No one should be allowed, for example, to ask for the card unnecessarily, as a means of harassing persons who look or sound "foreign." Requests should be confined to the workplace.

The country doesn't need or want the kind of identity papers used by totalitarian states. But a good case can be made for the Social Security card as a simple and reliable piece of worker identification.

Job applicants should have to prove they are in the country legally, and employers should have the right to ask for a document that says so.

The Providence Journal

Providence, R. I., July 15, 1980

One of the easy answers to the problems raised by thousands of illegal aliens in this country is the current proposal to require identification cards for all workers, including citizens as well as aliens. Such a proposal means that to keep track of possibly several million illegal aliens, everybody in the country would be put to the inconvenience and the dangers of a pervasive system of control.

Immigration officials obviously are having difficulties dealing with the wave of illegals who have been filtering into the country, mostly from Mexico, lured by the hope of jobs and improved income. Advocates of identity cards argue that without proper indentification, illegals would be unable to get work. Thus they would be blocked from taking jobs that otherwise might go to citizens or legal aliens.

Forgery-proof cards — perhaps glorified Social Security cards, with pictures and laminated to prevent tampering — are suggested as the method for proving identity. That would mean everyone of employable age in the country would have to carry such a card, nearly 200 million of us.

Social Security numbers are used today for keeping track of workers' earnings, contributions to the system and tax withholdings. They are used by some organizations, such as banks, credit bureaus and hospitals, for coding in automated data systems. But no one is required to carry a Social Security card. And, anyway, the standard card is easily reproduced or forged.

Civil rights defenders are quick to bristle at any suggestion of curtailing traditional American freedom from government surveillance of any kind. Studies in other connections have consistently rejected the idea of a national identification system — in 1971, 1973, and 1976. In addition, the Privacy Protection Study Commission, presidentially appointed, recommended against a "standard universal label for individuals" until privacy safeguards had been enacted into law.

If illegal aliens are, in effect, underground now, a stricter system to sift them out might only drive them further underground. They would then be forced to try new schemes to get fake cards or to get jobs outside the Social Security and tax systems entirely.

Employers who suspect new workers can always check with the Social Security system. In some areas of present-day American society, the illegal aliens do perform the least desirable kind of work, which is shunned by most legitimate workers. So it may be better to leave a kind of no-man's land in the labor market, to act as an equalizer.

At any rate, the millions of American citizens who value their personal freedoms should not be penalized in the efforts to control a relatively small group of aliens who have evaded the immigration laws. Identity cards for all would be another step toward the all-pervading government of George Orwell's book *1984*. Let's not make that prophecy come true in the very year it targeted for its warning.

The Chattanooga Times

Chattanooga, Tenn., March 3, 1981

The staff of the Select Commission on Immigration and Refugee Policy has revived an old controversy by recommending that the nation's workers be required to carry government identification cards. The suggestion is an effort to deal with a persistent problem — illegal aliens in the work force — but the ID card proposal is weighted down with shortcomings.

Under the staff's plan, all job applicants would be required to present to potential employers an identification card that bears their citizenship or immigration status. The measure, it is explained, is designed to help employers avoid hiring illegal aliens, and also contains penalties for employers who deliberately violate the law. But the proposal is a virtual invitation to abuse; worse, the possible results of error are awesome.

Upon a person's initial entry into the nation's work force, he or she would fill out the identification form and swear to its accuracy. In the paperwork tradition, the employer would retain a copy for his files and forward the original to the government, where some of the information would be fed into computer files. As a hedge against abuse of the information, the commission staff recommended safeguards to prevent the data from being released either to other government agencies or to private concerns.

That concern is commendable but somewhat naive, considering how easily confidential government information is leaked nowadays. Why should we expect the data bank for employee identification cards be any different?

More troublesome yet is the paperwork that would be created. The commission staff speculated that maintaining the identification card system would create a massive bureaucracy, the cost of which was estimated at nearly $3 billion for the first 15 years. But of course that figure not to increase. Finally, there is the enormous burden of paperwork that would be thrust upon business and industry.

The problem of illegal aliens' effect on the nation's work force is complicated; no easy solutions are in sight. But the recommendation by the Select Commission's staff carries the potential for more problems than the one it seeks to solve.

The Hartford Courant

Hartford, Conn., March 8, 1981

Bureaucrats in Washington occasionally have suggested a national identity card as a new way to discourage illegal immigration. If every American citizen has an identity card, it would be easier to flush out those immigrants, goes the argument.

The French experience with identity cards illustrates how easy it would be to abuse such a system, once it is established. Every French citizen is required to carry the card, without which he or she cannot marry, vote, get a passport or even receive registered mail. The registration system now has been computerized, ostensibly to combat crime.

This modernization allows police to conduct identity checks on the spot. A law is being formulated to actually authorize police to conduct such checks. Anyone without an identity card may be detained for six hours.

National identity cards do not belong in free societies.

A registration system is usually proposed with the best of intentions, but once established, the temptation to use it for non-intended purposes becomes great. Use turns into abuse.

The Washington Post

Washington, D. C., March 17, 1981

THERE IS a specter haunting the debate over illegal immigration, and his name is George Orwell. It is widely recognized, most recently by the Select Commission on Immigration and Refugee Policy, that any effective strategy to curb illegal immigration into the United States must focus on developing some means of distinguishing accurately between alien workers and legal residents. But the effort has stalled on the assertion that any form of national identity system would dangerously impair an entire series of privacy rights now enjoyed by Americans.

If the United States adopts a "universal identifier" while reforming its immigration laws, critics charge, the computerized record-keeping apparatus required to ensure its accuracy would usher in Mr. Orwell's totalitarian nightmare—*1984*. In this view, the cards would be used eventually as credit and police checks and, in other unspecified ways, would be perverted beyond their avowed purpose of verifying the employment eligibility of resident aliens. Worst-case arguments conjure up visions of all Americans being forced to produce the cards before registering at hotels, crossing state lines or for other abusive purposes unimagined today. Meanwhile, proposals to limit cards to aliens are denounced as both an assault on privacy and a blatant act of discrimination against the large number of Latins and Caribbean blacks among the illegal population.

The threat to privacy rights posed by a national identity card is real and is worthy of close scrutiny. But opponents have exaggerated it grossly. Even today, virtually every American uses daily a number of quasi-national (though not universal) identifiers, public and private: Social Security cards, drivers' licenses, Medicare and Medicaid numbers, armed forces identity cards and the familiar credit cards. A veritable army of government and private agencies collates and jostles these identifiers within their computer data banks constantly, using and abusing the data for purposes both benign and malevolent. Still, despite the warnings of civil libertarians, we have yet to fulfill our supposed rendezvous with an Orwellian destiny.

Why the fuss, then, about a more systematic identifier designed solely to deal with illegal immigration? The rights of illegals (including their privacy) would probably be strengthened through a national identity card system. The federal government would find it possible not only to identify provable abuses by employers or local authorities but also to extend legal protection and social services to workers whose presence in the United States had been legitimized by the new cards.

The system's main benefit, though, would be to allow the government to determine precisely and promptly the legal status of millions of alien workers who have inundated low-wage American labor markets. No humane and rational immigration policy stands a chance of success unless we reduce the currently uncontrollable rate of illegal entry.

Congress, while devising a national identity card system, should provide elaborate safeguards, possibly through amendments to the 1974 Privacy Act. Whether the identifier should be a forgery-proof Social Security card, a phone-in data bank, a new work identity card or some other proposed mechanism remains to be determined. Only through adopting such a system, however, can Americans reassert the primacy of *lawful* entry into this country. Endless and inappropriate evocations of George Orwell will not make the problem go away.

Sentinel Star

Orlando, Fla., March 13, 1981

MAKE NO mistake about it, Florida and a lot of other states have a real problem with illegal aliens. If it weren't so bad, surely Sen. Lawton Chiles — with the support of Gov. Bob Graham — would never have come up with the idea of issuing permanent identification cards to all U.S. workers so we can tell the legals from the illegals.

As bad as the problem is and as bold a political gambit as that may be, it is an idea whose time has not come. It runs headlong into fundamental American tenets of individual liberty and is something that most of us are never going to accept. Furthermore, the universal ID is riddled with potential problems.

Under the Chiles plan, an illegal alien applying for a job would have to produce the proper ID card or he, presumably, wouldn't be hired. Employers hiring cardless aliens would be subject to stiff fines and the illegal aliens supposedly would go back home and spread the word that finding work in the United States isn't quite as easy at it once was.

Such a card would almost necessarily require the bearer's picture and thumb print. But that is a tactic that comes dangerously close to the police state image that Americans have come to abhor. Rather than solving the problem, it shackles the law-abiding, freedom-loving U.S. citizen.

A secondary horror of mandatory ID cards would be the sprawling bureaucracy that would emerge to administer a program responsible for more than 200 million working-age Americans. That, alone, should give any lawmaker the chills.

That does not mean that the illegal alien problem is something that shouldn't be tackled.

But legal aliens are already required by law to carry identification cards, and they should be able to produce those cards for employment purposes. And an employer with questions about an applicant ought to ask for some sort of verification of citizenship. Employers who persist in using — and sometimes exploiting — an illegal alien work force ought to do it at the risk of stiff penalties.

That's a start, but proper enforcement eventually depends on a firm government policy and a more efficient and better-funded Immigration and Naturalization Service. Anyone thinking about sneaking across the U.S. border ought to know that there's a real chance of being caught.

Florida's leaders would best serve their country and their state by ensuring that INS gets the mandate and the money it needs. That's certainly less costly — and less risky — than asking millions of Americans to line up for fingerprinting.

SAN JOSE NEWS

San Jose, Calif., January 14, 1981

THERE are no counterfeit-proof documents. Any piece of "official" paper that can be produced by man can be forged, with varying degrees of skill and success, by other men.

This is the chief practical reason Congress should reject the national identity card concept narrowly embraced (on an 8-7 vote) by the Select Commission on Immigration and Refugee Policy last week. The bird won't fly.

Equally important, a "secure" national identity card raises philosophical, ethical and even ethnic concerns.

Congress, which will get the commission's laundry list of formal recommendations March 1, should have no trouble finding a variety of excellent reasons for rejecting this well-intentioned but dangerous and unsound "solution" to the vexing reality of illegal immigration.

The 16-member commission, created by Congress nearly three years ago to help it draft a new and more rational immigration and refugee policy, clearly sees illegal immigration — mostly temporary and overwhelmingly economic in motivation — as a problem. But, judging from its recommendations in this area, the commission is less sure about how serious the problem is and whether, in fact, it can be solved at all. The national identity card notion smacks of indecision and desperation.

The real goal of the commission is to make the United States less attractive to the economically deprived of other nations, particularly the migrant poor of Mexico.

The majority of illegal immigrants, or, as they prefer to be called, undocumented immigrants, come north from Mexico because they cannot find enough work at home to feed their families. There is work, much of it menial and almost all of it underpaid by American standards, in the United States.

The commission reasons that if there were no work here for these individuals, they would either stay home or go elsewhere. But there *is* work here, so how can the undocumented be prevented, or discouraged, from coming north?

By implication, the commission has written off physically sealing the 2,000-mile Mexican border. In terms of money and manpower, closing the border is a practical impossibility.

The next best approach, in the commission's view, is to make it illegal for American employers to hire illegal, or undocumented, immigrants. It is now illegal for undocumented workers to be here, but it is not illegal for Americans to hire them. Accordingly, the commission unanimously recommends civil and criminal sanctions against employers who "knowingly" hire undocumented workers.

This, of course, raises the fairness issue. How can a restaurateur, for example, be sure the Spanish-speaking dishwasher he has just hired (at below minimum wage likely as not) really came from San Ysidro, as he said, and not from Sinaloa? How can employers "know" they are hiring only citizens and resident aliens?

Simple, says the commission: Issue *everybody* a counterfeit-proof identity card (or provide employers with some electronic equivalent). Without the card, nobody works. What could be tidier?

In truth, very few things could be messier. As mentioned earlier, such documents could be, and most assuredly would be, forged. Bogus Immigration Service "green cards," California drivers' licenses and Social Security cards are hot items along the border now. A national identity card would just augment the forger's inventory and raise the cost of crossing the border illegally.

Hispanic-American groups oppose the work identity card on the ground that it will be used almost exclusively against Latinos and other "foreign-looking" individuals. They could be right. Employers who wanted to discriminate could always claim they doubted the validity of the individual's identity card.

Civil libertarians warn a national identity card could presage 1984 — with Big Brother government keeping tab on everybody's comings and goings. They fear, perhaps with justification, that the existence of such a card would invite abuse sooner or later. As they point out, the power to issue a work-identity card implies the power to alter it, make it conditional or withhold it as well.

The analogy is not precise, but it is nonetheless an unpleasant fact that the Soviet Union's internal passport system is founded on a national identity card that doubles as a work permit.

American employers should be held criminally liable for hiring undocumented aliens, but a national identity card isn't needed to do the job. Immigration sweeps through industries and fields known to be magnets for illegal workers have proved that it is possible to sift undocumented workers from citizens and resident aliens. It isn't easy. It is, in fact, slow, cumbersome and expensive, but it is possible — and without national identity cards.

Los Angeles Times
Los Angeles, Calif., January 8, 1981

The Select Commission on Immigration and Refugee Policy, created two years ago by Congress to thoroughly study the nation's immigration laws and practices, has decided by the narrowest of margins to recommend that this country develop a "secure system" that employers could use to verify that persons who apply for jobs are in the country legally.

Although controversial, this proposal is necessary.

The commission, composed of four House members, four senators, four Cabinet officers and four members of the public, will present its final report to Congress on March 1. Members of the panel have been meeting over the last month to vote on a list of proposed reforms in the way the United States handles both legal and illegal immigration. The recommendation for a secure identification system was approved 8 to 7, with one abstention.

In making their close call on this proposal, the majority of commissioners decided to override the concerns of civil libertarians, who fear that an identification system for work purposes could become a national identity card, and Latino civil-rights groups, which warn that any such system would inevitably be used only against Latinos, Asians and other foreign-looking or foreign-sounding citizens.

Those concerns are valid. But there is also a great public concern over the flow of illegal-immigrant workers into this country. The commission majority believes that an effective way to slow this migration is to penalize employers who hire these workers. This would theoretically dry up the jobs that lure many immigrants here. The only way such employer sanctions would be effective is with some kind of counterfeitproof document that all workers—and we emphasize all workers—would have to show when applying for a job to prove that they were in the country legally.

The commission did not indicate in its vote precisely what this secure identity system should be. We have suggested in the past that the Social Security card be made a more secure document. The final decision, of course, will be up to Congress, and to the incoming administration of Ronald Reagan.

San Francisco Chronicle
San Francisco, Calif., March 2, 1981

THE REAGAN administration has inherited, as did the Carter, Ford, Nixon, Johnson and Kennedy administrations before it, the thorny, complex and continuing problem of establishing an effective immigration policy for the nation. The fact that the latest formal effort to define the problem and formulate a policy to respond to it has ended in disarray is of little help to the new administration.

The Select Commission on Immigration and Refugee Policy spent two years attempting to deal with a problem it has officially found to be "out of control." The commission has recommended a modest increase in the number of legal immigrants to be allowed to settle in the country each year and has also urged the federal government to increase its efforts to stem the tide of illegal aliens coming across the notoriously leaky southern border.

While the commission agreed that it should be against the law to employ persons not legally entitled to be residents here, it failed to agree upon what we believe to be an essential element of such a policy: a secure, tamper-proof means of identification.

THE COMMISSION chairman, the Rev. Theodore Hesburgh, president of Notre Dame University, had urged his colleagues to recommend to the president and to Congress that all Americans and legal resident aliens be furnished with a counterfeit-proof, upgraded Social Security card as a means of establishing eligibility for employment. But in a sharply divided vote, the commission recommended only "some system of more secure identification."

The commission failed to approve the concept of a worker identification card because of civil liberty concerns and because some members felt it was an "overreaction" to the problem.

The failure of the commission to agree, after detailed study, hearings, discussion and reports, probably indicates that a national identification system would also face difficulties in winning approval in Congress. As long as this is so, we may anticipate that the Reagan administration will pass along the immigration problem to the administration that succeeds it.

FORT WORTH STAR-TELEGRAM
Fort Worth, Texas, January 19, 1981

One way of placing some kind of control on the illegal flow of Mexican nationals into this country is through documentation. We have been in favor of some form of documentation of Mexican workers, such as the old bracero program, to cut down the number of Mexicans in this country illegally.

The poverty and lack of employment in Mexico and the seeming abundance in the United States is the reason for the migration. Many who enter this country illegally from Mexico find work but they are underpaid and exploited, too.

It has been suggested that a national worker identification card be used and that anyone who does not have such a card not be hired. While such a national ID system smacks of police statism and can be abused, the idea may be workable in some form. For example, Social Security cards — which are already used by employees as a form of ID — might meet little resistance, and they could be made tamper-proof.

Recently the federal Select Commission on Immigration and Refugee Policy recommended use of worker ID cards after a provision was added to penalize employers who hire undocumented workers.

The penalty condition seems fair. It would do little good to require IDs if there were no penalty for hiring a person without ID. Unscrupulous employers would continue to hire and exploit undocumented workers, the same as they are doing now.

The ID requirement would make it more difficult for illegal immigrants to find work in the United States. A card — even a tamper-proof card — can be forged but Social Security numbers are easy to verify.

Illegal immigration from Mexico is one of the major domestic problems that will face the new administration. Caring for and educating the children of those Mexican nationals is a problem that the American taxpayer feels is unfair. If the workers who enter this country from Mexico are documented and gainfully employed, they can share in the expense of the care and education of their children.

The ID proposal is not the final answer to the illegal immigrant problem but it goes far in helping to alleviate the problem. It deserves serious thought.

Reagan Policy Proposals: 'Guest Workers,' Employer Fines

The Reagan Administration released a plan for immigration reform July 30, after reviewing the recommendations of the Select Commission on Immigration and Refugee Policy. The proposals included admitting Mexicans as temporary workers and fining employers who knowingly hired illegal aliens. An amnesty was planned for illegal aliens in the country before Jan. 1. They would be allowed to work and would have to pay taxes, but they would not receive government benefits and would have to wait 10 years before being eligible to apply for citizenship. (The normal waiting period for citizenship was five years.)

Declaring, "We have lost control of our borders," Attorney General William French Smith called for $40 million for stepped-up enforcement measures and $35 million for new detention facilities for aliens who entered without visas. He added that the government had called for the Coast Guard to intercept boats from Haiti. The two-year experimental "guest worker" program would allow 50,000 Mexicans a year to work in the U.S., he said. The quotas for immigration from Mexico and Canada would be doubled from the present 20,000 each, and Mexicans could take visas unclaimed by Canadians. Employers who hired illegal aliens would face fines of up to $1,000 for each illegal worker, but the administration flatly rejected identity cards. Instead, employers would have to rely on existing documents, such as driver's licenses, birth certificates, Social Security cards or draft cards.

THE ARIZONA REPUBLIC
Phoenix, Ariz., July 31, 1981

ALL the glowing rhetoric that Attorney General William French Smith employed in unveiling the Reagan administration's plan to control the flow of illegal aliens into the United States does not hide the fact that it will do nothing of the kind.

The key provision of the plan involves making it unlawful to hire illegal aliens. Employers of four or more persons found guilty of *knowingly* hiring illegal aliens would be subject to civil fines.

This is obviously unenforceable.

It would be all but impossible for the government to prove that an employer *knew* his employes were in the U.S. illegally. Moreover, in the rare cases in which it could be proved, the fines proposed — a maximum of $1,000 — are too small to deter anyone from knowingly breaking the law.

Some legislators have proposed that *everyone* applying for a job be forced to produce a forgery-proof card, issued by the government, attesting that he is either citizen or an legal alien.

This would make it possible to prove that an employer knowingly hired illegal aliens, but the administration plan does not include such a provision, and that's just as well.

It goes against the American grain.

The card would be too much like the internal passport that Soviet citizens are forced to carry. Making U.S. citizens carry them would be one small step to making this a police state.

Another key provision of the administration plan is the institution of a program under which 50,000 Mexican nationals would be permitted to enter the U.S. on a temporary basis annually to work in specific areas at specified types of jobs.

This would do nothing to stem the flow of hundreds of thousands of Mexican nationals into the U.S. every year.

Other provisions of the plan would regularize the status of aliens who entered the U.S. illegally before Jan. 1, 1980.

That would be a humanitarian act, but, again, it would not keep illegal aliens from continuing to pour into this country. On the contrary, it might work to encourage them.

It's time Americans faced reality.

Short of emulating the communists — short of requiring everyone to carry a sort of internal passport, and short of building a wall along the entire 2,000 miles of the U.S. border with Mexico and manning it with armed guards — there's nothing much we can do about the illeal alien problem beyond what we're doing now.

When illegals are caught, they are shipped back where they came from. If they return and are caught again, we send them home again.

It's a frustrating endeavor and, in the long run, futile.

However, the alternatives that might work are unthinkable.

THE ATLANTA CONSTITUTION
Atlanta, Ga., July 31, 1981

President Reagan has unveiled what he called a realistic immigration policy, one that combined the traditional open door to America with fairness to its own citizens. That's a worthy goal and one long overdue. Here's hoping it achieves that end.

Briefly, the policy includes:

• Legislation to punish, with fines of up to $1,000, employers of more than four people who knowingly hire illegal aliens.

• A temporary worker program for up to 50,000 Mexican nationals annually. Workers could bring in families but would not have access to welfare or food stamp assistance or be eligible for unemployment compensation.

• Legal status for qualifying illegal aliens in the United States as of Jan. 1, 1980. They could apply for "renewable term temporary resident" status and get it renewed every three years. After 10 years of continuous residency, those residents could apply for permanent resident status if they are not otherwise excludable and could demonstrate use of the English language.

• Increased enforcement of existing immigration and fair labor laws.

• International cooperation within the western hemisphere to enforce immigration laws and discourage illegal migration.

Traditionally, our country has been at the top of the list held by people wanting to leave their homeland. There is so much to say for our way of life. In times past the vastness between the Atlantic and Pacific and Canada and Mexico has provided homes, farms and other jobs for those who wanted to start over.

The aliens came here from all over the globe. They learned English and they fit in well. They were absorbed into the culture and were proud to be a part of America.

Our nation has grown and there aren't as many jobs available now for people who don't speak the language. Inflation and tough economic times have combined to make it hard for anyone trying to get started, even people who grew up here. The latest surge of refugees seemed to want to make matters worse by holding on to their native cultures and language, not wanting to blend in.

Something had to be done. The Reagan administration has made an effort. For the sake of citizens and aliens — those here now and those who will come later — we hope it works.

The Seattle Times
Seattle, Wash., July 31, 1981

DESPITE the efforts of heaven knows how many advisory committees and other study groups under several administrations, there has been no major immigration legislation for 15 years.

While succeeding administrations and Congresses have failed to come to grips with the problem, the flow of illegal aliens has crept up — no, snowballed — to the point where informed estimates of the total now in the country run from 3.5 million to 6 million.

The vast bulk of the "illegals" are here for jobs — at a time when some 7 million Americans are unemployed.

The other side of the coin, of course, is that many of the "illegals" gladly do stoop labor and other work that Americans, even though unemployed, won't touch. The same situation applies with "guest workers" in Western Europe.

It is pointed out with considerable validity that if it were not for the influx of alien labor, legal and illegal, much of America's agricultural produce would go unharvested.

Yesterday the Reagan administration unveiled its long-awaited immigration policy. It is a balanced program that attempts to get a grip on the problem while taking account of U.S. economic needs and the sensibilities of Uncle Sam's North American neighbors. But there is no certainty that it will work.

The program includes:
— Civil fines of up to $1,000 against employers of more than four persons who knowingly hire illegal aliens (a wrist-slap).

— An experimental temporary-worker program for up to 50,000 Mexican nationals annually — wisely targeted to specific areas and categories of jobs.

— Legal status for qualifying illegal aliens who were in the U.S. prior to January 1, 1980. These "illegals" could move in steps toward permanent-resident status.

The crux of the problem, as stated yesterday by Attorney General William French Smith, is that "we have lost control of our borders. We have pursued unrealistic policies. We have failed to enforce our laws effectively."

It remains to be seen whether the Reagan administration can succeed where its predecessors failed. But at least, in putting forward a package whose principles are designed, in the President's words, "to preserve our tradition of accepting foreigners to our shores, but to accept them in a controlled and orderly fashion," this administration will proceed from a proper perspective.

The Honolulu Advertiser
Honolulu, Ha., August 3, 1981

Most illegal immigration to this country is rooted in the poverty of places like northern Mexico, the Caribbean and parts of South America and the existence of employers in the U.S. willing (and even eager) to fill low-paying, undesirable jobs with undocumented aliens.

As long as these conditions persist people will be pressing to enter this country with or without official permission.

But economic hard times here, concern about the changing cultural climate in the West and in Florida and a backlash against recent refugees from Cuba, Vietnam and Haiti have increased pressure for action on this long unsolved problem.

PROPOSALS UNVEILED by the Reagan adminstration are similar to those of a special commission appointed by former president Carter. This points up the reality that there are few viable options.

The proposals reasonably begin by accepting the idea that it is impossible to deport millions of people who have already been in the country for years. A gradual amnesty will allow them to apply for permanent resident status after 10 years if they can speak English and have no criminal record.

The proposals call for legal action against employers who knowingly hire illegal aliens. This may have some impact in Hawaii since most of our undocumented aliens are visitors (generally from the Orient) who overstay tourist or student visas to look for work.

While this provision (somewhat unexpected from a Republican administration) will admittedly be hard to enforce, it acknowledges that illegal immigration cannot be stopped as long as some employers profit by it.

An experimental "guest worker" program should meet the needs both of employers (particularly in agriculture) who depend on seasonal labor and aliens who do not want to live in the U.S but only to work here. Still, it will have to be carefully monitored to avoid abuses of both the Mexican workers and the American labor force.

The whole package is to be held together by better funding and more personnel for the Immigration and Naturalization Service, which had been cut out of the Stockman budget.

WISELY, THE PLAN shies away from a so-called "counterfeit-proof" national identification card for everyone to carry. The whole notion is alien to American sensibilities about government interference and civil rights.

Further it would be quite expensive. Besides, as long as birth certificates, drivers' licenses, social security cards and other forms of identification can be improperly obtained, no national ID card could be fool-proof.

These proposals have been long awaited and now they will get a thorough going over by Congress. In general they appear to be a fair way for a nation of immigrants to deal with borders that have unfortunately gone out of control.

Nevada State Journal
Reno, Nev., July 20, 1981

The Reagan administration's plan to give Mexican aliens legal seasonal work status in this country does not sit well.

It does not sit well because it is no real answer to the illegal alien problem, and it does not meet the other needs of this nation.

Admittedly, the illegal alien problem is a difficult one. To seal off the border would require a massive and extremely costly effort. It would also strain relations with Mexico — which, of course, has oil that we need (isn't that always the case lately in international affairs?)

Placing the responsibility on employers is unrealistic; if they can hire cheaper labor, they will; and if Americans will not work at certain "unglamorous" or tedious jobs, then employers have no qualms about going to aliens.

Rounding up all the illegal aliens and shipping them home is a difficult and probably impossible task — especially when they will come streaming right back again.

And yet there must be better answers than the one reportedly being readied in Washington. This answer, as leaked by those who should know, includes legalizing the status of Mexican illegals who have been in this country for five years before Jan. 1, 1980, admitting other Mexicans as "guest workers," penalizing employers who hire illegal aliens, doubling the number of Mexicans (and Canadians as well) who can immigrate here each year, and encouraging neighboring countries to help prevent ships carrying potential illegals from setting forth for this country.

Numerous facets of the plan just do not seem workable. Legalizing five-year illegals does, perhaps, eliminate one part of the problem, but only by redefining it to say that it doesn't exist. Doubling the number of legal Mexican immigrants from 20,000 to 40,000 simply redefines and ignores the problem in another way. Penalizing employers will be difficult; no matter what laws are enacted, it still must be proved that employers knowingly hired illegals, and this is not necessarily easy. Neighboring countries might give lip service to programs to stem the flood, but real cooperation is

not likely. Countries overflowing with poor people have no desire to keep them, and they have every interest in seeing them leave.

At the same time, the United States has a considerable unemployment problem, which seems likely to get worse. So one must ask quite seriously if this is the time to legalize and in fact encourage a huge flood of illegal workers into this country (it is not known how many work cards would be issued, but early discussion has ranged from 500,000 to 1 million a year, far above the present 30,000).

Would it not be better to try to fill the waiting jobs with American workers rather than aliens? Particularly, could not jobless youths, especially from the big cities, be encouraged to take seasonal agricultural jobs? Opponents of this suggestion will say that this would involve massive relocation efforts, that big city youths would not go, and that they would not fit in on the farms. Certainly there would be difficulties, but if such a program were only partially successful it would do a great deal to help resolve the youth unemployment problem.

A similar program might also be effected for adults, particularly those on welfare. This would involve a hardship, especially for fathers who would have to leave home during the working season. But other fathers do the same: salesmen, sailors, construction workers. They do it for better work and the economic improvement of their families. So this would not be a particularly cruel or unusual thing to ask.

If the jobs were filled by Americans, if there were no jobs or fewer jobs waiting for aliens, then the flow of aliens would slow considerably.

And if these solutions do not work, perhaps there are other "in-house" answers.

The point, really, is this: The United States should do better than simply caving in to the illegal alien flow by legalizing what it cannot control. At least it should try to do better. And if it tries, it just might succeed.

THE BLADE

Toledo, Ohio, August 5, 1981

AMONG a number of reasonable proposals by the Reagan administration to reduce the flow of illegal aliens into this country is one that will push many American employers into the untenable position of being asked to comply with an inadequate federal law.

A key provision of the plan unveiled last week would impose civil penalties on those employers who knowingly hire illegal aliens. The law, which would not apply to firms that employ fewer than three workers, would impose a fine of between $500 and $1,000 for each such person arrested. The Blade has supported such a step as one way to discourage the hiring of undocumented aliens.

Missing from this approach, however, is a comparable requirement for some kind of universally recognized identity card — most likely a counterfeit-resistant Social Security card — that could serve as proof of citizenship. The absence of such a provision, even though it would be costly — Attorney General William French Smith said it would cost between $800 million and $2 billion — would leave employers without an assured way of knowing if they were obeying the law.

The plan would require job applicants to supply two pieces of identification (Social Security card, driver's license, birth certificate, or the like). The stumbling block is that those who now unlawfully cross the U.S.-Mexican border find forged documents of this sort easily obtainable.

Other parts of the overall plan have some merit. One element, to go into effect immediately, will allow U.S. Coast Guard ships to intercept suspicious-looking boats. The Administration also hopes to gain approval of a guest-worker plan, and it is supporting $75 million more for the Immigration and Naturalization Service to increase patrols of the U.S.-Mexican border.

The money, however, will do little to secure the 2,000-mile-long border. A better step is to reduce the economic incentive for crossing the border in the first place, and that will only work if employer sanctions and a counterfeit-proof identity card are imposed. Until that time, a sizable gap will exist in the Administration's effort to bring illegal immigration under control.

Houston Chronicle

Houston, Texas, August 2, 1981

The Reagan administration's proposed new immigration policy is fundamentally flawed by amnesty for illegal aliens.

It is not acceptable to reward illegality, nor to permanently burden the country's social, political and economic structure with perhaps up to 5 million people who have no right to be here. Neither is amnesty practical. There is no effective way to determine the truth of eligibility, and, as Chronicle Washington Bureau Chief Norman Baxter points out in a column on this page today, an amnesty will simply encourage more illegal aliens.

We believe the vast majority of Americans are sick and tired of this country's being unable to control who comes here, how long they stay and what they do. It is plain wrong to ask Americans to consent to the privilege of residency, and citizenship, for those who have violated the law with impunity.

In some of its elements other than amnesty, the administration's policy is more sensible than previous plans.

We have no objection to proposals to penalize employers who knowingly hire illegal aliens, so long as such laws do not have the effect of discriminating against citizens or legal residents who look or sound foreign and so long as employers will not be liable for innocent hiring of illegals. These two concerns seem addressed in the Reagan plan by giving employers an absolute defense against prosecution by making a good faith inspection of two forms of identification. This should eliminate employer reluctance to hire, out of fear of penalty, those who look or sound foreign, as well as protect employers who have no real way of knowing the true legal status of an applicant.

We support the president's request for new authority to crack down on those coming here illegally by sea from the Caribbean, such as from Haiti and Cuba. This cannot be allowed to continue and spread.

Also asked of Congress is an increase in the number of legal immigrants each year from Mexico. A case can be made for this, but only after getting the illegal immigration under control.

The president wants to try a formal temporary-worker program for two years; 50,000 Mexican nationals a year for stays of nine to 12 months, restricted to certain areas and types of jobs. Why not give it a try? If it works, fine; if not, get rid of it.

The Virginian-Pilot

Norfolk, Va., August 2, 1981

The personnel office—more so than the border—is the point at which illegal immigrants to United States could best be spotted and turned back. Most of the swarms of "illegals"—from Mexico, the West Indies, South America, and Hong Kong—slipping into this land are in search of jobs. Besides, there is simply too much border to police; many of the "illegals" come in through Canada these days. So by declining to sponsor a counterfeit-resistant Social Security or worker-identity card, the White House has fatally undercut its proposed new immigration policy.

Going along with a recommendation by President Carter's select committee on immigration, the administration urges penalties for employers who knowingly hire illegal aliens. That's a good start. But any employer who hires an "illegal" on the basis of a phony birth certificate and phony driver's license or Social Security card—production of such documents is a flourishing industry—could plead that he thought the applicant was lawfully in the U.S.

Attorney General William French Smith says the adminis-tration decided not to recommend the institution of a national worker identity card system because it would cost $2 billion. But identity cards could be issued over several years, starting, say, with the youngest age groups; that would spread out the expense. Mr. French asserts that the U.S. has lost control of its borders, which is obvious enough. But how can control be regained without a reliable means of identifying persons improperly here?

The U.S. is wide open to all comers. Between 6 million and 10 million illegals are mixed into the population. President Reagan's plan to confer citizenship on them recognizes the impossibility of returning them to their homeland without a draconian law-enforcement effort. It also recognizes the contributions that these millions have made to the national economy by working at jobs that many natives scorn.

Nothing about the administration's immigration program suggests it can be very effective. Letting in an additional 50,000 guest workers annually for the next two years has merit as far as it goes. The trouble is that de-mand for Mexican labor in the U.S. job market is greater than could be satisfied by 100,000 guest workers; the desperate still will have an incentive to cross the border.

The Border Patrol meanwhile is hopelessly outnumbered, and the additional $75 million a year that the administration asks for the U.S. Immigration and Naturalization Service will provide only feeble reinforcement.

Perhaps neither the administration nor Americans generally truly want to shut the golden door on job-hungry hordes seeking a fresh start. And worker-identity cards—however normal in Europe—are not to American tastes. But if we are serious about restraining the immigrant flood, which strains the fabric of American society, we must devise a sure means of personal identification. No other nation in which millions of workers were jobless would tolerate the immigration that the U.S. virtually welcomes—more than 800,000 legals and illegals last year. Whatever its stated intent, the administration has prescribed an immigration remedy that will not work.

THE SUNDAY OKLAHOMAN

Oklahoma City, Okla., August 2, 1981

INITIAL reaction from Congress suggests that President Reagan may get some but not all of the changes he has requested in U.S. immigration policy.

Which is just as well, since some of the recommendations are seriously flawed and sure to arouse bitter controversy on all sides.

Few will quarrel with measures designed to prevent any recurrence of Castro's mass dumping of some 125,000 Cubans on our shores last year, or preventive action on the high seas to intercept the continuing flood of Haitians into Florida. All of them are illegal, and none should ever have been allowed to stay in the first place.

Similarly, some sort of sanctions should be authorized against employers who knowingly hire illegal aliens. This has been suggested by nearly all immigration policy studies.

Nor is there any good argument against restoration of a "guest worker" program similar to the old bracero program that was ended in 1964. This would assure legal protection and return to their native countries (principally Mexico) of legal entrants who would supplant the illegals now working in agriculture and performing other menial jobs.

Protests of "exploitation" to the contrary, the foreigners work willingly and diligently at jobs most Americans won't take, especially when they can get welfare, food stamps and medical care without working.

But the proposal under which an undetermined number of illegals already here could gain work status leading to permanent legal residency is something else.

Upwards of six million illegals would be affected. Any way you slice it, this amounts to legalizing the illegal. Nor is it realistic. Illegals who claimed the new status would have to pay taxes but could not bring in other family members or be eligible for any welfare assistance. Under those conditions, many of them would prefer to remain illegal.

Even more disappointing is the administration's failure to address the basic assumptions upon which U.S. immigration policy has traditionally been based.

Does the United States have a permanent, unchanging moral obligation to accept a continuing influx of people, regardless of where they come from or the circumstances that prompted their departure? Most Americans today would say no.

Given the finite extent of our resources and societal absorption capacity, is there a point at which all immigration should be drastically curtailed? Again, most Americans would answer yes.

The immigration issue will continue to fester until these questions are answered by a majority consensus. Otherwise, we hasten the arrival of a polyglot, multi-lingual and Balkanized America that will bear little resemblance to the country we have today.

The San Diego Union

San Diego, Calif., August 5, 1981

It is important to realize that President Reagan's immigration reform program, which he submitted to Congress last Thursday, is not a comprehensive, final solution. Rather, it should be viewed as no more than an initial step in what is certain to be a long, difficult process.

The Reagan administration generally improved upon the recommendations of the Select Commission on Immigration and Refugee Policy, which was named more than two years ago by President Carter. In some cases, however, the Reagan proposals do not reach the Commission's more vigorous remedies. Sharp differences within the administration resulted in compromises and a far smaller guest worker program than proposed either by the Commission or by pending legislation in Congress.

But even the scaled-down Reagan plan has stirred howls from those who protest that it goes too far as well as from those who argue it doesn't go far enough. Politics being the art of the possible, this early outcry from both extremes of the spectrum suggests the administration, with redeeming realism, has taken the high middle ground on this complex issue and, therefore, has a good chance of prevailing in the long, hard struggle for enactment.

Basically, the reforms proposed last week confirm earlier White House reports. They would: Bestow legal status, or grant amnesty, to as many as 6 million aliens who entered this country illegally and have resided here since Jan. 1, 1980; fine employers of four or more persons up to $1,000 for each illegal alien knowingly hired; admit up to 50,000 Mexican guest workers annually for a two-year test period; double the annual immigration quota for Mexico and Canada to 40,000; legalize refugees from Cuba and Haiti within five years; and provide a slight increase in the Border Patrol.

A major concern with the program is that the administration's amnesty plan is so complicated as perhaps to defy enforcement. Aliens residing continuously in this country for five years are immediately eligible for permanent-resident status; those here for three years could apply for temporary-worker status and then permanent residency after five years; those here less than three years prior to Jan. 1, 1980, would be required to spend 10 years as "renewable-term temporary residents." The alien would have to renew his status every three years, would have to pay Social Security and other taxes, but be ineligible for welfare, unemployment compensation, subsidized housing, or food stamps. Moreover, the alien would not be permitted to bring in a spouse or children. Verifying continuous residence over such time periods obviously will be a formidable problem.

With a special nod to Mexico, the administration would permit the unused visas from Canada to be claimed by Mexicans. Because only 10,000 Canadians immigrate annually to the United States, this means the Mexican quota would be increased by 30,000 to 70,000 — a quantum leap from the current 20,000 limit.

On the other hand, the 50,000 guest worker figure is widely considered to be preposterously small. Gov. William Clements of Texas believes the figure should be at least 500,000, and Sen. S.I. Hayakawa, noting that 120,000 workers are needed just to harvest Fresno County's raisin crop, is the co-author of legislation for a guest-worker program of 1 million.

The most disturbing disappointment is the proposal to add only $40 million to the 1982 budget of the Immigration and Naturalization Service and Border Patrol. This means only 236 more officers are scheduled for the border. So slight an increase is ineffective tokenism, considering that at least 1,000 more officers are needed, by all accounts, to maintain some semblance of border control.

Despite its limitations and some of its troublesome provisions, the Reagan administration's immigration package is, overall, humane and generous. And, moreover, in singling Mexico out for special treatment, it goes beyond the recommendations of any commission or previous administration. But its real significance is that, whereas other administrations have debated, delayed, and done little or nothing to uphold U.S. immigration laws, the Reagan administration has taken this all-important first step. After enactment, experience can prove where future changes should be made to bring this situation into balance.

The alternative of doing nothing has become increasingly unacceptable, because the United States alone simply cannot solve the population and economic problems of this planet.

ALBUQUERQUE JOURNAL

Albuquerque, N. M., August 2, 1981

Ronald Reagan's proposed solutions to the nation's immigration problems are no better than solutions offered in the past. This lack of vision is important to New Mexico, across whose southern border many Mexicans illegally cross.

Reagan wants to beef up the Border Patrol. But one U.S. official says that, at even three times present strength, the 2,000-mile border still could not be sealed and we still wouldn't know how many "indocumentados" are crossing. He also wants an "experimental" guest-worker program importing 50,000 Mexicans a year, apparently to gather data for a study.

Other features are stiff fines for employers who knowingly hire illegals, a Coast Guard interception program for the Caribbean, and a two-track legalization program that sets up a new "renewable-term temporary resident" status. All the proposals were, at least in part, products of a study made by the presidentially appointed Hesburgh Commission.

Sen. Harrison Schmitt, R-N.M., quickly characterized the program as a "warmed over" version of the old Carter administration policy. Schmitt is right, but only to a degree. Carter at least tried to push U.S. help to ease conditions in other countries which made their people want to emigrate to the United States. Reagan does not address that matter.

Leaders like Schmitt and Democratic Gov. Richard Lamm of Colorado have been concerned about the long-term demographics vis-a-vis Mexican immigration. Gov. Lamm notes that half the nation's immigrants, legal and illegal, are from Mexico. Schmitt notes that however bad illegal immigration is now — estimates vary, but they sound high — it is going to be a lot worse by the year 2000, particularly if no major changes are made in U.S. policy.

All this is fine, but what changes can be made that will be acceptable politically, economically, socially? Former Carter aide Abelardo L. Valdez has suggested a free trade zone extending 200 miles on either side of the U.S.-Mexico border. The idea is a major departure from most other ideas, but it, too, has its problems. For one thing, it limits itself to trade and manufacturing matters, leaving illegal aliens, for example, out of it.

Then there's Anthony P. Maingot, a resident alien from Trinidad teaching at Florida International University. He says the hemisphere's immigration problems cannot be "solved through immigration policies alone — and certainly not an isolated American policy, no matter how wise and clear." That may be true, but it doesn't respond to Schmitt's longer-term worries.

Domestic political pressure obstructs any major change in policy. Also, the old American value of sharing our freedom has collided with economic and social conditions that undermine American conviction in that value.

Reagan, in these conditions, might take a page out of his supply-side economics. The supply, in immigration, is coming from many have-not countries, including one teeming with jobless, hungry people on our southern border. By giving people incentives to stay in their home countries — through economic and technical aid that leads to jobs — they may be less inclined, in their eagerness to find freedom and prosperity, to saddle this country with a major and worsening problem for which we have not yet found a workable solution.

DESERET NEWS

Salt Lake City, Utah, July 31, 1981

U.S. immigration policy long has been labeled by those familiar with the problem as "chaotic" or "out of control."

One reason is that world conditions change so rapidly last year's policy may not fit this year's realities. For example, the ink was hardly dry on the Refugee Act of 1980 when some 155,000 Cubans and Haitians began arriving — uninvited — on U.S. shores. Unable to cope with the emergency, the Carter administration coined a new status — administration plan for dealing with the situation. Among other things, that plan would:

In addition to the thousands of immigrants who arrive yearly fleeing political upheaval, poverty, or religious persecution, there are tens of thousands who slip across the borders illegally. The Census Bureau estimates that between 3.5 million and 6 million persons are illegally in the country at any one time.

This week, Attorney General William French Smith outlined the long-awaited administration plan. Among other things, that plan would:

— Grant amnesty to illegal aliens already living in the United States who arrived before Jan. 1, 1980.

— Allow as many as 50,000 Mexican nationals a year to enter the United States for specific areas and job categories.

— Fine employers of more than four employees up to $1,000 each for knowingly hiring illegal aliens.

That plan answers many, but not all, of the criticisms of the present program. For instance, it attempts to prevent formation of a substantially large underclass of illegal citizens, which current law has been unable to cope with. It attempts to remove incentives for exploitation of illegal immigrants by unscrupulous employers. And it preserves the American tradition of humane treatment of and sanctuary for the oppressed.

How well it will protect American work and living standards remains to be seen. But certainly those standards will not be appreciably worse for legalizing the aliens who are already here, nor for the 50,000 Mexican nationals who will be permitted to work at specific jobs in this country.

The trouble is that the amnesty provision is, in effect, a reward for breaking the law as long as one gets away with it long enough. That's no way to inspire respect for this or any other law.

When President Carter proposed a similar amnesty bill for illegal immigrants in 1978, Congress quickly killed the idea. But four of the 16 commissioners on the Select Commission on Immigration and Refugee Policy are elected Republicans and four are cabinet secretaries. That commission, set up by Congress after the Carter amnesty proposal, made recommendations for overhauling immigration policy. And presumably its members will lobby for passage of a plan that includes many of their recommendations.

The administration plan walks a tight line between closing the door to illegal immigration and recognizing the many aliens who long have lived in the country. It deserves Congress' careful attention.

SYRACUSE HERALD-JOURNAL

Syracuse, N. Y., August 3, 1981

The "national identification card" has a ring of "Big Brother" to it, and the Reagan administration has disavowed the idea unequivocally, but we must interject that if Social Security is not a system of national identity, we don't know what it is.

Of course, in dealing with the problems of immigration, legal and illegal, the Social Security card was considered only briefly for ID purposes because of its obvious counterfeitability. To make the SS card uncopyable would be a $2 billion project, we're told.

But President Reagan has proposed a number of changes in our immigration laws, and without some way of separating the legal immigrants from the illegals, the reforms will not be entirely workable.

For practical reasons, he suggests the 3 million to 6 million illegal aliens now living in the United States be given limited amnesty, subject to eventual citizenship.

We still will have no way of identifying those who choose, perhaps through ignorance of the law, to maintain their illegal status, or those who enter the country illegally after the law is implemented.

He proposes sanctions against employers who "knowingly" employ illegal aliens. Presumably, an employer who claims he "didn't know" the employee was illegal will be let off the hook.

Should an employer who suspects a prospective worker is in this country illegally turn that person away, regardless of the ID the person shows? We think not. But how will the employer prove he didn't know the employee was an illegal alien without being able to refer back to some kind of standardized ID?

Amnesty for those illegal aliens in this country now is both practical and humane. The 10-year waiting period for citizenship is not, however, since permanent residents normally are eligible to apply for citizenship after five years.

Additional funding for enforcement, including more Border Patrol agents and new detention facilities, is long overdue, but the $75 million the president has recommended probably is nowhere near the amount it will take to do the job.

The program has its weaknesses. We expect the Congress will fine tune it and plug the gaps.

The Philadelphia Inquirer
Philadelphia, Pa., August 7, 1981

Illegal immigration to the United States, in flood-tide proportions along the Mexican border, in flotillas from Haiti and Cuba, and in substantial numbers from many other countries, is a serious problem the nation has ignored too long. The Reagan administration has given early recognition to the need for remedies and deserves congressional and public support in its over-all objectives to enforce the nation's immigration laws. Some of the details in the President's plan are open to grave doubts, however, as to their practicality and desirability.

National policy, as Mr. Reagan said, should "be fair to our own citizens while it opens the door of opportunity to those who seek a new life in America." Attorney General William French Smith put it more succinctly: "We have lost control of our borders." More than 700,000 Mexicans were taken into custody by the Border Patrol last year attempting to enter illegally, but at least that many more got through undetected. In toto, it is estimated conservatively that more than 800,000 aliens entered the United States in 1980, and the number might have been over a million. No one knows how many. More than six million illegal aliens currently reside in this country and, again, that is a conservative estimate.

Under the Reagan proposals illegal aliens who can prove they have been in the United States 10 years or more would be eligible to apply for U. S. citizenship. Illegals who arrived before Jan. 1, 1980, could get "temporary resident" status and apply for citizenship after 10 years of residence. These provisions recognize the futility of trying to deport millions of illegal aliens who have been in this country for some time. The need is to make a fresh start to curb illegal entry in the future.

Besides stepped-up Border Patrol vigilance, Mr. Reagan proposes subjecting employers to fines up to $1,000 for each illegal alien hired. Employers would not be subject to a fine if they could show a good-faith effort was made to comply with the law by requiring two means of identification such as a Social Security card and birth certificate or driver's license. The President wisely rejected suggestions that every American be required to carry an identification card, on grounds that it would be too costly and would smack of totalitarianism.

Although the proposed safeguards against hiring illegal aliens may not be stringent enough, it is necessary to avoid measures that would discriminate against minority U.S. citizens seeking jobs. Hispanic organizations rightly are concerned about Americans of Mexican descent, particularly in the southwestern states, who might encounter difficulty obtaining work if prospective employers suspected they were illegal aliens and did not want to risk fines.

A highly questionable Reagan proposal would allow up to 50,000 Mexicans a year to enter the United States as "guest workers" during a two-year experimental period. With serious unemployment problems in this country, importing low-wage labor may be difficult to justify.

Another part of the Reagan plan, which would authorize the Coast Guard to intercept vessels in international waters and force them to turn away from U.S. shores — a proposal aimed principally at the "boat people" from Haiti and Cuba — seems unnecessarily harsh and in conflict with international law governing rights of passage on the high seas. Whatever action is taken could await entry into U.S. waters.

Immigration laws must be enforced in a way that respects human rights and provides neither incentives nor excuses for discrimination against Americans of any race or ethnic background. It will be a difficult task at best, long overdue, and President Reagan's proposals are a beginning.

Los Angeles Times
Los Angeles, Calif., August 2, 1981

The Reagan Administration's package of immigration-law reforms will not do the job that needs to be done. Some of them are sensible, but sharp differences within the Administration were compromised to the point that the reforms are bits and pieces rather than parts of a coherent whole.

The inability to produce a comprehensive immigration program is not unique to this Administration—its predecessors failed, too. Immigration policy, politically, seems to be an intractable problem.

The most notable example of incoherence was the Administration's decision to water down a proposal for new laws to penalize employers who knowingly hire illegal-immigrant workers. Proponents of such measures plausibly argue that they would help discourage illegal immigrants. But the idea is strongly opposed by some of President Reagan's strongest political supporters in the business community and the agricultural industry.

Although the Reagan immigration package does include provisions for employer sanctions, mostly civil fines, its biggest flaw is the failure to include a secure worker identity card to help enforce the sanctions.

The only way in which employer sanctions could be enforced in a non-discriminatory manner would be for all job-seekers to have some way to prove that they can legally work in this country. The Reagan package would allow employers to use routine forms of identification, such as birth certificates and drivers' licenses, as proof of legal residence. That is not enough. We have suggested before that the best tool would be a counterfeit-proof Social Security card that all workers would have to show when applying for a job. Otherwise, unscrupulous or overly cautious employers could use an employer-sanctions law to discriminate against Latinos, Asian-Americans and other "foreign"-looking residents.

The Administration package also brushes too quickly over the question of stricter border enforcement, recommending token budget increases for the Immigration and Naturalization Service and U.S. Border Patrol. Reagan is trying to limit federal spending wherever he can, so he is obviously not willing to spend the large amounts of money that would be needed to seal this country's borders.

But we are surprised that this Administration has not taken a more serious look at a sensible proposal that was considered by both former Presidents Richard M. Nixon and Jimmy Carter. They talked of consolidating the Border Patrol and other federal law-enforcement agencies that now police the borders into a single border-management agency. Although unions representing federal employees oppose the idea, it would be more economical and efficient than the current border situation—and, we think, more humane.

We have long argued that the best place to try to stem the flow of illegal immigrants into this country is right at the border or ports of entry. That is preferable to having immigration agents raid factories and other workplaces, and even ethnic neighborhoods. These raids net comparatively few illegal immigrants while terrorizing whole communities.

One notable proposal that the Reagan package does include is a guest-worker program for Mexican laborers, who make up about half the illegal immigrants in this country. The plan is smaller than expected—a two-year pilot program of 50,000 workers a year. That is better than a massive plan, because it would give planners a chance to determine if a guest-worker program could be operated without all the problems and abuses that existed in the old bracero program.

Reagan also proposed an increase in the annual allotment of immigrant visas for Mexico and Canada—a move that should help alleviate the pressure that leads many Mexicans, who are otherwise eligible for legal entry, to sneak into the country illegally while awaiting issuance of their visas.

The Administration package has a somewhat complicated plan to grant amnesty to illegal immigrants who have been in the country for some time. Although it appears generous on the surface, it may not prove to be very attractive to the persons it is intended to help.

People residing continuously in the United States for five years could apply immediately for permanent-resident status. Those living here for three years could apply for temporary-worker status, then permanent residency after five years.

People who have been in the country less than three years, but who entered before Jan. 1, 1980, would have to spend 10 years in the status of "renewable-term temporary resident." They could apply for permanent residency after their long wait. In the meantime, they could work and pay taxes, but would not be eligible for Social Security benefits, disability insurance or other government benefits, except for medical care. They could also not bring spouses or children into the country.

There are legal questions about the constitutionality of this transient status, and also philosophical problems. In the past, Latino spokesmen have argued that such status could create a legal underclass of foreign workers with no rights or protections. Some have even likened such proposals to legalized slavery. That is a strong term to use, but it does seem to us that this idea could be dehumanizing and degrading to the workers involved.

We worry that some employers might cynically encourage young, unmarried immigrants to apply for this amnesty just so that they could stay in the country and work a few years. Even some workers might be tempted to abuse this provision, figuring that they could earn more money here in a few years than they could earn at home, even after paying U.S. taxes. If manipulated in this way, this provision could become a de facto guest-worker program on a massive and uncontrolled scale.

Like other parts of the Reagan immigration proposals, the amnesty provisions should be revised.

The Charlotte Observer

Charlotte, N. C., August 2, 1981

President Reagan's proposal last week to revise and strengthen United States immigration laws was a useful step forward. It wisely includes new diplomatic efforts to win help from Mexico and other U.S. neighbors in dealing with undocumented workers.

Yet the weakness in the administration's proposal may be inadequate measures here at home.

For example, the administration rejected the proposal to create an identity card to replace Social Security cards for all workers because such a project could cost $850 million to $2 billion.

But of what use is the administration's tough decision to seek fines for employers who hire illegal immigrants, unless the government provides more secure means of identification than forgeable birth certificates and Social Security cards? At best, the administration is inviting harassment of Asian and Hispanic Americans who simply "look different." At worst, the business of border document counterfeiters will boom.

Wisely, the administration wants to add about $75 million more to the budget of the Immigration and Naturalization Service, including $40 million for new enforcement efforts such as more Border Patrol officers. But right now the Border Patrol has only 350 officers on duty at a time. Experts say the service would need 2.5 million more officers, standing shoulder-to-shoulder along the 2,000-mile Mexican border, to stop the influx there. And that would ignore the problem of refugees entering from other points.

Mr. Reagan's ideas are useful. But if Attorney General William French Smith is correct in his assessment that we have "lost control of our borders," the Reagan plan is not complete enough to secure those borders.

The Des Moines Register

Des Moines, Iowa, August 6, 1981

Attorney General William French Smith was stating the obvious when he said, "We have lost control of our borders." Last year, 1 million to 1.5 million aliens entered illegally. Not all stayed, but the Reagan administration estimates that the number of resident illegal aliens grows by as much as 500,000 a year. The total number who have established permanent residence is estimated by the Census Bureau at 3.5 million to 6 million.

The Reagan administration last week released its proposals for regaining control of the nation's borders while improving the lot of illegal aliens already here. The goals are laudable, but the proposed measures fall short of what is needed.

One obvious remedy is to strengthen the Border Patrol, which has fewer agents on the hundreds of miles of U.S.-Mexican border than there are guards at federal buildings in Washington. The administration proposed an additional $75 million for enforcement measures. That will not be enough, and it will do nothing about the thousands of aliens who enter the country legally on temporary visas and then just stay.

Most authorities agree that the best hope of discouraging illegal immigration is to crack down on employers hiring illegal aliens. The administration proposed to make this unlawful, but the suggested penalties would be no more than $1,000 per illegal alien — not enough to discourage most companies that benefit from cheap immigrant labor.

The administration failed to come up with an adequate method for employers to determine the status of an alien job-seeker. Under the proposal, employers are supposed to demand either documentation issued by the Immigration and Naturalization Service or any two of the following: birth certificate, drivers license, Social Security card or Selective Service registration card.

This would be futile. Counterfeit drivers licenses and birth certificates are readily available along the Mexican border. What is needed is a forgery-proof Social Security card or labor permit without which no one, native or alien, could be hired.

The administration concluded — as have most experts — that there is no hope of rounding up and deporting the millions of illegal aliens who already live here. So the administration wisely proposed an amnesty. But the conditions are so unattractive that many illegal aliens would refuse to take advantage of it.

Under the proposal, they would pay taxes but would not be eligible for unemployment benefits or various welfare programs. They would not be granted permanent resident-alien status — a step toward U.S. citizenship — for 10 years (five years for Cubans and Haitians). In the meantime, they could bring neither spouse nor children to this country to live with them.

A more liberal amnesty program that allowed illegal aliens to bring in their immediate relatives would be more effective and more humane.

We are bothered by the administration's proposal to admit up to 100,000 Mexicans to work under an experimental "guest worker" program. This program would be too small to have any impact on Mexican unemployment, yet those Mexicans who took advantage of it would be subject to second-class status and exploitation by cheap-labor employers.

The United States obviously cannot afford to admit everyone who wants to live here, but those aliens who are allowed to enter and remain should be given the kind of fair treatment that has made this country a beacon for immigrants.

The Dallas Morning News

Dallas, Texas, August 1, 1981

FLUSHED with his tax-cut victory, President Reagan has turned his guns on what may be a harder target to hit: immigration law reform.

The plan revealed by U.S. Atty. Gen. William French Smith covers all immigration, but the heart of the proposal most directly affects Mexican workers who come to this country, legally or illegally.

For a decade, a swelling tide of illegal immigration from Mexico has rolled into this country. Washington's reaction — or lack of reaction — to this fact has become a national disgrace. The Immigration and Naturalization Service has been underfunded and ill-equipped to handle the flow. But with the problem steadily growing worse, Congress has chosen to simply ignore it.

Former President Carter made halting gestures to deal with it, but as was his wont, he backed off before anything was accomplished. President Reagan should not, and let us hope will not, follow that bad example.

Most controversial of the provisions in the proposed law will be the civil penalties levied against employers who follow a "pattern or practice" of hiring illegal aliens. Rhetoric already has started to flow claiming this would make Mexican-Americans second-class citizens.

Bunk. Most of the major employers of illegal Mexican aliens know exactly what they are doing; indeed, many all but run recruiting services seeking Mexican nationals. No program to control illegal immigration will work until the attraction of jobs is brought under control, and that means penalizing those employers who hire the illegals.

Some Americans, too, will complain about providing special status for aliens who entered the country illegally and have stayed to become productive citizens. But this isn't a new action. Three times since 1924, similar gestures have been made to long-term aliens. The government simply recognizes that for whatever reason it failed to properly enforce the immigration laws, and those aliens who have become law-abiding members of the community are allowed to seek citizenship if they so desire.

It is good to see that Gov. Bill Clements is getting considerable credit for influencing the President's proposal. Farmers and ranchers in the state played a major role in the adoption of the so-called Texas Proviso in 1952 that prohibited the prosecution of employers of illegal aliens. And that provision has made enforcement of the immigration laws difficult, if not impossible.

As the bill is debated, especially in relation to Mexico, it must be kept in mind that the United States has benefited from Mexican labor during both world wars and during periods of economic growth. Too often our attitudes have not recognized the positive contribution Mexican workers have made.

Reagan's proposal extends this long-delayed recognition. It offers a practical way to solve a serious problem. It should be adopted.

Sentinel Star

Orlando, Fla., August 9, 1981

DESPITE the hoopla, it is unlikely that six months or a year from now, there will be any appreciable change in the crisis that is our immigration situation.

The reason for this pessimistic prognosis is that changing immigration policy involves more than a series of announcements by the president and his attorney general: There is a massive bureaucracy that must be stirred out of its inertia if the impotent Immigration and Naturalization Service is ever to gain the upper hand in the effort to control the nation's borders.

Many of the plans and proposals recently announced by President Reagan sound good and look good on paper. They appear to be based on common sense and pragmatic politics. But the fact is that, like all of the plans announced by past presidents, the Reagan immigration policy must be put into effect if it is to do any good.

It makes sense to admit the futility of trying to deal effectively with the millions of illegal aliens already here. It makes sense to grant resident alien status to those who can prove they have been here for more than two years. It makes sense to prepare detailed contingency plans for dealing with another exodus of Cuban refugees, such as last year's Mariel experience.

It makes sense to place some of the burden for determining who is legal and who is not on the potential employer, although it would have helped if the president had given him more concrete guidelines on what identity papers he may legally demand. And until there is some sort of foolproof ID card, employers will always have a loophole to escape prosecution.

It also makes sense to put the priority on high seas interdiction of boats full of aliens bound for illegal entry of American territory.

Once illegal aliens set foot in the United States, they become wards of the court insofar as their rights to due process of American law. For that reason, it is unrealistic to believe that judicial review of their status can be significantly expedited. While there is an obvious need to set down what the procedures will be and to work with the judiciary to see that the process is streamlined in every way possible, that will not solve the problem.

The current desperate situation warrants desperate measures, and interdiction fits that bill. It is tricky, potentially dangerous and might well, as critics charge, bring howls of outrage from other nations.

Tough.

No other nation has seen fit to cooperate with the United States when we attempted to enlist aid in coping with the refugee problem. The merits of their protestations are directly proportionate to their willingness to get involved.

The key to President Reagan's immigration policy lies with the effectiveness of its enforcement. The path to the present state of America's immigration situation is littered with hollow policies grandly announced and then left to wither with neither the muscle nor the guts to tackle a totally nasty problem.

If Mr. Reagan is willing to push his specific proposals in the face of stinging domestic and foreign criticism, then there is a chance that control of American immigration policy will be returned to the White House and wrested from anyone who wishes to challenge it.

If not, then things will simply get progressively worse.

SAN JOSE NEWS

San Jose, Calif., August 4, 1981

PRESIDENT Reagan has put forward an immigration policy that angers as many individuals and groups as it pleases but, because it plays to a growing national xenophobia, may be enacted by Congress relatively intact.

That is not to say the Reagan program will necessarily make sense of the existing chaos which passes for a national immigration policy or that it will significantly diminish illegal immigration. It probably won't do either.

It will, if Congress puts its money where its loudest mouths are, expand the Border Patrol on the one hand (with a $75 million increase in the budget of the patrol's parent agency, the Immigration and Naturalization Service) while encouraging continued illegal immigration on the other by failing to attack the econmomic causes of that immigration.

It will also tender the carrot of permanent resident status to an estimated 3 million to 5 million illegal immigrants who arrived here before Jan. 1, 1980 provided they work here for 10 more years, learn a little English and pay taxes. They will not, however, be eligible for any public services save Medicaid.

Already, Hispanic-American groups are calling this portion of the Reagan proposal a recipe for peonage, and they have a point. Whoever pays taxes to a government, citizen or not, should be able to call on that government for the full range of its common services.

The worst feature of the Reagan immigration program, however, is that it lacks focus: It can't make up its mind what it really wants to do. Consequently, it will probably end up perpetuating the status quo, which as the late Select Commission on Immigration and Refugee Policy concluded last spring, is a mess.

In its final report, the commission pronounced illegal immigration to be "out of control" and proposed some, but by no means all, of the remedies included in the Reagan program. For example, both the commission and the president think that employers should be punished for knowingly hiring illegal immigrants. The commission recommended some form of tamper-proof identification be issued to all workers, to protect employers and employees alike.

The president accepted the employer sanctions but rejected the notion of secure identity cards.

The commission recommended against a guest worker program, pointing out that its predecessor, the bracero farmworker program, had actually encouraged illegal immigration.

The president wants Congress to give him a two-year trial program which will admit 50,000 guest workers from Mexico each year. The Mexican government thinks, informally at any rate, that this isn't nearly enough, a sentiment shared by many employers in the West and Southwest who depend on cheap, docile — and transient — labor from Mexico.

This, of course, is the crux of the illegal immigration problem. Mexico, despite burgeoning oil revenues, remains a country full of social inequity. A relatively small number of individuals control a disproportionate share of the wealth, and the Mexican government has traditionally preferred to see the poor trek north for jobs rather than try to reduce the number of poor at home. It is a policy that dovetails neatly with the economic interests of American employers who are not wildly enthusiastic about minimum wage laws and the Occupational Safety and Health Act.

The Reagan immigration proposals do nothing to encourage job creation in Mexico, which would be one way of easing pressure on the border; neither do they seek to legalize what they can't control, which would be another means to the same end.

For example, the president proposes that Mexico and Canada each be granted 40,000 immigrant visas a year — with one country picking up the other's unused quotas. Even assuming that no Canadians wanted to move to the United States, 80,000 Mexicans could emigrate here annually; however, the State Department reports that of Jan 1, 1980, it had on file 274,838 active visa applications from Mexicans wanting to live here permanently.

The president's proposals fail to deal seriously with tide of illegal immigration that continues to sweep over our 1,900-mile border with Mexico. Maybe, in fact, there is no adequate way to deal with it. Closing the border physically is probably impossible, but even if it could be sealed off, important and powerful elements in both countries want it kept open.

On balance, the Reagan immigration proposals are narrow and disappointing. When he was still a presidential candidate, Reagan talked about a North American Accord, a common market approach to immigration, economic and energy concerns of the United States, Mexico and Canada. Whatever happened to that concept?

Index